T0326283

Numerical Methods and Optimization in Finance

Numerical Methods and Optimization in Finance

Manfred Gilli

University of Geneva and Swiss Finance Institute

Dietmar Maringer

University of Basel and University of Geneva

Enrico Schumann

VIP Value Investment Professionals AG, Switzerland

AMSTERDAM • BOSTON • HEIDELBERG • LONDON
NEW YORK • OXFORD • PARIS • SAN DIEGO
SAN FRANCISCO • SINGAPORE • SYDNEY • TOKYO

Academic Press is an imprint of Elsevier

Academic Press is an imprint of Elsevier
225 Wyman Street, Waltham, MA 02451, USA
525 B Street, Suite 1900, San Diego, CA 92101-4495, USA
The Boulevard, Langford Lane, Kidlington, Oxford, OX5 1GB, UK

Library of Congress Cataloging-in-Publication Data
Application submitted

British Library Cataloguing-in-Publication Data
A catalogue record for this book is available from the British Library.

ISBN: 978-0-12-375662-6

For information on all Academic Press publications,
visit our website: *www.elsevierdirect.com*

Printed and bound in the United States of America
11 12 13   9 8 7 6 5 4 3 2 1

Working together to grow
libraries in developing countries

www.elsevier.com | www.bookaid.org | www.sabre.org

ELSEVIER   BOOK AID
International   Sabre Foundation

Contents

List of Algorithms

Acknowledgements

This book would not have been possible without the help of many people. First, we thank Peter Winker who was a teacher to all of us (in one way or another). Peter coordinated the COMISEF (Computational Optimization in Statistics, Econometrics and Finance) project; much of the research described in this book has grown out of this project. We are grateful to the EU for having financed COMISEF (Project MRTN-CT-2006-034270). Also, we would like to thank all the members of COMISEF for providing a fruitful network.

Next, there is Karen Maloney from Elsevier who initiated this endeavor. Without her, the book would never have been written. Many thanks also go to Scott Bentley for managing our project. Then, there is Evis Këllezi, who has been contributing for many years to the research that went into this book, and, not least, she read and commented on many drafts.

There are many other people whom we want to thank. They contributed in many ways: critical suggestions and comments, moral support, patient technical help, inspiration, and proofreading. Thanks go to Gerda Cabej, Giacomo di Tollo, Alain Dubois, Stefan Große, Benoît Guilleminot, Marc Hofmann, Hilda Hysi, Susan Kriete-Dodds, Yvan Lengwiler, Jonela Lula, Alfio Marazzi, Christian Oesch, Ilir Roko, Giorgio Pauletto, Evdoxia Pliota, Tikesh Ramtohul, Gregor Reich, Jin Zhang, and many more.

And finally, one of the authors would like to thank Caroline and Walter, who allowed him to work in the inspiring environment of Chalet Dagobert in Verbier from which the book greatly benefitted.

Manfred Gilli
Dietmar Maringer
Enrico Schumann

Geneva, Basel, Lucerne
January 2011

## CHAPTER ONE

Introduction

1.1. About this book

The origin of this book lies in the city of Geneva in Switzerland, so it seems only appropriate to start there. In case you do not know Switzerland, here is a map.

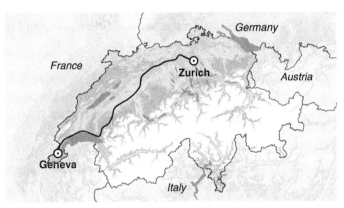

Imagine you stand at the wonderful lakefront of Geneva, with a view on Mont Blanc, and you decide to take a run to Lake Zurich. We admit that this is unlikely, given that the distance is 250 km. But it is just an example. Also, imagine you could run the whole distance with a speed of 20 km per hour which is about the speed that a world-class marathon runner could manage (we ignore the fact that Switzerland is quite a mountainous region). It would still take you more than 12 hours to arrive in Zurich. Now, imagine you took a plane with an average speed of 800 km per hour. This is about 40 times faster, and you would arrive in less than half an hour. What is our point? First, few people would run from Geneva to Zurich. But what we wanted to give you is an idea of speedup. It is just forty in this case, not a large number, but it makes a difference.

This book is not about traveling but about quantitative methods in a specific field, computational finance. Quantitative analysis has become ever more important in scientific research and the industry over the last decades,

1

and in our view, it has much changed. On the one hand, ever more data is collected and stored today, waiting to be analyzed. At the same time, computing power has increased dramatically. If we measure the speed of a computer by the number of operations it can perform in a second, then computers have improved by a factor of perhaps 1,000,000 since the early 1980s.[1] If traveling had matched this speedup, we could go from Geneva to Zurich in 4/100 of a second. Better yet, we do not talk about supercomputers here but about the kind of computers we have on our desktops. (And at least in the past, the power of what was called a supercomputer at one point in time was available for private users only a few years later.)

Computational finance is not a well-defined discipline. It is the intersection of financial economics, scientific computing, econometrics, software engineering, and many other fields. Its goal is to better understand prices and markets (if you are an academic), and to make money (if you are more practically inclined). This book is about tools for computational finance, with an emphasis on optimization techniques. In fact, we will focus on a particular type of optimization methods: heuristics. The theme of the book is the practical, computational application of financial theory; we do not deal with the theory itself; in some cases, there may not even be much established theory. Hence, we will not develop ideas theoretically but consider quantitative analysis as a primarily computational discipline, in which applications are put into software form and tested empirically. For every topic in this book, we discuss the implementation of methods; algorithms will be given in pseudocode, Matlab or R code will be provided for all important examples.[2]

The readers we have in mind are students (Master or PhD level) in programs on quantitative and computational finance, and researchers in finance but also practitioners in banks and other financial companies. The book could be the main reference for courses in computational finance programs or an additional reference for quantitative or mathematical finance courses. Many of the chapters have the flavor of case studies. From a pedagogical view, this allows students to learn the required steps for tackling specific problems; these steps can then be applied to other problems. From the practical side the selected problems will, we hope, be relevant enough to make the book a reference on how to implement a given technique. In fact, the ideal, prototypic kind of reader that we have in mind—let us call him "the analyst"—does not only work on theory, but his job requires a close interaction between theoretical ideas and computation with data.

---

[1] The first IBM PC in the early 1980s did about 10 or 20 Kflops (one flop is one floating point operation per second, see page 32). And this does not take into account improvements in algorithms.

[2] Matlab and R are sufficiently similar so that code from one language can be translated into the other.

The book is structured into three parts. The first part, "Fundamentals," begins with an introduction to numerical analysis, so we discuss computer arithmetic, approximation errors, how to solve linear equations, how to approximate derivatives, and other topics. These discussions will serve as a reference to which later chapters often come back. For instance, the Greeks for option pricing models can often be computed by finite differences. Numerical methods are rarely discussed in standard finance books (Brandimarte, 2006, is an exception), even though they are the basis for empirically applying and testing models. Beyond the initial chapters, our book will not discuss numerical methods in an abstract way. For a general treatment see, for instance, Heath (2005) or the concise and very recommended summary given by Trefethen (2008b); we will only discuss numerical aspects that are relevant to our applications. Further chapters will explain deterministic numerical methods to price instruments, namely trees and finite difference methods, and their application to standard products.

The second part, "Simulation," starts with chapters on how to generate random numbers and how to model dependence. Chapter 8 discusses how time series processes, simple assets, and portfolios can be simulated. There is also a short example on how to implement an agent-based model. By means of several case studies, applications will illustrate how these models can be used for generating more realistic price processes and how simulation can help to develop an intuitive understanding of econometric models and solve practical problems.

The third part, "Optimization" deals with optimization problems in finance. Many relevant optimization models cannot be solved with standard methods that are readily available in software packages. Hence, standard methods will only be briefly touched. We will rather show how to apply another class of techniques, so-called heuristics. Chapter 11 will detail building blocks of numerical optimization algorithms. Though this includes gradient-based techniques like Newton's method, emphasis will be put on more robust techniques like direct search. Chapter 12, "Heuristic Methods in a Nutshell," will then move from these building blocks to specific techniques, and give an overview of heuristic methods. The remaining chapters will deal with specific problems from portfolio optimization, the estimation of econometric models, and the calibration of option pricing models.

1.2. Principles

We start with some principles, or guidelines, for the applications in the book.

1. *We don't know much in finance.* No, we are not being modest here. "We" does not only refer to the authors, but to finance and the people working in finance in general (which includes us). A number of people may object

to this statement, so let us clarify: what we mean by "not knowing much" is that there is little empirically founded and tested, objective knowledge in finance that can be confidently exploited in practical applications. True, there is a vast body of theory. But when we look at the empirical track record of much of this theory—let us say there remains room for improvement.

This has an important implication: when it comes to empirical applications, it is difficult in finance to give general statements like "this model is better than that model" or "this method is better than that method." This is less of a problem in numerical analysis, where we can quite objectively compare one method with another. But in finance, we really don't know much. This makes it difficult to decide what model or technique is the appropriate one for a specific purpose.

There is a second, related implication. If it is so difficult to tell what a good model is, then all that is said must reflect opinion, as opposed to facts. Books—like this one—reflect opinion. In fact, we use the "we" throughout, but this book is written by three authors, and the "we" does not mean that we always agree. Everything in this book reflects the opinion of at least one of us. We cannot claim that the techniques we discuss are the best and final answers, but all results come from extensive analyses, and we have found the methods useful.

We really want to stress this point. Some textbooks in finance give the impression that, for example, "if you want to do portfolio optimization, this is what you need to do." No, please. It should be "This is one possibility, and if you have a better idea, please try." This is all the more true since many models in finance were not motivated by empirical usefulness, but rather mathematical elegance or mere tractability. We will argue in this book that modern computing power (which we all have on our desktops) allows us to give up the need to adhere to rigid mathematical structures (no, an objective function need not be quadratic).

2. *Don't be scared.*[3] Academic finance and economics has become ever more formal and mathematical over the last three decades or so. In our experience, this can be intimidating, and not just to students. One way to overcome this is to show that even complicated models may be only a few lines of computer code and, thus, manageable. (So even for seemingly standard material like binomial trees, we will detail implementation issues which, to our knowledge, are rarely discussed in detail in other books.) Implementing a model gives more intuition about a model than only manipulating its equations. The reason: we get a feel of magnitude of possible errors; we see which difficulties are real, and which ones

---

[3] We should have written it on the cover and made the book slightly less expensive than its competitors; see Adams (1979).

we need not bother with. And implementing a model is anyway the necessary first step to a test whether the model makes practical sense. The purpose of computational finance as stated above (both academic and practical) means that the goal is neither to write beautiful equations nor to write beautiful code, but to get applications to run. Writing reliable software is often important here, but reliable means that the software fulfills its purpose.

3. *Judge the quality of a solution with respect to the application.* We are interested in methods for computational finance. And in our definition of computational finance, the relevance of a model is determined by whether it fulfills its purpose. So it should never be judged by

   (i) how elegant the mathematics is,

   (ii) whether it nicely fits into a theoretical framework (e.g., if a model is built to help forecast interest rates, our concern should not be whether the model excludes arbitrage opportunities),

   (iii) how elegantly the code is written (of course, if the purpose of a program is to compute an answer fast, efficiency becomes a goal).

4. *Don't translate math literally into computer code.* Mathematically, for a vector e, computing $\sum_i e_i^2$ may be equivalent to computing $e'e$, but this need not be the case on a computer. While rounding errors are rarely relevant (see the previous rule and Chapter 2), there may be substantial differences in necessary computing time, which may in turn compromise the performance of a model.

5. *Go experiment.* When you implement an idea, try things, experiment, work with your data, be wild. The tools described in this book will, we hope, help to better test and implement ideas. Eventually, it is the applications that matter; not the tools. We do not need a perfect hammer, the question is where to put the nail.

1.3. On software

We deal with the practical application of numerical methods, so we need to discuss software. The languages of choice will be Matlab and R, sample code will be given in the text when it is discussed. All code can be downloaded from our website http://www.nmof.net. For R we have created a package NMOF that contains most of the code.[4]

We needed to make a decision how to present code. The main purpose of giving sample programs is to motivate readers to use the code, to experiment with it, to adapt it to their own problems. This is not a book on software

---

[4] One should always check if chosen acronyms are used in different contexts; this may spare some quite embarrassing situations. Apparently, for scuba divers, NMOF means "no mask on forehead", as opposed to MOF. Sharing the package's name with this abbreviation seems acceptable.

engineering, it is a book on the application of numerical methods in finance. We will thus rarely discuss design issues like reusability of code (if you are interested in such topics, we suggest you visit the QuantLib project at http://quantlib.org or have a look at Joshi, 2008). The concern of our prototypical analyst (see page 2) is not how to design software, but to investigate problems and data. So our goal is not to provide code that can be used without thinking of what the code does or if it is appropriate for a given problem. In particular, we rarely discuss one crucial element of design: error handling. Not because we deem it unimportant, but because with respect to our goals it obscures the code.

At many places throughout this book we will give suggestions how to make code faster.[5] We are aware that such suggestions are dangerous. Hardware changes, and software as well. For example, if you want to implement binomial trees, we suggest Chapter 5, but also Higham (2002). Higham compares various implementations of a binomial tree with Matlab; his files can be downloaded from http://personal.strath.ac.uk/d.j .higham/algfiles.html. A straightforward version of a tree uses two loops, one over prices and one over time. Higham finds that when the inner loop of the tree (going through the prices) is vectorized, he gets a speedup of 25 or so. When we run the programs today, the speedup is still impressive (say, 2–4, depending on the number of time steps), but clearly less than 25. Why is that? Matlab since version 6.5 includes the Just-In-Time (JIT) compiler (MathWorks, 2002) which accelerates loops, often to the point where vectorization does not give an advantage anymore. If you want to get an idea of the original speed, use

```
feature accel off
% run code here
feature accel on
```

and Higham's programs. The moral of this example is that (i) Higham knew what he wrote about, and (ii) memorizing rules cannot replace experimentation.

So we want efficient code, but does this not go against Rule 3? Not necessarily. True, efficiency (in the sense of fast programs) is a constraint, not a goal per se. If we need to compute a solution to some problem within 2 minutes, and we have a program that achieves this, there is no need to spend days (or more) to make the program run in 5 seconds. But there is one application that is crucial in finance for which a lack of speed becomes a hindrance: testing. We will rarely devise a model, implement it, and start to use it; we will start by testing a model on historic data. The faster the programs work, the more we can test. Also, we may want to scale up

---

[5] When testing code, we mostly used the following equipment: PC: Intel Core 2 Duo P8700 with 2.53 GHz, 2 GB RAM, Windows XP; Matlab: 7.8.0.347 (R2009a); R: 2.10.1, December 14, 2009.

the model later on, maybe with more data or more assets, hence efficient implementations become important.

But then, if we are interested in efficient code, why did we not use lower-level languages like C in the first place? Several reasons: first, it is a matter of taste and path dependency.[6] Second, for the applications that we looked into, Matlab and R were always fast enough. Third, if our goal is exploration, then the time to implement a workable version of an algorithm matters. And here we think that Matlab and R are superior. In any case, we will present many algorithms as pseudocode in which we do not use high-level language (e.g., a loop will always be written as a loop, not as a vectorized command), hence coding is possible for other languages as well.

We will not implement all methods from scratch. A rule in programming is not to rewrite algorithms that are available in implementations of sufficient quality. Still, even available algorithms should be understood theoretically. Examples of this type of software include solvers for linear equations and other routines from linear algebra, collected in libraries such as LAPACK. To be concrete, let us give an example why it makes sense to know how an algorithm works. Suppose we wanted to find the Least Squares solution for an overidentified linear system

$$X\theta \approx y, \tag{1.1}$$

that is, we try to find θ that minimizes $\|X\theta - y\|_2$. Solving such equations is discussed in Chapter 3. X is a matrix of size $m \times n$ with $m > n$, y is a vector of length m, and θ is the parameter vector of length n. The Least Squares solution is given by solving the normal equations

$$X'X\theta = X'y,$$

but we need not explicitly form $X'X$. Rather, we compute the QR decomposition of X, where Q is $m \times m$ and R is $m \times n$. Suppose we need a fast computation—maybe we have to solve Eq. (1.1) many times—and m is far greater than n. Then working with the normal equations (i.e., really computing $X'X$ and $X'y$) may be more practical (see Section 3.4). Importantly, both approaches are equivalent mathematically, but not numerically. The following code examples for Matlab and R show that there are sometimes substantial performance differences between methods.

Listing 1.1. C-Introduction/M/equations.m

```
1 % equations.m -- version 2011-01-02
2 m = 10000; n = 10; trials = 100;
3 X = randn(m,n); y = randn(m,1);
```

---

[6] It is safe to say that all three of us are Matlab fans. One of us bought his first license in 1985 and has used Matlab ever since.

```
 4
 5 % QR
 6 tic
 7 for r=1:trials
 8     sol1 = X\y;
 9 end
10 toc
11
12 % form (X'X) and (X'y)
13 tic
14 for r=1:trials
15     sol2 = (X'*X)\(X'*y);
16 end
17 toc
18
19 % check
20 max(abs(sol1(:)-sol2(:)))
```

Listing 1.2. C-Introduction/R/equations.R

```
 1 # equation.R -- version 2011-01-03
 2 m <- 10000; n <- 10; trials <- 100
 3
 4 X <- array(rnorm(m * n), dim = c(m, n))
 5 y <- rnorm(m)
 6
 7 # QR
 8 system.time({
 9     for (r in seq(trials)) sol1 <- qr.solve(X, y)
10 })
11
12 # form (X'X) and (X'y)
13 system.time({
14     for (r in seq(trials))
15         sol2 <- solve(crossprod(X),crossprod(X,y))
16 })
17
18 # cholesky
19 system.time({
20     for (r in seq(trials)) {
21         C <- chol(crossprod(X))
22         rhs <- crossprod(X,y)
23         sol3 <- backsolve(C,forwardsolve(t(C),rhs))
24     }
25 })
26
27 # check
28 all.equal(as.numeric(sol1),as.numeric(sol2))
29 all.equal(as.numeric(sol2),as.numeric(sol3))
```

Another example for software that should not be written from scratch are random number generators, in particular for uniform variates (which are the basis for other distributions). Knowledge of how variates are generated is helpful, but the rule is to trust Matlab and R (meanwhile, both use the

Mersenne Twister method). This does not mean that such implementations are necessarily bug-free;[7] but they have been tested extensively, and it is more likely that programming our own generators leads to errors.

Nevertheless, we will often need to write our own software. This may include pricing equations, trees, or lattices for pricing financial instruments, for instance in proprietary software; but in particular the optimization algorithms described in Part 3.

1.4. On approximations and accuracy

Many of the models discussed in this book are optimization models. Essentially, any financial model can be rewritten as an optimization problem, since a model's solution is always the entity that best fulfills some condition. (Of course, just because we can rewrite a model as an optimization problem does not mean that handling it like an optimization problem needs to be the most convenient way to solve it.) In setting up and solving such a model, we necessarily commit a number of approximation errors. "Errors" does not mean that something went wrong; these errors will occur even if all procedures work as intended. In fact, the essence of numerical analysis is sometimes described as approximating complicated problems with simpler ones that are easier to solve. But this does not mean that we lose something. The notion of an "approximation error" is meaningless if we do not evaluate its magnitude. This book is not a text on generic numerical methods, but on financial models, and how they are solved. So we should compare the errors coming from the numerical techniques to solve models with the overall quality of the model.

Let us discuss these errors in more detail. (A classic reference on the analysis of such errors is von Neumann and Goldstine, 1947. The discussion in Morgenstern, 1963, Chapter 6, goes along the same lines.) The first approximation error comes when we move from the real problem to the model. For instance, we may move from actual prices in actual time to a mathematical description of the world, in which both prices and time are continuous (i.e., infinitely-small steps are possible). Or we may characterize an investment portfolio as a random variable whose distribution is influenced by the chosen asset weights, and we try to select weights such that we obtain a favorable distribution. But this leaves out many details of the actual investment process.

Any such model, if it is to be empirically meaningful, needs a link to the real world: this link comes in the form of data, or parameters that have to be forecast, estimated, simulated or approximated in some way. Again, we have

---

[7] Excel's random number generator has a particularly bad reputation. In Excel 2003, for instance, the initial version generated negative uniform variates.

another source of error, for the available data may or may not well reflect the true, unobservable processes in which we are interested.

When we solve such models on a computer, we approximate a solution; such approximations are the essence of numerical analysis. At the lowest level, errors come with the mere representation of numbers. For instance, Matlab or R may agree with

```
0.1 + 0.1 == 0.2
```

but at the same time consider

```
0.1 + 0.1 + 0.1 == 0.3
```

as FALSE. A computer can only represent a finite set of numbers exactly. Any other number has to be rounded to the closest representable number, hence we have what is called roundoff error, explained in more detail in Chapter 2.

Next, many functions (e.g., the logarithm) cannot be computed exactly on a computer, but need to be approximated. Operations like differentiation or integration, in mathematical formulation, require a going-to-the-limit, that is, we let numbers tend to zero or infinity. But that is not possible on a computer, any quantity must remain finite. Hence, we have so-called truncation error. For optimization models, we may incur a specific variety of this error: some algorithms, in particular the methods that we describe in Part 3, are stochastic, hence we do not (in finite time) obtain the model's exact solution, but only an approximation (notwithstanding other numerical errors).

In sum, we can roughly divide our modeling into two steps: from reality to the model, and then from the model to its numerical solution. Unfortunately, large parts of the computational finance literature seem only concerned with assessing the quality of the second step, from model to implementation, and attempt to improve here. In the past, a certain division of labor may have been necessary: the economist created his model, and the computer engineer put it into numerical form. But today, there remains little distinction between the researcher who creates the model, and the numerical analyst who implements it. Modern computing power allows us to solve incredibly complex models on our desktops: John von Neumann and Herman Goldstine, in the above-cited paper, describe the inversion of "large" matrices where large meant $n > 10$. In a footnote (fn. 12), they "anticipate that $n \sim 100$ will become manageable." Today, Matlab inverts a 100×100 matrix on a normal desktop PC in $1/1000$ of a second. But see Chapter 3 before you really invert a matrix.

If the analyst is now both modeler and computer engineer, then of course, the responsibility to check the reasonableness of the model and its solution lies—at all approximation steps—with the analyst, and then only evaluating problems at the second step, from model to implementation, falls short of what is required: any error in this step must be set into context, we need to compare it with the error introduced in the first step, when setting up the model. Admittedly, this is much more difficult, but it is necessary.

To give a concrete example: when we simulate a stochastic differential equation (SDE) on a computer, we will approximate it by a difference equation. Thus, we will generally introduce a discretization error (except for the rare cases in which we have a solution for the SDE). A typical application of such SDEs is option pricing with the Monte Carlo method (see Section 9.3). It is then sometimes stressed that in such cases, we can accept a less-precise result from the Monte Carlo procedure because we anyway have a discretization error. It is rarely stressed that we can also accept a less-precise result because the SDE may be a poor approximation of the true process in the first place.

Suppose we accept a model as "true," then the quality of the model's solution will always be limited by the attainable quality of the model's inputs. Appreciating these limits helps to decide how "exact" a solution we actually need. This decision is relevant for many problems in financial engineering: We generally face a trade-off between the precision of a solution and the effort required (most apparently, computing time). Surely, the numerical precision with which we solve a model matters; we need reliable methods. Yet, empirically, there must be an adequate precision threshold for any given problem. Any improvement beyond this level cannot translate into gains regarding the actual problem any more; only in costs (increased computing time or development costs). For many finance problems, we guess, this required precision is not high.

Example 1.1

We often work with returns instead of prices. Given a financial instrument's price S_t (where the subscript denotes time), the discrete return r_{t+1} between t and $t+1$ is defined as

$$r_{t+1}^{\text{discr}} = \frac{S_{t+1} - S_t}{S_t} = \frac{\Delta S_{t+1}}{S_t}$$

where $\Delta S_{t+1} \equiv S_{t+1} - S_t$. Log returns are given by

$$r_{t+1}^{\log} = \log S_{t+1} - \log S_t.$$

When we compute portfolio returns, we can aggregate the returns of single assets on the portfolio level by working with discrete returns; for log returns this is not true. But practically, the difference between the returns is small. We have

$$\frac{\Delta S_{t+1}}{S_t} - \log\left(\frac{\Delta S_{t+1}}{S_t} + 1\right) = \frac{\Delta S_{t+1}}{S_t} - \left[\frac{\Delta S_{t+1}}{S_t} - \frac{1}{2}\left(\frac{\Delta S_{t+1}}{S_t}\right)^2 + \frac{1}{3}\left(\frac{\Delta S_{t+1}}{S_t}\right)^3 - \cdots\right]$$

$$= \frac{1}{2}\left(\frac{\Delta S_{t+1}}{S_t}\right)^2 - \mathscr{O}\left[\left(\frac{\Delta S_{t+1}}{S_t}\right)^3\right].$$

We have used the fact that the Taylor expansion of $\log(1 + x)$ is

$$x - \frac{x^2}{2} + \frac{x^3}{3} - \frac{x^4}{4} + \cdots$$

For all practical purposes there is no difference between log returns and discrete returns; any error arising from choosing the wrong method will be swamped by estimation error; see the next example.

Example 1.2

In numerical analysis, the sensitivity of a problem is defined as follows (see Chapter 2): if we perturb an input of a model, the change in the model's output should be proportional. If the impact is far larger, the problem is called sensitive. Sensitivity often is not a numerical problem; it rather arises from the model or the data. In finance, models are sensitive. Fig. 1.1 shows the 253 daily closing prices of the S&P 500 from December 31, 2008, to December 31, 2009. The index level rose by 23%. By 23.45%, to be more precise, from 903.25 to 1115.10. But does it make sense to report this number to such a precision?

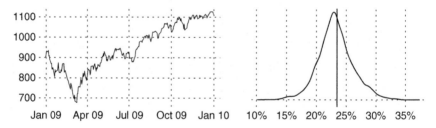

Figure 1.1 Left: The S&P 500 in 2009. Right: Annual returns after jackknifing two observations. The vertical line gives the realized return.

We randomly pick two observations—less than one percent of the daily returns—and delete them; then we compute the yearly return again. Repeating this jackknifing 5000 times, we end up with a distribution of returns; it is pictured in the right panel of Fig. 1.1. The median return is about 23%, but the 10th quantile is 20%, the 90th quantile is 27%, the minimum is only about 11%, the maximum is 34%! Apparently, tiny differences like adding or deleting a couple of days cause very meaningful changes.

This sensitivity has been documented in the literature (for instance in Acker and Duck, 2007; Dimitrov and Govindaraj, 2007), but it is often overlooked or ignored. Hence the precision with which point estimates are sometimes reported must not be confused with accuracy. We may still be able to state qualitative ("This strategy performed better than that strategy.") and quantitative ("How much better? About 2% per year.") results, but we should not make single numbers overly precise. We need robustness checks. Returns are the empirical building blocks of many models. If these simple calculations are already that sensitive, we should not expect more complex computations to be more accurate.

Example 1.3

The theoretical pricing of options, following the papers of Black, Scholes, and Merton in the 1970s, is motivated by an arbitrage argument according to which we can replicate an option by trading in the underlier and a risk-free bond. A replication strategy prescribes to hold a certain quantity of the underlier, the Delta. The Delta is changing with time and with moves in the underlier's price, hence the options trader needs to rebalance his positions. Suppose you live in a Black–Scholes world. You just sold a one-month call (strike and spot price are 100, no dividends, risk-free rate is at 2%, volatility is constant at 30%), and you wish to hedge the position. There is one deviation from Black–Scholes, though: you cannot hedge continuously, but only at fixed points in time (see Kamal and Derman, 1999).

We simulate 100,000 paths of the stock price, and Delta-hedge along each path (see Higham, 2004). We compute two types of Delta: one is the delta as precise as Matlab can do; one is rounded to two digits (e.g., 0.23 or 0.67). The following table shows the volatility of the hedging error (i.e., the difference between the achieved payoff and the contractual payoff), in % of the initial option price. (It is often helpful to scale option prices, for example, price to underlier, or price to strike.) Fig. 1.2 shows replicated option payoffs.

Frequency of rebalancing	With exact Delta	With Delta to two digits
Once per day	18.2%	18.2%
Five times per day	8.3%	8.4%

The volatility of the profit-and-loss is practically the same, so even in the model world, nothing is lost by not computing Delta to a high precision. Yet in research papers and books on option pricing, we often find prices and Greeks to 4 or even 6 decimals. Here is the typical counterargument: "True, for one option we don't need much precision. But what if we are talking about one million options? Then small differences matter." We agree; but the question is not whether differences matter, but whether we can meaningfully compute them. If your

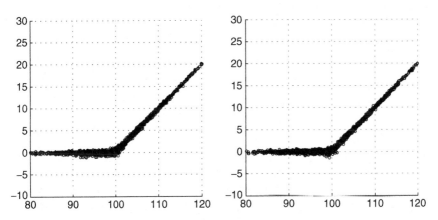

Figure 1.2 Payoff of replicating portfolios with Delta to double precision (left), and Delta to two digits (right).

accountant disagrees, suggest the following rule: whenever you sell an option, round up; when you buy, round down. Between buying one option or buying one million options, there is an important difference: you simply take more risk.

1.5. Summary: the theme of the book

So what to make of it all? Here is our opinion:

- Quantitative models are useful in finance. Certainly, not for every purpose, but in general we think that finance is better off with quantitative methods. Properly applying such methods requires sound implementations.
- But: we think that we should not go overboard with it. The perfectionism that numerical analysts employ to refine methods is not just unnecessary in finance, it is misplaced. In principle, there would seem little cost in being as precise as possible. But there is. First, highly precise or "exact" solutions give us a sense of certainty that is never justified by a model. Secondly, computing more-precise solutions will require more resources. This does not just mean more computing time, but often also more time to develop, implement, and test a particular method, and hence— economist!—it is simply a misallocation of resources.
- This is actually good news. It means that when we are pondering ideas and possible models, we should not be too much concerned with whether we can eventually solve a model with high precision. In sum, with all the things said before as a caveat: we can numerically solve any financial model, or—to put it the other way around—we doubt that there is any financial model that failed because it could not be handled numerically with sufficient precision.

> Numerical issues are not the main source of trouble in finance (they can be a nuisance, though). All we require are solutions that are good enough. And good enough seems quickly achieved in finance. So as a general rule: do not despair when it comes to numerical issues, but compare them with the accuracy of the actual model. If the model's quality is already limited, then do not waste your time thinking about fourth decimals. Think of quantitative finance as gardening; we need sturdy tools for it, but no surgical instruments.

## PART ONE

Fundamentals

CHAPTER TWO

Numerical analysis in a nutshell

2.1. Computer arithmetic

"All the trouble" in numerical computation comes from the fact that during computation, it can happen that $1 + \epsilon = 1$ for $\epsilon \neq 0$. In other words, a computer, generally, cannot perform exact real number arithmetic.

There are two sources of errors appearing systematically in numerical computation. One is related to the simplification of the mathematical model behind the problem to be solved, as for instance the replacement of a derivative by a finite difference or other discretizations of a continuous problem. These errors are termed truncation errors. The second source is due to the fact that it is impossible to represent real numbers exactly in a computer, which leads to rounding errors.

The support for all information in a computer is a "word" constituted by a sequence of generally 32 bits,[1] a bit having a value of 0 or 1.

$$2^{31} \quad 2^{30} \qquad\qquad\qquad 2^3 \quad 2^2 \quad 2^1 \quad 2^0$$

0	0	0	0	$\cdots$	$\cdots$	0	0	1	0	1	0

This sequence of bits is interpreted as the binary representation of an integer. Integers can thus be represented exactly in a computer. If all computations can be made with integers, we are dealing with integer arithmetic. Such computations are exact.

Representation of real numbers

In a computer, a real variable $x \neq 0$ is represented as[2]

$$x = \pm n \times b^e$$

---

[1] This is why computers are also called binary machines. More recent technology is moving toward 64 bits.

[2] The standards for the representation of real numbers have been set by the IEEE Standards Association, and we only present the basics.

where n is the mantissa (or fractional part), b is the base (always 2), and e is the exponent. For instance, the real number 91.232 is expressed as 0.71275×2^7 (or with base 10, we have 0.91232×10^2).

In order to code this number, we partition the word in three parts, one containing the exponent e, the other the mantissa n, and the first bit from the left indicates the sign.

Whatever the size of the word, we dispose of only a limited number of bits for the representation of the integers n and e. As a consequence, it is impossible to represent all real numbers exactly.

In order to keep the illustration manageable, let us illustrate this fact by considering a word with 6 bits, in which $t = 3$ is the number of bits reserved for the mantissa and $s = 2$ is the number of bits reserved for the exponent. One bit is needed for the sign.

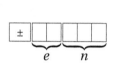

$$
e = \begin{array}{|c|c|c|} \hline 0 & 0 & 0 \\ \hline 0 & 1 & 1 \\ \hline 1 & 0 & 2 \\ \hline 1 & 1 & 3 \\ \hline \end{array}
\qquad
n = \begin{array}{|c|c|c|c|} \hline 1 & 0 & 0 & 4 \\ \hline 1 & 0 & 1 & 5 \\ \hline 1 & 1 & 0 & 6 \\ \hline 1 & 1 & 1 & 7 \\ \hline \end{array}
$$

Normalizing the mantissa, that is imposing the first bit from the left being 1, we have $n \in \{4, 5, 6, 7\}$ and defining the offset of the exponent as $o = 2^{s-1} - 1$, we have

$$(0 - o) \le e \le (2^s - 1 - o),$$

that is $e \in \{-1, 0, 1, 2\}$. The real number x then varies between

$$(2^{t-1} \le n \le 2^t - 1) \times 2^e.$$

Adding 1 to the right of $(2^{t-1} \le n \le 2^t - 1) \times 2^e$ we get $n < 2^t$, and multiplying the whole expression by 2^{-t}, we obtain

$$(2^{-1} \le n < 1) \times 2^{e-t}.$$

The following table reproduces the set of positive real numbers $f = n \times 2^{e-t}$ for a word with 6 bits, $t = 3$ and $s = 2$.

n	2^{e-t}			
	$e=-1$	$e=0$	$e=1$	$e=2$
	$1/16$	$1/8$	$1/4$	$1/2$
$\boxed{1}\,\boxed{0}\,\boxed{0}=2^2=4$	$1/4$	$1/2$	1	2
$\boxed{1}\,\boxed{0}\,\boxed{1}=2^2+2^0=5$	$5/16$	$5/8$	$5/4$	$5/2$
$\boxed{1}\,\boxed{1}\,\boxed{0}=2^2+2^1=6$	$3/8$	$3/4$	$3/2$	3
$\boxed{1}\,\boxed{1}\,\boxed{1}=2^2+2^1+2^0=7$	$7/16$	$7/8$	$7/4$	$7/2$

Moreover, we observe that the representable real numbers are not equally spaced, indeed the grid becomes coarser when moving to larger numbers.

Modern software such as Matlab uses double precision (64-bit words) with $t = 52$ bits for the mantissa and $e \in [-1023, 1024]$, the range of integers for the exponent.

The range of the set f of representable real numbers is then given by $m \le f \le M$ with $m \approx 2.22 \times 10^{-308}$ and $M \approx 1.79 \times 10^{308}$. This is a quite impressive range (just for comparison, the number of electrons in the observable universe is estimated to be of the order of 10^{80}).

If the result of an expression is smaller than m, we get an underflow, which then results into a zero value.[3] If the result of a computation is larger than M, we are in a situation of overflow that then results into an Inf that in most cases will destroy subsequent computations.

The notation float($\cdot$) represents the result of a floating point computation. A computer using the arithmetic of the preceding example ($t = 3$ and $s = 2$) would produce with chopping[4] the following numbers, float(1.74) = 1.5 and float(0.74) = 0.625.

The result for float(1.74 − 0.74) = 0.875 illustrates that even if the exact result is in the set of representable numbers, its representation might be different.

---

[3] Matlab denormalizes small numbers and handles expressions until 10^{-324}.

[4] As opposed to perfect rounding, chopping consists of cutting digits beyond a given position.

Machine precision

The precision of floating point arithmetic is defined as the smallest positive number ϵ_{mach} such that

$$\text{float}(1 + \epsilon_{\text{mach}}) > 1.$$

The machine precision ϵ_{mach} can be computed with the following algorithm:

1: $e = 1$
2: **while** $1 + e > 1$ **do**
3:     $e = e/2$
4: **end while**
5: $\epsilon_{\text{mach}} = 2e$

With Matlab we have $\epsilon_{\text{mach}} \approx 2.2 \times 10^{-16}$, that is, digits beyond the 16th position on the right are meaningless.

Note that floating point computation is not associative. Indeed for $e = \epsilon_{\text{mach}}/2$, we obtain the following results:

$$\text{float}\left(\text{float}(1 + e) + e\right) = 1,$$

$$\text{float}\left(1 + \text{float}(e + e)\right) > 1.$$

Example of limitations of floating point arithmetic

Sometimes the approximation obtained with floating point arithmetic can be surprising. Consider the expression

$$\sum_{k=1}^{\infty} 1/k = \infty.$$

Computing this sum will, of course, produce a finite result. What might be surprising is that this sum is certainly smaller than 100. The problem is not generated by an underflow of $1/k$ or an overflow of the partial sum $\sum_{k=1}^{n} 1/k$ but by the fact that for n satisfying

$$\frac{1/n}{\sum_{k=1}^{n-1} 1/k} < \epsilon_{\text{mach}}$$

the sum remains constant. To show this, we consider $e < \epsilon_{\text{mach}}$ and we can write

$$\text{float}\left(\quad 1 \quad + \quad e \quad \right) = \quad 1$$

$$\text{float}\left(\sum_{k=1}^{n-1} 1/k \quad + \quad 1/n \quad \right) = \sum_{k=1}^{n-1} 1/k$$

$$\text{float}\left(\quad 1 \quad + \quad \frac{1/n}{\sum_{k=1}^{n-1} 1/k} \quad \right) = \quad 1.$$

In the figure below, we show how the function $\sum_{k=1}^{n-1} 1/k$ grows for n going up to 10^7.

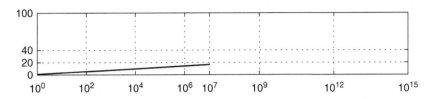

We can conclude that $\sum_{k=1}^{n-1} 1/k < 100$ for values of n that can be considered in practice. Given that $\epsilon_{\mathrm{mach}} \approx 2 \times 10^{-16}$, we establish

$$\frac{1/n}{100} = 2 \times 10^{-16}$$

from which we conclude that n is of order 2×10^{14}. For a computer with a performance of 1 Gflops, the sum will stop to increase after $(2 \times 2 \times 10^{14})/10^9 = 4 \times 10^5$ seconds, that is more than 4 days of computing without exceeding the value of 100.

2.2. Measuring errors

In numerical computations, frequently, one has to measure the error e between an approximated value $\hat{x}$ and an exact value x or, for instance, the distance between two successive values in an iterative algorithm. The absolute error defined as

$$|\hat{x} - x|$$

is a very natural way to do this. However, this is not suitable for all situations. Consider the case in which $\hat{x} = 3$ and $x = 2$; we have an absolute error of 1, which cannot be considered "small." On the contrary for $\hat{x} = 10^9 + 1$ and $x = 10^9$, an absolute error of 1 can be considered "small" with respect to x.

The relative error defined as

$$\frac{|\hat{x} - x|}{|x|}$$

for $x \neq 0$ avoids the problem illustrated earlier. The relative error for the previous example is 0.5 and 10^{-9}.

If $x = 0$ (or very close to zero), the absolute error will do the job, but the relative error will not. It is possible to combine absolute and relative errors with the following expression

$$\frac{|\hat{x} - x|}{|x| + 1}.$$

This definition then avoids the problems if x is near zero; it has the properties of the relative error if $|x| \gg 1$ and the properties of the absolute error if $|x| \ll 1$.

2.3. Approximating derivatives with finite differences

Instead of working with the analytical derivative of a function, it is possible to compute a numerical approximation considering finite increments of the arguments of the function. Such approximations are easy to compute, their precision is generally sufficient, and, therefore, they are very convenient in numerical computations.

We consider a continuous function $f : \mathbb{R} \to \mathbb{R}$, the derivative of which is

$$f'(x) = \lim_{h \to 0} \frac{f(x+h) - f(x)}{h}. \tag{2.1}$$

If, instead of letting h go to zero, we consider "small" values for h, we get an approximation for $f'(x)$. An immediate question is then: How to choose h to get a good approximation if we work with floating point arithmetic?

We consider f with derivatives of order $n+1$. For finite h, the Taylor expansion writes

$$f(x+h) = f(x) + hf'(x) + \frac{h^2}{2}f''(x) + \frac{h^3}{6}f'''(x) + \cdots + \frac{h^n}{n!}f^{(n)}(x) + R_n(x+h)$$

with the remainder

$$R_n(x+h) = \frac{h^{n+1}}{(n+1)!}f^{(n+1)}(\xi), \qquad \xi \in [x, x+h],$$

where ξ is not known.

Thus, Taylor series allow the approximation of a function with a degree of precision that equals the remainder.

Approximating first-order derivatives

Now, consider Taylor's expansion up to order two,

$$f(x+h) = f(x) + hf'(x) + \frac{h^2}{2}f''(\xi) \quad \text{with} \quad \xi \in [x, x+h],$$

from which we get

$$f'(x) = \frac{f(x+h) - f(x)}{h} - \frac{h}{2}f''(\xi). \tag{2.2}$$

Expression (2.2) decomposes $f'(x)$ into two parts, the approximation of the derivative and the truncation error. This approximation is called forward difference. The approximation by backward difference is defined as

$$f'(x) = \frac{f(x) - f(x-h)}{h} + \frac{h}{2}f''(\xi). \tag{2.3}$$

Consider $f(x+h)$ and $f(x-h)$:

$$f(x+h) = f(x) + hf'(x) + \tfrac{h^2}{2}f''(x) + \tfrac{h^3}{6}f'''(\xi_+) \quad \text{with} \quad \xi_+ \in [x, x+h],$$

$$f(x-h) = f(x) - hf'(x) + \tfrac{h^2}{2}f''(x) - \tfrac{h^3}{6}f'''(\xi_-) \quad \text{with} \quad \xi_- \in [x-h, x],$$

then the difference $f(x+h) - f(x-h)$ is

$$f(x+h) - f(x-h) = 2hf'(x) + \tfrac{h^3}{6}\Big(f'''(\xi_+) + f'''(\xi_-)\Big).$$

If f''' is continuous, we can replace $\frac{f'''(\xi_+)+f'''(\xi_-)}{2}$ by the mean $f'''(\xi)$, $\xi \in [x-h, x+h]$ and we get

$$\frac{h^3}{3}\Big(f'''(\xi_+) + f'''(\xi_-)\Big) = \frac{2h^3}{3}\underbrace{\frac{f'''(\xi_+) + f'''(\xi_-)}{2}}_{f'''(\xi)}$$

$$f'(x) = \frac{f(x+h) - f(x-h)}{2h} - \frac{h^2}{3}f'''(\xi),$$

which defines the approximation by central difference. We observe that this approximation is more precise as the truncation error is of order $O(h^2)$.

Approximating second-order derivatives

Developing the sum $f(x+h) + f(x-h)$ in which

$$f(x+h) = f(x) + hf'(x) + \tfrac{h^2}{2}f''(x) + \tfrac{h^3}{6}f'''(\xi_+) \quad \text{with} \quad \xi_+ \in [x, x+h],$$

$$f(x-h) = f(x) - hf'(x) + \tfrac{h^2}{2}f''(x) - \tfrac{h^3}{6}f'''(\xi_-) \quad \text{with} \quad \xi_- \in [x-h, x],$$

we get

$$f''(x) = \frac{f(x+h) - 2f(x) + f(x-h)}{h^2} - \frac{h^2}{3}f'''(\xi) \quad \text{with} \quad \xi \in [x-h, x+h].$$

There exist several different approximation schemes, also of higher order (see Dennis and Schnabel, 1983).

Partial derivatives

The approximation by a central difference of the partial derivative with respect to x of a function $f(x, y)$ is

$$f_x = \frac{f(x+h_x, y) - f(x-h_x, y)}{2h_x}.$$

Approximating the derivative of f_x with respect to y with a central difference, we get the approximation for f_{xy},

$$f_{xy} = \frac{\frac{f(x+h_x,y+h_y)-f(x-h_x,y+h_y)}{2h_x} - \frac{f(x+h_x,y-h_y)-f(x-h_x,y-h_y)}{2h_x}}{2h_y}$$

$$= \tfrac{1}{4h_x h_y} \left(f(x+h_x,y+h_y) - f(x-h_x,y+h_y) \right.$$

$$\left. -f(x+h_x,y-h_y) + f(x-h_x,y-h_y) \right).$$

How to choose h

How to choose h if we use floating point arithmetic? To reduce the truncation error, we would be tempted to choose h to be as small as possible. However, we also must take into consideration the rounding error.

If h is too small, we have float$(x+h) = $ float(x) and even if float$(x+h) \neq$ float(x), we can have float$\left(f(x+h)\right) = $ float$\left(f(x)\right)$ if the function varies very slowly.

Truncation error for forward difference

Denote

$$f'_h(x) = \frac{f(x+h) - f(x)}{h}$$

as the approximation of the derivative corresponding to a given value of h. If we accept that in the truncation error $-\frac{h}{2}f''(\xi)$ we have for a number M and all t in the domain of our application,

$$|f''(t)| \leq M$$

then we get the following bound for the truncation error

$$|f'_h(x) - f'(x)| \leq \tfrac{h}{2}M$$

indicating that we can reach any precision, given h is chosen to be sufficiently small. However, in floating point arithmetic, it is not possible to evaluate $f'_h(x)$ exactly because of rounding errors.

Consider that the rounding error for evaluating $f(x)$ has the following bound

$$|\text{float}\left(f(x)\right) - f(x)| \leq \epsilon.$$

Then, the rounding error (for finite precision computations) for a forward difference approximation is bounded by

$$|\text{float}\left(f'_h(x)\right) - f'_h(x)| \leq \tfrac{2\epsilon}{h}$$

$$\text{float}\left(f_h'(x)\right) = \text{float}\left(\frac{f(x+h) - f(x)}{h}\right)$$

$$= \frac{\text{float}\left(f(x+h)\right) - \text{float}\left(f(x)\right)}{h}$$

$$= \frac{\epsilon + \epsilon}{h}.$$

Finally, the upper bound for the sum of both sources of errors is

$$|\text{float}\left(f_h'(x)\right) - f'(x)| \le \tfrac{2\epsilon}{h} + \tfrac{M}{2}h.$$

A compromise between the reduction of the truncation error and that of the rounding error becomes necessary. As a consequence, the precision we can achieve is limited.[5] The optimal value for h corresponds to the minimum for $g(h) = \tfrac{2\epsilon}{h} + \tfrac{h}{2}M$. From the first-order conditions,

$$g'(h) = -\tfrac{2\epsilon}{h^2} + \tfrac{M}{2} = 0,$$

we compute that the bound reaches its minimum for

$$h = 2\sqrt{\tfrac{\epsilon}{M}}.$$

In practice, ϵ corresponds to the machine precision ϵ_{mach}, and if we admit that M is of order one, then setting $M = 1$ we get

$$h = 2\sqrt{\epsilon_{\text{mach}}}.$$

In Matlab, we have $\epsilon_{\text{mach}} \approx 2 \times 10^{-16}$ and $h \approx 10^{-8}$.

In the case of central differences, we have $g(h) = \tfrac{2\epsilon}{h} + \tfrac{h^2}{3}M$. The first-order condition is

$$g'(h) = -\tfrac{2\epsilon}{h^2} + \tfrac{2Mh}{3} = 0$$

from which we get $h = (3\epsilon/M)^{1/3}$. Replacing ϵ and M gives

$$h \approx 10^{-5}.$$

Example 2.1

To illustrate the influence of the choice of h on the precision of the approximation of the derivative, we consider the function $f(x) = \cos(x^x) - \sin(e^x)$ and its derivative

$$f'(x) = -\sin(x^x)x^x\left(\log(x) + 1\right) - \cos(e^x)e^x.$$

Fig. 2.1 shows the relative error for the numerical approximation of the derivative evaluated at $x = 1.5$, as a function of the step size h in the range of 10^{-16} to 1. For the central difference approximation, the minimum error is achieved around $h = 10^{-5}$, and for the forward difference approximation, the optimal value is $h = 10^{-8}$ according to our previous results.

---

[5] h is chosen as a power of 2 and therefore can be represented without rounding error.

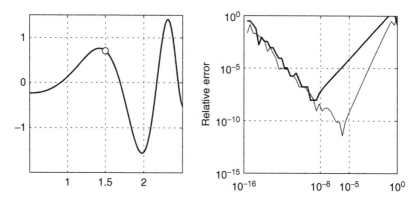

Figure 2.1 Function $f(x) = \cos(x^x) - \sin(e^x)$ (left panel) and relative error of the numerical approximation of the derivative at $x = 1.5$ for forward difference (thick line) and central difference (thin line).

2.4. Numerical instability and ill-conditioning

In Section 2.1, it has been shown that binary machines can represent only a subset of the real numbers, introducing rounding errors that may seriously affect the precision of the numerical solution. If the "quality" of a solution is not acceptable, it is important to distinguish between the following two situations:

  i. Rounding errors are considerably amplified by the algorithm. This situation is called numerical instability.

  ii. Small perturbations of data generate large changes in the solution. This is termed an ill-conditioned (or sensitive) problem.

In the following we give illustrations of numerical instability and of an ill-conditioned problem.

Example of a numerically unstable algorithm

Consider the second-order equation $ax^2 + bx + c = 0$ and its analytical solutions

$$x_1 = \frac{-b - \sqrt{b^2 - 4ac}}{2a} \qquad x_2 = \frac{-b + \sqrt{b^2 - 4ac}}{2a}.$$

The following algorithm simply translates the analytical solution:

1: $\Delta = \sqrt{b^2 - 4ac}$
2: $x_1 = (-b - \Delta)/(2a)$
3: $x_2 = (-b + \Delta)/(2a)$

    For $a = 1$, $c = 2$, and floating point arithmetic with 5 digits of precision, the algorithm produces the following solutions for different values of b:

b	Δ	float (Δ)	float (x_2)	x_2	$\frac{\|\text{float}(x_2)-x_2\|}{\|x_2\|+1}$
5.2123	4.378135	4.3781	-0.41708	-0.4170822	1.55×10^{-6}
121.23	121.197	121.20	-0.01500	-0.0164998	1.47×10^{-3}
1212.3	1212.2967	1212.3	0	-0.001649757	Catastrophic cancelation

Note that $\text{float}(x_2) = \left(-b + \text{float}(\Delta)\right)/(2a)$

Let us now consider an alternative algorithm exploiting the relation $x_1 x_2 = c/a$ satisfied by the solutions according to Viète's theorem:

1: $\Delta = \sqrt{b^2 - 4ac}$
2: **if** $b < 0$ **then**
3: $\qquad x_1 = (-b + \Delta)/(2a)$
4: **else**
5: $\qquad x_1 = (-b - \Delta)/(2a)$
6: **end if**
7: $x_2 = c/(a x_1)$

This algorithm avoids catastrophic cancelation, that is, loss of significant digits when computing a small number by subtracting two large numbers. Solving for $b = 1212.3$, we get an astonishingly precise result considering that we use only 5 digits of precision.

b	float (Δ)	float (x_1)	float (x_2)	x_2
1212.3	1212.3	-1212.3	-0.0016498	-0.001649757

Example of an ill-conditioned problem

We consider the following linear system for which we easily verify that the exact solution is $x = [1 \ -1]'$. Note that in practice, one almost never knows the solution. In our case, it has been obtained by construction.

$$A = \begin{bmatrix} 0.780 & 0.563 \\ 0.913 & 0.659 \end{bmatrix} \qquad b = \begin{bmatrix} 0.217 \\ 0.254 \end{bmatrix}. \tag{2.4}$$

Solving this linear system with Matlab, we obtain

$$x = A\backslash b = \begin{bmatrix} 0.99999999991008 \\ -0.99999999987542 \end{bmatrix}. \tag{2.5}$$

Despite the seemingly high precision of the solution, this is an ill-conditioned problem. Consider the matrix

$$E = \begin{bmatrix} 0.001 & 0.001 \\ -0.002 & -0.001 \end{bmatrix}$$

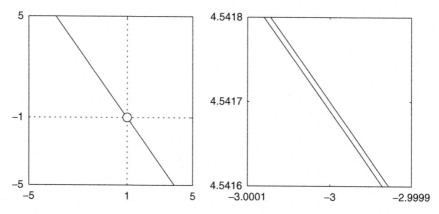

Figure 2.2 Left panel: graphical solution of linear system (2.4). Right panel: details around the coordinate $(-3, 4.54)$ of the straight lines defining the linear system.

and the perturbed system $(A + E)x_E = b$. The new solution is then

$$x_E = \begin{bmatrix} -5.0000 \\ 7.3085 \end{bmatrix},$$

which deviates an order of magnitude from the original solution with respect to the perturbation in matrix A. The solution of the linear system (2.4) corresponds to the intersection of the two lines corresponding to the equations. This is shown in the left panel of Fig. 2.2, in which only one line is visible as the lines are very close to being parallel. The right panel illustrates the zoomed-in region around the coordinate $(-3, 4.54)$, which clearly shows the existence of the two distinct lines. Thus, a very small perturbation of the coefficients defining the lines leads to a substantial shift of the intersection.

2.5. Condition number of a matrix

The sensitivity of the solution of a problem $f(x)$ with respect to a perturbation of the data x is called the condition of the problem. It can be considered as the absolute value of the elasticity

$$\text{cond}\left(f(x)\right) \approx \frac{|x f'(x)|}{|f(x)|}.$$

If this elasticity is large, the problem is referred to as ill-conditioned. Note that we can distinguish three situations in which the condition number can become large:

- $f'(x)$ very large with x and $f(x)$ normally sized
- x very large with $f(x)$ and $f'(x)$ normally sized
- $f(x)$ very small with x and $f'(x)$ normally sized

The condition number of a problem is generally difficult to estimate. However, for a linear system, the condition number of the coefficient matrix A is defined as

$$\kappa(A) = \|A^{-1}\| \, \|A\|,$$

which can be computed efficiently in Matlab with the function `cond`. For our example we have $\text{cond}(A) = 2.2 \times 10^6$.

As a rule of thumb, if $\text{cond}(A) > 1/\sqrt{\text{eps}}$, we should worry about our numerical results. In Matlab, we have $\text{eps} = 2.2 \times 10^{-16}$ which gives $1/\sqrt{\text{eps}} = 6.7 \times 10^8$, which means that in solving a problem with a condition number of the order 10^8, we lose, in the results, half of the significant digits. Of course, we may become suspicious even if we encounter smaller condition numbers depending on the kind of problem.

Example 2.2

In practical applications, we may well find situations with perfectly acceptable condition numbers, but, nevertheless, we should not trust the solutions too much. In other words, we may encounter settings for which we can numerically compute a solution without a problem, but should be careful in interpreting the results.

An example: in a linear regression model, the Jacobian is the data matrix. The condition number of this matrix can be acceptable even though high correlation between the columns may prohibit any sensible inference regarding single coefficients. The following Matlab script sets up a linear regression model with extremely correlated regressors.

```
% -- set number of observations, number of regressors
nObs = 150; nR = 5;

% -- set up correlation matrix
C = ones(nR,nR) * 0.9999; C( 1:(nR+1):(nR*nR) ) = 1;

% -- create data
X = randn(nObs,nR); C = chol(C); X = X*C; bTrue = randn(nR,1);
y = X*bTrue + randn(nObs,1)*0.2;
plotmatrix(X)
```

The regression X\y can be computed[6] without numerical problems, though we had better not interpret the coefficients.

Comments and examples

The condition number represents a measure of the upper bound for the problems one may encounter when solving a system of equations. As another example, consider the system of equations with

$$A = \begin{bmatrix} 10^{-10} & 0 \\ 0 & 10^{10} \end{bmatrix}$$

---

[6] The workings of Matlab's backslash operator are explained on page 67.

and any value for b. The condition number of matrix A is $\mathrm{cond}(A) = 10^{20}$ but we can compute the solution $x_i = b_i / A_{ii}$ without any numerical problem.

Given a linear system $Ax = b$ and its computed solution x_c, the quantity $r = Ax_c - b$ is called residual error. One might think that the residual error is an indicator for the precision of the computation. This is only the case if the problem is well-conditioned. As an illustration, we take the example from page 27 and consider two candidates x_c for the solution and their associated residual error:

$$x_c = \begin{bmatrix} 0.999 \\ -1.001 \end{bmatrix} \quad r = \begin{bmatrix} -0.0013 \\ -0.0016 \end{bmatrix} \quad \text{and} \quad x_c = \begin{bmatrix} 0.341 \\ -0.087 \end{bmatrix} \quad r = \begin{bmatrix} 10^{-6} \\ 0 \end{bmatrix}.$$

We observe that a much smaller residual error is produced by the candidate that is by far of lower quality. Hence, we conclude that for ill-conditioned systems, the residual error is not suited to give us information about the quality of the solution.

A matrix can be well-conditioned for the solution of the associated linear system and ill-conditioned for the identification of its eigenvalues, and vice versa. This is illustrated by the following examples.

As a first example, we take $A = \texttt{triu(ones(20))}$, that is, an upper triangular matrix with all its entries equal to one. A is ill-conditioned for the computation of its eigenvalues. With Matlab's function $\texttt{eig}$, we compute

$$\lambda_1, \ldots, \lambda_{20} = 1,$$

and setting $A_{20,1} = 0.001$, we get

$$\lambda_1 = 2.77, \ldots, \lambda_{20} = 0.57 - 0.08i.$$

However, A is well-conditioned for solving a linear system as $\texttt{cond(A)}$ is 26.03.

As a second example, we take the matrix

$$A = \begin{bmatrix} 1 & 1 \\ 1 & 1+\delta \end{bmatrix},$$

which poses no problem for the computation of its eigenvalues. For $\delta = 0$, we get the following two eigenvalues

$$\lambda_1 = 0 \quad \text{and} \quad \lambda_2 = 2,$$

and setting $\delta = .001$, we get

$$\lambda_1 = 0.0005 \quad \text{and} \quad \lambda_2 = 2.0005.$$

In turn, A is ill-conditioned for the solution of a linear system. For $\delta = 0$, A is singular, that is, $\texttt{cond(A)}$ is $\texttt{Inf}$. For $\delta = 0.001$, we obtain $\texttt{cond(A)}$ is 4002.

To conclude, we recall that if we want to obtain sound numerical results with a computer, we need to make sure that we have:
- a well-conditioned problem
- a numerically stable algorithm if executed with finite precision
- software that is a good implementation of the algorithm

Finally, a numerically stable algorithm will never be able to solve an ill-conditioned problem with more precision than the data contain. However, a numerically unstable algorithm may produce bad solutions even for well-conditioned problems.

2.6. A primer on algorithmic and computational complexity

The analysis of the computational complexity of an algorithm provides a measure of the efficiency of an algorithm and is used for comparison and evaluation of the performance of algorithms. Only a few elements relevant for characterizing the properties of the algorithms presented in this book will be discussed.[7]

The definition of the problem size is central as the computational effort of an algorithm should be a function of it. Generally, the size is expressed as roughly the number of elements the algorithm has to process (amount of data). In the case of the computation of the solution of a linear system $Ax = b$, the size of the problem is given by the order n of the matrix A. For a matrix multiplication, the size is defined by the dimension of the two matrices.

2.6.1. Criteria for comparison

A detailed comparison is generally difficult to perform and mostly not very useful. The most important criterion for comparison is the execution time of the algorithm. In order to be practical, the measure has to be computed easily and has to be independent of the computational platform. Therefore, the execution time is measured in number of elementary operations. Thus, the complexity of an algorithm is defined as the number of elementary operations to solve a problem of size n.

Consider an algorithm that sequentially seeks a particular item in a list of length n. Its computation time is then $C(n) \leq k_1 n + k_2$, where $k_1 \geq 0$ and $k_2 \geq 0$ are two constants independent of n characterizing a particular implementation. Generally, the worst case $C(n) = k_1 n + k_2$ is considered.[8]

Other criteria are the so-called space complexity, that is, the amount of fast memory necessary to execute the algorithm, and the simplicity of the

---

[7] Practically, the specific implementation of an algorithm also matters.
[8] Another way is to consider the average number of operations, which generally has to be evaluated by simulation. Some algorithms that behave very badly in the worst case perform efficiently on average. An example is the simplex algorithm for the solution of linear programs.

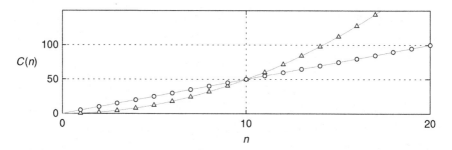

Figure 2.3 Operation count for algorithm A_1 (triangles) and A_2 (circles).

coding. The former tends to be less of a problem with modern computing technology but the latter should not be underestimated.

Order of complexity and classification

As mentioned earlier we do not want to measure the complexity in detail. Generally, and in particular for matrix computation, we only count the number of elementary operations consisting of addition, subtraction, multiplication, and division. These operations are termed flop (floating point operation).[9] Also, only the order of the counting function will be considered. As an illustration consider two algorithms A_1 and A_2 in which the function counting the elementary operations is $C_{A_1}(n) = 1/2 \, n^2$ for the first algorithm and $C_{A_2}(n) = 5n$ for the latter.

In Fig. 2.3, we observe that for $n > 10$, Algorithm A_2 is faster than Algorithm A_1. As computing time becomes critical for growing values of n, it is only the order[10] of the counting function which determines the complexity. Hence, the complexity of algorithm A_1 is $\mathcal{O}(n^2)$ and algorithm A_2 has a complexity of $\mathcal{O}(n)$. The complexity of an algorithm with $1/3 \, n^3 + n^2 + 2/3 \, n$ elementary operations is of order $\mathcal{O}(n^3)$.

Algorithms are classified into two main groups according to the order of the function counting elementary operations:

- Polynomial time algorithms, that is, the operation count is a polynomial function of the problem size.
- Non-polynomial time algorithms.

Only algorithms from the polynomial time class can be considered as efficient.

The performance of computers is measured in flops per second. Personal computers evolved from a few Kflops (10^3 flops) in the early 1980s to several

---

[9] An example of the count of elementary operations for an algorithm is given on page 42.

[10] The order of a function is formalized with $\mathcal{O}(\cdot)$ notation, which is defined as follows: a function $g(n)$ is $\mathcal{O}(f(n))$ if there exist constants c_0 and n_0 such that $g(n)$ is smaller than $c_0 f(n)$ for all $n > n_0$.

Gflops (10^9 flops) at the end of the first decade of 2000. The size of available fast memory increased by the same factor.

Note that faster computers will not remove non-polynomial algorithms from the class of non-efficient algorithms. To illustrate this, consider, for instance, an algorithm with complexity 2^n and assume N to be the size of the largest problem instance one can solve in an acceptable amount of time. Increasing the computation speed by a factor of 1024 will increase the size of the problem computed in the same time to $N + 10$.

2.A. Operation count for basic linear algebra operations

Each of the elementary operations –addition, subtraction, multiplication and division– counts for one flop. Given the vectors x, $y \in \mathbb{R}^n$, $z \in \mathbb{R}^m$ and the matrices $A \in \mathbb{R}^{m \times r}$ and $B \in \mathbb{R}^{r \times n}$, we have:

Operation	flops	
$x + y$	n	
$x' x$	$2n$	$(n > 1)$
$x z'$	nm	
AB	$2mrn$	$(r > 1)$

CHAPTER THREE

Linear equations and Least Squares problems

Systems of linear equations arise very frequently in numerical problems, and therefore, the choice of an efficient solution method is of great importance. Formally, the problem consists in finding the solution of $Ax = b$, where A is the coefficient matrix, b the so-called right-hand-side vector, and x the unknown solution vector. In other words, we have to find the solution for the following system of equations

$$
\begin{aligned}
a_{11}x_1 + a_{12}x_2 + \cdots + a_{1n}x_n &= b_1 \\
a_{21}x_1 + a_{22}x_2 + \cdots + a_{2n}x_n &= b_2 \\
&\vdots \\
a_{n1}x_1 + a_{n2}x_2 + \cdots + a_{nn}x_n &= b_n
\end{aligned}
\equiv
\underbrace{\begin{bmatrix} a_{11} & a_{12} & \cdots & a_{1n} \\ a_{21} & a_{22} & \cdots & a_{2n} \\ \vdots & \vdots & \ddots & \vdots \\ a_{n1} & a_{n2} & \cdots & a_{nn} \end{bmatrix}}_{A}
\underbrace{\begin{bmatrix} x_1 \\ x_2 \\ \vdots \\ x_n \end{bmatrix}}_{x}
=
\underbrace{\begin{bmatrix} b_1 \\ b_2 \\ \vdots \\ b_n \end{bmatrix}}_{b}.
$$

The expression on the right side is the equivalent formalization in matrix form.

A few preliminary remarks: The solution exists and is unique if and only if the determinant of A satisfies $|A| \neq 0$. The algebraic notation for the solution $x = A^{-1}b$ might suggest that we need to compute the inverse A^{-1}. However, an efficient numerical method computes neither the inverse A^{-1} to solve the system nor the determinant $|A|$ to check whether a solution exists.

A word of caution: The intention of the presentation of the algorithms that follow is not to instruct the user to write their own code for solving linear systems. It would be very hard to beat the code implemented in most of the popular softwares. The target of this presentation is to provide understanding and help to make the appropriate choices among the available techniques. For all details, see Golub and Van Loan (1989).

Choice of method

The choice of the appropriate method to solve a linear system depends on the structure and the particular quantification of the matrix A. With respect to the properties of the structure of the matrix A, we distinguish the case where the matrix is

- dense, that is, almost all of the elements are nonzero
- sparse, that is, only a small fraction of the n^2 elements of the matrix are nonzero
- banded, that is, the nonzero elements of the matrix are concentrated near the diagonal (the bandwidth b is defined as $a_{ij} = 0$ if $|i - j| > b$; a diagonal matrix has $b = 0$ and a tridiagonal matrix has $b = 1$)
- triangular or has a block structure

Particular matrices with respect to their content are, among others, symmetric matrices ($A = A'$) and more importantly positive-definite matrices ($x'Ax > 0, \forall x \neq 0$). As a rule, if a matrix has structure, this can (in principle) be exploited.

There exist two broad categories of numerical methods for solving linear systems:

- Direct methods which resort to factorization
- Iterative methods (stationary and non stationary).

3.1. Direct methods

Direct methods transform the original problem into an easy-to-solve equivalent problem. For instance, a system $Ax = b$ is transformed into $Ux = c$ with matrix U triangular or diagonal, which makes it easy to compute x. Another approach consists in the transformation $Qx = c$ with Q orthogonal which again allows recovery of x immediately from $x = Q'c$.

3.1.1. Triangular systems

As triangular systems play an important role in the solution of linear systems, we briefly present the methods for solving them. Consider the lower triangular system

$$\begin{bmatrix} \ell_{11} & 0 \\ \ell_{21} & \ell_{22} \end{bmatrix} \begin{bmatrix} x_1 \\ x_2 \end{bmatrix} = \begin{bmatrix} b_1 \\ b_2 \end{bmatrix}.$$

If the elements satisfy $\ell_{11}, \ell_{22} \neq 0$, the unknowns can be computed sequentially as

$$x_1 = b_1 / \ell_{11}$$
$$x_2 = (b_2 - \ell_{21}x_1)/\ell_{22}.$$

Forward substitution

For a system $Lx = b$, with L a lower triangular matrix, the solution for the ith equation can be written as

$$x_i = \left(b_i - \sum_{j=1}^{i-1} \ell_{ij} x_j \right) / \ell_{ii}$$

This procedure is called forward substitution. Note that the element b_i is only used for the computation of x_i (see also the above figure), and thus, we can overwrite b_i with x_i in vector b. Algorithm 1 solves the lower triangular system $Lx = b$ of order n by forward substitution and overwrites b with the solution x. The algorithm necessitates $n^2 + 3n - 4$ flops.

Algorithm 1 Forward substitution.

1: $b_1 = b_1 / L_{1,1}$
2: **for** $i = 2 : n$ **do**
3:      $b_i = (b_i - L_{i,1:i-1} \, b_{1:i-1})/L_{ii}$
4: **end for**

Back-substitution

For an upper triangular system $Ux = b$ we proceed in an analogous way as done before, that is,

$$x_i = \left(b_i - \sum_{j=i+1}^{n} u_{ij} x_j \right) / u_{ii}$$

This procedure is called back-substitution. Again the element b_i can be overwritten by x_i. Algorithm 2 solves the upper triangular system $Ux = b$ by back-substitution and overwrites b with the solution x. The operation count is identical to the one of Algorithm 1.

3.1.2. LU factorization

LU factorization is the method of choice if matrix A is dense and has no particular structure. Matrix A is factorized into a product of two matrices

---

Algorithm 2 Back-substitution.

1: $b_n = b_n / U_{n,n}$
2: **for** $i = n - 1 : -1 : 1$ **do**
3:     $b_i = (b_i - U_{i,i+1:n} \, b_{i+1:n}) / U_{ii}$
4: **end for**

L and U, which are lower and upper triangular, respectively. In $Ax = b$, we replace A by its factorization LU and solve the transformed system $LUx = b$ in two steps, each involving the solution of a triangular system. This is illustrated in the following figure where y is an intermediate vector.

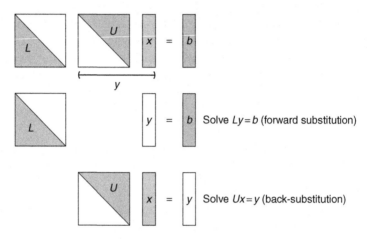

LU factorization necessitates $2/3\,n^3 - 1/2\,n^2 - 1/6\,n + 1$ elementary operations, and therefore, its complexity is $\mathcal{O}(n^3)$.

LU factorization with **Matlab**

Matlab uses the syntax x = A\b to solve $Ax = b$ no matter what type A is.[1] Let us illustrate the three steps of the procedure presented above.

The Matlab command [L,U] = lu(A) computes L and U, but L is a permuted triangular matrix which cannot be used as such in the forward substitution. Therefore, we execute the command

```
[L,U,P] = lu(A)
```

that produces a triangular matrix L, and a permutation matrix P such that $LU = PA$, which means that L and U correspond to the LU factorization of a permuted system of equations. The lines of code that follow illustrate the procedure. Forward and back-substitutions are executed with the backslash operator, and the vector y is not explicitly computed.

---

[1] The workings of the backslash operator \ in Matlab are explained on page 67.

```
n = 5; x = ones(n,1); A = unidrnd(40,n,n); b = A*x;
[L,U] = lu(A);
x1 = L\(U\b);
[L,U,P] = lu(A);
x2 = U\(L\P*b);
x3 = A \ b;
```

The output produced is given below. We observe that x1, which is computed without taking into consideration the permutation, produces a wrong result.

```
disp([x1 x2 x3])

    17.2973      1.0000      1.0000
     4.0528      1.0000      1.0000
   -19.1852      1.0000      1.0000
    -5.4929      1.0000      1.0000
   -11.7563      1.0000      1.0000
```

If the system has to be solved several times for different right-hand-side vectors, the factorization has to be computed only once.

```
n = 300; R = 1000; A = unidrnd(40,n,n); B = unidrnd(50,n,R);
tic
X = zeros(n,R);
[L,U,P] = lu(A);
for k = 1:R
    X(:,k) = U\(L\P*B(:,k));
end
toc
```

The corresponding output is:[2]

```
Elapsed time is 17.596900 seconds.
```

Note that this can be coded in a more efficient way by applying the permutation to the whole matrix in one step and by overwriting B with the solution. The matrices A and B are taken from the previous code.

```
tic
[L,U,P] = lu(A);
B = P*B;
for k = 1:R
    B(:,k) = U\(L\B(:,k));
end
toc
```

```
Elapsed time is 0.836405 seconds.
```

According to the elapsed time, we have an improvement of about 20 times. However, the most efficient way to code the problem is to apply the backslash operator to the right-hand matrix. This is about 135 times faster than our initial code.

---

[2] The Matlab command tic starts a stopwatch timer and toc reads the timer.

```
tic
X = A \ B;
toc
```

```
Elapsed time is 0.129231 seconds.
```

3.1.3. Cholesky factorization

If the matrix A is symmetric and positive-definite, we use the Cholesky factorization. A matrix $A \in \mathbb{R}^{n \times n}$ is positive-definite if for any vector $x \in \mathbb{R}^n$, $x \neq 0$, we have $x'Ax > 0$. This is, among others, the case for $A = X'X$ with matrix X having full column rank, a very frequent situation in econometric and statistical analysis.

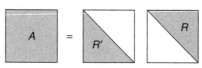

This factorization necessitates fewer computations as it produces only one triangular matrix R. Its operation count is $1/3\,n^3 + n^2 + 8/3\,n - 2$ flops. To solve a linear system $Ax = b$, we again replace A by its factorization $R'R$ and proceed with the forward and back-substitutions as done with the LU factorization.

The Cholesky decomposition is also appropriate to test numerically whether a matrix A is positive-definite. In Matlab this is done by calling the function chol which computes the Cholesky factorization with two output arguments [R,p] = chol(A). If the function returns $p \neq 0$, the submatrix A(1:p-1,1:p-1) is positive-definite. The following Matlab code illustrates the use of the Cholesky factorization for the solution of a linear system with a symmetric and positive-definite coefficient matrix A.

```
n = 5; m = 20;
X = unidrnd(50,n,n); A = X'*X; x = ones(n,1); b = A*x;
[R,p] = chol(A);
if p > 0, error('A not positive-definite'); end
x1 = R\(R'\b);
```

The Cholesky factorization can also be used to generate very cheaply multivariate random variables. A random vector x with given desired variance–covariance matrix Σ is generated with the product

$$x = R'u,$$

where $R'R = \Sigma$ is the Cholesky factorization and $u \sim N(0, I)$ is an i.i.d. normal vector. The variance–covariance matrix of x then satisfies (see Section 7.1.1)

$$E(xx') = E(R'\underbrace{uu'}_{I}R) = R'R = \Sigma.$$

The **Matlab** code given below generates 1000 observations of three normally distributed vectors with variance–covariance Q and then re-estimates their variance–covariance matrix.[3]

```
Q = [400   40  -20
      40   80  -10
     -20  -10  300];
[R,p] = chol(Q);
if p ~= 0, error('Q not positive-definite'); end
n = 1000; U = randn(3,n);
Z = R'*U;
disp(fix(cov(Z')))
```

```
 407    42   -33
  42    82   -15
 -33   -15   284
```

The Cholesky algorithm

In order to explain how the Cholesky matrix can be computed, we consider the jth step in the factorization $A = GG'$, where the first $j - 1$ columns of G are already known. In the following scheme the light gray area corresponds to the elements already computed and the dark one to the elements computed at step j. (The unknown element G_{jj} has been left uncolored.)

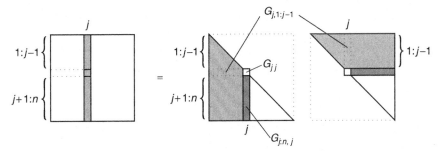

Column j of the product then corresponds to a combination of the j columns of matrix $G_{1:n,1:j}$, that is,

$$A_{1:n,j} = \sum_{k=1}^{j} G_{jk} \, G_{1:n,k}$$

from where we can isolate

$$G_{jj} \, G_{1:n,j} = A_{1:n,j} - \sum_{k=1}^{j-1} G_{jk} \, G_{1:n,k} \equiv v$$

---

[3] Note that the smaller the value n, the larger the deviations between the variance–covariance matrix of the data-generating process and the empirical variance–covariance matrix will become.

and as $G_{1:n,1:j-1}$ is known, we can compute v. We then consider the expression $G_{jj}\, G_{1:n,j} = v$; the components of vector $G_{1:j-1,j}$ are zero as G is a lower triangular matrix. Element j of this vector is $G_{jj}\, G_{jj} = v_j$ from where we get that $G_{jj} = \sqrt{v_j}$. The solution for vector $G_{j:n,j}$ is then

$$G_{j:n,j} = v_{j:n} / \sqrt{v_j}$$

from which we can derive the following algorithm:

---

for $j = 1 : n$ **do**
$\quad v_{j:n} = A_{j:n,j}$
$\quad$ **for** $k = 1 : j - 1$ **do**
$\quad\quad v_{j:n} = v_{j:n} - G_{jk}\, G_{j:n,k}$
$\quad$ **end for**
$\quad G_{j:n,j} = v_{j:n} / \sqrt{v_j}$
end for

It is possible to formulate the algorithm so as to overwrite the lower triangle of matrix A by matrix G. Given a positive-definite matrix $A \in \mathbb{R}^{n \times n}$ Algorithm 3 computes a lower triangular matrix $G \in \mathbb{R}^{n \times n}$ such that $A = GG'$. For $i \geq j$, this algorithm overwrites A_{ij} by G_{ij}.

Algorithm 3   Cholesky factorization.

1: $A_{1:n,1} = A_{1:n,1} / \sqrt{A_{11}}$
2: **for** $j = 2 : n$ **do**
3: $\quad A_{j:n,j} = A_{j:n,j} - A_{j:n,1:j-1}\, A'_{j,1:j-1}$
4: $\quad A_{j:n,j} = A_{j:n,j} / \sqrt{A_{jj}}$
5: **end for**

The operation count for Algorithm 3 is $1/3\, n^3 + n^2 + 8/3\, n - 2$ flops.

Example 3.1

For illustration purposes, we detail the operation count for Algorithm 3. We have $n + 1$ operations in Statement 1 (n divisions and one square root). For Statement 3, we count:

- $2(n - j + 1)(j - 1)$ operations for the product $A_{j:n,1:j-1}\, A'_{j,1:j-1}$
- $n - j + 1$ operations for the subtraction
- 2 operations for the computation of indices $(j - 1)$

Total for Statement 3 is $2(n - j + 1)(j - 1) + n - j + 1 + 2$ which simplifies to $(n - j + 1)(2(j - 1) + 1) + 2$.

Statement 4 necessitates $(n - j + 1) + 1$ operations ($n - j + 1$ divisions and one square root).

Statements 3 and 4 together total $(n - j + 1)(2(j - 1) + 2) + 3$ operations. To compute the sum of these operations for $j = 2, \ldots, n$, we use Matlab's symbolic computation facilities. To the sum, we add the $n + 1$ operations occurring in Statement 1 and simplify the result.

```
syms n j
fljg1 = symsum((n-j+1)*(2*(j-1)+2)+3,j,2,n);
flops = simplify(fljg1 + n + 1)

flops = 8/3*n-2+1/3*n^3+n^2
```

3.1.4. QR decomposition

If $A \in \mathbb{R}^{m \times n}$ is square or rectangular and has full column rank, we can compute the QR decomposition. The following scheme illustrates the decomposition for a rectangular matrix.

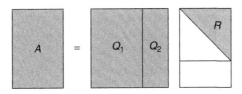

Q is an orthogonal matrix, that is, $Q'Q = I$. In the case matrix A is square, Q_2 vanishes in the partition of Q. R is triangular. The QR decomposition is computationally more expensive; the highest term in the operation count is $4m^2 n$.

To solve a linear system $Ax = b$ we again replace A by its decomposition, multiply the system from the left by Q', and solve the resulting triangular system by back-substitution.

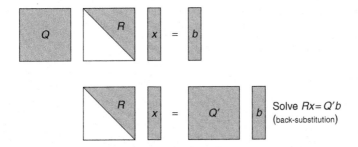

Solve $Rx = Q'b$
(back-substitution)

The Matlab function qr computes the decomposition, and the solution of the triangular system is again coded with the backslash operator.

```
[Q,R] = qr(A);
x = R \ (Q'*b);
```

3.1.5. Singular value decomposition

The numerically most stable decomposition is the singular value decomposition (SVD), but it is also the most expensive computationally ($4\,m^2\,n + 8\,m\,n^2 + 9\,n^3$ flops). Given a matrix $A \in \mathbb{R}^{m\times n}$ this decomposition computes two orthogonal matrices $U \in \mathbb{R}^{m\times m}$ and $V \in \mathbb{R}^{n\times n}$, of left and right singular vectors, respectively, such that

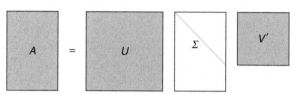

where $\Sigma = \mathrm{diag}(\sigma_1,\dots,\sigma_p) \in \mathbb{R}^{m\times n}$ and $p = \min(m,n)$. The σ_i are called the singular values, and they satisfy $\sigma_1 \geq \sigma_2 \geq \cdots \geq \sigma_p \geq 0$.

This decomposition is among others used to compute the pseudoinverse.[4] An important use of SVD is the computation of the numerical rank of a matrix. This is accomplished by searching the number of singular values greater than a given tolerance. Matlab computes the decomposition with the command [U,S,V] = svd(A). If the function is called with a single output argument, svd returns the vector of singular values. The Matlab function eps with argument x computes the distance from x to the next larger floating point number.

```
s = svd(A);
tol = max(size(A)) * eps(s(1));
rank = sum(s > tol);
```

3.2. Iterative methods

If we ignore rounding errors, a direct method produces an exact solution after a number of finite and known elementary operations. In contrast, iterative methods generate a sequence of approximations to the solution in an infinite number of operations. However, in practice, the approximation is satisfactory after a relatively small number of iterations.

Iterative methods simply proceed by matrix vector products and are, therefore, very easy to program. Given that the complexity of direct methods is $\mathscr{O}(n^3)$, there is a limit for the size of manageable problems. However, large systems are generally sparse, that is, only a small fraction of the n^2 elements is nonzero. In such situations an iterative method can very easily exploit this sparse structure by simply taking into account the nonzero elements in the matrix vector product.[5] However, this comes with the inconvenience

---

[4] See page 66.

[5] Nowadays, direct methods exist that efficiently exploit a sparse structure. However, their implementation is more complex.

that efficiency depends on the speed of convergence, which is generally not guaranteed.

If we use an iterative method to solve a sparse system, we have to verify the existence of a normalization of the equations. This corresponds to the existence of a permutation of the rows and columns of the matrix such that all elements on the diagonal are nonzero. The problem of finding a normalization in a sparse matrix is discussed in Section 3.3.3.

Iterative methods can be partitioned into two classes, stationary methods relying on information remaining invariant from iteration to iteration and nonstationary methods relying on information from the previous iteration. Stationary iterative methods go back to Gauss, Liouville, and Jacobi whereas nonstationary methods, also often referred to as Krylov subspace methods, have been developed from around 1980. An overview can be found in Barrett et al. (1994) and Saad (1996). They are among the most efficient methods available for large[6] sparse linear systems. The following presentation focuses on stationary iterative methods only.

3.2.1. Jacobi, Gauss–Seidel, and SOR

Given a linear system $Ax = b$, we choose a normalization,[7] indicated in gray below,

$$
\begin{aligned}
a_{11}\, x_1 + a_{12}x_2 + a_{13}x_3 &= b_1 \\
a_{21}x_1 + a_{22}\, x_2 + a_{23}x_3 &= b_2 \\
a_{31}x_1 + a_{32}x_2 + a_{33}\, x_3 &= b_3,
\end{aligned}
$$

isolate the variables associated to the normalization and rewrite the system as

$$
\begin{aligned}
x_1 &= (b_1 - a_{12}x_2 - a_{13}x_3)\,/\,a_{11} \\
x_2 &= (b_2 - a_{21}x_1 - a_{23}x_3)\,/\,a_{22} \\
x_3 &= (b_3 - a_{31}x_1 - a_{32}x_2)\,/\,a_{33}.
\end{aligned}
$$

The variables x_i on the right-hand-side are unknown, but we can consider that $x^{(k)}$ is an approximation for the solution of the system, which allows us to compute a new approximation in the following way:

$$
\begin{aligned}
x_1^{(k+1)} &= \left(b_1 - a_{12}x_2^{(k)} - a_{13}x_3^{(k)}\right)/a_{11} \\
x_2^{(k+1)} &= \left(b_2 - a_{21}x_1^{(k)} - a_{23}x_3^{(k)}\right)/a_{22} \\
x_3^{(k+1)} &= \left(b_3 - a_{31}x_1^{(k)} - a_{32}x_2^{(k)}\right)/a_{33}.
\end{aligned}
$$

---

[6] Allowing an efficient solution of a system of equations going into the order of millions of variables.

[7] For large and sparse matrices with irregular structure, it might not be trivial to find a normalization. For a discussion see Gilli and Garbely (1996).

This defines the Jacobi iteration that is formalized with the pseudocode given in Algorithm 4.

Algorithm 4   Jacobi iteration.

1: give initial solution $x^{(0)} \in \mathbb{R}^n$
2: **for** $k = 0, 1, 2, \ldots$ `until` convergence **do**
3:    **for** $i = 1 : n$ **do**
4:       $x_i^{(k+1)} = \left(b_i - \sum_{j \neq i} a_{ij} x_j^{(k)} \right) / a_{ii}$
5:    **end for**
6: **end for**

If we use the computed approximation on the left-hand-side as soon as it is available in the succeeding equations, we have the Gauss–Seidel iteration

$$x_1^{(k+1)} = \left(b_1 - a_{12} x_2^{(k)} \qquad - a_{13} x_3^{(k)} \right) / a_{11}$$

$$x_2^{(k+1)} = \left(b_2 - a_{21}\, x_1^{(k+1)} - a_{23} x_3^{(k)} \right) / a_{22}$$

$$x_3^{(k+1)} = \left(b_3 - a_{31} x_1^{(k+1)} - a_{32} x_2^{(k+1)} \right) / a_{33}.$$

With the Gauss–Seidel iteration, we do not need to store the past and current solution vector as we can successively overwrite the past solution vector x with the current solution. The corresponding pseudocode is given in Algorithm 5 where we also sketch how the solution vector is successively overwritten. For $j < i$, the elements in array x have already been overwritten by the newly computed $x_j^{(k+1)}$ and for $j > i$, the elements correspond to the $x_j^{(k)}$ of the previous iteration.

Algorithm 5   Gauss–Seidel iteration.

1: give initial solution $x \in \mathbb{R}^n$
2: **while** not converged **do**
3:    **for** $i = 1 : n$ **do**
4:       $x_i = \left(b_i - \sum_{j \neq i} a_{ij} x_j \right) / a_{ii}$
5:    **end for**
6: **end while**

Successive overrelaxation

The convergence of the Gauss–Seidel method can be improved by modifying Statement 4 in the Gauss–Seidel algorithm in the following way

$$x_i^{(k+1)} = \omega\, x_{GS,i}^{(k+1)} + (1 - \omega) x_i^{(k)}, \tag{3.1}$$

where $x_{GS,i}^{(k+1)}$ is the value of $x_i^{(k+1)}$ computed with a Gauss–Seidel step and ω is the relaxation parameter. Hence, successive overrelaxation (SOR) is a linear combination of a Gauss–Seidel step and the past SOR step.

We will now show how the SOR iteration (3.1) can be simplified. Indeed, it is not necessary to explicitly compute the Gauss–Seidel solution $x_{GS,i}^{(k+1)}$. We recall the generic Gauss–Seidel iteration

$$x_i^{(k+1)} = \left(b_i - \sum_{j=1}^{i-1} a_{ij} x_j^{(k+1)} - \sum_{j=i+1}^{n} a_{ij} x_j^{(k)} \right) / a_{ii} \qquad (3.2)$$

and the fact that an array x can store the relevant elements of $x^{(k)}$ and $x^{(k+1)}$ simultaneously. We visualize this in the following scheme for the ith component of $x^{(k+1)}$.

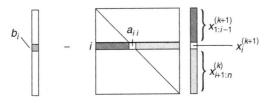

This is the reason why in Statement 4 of Algorithm 5 we drop the upper indices and merge both arrays into a single array and write

$$x_i = \left(b_i - \sum_{j \neq i} a_{ij} x_j \right) / a_{ii}.$$

Expression (3.1) can be rewritten as

$$x_i^{(k+1)} = \omega \left(x_{GS,i}^{(k+1)} - x_i^{(k)} \right) + x_i^{(k)}. \qquad (3.3)$$

We consider the expression $\left(x_{GS,i}^{(k+1)} - x_i^{(k)} \right)$, where we replace $x_{GS,i}^{(k+1)}$ with the expression given in (3.2) and multiply the term $x_i^{(k)}$ on the right by a_{ii}/a_{ii}.

$$x_i^{(k+1)} = \frac{b_i - \sum_{j=1}^{i-1} a_{ij} x_j^{(k+1)} - \sum_{j=i+1}^{n} a_{ij} x_j^{(k)}}{a_{ii}} - \frac{a_{ii} x_i^{(k)}}{a_{ii}}.$$

Including $a_{ii} x_i^{(k)}$ in the second sum, we get

$$x_i^{(k+1)} = \left(b_i - \sum_{j=1}^{i-1} a_{ij} x_j^{(k+1)} - \sum_{j=i}^{n} a_{ij} x_j^{(k)} \right) / a_{ii}$$

and given that $x_i^{(k)}$ and $x_i^{(k+1)}$ can be stored in the same array, (3.3), which is equivalent to (3.1), can be written as

$$x_i = \omega (b_i - A_{i,1:n} x)/a_{ii} + x_i,$$

given that x is initialized with $x^{(k)}$. This is then the generic iteration of the successive overrelaxation method (SOR), which is summarized in Algorithm 6.

Algorithm 6   SOR method.

1: give starting solution $x \in \mathbb{R}^n$
2: **while** not converged **do**
3:     **for** $i = 1 : n$ **do**
4:         $x_i = \omega(b_i - A_{i,1:n}x)/a_{ii} + x_i$
5:     **end for**
6: **end while**

The relaxation parameter ω is defined in the interval $0 < \omega < 2$.[8] We see that SOR is a generalization in which, for $\omega = 1$, we have the Gauss–Seidel method. If $\omega < 1$ we have the damped Gauss–Seidel method which can be used to help establish convergence for diverging iterations. For $\omega > 1$, we have a speedup of convergence.

Illustrations of the application of the SOR method are given in the Example on page 50 and for the pricing of American put options on page 92.

3.2.2. Convergence of iterative methods

The choice of the normalization of the equations influences the convergence behavior of all methods. The order in which the equations are iterated is of importance only for Gauss–Seidel and SOR. For a formal analysis of the convergence, we decompose the coefficient matrix A into the following sum

$$A = L + D + U,$$

where L is lower triangular, D is diagonal, and U is upper triangular. We then generalize the iteration equations as

$$Mx^{(k+1)} = Nx^{(k)} + b.$$

For the different methods, the matrices M and N are
- $M = D$ and $N = -(L + U)$ for Jacobi
- $M = D + L$ and $N = -U$ for Gauss–Seidel
- $M = D + \omega L$ and $N = (1 - \omega)D - \omega U$ for SOR

An iteration scheme then converges if the spectral radius ρ of the matrix $M^{-1}N$ is smaller than 1. It can easily be shown that in the case of the SOR method, the spectral radius of $M^{-1}N$ is smaller than one only if $0 < \omega < 2$.

---

[8] An example about how to explore the optimal value is given on page 50.

To derive this result, we consider that according to the definition of M and N, we have $A = M - N$ and substituting $M - N$ in $Ax = b$ gives $Mx = Nx + b$. Denoting the error at iteration k by $e^{(k)} = x^{(k)} - x$, we write

$$Mx = Nx + b = N\left(x^{(k)} - e^{(k)}\right) + b = \underbrace{Nx^{(k)} + b}_{Mx^{(k+1)}} - Ne^{(k)}$$

$$M\underbrace{(x^{(k+1)} - x)}_{e^{(k+1)}} = Ne^{(k)}$$

$$e^{(k+1)} = M^{-1}Ne^{(k)} = (M^{-1}N)^k e^{(0)},$$

and we know that $(M^{-1}N)^k \to 0$ if and only if $\rho(M^{-1}N) < 1$.

Often, this condition is not practical as it involves much more computation than the original problem of solving the linear problem. However, in situations where the linear system has to be solved repeatedly, it is worthwhile to search the optimal value for the relaxation parameter ω. Such a search is illustrated in the example given on page 50.

There are a few cases in which convergence is guaranteed. For Jacobi, diagonal dominance[9] is a sufficient condition to converge. For Gauss–Seidel, we can show that the iterations always converge if matrix A is symmetric positive-definite.

3.2.3. General structure of algorithms for iterative methods

Iterative methods converge after an infinite number of iterations, and therefore, we must provide a stopping criterion. In general, iterations will be stopped if the changes in the solution vector, that is, the error, become sufficiently small. As already suggested in Section 2.2, we choose a combination between absolute and relative error, that is, we stop the iterations if the following condition is satisfied

$$\frac{|x_i^{(k+1)} - x_i^{(k)}|}{|x_i^{(k)}| + 1} < \varepsilon \qquad i = 1, 2, \ldots, n,$$

where ε is a given tolerance. An implementation of this condition with Matlab is given with the function `converged`. Moreover, it is good practice

---

[9] A matrix $A \in \mathbb{R}^{n \times n}$ is strictly diagonal dominant if

$$|a_{ii}| > \sum_{\substack{j=1 \\ j \neq i}}^{n} |a_{ij}| \quad i = 1, \ldots, n$$

hence satisfying

$$\rho(M^{-1}N) \leq \| D^{-1}(L+U) \|_\infty = \max_{1 \leq i \leq n} \sum_{\substack{j=1 \\ j \neq i}}^{n} \left| \frac{a_{ij}}{a_{ii}} \right| < 1.$$

to prevent the algorithm from exceeding a given maximum number of iterations. This is done in Statement 5 in Algorithm 7.

Algorithm 7   General structure of iterative methods.

1: initialize $x^{(1)}$, $x^{(0)}$, ε and `maxit`
2: **while** not$\big($converged$(x^{(0)}, x^{(1)}, \varepsilon)\big)$ **do**
3:     $x^{(0)} = x^{(1)}$ # Store previous iteration in $x^{(0)}$
4:     compute $x^{(1)}$ with Jacobi, Gauss–Seidel, or SOR
5:     stop if number of iterations exceeds `maxit`
6: **end while**

Listing 3.1. C-LinEqsLSP/M/converged.m

```
1 function  res = converged(x0,x1,tol)
2 % converged.m  -- version 2007-08-10
3 res = all( abs(x1-x0) ./ (abs(x0) + 1) < tol );
```

Note that, as mentioned earlier, the convergence of Jacobi iterations is sensitive to the normalization of the equations, whereas the convergence of Gauss–Seidel iterations is sensitive to the normalization and the ordering of the equations. In general, no practical method for checking the convergence of either method exists.

Example 3.2

We give an example about how to solve a linear system with the SOR method. We set a seed for the random generator and generate a matrix X from which we compute A which is positive-definite by construction. The optimal value for the relaxation parameter ω is computed with the Matlab code `OmegaGridSearch.m`. First, the SOR method, given in the code `SOR.m`, is executed for $\omega = 1$, which corresponds to a Gauss–Seidel iteration. Second, the optimal value for ω is used in the input for the SOR. The number of iterations for each execution is printed, and we observe the faster convergence when we use the optimal value for SOR.

Figure 3.1 shows the graphic produced by the function `OmegaGridSearch.m` and we observe that $\omega \approx 1.17$ minimizes the spectral radius of $M^{-1}N$, which governs the convergence of the SOR method.

```
randn('state',999);
n = 100; m = 30; X = [ones(n,1) randn(n,m-1)]; A = X'*X;
x = ones(m,1);  b = A*x; x1 = 2*x;
maxit = 80; tol = 1e-4;
wopt = OmegaGridSearch(A);
omega = 1;
[sol1,nit1] = SOR(x1,A,b,omega,tol,maxit);
omega = wopt;
[sol2,nit2] = SOR(x1,A,b,omega,tol,maxit);
fprintf('\n  nit1 = %i   nit2 = %i\n',nit1,nit2);

nit1 = 14   nit2 = 10
```

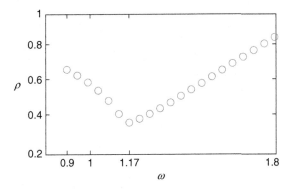

Figure 3.1 Grid search for optimal ω.

Listing 3.2. C-LinEqsLSP/M/OmegaGridSearch.m

```
1  function [w,r] = OmegaGridSearch(A,winf,wsup,npoints)
2  % OmegaGridSearch.m  -- version  2010-10-28
3  % Grid search for optimal relaxation parameter
4  if nargin == 1, npoints = 21;  winf = .9; wsup = 1.8; end
5  D = diag(diag(A)); L = tril(A,-1); U = triu(A,1);
6  omegavec = linspace(winf,wsup,npoints);
7  for k = 1:npoints
8      w = omegavec(k);
9      M = D + w*L;
10     N = (1-w)*D - w*U;
11     v = eig(inv(M)*N);
12     s(k) = max(abs(v));
13 end
14 [smin,i] = min(s);
15 w = omegavec(i);
16 plot(omegavec,s,'o','MarkerSize',5,'Color',[.5 .5 .5])
17 set(gca,'xtick',[winf 1 w wsup]);
18 ylabel('\rho','Rotation',0); xlabel('\omega')
19 if nargout == 2, r = smin; end
```

Listing 3.3. C-LinEqsLSP/M/SOR.m

```
1  function [x1,nit] = SOR(x1,A,b,omega,tol,maxit)
2  % SOR.m  -- version 2010-10-25
3  % SOR for Ax = b
4  if nargin == 3, tol=1e-4; omega=1.2; maxit=70; end
5  it = 0; n = length(x1); x0 = -x1;
6  while ~converged(x0,x1,tol)
7      x0 = x1;
8      for i = 1:n
9          x1(i) = omega*( b(i)-A(i,:)*x1 ) / A(i,i) + x1(i);
10     end
11     it=it+1; if it>maxit, error('Maxit in SOR'), end
12 end
13 if nargout == 2, nit = it; end
```

3.2.4. Block iterative methods

Certain sparse systems of equations can be rearranged such that the coefficient matrix A has an almost block diagonal structure, that is, with relatively dense matrices on the diagonal and very sparse matrices off-diagonal. In economic analysis, this is the case for multi-country macroeconomic models in which the different country models are linked together by a relatively small number of trade relations.

A block iterative method is then a technique where one iterates over the subsystems defined by the block diagonal decomposition. The technique to solve the subsystems is free and not relevant for the discussion.

Let us consider a linear system $Ax = b$ and a partition of A in the form

$$
A = \begin{bmatrix}
A_{11} & A_{12} & \cdots & A_{1N} \\
A_{21} & A_{22} & \cdots & A_{2N} \\
\vdots & \vdots & & \vdots \\
A_{N1} & A_{N2} & \cdots & A_{NN}
\end{bmatrix},
$$

where the diagonal blocks A_{ii}, $i = 1,\dots,N$ are square. Writing the system $Ax = b$ under the same partitioned form, we have

$$
\begin{bmatrix}
A_{11} & \cdots & A_{1N} \\
\vdots & \vdots & \vdots \\
A_{N1} & \cdots & A_{NN}
\end{bmatrix}
\begin{bmatrix}
x_1 \\
\vdots \\
x_N
\end{bmatrix}
=
\begin{bmatrix}
b_1 \\
\vdots \\
b_N
\end{bmatrix}
\quad \text{or} \quad \sum_{j=1}^{N} A_{ij} x_j = b_i \quad i = 1,\dots,N.
$$

If the matrices A_{ii}, $i = 1,\dots,N$ are nonsingular, Algorithm 8 can be applied. As mentioned earlier, the linear system in Statement 4 can be solved with any method.

Algorithm 8   Block Jacobi method.

1: give initial solution $x^{(0)} \in \mathbb{R}^n$
2: **for** $k = 0,1,2,\dots$ until convergence **do**
3:    **for** $i = 1 : N$ **do**
4:       solve $\quad A_{ii} x_i^{(k+1)} = b_i - \displaystyle\sum_{\substack{j=1 \\ j \neq i}}^{N} A_{ij} x_j^{(k)}$
5:    **end for**
6: **end for**

Modifying Statement 4 in Algorithm 8 in the following way,

$$
\text{solve} \quad A_{ii} x_i^{(k+1)} = b_i - \sum_{j=1}^{i-1} A_{ij} x_j^{(k+1)} - \sum_{j=i+1}^{N} A_{ij} x_j^{(k)},
$$

leads to the block Gauss–Seidel method.

There exist many variants of block methods according to the choice of the decomposition and the way the block is solved. A particular variant consists of choosing $N = 2$ with A_{11} being a lower triangular matrix, that is, easy to solve, and A_{22} arbitrary but of significantly smaller size, which will be solved with a direct method.

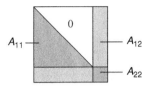

In such a situation, the variables in A_{22} are called minimal feedback vertex set.[10] If the systems in Statement 4 are solved only approximatively, the method is called incomplete inner loops.

As explained for the iterative methods on page 48, the convergence of the block iterative methods depends on the spectral radius of matrix $M^{-1}N$.

3.3. Sparse linear systems

Any matrix with a sufficient number of zero elements such that there is a gain from avoiding redundant operations and storage is a sparse matrix. Very large but sparse linear systems arise in many practical problems in economics and finance. This is, for instance, the case when we discretize partial differential equations. These problems cannot be solved without resorting to appropriate algorithms.

3.3.1. Tridiagonal systems

A simple case of a sparse system is a linear system with a banded matrix of bandwidth $bw = 1$ ($a_{ij} = 0$ if $|i - j| > bw$). Such a matrix is termed tridiagonal, and its storage necessitates only three arrays of length n respectively $n - 1$. The LU factorization of a tridiagonal matrix A can be readily derived by sequentially developing the product $LU = A$

$$
\underbrace{\begin{bmatrix} 1 & & & & \\ \ell_1 & 1 & & & \\ & \ell_2 & 1 & & \\ & & \ell_3 & 1 & \\ & & & \ell_4 & 1 \end{bmatrix}}_{L}
\underbrace{\begin{bmatrix} u_1 & r_1 & & & \\ & u_2 & r_2 & & \\ & & u_3 & r_3 & \\ & & & u_4 & r_4 \\ & & & & u_5 \end{bmatrix}}_{U}
=
\underbrace{\begin{bmatrix} d_1 & q_1 & & & \\ p_1 & d_2 & q_2 & & \\ & p_2 & d_3 & q_3 & \\ & & p_3 & d_4 & q_4 \\ & & & p_4 & d_5 \end{bmatrix}}_{A}.
$$

Algorithm 9 details the factorization of a tridiagonal matrix A with p_i, $i = 1, \ldots, n - 1$ for the lower diagonal, d_i, $i = 1, \ldots, n$ for the main diagonal,

---

[10] See Gilli (1992) for more details.

and q_i, $i = 1, \ldots, n - 1$ for the upper diagonal. We verify that $r_i = q_i$, $i = 1, \ldots, n - 1$ and only the lower diagonal of L and the main diagonal of U have to be computed. The operation count for Algorithm 9 is $4n - 4$ flops.

Algorithm 9   Factorization of tridiagonal matrix.

1: $u_1 = d_1$
2: **for** $i = 2 : n$ **do**
3:     $\ell_{i-1} = p_{i-1}/u_{i-1}$
4:     $u_i = d_i - \ell_{i-1} q_{i-1}$
5: **end for**

Forward and back-substitution for these particular triangular systems are given in Algorithm 10. Given the lower diagonal ℓ, the diagonal u, and the upper diagonal q, the algorithm overwrites the right-hand-side vector b with the solution. The operation count is $7n - 5$ flops.

Algorithm 10   Forward and back-substitution for tridiagonal system.

1: give ℓ, u, q and b
2: **for** $i = 2 : n$ **do**
3:     $b_i = b_i - \ell_{i-1} b_{i-1}$
4: **end for**
5: $b_n = b_n/u_n$
6: **for** $i = n - 1 : -1 : 1$ **do**
7:     $b_i = (b_i - q_i b_{i+1})/u_i$
8: **end for**

Example 3.3

We generate a tridiagonal linear system of size $n = 500$ and solve it $m = 100,000$ times using first Matlab's built-in sparse matrix computations facilities, and then using the sparse code lu3diag.m and solve3diag.m. We observe that execution speed is slightly in favor of the sparse Matlab code, but with respect to the complexity of the built-in code, the suggested implementation is very simple.

```
n = 500; m = 100000;
c = (1:n+1) / 3; d = ones(n,1); x = ones(n,1);
p = -c(2:n); q = c(1:n-1);
A = spdiags([[p NaN]' d [NaN q]'],-1:1,n,n);
b = A*x;
%
tic
[L,U] = lu (A);
for k = 1:m
    s1 = U\ (L\b);
end
```

```
fprintf('\n Sparse Matlab %i (sec)',fix(toc));
tic
[l,u] = lu3diag(p,d,q);
for k = 1:m
    s2 = solve3diag(l,u,q,b);
end
fprintf('\n   Sparse code %i (sec)\n',fix(toc));
```

```
Sparse Matlab 5 (sec)
  Sparse code 9 (sec)
```

Listing 3.4. C-LinEqsLSP/M/solve3diag.m

```
 1  function b = solve3diag(l,u,q,b)
 2  % solve3diag.m  -- version 1999-05-11
 3  % Back and forward substitution for tridiagonal system
 4  n = length(b);
 5  for i = 2:n
 6      b(i) = b(i) - l(i-1) * b(i-1);
 7  end
 8  b(n) = b(n) / u(n);
 9  for i = n-1:-1:1
10      b(i) = ( b(i) - q(i) * b(i+1) ) / u(i);
11  end
```

3.3.2. Irregular sparse matrices

There exist different storage schemes, the choice of which is problem dependent. Matlab stores the nonzero elements of a matrix column wise. For a matrix A with $n = 3$ columns and containing $nnz = 4$ nonzero elements, Matlab uses the following representation:

$$A = \begin{bmatrix} 0 & 1 & 0 \\ 2 & 0 & 3 \\ 4 & 0 & 0 \end{bmatrix}$$

Columns
1 2 3

Column pointers: | 1 | 3 | 4 | × | $n+1$

1 2 3 4

Row index: | 2 | 3 | 1 | 2 | nnz

Elements: | 2 | 4 | 1 | 3 | nnz

This storage scheme needs $n+1$ integers for the column pointers, nnz integers for the row indices, and nnz real numbers for the matrix elements.

An integer number is represented with 4 bytes and a real number with 8 bytes. The total amount of bytes to store a matrix with n columns and nnz nonzero elements is then $12\,nnz + 4\,n + 4$ bytes.[11]

---

[11] Matlab's whos function might return a larger number due to automatic preallocation of storage space.

Sparse matrices in **Matlab**

The conversion to a sparse matrix is not automatic in **Matlab**. The user must execute an explicit command. However, once initialized, the sparse storage is propagated, that is, an operation with a sparse matrix produces a sparse result, except for addition and subtraction. The conversion is obtained with the functions `sparse` and `full`.

```
A = [0 1 0; 2 0 3; 4 0 0];
B = sparse(A)
C = full(B)
B =
    (2,1)        2
    (3,1)        4
    (1,2)        1
    (2,3)        3
C =
    0      1      0
    2      0      3
    4      0      0
```

It would not be practical to create a sparse matrix by converting a full matrix. Therefore, it is possible to create a sparse matrix directly by specifying the list of nonzero elements and their corresponding indices. The command

```
S = sparse(i,j,e,m,n,nzmax);
```

creates a sparse matrix S of size $m \times n$ with $S_{i(k),j(k)} = s(k)$ with preallocated memory for `nzmax` elements. The preallocation of memory is a good practice to speed up the code but is not mandatory. In the example below, we code the 3×3 matrix A given above without preallocating memory.

```
i = [2 3 1 2]; j = [1 1 2 3]; e = [2 4 1 3];
S = sparse(i,j,e,3,3);
[i,j,e] = find(S)
i =
    2
    3
    1
    2
j =
    1
    1
    2
    3
e =
    2
    4
    1
    3
```

Note that if a matrix element appears more than once in the list, it is not overwritten, but the elements are summed.

Particular sparse matrices can be created with the commands `speye`, `spdiags`, `sprandn`, etc. The command `help sparfun` lists the functions which are specific to sparse matrices.

3.3.3. Structural properties of sparse matrices

For sparse matrices we can investigate certain properties depending only on the sparsity structure, that is, the information about what elements are different from zero regardless of their numerical value. This analysis is particularly relevant for irregular sparse matrices where zero elements can be present on the main diagonal. In order to analyze these properties, it is convenient to associate an incidence matrix to the matrix under consideration. The incidence matrix M of a matrix A is defined as

$$m_{ij} = \begin{cases} 1 & \text{if } a_{ij} \neq 0 \\ 0 & \text{otherwise} \end{cases}.$$

In the following, the structural properties are investigated by analyzing the incidence matrix.

Structural rank

Recall that the determinant of a square matrix $M \in \mathbb{R}^{n \times n}$ can be formalized as

$$\det M = \sum_{p \in P} \text{sign}(p) m_{1p_1} m_{2p_2} \cdots m_{np_n}, \tag{3.4}$$

where P is the set of $n!$ permutations of the elements of the set $\{1, 2, \ldots, n\}$ and $\text{sign}(p)$ is a function taking the values $+1$ and -1. From Eq. (3.4) we readily conclude that a necessary condition for the determinant being nonzero is the existence of at least one nonzero product in the summation, which then corresponds to the existence of n nonzero elements in M, each row and column containing exactly one of these elements. This is equivalent to the existence of a permutation of the columns of M such that all elements on the main diagonal are nonzero. Such a set of elements is called a normalization of the equations or a matching. For more details see Gilli (1992) or Gilli and Garbely (1996). So, the existence of a normalization is a necessary condition for a matrix being nonsingular.

The Matlab function `dmperm`[12] searches a matching W of maximal cardinality. The command `p = dmperm(M)` returns an array p defined as $p_i = j$ if $m_{ij} \in W$ and 0 elsewhere. For a complete matching, that is, of cardinality n, the permutation `M(p,:)` produces a matrix with nonzero elements on the diagonal.

---

[12] This function implements the algorithm by Dulmage and Mendelsohn (1963).

The maximum cardinality of a matching is called the structural rank of a matrix and corresponds to the number of nonzero elements returned by dmperm. The Matlab function sprank computes this number as

```
r = sum(dmperm(M) > 0);
```

Block triangular decomposition

A sparse matrix might be decomposable, that is, there exists a permutation of the rows and columns such that the matrix has a block triangular shape with each matrix on the diagonal being square and indecomposable. If such a decomposition does not exist, the matrix is indecomposable. For a decomposable matrix, we can solve the subsystems recursively. In Fig. 3.2, we present a small example of a decomposable matrix. The Matlab command dmperm computes the row permutation vector p and the column permutation vector q. The vectors r and s contain the row and column pointers for the indecomposable square matrices on the diagonal. The pointers correspond to the starting row/column of a block. So $r_1 = 1$ indicates that the first block starts at row 1 (same for the column) and $r_2 = 2$ indicates that block 2 starts at row/column 2, hence the first block is composed by a single element. This is also the case for blocks 2 to 4. Block 5 then starts at row/column 5 ($r_5 = 5$) and the succeeding block at row/column 9 ($r_6 = 9$), which defines a block of order 4, and so on.

```
[p,q,r,s] = dmperm(A)

p =
    11   9   2   5   12  13  10   1   7   6   3   4   8
q =
     1  13   2   8    3   4  11  12   6   7   9   5  10
```

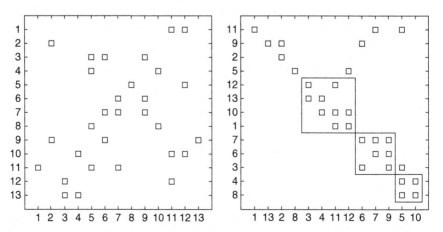

Figure 3.2 Example of a decomposable matrix (left) and its block triangular form (right).

```
r =
    1    2    3    4    5    9   12   14
s =
    1    2    3    4    5    9   12   14
```

`spy(A(p,q))`

The Matlab command `spy` produces a graph of the incidence matrix. In Fig. 3.2, rows and columns are labeled with the vectors p respectively q. In the right panel of the figure, blocks are framed, but frames are not produced by `spy`.

Structurally singular matrices

If a sparse matrix of order n is structurally singular, that is, with structural rank $k < n$, it might be of relevance to know where new nonzero elements have to be introduced in order to increase its rank. It can be shown (Gilli and Garbely, 1996) that the rows and columns of a structurally singular matrix can be permuted so as to bring out a submatrix of zeros of dimension $v \times w$ with $v + w = 2n - k$. To augment the structural rank, nonzero elements must then be introduced into this submatrix. Below, an example of a matrix of order 8 with structural rank 6. Figure 3.3 exhibits the original matrix and the permutation showing the 6×4 zero submatrix.

```
A = sparse(8,8);
A(1,1:5) = 1;       A(2,[3 6]) = 1;
A(3,[3 7]) = 1;     A(4,[1 2 4 6 7 8]) = 1;
A(5,[5 6]) = 1;     A(6,[6 7]) = 1;
A(7,[3 7]) = 1;     A(8,[3 5]) = 1;
[p,q,r,s] = dmperm(A)
p =
    1    4    2    5    6    3    7    8
q =
    4    8    1    2    3    5    6    7
```

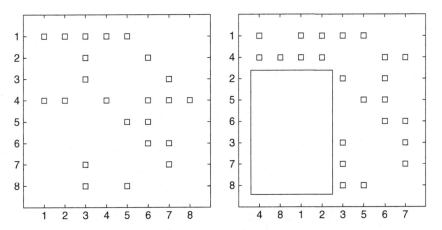

Figure 3.3 Example of a matrix of order 8 with structural rank 6 and the corresponding 6×4 zero submatrix (right panel).

```
r =
     1    3    9
s =
     1    5    9

spy(A(p,q))
```

3.4. The Least Squares problem

Fitting a model to observations is among the most fundamental problems in empirical modeling. We will discuss the case in which the number of observations is greater than the number of parameters. According to the choice of the model, this will involve the solution of a linear system.

The "best" solution can be determined in several ways. Let us recall the usual notation in statistics (and econometrics), where y are the observations of the dependent variable, X the independent variables, and $f(X, \beta)$ the model with β the vector of parameters. The solution chosen then corresponds to the minimization problem

$$\min_{\beta} \| f(X, \beta) - y \|_2^2.$$

In numerical methods, a different notation is used. The problem is written as $Ax = b$, where b are the observations,[13] A the independent variables, and x is the vector of parameters. Such a system with $A \in \mathbb{R}^{m \times n}$, $m > n$ is called an overidentified system. Generally, such a system has no exact solution, and we define the vector of residuals as

$$r = Ax - b.$$

The Least Squares solution is then obtained by solving the following minimization problem

$$\min_{x \in R^n} g(x) = \frac{1}{2} r(x)' r(x) = \frac{1}{2} \sum_{i=1}^{m} r_i(x)^2, \tag{3.5}$$

with $r(x)$ the vector of residuals as a function of the parameters x.

The particular choice of minimizing the Euclidean norm of the residuals is motivated by two reasons: i) in statistics such a solution corresponds, in the case of the classical linear model with i.i.d. residuals, to the best linear unbiased estimator (BLUE); ii) the solution can be obtained with relatively simple and efficient numerical procedures.

The Least Squares approach is attributed to Gauss who in 1795 (at the age of 18) discovered the method. The development of modern numerical

---

[13] Another common notation is $Ax \approx b$ that serves as a reminder that there is, in general, no equality between the left- and right-hand vectors.

procedures for the solution of Least Squares has taken place in the 1960s with the introduction of the QR and SVD decompositions and more recently with the development of methods for large and sparse linear systems.

Often, and particularly for problems arising in statistics and econometrics, we are not only interested in the solution x of the Least Squares problem $Ax = b$ but we also want to compute the variance–covariance matrix $\sigma^2(A'A)^{-1}$. Therefore, we need to evaluate $\|b - Ax\|_2^2$ at the solution as this quantity appears in the evaluation of $\sigma^2 = \|b - Ax\|_2^2/(m-n)$, and we also need an efficient and numerically stable method to compute $(A'A)^{-1}$ or a subset of elements of this matrix.

In the following sections, we will explain how to perform this for the different chosen approaches.

3.4.1. Method of normal equations

The solution for the problem defined in Eq. (3.5) can be obtained in different ways. One way is to derive Eq. (3.5) with respect to x and write the first-order condition for a minimum, that is,

$$2A'Ax - 2A'b = 0,$$

which corresponds to the linear system

$$A'Ax = A'b,$$

called the system of normal equations.

The system of normal equations can also be derived by geometrical considerations. The closest solution b to Ax is given by the orthogonal projection of b into the space generated by the columns of A.

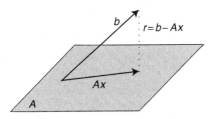

The condition for the projection to be orthogonal is

$$A'r = A'(b - Ax) = 0$$

from where we again obtain the system of normal equations $A'Ax = A'b$.

If the matrix A is of full rank, $A'A$ is positive-definite and the system of normal equations can be solved by resorting to the Cholesky factorization (see Algorithm 11).

Computation of $\|r\|_2^2$

If the sum of residuals $\|r\|_2^2$ is needed, we form the bordered matrix

$$\overline{A} = \begin{bmatrix} A & b \end{bmatrix}$$

and consider the Cholesky factorization of the matrix $\overline{C} = \overline{A}'\overline{A}$,

$$\overline{C} = \begin{bmatrix} C & c \\ c' & b'b \end{bmatrix} = \overline{G}\,\overline{G}' \quad \text{with} \quad \overline{G} = \begin{bmatrix} G & 0 \\ z' & \rho \end{bmatrix}.$$

The solution x and the norm of the residuals are then computed as[14]

$$G'x = z \quad \text{and} \quad \|Ax - b\|_2 = \rho.$$

Computation of $(A'A)^{-1}$

The matrix $S = (A'A)^{-1}$ can be computed avoiding the direct inversion of $A'A$ by considering that

$$\begin{aligned} S &= (A'A)^{-1} \\ &= (GG')^{-1} \\ &= G'^{-1}G^{-1} \end{aligned}$$

which necessitates only the computation of the inverse of a triangular matrix $T = G^{-1}$ and the computation of the lower triangle of the product $T'T$. The inverse T of a lower triangular matrix G is computed as

$$t_{ij} = \begin{cases} 1/g_{ii} & i = j \\ -1/g_{ii} \sum_{k=j}^{i-1} g_{ik} t_{kj} & i \neq j \end{cases}$$

and needs $n^3/3 + 3/2 n^2 - 5/6 n$ elementary operations.[15]

---

[14] To demonstrate this result, we develop the expressions for $\overline{A}'\overline{A}$ and $\overline{G}\,\overline{G}'$

$$\begin{bmatrix} C & c \\ c' & b'b \end{bmatrix} = \begin{bmatrix} G & 0 \\ z' & \rho \end{bmatrix} \begin{bmatrix} G' & z \\ 0 & \rho \end{bmatrix} = \begin{bmatrix} GG' & Gz \\ z'G' & z'z + \rho^2 \end{bmatrix}$$

where we recognize that G corresponds to the Cholesky matrix of $A'A$ and

$$Gz = c \quad \text{and} \quad b'b = z'z + \rho^2.$$

As $r = b - Ax$ is orthogonal to Ax, we have

$$\|Ax\|_2^2 = (r + Ax)'Ax = b'Ax = \underbrace{b'AG'^{-1}}_{z'} z = z'z$$

from which we derive

$$\|Ax - b\|_2^2 = \underbrace{x'A'Ax}_{z'z} - 2\underbrace{b'Ax}_{z'z} + b'b = b'b - z'z = \rho^2.$$

[15] It is also possible to compute matrix S without inverting matrix G (cf. Björck, 1996, p. 119, and Lawson and Hanson, 1974, pp. 67–73).

If only the diagonal elements of S were needed, it would be sufficient to compute the square of the Euclidean norm of the vectors of T, that is,

$$s_{ii} = \sum_{j=i}^{n} t_{ij}^2 \qquad i = 1, 2, \ldots, n.$$

Algorithm 11 summarizes the solution of the Least Squares problem with normal equations.

Algorithm 11   Least Squares with normal equations.

1: compute $C = A'A$ # (only lower triangle needed)

2: form $\overline{C} = \begin{bmatrix} C & A'b \\ b'A & b'b \end{bmatrix}$

3: compute $\overline{G} = \begin{bmatrix} G & 0 \\ z' & \rho \end{bmatrix}$ # (Cholesky matrix)

4: solve $G'x = z$ # (upper triangular system)

5: $\sigma^2 = \rho^2/(m-n)$

6: compute $T = G^{-1}$ # (inversion of triangular matrix)

7: $S = \sigma^2 T'T$ # (variance–covariance matrix)

The method of normal equations is appealing as it relies on simple procedures such as the Cholesky factorization, matrix multiplications and forward and back-substitutions. Moreover, the initial matrix A of dimensions $m \times n$ is compressed into an $n \times n$ matrix which might constitute an advantage in situations where $m \gg n$.

Below a small example with the corresponding results and the Matlab code to solve it with the normal equations approach are given.

Listing 3.5. C-LinEqsLSP/M/ExNormalEquations.m

```
1  % ExNormalEquations.m   -- version 2003-11-12
2  A=[1 1; 1 2; 1 3; 1 4]; b=[2 1 1 1]';
3  [m,n] = size(A);
4  C = A'*A; c = A'*b; bb = b'*b;
5  Cbar = [C c; c' bb];
6  Gbar = chol(Cbar)';
7  G = Gbar(1:2,1:2); z = Gbar(3,1:2)'; rho = Gbar(3,3);
8  x = G'\z
9  sigma2 = rho^2/(m-n)
10 T = trilinv(G);      % Inversion of triangular matrix
11 S = T'*T;
12 Mcov = sigma2*S
```

```
x =
    2.0000
   -0.3000
```

```
sigma2 =
      0.1500
Mcov =
      0.2250   -0.0750
     -0.0750    0.0300
```

The following Matlab code overwrites a lower triangular matrix by its inverse.

Listing 3.6. C-LinEqsLSP/M/trilinv.m

```
1 function L = trilinv(L)
2 % trilinv.m  -- version 1995-03-25
3 for i = 1:length(L(:,1))
4     for j = 1:i-1
5         L(i,j) = -L(i,j:i-1)*L(j:i-1,j) / L(i,i);
6     end
7     L(i,i) = 1/L(i,i);
8 end
```

The diagonal, or single elements of the variance–covariance matrix can be computed with the code

```
for i = 1:n
    s(i) = T(i:n,i)' * T(i:n,i) * sigma2;
end
```

3.4.2. Least Squares via QR factorization

An orthogonal transformation of a vector does not modify its length. This property is exploited when solving the Least Squares problem which necessitates the minimization of the length of the residual vector. For the discussion that follows it is convenient to partition the matrices Q and R of the QR decomposition as shown below.

The length of the vector of residuals r to be minimized is

$$\| \underbrace{Ax - b}_{r} \|_2^2.$$

We replace matrix A by its factorization QR and apply to the vector of residuals r an orthogonal transformation by multiplying it by Q', which gives $\| Q'QRx - Q'b \|_2^2$, and as mentioned earlier, the length of r is not affected. Considering the partition of the matrices Q and R,

$$\left\| \begin{bmatrix} R_1 \\ 0 \end{bmatrix} x - \begin{bmatrix} Q_1' \\ Q_2' \end{bmatrix} b \right\|_2^2,$$

and rewriting the expression, we get

$$\| R_1 x - Q_1' b \|_2^2 + \| Q_2' b \|_2^2.$$

Solving the upper triangular system $R_1 x = Q_1' b$, we obtain the solution x, and the sum of squared residuals $g(x)$ corresponds to $\| Q_2' b \|_2^2$.

In practice, we do not store matrix Q, but the columns are computed bit by bit as they are needed. Note that due to the orthogonality of Q, we have $A'A = R'Q'QR = R'R$, and, therefore, for the computation of $(A'A)^{-1}$, we can proceed as we have done previously for the Cholesky factorization.

We reconsider the same example we used for the normal equations approach and illustrate the solution via the QR factorization.

Listing 3.7. C-LinEqsLSP/M/ExLSQR.m

```
1  % ExLSQR.m  -- version 1995-11-25
2  A=[1 1; 1 2; 1 3; 1 4]; b=[2 1 1 1]';
3  [m,n]  = size(A);
4  [Q,R]  = qr(A);
5  R1 = R(1:n,1:n); Q1 = Q(:,1:n); Q2 = Q(:,n+1:m);
6  x = R1\(Q1'*b)
7  r = Q2'*b;
8  sigma2 = r'*r/(m-n)
9  T = trilinv(R1');
10 S = T'*T;
11 Mcov = sigma2*S
```

```
x =
      2.0000
     -0.3000
sigma2 =
      0.1500
Mcov =
      0.2250    -0.0750
     -0.0750     0.0300
```

3.4.3. Least Squares via SVD decomposition

As is the case for the QR decomposition, we exploit the property that the length of a vector is invariant to orthogonal transformations. The SVD approach can handle situations in which the columns of matrix $A \in \mathbb{R}^{m \times n}$ do not have full rank, that is, the rank r of matrix A satisfies

$r \le p = \min(m, n)$. We have

$$x = V \begin{bmatrix} \Sigma_r^{-1} & 0 \\ 0 & 0 \end{bmatrix} U'b \quad \text{or} \quad x = \sum_{i=1}^{r} \frac{u_i'b}{\sigma_i} v_i, \qquad (3.6)$$

$$\underbrace{\phantom{V \begin{bmatrix} \Sigma_r^{-1} & 0 \\ 0 & 0 \end{bmatrix} U'b}}_{A^+}$$

where the matrices V, Σ, and U are matrices of the singular value decomposition $A = U\Sigma V'$. Matrix A^+ is the so-called pseudoinverse. Denote

$$z = V'x = \begin{bmatrix} z_1 \\ z_2 \end{bmatrix} \quad \text{and} \quad c = U'b = \begin{bmatrix} c_1 \\ c_2 \end{bmatrix},$$

with z_1 and $c_1 \in \mathbb{R}^r$. We now consider the vector of residuals (and its Euclidean norm) and apply an orthogonal transformation to the vector of residuals

$$\| b - Ax \|_2 = \| U'(b - AVV'x) \|_2$$

$$= \left\| \begin{bmatrix} c_1 \\ c_2 \end{bmatrix} - \begin{bmatrix} \Sigma_r & 0 \\ 0 & 0 \end{bmatrix} \begin{bmatrix} z_1 \\ z_2 \end{bmatrix} \right\|_2$$

$$= \left\| \begin{matrix} c_1 - \Sigma_r z_1 \\ c_2 \end{matrix} \right\|_2.$$

The vector x as defined in Eq. (3.6) minimizes the sum of squared residuals given that $c_1 - \Sigma_r z_1 = 0$ and therefore SSR $= \sum_{i=r+1}^{m} (u_i'b)^2$. Note that Eq. (3.6) produces a solution even in the case when the columns of A do not have full rank.

From the singular value decomposition of matrix A, we derive that $(A'A)^{-1} = V\Sigma_r^{-2}V'$, where Σ_r is the square submatrix of Σ. Then, we are able to express particular elements of matrix $S = (A'A)^{-1}$ as

$$s_{ij} = \sum_{k=1}^{n} \frac{v_{ik}v_{jk}}{\sigma_k^2}.$$

Again we consider the example already used for the normal equation approach and the QR factorization to illustrate the solution via the SVD decomposition.

Listing 3.8. C-LinEqsLSP/M/ExLSsvd.m

```
1 % ExLSsvd.m  -- version 1995-11-27
2 A = [1 1; 1 2; 1 3; 1 4]; b = [2 1 1 1]';
3 [m,n] = size(A);
4 [U,S,V] = svd(A);
5 c = U'*b;  c1 = c(1:n);  c2 = c(n+1:m);
6 sv = diag(S);
7 z1 = c1./sv;
8 x = V*z1
```

```
 9 sigma2 = c2'*c2/(m-n)
10 S = V*diag(sv.^(-2))*V';
11 Mcov = sigma2*S
```

```
x =
    2.0000
   -0.3000
sigma2 =
    0.1500
Mcov =
    0.2250   -0.0750
   -0.0750    0.0300
```

3.4.4. Final remarks

The solution via SVD decomposition is the most expensive but also the most accurate numerical procedure to solve the Least Squares problem: an accuracy that is seldom needed in problems related to empirical finance. In modern software, the method of choice for the solution of the Least Squares problem is via QR factorization. However, if $m \gg n$, the normal equations approach necessitates about half the operations and memory space. In Matlab, the backslash operator solves the problem via QR.

The backslash operator in Matlab

Algorithm 12 illustrates how $\backslash$ works with full matrices:

Statement 1 tests whether A is square, Statement 3 verifies if A is lower triangular and Statement 6 tests for the upper triangular case. If the condition in Statement 10 is true, A is symmetric and Statement 13 checks whether A is positive-definite. Finally, in Statement 22, a rectangular matrix A is identified and a Least Squares problem is solved via QR factorization (see Section 3.4.2).

As mentioned previously, one should always avoid to compute the inverse of a matrix. This is approximately twice as expensive as the methods presented to solve linear systems. The solution X of the set of linear systems $AX = I$ corresponds to A^{-1}.

If an inverse appears in an expression, generally, it hides the solution of a linear system. For instance, in the bilinear form $s = q'A^{-1}r$, $A^{-1}r$ is the solution of $Ax = r$, and, therefore, we can code

```
s = q' * (A\r)
```

Algorithm 12 Pseudocode for how $\backslash$ works in **Matlab**.

```
 1: if size(A,1) == size(A,2) then
 2:     % A is square
 3:     if isequal(A,tril(A)) then
 4:         % A is lower triangular
 5:         x = A \ b;                                  # forward substitution on b
 6:     else if isequal(A,triu(A)) then
 7:         % A is upper triangular
 8:         x = A \ b;                                  # back-substitution on b
 9:     else
10:         if isequal(A,A') then
11:             % A is symmetric
12:             [R,p] = chol(A);
13:             if (p == 0) then
14:                 % A is symmetric positive-definite
15:                 x = R \ (R' \ b);                   # forward and back-substitution
16:                 return
17:             end if
18:         end if
19:         [L,U,P] = lu(A);                            # A is a general square matrix
20:         x = U \ (L \(P*b));                         # forward and back-substitution
21:     end if
22: else
23:     % A is rectangular
24:     [Q,R] = qr(A);
25:     x = R \ (Q' * b);                               # back-substitution on Q'b
26: end if
```

## CHAPTER FOUR

Finite difference methods

This chapter is intended as a simple introduction to finite difference methods for financial applications. For a comprehensive introduction about these methods, we suggest[1] Farlow (1982) or Smith (1985).

4.1. An example of a numerical solution

Let us consider the following differential equation

$$\frac{\partial f}{\partial x} = -f(x)/x, \tag{4.1}$$

which is a so-called ordinary differential equation as f is a function of a single variable. Solving a differential equation means finding a function $f(x)$ that satisfies Eq. (4.1). For this simple case, we easily find that the general solution is

$$f(x) = \frac{C}{x}. \tag{4.2}$$

Indeed, the derivative of Eq. (4.2) is $\frac{\partial f}{\partial x} = -\frac{C}{x^2}$ and replacing $f(x)$ in Eq. (4.1), we obtain the expression for the derivative

$$-\frac{\frac{C}{x}}{x} = -\frac{C}{x^2}.$$

The solution (4.2) contains an arbitrary constant C that disappears when we take its first derivative. This means that there exists an infinite choice for C satisfying Eq. (4.1). In order to find a particular solution we have to impose some constraints to Eq. (4.2), as, for instance, that a given point has to belong to it. These are called initial conditions. For example, consider the initial condition $f(2) = 1$, generally written as $x_0 = 2$ and $y_0 = 1$, and from which we derive that $1 = C/2$ and $C = 2$. Below, you find the graph of the particular solution $f(x) = 2/x$.

[1] Presentations of finite difference methods in finance books often lack simplicity.

Numerical Methods and Optimization in Finance
© 2011 Elsevier Inc. All rights reserved.

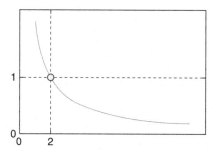

Three approaches can be considered to get the solution of a differential equation:

- Search for an analytical solution; difficult in most situations and, worse, an analytical solution may often not exist.
- Search for an approximation of the analytical solution. Generally, this involves great effort for finally having only an approximation, the precision of which may be hard to evaluate.
- Resort to a numerical approximation, which allows us to easily tackle any differential equation. A numerical method approximates the function satisfying the differential equation in a given finite number of points. Thus, while the analytical solution is a formula, a numerical solution is a table of approximations for given values of the independent variable.

A first numerical approximation

Let us use a numerical method to find the solution for the previous example. By replacing the derivative with a forward approximation, the differential equation $\frac{\partial f}{\partial x} = -f(x)/x$ becomes

$$\frac{f(x + \triangle_x) - f(x)}{\triangle_x} = -f(x)/x$$

from which we get

$$f(x + \triangle_x) = f(x)\left(1 - \frac{\triangle_x}{x}\right).$$

Starting from $x_0 = 2$, where we have $f(x_0) = 1$, we can determine the value of the function at $x_0 + \triangle_x$ numerically. This defines the so-called explicit method.[2] The Matlab code that follows implements this method. In the code, function values $f(x_i)$ are denoted y_i and a constant has been added to the index. The reason for this is that in Matlab, as in some other languages (but not in C), the first element of an array is indexed with 1. In order to enhance the reading of the code, it would be preferable to have x_0 correspond to the address 0. This can be achieved with the following construction:

[2] More generally, a method is called explicit whenever we compute the function value at a grid node directly from other nodes whose values are known.

- define f7=1 (*offset*)
- shift indexing by f7
- x(f7+i) $i = 0, 1, \ldots, N$

i	0	1			N
address	1	2			$N+1$
x	x_0	x_1	$\cdots$	$\cdots$	x_N

Listing 4.1. C-FiniteDifferences/M/ODE1a.m

```
1  % ODE1a.m   -- version 1997-12-09
2  f7  =   1;
3  x0  =   2; y0 = 1;
4  xN  = 10; N  = 10;
5  dx  = (xN - x0)/N;
6  x   = linspace(x0,xN,N+1); y = zeros(1,N+1);
7  y(f7+0) = y0;
8  for i = 1:N
9      y(f7+i) = y(f7+i-1) * ( 1 - dx/x(f7+i-1) );
10 end
```

Figure 4.1 plots the numerical approximation of the solution of the differential equation given in Eq. (4.1) computed with the code ODE1a.m. Note that the solution is computed only for N points. Also, we observe how the precision depends on increasing values of N.

A second numerical approximation

We may also approximate the derivative in the differential equation given in Eq. (4.1) by a central difference

$$\frac{f(x+\triangle_x) - f(x-\triangle_x)}{2\,\triangle_x} = -f(x)/x.$$

Isolating $f(x)$ we get

$$f(x) = \frac{x}{2\,\triangle_x}\Big(f(x-\triangle_x) - f(x+\triangle_x)\Big).$$

To solve this expression, we need to know two points of the solution, that is, $f(x-\triangle_x)$ and $f(x+\triangle_x)$, thus introducing an additional initial condition.

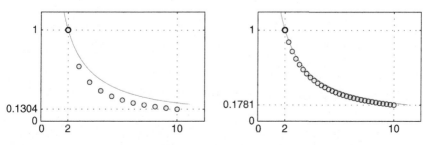

Figure 4.1 Numerical approximation with the explicit method (circles) of the differential equation defined in Eq. (4.1) for $N = 10$ (left panel) and $N = 30$ (right panel).

Let us write the approximation for four successive points (x_1, y_1), (x_2, y_2), (x_3, y_3), and (x_4, y_4):

$$y_1 = x_1(y_0 - y_2)/(2\Delta_x)$$

$$y_2 = x_2(y_1 - y_3)/(2\Delta_x)$$

$$y_3 = x_3(y_2 - y_4)/(2\Delta_x)$$

$$y_4 = x_4(y_3 - y_5)/(2\Delta_x)$$

Note that this is a linear system. In matrix form, we have

$$\begin{bmatrix} 1 & c_1 & & \\ -c_2 & 1 & c_2 & \\ & -c_3 & 1 & c_3 \\ & & -c_4 & 1 \end{bmatrix} \begin{bmatrix} y_1 \\ y_2 \\ y_3 \\ y_4 \end{bmatrix} = \begin{bmatrix} c_1 y_0 \\ 0 \\ 0 \\ -c_4 y_5 \end{bmatrix}$$

with $c_i = x_i/(2\Delta_x)$, and we can solve the system if y_0 and y_5 are known. This method is called the implicit method.[3] In this particular case, the initial condition is easy to determine; for the final condition, we choose zero, as we already know that the function tends to zero. If we are "far enough to the right," the precision of such an approximation is acceptable. The Matlab code that implements the implicit method in which the derivative is approximated with a central difference is given below.[4] The Matlab function spdiags, used in the code, is explained in more details on page 101.

Listing 4.2. C-FiniteDifferences/M/ODE1b.m

```
1  % ODE1b.m  -- version 1997-12-09
2  f7 = 1;
3  x0 = 2;   y0 = 1;   % Initial condition
4  xN = 30;  yN = 0;   % Final condition
5  N  = 30;            % Number of points
6  dx = (xN - x0)/N;
7  x  = linspace(x0,xN,N+1);
8  y(f7+0) = y0;
9  x(f7+0) = x0;
10 for i = 1:N
11     c(i) = x(f7+i)/(2*dx);
12 end
13 A=spdiags([[-c(2:N) NaN]' ones(N,1) [NaN c(1:N-1)]'],-1:1,N,N);
14 b = [c(1)*y0  zeros(1,N-2)  -c(N)*yN]';
15 y(f7+(1:N)) = A\b;
```

Figure 4.2 shows approximations for different final conditions and number of steps. From the two examples, it clearly appears that the choice of the numerical method, as well as the step length, and final conditions for

---

[3] More generally, an implicit method is one in which a node is computed as the solution of a system of equations. The explicit and implicit methods are also called explicit and implicit Euler methods.

[4] An alternative method to solve the tridiagonal linear system of the example is given on page 54.

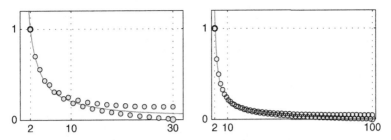

Figure 4.2 Numerical approximation with the implicit method (circles) of the differential equation defined in Eq. (4.1) for $x_N = 30$ and $N = 30$ (left panel) and $x_N = 100$ and $N = 80$ (right panel).

the implicit method, determine the quality of the approximation and the computational complexity. In particular for the implicit method, the smaller the step size, the larger the linear system we have to solve.

4.2. Classification of differential equations

Let $u(x, y)$ be a function of x and y, and let the partial derivatives of u be indicated by subscripts, that is, $u_x \equiv \frac{\partial u(x)}{\partial x}$ and $u_{xy} \equiv \frac{\partial u(x,y)}{\partial x \partial y}$. We distinguish two classes of differential equations:

- Ordinary differential equations (ODE), characterized by a function with a single independent variable
- Partial differential equations (PDE). In this case, the function has several independent variables

Partial differential equations are also classified according to the following criteria (e.g., for a function $u(x, y)$):

- Highest degree of derivative
- Linear function of derivatives with constant coefficients, for example,

$$u_{xx} + \boxed{3}\; u_{xy} + u_{yy} + u_x - u = e^{x-y}$$

- Linear function of derivatives with variable coefficients, for example,

$$\boxed{\sin(xy)}\; u_{xx} + \boxed{3x^2}\; u_{xy} + u_{yy} + u_x - u = 0$$

- Nonlinear function of derivatives, for example,

$$u_{xx} + 3u_{xy} + u_{yy} + \boxed{u_x^2} - u = e^{x-y}$$

A particular class encapsulates linear two-dimensional partial differential equations of degree two, that is, of the form

$$\boxed{a}\; u_{xx} + \boxed{b}\; u_{xy} + \boxed{c}\; u_{yy} + d u_x + e u_y + f u + g = 0,$$

which again, according to the value of the discriminant, is partitioned into

$$b^2 - 4ac \begin{cases} > 0 & \text{hyperbolic equation} \\ = 0 & \text{parabolic equation} \\ < 0 & \text{elliptic equation.} \end{cases}$$

Note that with variable coefficients we can shift from one situation to another. Examples of linear two dimensional PDEs of degree two are follows:

- Hyperbolic PDEs for time processes, for example, wave motion,

$$u_{xx} - u_{tt} = 0.$$

- Parabolic PDEs for propagation, for example, heat propagation,

$$u_t - u_{xx} = 0.$$

- Elliptic PDEs for modeling systems in equilibrium, for example, Laplace equation,

$$u_{xx} + u_{yy} = 0.$$

There are three components when working with a PDE:
- The PDE
- The spatial and temporal domains the PDE has to satisfy
- The initial conditions (at time 0) and the conditions at the boundary of the domain

4.3. The Black–Scholes equation

The Black–Scholes equation is a basic model used to price European style options. The equation writes

$$V_t + \frac{1}{2}\sigma^2 S^2 V_{SS} + (r - q)S V_S - r V = 0,$$

where V is the option price, S and σ are the price and the volatility of the underlying asset, respectively, r is the annualized continuously compounded risk-free rate of return, and q is the annualized continuously compounded yield of the underlying. V_t is the derivative with respect to time. V_S and V_{SS} are the first- and second-order derivatives with respect to the price of the underlying. Time is measured in years.

The Black–Scholes equation is a PDE with the following characteristics:
- Linear with variable coefficients
- First order in time
- Second order in space (that is, the stock price)
- Parabolic PDE ($b = 0$ and $c = 0$ in the discriminant)

One reason for the popularity of the Black–Scholes equation is the existence of an analytical solution. For the call, this solution is

$$C(S,t) = S e^{-q(T-t)} N(d_1) - X e^{-r(T-t)} N(d_2),$$

where X is the exercise or strike price of the option and $N(z) = \frac{1}{\sqrt{2\pi}} \int_{-\infty}^{x} e^{-z^2/2} dz$ is the standard normal cumulative distribution function with the arguments

$$d_1 = \frac{\log(S/X) + (r - q + \sigma^2/2)(T - t)}{\sigma\sqrt{T - t}} \quad \text{and} \quad d_2 = d_1 - \sigma\sqrt{T - t}.$$

Substituting the expression for the call in the put-call parity, we get the solution for the put

$$P(S,t) = C(S,t) - S e^{-q(T-t)} + X e^{-r(T-t)}$$

$$= S e^{-q(T-t)} N(d_1) - X e^{-r(T-t)} N(d_2) - S e^{-q(T-t)} + X e^{-r(T-t)}$$

$$= X e^{-r(T-t)} \left(1 - N(d_2)\right) - S e^{-q(T-t)} \left(1 - N(d_1)\right)$$

$$= X e^{-r(T-t)} N(-d_2) - S e^{-q(T-t)} N(-d_1).$$

The call and put formulæ are implemented in the Matlab code BScall.m and BSput.m. The standard normal cumulative distribution is computed with the Matlab function normcdf. Note that element-by-element multiplications and divisions have been coded so that it will be possible to provide a particular input argument as an array for which the function will then return the corresponding array of prices.

Listing 4.3. C-FiniteDifferences/M/BScall.m

```
1 function C = BScall(S,X,r,q,T,sigma)
2 % BScall.m  -- version  2007-04-05
3 % Pricing of European call with Black-Scholes
4 d1 = (log(S./X) + (r-q+sigma.^2 /2) .* T) ./ (sigma.*sqrt(T));
5 d2 = d1 - sigma .* sqrt(T);
6 C  = S .* exp(-q .* T) .* normcdf(d1) - ...
7      X .* exp(-r .* T) .* normcdf(d2);
```

Listing 4.4. C-FiniteDifferences/M/BSput.m

```
1 function P = BSput(S,X,r,q,T,sigma)
2 % BSput.m  -- version  2004-04-23
3 % Pricing of European put with Black-Scholes
4 d1 = (log(S./X) + (r-q+sigma.^2 /2) .* T) ./ (sigma.*sqrt(T));
5 d2 = d1 - sigma .* sqrt(T);
6 P  =  X .* exp(-r .* T) .* normcdf(-d2) - ...
7       S .* exp(-q .* T) .* normcdf(-d1);
```

```
S = 10; X = 8; r = 0.03; q = 0; sigma = 0.20; T = 2;
C = BScall(S,X,r,q,T,sigma)
```

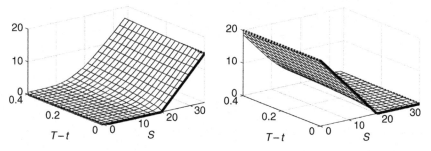

Figure 4.3 Price of call option (left panel) and price of put option (right panel) for $X = 20$, $r = 0.10$, $q = 0$ and $\sigma = 0.60$.

```
C =
    3.3590

P = BSput(S,X,r,q,T,sigma)

P =
    2.5748
```

Figure 4.3 plots the prices computed with the Black–Scholes equation for the call (left panel) and the put (right panel) options as a function of the price S of the underlying asset and the time $T - t$ to maturity. For the remaining parameters we have chosen exercise price $X = 20$, interest rate $r = 10\%$, dividend yield $q = 0$, and volatility $\sigma = 60\%$.

4.3.1. Explicit, implicit, and θ-methods

In the following, the option prices will be computed with a numerical method, and the analytical prices will serve as a benchmark. As already mentioned, in order to apply a numerical method, we need to define the domain, that is, the range of the variables t and S, for which we want to solve the PDE and specify the initial and boundary conditions. In Fig. 4.3, the initial or terminal conditions (see footnote 5), plotted with a solid line, correspond to the option price at expiration. These prices are known exactly. The boundary conditions, plotted in dash dot in Fig. 4.3, correspond to the prices of the option at the limits of the domain defined for S. The numerical method will then approximate the prices on the nodes of a grid which also has to be specified.

4.3.2. Initial and boundary conditions and definition of the grid

The initial and boundary conditions for a European call are

$$V(S,T) = \max(S - X, 0)$$

$$V(0,t) = 0$$
$$\lim_{S \to \infty} V(S,t) = S,$$

while the initial and boundary conditions for a put are

$$V(S,T) = \max(X - S, 0)$$
$$V(0,t) = X e^{-r(T-t)}$$
$$\lim_{S \to \infty} V(S,t) = 0$$

with X as the exercise price.

The space domain is specified by the interval $[S_{\min}, S_{\max}]$ for the underlying and the number N of grid points for which we want to compute the numerical approximation. For the time domain, the elapsed time goes from 0 to T in M steps, but as in a binomial tree, we will walk backward from T to $0.$[5] The length of the space steps is then $\triangle_S = (S_{\max} - S_{\min})/N$, and the length of the time steps is $\triangle_t = T/M$. The numerical approximations of $V(S,t)$ will be (only) computed at the grid points at the following rows and columns

$$S_i = S_{\min} + i \triangle_S \qquad i = 0,\dots,N$$
$$t_j = j \triangle_t \qquad j = 0,\dots,M.$$

The nodes in the grid are denoted v_{ij}, and we also have

$$v_{ij} = V(S_{\min} + i\triangle_S, j\triangle_t), \qquad i = 0,\dots,N, \quad j = 0,\dots,M,$$

the values of $V(S,t)$ at the $(N+1) \times (M+1)$ grid points. The time grid could also have been defined as $t_j = t_0 + j \triangle_t$. However, as we always have $t_0 = 0$, contrarily to $S_{\min}$ for which we can also have $S_{\min} > 0$, we simply write $t_j = j \triangle_t$. Figure 4.4 illustrates the grid.

Terminal conditions correspond to the nodes in dark in column M, and boundary conditions correspond to the gray nodes in row 0 and N. The other (unknown) nodes will be evaluated starting from right (the terminal conditions) to left.

Considering only function evaluations at the grid points v_{ij}, $i = 0,\dots,N$, $j = 0,\dots,M$, we approximate the partial derivatives with respect to time and space in the Black–Scholes equation. The derivative V_t of the option with respect to time is approximated with a backward difference, and the derivative of the option with respect to the stock price is approximated with

---

[5] A typical parabolic PDE is a function of time and space. Such an equation is then solved forward, that is, given the spatial boundary conditions, we start from some initial condition at time $t = 0$ and step forward in time. The Black–Scholes equation is such a PDE; the space variable is the underlier's price. The equation can be transformed in various ways; in fact, it is equivalent to the heat equation in physics; see, for instance, Wilmott, Dewynne, and Howison (1993). In this chapter, we will not transform the equation but leave it in its original form. We do not need to understand anything about PDEs to see that now we cannot solve the equation forward in time, simply because we have no initial conditions. We could now transform time to run backward (that is, switch from calendar time t to remaining lifetime $T - t$). But a conceptually much simpler approach is to solve the equation backward. As in a binomial tree, we start from the terminal condition (the payoff at T), and then step backward through the grid, from time T to time 0.

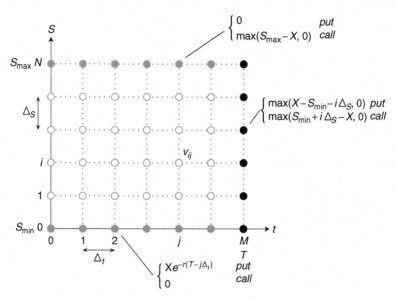

Figure 4.4 Finite difference grid with terminal conditions (dark circles) and boundary conditions (gray circles).

a central difference

$$V_t\big|_{t=j\Delta_t} \approx \frac{v_{ij}-v_{i,j-1}}{\Delta_t} \qquad V_S\big|_{S=S_{\min}+i\Delta_S} \approx \frac{v_{i+1,j}-v_{i-1,j}}{2\Delta_S}.$$

The second-order derivative of the option with respect to the stock price is approximated with

$$V_{SS}\big|_{S=S_{\min}+i\Delta_S} \approx \frac{v_{i+1,j}-2v_{ij}+v_{i-1,j}}{\Delta_S^2}.$$

We observe that four grid points are involved in the numerical approximation of the derivatives of v_{ij}. These four grid points are marked in Fig. 4.5.

We now write the Black–Scholes equation

$$V_t + \frac{\sigma^2}{2}S^2 V_{SS} + (r-q)S V_S - r V = 0$$

for a given node (i,j) in the grid by replacing V by v_{ij} and the derivatives by the approximations introduced before

$$\frac{v_{ij}-v_{i,j-1}}{\Delta_t} + \frac{\sigma^2}{2}S_i^2 \frac{v_{i+1,j}-2v_{ij}+v_{i-1,j}}{\Delta_S^2}$$

$$+(r-q)S_i \frac{v_{i+1,j}-v_{i-1,j}}{2\Delta_S} - r\,v_{ij} = 0.$$

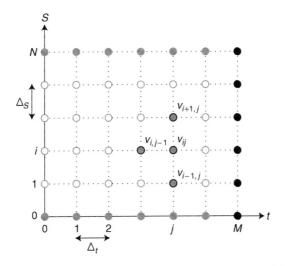

Figure 4.5 Four points involved in the numerical approximation of the derivatives of v_{ij}.

Denoting $a_i = \frac{\Delta_t \sigma^2 S_i^2}{2\Delta_S^2}$ and $b_i = \frac{\Delta_t (r-q) S_i}{2\Delta_S}$ and multiplying by Δ_t, we rewrite the equation as

$$v_{ij} - v_{i,j-1} + a_i \left(v_{i+1,j} - 2v_{ij} + v_{i-1,j} \right) + b_i \left(v_{i+1,j} - v_{i-1,j} \right) - \Delta_t \, r \, v_{ij} = 0.$$

By factoring identical nodes, we get

$$v_{ij} - v_{i,j-1} + \underbrace{(a_i - b_i)}_{d_i} v_{i-1,j} + \underbrace{(-2a_i - \Delta_t \, r)}_{m_i} v_{ij} + \underbrace{(a_i + b_i)}_{u_i} v_{i+1,j} = 0.$$

$$(4.3)$$

The $N-1$ equations involving the $N-1$ nodes v_{ij}, $i = 1, \ldots, N-1$, of column j in the grid, are then

$$
\begin{aligned}
v_{1,j} &- v_{1,j-1} &+ d_1 v_{0,j} &+ m_1 v_{1,j} &+ u_1 v_{2,j} &= 0 \\
v_{2,j} &- v_{2,j-1} &+ d_2 v_{1,j} &+ m_2 v_{2,j} &+ u_2 v_{3,j} &= 0 \\
&\vdots & \vdots & \vdots & \vdots & \vdots \\
v_{i,j} &- v_{i,j-1} &+ d_i v_{i-1,j} &+ m_i v_{i,j} &+ u_i v_{i+1,j} &= 0 \\
&\vdots & \vdots & \vdots & \vdots & \vdots \\
v_{N-1,j} &- v_{N-1,j-1} &+ d_{N-1} v_{N-2,j} &+ m_{N-1} v_{N-1,j} &+ u_{N-1} v_{N,j} &= 0.
\end{aligned}
$$

Before discussing how to solve for the unknown values on the grid nodes, we proceed with some reformulation of the presentation of the problem. First, we resort to a matrix notation

$$v_{1:N-1,j} - v_{1:N-1,j-1} + P \, v_{0:N,j} = 0,$$

$$(4.4)$$

where matrix P is as follows:

$$P = \begin{bmatrix} d_1 & m_1 & u_1 & 0 & \cdots & & \cdots & 0 \\ 0 & d_2 & m_2 & u_2 & & & & \vdots \\ \vdots & & d_3 & m_3 & \ddots & & & \vdots \\ \vdots & & & \ddots & \ddots & u_{N-2} & & 0 \\ 0 & \cdots & & & 0 & d_{N-1} & m_{N-1} & u_{N-1} \end{bmatrix}.$$

Second, we introduce a set notation for the indices of the vectors by denoting the rows of the grid by the set $\overline{\Omega}$ for which we consider the following partition:

$$\overline{\Omega} = \Omega \cup \partial\Omega \quad \text{and} \quad \Omega \cap \partial\Omega = \emptyset.$$

Ω is set of interior points, that is, $i = 1, \ldots, N-1$, and $\partial\Omega$ is the set of points lying on the border, that is, $i = 0, N$ of the grid. Applying this partition to the columns of P defines two matrices A and B (columns forming matrix B in gray tone)

$$P = \begin{bmatrix} d_1 & m_1 & u_1 & 0 & \cdots & & \cdots & 0 \\ 0 & d_2 & m_2 & u_2 & & & & \vdots \\ \vdots & & d_3 & m_3 & \ddots & & & \vdots \\ \vdots & & & \ddots & \ddots & u_{N-2} & & 0 \\ 0 & \cdots & & & 0 & d_{N-1} & m_{N-1} & u_{N-1} \end{bmatrix} \equiv \begin{bmatrix} B_{\cdot,1} & A & B_{\cdot,2} \end{bmatrix}.$$

Note that the columns of P correspond to the rows of the grid (first column is row zero). The following notation

$$P v_{\overline{\Omega}}^j = A v_{\Omega}^j + B v_{\partial\Omega}^j,$$

where

$$v_{\overline{\Omega}}^j \equiv v_{ij}, \, i = 0, 1, \ldots, N,$$

$$v_{\Omega}^j \equiv v_{ij}, \, i = 1, \ldots, N-1,$$

$$v_{\partial\Omega}^j \equiv v_{ij}, \, i = 0, N,$$

then corresponds to the product $P v_{0:N,j}$ in Eq. (4.4). Substituting this product, we get

$$v_{\Omega}^j - v_{\Omega}^{j-1} + A v_{\Omega}^j + B v_{\partial\Omega}^j = 0. \tag{4.5}$$

Different approaches can be considered to compute the solution v_{Ω}^0 which is the value of the nodes in the leftmost column ($j = 0$) of the grid.

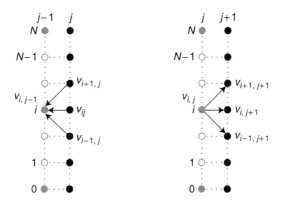

Figure 4.6 Explicit method (left) and implicit method (right).

The explicit method proceeds in isolating v_Ω^{j-1} in Eq. (4.5),

$$v_\Omega^{j-1} = (I + A)\, v_\Omega^j + B\, v_{\partial\Omega}^j,$$

and then solving the equation for $j = M, M-1, \ldots, 1$. The left panel in Fig. 4.6 highlights the grid nodes involved when solving for node $v_{i,j-1}$. Note that the explicit method only involves matrix vector products.

If we approximate V_t, the derivative of V with respect to time, with a forward difference

$$V_t \big|_{t=j\Delta_t} \approx (v_{i,j+1} - v_{i,j})/\Delta_t$$

Eq. (4.5) becomes

$$v_\Omega^{j+1} - v_\Omega^j + A\, v_\Omega^j + B\, v_{\partial\Omega}^j = 0, \qquad (4.6)$$

and the solution v_Ω^0 is obtained by successively solving the linear system

$$(I - A)\, v_\Omega^j = v_\Omega^{j+1} + B\, v_{\partial\Omega}^j$$

for $j = M-1, \ldots, 1, 0$. This defines the implicit method. The right panel in Fig. 4.6 highlights the grid nodes involved when solving for v_{ij}.

The explicit and the implicit method can be combined by considering Eq. (4.6) at time step j

$$v_\Omega^{j+1} - v_\Omega^j + A\, v_\Omega^j + B\, v_{\partial\Omega}^j = 0,$$

and Eq. (4.5) at time step $j+1$

$$v_\Omega^{j+1} - v_\Omega^j + A\, v_\Omega^{j+1} + B\, v_{\partial\Omega}^{j+1} = 0.$$

We now write a linear combination of the two previous equations:

$$\theta\, (v_\Omega^{j+1} - v_\Omega^j + A v_\Omega^j + B v_{\partial\Omega}^j) + (1 - \theta)\, (v_\Omega^{j+1} - v_\Omega^j + A v_\Omega^{j+1} + B v_{\partial\Omega}^{j+1}) = 0$$

with $\theta \in [0, 1]$. Rearranging, we obtain

$$A_m \, v_\Omega^j = A_p \, v_\Omega^{j+1} + \theta \, B \, v_{\partial\Omega}^j + (1 - \theta) \, B \, v_{\partial\Omega}^{j+1}, \qquad (4.7)$$

where $A_m = I - \theta A$ and $A_p = I + (1 - \theta)A$. The solution v_Ω^0 is computed by solving the linear system (4.7) for $j = M - 1, \ldots, 1, 0$. This defines the θ-method. The particular case in which $\theta = \frac{1}{2}$ defines the Crank–Nicolson method. Algorithm 13 summarizes the θ-method, and the following table shows how the θ-method generalizes all methods.

θ	Method	A_m	A_p
0	Explicit	I	$I + A$
1	Implicit	$I - A$	I
$\frac{1}{2}$	Crank–Nicolson	$I - \frac{1}{2}A$	$I + \frac{1}{2}A$

Algorithm 13 θ-method.

1: define terminal and boundary conditions v_Ω^M, $v_{\partial\Omega}^{0:M-1}$, and θ
2: compute A_m, A_p, and B
3: **for** $j = M - 1 : -1 : 0$ **do**
4:     solve $A_m \, v_\Omega^j = A_p \, v_\Omega^{j+1} + \theta \, B \, v_{\partial\Omega}^j + (1 - \theta) \, B \, v_{\partial\Omega}^{j+1}$
5: **end for**

4.3.3. Implementation of the θ-method with Matlab

As illustration of the θ-method, we suggest the evaluation of a European put option[6] with the Matlab code FDM1DEuPut. Following Algorithm 13, the implementation of the θ-method essentially consists of two steps, computing the matrices A_m, A_p, and B (Statement 2) and the solution of the linear systems in Statement 4.

For the first step, we suggest the Matlab code GridU1D.m which implements a discretization using a uniform grid. S_{min} and S_{max} define the interval for the space variable, and M and N define the number of time and space steps, respectively. The generated matrices A_m, A_p, and B are sparse matrices. The array S stores the values of the underlying on the grid nodes.

Listing 4.5. C-FiniteDifferences/M/GridU1D.m

```
1 function [Am,Ap,B,S] = GridU1D(r,q,T,sigma,Smin,Smax,M,N,theta)
2 % GridU1D.m  -- version  2004-04-14
3 % Uniform grid in original variables
4 f7 = 1;  dt = T/M;
5 S  = linspace(Smin,Smax,N+1)';
6 dS = (Smax - Smin) / N;
```

---

[6] An application with higher space dimensions can be found in Gilli, Këllezi, and Pauletto (2002), where option prices are computed on the maximum of three underlying assets.

```
7  a = (dt*sigma^2*S(f7+(1:N-1)).^2) ./ (2*dS^2);
8  b = (dt*(r-q)*S(f7+(1:N-1))) / (2*dS);
9  d = a - b;    m = - 2*a - dt*r;    u = a + b;
10 P = spdiags([d m u], 0:2, N-1, N+1);
11 Am = speye(N-1) -     theta *P(:,f7+(1:N-1));
12 Ap = speye(N-1) + (1-theta)*P(:,f7+(1:N-1));
13 B  = P(:,f7+[0 N]);
```

For the second step, we observe that for the successive computations for the solution of the linear system, we only address nodes from columns j and $j + 1$. Thus, in the code, we use two arrays, V0 for storing column j and V1 for column $j + 1$. Once V0 is computed, it is copied to V1 for the next iteration. For the row indices, we recall that, according to the definition introduced on page 80, Ω stands for $i = 1, \ldots, N - 1$ and $\partial\Omega$ for $i = [0, N]$. V0 is initialized in Statement 5 with the terminal conditions for the put. The boundary conditions for $i = 0$ are computed in Statement 10, and for $i = N$, we propagate the terminal condition for that node when we copy V0 to V1 in Statement 9. Note that the coefficient matrix A_m is factorized only once (Statement 7) and that we proceed with forward and back-substitutions (Statement 13). The illustration below explains how the set notation for the indices maps into the nodes of the grid.

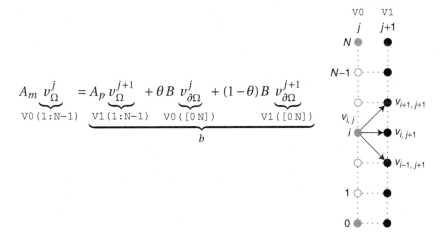

$$A_m \underbrace{v_\Omega^j}_{\text{V0 (1:N-1)}} = A_p \underbrace{v_\Omega^{j+1}}_{\text{V1 (1:N-1)}} + \theta B \underbrace{v_{\partial\Omega}^j}_{\text{V0 ([0 N])}} + (1-\theta) B \underbrace{v_{\partial\Omega}^{j+1}}_{\text{V1 ([0 N])}}$$

Listing 4.6. C-FiniteDifferences/M/FDM1DEuPut.m

```
1  function [P,Svec] = FDM1DEuPut(S,X,r,q,T,sigma,Smin,Smax,M,N,
        theta)
2  %    FDM1DEuPut.m  -- version  2006-06-12
3  %   Finite difference method for European put
4  [Am,Ap,B,Svec] = GridU1D(r,q,T,sigma,Smin,Smax,M,N,theta);
5  V0 = max(X - Svec,0);    % Initial conditions
6  % Solve linear system for succesive time steps
7  [L,U] = lu(Am);    f7 = 1;    dt = T/M;
8  for j = M-1:-1:0
9      V1 = V0;
10     V0(f7+0) = (X-Svec(f7+0))*exp(-r*(T-j*dt)));
11     b = Ap*V1(f7+(1:N-1)) + theta *B*V0(f7+[0 N]) ...
```

```
12                              + (1-theta)*B*V1(f7+[0 N]);
13     V0(f7+(1:N-1)) = U\(L\b);
14 end
15 if nargout==2, P=V0; else P=interp1(Svec,V0,S,'spline'); end
```

FDM1DEuPut.m returns two output arguments, that is, Svec, which is the array of $N + 1$ values of the underlying on the grid going from S_{min} to S_{max}, and the corresponding prices P of the option. If the function is called with a single output argument, the price corresponding to an arbitrary value of S, not necessarily lying in the grid, is computed by interpolation. This is done in Statement 15.

In the following, we give numerical results for a European put with underlying $S = 50$, strike $X = 50$, risk-free rate $r = 0.10$, time to maturity $T = 5/12$, volatility $\sigma = 0.40$, and dividend yield $q = 0$. The space grid goes from $S_{min} = 0$ to $S_{max} = 150$; time and space steps are, respectively, 100 and 500. The parameter θ has been successively set to $1/2$, 0, and 1, thus producing results for the Crank–Nicolson, explicit, and implicit methods. The Black–Scholes price has been computed as a benchmark.

```
S = 50; X = 50; r = 0.10; T = 5/12; sigma = 0.40; q = 0;
P = BSput(S,X,r,q,T,sigma)

P =
    4.0760

Smin = 0; Smax = 150; M = 100; N = 500; theta = 1/2;
P = FDM1DEuPut(S,X,r,T,sigma,q,Smin,Smax,M,N,theta)

P =
    4.0760

theta = 0;
P = FDM1DEuPut(S,X,r,T,sigma,q,Smin,Smax,M,N,theta)

P =
   -2.9365e+154

theta = 1;
P = FDM1DEuPut(S,X,r,T,sigma,q,Smin,Smax,M,N,theta)

P =
    4.0695
```

We observe reasonable accuracy for the Crank–Nicolson and implicit methods; however, the explicit method fails. With $M = 1000$ time steps and $N = 100$ space steps, the explicit method achieves a good result.

```
theta = 0; M = 1000; N = 100;
P = FDM1DEuPut(S,X,r,T,sigma,q,Smin,Smax,M,N,theta)

P =
    4.0756
```

4.3.4. Stability

The precision for finite difference methods depends, among other things, on the number of time and space steps. These issues are known as the problem of stability that is caused by an ill-conditioned linear system. We will not discuss this problem in detail but simply give some intuition. We have to be aware that increasing the number of space steps increases the size of the linear system, and the number of time steps defines how often the linear system has to be solved. Also, the parameters like volatility σ and risk-free rate r influence the conditioning of the linear system.

In Fig. 4.7, we compare the results for increasing time steps and observe that the three methods converge to identical precision. Errors are plotted as the difference between the analytical Black–Scholes prices and the finite difference prices. Note that errors are largest at-the-money.

In Fig. 4.8, we compare the results for varying values of σ. The explicit method first produces the most accurate results but becomes unstable, that is, strongly oscillates (appearing as gray grid) if σ is increased.

Another illustration of the unstable behavior of the explicit method is given in Fig. 4.9 where, first, for a given number of space steps, the explicit method is the most accurate. Increasing the space steps improves accuracy of the implicit and Crank–Nicolson methods but destroys the results for the explicit method (gray grid of oscillations).

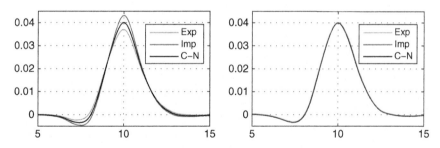

Figure 4.7 $M = 30$ (left panel) and $M = 500$ (right panel). Common parameters: $N = 100$, $\sigma = 0.20$, $r = 0.05$, $q = 0$, $X = S = 10$.

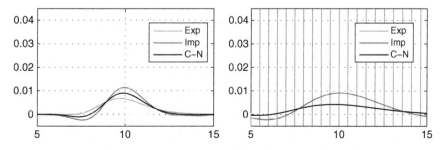

Figure 4.8 $\sigma = 0.20$ (left panel) and $\sigma = 0.40$ (right panel). Common parameters: $N = 100$, $M = 30$, $r = 0.05$, $q = 0$, $X = S = 10$.

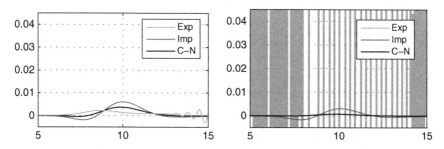

Figure 4.9 $N = 310$ (left panel) and $N = 700$ (right panel). Common parameters: $M = 30$, $\sigma = 0.20$, $r = 0.05$, $q = 0$, $X = 10$.

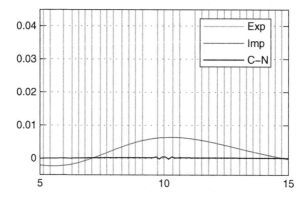

Figure 4.10 $N = 700$, $M = 30$, $\sigma = 0.50$, $r = 0.05$, $X = 10$.

Finally, in Fig. 4.10, we see that the accuracy of the Crank–Nicolson method remains almost unchanged for an increased value of σ. The conclusion we draw from these comparisons is that the behavior of the Crank–Nicolson method is the most stable as its accuracy increases monotonically with the number of space steps N.

Example 4.1

We give an example of an exotic option that can be conveniently priced with a finite difference method. We consider barrier options that are path dependent as they are activated or null if the underlying crosses a certain predetermined level. We consider the particular case of a down-and-out put which becomes void if the price of the underlying crosses a given barrier S_b in a down movement. At the beginning of the option's life, the price S_0 of the underlying and the exercise price X satisfy

$$S_0 > S_b \quad \text{and} \quad X > S_b.$$

We consider the domain $S > S_b$ with the boundary conditions

$$V(S_b, t) = 0 \qquad \text{and} \qquad \lim_{S \to \infty} V(S, t) = 0$$

and the terminal condition

$$V(S,T) = \max(X - S, 0).$$

Modifying the boundary condition and setting $S_{min} = S_b$ in the code `FDM1DEuPut.m` will then solve the problem. Below, you find the modified code `FDDownOutPut.m`. In place of Statement 10 in `FDM1DEuPut.m` the new boundary conditions are specified in Statement 7 and they propagate when copying `V0` onto `V1` in Statement 11.

Listing 4.7. C-FiniteDifferences/M/FDDownOutPut.m

```
1  function [P,Svec] = FDDownOutPut(S,X,r,q,T,sigma,Smin,Smax,M,N,
      theta)
2  % FDDownOutPut.m  -- version  2010-11-06
3  %  Finite difference method for down and out put
4  [Am,Ap,B,Svec] = GridU1D(r,q,T,sigma,Smin,Smax,M,N,theta);
5  f7 = 1;
6  V0 = max(X - Svec,0); % Initial conditions
7  V0(f7+0) = 0;          % Boundary condition for down and out put
8  % Solve linear system for succesive time steps
9  [L,U] = lu(Am);
10 for j = M-1:-1:0
11     V1 = V0;
12     b = Ap*V1(f7+(1:N-1)) + theta *B*V0(f7+[0 N]) ...
13                    + (1-theta)*B*V1(f7+[0 N]);
14     V0(f7+(1:N-1)) = U\(L\b);
15 end
16 if nargout==2, P=V0; else P=interp1(Svec,V0,S,'spline'); end
```

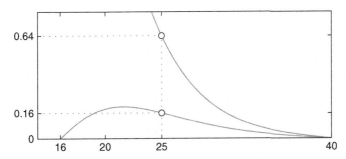

Figure 4.11 Price of down-and-out put (lower line) and European put (upper line) as a function of the price of the underlying at the beginning of the option's life.

Below you find the numerical results for a down-and-out put with barrier $S_b = 16$, $S_0 = 25$, strike $X = 20$, interest rate $r = 5\%$, time to expiry $T = 6/12$, volatility $\sigma = 40\%$, and dividend yield $q = 0$. We compute also the price for a European put. Figure 4.11 compares the down-and-out put with a European put.

```
S0 = 25; X = 20; r = 0.05; T = 6/12; sigma = 0.40; q = 0;
Smin = 16; Smax = 40; N = 100; M = 50; theta = 1/2;

P = FDDownOutPut(S0,X,r,q,T,sigma,Smin,Smax,M,N,theta);
```

```
fprintf('\n Down-and-out put: %5.3f\n',P);

Down-and-out put: 0.162

Smin = 0; P = FDM1DEuPut(S,X,r,q,T,sigma,Smin,Smax,M,N,theta);
fprintf('\n    European put: %5.3f\n',P);

European put: 0.649
```

4.3.5. Coordinate transformation of space variables

In the discussion in Section 4.3.4 we saw that the precision of the Crank–Nicolson method diminishes around the exercise price but can be improved with a finer space grid. However, there are two arguments against fine space grids. First, it increases the computational complexity as the size of the linear system grows, and second, in regions further away from the strike price, a fine grid is not needed as the precision is already very good.

Even though in our opinion the precision of the Crank–Nicolson method is sufficient for most practical applications, one could think to use an irregularly spaced grid, dense around the exercise price and coarser when moving away. In the following, we present some simple ideas on how to produce variable space grids by means of coordinate transformations in the Black–Scholes equation.

We consider a transformation of the underlying S,

$$S = S(x),\tag{4.8}$$

substitute the transformation given in Eq. (4.8) in the pricing equation, and solve it by applying a uniform grid on the variable x. As an example, we consider the Black–Scholes equation $V_t + \frac{1}{2}\sigma^2 S^2 V_{SS} + (r-q)S V_S - rV = 0$, where we replace S by $S(x)$, compute the first-order derivative of $V(S(x))$ with respect to x,

$$V_x = \frac{\partial V}{\partial S}\frac{\partial S}{\partial x} = V_S J(x) \quad\text{and}\quad V_S = \frac{V_x}{J(x)},$$

and the second-order derivative

$$\frac{\partial}{\partial x}\left(V_S\right) = V_{SS} J(x) \quad\text{and}\quad V_{SS} = \frac{1}{J(x)}\frac{\partial}{\partial x}\underbrace{\left(\frac{V_x}{J(x)}\right)}_{V_S}.$$

We can now write the Black–Scholes equation as a function of x,

$$V_t + \frac{\sigma^2 S^2(x)}{2J(x)}\frac{\partial}{\partial x}\left(\frac{V_x}{J(x)}\right) + (r-q)\frac{S(x)}{J(x)}V_x - rV = 0,$$

and use the following approximations:

$$J(x) \approx \frac{J\left(x + \frac{\Delta_x}{2}\right) + J\left(x - \frac{\Delta_x}{2}\right)}{2}$$

$$J\left(x + \frac{\Delta_x}{2}\right) \approx \frac{S(x + \Delta_x) - S(x)}{\Delta_x}$$

$$V_x \approx \frac{V(x + \Delta_x) - V(x - \Delta_x)}{2\,\Delta_x}$$

$$\frac{\partial}{\partial x}\left(\frac{V_x}{J(x)}\right) \approx \left(\frac{V(x + \Delta_x) - V(x)}{J\left(x + \frac{\Delta_x}{2}\right)\Delta_x^2} - \frac{V(x) - V(x - \Delta_x)}{J\left(x - \frac{\Delta_x}{2}\right)\Delta_x^2}\right).$$

As done previously for the implicit method, we use a forward difference to approximate V_t and obtain

$$\frac{v_{i,j+1} - v_{ij}}{\Delta_t} + \frac{\sigma^2 S_i^2}{2J_i}\left(\frac{v_{i+1,j} - v_{ij}}{\Delta_x^2 J_{i+\frac{1}{2}}} - \frac{v_{ij} - v_{i-1,j}}{\Delta_x^2 J_{i-\frac{1}{2}}}\right) +$$

$$(r - q)\frac{S_i}{J_i}\left(\frac{v_{i+1,j} - v_{i-1,j}}{2\,\Delta x}\right) - r\,v_{ij} = 0.$$

Substituting $J_{i+\frac{1}{2}} = \frac{S_{i+1} - S_i}{\Delta x}$, $J_{i-\frac{1}{2}} = \frac{S_i - S_{i-1}}{\Delta x}$ and $J_i = \frac{S_{i+1} - S_{i-1}}{2\Delta x}$, we obtain

$$v_{i,j+1} - v_{ij} + \frac{\sigma^2 S_i^2 \,\Delta_t}{S_{i+1} - S_{i-1}}\left(\frac{v_{i+1,j} - v_{ij}}{S_{i+1} - S_i} - \frac{v_{ij} - v_{i-1,j}}{S_i - S_{i-1}}\right)$$

$$+(r - q)\frac{S_i \,\Delta_t}{S_{i+1} - S_{i-1}}(v_{i+1,j} - v_{i-1,j}) - \Delta_t\,r\,v_{ij} = 0.$$

In order to compact the presentation, we denote $a_i = \frac{S_i \Delta_t}{S_{i+1} - S_{i-1}}$, $b_i = \frac{\sigma^2 S_i a_i}{S_{i+1} - S_i}$, $c_i = \frac{\sigma^2 S_i a_i}{S_i - S_{i-1}}$, and $e_i = (r - q)a_i$, and we get the $i = 1, \ldots, N - 1$ equations

$$v_{i,j+1} - v_{ij} + b_i(v_{i+1,j} - v_{ij})$$

$$-c_i(v_{ij} - v_{i-1,j}) + e_i(v_{i+1,j} - v_{i-1,j}) - \Delta_t\,r\,v_{ij} = 0.$$

Collecting the identical terms, we get the following expression:

$$v_{i,j+1} - v_{ij} + \underbrace{(c_i - e_i)}_{d_i}v_{i-1,j} + \underbrace{(-b_i - c_i - \Delta_t\,r)}_{m_i}v_{ij} + \underbrace{(b_i + e_i)}_{u_i}v_{i+1,j} = 0,$$

which is very similar to Eq. (4.3) except for the forward difference approximation used for the time derivative and the difference in the definition of the coefficients. The corresponding matrix notation is

$$v_\Omega^{j+1} - v_\Omega^j + P\,v_\Omega^j = 0,$$

where matrix P is the one defined on page 80. We apply the same partition to P as done previously and compute the matrices A_m, A_p, and B needed to implement the θ-method.

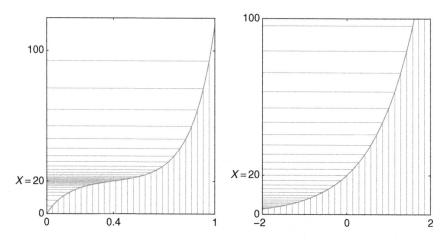

Figure 4.12 Coordinate transformations for $N = 29$ and $X = 20$. Left panel: Sine hyperbolic function with $\lambda = 10$ and $p = 0.4$. Right panel: Logarithmic transformation with $I = 2$.

We briefly discuss two potential transformations. The first is a logarithmic transformation

$$S = X e^x,$$

where X is the exercise price and $x \in [-I, I]$ is defined in a symmetric interval around zero of length $2I$. The inverse of the transformation is $x = \log(S/X)$. The right panel in Fig. 4.12 shows the corresponding grid in the S variable. We observe that the grid becomes finer when approaching $S = 0$ and not around $S = X$.

The second transformation uses a sine hyperbolic function

$$S = X \left(\exp(ux - c) - \exp(-(ux - c)) \right) / 2\lambda + X,$$

with $x \in [0,1]$, λ a shape parameter defining $c = \log(\lambda + \sqrt{\lambda^2 + 1})$, and $u = Nc/(\lfloor pN \rfloor + 1/2)$. N is the number of grid points, and p defines the value of x corresponding to X. The left panel in Fig. 4.12 shows that the grid computed with this transformation is finest around $S = X$.

Finally, Fig. 4.13 compares the absolute error with respect to the Black–Scholes solution for prices computed with the logarithmic transformation and the transformation using the sine hyperbolic function for increasing numbers of grid nodes N.

4.4. American options

An American option can be exercised at any time. Therefore, it follows that the price must satisfy the following PDE

$$V_t + \tfrac{1}{2}\sigma^2 S^2 V_{SS} + (r - q)S V_S - r V \geq 0, \tag{4.9}$$

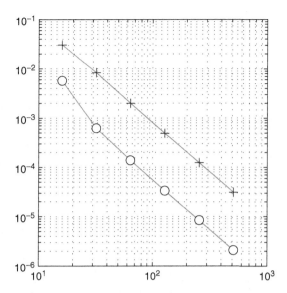

Figure 4.13 Absolute errors for the sine hyperbolic transformation (circles) and the logarithmic transformation (plus signs).

and in order to exclude arbitrage opportunities, the option price at any time must satisfy

$$V(S,t) \geq \max(X - S(t), 0).\tag{4.10}$$

Terminal and boundary conditions for the put are

$$V(S,T) = \max(X - S(T), 0) \quad \text{and} \quad V(0,t) = X, \quad \lim_{S \to \infty} V(S,t) = 0.$$

We denote $S_f(t)$ as the largest value of S, at time t, for which

$$V(S_f(t), t) = X - S_f(t),$$

which then defines the early exercise boundary, that is, the price of the underlying at time t for which it is optimal to exercise the option.

The solution of Eq. (4.9) is formalized with the following equation and inequalities[7]

$$\mathcal{L}_{BS}(V)\left(V(S,t) - V(S,T)\right) = 0$$

$$\mathcal{L}_{BS}(V) \geq 0 \quad \text{and} \quad \left(V(S,t) - V(S,T)\right) \geq 0$$

which constitutes a sequence of linear complementary problems. Using the notation introduced for the formalization of the θ-method, this

---

[7] $\mathcal{L}_{BS}(V) \stackrel{\text{def}}{=} V_t + \frac{1}{2}\sigma^2 S^2 V_{SS} + r S V_S - r V$ is the Black–Scholes differential operator.

translates into

$$\left(A_m v_\Omega^j - b^j\right) \dot{\times} \left(v_\Omega^j - v_\Omega^M\right) = 0,$$

$$A_m v_\Omega^j \geq b^j \qquad \text{and} \qquad v_\Omega^j \geq v_\Omega^M, \tag{4.11}$$

where v_Ω^M is the payoff, $A_m = I - \theta A$, $A_p = I + (1-\theta)A$, and $b^j = A_p v_\Omega^{j+1} + \theta B v_{\partial\Omega}^j + (1-\theta) B v_{\partial\Omega}^{j+1}$. The notation $\dot{\times}$ designates an element by element product.

The solution for the two inequalities in (4.11) can be approached by solving the linear system $A_m x = b^j$ with an iterative method and, if necessary, truncate the elements of vector x as soon as they are computed in the following way: $x_i = \max(x_i, v_i^\Omega)$. This can be achieved with a modification of the SOR method presented in Section 3.2.1. This modified method, called projected successive overrelaxation (PSOR), for the solution of time step j is given in Algorithm 14.

Algorithm 14 Projected successive overrelaxation (PSOR).

1: give starting solution $x \in \mathbb{R}^n$
2: **while** not converged **do**
3:     **for** $i = 1 : n$ **do**
4:         $x_i = \omega (b_i^j - A_{i,1:n} x)/a_{ii} + x_i$
5:         $x_i = \max(x_i, v_i^\Omega)$
6:     **end for**
7: **end while**
8: $v_\Omega^j = x$

Algorithm 14 is implemented with the Matlab code PSOR.m. The input arguments are the starting solution x1, the matrix A and vector b corresponding to period j, and the payoff. It is also possible to overwrite the default option for the relaxation parameter ω, the tolerance for the convergence test, and the maximum number of iterations.

Listing 4.8. C-FiniteDifferences/M/PSOR.m

```
 1 function x1 = PSOR(x1,A,b,payoff,omega,tol,maxit)
 2 % PSOR.m  -- version  2004-05-03
 3 % Projected SOR for Ax >= b and x = max(x,payoff)
 4 if nargin == 4, tol = 1e-4; omega = 1.7; maxit = 70; end
 5 it = 0; N = length(x1); x0 = -x1;
 6 while not( converged(x0,x1,tol) )
 7    x0 = x1;
 8    for i = 1:N-1
 9        x1(i) = omega*( b(i)-A(i,:)*x1 ) / A(i,i) + x1(i);
10        x1(i) = max(payoff(i), x1(i));
11    end
12    it=it+1; if it>maxit, error('Maxit in PSOR'), end
13 end
```

Another approach for the solution of the two inequalities in (4.11) consists in computing first the solution x of the linear system

$$A_m x = b^j$$

with a direct method, and then deriving v_Ω^j by truncating x,

$$v_\Omega^j = \max(x, v_\Omega^M),$$

with max a component-wise operation in order to satisfy the inequality (4.11). This defines the explicit payout (EP) method. Algorithm 15 summarizes the procedure which terminates with the solution v_Ω^0.

Algorithm 15 Explicit payout method (EP).

1: $v_\Omega^M = \max(X - S, 0)$

2: **for** $j = M - 1 : -1 : 0$ **do**

3: $\quad b^j = A_p v_\Omega^{j+1} + \theta B v_{\partial\Omega}^j + (1 - \theta) B v_{\partial\Omega}^{j+1}$

4: $\quad$ solve $\quad A_m v_\Omega^j = b^j$

5: $\quad v_\Omega^j = \max(v_\Omega^j, v_\Omega^M)$

6: **end for**

The complete procedure for pricing American put options either with the projected SOR (PSOR) or the explicit payout (EP) method is implemented with the Matlab code FDM1DAmPut.m.

Listing 4.9. C-FiniteDifferences/M/FDM1DAmPut.m

```
1  function [P,Sf] = FDM1DAmPut(S,X,r,q,T,sigma,Smin,Smax,M,N,
        theta,method)
2  % FDM1DAmPut.m   -- version: 2007-05-28
3  % Finite difference method for American put
4  f7 = 1;   Sf = NaN(M,1);
5  [Am,Ap,B,Svec] = GridU1D(r,q,T,sigma,Smin,Smax,M,N,theta);
6  V0 = max(X - Svec,0);
7  Payoff = V0(f7+(1:N-1));
8  % Solve linear system for succesive time steps
9  [L,U] = lu(Am);
10 for j = M-1:-1:0
11     V1 = V0;
12     V0(f7+0) = X - Svec(f7+0);
13     b = Ap*V1(f7+(1:N-1)) +    theta *B*V0(f7+[0 N])...
14                           + (1-theta)*B*V1(f7+[0 N]);
15     if strcmp(method,'PSOR')
16         V0(f7+(1:N-1)) = PSOR(V1(f7+(1:N-1)),Am,b,Payoff);
17         p = find(Payoff - V0(f7+(1:N-1)));
18         Sf(f7+j) = Svec(p(1));
19     elseif strcmp(method,'EPOUT') % Explicit payout
20         solunc = U\(L\b);
21         [V0(f7+(1:N-1)),Imax] = max([Payoff solunc],[],2);
22         p = find(Imax == 2);
```

```
23        i = p(1)-1; % Grid line of last point below payoff
24        Sf(f7+j) = interp1(solunc(i:i+2)-Payoff(i:i+2),...
25                            Svec(f7+(i:i+2)),0,'cubic');
26     else error('Specify method (PSOR/EPOUT)');
27     end
28 end
29 if ~isempty(S),
30     P = interp1(Svec,V0,S,'spline');
31 else
32     P = [Svec(2:end-1) V0(f7+(1:N-1))];
33 end
```

We first discuss the results for the PSOR method with an example in which $X = 50$, $r = 0.10$, $T = 5/12$, $\sigma = 0.40$, and $q = 0$. For the grid parameters, the values are $S_{min} = 0$, $S_{max} = 80$, $N = 40$, $M = 50$, and $\theta = 1/2$.

If for the input argument of FDM1DAmPut.m we specify a value for the underlying S, the function returns the corresponding option price in the output argument P. If S is specified as an empty array [], P will be a matrix where column one holds the value of the underlying on the grid and column two the corresponding option prices. Below is computed the option price corresponding to the underlying with price $S = 55$. Note that the starting solution provided to PSOR in Statement 16 corresponds to the solution of the preceding time step.

```
S = 55; X = 50; r = 0.10; T = 5/12; sigma = 0.40; q = 0;
Smin = 0; Smax = 80; N = 40; M = 50; theta = 1/2;

[P,Sf] = FDM1DAmPut(S,X,r,T,sigma,q,Smin,Smax,M,N,theta,'PSOR')

P =
    2.5769
```

The early exercise boundary is defined by the borderline between option prices above and below the options payoff. This is illustrated in the left panel in Fig. 4.14 in which we reproduce the grid for the previous example. The nodes in which the option price is above the payoff are in dark.

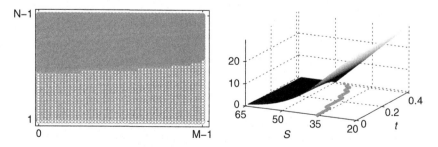

Figure 4.14 Finite difference grid for $S_{min} = 0$, $S_{max} = 80$, $N = 40$, $M = 50$, and $\theta = \frac{1}{2}$. Left panel: Dark nodes indicate option price greater than payoff. Right panel: Option prices and early exercise boundary.

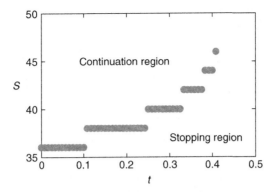

Figure 4.15 Early exercise boundary (same setting as in Figure 4.14).

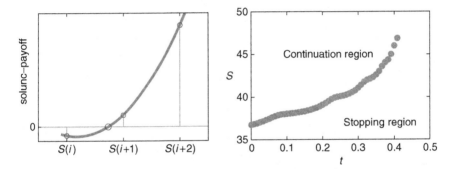

Figure 4.16 Left panel: Grid nodes used for interpolation. Right panel: Early exercise boundary resulting from interpolation of the solutions obtained with the explicit payout method.

We observe that, due to the discrete character of the grid, the early exercise boundary is a step function. In Fig. 4.15, we map the boundary to the corresponding value of the underlying. The area below the curve is called the stopping region, and the area above is the continuation region.

With the explicit payout method, all elements of v_Ω^j are available when the solution is truncated. This makes it possible to proceed with an interpolation between the elements above and below the payoff. We use one point below the payoff and two points above for interpolation. This is implemented in Statements 22–25. The left panel in Fig. 4.16 illustrates the procedure, and the right panel shows the early exercise boundary computed from the interpolated unconstrained solution of the explicit payout method. We observe that the function no longer contains steps.

A finer grid produces smoother early exercise boundaries. Fig. 4.17 shows the boundaries for both methods with a finer space grid. Prices are not significantly different, but execution times are.[8]

---

[8] Execution time for the explicit payout method is in the order of 1/10 of a second.

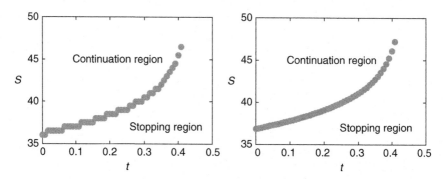

Figure 4.17 Computation of early exercise boundaries with finer grid ($S_{max} = 150$, $N = 300$, and $M = 50$). PSOR (left panel) and EP (right panel).

Matrix A_m has to be factorized only once (Statement 9 in FDM1DAmPut.m), and Matlab solves the sparse linear systems very efficiently.[9]

```
S = 55; E = 50; r = 0.10; T = 5/12; sigma = 0.40; q = 0;
Smin = 0; Smax = 150; N = 300; M = 50; theta = 1/2;

tic
[P,Sf1]=FDM1DAmPut(S,E,r,q,T,sigma,Smin,Smax,M,N,theta,'PSOR');
fprintf('\n PSOR:  P = %5.3f (%i sec)\n',P,fix(toc));

  PSOR:  P = 2.593 (7 sec)

tic
[P,Sf2]=FDM1DAmPut(S,E,r,q,T,sigma,Smin,Smax,M,N,theta,'EPOUT')
fprintf('\n EPout: P = %5.3f (%i sec)\n',P,fix(toc));

  EPout: P = 2.591 (0 sec)
```

In the code PSOR.m, the default value for the relaxation parameter ω has been set to 1.7. This value has been computed using a grid search. The coefficient matrix A_m needed for the search is computed in FDM1DAmPut.m by GridU1D.m. In order to make this matrix available we suggest setting a breakpoint in FDM1DAmPut.m and saving the matrix with the Matlab command save tempAm Am. We than use the function OmegaGridSearch.m. Figure 4.18 illustrates the search for optimal omega.

```
load tempAm
A = full(Am);
D = diag(diag(A)); L = tril(A,-1); U = triu(A,1);

winf = 0.9; wsup = 1.9; npoints = 21;
[w,r] = OmegaGridSearch(A,winf,wsup,npoints)
```

---

[9] In the following example, we present a modified implementation in which we use the algorithms for solving tridiagonal systems introduced in Section 3.3.1.

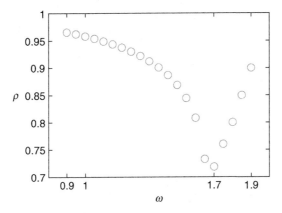

Figure 4.18 Grid search for the optimal omega in the PSOR algorithm.

```
w =
     1.7000
r =
     0.7185
```

Example 4.2

The sparse linear system in the explicit payout method has been solved with Matlab's built-in sparse matrix-handling capabilities. However, we have presented in Section 3.3.1 algorithms and code designed to exploit the sparsity of tridiagonal linear systems. This code can also be used for the explicit payout method and is implemented in FDM1DAmPutsc.m. The function GridU1Dsc.m called in Statement 5 computes matrices A_m and A_p that store the three diagonals of our system columnwise as shown hereafter

$$\begin{bmatrix} 0 & m_1 & u_1 \\ d_2 & m_2 & u_2 \\ \vdots & \vdots & \vdots \\ d_{N-2} & m_{N-2} & u_{N-2} \\ d_{N-1} & m_{N-1} & 0 \end{bmatrix} \begin{bmatrix} x_0 \\ x_1 \\ x_2 \\ \vdots \\ x_{N-2} \\ x_{N-1} \\ x_N \end{bmatrix} = \begin{bmatrix} m_1 x_1 + u_1 x_2 \\ d_2 x_1 + m_2 x_2 + u_2 x_3 \\ \vdots \\ d_{N-2} x_{N-3} + m_{N-2} x_{N-2} + u_{N-2} x_{N-1} \\ d_{N-1} x_{N-2} + m_{N-1} x_{N-1} \end{bmatrix}$$

In Statement 10 of FDM1DAmPutsc.m, we compute the vectors ℓ and u of the LU factorization, and in Statement 14, the function buildb.m computes the right-hand-side vector of the linear system to solve. Given the storage scheme used for the tridiagonal matrix, the matrix vector product is coded in buildb.m as

$$A_{i,[1\,2\,3]} x_{[i-1\,i\,i+1]} \qquad i = 1,\dots,N.$$

Back- and forward substitutions are executed in Statement 16 by solve3diag.

Execution is about four times slower compared with the the built-in sparse code of Matlab but still remains in the order of tenths of seconds for problem sizes relevant in our applications.

Listing 4.10. C-FiniteDifferences/M/FDM1DAmPutsc.m

```
 1 function [P,Sf] = FDM1DAmPutsc(S,X,r,q,T,sigma,Smin,Smax,M,N,
      theta)
 2 % FDM1DAmPutsc.m  -- version: 2010-10-30
 3 % Finite difference method for American put (sparse code)
 4 f7 = 1;  Sf = NaN(M,1);
 5 [Am,Ap,B,Svec] = GridU1Dsc(r,q,T,sigma,Smin,Smax,M,N,theta);
 6 V0 = max(X - Svec,0);
 7 Payoff = V0(f7+(1:N-1));
 8 % Solve linear system for succesive time steps
 9 p = Am(2:N-1,1); d = Am(:,2); q = Am(1:N-1,3);
10 [l,u] = lu3diag(p,d,q);
11 for j = M-1:-1:0
12     V1 = V0;
13     V0(f7+0) = X - Svec(f7+0);
14     b = buildb(Ap,B,theta,V0,V1);
15     % Explicit payout
16     solunc = solve3diag(l,u,q,b);
17     [V0(f7+(1:N-1)),Imax] = max([Payoff solunc],[],2);
18     p = find(Imax == 2);
19     i = p(1)-1; % Grid line of last point below payoff
20     Sf(f7+j) = interp1(solunc(i:i+2)-Payoff(i:i+2),...
21                        Svec(f7+(i:i+2)),0,'cubic');
22 end
23 if ~isempty(S),
24     P = interp1(Svec,V0,S,'spline');
25 else
26     P = [Svec(2:end-1) V0(f7+(1:N-1))];
27 end
```

Listing 4.11. C-FiniteDifferences/M/GridU1Dsc.m

```
 1 function [Am,Ap,B,S] = GridU1Dsc(r,q,T,sigma,Smin,Smax,M,N,
      theta)
 2 % GridU1Dsc.m  -- version  2011-05-14
 3 % Uniform grid in original variables (sparse code)
 4 f7 = 1;  dt = T/M;
 5 S = linspace(Smin,Smax,N+1)';
 6 dS = (Smax - Smin) / N;
 7 a = (dt*sigma^2*S(f7+(1:N-1)).^2) ./ (2*dS^2);
 8 b = (dt*(r-q)*S(f7+(1:N-1))) / (2*dS);
 9 d = a - b;  m = - 2*a - dt*r;  u = a + b;
10 %
11 tta = theta;
12 Am = [[0;  -tta*d(2:N-1)]     1-tta*m [  -tta*u(1:N-2);0]];
13 Ap = [[0;(1-tta)*d(2:N-1)] 1+(1-tta)*m [(1-tta)*u(1:N-2);0]];
14 B = [d(1) u(N-1)];
```

Listing 4.12. C-FiniteDifferences/M/buildb.m

```
1  function b = buildb(Ap,B,theta,V0,V1)
2  % buildb.m  -- version  2010-10-30
3  % Builds right-hand side vector for theta method
4  n = size(Ap,1);
5  b = zeros(n,1); f7 = 1; N = n+1;
6  for i = 1:n
7      b(i) = Ap(i,:)*V1(f7+(i-1:i+1));
8  end
9  b(1) = b(1) + theta*B(1)*V0(f7+0) + (1-theta)*B(1)*V1(f7+0);
10 b(n) = b(n) + theta*B(2)*V0(f7+N) + (1-theta)*B(2)*V1(f7+N);
```

Example 4.3

The code FDM1DAmPut.m can be easily adapted to price a variety of options. We illustrate this with an American strangle[10] which combines a put with exercise price X_1 with a call with exercise price X_2 such that $X_1 < X_2$. This then corresponds to the following payoff (or terminal conditions, see dotted line in the graph of Fig. 4.19)

$$V(S,T) = \begin{cases} \max(X_1 - S, 0) & \text{if} \quad S < X_2 \\ \max(S - X_2, 0) & \text{if} \quad S > X_1 \end{cases}$$

and boundary conditions

$$V(0,t) = X_1 e^{-r(T-t)}$$

$$V(S,t) = (S - X_2) e^{-r(T-t)} \quad S > X_2.$$

In the modified code FDAmStrangle.m, the terminal conditions are coded in Statements 6–9 and the boundary conditions in Statements 14 and 15. All remaining code, except the additional exercise price in the input arguments, is identical with FDM1DAmPut.m.

Listing 4.13. C-FiniteDifferences/M/FDAmStrangle.m

```
1  function [P,Sf] = FDAmStrangle(S,X1,X2,r,q,T,sigma,Smin,Smax,M,
       N,theta,method)
2  % FDAmStrangle.m  -- version  2010-11-07
3  % Finite difference method for American strangle
4  f7 = 1;  dt = T/M;  Sf = NaN(M,1);
5  [Am,Ap,B,Svec] = GridU1D(r,q,T,sigma,Smin,Smax,M,N,theta);
6  V0 = max(X1 - Svec,0);
7  I  = find(Svec >= X2);
8  V0(I) = Svec(I) - X2;
9  Payoff = V0(f7+(1:N-1));
10 % Solve linear system for succesive time steps
11 [L,U] = lu(Am);
12 for j = M-1:-1:0
13     V1 = V0;
```

---

[10] For other approaches to price American strangles, see, for instance, Chiarella and Ziogas (2005).

```
14    V0(f7+0) = exp(-r*(T-j*dt))*(X1 - Smin);
15    V0(f7+N) = exp(-r*(T-j*dt))*(Smax - X2);
16    b = Ap*V1(f7+(1:N-1)) +    theta *B*V0(f7+[0 N])...
17                          + (1-theta)*B*V1(f7+[0 N]);
18    if strcmp(method,'PSOR')
19        V0(f7+(1:N-1)) = PSOR(V1(f7+(1:N-1)),Am,b,Payoff);
20        p = find(Payoff - V0(f7+(1:N-1)));
21        Sf(f7+j) = Svec(p(1));
22    elseif strcmp(method,'EPOUT') % Explicit payout
23        solunc = U\(L\b);
24        [V0(f7+(1:N-1)),Imax] = max([Payoff solunc],[],2);
25        p = find(Imax == 2);
26        i = p(1)-1; % Grid line of last point below payoff
27        Sf(f7+j) = interp1(solunc(i:i+2)-Payoff(i:i+2),...
28                           Svec(f7+(i:i+2)),0,'cubic');
29    else error('Specify method (PSOR/EPOUT)');
30        end
31 end
32 if ~isempty(S),
33     P = interp1(Svec,V0,S,'spline');
34 else
35     P = [Svec(2:end-1) V0(f7+(1:N-1))];
36 end
```

Figure 4.19 shows the price of an American strangle with $X_1 = 100$, $X_2 = 150$, $r = 5\%$, $T = 1$, $\sigma = 40\%$, and $q = 10\%$. The grid was specified with $S_{\min} = 0$, $S_{\max} = 250$, $N = 200$, $M = 100$, $\theta = 1/2$, and the explicit payout method has been selected.

```
S0 = 165; X1 = 100; X2 = 150; r=0.05; T=1; sigma=0.40; q=0.10;
Smin = 0; Smax = 250; N = 200; M = 100; theta = 1/2;

[P,Svec] = FDAmStrangle(S0,X1,X2,r,q,T,sigma,Smin,Smax,M,N,
    theta,'EPOUT');
fprintf('\n    European put: %5.3f\n',P);

American strangle: 31.452
```

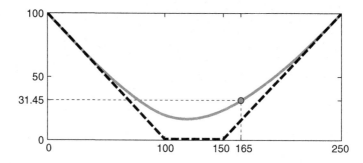

Figure 4.19 Price of American strangle (dashed line is the payoff).

4.A. A note on Matlab's function `spdiags`

Matlab provides a very convenient way to construct sparse diagonal matrices. This is achieved with the function `spdiags`. We briefly explain its usage. Consider the command `D = spdiags(B,d,m,n);` B is a matrix in which diagonals are stored column by column (all of same length). The argument d specifies the location of the diagonals. As an example, take

$$B = \begin{bmatrix} 1 & 6 & 11 \\ 2 & 7 & 12 \\ 3 & 8 & 13 \\ 4 & 9 & 14 \\ 5 & 10 & 15 \end{bmatrix} \quad \text{and} \quad d = \begin{bmatrix} -2 & 0 & 1 \end{bmatrix}.$$

Then, the diagonals are placed into a matrix at rows as indicated in vector d. The number of columns is defined by the number of rows in B. This is shown in the leftmost figure in the picture below.

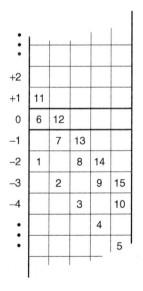 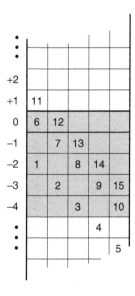

The arguments m and n in the function call specify the size of a submatrix from this matrix, where m is the number of rows starting from row 0 and going down $(0, -1, -2, \ldots)$ and n is the number of columns starting from the leftmost column (column 1). The submatrix can be rectangular, and n, the number of columns, does not have to match the length of the diagonal. The figure at right shows the submatrix corresponding to $m = 5$

and $n = 5$. We note that the last two elements in the first diagonal and the first element in the third diagonal are not included in the submatrix. Therefore, matrix B could be specified as

$$
B = \begin{bmatrix} 1 & 6 & \text{NaN} \\ 2 & 7 & 12 \\ 3 & 8 & 13 \\ \text{NaN} & 9 & 14 \\ \text{NaN} & 10 & 15 \end{bmatrix}.
$$

## CHAPTER FIVE

Binomial trees

5.1. Motivation

Binomial trees serve as an intuitive approach to explain the logic behind option pricing models and also as a versatile computational technique. This chapter describes how to implement such models. All algorithms are given in pseudocode; some sample codes are given for Matlab and R. We start with the Black–Scholes option pricing model: first, this gives us a natural benchmark to judge the quality of our trees; second, it is easy then to demonstrate the flexibility of tree-models.

The binomial model assumes that, over a short period of time Δ_t, a financial asset's price S either rises by a small amount or goes down a small amount, as pictured below. The probability of an uptick is p, while a downtick occurs with probability $1 - p$. (Probabilities here are generally risk-neutral ones.)

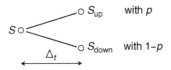

Such a model for price movements may either be additive (i.e., absolute movements) or multiplicative (i.e., relative movements). "Additive" and "multiplicative" here refers to units of the observed price; computationally, a multiplicative model can be changed into an additive one by taking logarithms. There are two objections against additive models: a price could become negative, and the magnitude (in currency units) of a price change does not depend on the current price. Hence, a 1-unit move is as likely for a stock with price 5 as for a stock with price 500, which, empirically, is not the case. Still, for very short periods of time, an additive model may be just as good as a multiplicative one. In fact, the additive model may be even better at capturing market conventions (e.g., prices in certain markets may move by fixed currency amounts) or institutional settings (e.g., when modeling central banks' interest rate setting). Nevertheless, we will discuss multiplicative models; the implementation of additive models requires only minor changes in the procedures described below. We will assume that S is a share price, even though the model may be applied to other types of securities as well. We want to find the price, and later on the Greeks, of plain vanilla call and put options. Now is time 0; the option expires at T. The time until expiration is divided into a number M of periods; with $M = 1$, we have $\triangle_t = T$, else $\triangle_t = T/M$. The subscript t differentiates the symbol for a short period of time from the symbol for Delta, Δ, that will be used later.

Matching moments

We start with a tree for a Black–Scholes world, thus we want to match the mean and variance of the returns of S in our tree to a given mean and variance σ^2 in a continuous-time world. Let u and d be the gross returns of S in case of an uptick and downtick, respectively. With $M = 1$ and the current price S_0, we have

$$E\left(\frac{S_{\triangle_t}}{S_0}\right) = pu + (1-p)d, \tag{5.1}$$

$$Var\left(\frac{S_{\triangle_t}}{S_0}\right) = \frac{1}{S_0^2}Var(S_{\triangle_t}) = pu^2 + (1-p)d^2 - \left(pu + (1-p)d\right)^2 \tag{5.2}$$

where we have used

$$Var(S_{\triangle_t}) = \underbrace{S_0^2\left(pu^2 + (1-p)d^2\right)}_{E(S_{\triangle_t}^2)} - \underbrace{S_0^2\left(pu + (1-p)d\right)^2}_{(ES_{\triangle_t})^2}$$

to obtain Eq. (5.2). $E(\cdot)$ and $Var(\cdot)$ are the expectations and variance operator, respectively. In a risk-neutral world with continuous time, the mean gross return is $e^{r\triangle_t}$, where r is the risk-free rate. So with Eq. (5.1),

$$pu + (1-p)d = e^{r\triangle_t}. \tag{5.3}$$

Thus we have an equation that links our first target moment, the mean return, with the tree parameters p, u, and d. In the Black–Scholes model, we have lognormally distributed stock prices with variance

$$Var(S_{\triangle_t}) = S_0^2 e^{2r\triangle_t}(e^{\sigma^2\triangle_t} - 1) = S_0^2(e^{2r\triangle_t + \sigma^2\triangle_t} - e^{2r\triangle_t}).$$

Dividing by S_0^2 and equating to Eq. (5.2), we obtain

$$pu^2 + (1-p)d^2 = e^{2r\triangle_t + \sigma^2\triangle_t}, \tag{5.4}$$

which links our second target moment, σ^2, with our tree parameters. We now have two equations, (5.3) and (5.4), from which we try to infer the values for p, u, and d, hence there is an infinity of possible specifications for the tree. Different authors introduce different restrictions to obtain a solution. One possible (and probably the best-known) assumption, made by Cox, Ross, and Rubinstein (1979), is that

$$ud = 1.$$

We obtain

$$p = \frac{e^{r\Delta t} - d}{u - d}$$

from Eq. (5.3); for u and d, Cox, Ross, and Rubinstein (1979) suggest the approximative solutions

$$u = e^{\sigma\sqrt{\Delta t}},$$

$$d = e^{-\sigma\sqrt{\Delta t}}.$$

These parameter settings ensure that Eq. (5.3) is satisfied exactly and Eq. (5.4) approximately (with the approximation improving for decreasing Δt and becoming exact in the limit). See Jabbour, Kramin, and Young (2001) for a discussion of these and other possible parameter settings.

5.2. Growing the tree

When we increase the number of periods, $\Delta t = T/M$ becomes smaller. The following figure shows the resulting prices for $M = 4$.

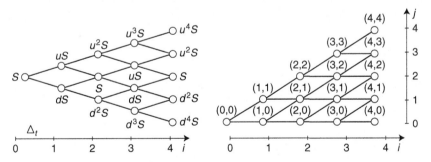

The right side of the figure above gives a convenient form to visualize and work with the resulting tree. The node (i, j) represents the asset price after i periods and j upticks, that is

$$S_{i,j} = Su^j d^{i-j}.$$

A point in time on the grid is labeled i, which translates into a point in "real" time as

$$t = T\frac{i}{M} = i\,\Delta t.$$

Note that there is also an equally shaped tree for the option prices in which every node corresponds exactly to a node in the stock price tree. Furthermore, in this tree here, the parameters (u, d, p) stay unchanged at every node. Thus, the volatility (i.e., the volatility that is inserted in Eq. (5.2) to obtain the model parameters) is constant, as in the Black–Scholes model. (The volatility at a certain node is also called "local volatility.")

5.2.1. Implementing a tree

We start with computing the current price C_0 of a European call; Algorithm 16 gives the procedure for given values of the spot price S, the strike X, the volatility σ, the risk-free rate r, and time to maturity T.

Algorithm 16 European call for S, X, r, σ, T, and M time steps.

1: initialize $\Delta_t = T/M$, $\quad S_{0,0} = S$, $\quad v = e^{-r\Delta_t}$
2: compute $u = e^{\sigma\sqrt{\Delta_t}}$, $\quad d = 1/u$, $\quad p = (e^{r\Delta_t} - d)/(u - d)$
3: $S_{M,0} = S_{0,0} d^M$
4: **for** $j = 1 : M$ **do**
5: $\quad\quad S_{M,j} = S_{M,j-1}\, u/d$ # initialize asset prices at maturity
6: **end for**
7: **for** $j = 0 : M$ **do**
8: $\quad\quad C_{M,j} = \max(S_{M,j} - X, 0)$ # initialize option values at maturity
9: **end for**
10: **for** $i = M - 1 : -1 : 0$ **do**
11: $\quad\quad$ **for** $j = 0 : i$ **do**
12: $\quad\quad\quad C_{i,j} = v\left(p\, C_{i,j+1} + (1 - p)\, C_{i,j}\right)$ # step back through the tree
13: $\quad\quad$ **end for**
14: **end for**
15: $C_0 = C_{0,0}$

For the price of a put, we only have to replace $\max(S_{M,j} - X, 0)$ in Statement 8 by $\max(X - S_{M,j}, 0)$.

Numerical implementation

An implementation with Matlab may look as follows.

Listing 5.1. C-BinomialTrees/M/EuropeanCall.m

```
1  function C0 = EuropeanCall(S0,X,r,T,sigma,M)
2  % EuropeanCall.m -- version 2010-12-28
3  % compute constants
4  f7 = 1;   dt = T / M;   v = exp(-r * dt);
5  u = exp(sigma*sqrt(dt));   d = 1 /u;
6  p = (exp(r * dt) - d) / (u - d);
7
8  % initialize asset prices at maturity (period M)
9  S = zeros(M + 1,1);
```

```
10  S(f7+0) = S0 * d^M;
11  for j = 1:M
12      S(f7+j) = S(f7+j - 1) * u / d;
13  end
14
15  % initialize option values at maturity (period M)
16  C = max(S - X, 0);
17
18  % step back through the tree
19  for i = M-1:-1:0
20      for j = 0:i
21          C(f7+j) = v * (p * C(f7+j + 1) + (1-p) * C(f7+j));
22      end
23  end
24  C0 = C(f7+0);
```

A few remarks: Several of the loops in Algorithm 16 count from or to 0, which is a convenient way for notation, but does not conform well with how vectors and matrices are indexed in Matlab or R. A helpful "trick" is to use an offsetting constant ($f7$). This is added to an iterator and allows us to quickly code an algorithm while reducing errors (later on one may dispose of the constant). It is not necessary to store the complete matrices of stock and option prices; it is enough to keep one vector that is updated while stepping through the tree. Note in particular that we do not need to update the stock prices, only the option prices are computed afresh in every time step. The algorithm could be accelerated by also precomputing quantities like $(1 - p)$ or, since we discount in every period by $e^{-r \Delta t}$, by leaving out the periodic discount factor v and instead discounting $C0$ by e^{-rT}. Such changes would, however, only marginally improve the performance while rather obscuring the code; thus, we leave them out here.

5.2.2. Vectorization

We do not exploit any special structure in Matlab (i.e., we do not vectorize), even though the inner loop could be avoided by realizing that for every time step i, we have

$$
e^{r \Delta t} \underbrace{\begin{bmatrix} C_{i,i} \\ C_{i,i-1} \\ \vdots \\ C_{i,1} \\ C_{i,0} \end{bmatrix}}_{V} = p \underbrace{\begin{bmatrix} C_{i+1,i+1} \\ C_{i+1,i} \\ \vdots \\ C_{i+1,2} \\ C_{i+1,1} \end{bmatrix}}_{V^+} + (1-p) \underbrace{\begin{bmatrix} C_{i+1,i} \\ C_{i+1,i-1} \\ \vdots \\ C_{i+1,1} \\ C_{i+1,0} \end{bmatrix}}_{V^-},
$$

which is illustrated below for $i = 2$.

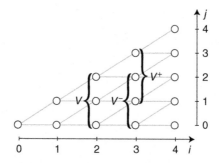

Some testing showed that implementing this approach does not substantially improve performance (in current versions of Matlab), even though in older versions of Matlab it did (see Higham, 2002). Hence, we keep the double-loop structure. The same does not hold for R; here the nested loops are much slower than the vectorized version.

Listing 5.2. C-BinomialTrees/R/EuropeanCall.R

```
 1  # EuropeanCall.R -- version 2010-12-28
 2  EuropeanCall <- function(S0,X,r,T,sigma,M) {
 3      # compute constants
 4      f7 <- 1;  dt <- T/M; v <- exp(-r * dt)
 5      u  <- exp(sigma * sqrt(dt)); d <- 1/u
 6      p  <- (exp(r * dt) - d) / (u - d)
 7
 8      # initialize asset prices at maturity (period M)
 9      S <- numeric(M + 1)
10      S[f7+0] <- S0 * d^M
11      for (j in 1:M) S[f7+j] <- S[f7+j - 1] * u / d
12
13      # initialise option values at maturity (period M)
14      C <- pmax(S - X, 0)
15
16      # step back through the tree
17      for (i in seq(M-1,0,by=-1)) {
18          C <- v * (p * C[(1+f7):(i+1+f7)] +
19              (1 - p)* C[(0+f7):(i+f7)])
20      }
21      return(C)
22  }
```

The prices at period M (Statements 10–14 in the R-code) could be initialized by the more efficient vectorized command `S <- S0 * u^(0:M) * d^(M:0)`.

5.2.3. Binomial expansion

Algorithm 16 only uses the stock prices at T. These prices are, in turn, computed from the current price, $S_{0,0}$. Since the number of stock paths reaching final node j is given by

$$\binom{M}{j} = \frac{M!}{(M-j)!j!}$$

we can write

$$C_{0,0} = e^{-rT} \sum_{k=0}^{M} \binom{M}{k} p^k (1-p)^{M-k} C_{M,k} \tag{5.5}$$

where $C_{M,k} = \max(u^k d^{M-k} S - X, 0)$ is the payoff of the call option, evaluated at the respective final node. There is, in fact, no need to sum over all end nodes, but it suffices to select those where the option expires in the money. Such an implementation of a "tree" loses the possibility of including early exercise features (see below). It demonstrates the flexibility of the binomial method, though, since nothing limits us to plain vanilla payoffs $\max(S - X, 0)$ (or $\max(X - S, 0)$ for the put). An example may be a "power option" whose payoff (for the call) is given by

$$\max(S_T^z - X, 0)$$

where z is a real number (usually an integer) greater than one.

Numerical implementation

A straightforward implementation of Eq. (5.5) may lead to an overflow since, as the number of time steps grows, ever larger integers are required for the binomial coefficient (see Higham, 2002, for a detailed discussion of ways to circumvent these problems in Matlab; see Staunton, 2003, for Excel experiences). The following Matlab and R implementations are based on Higham (2002).

Listing 5.3. C-BinomialTrees/M/EuropeanCallBE.m

```
1  function C0 = EuropeanCallBE(S0,X,r,T,sigma,M)
2  % EuropeanCallBE.m  -- version: 2011-05-15
3  % compute constants
4  dt = T / M;
5  u = exp(sigma*sqrt(dt));    d = 1 /u;
6  p = (exp(r * dt) - d) / (u - d);
7
8  % initialise asset prices at maturity (period M)
9  C = max(S0*d.^((M:-1:0)').*u.^((0:M)') - X,0);
10
11 % log/cumsum version
12 csl = cumsum(log([1; [1:M]']));
13 tmp = csl(M+1) - csl - csl(M+1:-1:1) + log(p)*((0:M)') + ...
14      log(1-p)*((M:-1:0)');
15 C0 = exp(-r*T)*sum(exp(tmp).*C);
```

Listing 5.4. C-BinomialTrees/R/EuropeanCallBE.R

```
1  # EuropeanCallBE.R -- version 2011-05-15
2  EuropeanCallBE <- function(S0,X,r,T,sigma,M) {
3      # compute constants
4      dt <- T/M
5      u <- exp(sigma*sqrt(dt))
6      d <- 1/u
7      p <- (exp(r * dt) - d) / (u - d)
8
9      # initialize asset prices at maturity (period M)
10     C <- pmax(S0 * d^(M:0) * u^(0:M) - X, 0)
11
12     # log/cumsum version
13     csl <- cumsum(log(c(1,1:M)))
14     tmp <- csl[M+1] - csl - csl[(M+1):1] +
15            log(p)*(0:M) + log(1-p)*(M:0)
16     C0 <- exp(-r*T)*sum(exp(tmp)*C)
17     return(C0)
18 }
```

5.3. Early exercise

Early exercise features are easily implemented in the binomial method; the original paper by Cox, Ross, and Rubinstein (1979) advocated the method exactly because of this possibility. What is required is that when we compute the new option price at a specific node, we check whether the payoff from exercising is greater than the current value of the option. Thus we need to go through the tree; we cannot use the binomial expansion. It is also necessary to update the spot price at every node. Algorithm 17 details the necessary changes in the procedure.

Algorithm 17 Testing for early exercise: An American put.

$\cdots$

for $i = M - 1 : -1 : 0$ **do**
    for $j = 0 : i$ **do**
        $C_{i,j} = v \left(p \, C_{i,j+1} + (1-p) \, C_{i,j} \right)$
        $S_{i,j} = S_{i,j}/d$
        $C_{i,j} = \max(C_{i,j}, X - S_{i,j})$
    end for
end for
$\cdots$

The following Matlab code can be used to price an American put.

Listing 5.5. C-BinomialTrees/M/AmericanPut.m

```
1  function P0 = AmericanPut(S0,X,r,T,sigma,M)
2  % AmericanPut.m -- version 2010-12-28
```

```
 3 f7 = 1;   dt = T / M;   v = exp(-r * dt);
 4 u = exp(sigma * sqrt(dt));   d = 1 / u;
 5 p = (exp(r * dt) - d) / (u - d);
 6
 7 % initialize asset prices at maturity (period M)
 8 S = zeros(M + 1,1);
 9 S(f7+0) = S0 * d^M;
10 for j = 1:M
11     S(f7+j) = S(f7+j - 1) * u / d;
12 end
13
14 % initialize option values at maturity (period M)
15 P = max(X - S, 0);
16
17 % step back through the tree
18 for i = M-1:-1:0
19     for j = 0:i
20         P(f7+j) = v * (p * P(f7+j + 1) + (1-p) * P(f7+j));
21         S(f7+j) = S(f7+j) / d;
22         P(f7+j) = max(P(f7 + j),X - S(f7+j));
23     end
24 end
25 P0 = P(f7+0);
```

5.4. Dividends

Continuous dividends

If the dividend of the asset can be approximated by a continuous dividend yield q, the algorithms need only be slightly changed. In a risk-neutral world, the drift of a dividend-paying asset changes from r to $r - q$; hence, we replace any r with $r - q$ in the tree parameters u, d, and p.

Discrete dividends

Assume the asset pays a discrete dividend, that is a fixed currency amount D, at some future time T_D (with $0 < T_D < T$). Algorithm 18 describes how to implement the "escrowed dividend model" for an American call option.

The dividend's present value D^* only depends on time (the outer loop), not on the level of S. With Matlab:

Listing 5.6. C-BinomialTrees/M/AmericanCallDiv.m

```
1 function C0 = AmericanCallDiv(S0,X,r,T,sigma,D,TD,M)
2 % AmericanCallDiv.m -- version 2010-12-28
3 % compute constants
4 f7 = 1; dt = T/M; v = exp(-r * dt);
5 u = exp(sigma*sqrt(dt)); d = 1 /u;
6 p = (exp(r * dt) - d)/(u - d);
7
8 % adjust spot for dividend
9 S0 = S0 - D * exp(-r * TD);
```

```
10
11 % initialize asset prices at maturity (period M)
12 S = zeros(M + 1,1);
13 S(f7+0) = S0 * d^M;
14 for j = 1:M
15     S(f7+j) = S(f7+j - 1) * u / d;
16 end
17
18 % initialize option values at maturity (period M)
19 C = max(S - X, 0);
20
21 % step back through the tree
22 for i = M-1:-1:0
23     % compute present value of dividend (dD)
24     t = T * i / M;
25     dD = D * exp(-r * (TD-t));
26     for j = 0:i
27         C(f7+j) = v * ( p * C(f7+j + 1) + (1-p) * C(f7+j));
28         S(f7+j) = S(f7+j) / d;
29         if t > TD
30             C(f7+j) = max(C(f7 + j), S(f7+j) - X);
31         else
32             C(f7+j) = max(C(f7 + j), S(f7+j) + dD - X);
33         end
34     end
35 end
36 C0 = C(f7+0);
```

Algorithm 18 American call for $S, X, r, \sigma, T, T_D, D$ and M time steps.

1: initialize $\Delta_t = T/M, \quad S_{0,0} = S, \quad v = e^{-r\Delta_t}$
2: compute $u = e^{\sigma\sqrt{\Delta_t}}, \quad d = 1/u, \quad p = (e^{r\Delta_t} - d)/(u - d)$
3: compute $S_{0,0} = S - De^{-rT_D}$ # adjust spot for dividend
4: $S_{M,0} = S_{0,0}d^M$
5: **for** $j = 1 : M$ **do**
6:     $S_{M,j} = S_{M,j-1}u/d$
7: **end for**
8: **for** $j = 0 : M$ **do**
9:     $C_{M,j} = \max(S_{M,j} - X, 0)$
10: **end for**
11: **for** $i = M - 1 : -1 : 0$ **do**
12:     compute $t = iT/M$ # compute current time
13:     compute $D^* = De^{-r(T_D-t)}$ # compute present value of dividend
14:     **for** $j = 0 : i$ **do**
15:         $C_{i,j} = v\left(p\,C_{i,j+1} + (1-p)\,C_{i,j}\right)$
16:         $S_{i,j} = S_{i,j}/d$
17:         **if** $t < T_D$
18:             $C_{i,j} = \max(C_{i,j}, S_{i,j} + D^* - X)$ # before dividend
19:         **else**
20:             $C_{i,j} = \max(C_{i,j}, S_{i,j} - X)$ # after dividend
21:         **end if**
22:     **end for**
23: **end for**
24: $C_0 = C_{0,0}$

5.5. The Greeks

The Black–Scholes option price is a function f of the spot price S, the strike X, the (constant) volatility σ, the risk-free rate r and time to maturity T. (If the underlier pays dividends, these will also affect the value of f.) A Taylor series expansion can be used to estimate the sensitivity of f to a given change in one of the parameters. The change in the option price is then a function of the (mathematical) derivatives of f, evaluated at the current values of the arguments. These derivatives are known as the "Greeks," and for Black–Scholes the most common ones are available in closed form. For the binomial model, the Greeks need in general be approximated by finite differences; see Chapter 2. One advantage of this approach over the analytical expressions is that we can use a meaningful change in the respective argument of f. For instance, the Θ may be computed for one day hence, which may be more reasonable (and easier to communicate to a trader) than a change of infinitesimally small size. Unfortunately, such a straightforward implementation of finite differences requires to step through the tree two or even three times. If time is of the essence, some Greeks can also be approximated directly from the original tree. (These direct approximations are again finite differences.)

Greeks from the tree

Delta Δ
The Δ is the change in the option price for a given small change in S. An estimate of Δ can be read directly from the tree:

$$\Delta_{0,0} = \frac{C_{1,1} - C_{1,0}}{S_{1,1} - S_{1,0}} \tag{5.6}$$

where we have used a subscript to Δ to indicate the node for which it is computed (here the root node, i.e., now). The following figure shows the nodes required to compute the value (left is the stock price tree, right the option price tree).

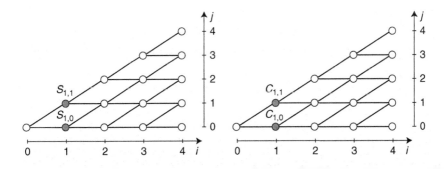

For an arbitrary node (i, j), we have

$$\Delta_{i,j} = \frac{C_{i+1,j+1} - C_{i+1,j}}{S_{i+1,j+1} - S_{i+1,j}}.$$ (5.7)

Gamma Γ

The Γ is the change in the Δ given a small change in the spot price S. Thus, the current Γ may be approximated as

$$\Gamma_{0,0} = \frac{\Delta_{1,1} - \Delta_{1,0}}{S_{1,1} - S_{1,0}} \quad \text{or} \quad \Gamma_{0,0} = \frac{\Delta_{1,1} - \Delta_{1,0}}{\frac{1}{2}(S_{2,2} - S_{2,0})}$$ (5.8)

where the second possibility uses the midpoint of the prices after two upticks and two downticks, respectively. The Δ-values, following Eq. (5.7), are

$$\Delta_{1,1} = \frac{C_{2,2} - C_{2,1}}{S_{2,2} - S_{2,1}} \quad \text{and} \quad \Delta_{1,0} = \frac{C_{2,1} - C_{2,0}}{S_{2,1} - S_{2,0}}.$$

Hence we obtain

$$\Gamma_{0,0} = \frac{\frac{C_{2,2} - C_{2,1}}{S_{2,2} - S_{2,1}} - \frac{C_{2,1} - C_{2,0}}{S_{2,1} - S_{2,0}}}{\frac{1}{2}(S_{2,2} - S_{2,0})},$$ (5.9)

where we have used the second approach from Eq. (5.8) to approximate a small change in S. The figure below shows the nodes that are required to compute the Γ.

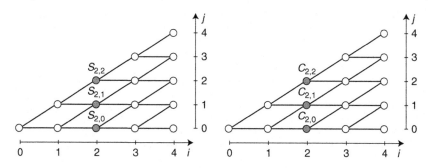

Theta Θ

The Θ is the change in the price of the option for a small change in T. Since the remaining lifetime of the option naturally decreases, the sign is usually switched for the analytical derivative. So for a long position in an option, the Θ is negative. This sign change is not necessary for a finite difference method if we let h be a small negative quantity. If the tree fulfills the condition $ud = 1$ (as is the case for Cox, Ross, and Rubinstein, 1979), the spot price will arrive at its initial value at time step 2. Thus, a simple method to approximate Θ is

$$\Theta_{0,0} = \frac{C_{2,1} - C_{0,0}}{2\,\Delta_t}. \tag{5.10}$$

The following figure indicates the required nodes.

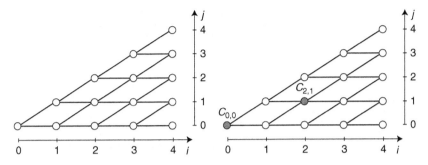

If the "centering on the spot" condition $ud = 1$ is not fulfilled, then Θ may either be approximated by a standard finite difference or, as suggested by Rubinstein (1994), by

$$\Theta_{0,0} = rC_{0,0} - rS_{0,0}\Delta_{0,0} - \frac{1}{2}\sigma^2 S_{0,0}^2 \Gamma, \tag{5.11}$$

which uses the Black–Scholes differential equation. The Δ and Γ can be taken from the tree as described above, hence one loop through the tree suffices to obtain Θ. Some remarks: When computing the Greeks, the spot price must be updated in the tree. If there is a discrete dividend, it must be added back to the spot (as in the case of early exercise). A Matlab program (we chose a European call to make comparison with the analytical Greeks easier):

Listing 5.7. C-BinomialTrees/M/EuropeanCallGreeks.m

```
1  function [C0,deltaE,gammaE,thetaE] = EuropeanCallGreeks(S0,X,r,
       T,sigma,M)
2  % EuropeanCallGreeks.m -- version 2010-12-28
3  % compute constants
4  f7 = 1;   dt = T/M;   v = exp(-r * dt);
5  u = exp(sigma*sqrt(dt));   d = 1 /u;
6  p = (exp(r * dt) - d)/(u - d);
7
8  % initialize asset prices at maturity (period M)
9  S = zeros(M + 1,1);
10 S(f7+0) = S0 * d^M;
11 for j = 1:M
12     S(f7+j) = S(f7+j - 1) * u / d;
13 end
14
15 % initialize option values at maturity (period M)
16 C = max(S - X, 0);
17
```

```
18 % step back through the tree
19 for i = M-1:-1:0
20     for j = 0:i
21         C(f7+j) = v * ( p * C(f7+j + 1) + (1-p) * C(f7+j));
22         S(f7+j) = S(f7+j) / d;
23     end
24     if i==2
25       %gamma
26       gammaE = ((C(2+f7) - C(1+f7)) / (S(2+f7) - S(1+f7)) - ...
27                 (C(1+f7) - C(0+f7)) / (S(1+f7) - S(0+f7)))/ ...
28                 (0.5 * (S(2+f7) - S(0+f7)));
29         %theta (aux)
30         thetaE = C(1+f7);
31     end
32     if i==1
33         %delta
34         deltaE = (C(1+f7) - C(0+f7)) / (S(1+f7) - S(0+f7));
35     end
36     if i==0
37         %theta (final)
38         thetaE = (thetaE - C(0+f7)) / (2 * dt);
39     end
40 end
41 C0 = C(f7+0);
```

PART TWO

Simulation

CHAPTER SIX

Generating random numbers

6.1. Monte Carlo methods and sampling

6.1.1. How it all began

Monte Carlo, an area in the Principality of Monaco, is probably best known for its casino—and, among quants, for lending its name to a broad range of methods and techniques that involve random numbers to crack numerical problems. One of the pioneers for the latter was Stan Ulam who, in the 1940s, wondered whether there is a practical way of finding the odds for certain outcomes in the game of solitaire that do not require cumbersome combinatorics. His idea was to just draw a series of samples and evaluate them. Together with John von Neumann, he then extended this approach to solve demanding numerical problems in physics using electronic computers.[1] However, much earlier examples for similar experiments can be found.

French mathematician Georges Louis Leclerc Comte de Buffon considered the following problem. Assume that on a piece of paper there are parallel lines with a distance of t. Now, if one drops a needle of length ℓ onto this sheet of paper,[2] what are the chances that it touches one of the lines? After many experiments, he found the relationship

$$2 \times \frac{\text{number of drops}}{\text{number of hits}} \times \frac{\ell}{t} \approx \pi,$$

where $\pi = 3.14\ldots$ is the constant ratio between diameter and circumference of any circle. In his honor, this method to estimate π is called Buffon's algorithm. A variant of this method will be introduced later in the text.[3]

---

[1] See Ulam, Richtmyer, and von Neumann (1947) and Metropolis and Ulam (1949).
[2] Legend has it that he was also seen throwing bread sticks, *baguettes*, over his shoulder to perform experiments on a slightly larger scale.
[3] Impatient readers are referred to page 131.

6.1.2. Financial applications

In finance and economics, Monte Carlo methods are used to find approximate solutions to demanding problems. One of their advantages is that the quality of approximation can be improved simply by increasing the number of drawn samples—obviously provided that the model is correctly specified and the samples have the required statistical properties. Apart from cracking challenging numerical problems such as derivative pricing, they are also used to generate scenarios for future outcomes, produce values that are substituted for real observations, or evaluate the magnitude when factors in complex systems change, to name just a few.

Key ingredients are the models, the relationships, and the random numbers employed. This chapter deals with the latter. Several alternatives exist, the main ones are as follow:

- Genuine *random numbers* in the strictest sense can only be produced by physical and real-world processes, such as radioactive decay—or the outcomes from a fair casino roulette table. If the efficient market hypothesis holds, one might argue that asset prices, too, contain genuine randomness; even when properties and underlying principles are understood and known, the actual outcome cannot be perfectly predicted and must, therefore, be considered random. (Genuine) random numbers coming from computers are rare if not impossible; devices that measure physical activities (e.g., background radiation) could do the trick here.

- Random numbers from software might look genuinely random at first glance, yet they do come from a deterministic algorithm. Therefore, they are called *pseudorandom numbers*. This might seem like a limitation, but actually, numbers from a reliable deterministic random number generator can have great benefits. The two most important advantages are: (i) they can be reproduced; this facilitates controlled and replicable experiments; and (ii) one can accommodate the type of distribution and properties.

- *Quasirandom numbers* are constructed to maximize some goodness-of-fit measure. Usually, they are too "perfect" to look random, but they satisfy the relevant theoretical properties as well as possible. These methods can be efficient in areas such as numerical integration but are often inadequate for a series of repeated independent experiments.

- *Bootstrap* methods resample from a given data set. Their advantage is that no assumptions about parametric distributions are required, but they do rely on a representative set of available observation.

For our purposes, pseudorandom numbers will be the most important type. In the sense of brevity, the prefix "pseudo" will mostly be dropped, and terms such as "random variables," "random variates," and "random numbers" will refer to this group unless stated otherwise. Again, their main property is that they are generated by some deterministic processes, but they should not be distinguishable from genuine random numbers. A lot of discussion and work has gone into creating such processes. Since pseudorandom numbers are one of the key ingredients for simulation, it is worthwhile to look at some of the standard algorithms.

6.2. Uniform random number generators

6.2.1. Congruential generators

When it comes to designing a (pseudo)random number generator (RNG), most effort has gone into methods for uniform random numbers. The reason for this is simple: it is relatively easy to transform uniform variates into other distributions. Therefore, getting the main building block of a uniform RNG right is crucial.

As discussed in Section 2.1, computers operate in discrete rather than continuous space. Hence, when b bits are used to represent a number, 2^b distinct values can be created. Uniform random numbers take any value within the range $[\ell, h]$ with equal probability. For practical reasons, however, uniform numbers within the range $[0, 1]$ are considered. The transformation is straightforward:

$$u \sim U(0,1) \iff \ell + (h - \ell)u \sim U(\ell, h). \qquad (6.1)$$

Hence, if one can produce uniformly distributed integers within the range $[0, 2^b - 1]$, interpreting these values as the mantissa immediately gives us (close enough to) continuous values in the range $[0, 1)$.

A widely used type of RNGs are *sequential congruential generators* in which each new number u_i is a function of the previous l numbers and parameters π:

$$u_i = f(u_{i-1}, \ldots, u_{k-l}; \pi).$$

To generate a sequence of integers, a simple case would be a *linear congruential generator*

$$u_i = (au_{i-1} + c) \mod m, \qquad (6.2)$$

where the parameters a, c, and m are integers (see Algorithm 19). Provided the initial value (or *seed*) u_0, this method can produce values $u_i \in \{0, \ldots, m - 1\}$. For example, if $m = 10$, then possible values for u_i are the integers from zero to nine. With m sufficiently large, the u_is can then be converted into rational numbers $f_i \in [0; 1)$ according to $f_i = u_i / m$. If, for example,

$m = 10^p$, we would end up with values that could be considered real valued with a precision of p digits after the decimal point.[4]

Algorithm 19 Linear congruential random number generator.

1: provide modulus m, multiplier a, $0 < a < m$, increment c, $0 < c < m$ and seed u_0
2: **for** $i = 1 : n$ **do**
3:     $u_i = (a u_{i-1} + c) \mod m$
4:     $f_i = u_i / m$
5: **end for**

Listing 6.1. C-RandomNumberGeneration/M/LinearCongruential.m

```
 1 function u = LinearCongruential(a,b,m,seed,N);
 2 % LinearCongruential.m  -- version 2011-01-06
 3 %    linear congruential random number generator
 4 %    a, c, m ... parameters
 5 %    seed ...... seed
 6 %    N ......... number of samples
 7
 8 % -- initialize
 9 if nargin<5, N = 1;   end;
10 u = nan(N+1,1);
11 u(1) = seed;
12 if u(1)<1
13     u(1) = floor(u(1)*m);
14 end
15
16 % -- generate variates
17 for i = 2:(N+1)
18     u(i) = mod( (a*u(i-1) + c) , m);
19 end
20 u(1) = [];
21 u = u/m;
```

An obvious feature of this method is that the sequence will exhibit cycles: since the parameters are fixed and only the immediate predecessor is used, a certain realization u_{i-1} will always have the same successor u_i. In other words, the sequence will be periodic: when a certain integer is drawn for the second time, it will be followed by the same number (and, consecutively, sequence of numbers) as in the first time. Even more importantly, with inappropriate parameter values a and c, not all of the integers within the range will be drawn; and if an integer is missed out in the first round, it will never occur in later rounds either. Both cases can easily be illustrated for small ranges (i.e., with small m), see Table 6.1.

---

[4] Since computers function with a binary system, a choice of $m = 2^{p_b}$ is more common. Since several binary digits are required to represent one decimal digit, p_b has to be higher than its decimal equivalent p; $p_b = \left\lceil \frac{\log(10)}{\log(2)} p \right\rceil$ to be precise. The effect, however, is the same.

Table 6.1 Series of pseudorandom numbers from a linear congruential RNG, where $u_i = (a\,u_{i-1}) \mod 7$ and $u_0 = 1$ and different multipliers a.

					a						
	113	114	115	116	117	118	119	120	121	122	123
u_1	1	2	3	4	5	6	0	1	2	3	4
u_2	1	4	2	2	4	1	0	1	4	2	2
u_3	1	1	6	1	6	6	0	1	1	6	1
u_4	1	2	4	4	2	1	0	1	2	4	4
u_5	1	4	5	2	3	6	0	1	4	5	2
u_6	1	1	1	1	1	1	0	1	1	1	1
u_7	1	2	3	4	5	6	0	1	2	3	4
u_8	1	4	2	2	4	1	0	1	4	2	2
u_9	1	1	6	1	6	6	0	1	1	6	1
u_{10}	1	2	4	4	2	1	0	1	2	4	4

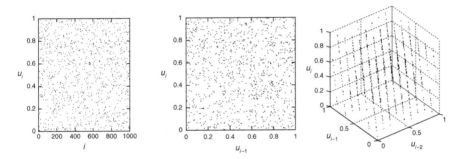

Figure 6.1 Random numbers from the `randu` function, where $u_i = (65539\,u_{i-1}) \mod 2^{31}$.

For larger values of m, this issue is harder to spot. Therefore, it took some time to recognize that the then widely used random number generator suffered from this problem: famously (or rather infamously), IBM's `randu` routine used the values $a = 65539$, $c = 0$, and $m = 2^{31}$. Plotting the sequence of the u_is gives a noisy picture (as one might expect from a RNG), and so does a two-dimensional scatterplot of u_i on the y-axis against u_{i-1} on the x-axis. A three-dimensional scatterplot of subsequent values u_{i-2}, u_{i-1}, and u_i, however, reveals that all points sit on one of 15 two-dimensional planes (see Fig. 6.1).

This phenomenon is an inherent property of this type of generator: when sequences of generated numbers are considered, they seem to arrange themselves in a rather distinct "lattice structure" or start exhibiting patterns. Also, setting $c = 0$ is not a good choice since $u_i = 0$ is an absorbent state, where all the subsequent numbers are also zero.[5] Good parameter calibration is, therefore, paramount when using this type of RNG. An example for a suitable choice of parameters, provided by Jones, Maillardet, and Robinson (2009, p. 332), would be $a = 1,664,525$ for the multiplier, $c = 1,013,904,223$ for the increment, and $m = 2^{32}$ for the modulus. Alternatively, other types of generators can also be used. Simple variants to the linear version include the multiple recursive generator,

$$u_i = \left(\sum_{j=1}^{\ell} a_j u_{i-j} \right) \mod m,$$

the lagged Fibonacci generator,

$$u_i = (u_{i-j} + u_{i-k}) \mod m,$$

and the inversive congruential generator,

$$u_i = (a u_{i-1}^{-1} + c) \mod m,$$

where u_{i-1}^{-1} is the modular multiplicative inverse of u_{i-1} (i.e., $u_{i-1}^{-1} u_{i-1} = 1$ mod m). For the inversive congruential generator, if $m = 1$, $u_0 \in (0,1)$ and noninteger values for a and c results in values in the range $(0,1)$. For the multiple recursive and lagged Fibonacci generators, the previously mentioned scaling (or shift of the decimal point) maps the u_is into the $(0,1)$ range.

It is important to note that for all approaches, independent multivariate random numbers can be generated by using subsequent values.

6.2.2. Mersenne Twister

Software like R and, in the more recent versions, Matlab provide the *Mersenne Twister* as standard. The name already indicates that one of its key ingredients is a Mersenne number, $M_p = 2^p - 1$, which, when written in binary notation, is a bit string of length p with all bits set to 1. For example, the binary representation of $M_4 = 2^4 - 1 = 15$ is 1111_2. In other words, M_p is the highest integer that can be represented with a bit string of length p. This method uses more than one previously generated number and performs bitwise operations. Its properties are similar to those of linear congruential generators, yet its period length is M_p. The commonly used version for 32-bit platforms, MT19937, has a period length of 2^{19937}; in other words, it takes a sequence of more than 10^{6000} draws until it becomes repetitive. Also, sequences of all lengths up to 623 are equally probable, so there should be no obvious lattice issues. For most applications (and certainly for those discussed in this book), this seems to be a safe enough choice.

---

[5] A linear congruential generator with $c = 0$ is also called *multiplicative congruential generator*.

There exists a large variety of approaches that test the quality of random numbers. One of the well-known sets of such tests are the diehard tests by George Marsaglia (see Marsaglia, 1995).

6.3. Nonuniform distributions

6.3.1. The inversion method

As mentioned, uniform random numbers can be used to generate variables that follow any arbitrary distribution. The most general approach for this is the inversion method. The idea behind this is relatively simple but extremely powerful: Assume X has a continuous cumulative distribution function (CDF) $F(X)$, and x_i is a random draw. Then $F(x_i)$ is uniformly distributed, $F(x_i) \sim U(0,1)$.

To grasp this idea intuitively, let us assume X is standard normally distributed, $X \sim N(0,1)$. In this case, there is a 50–50 chance that a random draw will bring a positive or negative value since the median for a standard normal variable is 0. Any negative realization will come with a probability of $F(x_i) \in [0, 0.5)$ $\forall x_i < 0$, whereas a positive draw (or the draw of $x_i = 0$) comes with a density above 0.5, $F(x_i) \in [0.5, 1]$ $\forall x_i > 0$. If we repeat this experiment n times, then half of the draws will be positive, the other half negative, and their respective densities $F(x_i)$ will be half of the times above 0.5, half of the times below. Plotting a histogram of the $F(x_i)$s with just two bins ($[0, 0.5)$ and $[0.5, 1]$) should, therefore, provide two bars of equal height; deviations are due to sampling error and should vanish when more samples are drawn. If we check not only at the median but also at the quartiles,[6] chances for a standard normal to be -0.67449 or less are $F(-0.67449) = 0.25$; accordingly, $F(+0.67449) = 0.75$, and we already know that $F(0) = 0.5$. Hence, there is a 25% chance that x_i is within $[\infty, -0.67449]$, another 25% chance that it falls within $[-0.67449, 0]$, and so on. The histogram of the $F(x_i)$s for these new bins should again have bars of equal height and contain $n/4$ observations each. It is easy to see where this example leads: there is a 10% chance that an observation falls into any of the 10 equally spaced quantiles of $F(x_i)$, a 1% chance for any of the 100 equally spaced intervals $[0, 0.01]$, $[0.01, 0.02]$, etc. Making the bins increasingly finer eventually approaches a continuous uniform distribution.

The inversion method now reverses this principle: It draws a uniform number $u_i \sim U(0,1)$ and checks which x_i has the corresponding $F(x_i)$.

---

[6] As a quick reminder, q_α is called the quantile for probability α if it has a cumulative distribution of $F(q_\alpha) = \alpha$. In other words, with a probability of α, random draws should produce values that are q_α or less. The quartiles $q_{25\%}$, $q_{50\%}$, and $q_{75\%}$ are special cases of quantiles.

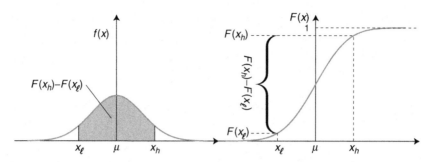

Figure 6.2 Confidence bands and probabilities for realizations within a region (x_ℓ, x_h).

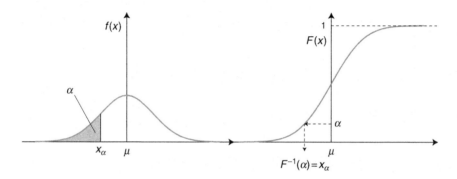

Figure 6.3 Inversion principle.

In our example, this is like picking the bin for the histogram first and then searching the x_i that belongs to that bin. Therefore, x_i corresponds to the u_i quantile of F. Figures 6.2 and 6.3 illustrate this.

More technically, let $F^{-1}(\alpha) = q_\alpha$ be the inverse (or quantile) function for a CDF $F(X)$ and u_i a uniform random number, $u_i \sim U(0,1)$. Then, $x_i = F^{-1}(u_i)$ is a random draw for $X \sim F(X)$. Graphically, $F^{-1}(X)$ switches the x- and y-axis. Analytically, one needs to solve the definition of $F(X)$ for X. This is possible for some distributions but not for all.

More frequently, however, numerical methods have to be employed to crack this problem. According to the method, the objective is to find the value x such that the CDF takes the value u: $F(x) = u$. This is equivalent to the zero-finding problem $F(x) - u = 0$; Chapter 11 discusses appropriate methods. The advantage of this approach is that it is the most generic one; basically, it works as long as the CDF $F(x)$ can be computed for any given x. If one needs to generate many draws, this approach can be slow; in that case, analytical approximations for the inverse can be helpful. Section 6.4 provides some examples for this.

6.3.2. Acceptance–rejection method

To draw samples x with a density f_X when the inverse of the CDF, F_X^{-1}, is not available, the acceptance–rejection method can be used. The main idea here is to take samples z from a manageable distribution with the same support and accept (or reject) and compare the two densities at this point. z is randomly accepted as a sample for x with probability $f_X(z)/(cf_Z(z))$. The scaling constant c ensures that this ratio never exceeds 1; in other words, the scaled density of z is always above that of f_X, $cf_Z \geq f_X$; this is why cf_Z is called the majorizing function.

To illustrate this principle, assume one wants to draw samples x from a standard normal distribution, $f_X = \phi(x)$. The maximum density is reached at $\phi(0) = 0.40$. For the sake of simplicity, we assume that we can ignore values below -5 and above $+5$. For the majorizing density, one can choose a uniform distribution for the same support, $z \sim U(-5, +5)$, and according to Eq. (6.1), it can be a transformed $U(0, 1)$ uniform. Its density in this range is a constant $f_Z = 1/10$; hence, $c \geq \frac{\max f_X}{f_Z} = \frac{0.40}{0.1} = 4$.

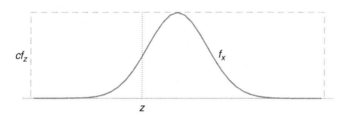

Strictly speaking, in this example f_X is a truncated density and should, therefore, be adjusted slightly. However, this would be perfectly offset by the adjusted c. With $r = \frac{f_X(z)}{cf_Z(z)} = \frac{f_X(z)}{4 \times 0.1}$, the Matlab sampling procedure reads as follows:

```
while true
    z = rand * 10 - 5;
    r = normpdf(z) / ( 4 * 0.1 );
    if rand < r;
        x = z;
        break;
    end
end
```

Obviously, the lower (higher) the density $f_X(z)$, the lower (higher) the probability that z is actually accepted as a sample for x; therefore, the algorithm should produce samples that resemble the distribution f_X.

The uniform distribution is arguably not the best choice for a majorizing density here. The main downside is that it requires truncation. If one is also interested in extreme values, this is not a good thing. We could increase the support, but then there will be broad regions where the chances of acceptance are very small, and we would have to draw an increasing number of samples until a sample is accepted. Therefore, it might be more efficient to choose another majorizing density that roughly resembles the shape of the actual density of interest.

For example, assume one wants to generate Gaussian variates x by sampling and accepting/rejecting exponentials. For the Gaussian, we have density

$$\phi(x) = \frac{1}{\sqrt{2\pi}} e^{-x^2/2}.$$

We only look at positive values of the distribution (and later flip a coin to get the sign); hence, $f_X(x) = 2\phi(x)$ is actually twice the Gaussian density. The density of the exponential distribution with unit mean is

$$f_Z = e^{-z}.$$

The ratio is

$$\frac{2\phi(z)}{e^{-z}} = \frac{\sqrt{2}}{\sqrt{\pi}} e^{z - z^2/2}.$$

This expression times $1/c$ will be an acceptance probability; hence, c should be chosen such that the ratio will not take values above 1. The maximum for the ratio is found for $z = 1$, so we need to fix c as follows:

$$c^* = \frac{\sqrt{2}}{\sqrt{\pi}} e^{1/2} \simeq 1.32.$$

Any other $c > c^*$ would work as well, but it would be less efficient, since we would reject more often. The following figures illustrates this.

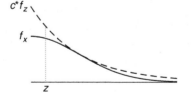
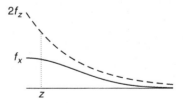

The y-scale of these densities does not matter (only their ratio); hence, we omit the y-axis. In the left panel, c^* is used. Suppose we draw a z of 0.3; the probability of acceptance is about 80%. In the right panel, we use a c of 2; the probability of acceptance drops to about 50%. Thus, we are much more likely to go through the loop without returning a random variate x. This scheme can be further simplified (Devroye, 1986, pp. 44–45); then, we obtain Algorithm 20.

Algorithm 20 Simplified acceptance–rejection for standard normal variates.

1: **repeat**
2: generate exponential sample Z
3: generate $(0,1)$ uniform sample U and set $V = 2U - 1$
4: **until** $(Z - 1)^2 \leq -2 \log(|V|)$
5: set $Y = \mathrm{sign}(V) Z$

Listing 6.2. C-RandomNumberGeneration/M/NormalAcceptReject.m

```
1  function x = NormalAcceptReject(n)
2  % NormalAcceptReject.m  -- version 2011-01-06
3  %       generate n standard normal variates x
4  x = NaN(n,1);
5  for i = 1:n
6      while isnan( x(i) )
7          z = -log(rand);
8          r = normpdf(z) / ( 1.32*exp(-z) );
9          if rand < r
10             x(i) = z * sign(rand - 0.5);
11         end
12     end
13 end
```

A special variant of the acceptance–rejection method is the ziggurat algorithm by Marsaglia and Tsang (2000), where the density is split into layers; a draw consists of first picking a layer and then an observation that falls within this segment.

6.4. Specialized methods for selected distributions

6.4.1. Normal distribution

The Box–Muller method
A widely popular algorithm to generate variates that are $N(0,1)$ distributed has been suggested by Box and Muller (1958). Its beauty lies in several aspects: the approach is remarkably simple and fast, and it produces two uncorrelated draws.[7] The idea is to use two (independent) uniform random numbers from the unit square, $u_1, u_2 \sim U(0,1)$, and to convert them into $z_1, z_2 \sim N(0,1)$:

$$z_1 = \underbrace{\sqrt{-2 \log(u_1)}}_{r}\ \underbrace{\cos(2\pi u_2)}_{c_x}$$

$$z_2 = \underbrace{\sqrt{-2 \log(u_1)}}_{r}\ \underbrace{\sin(2\pi u_2)}_{c_y}.$$

---

[7] How to generate variates that do exhibit correlation and other forms of dependencies will be presented in Chapter 7.

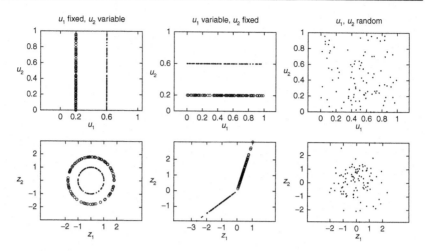

Figure 6.4 Numbers within the unit square before (top panel) and after (bottom panel) Box–Muller transformation.

Let us start with the second part of the equations. For any value $u_2 \in [0,1]$, the transformations $c_x = \cos(2\pi u_2)$ and $c_y = \sin(2\pi u_2)$ produce the coordinates for a point on the unit circle. The first part, $r = \sqrt{2\log(u_1)}$, produces a value in the range of $(0, \infty)$: if u_1 goes to zero, r goes to $-\infty$, and if u_1 goes to 1, r converges to zero. Multiplied with c_x and c_y, r scales the coordinates. Consequently, z_1 and z_2 are now sitting on a circle of random radius r. Fig. 6.4 illustrates this.

Listing 6.3. C-RandomNumberGeneration/M/GaussianBoxMullerSim.m

```
1  function [z1,z2] = GaussianBoxMullerSim(N_samples)
2  % GaussianBoxMullerSim.m  -- version 2011-01-06
3  if nargin < 1, N_samples=1; end;
4  u = rand(N_samples,2);
5  z1 = sqrt(-2*log(u(:,1))) .* cos(2 * pi * u(:,2));
6  z2 = sqrt(-2*log(u(:,1))) .* sin(2 * pi * u(:,2));
```

Alternatively, one could also argue that first the radius of the circle, r, is picked randomly (via u_1), and then a random point (z_1, z_2) on this circle is chosen (via u_2). Note that, by construction, any point (z_1, z_2) has the same chance of being picked. This ensures that z_1 and z_2 will be linearly uncorrelated.[8] In other words, $z_i \sim N(0,1)$ and $\mathrm{Cov}(z_1, z_2) = 0$. In a passing note, the Box–Muller transformation *always* requires two random uniform numbers, even if only one normal variate is to be produced. Fixing either u_1 or u_2 will cause neither z_1 nor z_2 to be normally distributed.

---

[8] Recipes for generating related variates will be presented in Chapter 7.

Marsaglia's polar method

Based on the Box–Muller transformation, George Marsaglia's polar method avoids trigonometric functions that used to be computationally time-consuming (see Marsaglia, 1991). The basic idea is to pick a point (a_1, a_2) from within the unit circle and transform its coordinates. The unit circle stretches both horizontally and vertically from -1 to $+1$; this means $a_1, a_2 \in [-1, 1]$. To achieve this, one can draw two uniform numbers and scale them according to Eq. (6.1):

$$a_i = -1 + \big(1 - (-1)\big)u_i = -1 + 2u_i \quad \text{for} \quad i = 1, 2 \quad \text{and} \quad u_i \sim U(0, 1).$$

Obviously, the point (a_1, a_2) could also be very close to one of the corners of the square enclosing the unit circle; $(0.9, 0.9)$ would be an example for such a case. To check whether the point actually is at or within the unit circle, we can use the Pythagorean theorem: the distance to the origin of point (a_1, a_2) is

$$r = \sqrt{a_1^2 + a_2^2}.$$

The unit circle, with its center right at the origin, is defined by r being exactly one. So to meet the "at-or-within-the-unit-circle" rule, points with $r > 1$ cannot be used and must be replaced with another random draw of a_is. In passing note, we have just touched a Monte Carlo method of estimating the value of π.

Example 6.1

The area of a circle of radius r is $A_c = 2r\pi$; the area of the square enclosing it is $A_s = (2r)^2$. Therefore, the area of the unit circle with $r = 1$ is exactly $A_c = \pi$; the square enclosing it has a side length of $2r = 2$ and an area of $A_s = 4$. The ratio of the two areas is, therefore, $A_c/A_s = \pi/4$. Now, this implies that a randomly picked point (a_1, a_2) with $a_i \in [-1, 1]$ should have a $\pi/4$ chance to fall at or within the unit circle, that is, to sit on a circle with radius $r \leq 1$. For n draws, one would expect the number of points within the circle to be $E(n_w) = n \cdot \pi/4$. Solving this equation, we get an approximation for π: $\pi = 4E(n_w)/n$. PiBySimulation.m uses this principle. Note how larger sample sizes n give estimates closer to the actual value of $\pi = 3.14159\ldots$

Listing 6.4. C-RandomNumberGeneration/M/PibySimulation.m

```
1  function piEst = PibySimulation(N_samples)
2  % PibySimulation.m  -- version 2011-01-06
3
4  a = rand(N_samples,2)*2 - 1;
5  r = sqrt(a(:,1).^2 + a(:,2).^2);
6  within_unit_circle = (r<=1);
7  piEst = 4 * sum(within_unit_circle)/N_samples;
```

Once a "valid" point with $r \leq 1$ is found, it can be transformed into a standard normal according to

$$z_1 = \sqrt{-2\log(r^2)}\frac{a_1}{r} \quad \text{and} \quad z_2 = \sqrt{-2\log(r^2)}\frac{a_2}{r}.$$

Again, z_1 and z_2 have no linear correlation, so

$$z_i \sim N(0,1) \quad \text{and} \quad \text{Cov}(z_1, z_2) = 0.$$

Listing 6.5. C-RandomNumberGeneration/M/GaussianPolarSim.m

```
 1 function [z1,z2] = GaussianPolarSim(N_samples)
 2 % GaussianPolarSim.m  -- version 2011-01-06
 3
 4 if nargin < 1, N_samples = 1; end
 5 a = rand(N_samples,2) * 2 - 1;
 6 s = a(:,1).^2 + a(:,2).^2;
 7
 8 % --check for "at-or-within-unit-circle" criterion
 9 outside = s > 1;
10 while sum(outside) > 0
11     a(outside,:) = rand(sum(outside),2) * 2 - 1;
12     s(outside,:) = a(outside,1).^2 + a(outside,2).^2;
13     outside = s > 1;
14 end
15
16 % --perform transformation
17 f  = sqrt(-2*log(s)./s);
18 z1 = f .* a(:,1);
19 z2 = f .* a(:,2);
```

By definition, any Gaussian variable, $X \sim N(\mu, \sigma^2)$, can be standardized by first demeaning it and then dividing it by its standard deviation,

$$X \sim N(\mu, \sigma^2) \iff Z \sim N(0,1) \quad \text{where} \quad Z = \frac{X - \mu}{\sigma}.$$

Considering the opposite route, a standard normal variable can be transformed into any arbitrary normal distribution by scaling it with the required standard deviation σ and shifting it by adding the location parameter (for this distribution equal to the expected value) μ:

$$Z \sim N(0,1) \iff X \sim N(\mu, \sigma^2), \quad \text{where} \quad X = Z\sigma + \mu.$$

Therefore, it is sufficient to have a generator for standard normal variables; all others can be derived by transformation.

6.4.2. Higher order moments and the Cornish–Fisher expansion

By definition, the normal distribution is symmetric and has a kurtosis of 3. In finance, we often find that empirical data have distributions that are (somewhat) bell shaped, but are heavy tailed and skewed. One way of dealing with this is the choice of alternative parametric distributions that share these properties, another one to transform the data. A simple way to do so is the Cornish–Fisher expansion. The idea is to shift the quantile of the normal distribution, $u_\alpha = N^{-1}(\alpha)$, according to

$$\Omega_\alpha = u_\alpha + \frac{S}{6}\left(u_\alpha^2 - 1\right) + \frac{K-3}{24}\left(u_\alpha^3 - 3u_\alpha\right) - \frac{S^2}{36}\left(2u_\alpha^3 - 5u_\alpha\right),$$

where S and K are the skewness and kurtosis, respectively. Given mean μ and standard deviation σ, the critical α quantile can then be computed by

$$q_\alpha^{\mathrm{CF}} = \mu + \Omega_\alpha \sigma.$$

A simple Matlab function is provided below.

Listing 6.6. C-RandomNumberGeneration/M/CornishFisher.m

```
1  function q = CornishFisher(r,alpha)
2  % CornishFisher.m  -- version 2011-01-06
3
4  S = skewness(r);
5  K = kurtosis(r);
6  u = norminv(alpha);
7  Omega = u + S/6*(u^2-1) + (K-3)/24 *(u^3 - 3*u) ...
8          - S^2/36 * (2*u^3-5*u);
9  q = mean(r) + Omega * std(r);
```

Similar to using kernel density estimates (see Section 6.7.2) rather than the raw empirical distribution, the Cornish–Fisher expansion can smooth the ragged nature of observations (in particular, in the tails of the distribution) and allow α quantiles that would otherwise not be permitted by the granularity of the data (e.g., estimate the 0.1% VaR based on just 250 observations).

In return, this approach can also be used for simulating data that are more or less normally distributed, yet with some skewness and/or excess kurtosis.

Listing 6.7. C-RandomNumberGeneration/M/CornishFisherSimulation.m

```
1  function X = CornishFisherSimulation(mu,sigma,skew,kurt,N);
2  % CornishFisherSimulation.m  version 2011-01-06
3  alpha = rand(N,1);
4  u = norminv(alpha);
5  Omega = u + skew/6*(u.^2-1) + (kurt-3)/24 *(u.^3 - 3*u) ...
6          - skew^2/36 * (2*u.^3-5*u);
7  X = mu + sigma * Omega;
```

However, note that this only works for reasonably small deviations from the normal distribution. Fig. 6.5 illustrates this: requiring a skewness within ± 0.5 works reasonably well, more extreme values are hardly possible. For excess kurtosis, the expansion tends to overreact, and samples have often higher kurtosis than required.

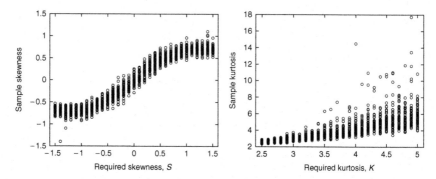

Figure 6.5 Required skewness (left panel) and kurtosis (right panel), and sample moments with 500 observations per sample.

6.4.3. Further distributions

For convenience, `rand` refers to a $(0,1)$ uniform random number generator and `randn` to the one for standard normals. Several important distributions can be traced back to the normal distribution or transformations of it.

Lognormal distribution X is lognormally distributed if $\log(X) \sim N(\mu, \sigma^2)$ is normally distributed. We will meet this distribution again on several occasions since it is a popular choice for stock prices.

```
z = randn*sigma + mu;
x = exp(z);
```

χ^2 **distribution** The sum of v squared normally distributed variables follows a chi-squared distribution with v degrees of freedom; the usual way of writing is χ_v^2.

```
z = randn(1,nu);
x = z*z';
```

F **distribution** The ratio of two χ^2 distributed variables, $x_i \sim \chi_{v_i}^2$, is F distributed: $F_{v_1,v_2} = \frac{V_1/v_1}{V_2/v_2}$.

```
z1 = randn(1,nu(1));
z2 = randn(1,nu(2));
v = z1*z1' / (z2 * z2');
```

Student t distribution The t distribution with v degrees of freedom is defined as the distribution of the ratio $Z/\sqrt{V/v}$, where $Z \sim N(0,1)$ and $V \sim \chi_v^2$; Z and V are independent. In this incarnation, it has expected value 0 and variance 1. This distribution is important in statistical testing, and it is sometimes used as an alternative to the normal distribution to model asset returns because of its heavier tails: the lower v the higher the chances for extreme values compared with the normal distribution, and this is a feature that can also be found in empirical data.

As mentioned earlier, V could, in principle, be sampled as the sum of v squared Gaussian variates. This requires sampling $v + 1$ standard Gaussian variates to compute one t variate. A more efficient algorithm is given in Bailey (1994):

```
u = rand(1,2);
x = sqrt( nu * u(1)^(-2/nu)-1) * cos(2*pi*u(2));
```

Exponential The exponential distribution comes with only one parameter, λ, which is also its mean. It suffices to generate variates with unit mean (i.e., $\lambda = 1$), since the scaled variable, mX, will have mean m.

```
x = -log(rand);
```

Laplace A Laplace variate with $\mu = 0$ and $b = 1$ is an exponential with $\lambda = 1$, plus a random sign (which is why the Laplace distribution is also called the double exponential distribution).

```
u = rand(2,1);
x = -log(u(1)) * sign(u(2) - 0.5);
```

Cauchy The Cauchy distribution has a PDF of $f(X) = \frac{\sigma}{\pi(X^2+\sigma^2)}$ and a CDF of $F(X) = 1/2 + 1/\pi \arctan(X/\sigma)$. The inverse is $\sigma \tan\left(\pi(U - 1/2)\right)$, but because of the symmetry of the tangent, variates can be simulated with $\sigma \tan(\pi U)$.

```
u = rand;
x = sigma * tan(pi*rand);
```

Poisson The Poisson distribution has probability mass function

$$P(k) = \frac{e^{-\mu}\mu^k}{k!} \quad \text{for} \quad k = 0,1,2,\ldots$$

For small μ, we can use the following algorithm (Ripley, 1987, Alg. 3.3):

```
P = 1;
N = 0;
c = exp(-mu);
while P > c
     P = P * rand;
     N = N+1;
end
x = N;
```

Poisson variates are often used to model the occurrence of independent events (in finance: jumps). For recipes to generate jumps over time, see Devroye (1986, Chapter 6).

Bernoulli Success ($x = 1$) has probability p, otherwise $x = 0$.

```
x = rand < p;
```

Binomial In a series of n draws, each time the probability of success is p. The probability of k successes is

$$\binom{n}{k} p^k (1-p)^{n-k}. \tag{6.3}$$

The binomial distribution gives the distribution of successes, that is, Eq. (6.3) for $0 \leq k \leq n$. The simplest (but practical only for small n) idea is to generate n Bernoulli variates, and to sum them.

```
x = sum(rand(n,1) < p);
```

6.5. Sampling from a discrete set

6.5.1. Discrete uniform selection

In several of the nondeterministic methods covered in this book, one needs to randomly pick one or several elements out of a given set. Assume that the n elements of this set are indexed $i = 1 \ldots n$. If any element can be picked with the same probability of $1/n$, this can be done in a simple fashion using uniform random numbers. Assume that $n = 2$, then the rule could be as follows: if a $(0,1)$ uniform random number u is within the range $[0, 0.5)$, the first element is picked; if it is within the range $[0.5, 1)$, the second element is chosen.[9] Multiplying u by n increases the ranges to $[0, 1)$ and $[1, 2)$. The integer part of $2u$ indicates which of the elements is chosen: 0 for the first and 1 for the second. Hence, rounding $2u$ up to the next integer will return the index number of the element. This generalizes for arbitrary $n \geq 1$. In Matlab,

```
ceil(rand*n)
```

will, therefore, produce a uniformly distributed discrete number from the set $\{1, 2, \ldots, n\}$.

If more than one draw is required, one needs to distinguish whether one element may be selected several times. If so,

```
u = ceil(rand(1,d)*n);
```

will produce a $1 \times d$ vector u containing the draws from the set $\{1, \ldots, n\}$, which may contain identical values. If an element may be drawn only once, there are several recipes. One would be to draw one element after the next one and ensure that it hasn't been picked previously. A Matlab implementation is as follows:

```
u = NaN(1,d);
for i = 1:d
```

---

[9] By construction, most uniform random number generators report neither the upper limit, 1, nor the lower limit, 0.

```
    while isnan(u(i))
        test = ceil(rand*n);
        if not(ismember(test,u(1:(i-1))))
            u(i) = test;
        end
    end
end
```

If d approaches n, this is probably not the most efficient way: for the later draws, only few valid options will be left, and an increasing number of invalid (and time-consuming) attempts are necessary to discover the remaining ones. In this case, a faster alternative is to shuffle the elements, place them in random order, and pick the first d elements:

```
rndList = randperm(n);
u = rndList(1:d);
```

Here, the Matlab function randperm(n) is used to produce a random permutation of the numbers $1,\ldots,n$. (For a homemade version of randperm, one can generate a vector of n uniform variates and use their ranks.) Alternatives will be presented in Section 6.5.3.

6.5.2. Roulette wheel selection

The implicit assumption in Section 6.5.1 was that all elements are picked with the same probability. If deviations from uniformity are required, then a different approach must be chosen. Consider a simple roulette wheel. The chance that the ball falls into any of the slots will depend on the slot's width: if one slot is wider, it will catch the ball more often. Assume the roulette wheel only had two slots, and one slot stretches over three-quarters of the wheel, the other one over just one-quarter. Then, the ball should have a 3/4 chance of landing in the first slot. Hence, if we standardize the circumference of the wheel with 1, then the first segment would stretch from 0 to 0.75, and the second one from 0.75 to 1. To simulate such a wheel, one could pick a $(0, 1)$ uniform numbers u and assign values below 0.75 to the first slot, those above 0.75 to the second. This is equivalent, by the way, to the approach chosen for simulating Bernoulli variables (see page 136): if the probability for success is p, then $u < p$ will give true if u falls within $[0, p)$ and false otherwise.

This principle can be generalized to an arbitrary number of possible outcomes. Each of the outcomes is assigned one slot, and the slot's width in proportion to the circumference reflects its probability of being chosen. The limits between the slots on a standardized roulette wheel (circumference = 1) are then at 0 and at the cumulative probabilities. For example, assume there are three alternatives, and they should be picked with chances $3 : 5 : 2$. Then, the (cumulative) probabilities are

Alternative	1	2	3
Probabilities	0.30	0.50	0.20
Cumulative probabilities	0.30	0.80	1.00

A $(0, 1)$ uniform random number has a 30% chance to fall into the first slot, $[0, 0.3)$, a 50% chance for the second slot, $[0.3, 0.8)$, and a remaining 20% chance for the third slot, $[0.8, 1)$. To make a draw, one can then pick a uniform random number, u, and determine the corresponding slot, that is, find the first slot where u does exceed the lower bound, but not the upper bound.

The Matlab code for roulette wheel selection is provided below. It accepts two arguments: the first is a vector of individual chances or propensities, the second (optional) is the number of draws.

Listing 6.8. C-RandomNumberGeneration/M/RouletteWheel.m

```
 1 function w = RouletteWheel(prop,N)
 2 % RouletteWheel.m  -- version 2011-01-06
 3 % roulette wheel selection
 4 % prop ... propensities for choosing an element ( > 0 )
 5 % N ...... number of draws
 6 if nargin < 2, N = 1; end
 7
 8 % -- compute (cumulative) probabilities
 9 prob = max(0,prop)/sum(max(prop,0));
10 cum_prob = cumsum(prob);
11
12 % -- perform draws
13 w = NaN(1,N);
14 for i = 1:N
15     u = rand;
16     w(i) = find(u < cum_prob,1);
17 end
```

6.5.3. Random permutations and shuffling

An integral part of some methods is to randomly (re-)arrange elements. What is a good method for this depends on how big the variations should be. If only minor variations in an existing sequence $\{x_i\}$ are required, one minor disturbance would be to randomly pick just two elements, i_1 and i_2, and swap them:

```
i = ceil(rand(1,2)*length(x));
while i(2) == i(1)
    i(2) = ceil(rand*length(x));
end
x(i) = x(i([2 1]));
```

Repeating this procedure adds disturbance; however, it is not the most efficient way of shuffling an entire sample. In that case, a random new order can be picked, and the elements arranged, accordingly. The Matlab function sort (u) returns two vectors, the sorted elements and the corresponding positions in the original, unsorted vector. Hence,

```
u = rand(1,n);
[ignore,i] = sort(u);
```

assigns i a random sequence of the numbers 1 to n. The Matlab function randperm(n) does exactly that.

In some circumstances, it might be helpful to move a subsequence of length s. A simple approach for this is to randomly select a sequence, find a new insertion point, and rearrange the parts.

Listing 6.9. C-RandomNumberGeneration/M/rearrange.m

```
1  function x = rearrange(x,s)
2  % rearrange.m  -- version 2011-01-06
3  %   x ... data sample
4  %   s ... length of segment to be moved
5
6  n  = length(x);
7  i_start = ceil(rand*(n-s+1));
8  i  = i_start + (0:(s-1));              % elements to be moved
9  t  = ceil(rand*(length(x)-s+1))-1;     % target position
10 chunk = x(i);
11 x(i) = [];                             % remove chunk
12 x  = [x(1:t) chunk x(t+1:end)];        % insert at new position
```

6.6. Sampling errors—and how to reduce them

6.6.1. The basic problem

Monte Carlo simulations heavily rely on the "law of large numbers": the distribution of (increasingly) large samples should converge to the distribution of the underlying population. Hence, when tossing a coin, say, $n = 1$ million times, then heads actually should come up approximately half of the time. With smaller sample sizes, however, this does not necessarily hold: for only 10 tosses, there is a reasonable chance (11.7% to be exact) to see seven heads and only three tails. Using this particular sample would then give us a biased picture due to the sampling error. Unfortunately, even when samples appear large, this Monte Carlo error can still be noticeable, for example, when sophisticated models are used or the analysis only focuses on certain parts of the distribution like the tails (neither of which is unusual in finance—just think of risk models for demanding portfolios or assets). More importantly, the number of draws cannot always be increased sufficiently to limit this error to an acceptable level; CPU time, memory, and other computational limitations are at the top of the list of potential restrictions.

There are different approaches to overcome this issue. They all have in common that they interfere with the way samples are drawn. In particular, they abandon the goal of producing (seemingly) independent draws. The following subsections discuss some of the more popular methods.

6.6.2. Quasi-Monte Carlo

General considerations...

Let us revisit the coin-flipping example for a minute. If we use the outcomes head (H) and tails (T) to represent a "yes/no" decision occurring with equal odds, the ideal outcome for n draws would be $n/2$ for either case. If one is only interested in frequencies and the sequence is irrelevant, a constructed solution for $n = 6$ draws that is "perfectly" distributed would simply assign one half the draws to "H" and the other half to "T." This "tailoring samples to fit the distribution" is, in essence, what quasi-Monte Carlo (QMC) does. Hence, a QMC solution here would be [H H H T T T], and another one [H T H T H T]. The latter has the advantage that discarding the last two observations would immediately provide the solution for $n = 4$ draws while the former wouldn't. In either case, serial patterns emerge that are highly unlikely in genuine random numbers.

Constructing a solution for continuous distributions is also feasible. Consider the $(0,1)$ uniform distribution. To evaluate the uniformness of the points, a discrepancy measure can be introduced that checks whether all observations are positioned equidistantly. When sorting the draws, $x_{(i)} \leq x_{(i+1)}\ \forall i = 1,\ldots,n-1$, uniform numbers should be equidistant; $x_{(i+1)} = x_{(i)} + \delta\ \forall i = 1,\ldots,n-1$. The tricky bit here is how to deal with the draws closest to the (lower and upper) limits, that is, $x_{(1)}$ and $x_{(n)}$. A wrap-around discrepancy measure would favor a solution where the distance to the limits is $\delta/2$; that is, $x_{(1)} = 0 + \delta/2$, $x_{(2)} = x_{(1)} + \delta = 3\delta/2$, and generally $x_{(i)} = x_{(i-1)} + \delta = (2i-1)\delta/2$.

To make this more tangible, if $n = 1$, then the only point will be ideally positioned at $x_{(1),n=1} = 0.5$. If $n = 2$, the distances between points ought to be $\delta_{n=2} = 0.5$, and the positions are $x_{(1),n=2} = 0.25$ and $x_{(2),n=2} = 0.75$, for $n = 3$: $\{1/6, 3/6, 5/6\}_{n=3}$; for $n = 10$: $\{0.05, 0.15, 0.25,\ldots,0.95\}_{n=10}$; and so on. For all of these cases, the expected value of the sequence is exactly 0.5; the variance, however, only converges to its theoretical value of $1/12$ if n is large. Therefore, alternative construction methods position the points such that higher moments also agree with their theoretical values as well as possible. For a comprehensive discussion, see Niederreiter (1992).

...and caveats

When looking at these examples more closely, one can already spot some limitations of these methods for financial applications.

- The optimal solution for $n+1$ is usually not found by taking the solution for n and adding one extra point. Likewise, choosing the values for high n but using only some of them (e.g., because one runs out of time) will lead to a (systematic) bias. Hence, the designer has to decide in advance how many samples he or she wants to evaluate.

- Determining the draws for the multivariate case can become a tough optimization problem in its own right—even (and in particular) when the draws must be orthogonal (i.e., uncorrelated) in all dimensions. Fang, Tang, Maringer, and Winker (2006) provide bounds and show how heuristics can help in tackling this problem.

- Repeated experiments generate exactly the same sequence. On the one hand, this is good as it simplifies replicability. On the other hand, this is not so good because if an interesting spot in the range is missed once, then repeated experiments will not cover it either. Even more importantly, it is difficult to judge how stable the results are: Results with pseudorandom numbers will vary from experiment to experiment, but should converge with increasing sample size. If results are close together, this could indicate stability; if they are all over the place, then the results are obviously not very robust. With quasi-Monte Carlo numbers, the results will be identical unless one changes n; and unless n changes dramatically (in particular when n is already high), the variations in the points could be modest. In finance, one is often interested in extreme risks and rare events, and generating draws with QMC might lead to biased and unreliable results.

- In financial applications, it is often not only the distribution of the numbers that matters, but also its sequence. Assume $n = 100$ uniform QMC numbers are used to generate returns. If the draws are constructed as in the example above, they will be sorted, and so will the returns. This might be fine if one is interested in a simulation of stock prices at one particular point in time; for example, the distribution at the maturity date of an option. However, if one is interested in a sample path over 100 days, it is a different story. To avoid undesirable sequential patterns, other construction methods have to be used. In short, not every QMC approach is equally suitable for all purposes.

Despite all these limitations, quasi-Monte Carlo can be a very useful and efficient tool for financial applications—when handled with care and if one is aware of their limitations. Section 8.2.3 will discuss this in the context of option pricing.

6.6.3. Stratified sampling

As mentioned earlier, Monte Carlo experiments with small samples can have the disadvantage that some important areas in the probability space could be left out. At the same time, there could be clusters of draws so that other areas are overrepresented. If quasi-Monte Carlo is inappropriate or too difficult to apply, then stratified sampling can be used to reduce the sampling error. The idea is to split the probability space into B segments of equal probability and draw N/B random samples from each of these segments. This ensures that the draws do not have too obvious clusters, while still preserving some of the Monte Carlo properties. If $B = 1$, then this is (usually) equivalent to "plain vanilla" Monte Carlo experiments; increasing $B \rightarrow N$ brings it closer to a quasi-Monte Carlo experiment.

There are many different versions to translate this general concept into an actual application. The first step always is to fix the number of segments or bins, B. Again, for the sake of simplicity, assume we want to draw $N = 100$ samples from a $(0, 1)$ uniform distribution. If one chooses $B = 5$, then the first bin would be $[0, 0.2)$, the next one $[0.2, 0.4)$, etc. The next steps can vary; the outcome, however, should be similar. To illustrate how to find solutions, consider the following three examples.

- In a rather systematic fashion, one could draw one number from each bin and repeat this exercise $N/B = 100/5 = 20$ times. Here is a simple Matlab implementation:

```
B = 5;
N = 100;
bin = repmat(1:B,1,ceil(N/B));
u = rand(1,N)/B + (bin-1)/B;
```

At this stage, the numbers will be piecewise sorted. Plotting the vector u will illustrate this. If sequence does matter, these numbers can be rearranged randomly or systematically; see page 138. Alternatively, one can permute the vector `bin` that contains the bin for each draw. The modified code then is:

```
bin = repmat(1:B,1,ceil(N/B));
bin = bin(randperm(length(bin)));
u   = rand(1,N)/B + (bin-1)/B;
```

- Another idea would be to draw N samples and check which bins are overrepresented and which are underrepresented. Excess observations from the former will be discarded and replaced with additional draws from the latter bins. Choosing which of the excess observations to keep and which ones to discard could be a deterministic or random decision.

- A third approach would be to use the roulette wheel principle and draw a sequence of N numbers. Initially, each bin should have the same probability of being chosen; over time, however, those bins with more elements in them should have a lower propensity of being chosen. In other words, the propensity should reflect the number of still available "free" slots in a bin. If each bin $b = 1, \ldots, B$ eventually contains at most $N_b^{\max}$ elements, then the number of free slots is $N_b^{\max} - N_b$, where N_b is the current number of elements in this bin. If all bins must eventually have the same number of elements, then $N_b^{\max} = N/B$ and the versions above would be more efficient implementations. However, if one allows for some variations and capacities (i.e., there is an upper limit on observations from one cluster and hence on clusters), then this could be reasonable. Likewise, one could design versions that ensure that a minimum amount of draws does come from each bin; the "cookbook recipe" then could be to first draw the necessary number of samples for each bin, and then fill it up with arbitrary draws; add permutation if necessary.

6.6.4. Variance reduction

Monte Carlo methods are based on the law of large numbers. Basically, it states that suitable samples should have properties similar to that of the population, and the larger the sample, the greater this similarity. Sometimes, dissimilarities are by design: a finite number of draws from a continuous space will never be exactly continuous, and, in particular, rare events will not be represented perfectly. More importantly, Monte Carlo methods use random variables—which makes the outcome a random sample; and the statistical signatures will also be random. Ideally, the reported statistics of the samples have little variance and are centered around the population's corresponding values. To decrease variance and "randomness" of results by experimental design, increasing the sample size helps (law of large numbers!) but is computationally costly. Alternatively, one can use a sampling process that favors fast variance reduction.

Quasi-Monte Carlo is targeting this issue for small samples by constructing variates that minimize the dissimilarity; they do come with other limitations, though (see Sections 6.6.2 and 9.3.4). Another approach would be to gear the generation of (pseudo)random numbers in a way that reduces the variance of the results.

Antithetic variables

To assess the magnitude of the sampling error, the central limit theorem (CLT) can help. Under certain (usually met) conditions, the mean of i.i.d. samples is approximately normally distributed, $\bar{x} \sim N(\mu_X, \sigma_X^2/n)$, where n is the sample size and μ_X and σ_X^2 are the mean and variance of the random variable X. The reason for this becomes obvious when looking at the definitions:

$$\mathsf{Var}(\bar{x}) = \mathsf{Var}\left(\sum_{i=1}^{n} \frac{1}{n} x_i\right) = \frac{1}{n}\mathsf{Var}(x_i) + \frac{n(n-1)}{n^2}\mathsf{Cov}(x_i, x_j)$$

if all samples x_i have the same variance and all pairs (x_i, x_j) have the same covariance. In other words, the sample mean will have a standard deviation of $\sigma_X/\sqrt{n}$. So, to reduce the sample mean's standard deviation by half when samples are uncorrelated, one needs four times as many independent samples; to reduce it by one order of magnitude (i.e., by a factor 10), n must be increased by a factor 100.

The decrease in the sample mean's variance could be accelerated if the samples had negative covariance; the most extreme case here would be a perfect negative correlation. Variance reduction with antithetic variables does exactly that: draw (or construct) samples that are perfectly negatively correlated. Assume $x_i \sim \mathrm{N}(0, 1)$. Then, $x_j = -x_i$ would be the perfect antithetic variable,[10] and the pair (x_i, x_j) would have exactly the desired mean of the underlying distribution: $\bar{x} = \mu = 0$. For $(0, 1)$ uniform variables, pairs (u_i, u_j), where $u_j = 1 - u_1$, would be the equivalent. These antithetic uniforms can then be used to generate samples for other distributions, for example, by using the inversion method.

The problem with this approach is that it is suitable only for certain parameters and statistics: the sample mean might converge very fast, but, for example, variance could be misrepresented. Therefore, antithetic variables are less useful in models where variance and/or higher moments are at least as important as the mean. Just think of pricing an out-of-the-money option: getting the expected price of the underlier correct is not sufficient to price derivatives.

Importance sampling

A major issue in financial simulations are rare and extreme events that have a great impact on the overall outcome. By definition, they should not occur too often, so in particular in small samples, one cannot really get it right: If they occur, they might be overrepresented; if they don't, they get completely ignored. Variance reduction (e.g., by antithetic variables) isn't a solution; just think of a call option at maturity: extreme positive events in the underlying's returns have a massive impact on the call when it is in-the-money, whereas differences in the prices below the strike price will make no difference, regardless of how extreme they are.

The idea of importance sampling is to prioritize sensitive regions and draw more samples there. The samples are then weighted appropriately to

---

[10] Note that for $x_i \sim \mathrm{N}(\mu, \sigma^2)$, $x_j = 2\mu - x_i$.

correct overrepresentation or underrepresentation. Intuitively, the weight should be the inverse of the factor of overrepresentation.

To illustrate this principle, assume S is lognormally distributed with $\log(S) \sim N(\mu, \sigma^2)$ and one is particularly concerned with extreme positive values. In that case, one could draw, say, three-quarters of all samples from the upper 10% quantile. In other words, $w\,n = 0.25 \cdot n$ of the samples should fall into the lower quantile, $q = F(s_i) \leq 0.9$.

```
% --setting
n  = 1000;  % number of samples
w  = 0.25;  % fraction of samples in lower quantile
q  = 0.90;  % lower quantile ends at

% --draw uniforms according to importance
u1 = rand(n*w,1)   * q;        % [0..q]
u2 = rand(n*(1-w))* (1-q) * q; % [q..1]
% --normal and log-normal variates, e.g., inversion method
s1 = norminv(u1,mu,sigma);   S1 = exp(s1);
s2 = norminv(u2,mu,sigma);   S2 = exp(s2);

% --compute mean
mean_S = ( sum(S1) * q/w + sum(S2) * (1-q)/(1-w) ) / n;
% --alternatively:
mean_S = mean(S1)*q  +  mean(S2)*(1-q);
```

The practical application of importance sampling can be hampered, though, when these samples are used as an ingredient for more sophisticated models. For a "plain vanilla" European option, the important areas of the underlier's distribution and the corresponding weights are easy to find; this might not be true for structured products.

6.7. Drawing from empirical distributions

6.7.1. Data randomization

Drawing from a given sample, that is, resampling, is an important issue in finance. For simulation purposes, empirical data can be used either directly (e.g., in bootstraps) or as basis for the calibration of parametric models (e.g., parametric bootstraps). At the same time, one ought to check how "typical" or unusual a data set is. There exists a variety of alternatives; some of them can be found in Gentle (2009, Chapter 12).

At this point, we only want to mention the jackknife, where a small number of observations are excluded from the sample. If the statistics of the remaining observations change noticeably, then the excluded observations are considered somewhat unusual. For financial data, jackknifing might also reveal something about robustness of results. Taking the daily returns from a year and ignoring the one or two best or worst days gives some indications what would have happened to a buy-and-hold investor who was (un)fortunate enough to be out of the market only on these days. Though rare, these extreme events tend to occur regularly and can have a substantial impact on the overall results. Fig. 1.1 in Section 1.4 illustrates this problem; Fig. 14.11 on page 483 provides a drastic example of how data errors can aggravate it; and Section 13.2.4 investigates the differences among true, estimated, and realized return properties of portfolios. At this stage, it is reasonable to assume that the available data are clean and representative.

6.7.2. Bootstrap

Basic concepts

A common problem in empirical work is that the true data-generating processes and underlying distributions are not observable, and only samples of observations are visible. These observations can be used to test hypotheses about assumed underlying models; they can also be used to calibrate these models. In other situations, it is opportune to use these data directly for simulations. In this case, one effectively samples from a sample. The basic principle here is to treat the available sample as if it was, more or less, the underlying population.

Obviously, there are some limitations and simplifying assumptions to it. The sample can (and almost always will) not be a perfect fit for the underlying distribution. The sample will be finite and discrete even if the underlying process is continuous. Nonetheless, the empirical distribution of a sample, F_e, is often the closest one can get to the actual underlying distribution F, and ideally, the estimator used on F_e produces the same results as if used on F itself. Given the focus of this book, a discussion of the underlying statistical theory is omitted; a good starting point is Gentle (2009, Chapter 13).

In finance, a popular application for bootstrap methods is the generation of returns. The simplest example here is the univariate case of assumed i.i.d. realizations of a single asset. Assume that a vector $\{r_i\}_{T\times 1}$ contains the available samples of the i.i.d. returns for a single period. Resampling n observations into a new vector $\{x\}_{n\times 1}$ can then be done by

```
j = ceil(rand(n,1)*T);
x = r(j);
```

Resampling should leave the basic statistics intact, and the bootstrapped samples x will have (approximately) the same mean, variance, and higher moments as the initial sample r.

Extending this to the multivariate case is straightforward. If $\{r_i\}_{T\times k}$ is a matrix where each column is for one asset and each row represents one observation of simultaneous returns of these k assets, then the code reads as follows:

```
j = ceil(rand(n,1)*T);
x = r(j,:);
```

In this case, the correlations, dependencies and co-moments[11] across assets should also remain in place. This approach can, therefore, be used when simulating n realizations for a single-period development of an entire portfolio.

When more than one period is of interest, things become slightly more challenging. In the absence of serial dependence within the data, the new sample $\{x\}$ can also be regarded as a series of subsequent i.i.d. returns. For empirical data, however, the assumption of independent returns often breaks down. Maintaining the time-series properties of returns is then important. If there is no (parametric) way to cater for this serial dependence, then a block bootstrap method can preserve at least some of the original properties. Rather than single data points, one picks blocks of b subsequent observations from the original sample $\{r\}$. For the multivariate case, one generic approach would be as follows:

```
for i = 1:b:(n-b)
    j = ceil(rand(n,1)*(T-(b-1)));
    x(i:(j+b-1),:) = r(j+(0:(b-1)),:);
end
```

This, however, causes the first and Tth observations to be picked only if j is 1 and $T - b + 1$, respectively, while an observation i somewhere in the center of the sample will be included in any block with starting point $j = (i - b + 1), \ldots, i$. In particular leaving out the most recent observations is not desirable for financial simulations, as they might be quite typical of what to expect next. Under the assumption of stationarity, the circular block bootstrap solves this problem by filling the $(T + d)$th position with observation d. The modulo function can be used for this:

```
j = mod(j-1,T) + 1;
```

The complete Matlab function for bootstrapping is provided here:

Listing 6.10. C-RandomNumberGeneration/M/bootstrap.m

```
1  function x = bootstrap(r,n,b)
2  % bootstrap.m  -- version 2011-01-06
3  %    r ... original data
4  %    n ... length of bootstrap sample x
5  %    b ... block length
6
7  if nargin < 3, b = 1; end
8  [T k] = size(r);
```

---

[11] Unlike the covariance, coskewness and cokurtosis are rarely used. If data follow a joint normal distribution, they contain no information, whereas they can contain interesting information for non-symmetric joint distributions. They are, however, numerically challenging and costly to compute. For details, see, for example, Konno and Suzuki (1995); Maringer (2008b); Maringer and Parpas (2009). Section 8.7.2 provides an example where higher order moments actually are an issue in real data.

```
 9 if b==1  % simple bootstrap
10     j = ceil(rand(n,1)*T);
11     x = r(j,:);
12 else   % circular block bootstrap
13     nb = ceil(n/b);              % number of bootstraps
14     js = floor(rand(nb,1)*T);  % starting points - 1
15     x = nan(nb*b,k);
16     for i = 1:nb
17         j = mod(js(i)+(1:b), T)+1; % positions in original data
18         s = (1:b) + (i-1)*b;
19         x(s,:) = r(j,:);
20     end
21     if (nb*n) > n              % correct length if nb*b > n
22         x((n+1):end,:) = [];
23     end
24 end
```

There is no universal solution for how to choose the block length *b*. Low values will break up the time structure, whereas high values will produce mostly identical resamples. Also, if there are very strong temporal patterns in the initial sample, cutting out chunks and arbitrarily stacking them together again can lead to unrealistically abrupt transitions. Bootstrap methods should, therefore, be used with caution.

Parametric and nonparametric bootstraps

By definition, the bootstrap method samples from a given data set. Problems can arise when the original data set either is small relative to the number of bootstrap samples or comes with rare events. The samples will be too similar and not necessarily represent the entire distribution. This can lead to bizarre behavior in the results and to overfitting,[12] and bigger sample sizes will only increase the computing time but not the quality of the simulation.

If one has a good idea of the data-generating process, he or she can try to fit a parametric model or distribution on the data and then sample from it. If, for example, one assumes that a stock price is lognormally distributed, all users need to do is to estimate the mean and standard deviation of the (normally) distributed log returns, sample corresponding normal variates, and transform them into prices. Chapter 8 demonstrates this in more detail. This "parametric bootstrap" reaches its limits, however, when not all crucial properties of the data are captured by the model—or if there is no obvious choice of model.

One "quick and dirty" fix would then be to jitter the data by adding some small noise, ε, to each sample. The usual suspect for this is Gaussian noise with standard deviation σ,

```
xs = x(j) + randn(size(j)) * sigma
```

---

[12] See, for example, Maringer (2005a).

This brings us to nonparametric methods. Assume one wants to generate random draws based on a finite sample of observations $\{x_i\}$ with unknown underlying density. Kernel density estimators can then be used to create a smoothed empirical probability density function (EPDF). For the univariate case, this can be done with

$$f_h(x) = \frac{1}{hn} \sum_{i=1}^{n} K\left(\frac{x - x_i}{h}\right),$$

where $K(\cdot)$ is the kernel, and h is the smoothing (or bandwidth) parameter. Early suggestions for kernels include the uniform, producing a shifted histogram (see Rosenblatt, 1956). Meanwhile, the Gaussian, the triangular, and the quadratic (or Epanechnikov) kernels have become very popular choices. For normally distributed data, Silverman (1986) shows that a bandwidth of $h = s\sqrt[5]{\frac{4}{3n}}$ is optimal for the Gaussian kernel, where s is the standard deviation of the sample. Table 6.2 provides the definitions of different kernels and sample fits. Once the EPDF has been estimated, samples can be drawn using, for example, the acceptance–rejection method (see Section 6.3.2).

Table 6.2 Popular kernels, $K(y)$, for kernel density estimation.

Type	$K(y)$	Example
Uniform	$\begin{cases} \frac{1}{2} & -1 \leq y \leq 1 \\ 0 & \text{otherwise} \end{cases}$	
Triangular	$\begin{cases} 1 - \lvert y \rvert & -1 \leq y \leq 1 \\ 0 & \text{otherwise} \end{cases}$	
Epanechnikov	$\begin{cases} \frac{3}{4}(1 - y^2) & -1 \leq y \leq 1 \\ 0 & \text{otherwise} \end{cases}$	
Gaussian	$\frac{1}{\sqrt{2\pi}} e^{-y^2/2}$	

Listing 6.11. C-RandomNumberGeneration/M/KDE.m

```
 1  function f_x = KDE(x,xi,h,Kernel)
 2  % KDE.m  -- version 2011-01-06
 3  %    kernel density estimation
 4  %    x ... points at which to estimate the density
 5  %    xi .. original sample
 6  %    h ... bandwidth, smoothing parameter
 7  %    Kernel .. name of kernel
 8
 9  if nargin < 4  % default function
10      Kernel = 'Gaussian';
11      if nargin < 3  % default value for h
12          h = (4/(3*length(xi)))^.2 * std(xi);
13      end
14  end
15
16  switch upper(Kernel)
17      case 'GAUSSIAN',
18          K = @(y) exp(-y.^2/2) / sqrt(2*pi);
19      case 'UNIFORM',
20          K = @(y) (abs(y) <1 )/2;
21      case 'TRIANGULAR',
22          K = @(y) max(0,(1-abs(y)));
23      case {'QUADRATIC','EPANECHNIKOV'}
24          K = @(y) max(0, 0.75*(1-y.^2)) ;
25      otherwise
26          error('Kernel not recognised')
27  end
28
29  f_x = zeros(size(x));
30  n = length(xi);
31  for j = 1:length(x)
32      y = (x(j) - xi(:))/h;
33      f_x(j) = ones(1,n) * K(y) / (h*n) ;
34  end
```

The choice of the smoothness parameter h can have a substantial impact. Again, consider the case of daily stock returns with one extreme event. If h is too low, f_x will have a narrow spike at this event; if h is too large, distinct features of the samples become smoothed out; Fig. 6.6 illustrates this.

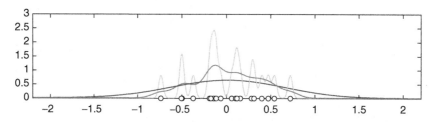

Figure 6.6 Gaussian kernel density estimates with smoothing parameters $h = 0.025$, 0.1, and 0.5, respectively (darker lines for larger h).

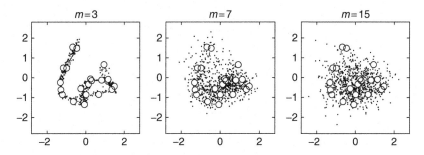

Figure 6.7 Samples generated with the Taylor–Thompson algorithm; original observations (circles) from a $(0, 1)$ Gaussian distribution.

Also, for multivariate data, the increasing number of dimensions can quickly increase the computational costs.

Taylor and Thompson (1986) suggest an alternative nonparametric approach that also takes "local" information into account but requires even less assumptions about the underlying density. Their algorithm randomly picks one observation x_j and its nearest neighbors (e.g., based on Euclidean distances), and a sample is created within their proximity. Intuitively speaking, if the neighbors are close, the new sample will be close to their center, whereas if they are dispersed over a large area, the new sample will also have higher variance. Algorithm 21 provides some additional technical details.

Algorithm 21 Taylor–Thompson algorithm.

1: randomly pick one observation x_{j_1}
2: find the $m - 1$ observations closest to x_{j_1}: $x_{j_2}, \ldots, x_{j_m}$
3: compute the mean $\bar{x}_s$ of the m observations $x_{j_i}, i = 1, \ldots, m$
4: generate random uniform samples $u_i \sim U\left(\frac{1}{m} - \sqrt{3(m-1)/m^2}, \frac{1}{m} + \sqrt{3(m-1)/m^2}\right)$
5: compute the linear combination $e = \sum_{i=1}^{m} u_i (x_{j_i} - \bar{x}_s)$
6: compute simulated value $x_s = \bar{x} + e$

Note that the weights u_i have expected value $1/m$ while their variance increases with increasing m to outbalance the loss of variance in the samples by averaging. Fig. 6.7 illustrates the effect of m: the fewer of the available observations are used, the more the new samples seem to cluster around or directly between the existing points; increasing m will produce samples from wider area.

Listing 6.12. C-RandomNumberGeneration/M/TaylorThompson.m

```
1 function Xs = TaylorThompson(X,N,m)
2 % TaylorThompson.m  -- version 2011-01-06
3 %   X ... original sample
```

```
 4 | %    N ... number of new samples to be drawn
 5 | %    m ... number of neighbors to be used
 6 |
 7 | [xr xc] = size(X);
 8 | % -- compute Euclidean distances
 9 | B = X * X';
10 | ED = sqrt(repmat(diag(B),1,xr) + repmat(diag(B)',xr,1) - 2*B);
11 |
12 | % -- limits for weights
13 | m = min(xr,m);
14 | uLim = 1/m + [-1 1] * sqrt(3*(m-1)/m.^2);
15 |
16 | % -- draw samples
17 | Xs = zeros(N,xc);
18 | for s = 1:N
19 |     j = ceil(rand*xr);
20 |     % -- m nearest neighbors:
21 |     [dnn inn] = sort(ED(:,j));
22 |     Xnn = X(inn(1:m),:);
23 |     % -- weights
24 |     u = rand(1,m) * (uLim(2)-uLim(1)) + uLim(1);
25 |     % -- form linear combinations
26 |     Xnn_bar = ones(1,m) * Xnn / m;
27 |     e = u * (Xnn - repmat(Xnn_bar,m,1));
28 |     Xs(s,:) = Xnn_bar + e;
29 | end
```

6.8. Controlled experiments and experimental design

6.8.1. Replicability and *ceteris paribus* analysis

Being able to control and reproduce variates is one of the major advantages of pseudorandom number generators: it allows the reproduction of previous experiments without having to store all generated variates. This is particularly valuable when previous results need to be reexamined, and effects due to sampling are to be investigated. Even more importantly, it allows for controlled experiments. Typical applications include cases where only a restricted number of variates are to be resampled for *ceteris paribus* experiments. Knowing the type of random number generator and the seeds used is enough to replicate the same variates and modify or substitute others.

Likewise, it facilitates easier comparisons and evaluations for variations in the data-generating model. Figures 8.5 and 8.7 will compare how different parametrization for time-series models produce signatures; reusing the same underlying random numbers helps isolating the effects. One of the advantages of the inversion method is that it allows direct comparison of simulations with slightly altered distribution properties. Consider the following example: Financial returns are often characterized by heavy tails; a simple means to achieve this is to use the Student t distribution instead of a normal distribution. To analyze how increasing kurtosis affects the outcome, *ceteris paribus*, one can generate a uniform sample, $\{u_i\}_{i=1}^{S}$, and then convert it into the corresponding normal or Student t value, $F_t^{-1}(\{u_i\}, v)$, for different degrees of freedom, v.

Similarly, it can be used to switch between distributions. Given, say, a standard normal sample $\{z_i\}_{i=1}^{S}$, the corresponding samples for a t distribution can be converted by first converting the normal variates into uniform ones via the CDF, $\{u_i\} = N(\{z_i\})$, which then are plugged into the inverse of the target CDF. More generally, to convert a sample x_i from distribution F_X to distribution F_Y, all one needs to do is $F_Y^{-1}(F_X(x_i))$. This helps to separate noise from effects due to changes in the model specification.

At the same time, controlling the experiments too heavily is not good either. Similar to variance reduction techniques, the "natural" variation in samples is reduced, and not all derived statistics will benefit equally. Also, seeding can undermine the quality of the random number generator itself, as the following sections illustrate for some of Matlab's random number generators.

6.8.2. Available random number generators in Matlab

Matlab offers three different types of RNGs for uniformly and two types for normally distributed numbers.[13] They can be invoked together with setting the seed to a certain value s:

`rand('seed',s)` for a multiplicative congruential algorithm (i.e., a linear congruential generator with parameter $c = 0$, see footnote 5; default in version 4);

`rand('state',s)` for Marsaglia's subtract with borrow algorithm (default in versions 5 through 7.3);

`rand('twister',s)` for the Mersenne Twister (default since version 7.4; widely regarded as the best).

Setting the seed for the uniform RNG also resets the RNG for other distributions, including the ones provided with the statistics toolbox. Standard normal pseudorandom variables have their own seeds, and the user can choose between different types of RNGs:

`randn('seed',s)` for the polar RNG (default in Version 4);

`randn('state',s)` for the ziggurat RNG (default since Version 5).

In its more recent versions (since 2008b, to be precise), Matlab also offers streaming: different variables can have individual streams of pseudorandom numbers (PRNs) with individual seeds and methods. However, with previous methods being well established and requiring less CPU time (in particular, when one requires to control many streams simultaneously),

---

[13] All descriptions of Matlab's RNGs are based on the documentation and help files for their 2008a and 2010a versions, which also provide details about and references for the different RNG algorithms in use. Help files and technical documentations are available online on www.mathworks.com.

not all users will see an immediate need to switch to this new approach. Also, previous methods have widely been used and provided the basis for a substantial body of literature in many different fields. This section, therefore, only addresses the "traditional" versions. Unfortunately, the functions `rand` and `randn` are opaque. Hence, no detailed comments can be made about how a seed is translated into the first PRN—nor can the user change it directly and make it suitable for his or her own requirements.

6.8.3. Uniform random numbers from Matlab's `rand` function

When performing a sequence of Monte Carlo experiments, it is often desirable that individual experiments be replicable and independent of the previous ones. Therefore, a simple approach would be to set the seed for the first experiment to some value s_1 and then just increase the seed by a fixed amount d, $s_i = s_{i-1} + d$, over experiments i. All this is under the—not unreasonable—assumption that different seeds always produce different and independent first draws.

Fig. 6.8 depicts $x_{1,s}$, the first PRNs drawn after the seed has been set to $s = 1, \ldots, 1000$. Obviously, `'seed'` produces patterns, and in `'state'`, clusters of samples with low values of $x_{1,s}$ appear to be generated only in certain regions of s: in the "southern" parts of the graph, clusters and gaps seem to alternate in regular intervals. This, however, is not particularly pronounced.

Plotting the first random numbers from subsequent seeds, $(x_{1,s}, x_{1,s+1})$, yields no surprises (Fig. 6.9): only the congruential RNG exhibits a linear relationship, whereas for the other two, no obvious pattern emerges. Seeding seems to be an issue mainly for the congruential RNG, which has long been supplemented with better alternatives. This also applies to RNGs for other distributions that use uniform PRNs, for example, via the inversion method. Only if a user is unaware that the command `rand('seed',s)` not only sets the seed but also switches to this unfavorable RNG, could this be a problem.

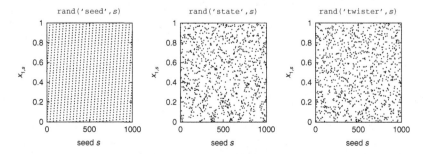

Figure 6.8 First uniform PRN drawn for different seeds and RNGs.

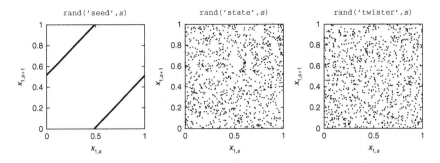

Figure 6.9 Scatterplots for first uniform PRNs drawn from seeds s and $s+1$.

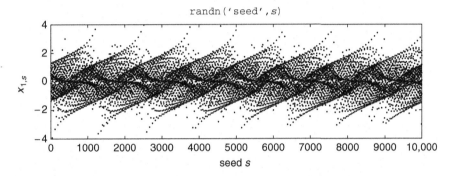

Figure 6.10 First normal PRN (polar) drawn for seeds $s = 1,\ldots,10,000$.

6.8.4. Gaussian random numbers from Matlab's `randn` function

For both RNGs for normal variates, things look completely different. For either method, one can easily spot patterns and dependencies between seed and first draw. Fig. 6.10 contains a scatterplot for seeds $s = 1,\ldots,10,000$ and the first draw, $x_{1,s}$ for the polar RNG. This algorithm, invoked with `randn('seed',s)`, was the default in Matlab version 4. It exhibits patterns where, for example, every 1200 seeds or so (at least) one value above 3 and one below -3 is produced.

From Matlab version 5 onwards, Marsaglia and Tsang's ziggurat algorithm is the default RNG for standard normal variates; the seed can be set by `randn('state',s)`. For this method, there are also clear patterns. Most obviously, there are long stretches of numbers with equal sign as can be seen from Fig. 6.11. All seeds in the range $s = 1,\ldots,447$ produce $x_{1,s} > 0$. For the following few seeds, the numbers are closely distributed around 0, and for $s = 464,\ldots,8383$, only negative $x_{1,s}$s are generated; the same is true for $s = 8448,\ldots,8704$. For seeds $s = 8704,\ldots,16,383$, on the other hand, not a single of the corresponding 7640 $x_{1,s}$s is negative. Within these long stretches of numbers with equal sign, the PRNs appear to fall within triangular shapes, implying that, for example, $x_{1,s} > 3$ (or $x_{1,s} < -3$ for that

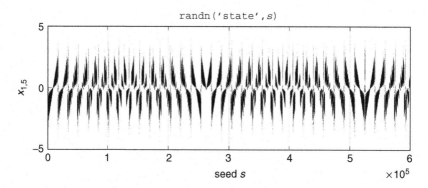

Figure 6.11 First normal PRN (ziggurat) drawn for seeds $s = 1, \ldots, 600{,}000$.

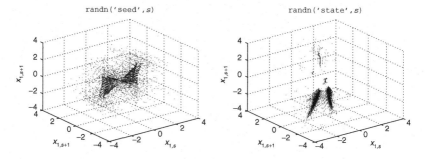

Figure 6.12 Scatterplot first draws from three subsequent seeds $s = 1, \ldots, 5000$.

matter) tends to occur in small regions. For higher seeds, these patterns sometimes get slightly more ragged; the main issues, however, persist.

In either case, this has implications on first draws when using subsequent seeds (Fig. 6.12). Increasing the intervals when picking seeds does not remedy the problem. Fig. 6.13 provides exemplary scatterplots for the first draws in which seeds are picked with step sizes of 100, 1000, and 10,000, respectively. Other step sizes provide similar patterns.

It must be emphasized again that this is not a problem of the respective RNG itself, but of how a provided seed s is translated into the first draw. This has consequences for controlled experiments: if in a series of (supposedly) independent runs or in subsequent iterations, the first step is to systematically set the seed for the normal RNG (or, with the argument 'seed', the uniform RNG), then their first normal PRNs can exhibit patterns and dependencies. If the first PRN picked is a relevant state variable, this can cause bias problems.

6.8.5. Remedies

Looking at later draws, these effects seem to vanish because the independence properties of the RNG itself take over. Hence, a quick fix for this

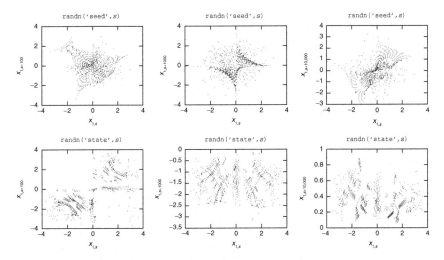

Figure 6.13 First PRN drawn for seeds $s = 1, \ldots, 1000$, $x_{1,s}$ plotted against $x_{1,s+d}$ with $d = 100$, 1000 and $10,000$ (left to right) for the polar (top panel) and ziggurat (bottom panel) RNGs.

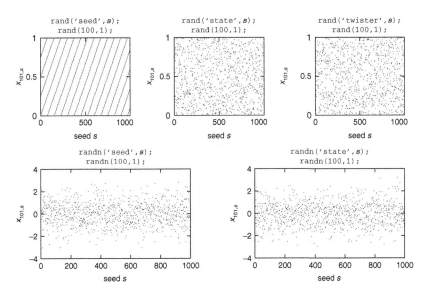

Figure 6.14 101st PRN drawn for seeds $s = 1, \ldots, 1000$, $x_{101,s}$ for the uniform (top panel) and normal (bottom panel) RNGs.

problem could be to draw n blank PRNs immediately after resetting the seed. This allows the RNG to burn in, and subsequent PRNs should be as well behaved as one can expect from this RNG. If n is prespecified and kept constant, this also preserves replicability. For example, after choosing $n = 100$, Fig. 6.14 contains the scatterplots for seeds and 101st draws for the three uniform and two normal RNGs. Comparing them to the corresponding graphs in Figures 6.8, 6.10, and 6.11 shows that the patterns have vanished; the only exception being the "usual suspect," that is, the congruential uniform RNG.

## CHAPTER SEVEN

Modeling dependencies

7.1. Transformation methods

7.1.1. Linear correlation

For many applications we need random variates that are dependent in a predetermined way. Our first aim is to generate a matrix X of size $N \times p$. For intuition, think of X as a sample of N observations of the returns of p assets. The variates in a given column of X should follow specific distributions (i.e., the marginal distributions of the specific asset), and the columns of X should be correlated.

The most-used measure of dependence is linear correlation. Assume two random variables Y and Z. Then for a sample of N paired observations $(y_1, z_1), (y_2, z_2), \ldots, (y_N, z_N)$ linear correlation ρ is computed as

$$\rho_{Y,Z} = \frac{\sum (y_i - m_Y)(z_i - m_Z)}{s_Y s_Z}. \tag{7.1}$$

m and s are the sample means and standard deviations, respectively. Linear correlation is invariant to linear transformations: changing two random variables into $a_1 + b_1 Y$ and $a_2 + b_2 Z$ will not change the linear correlation between them as long as b_1 and b_2 have the same sign (if they are of opposite sign, the sign of ρ will be reversed).

Now we have not just two but p random variables. It is convenient to treat them as a random vector Y of length p. To create X, we need to draw N times such a vector Y. Suppose Y should be distributed as:

$$Y \sim N(\mu, \Sigma).$$

μ is the vector of means with length p, and Σ is the $p \times p$ variance–covariance matrix. We start with a vector Y of i.i.d. standard Gaussian variates, so μ is a vector of zeros and Σ is the identity matrix of size p. The Matlab command `randn` creates a whole matrix, that is, N draws of Y, in one step.

```
% create uncorrelated Gaussian variates
p = 5;      % number of assets
N = 500;    % number of obs
X = randn(N, p);
% check
plotmatrix(X); corrcoef(X)
```

R's function `rnorm` always returns a vector. We can write a function that acts like `randn`.

Listing 7.1. C-ModelingDependencies/R/randn.R

```
1 # randn.R -- version 2010-12-10
2 randn <- function(m,n) array(rnorm(m*n), dim = c(m,n))
```

We scale the columns of X to have exactly zero mean and unit variance. This is not necessary, but it is most of the times harmless and convenient:[1]

  (i) If we transform a scalar Gaussian random variable Y with mean μ and variance σ^2 into $a + bY$, its mean will be $\mu + a$, and its variance will be $b^2\sigma^2$. Thus we can later on always enforce the desired means and variances.

 (ii) Linear correlation (in which we are interested here) is invariant to such linear transformations. So we can first make the columns of X be correlated as desired, and then later change the means and variances.

(iii) The rescaling simplifies computations: the correlation matrix is now equal to the variance–covariance matrix and can be computed as $\frac{1}{N}X'X$.

To generate correlated variates, we need two results. First, every variance–covariance matrix Σ is symmetric and real-valued. For now assume that the matrix is also positive-definite. If the matrix were semidefinite, it would not have full rank; this case is discussed below. In some pathological cases the matrix can also be indefinite; see page 396. Such a symmetric, real, and positive-definite matrix can always be decomposed into

$$\Sigma = LDL' = L\sqrt{D}\sqrt{D}L'$$

where L is a unit lower triangular matrix (i.e., it has ones on its main diagonal) and D is a diagonal matrix with strictly positive elements. $\sqrt{D}$ means that we take the square root of each diagonal element of D (which is always possible since all elements on the main diagonal of D are strictly positive). The matrix $L\sqrt{D}$ is a lower triangular matrix; a convenient choice to compute it is the Cholesky factorization.[2]

The second result is the following: suppose we generate a vector Y of uncorrelated Gaussian variates, that is, $Y \sim N(0,I)$. Whenever we

---

[1] The variance of variance across repeated samples will, of course, be zero.
[2] The Cholesky factorization is explained in detail in Section 3.1.3.

premultiply such a vector by a matrix B and add to the product a vector A, the resulting vector is distributed as follows:

$$BY + A \sim N(A, BIB').$$

So, let $B = L\sqrt{D}$, then we get

$$BIB' = BB' = L\sqrt{D}\sqrt{D}L' = \Sigma.$$

Thus, we obtain the desired result by premultiplying the (column) vector of uncorrelated random variates by the Cholesky factor. We want to create not only one vector Y, but a whole matrix of N observations, that is, each row in X is one realization of Y, so we postmultiply the whole matrix by B' (i.e., the upper triangular matrix):

$$X^c = XB'.$$

The columns of X^c are correlated as desired. Let us go through these steps with Matlab (see the script Gaussian2.m). We start with the matrix X.

Listing 7.2. C-ModelingDependencies/M/Gaussian2.m

```
1 % Gaussian2.m  -- version 2011-01-16
2 p = 5;      % number of assets
3 N = 500;    % number of obs
4 X = randn(N,p);
5 X = X * (diag(1./std(X)));
6 X = X - ones(N,1)*mean(X);
7 % check
8 plotmatrix(X); corrcoef(X)
```

Next we set up a correlation matrix. Matlab and R store matrices column-wise, and elements can also be addressed like in a stacked vector. In both Matlab and R, the Cholesky factor can be computed with the command chol; note that both Matlab and R return upper triangular matrices.

Listing 7.3. C-ModelingDependencies/M/Gaussian2.m

```
10 %% induce linear correlation
11 rho = 0.7;   % correlation between any two assets
12
13 % set correlation matrix
14 M = ones(p,p) * rho;
15 M(1 : (p+1) : (p*p)) = 1;
16
17 % compute cholesky factor
18 C = chol(M);
19
20 % induce correlation, check
21 Xc = X * C;
22 plotmatrix(Xc); corrcoef(Xc)
```

We can check the results by comparing the scatter plots of the columns of X and Xc, and by computing the correlation. The result of a call to Matlab's plotmatrix with $p = 3$ and $N = 200$ is shown in Fig. 7.1. The script Gaussian2.R shows the computations in R.

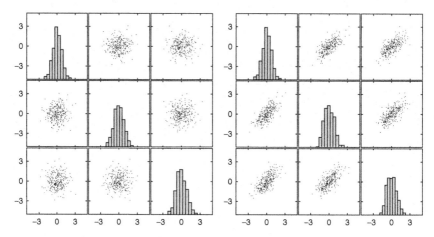

Figure 7.1 Left: scatter plot of three uncorrelated Gaussian variates. Right: scatter plot of three Gaussian variates with $\rho = 0.7$.

Listing 7.4. C-ModelingDependencies/R/Gaussian2.R

```
1  # Gaussian2.R -- version 2011-05-15
2  p    <- 5     # number of assets
3  N    <- 500   # number of obs
4  rho  <- 0.5   # correlation between two assets
5
6  ## create uncorrelated observations
7  X <- rnorm(N * p); dim(X) <- c(N, p)
8
9  ## check (see ?pairs)
10 panel.hist <- function(x, ...) {
11     usr <- par("usr"); on.exit(par(usr))
12     par(usr = c(usr[1:2], 0, 1.5))
13     h <- hist(x, plot = FALSE)
14     breaks <- h$breaks; nB <- length(breaks)
15     y <- h$counts; y <- y/max(y)
16     rect(breaks[-nB], 0, breaks[-1], y, ...)
17 }
18 pairs(X, xlim = c(-5,5), ylim = c(-5,5), labels = NA,
19       diag.panel = panel.hist, col = grey(0.4))
20 cor(X)
21
22 ## set correlation matrix
23 M <- array(rho, dim = c(p, p)); diag(M) <- 1
24
25 ## induce correlation, check
26 C <- chol(M); Xc <- X %*% C
27 pairs(Xc, xlim = c(-5, 5), ylim = c(-5, 5), labels = NA,
28       diag.panel = panel.hist, col = grey(0.4))
29 cor(Xc)
```

What if Σ does not have full rank? In Matlab, we can check the rank of Xc with the command `rank`. In R, we can use `qr(Xc)$rank` or the function `rankMatrix` from the `Matrix` package (Bates and Maechler, 2010). Here we stay with the Matlab example, so we type

```
rank(Xc)
```

and get

```
5
```

As a test, we replace the pth column of Xc with a linear combination of the other columns.

Listing 7.5. C-ModelingDependencies/M/Gaussian2.m

```
26  Xc(:,p) = Xc(:,1:(p-1))*rand(p-1,1);
```

Then, as expected, the call

```
rank(Xc)
```

will give us a

```
4
```

A correlation matrix is at its heart the cross-product of the data matrix X. The rank of $X'X$ can at most be the column rank of X (mathematically it will be the same rank; numerically $X'X$ could be of lower rank than X because of finite precision). Hence if X is rank deficient so is the correlation matrix. It is worth checking the scatter plots of the rank-deficient matrix Xc. It is not at all obvious that we have a redundant asset.

Listing 7.6. C-ModelingDependencies/M/Gaussian2.m

```
28  % check
29  plotmatrix(Xc); corrcoef(Xc)
30  M = corrcoef(Xc);
31  rank(M)
```

The Cholesky factorization requires full rank:

Listing 7.7. C-ModelingDependencies/M/Gaussian2.m

```
32  chol(M)
```

will (most of the time) result in

```
??? Error using ==> chol
Matrix must be positive definite.
```

(Just most of the time: in some cases Matlab may not give an error even though the matrix is not full rank.)

The theoretically best but often impractical approach is to check why there is rank deficiency. Sometimes, we can work with a reduced matrix. In our example, we know that the pth asset does not really have its own "stochastic driver," and hence we could compute its return as a combination of the returns of assets 1 to $p - 1$ (we could save a random variate). If that is not possible, we can instead think about the decomposition of Σ that we used. We required that

$$BB' = \Sigma$$

and the Cholesky factor was a convenient choice for B. But there are decompositions that do not require that Σ have full rank. One such alternative is the eigenvalue decomposition:

$$\Sigma = V\Lambda V'. \tag{7.2}$$

The $p \times p$ matrix V has in its columns the eigenvectors of Σ; Λ is diagonal and has as elements the eigenvalues of Σ. Since Σ is symmetric, the columns of V will be orthonormal, hence $V'V = I$, implying that $V' = V^{-1}$. (For a nonsymmetric matrix, we cannot just transpose V in Eq. (7.2).) Since Σ is nonnegative-definite, the eigenvalues cannot be smaller than zero. Hence, we can write Λ as $\sqrt{\Lambda}\sqrt{\Lambda}$ (with the root taken element-wise), and so get another symmetric decomposition. To induce correlations, just set $B = V\sqrt{\Lambda}$.

Listing 7.8. C-ModelingDependencies/M/Gaussian2.m

```
34 %% eigen decomposition
35 [V,D] = eig(M);
36 C = real(V*sqrt(D));
37 C = C';
38 Xcc = X * C;
39 plotmatrix(Xcc); corrcoef(Xcc)
```

In fact, we can also use the SVD (see page 44). The SVD decomposes a rectangular matrix X into

$$USV'.$$

Recall that we have scaled X so that each column has exactly zero mean, and unit standard deviation. In this case, the V in the eigenvalue decomposition and the SVD are the same—up to numerical precision, sorting, and sign; note that the Matlab help suggests

```
[U,S,V] = svd(X)
```

for the SVD, and

```
[V,D] = eig(A)
```

for the eigenvalue decomposition—the V in both cases is no coincidence. We have:

$$\Sigma = \frac{1}{N}X'X = \frac{1}{N}VS'U'USV'.$$

The U and V matrices are orthonormal, that is, $U'U = I$ and $V'V = I$. Hence we are left with

$$\frac{1}{N}X'X = \frac{1}{N}VS'SV'$$

and $\frac{1}{N}S'S = \Lambda$. That is, the squared singular values of X are the eigenvalues of $X'X$.

Listing 7.9. C-ModelingDependencies/M/Gaussian2.m

```
41  %% eigen v. svd
42  % eigen decomposition
43  M = corrcoef(X);
44  [V1,D] = eig(M);
45  C = real(V1*sqrt(D));
46  C = C';
47
48  % svd
49  [U,S,V2] = svd(X);
50
51  % ratio of sing values squared to eigenvalues
52  ((diag(S).^2)/(N-1)) ./ sort(diag(D),'descend')
```

7.1.2. Rank correlation

Linear correlation has a number of disadvantages: it may not capture certain nonlinear relationships, and it may make no sense at all for certain distributions. In fact, while it is true that correlation is bounded between -1 and $+1$, for many distributions these bounds are far tighter. Embrechts, McNeil, and Straumann (1999) give, as an example, the lognormal distribution. Lognormal variates can be obtained by creating Gaussian variates Z, and then transforming them with $\exp(Z)$. Here is a complete example:

Listing 7.10. C-ModelingDependencies/M/lognormals.m

```
1   % lognormals.m -- version 2010-01-08
2   %% uncorrelated Gaussian variates
3   p = 3; N = 200; X = randn(N,p);
4   X = X * (diag(1./std(X)));
5   X = X - ones(N,1)*mean(X);
6   figure(1)
7   plotmatrix(X); corrcoef(X)
8
9   %% induce linear correlation
10  rho = 0.5; M = ones(p,p) * rho;
11  M(1:(p + 1):(p * p)) = 1;
```

```
12 C = chol(M); Xc = X * C;
13 figure(2)
14 plotmatrix(Xc); corrcoef(Xc)
15
16 %% make exp
17 Z = exp(Xc);
18 figure(3)
19 plotmatrix(Z); corrcoef(Z)
```

When we compute the correlation of Xc:

```
corrcoef(Xc)
```

we get indeed:

```
ans =
    1.0000    0.5073    0.5093
    0.5073    1.0000    0.4763
    0.5093    0.4763    1.0000
```

But for the lognormals Z we get correlations like

```
ans =
    1.0000    0.3458    0.4098
    0.3458    1.0000    0.4131
    0.4098    0.4131    1.0000
```

So the correlations have shrunk.

Example 7.1

For lognormal variates, the attainable linear correlation is a function of the variances of the normals. Let Y_1 and Y_2 follow a Gaussian distribution and be linearly correlated with ρ, then the linear correlation between the associated lognormals can be computed analytically:

$$\text{linear correlation}(e^{Y_1}, e^{Y_2}) = \frac{e^{\rho\sigma_1\sigma_2} - 1}{\sqrt{(e^{\sigma_1^2} - 1)(e^{\sigma_2^2} - 1)}}.$$

What is more, if $\log(Y_1)$ has a Gaussian distribution with zero mean and unit variance, and $\log(Y_2)$ has a Gaussian distribution with zero mean and variance σ^2, then (McNeil, Frey, and Embrechts, 2005, Chapter 5)

$$\rho_{\min} = \frac{e^{-\sigma} - 1}{\sqrt{(e-1)(e^{\sigma^2} - 1)}} \quad \text{and} \quad \rho_{\max} = \frac{e^{\sigma} - 1}{\sqrt{(e-1)(e^{\sigma^2} - 1)}}.$$

As a test, we increase the standard deviation of the first column of Xc to 5:

Listing 7.11. C-ModelingDependencies/M/lognormals.m

```
20 %% change variance of Xc
21 sd = 5;
22 Xc(:,1) = sd*Xc(:,1);
23 Z = exp(Xc);
24 figure(4)
25 plotmatrix(Z); corrcoef(Z)
```

We get a correlation matrix like the following:

```
ans =
    1.0000    0.0130    0.0551
    0.0130    1.0000    0.4131
    0.0551    0.4131    1.0000
```

Thus, for certain distributions, linear correlation is not an appropriate choice to measure comovement. There are alternatives to linear correlation: we can use rank correlation.

The best-known rank correlation coefficient is that of Spearman. To compute Spearman correlation ρ^S between Y and Z, we replace the observations y_i and z_i by their ranks; then we can use Eq. (7.1). Spearman correlation is sometimes also defined as the linear correlation between $F_Y(Y)$ and $F_Z(Z)$ where $F_{(\cdot)}$ are the distribution functions of the random variables. This maps the realizations into $(0, 1)$; it is equivalent to the ranking approach in the population but not in the sample. To compute ranks with R, we can use the function rank.

Listing 7.12. C-ModelingDependencies/R/Spearman.R

```
1 Y <- rnorm(20)
2 Z <- rnorm(20)
3 cor(Y,Z, method = "spearman")
4
5 ranksY <- rank(Y)
6 ranksZ <- rank(Z)
7 cor(ranksY,ranksZ, method = "pearson")
```

Ranking the elements of a vector with Matlab is not so straightforward. Here is a small example. We have a vector Y, and we want to obtain the ranks, given in the column "ranks of Y."

Y	sorted Y	ranks of Y
4.9	0.0	5
3.2	1.5	4
0.0	2.7	1
2.7	3.2	3
1.5	4.9	2

The Matlab function sort returns a sorted vector and (optionally) a vector of indices. These indices are the sorting order for the original vector. Hence if

```
[sortedY,indexY] = sort(Y)
```

we have `sortedY` is the same as `Y(indexY)`. In the example, the index vector would be [3 5 4 2 1]'. (As a side note, such indexes can be used to create permutations of vectors; see page 139.) We want ranks, not indexes. So we need the indexes of the sorted indexes; see the following Matlab code.

Listing 7.13. C-ModelingDependencies/M/Spearman.m

```
 1 % spearman.m  version -- 2011-01-10
 2 Y = randn(20,1);
 3 Z = randn(20,1);
 4 corr(Y,Z,'type','Spearman')
 5 %
 6 [ignore, indexY] = sort(Y);
 7 [ignore, indexZ] = sort(Z);
 8 [ignore, ranksY] = sort(indexY);
 9 [ignore, ranksZ] = sort(indexZ);
10 corr(ranksY,ranksZ,'type','Pearson')
```

This only works if the elements in Y are all distinct, that is, there are no ties. In Matlab's Statistics Toolbox, the function `tiedrank` computes average ranks for cases with ties. R's `rank` also handles ties correctly.

Spearman correlation has a more general invariance property than linear correlation. Since it only uses ranks, it does not change under monotonically increasing transformations. Since distribution functions and their inverses have this property, the rank correlation stays the same. Try:

```
X = randn(10000,2);
M = [1 0.7; 0.7 1];
C = chol(M); X = X*C;
corr(X, 'type', 'Spearman')
corr(exp(X),'type','Spearman')     % a monotone transformation
corr(normcdf(X),'type','Spearman') % a monotone transformation
```

But how can we induce rank correlation between variates with specified marginal distributions? We need a sample of uniforms with a given rank correlation, then we can use the inversion method (Section 6.3.1). What we know is how to generate a sample of Gaussians with a specified linear correlation. It turns out this is all we need, since in the Gaussian case there exist explicit relations between rank and linear correlation (Hotelling and Pabst, 1936; McNeil, Frey, and Embrechts, 2005):[3]

$$\rho^{\text{linear}} = 2\sin(\pi/6\,\rho^S), \qquad\qquad \rho^S = {6}/{\pi}\arcsin(\rho/2) \qquad (7.3)$$

---

[3] An alternative rank correlation measure is Kendall's τ, defined as follows:

$$\tau = \text{prob}\big((Y_i - Y_j)(Z_i - Z_j) > 0\big) - \text{prob}\big((Y_i - Y_j)(Z_i - Z_j) < 0\big).$$

prob($\cdot$) stands for "probability that ($\cdot$)." For the Gaussian case, we also have an explicit relation between linear correlation and Kendall's τ:

$$\rho^{\text{linear}} = \sin(\pi/2\,\tau), \qquad\qquad \tau = {2}/{\pi}\arcsin\rho.$$

Algorithm 22 describes a procedure to create a random vector Y with marginal distribution F and rank correlation matrix Σ^{rank}. An example, creating lognormals with a rank correlation of 0.9, follows.

Algorithm 22 Generate variates with specific rank correlation.

1: set Σ^{rank} (rank correlation)
2: compute corresponding Σ (linear correlation) with Eq. (7.3)
3: generate Gaussian variates Z with linear correlation Σ
4: compute uniforms $U = F_{\text{Gaussian}}(Z)$ (which preserves rank correlation)
5: compute $Y = F^{-1}(U)$ (which preserves rank correlation)

Listing 7.14. C-ModelingDependencies/M/exRankcor.m

```
 1 % exRankcor.m -- version 2010-01-09
 2 %% example rank correlation
 3 p = 3; N = 1000;
 4 X = randn(N,p);
 5 X = X * (diag(1./std(X)));
 6 X = X - ones(N,1)*mean(X);
 7 plotmatrix(X); corrcoef(X)
 8
 9 %% induce rank correlation: Spearman
10 rhoS = 0.9;    % correlation between any two assets
11
12 % set rank correlation matrix
13 Mrank = ones(p,p) * rhoS;
14 Mrank(1:(p + 1):(p * p)) = 1;
15
16 % compute corresponding linear correlation matrix
17 M = 2*sin(pi/6.*Mrank);
18
19 % compute cholesky factor
20 C = chol(M);
21
22 % induce correlation, check
23 Xc = X * C;
24 plotmatrix(Xc);
25
26 % check
27 corr(Xc,'type','Pearson')
28 corr(Xc,'type','Spearman')
29
30 sd = 5; Xc(:,1) = sd * Xc(:,1);
31 Z = exp(Xc);
32 % check
33 corr(Z,'type','Pearson')
34 corr(Z,'type','Spearman')
```

The interesting bit happens in lines 30–34. exp() is a monotonous transformation, so the rank correlation remains. In fact, the inverse of the lognormal is $\exp(F^{-1}_{\text{Gaussian}}.)$ The linear correlation of the lognormals is reduced as before:

```
ans =
    1.0000      0.4516      0.4849
    0.4516      1.0000      0.8532
    0.4849      0.8532      1.0000
```

But the rank correlation stays where it is.

```
ans =
    1.0000      0.9037      0.9031
    0.9037      1.0000      0.9047
    0.9031      0.9047      1.0000
```

In fact, for Spearman we would not really have needed the adjustment in Eq. (7.3) since the maximum difference between ρ and ρ^S in the Gaussian case is less than 0.02. So when we compare the Matlab scripts lognormals.m and exRankcor.m, we have done nothing much different compared with the Gaussian case; if you look at the scatter plots, you find that they may still look awkward because of the right tails of the lognormal. The only thing that is different now is how we measure correlation, the actual results are almost the same.

As another example, we create rank-correlated triangular variates T. Such variates are often used in decision modeling since they only require the modeler to specify a range of possible outcomes (Min to Max) and the most likely outcome Mode. Triangular variates T can be simulated in a number of ways (Devroye, 1986). One possibility is

$$T = \text{Mode} + \big(\text{Min} + U_1(\text{Max} - \text{Min}) - \text{Mode}\big)\sqrt{U_2},$$

or we could use

$$T = \text{Mode} + \big(\text{Min} + U_1(\text{Max} - \text{Min}) - \text{Mode}\big)\max(U_2, U_3);$$

see Devroye (1996). The U_i are uniform variates. The R script tria.R implements both variants.

Listing 7.15. C-ModelingDependencies/R/tria.R

```
 1  # tria.R -- version 2010-12-16
 2  # variant 1
 3  Min <- 0; Max <- 3; Mode <- 0.75
 4  rtria1 <- function(u1, u2, Min, Max, Mode) {
 5      Mode + (Min + u1 * (Max - Min) - Mode) * sqrt(u2)
 6  }
 7  trials <- 1000
 8  T <- rtria1(runif(trials), runif(trials), Min,Max,Mode)
 9  hist(T)
10
11
12  # variant 2
```

```
13 Min <- 0; Max <- 3; Mode <- 0.75
14 rtria2 <- function(u1,u2,u3,Min,Max,Mode) {
15     Mode + (Min + u1 * (Max - Min) - Mode) * pmax(u2, u3)
16 }
17 trials <- 1000
18 T <- rtria2(runif(trials), runif(trials), runif(trials),
19              Min, Max, Mode)
20 hist(T, breaks = 100)
```

We can also use the inverse of the triangular distribution.

Listing 7.16. C-ModelingDependencies/R/tria.R

```
23 # inverse
24 triaInverse <- function(u,min,max,mode) {
25     range <- max-min
26     r <- ifelse(u <= (mode-min)/(range),
27            min + sqrt(  u  * range * (mode - min)),
28            max - sqrt((1-u) * range * (max  - mode)))
29     return(r)
30 }
31 trials <- 1000
32 u <- runif(trials)
33 Min <- 0; Max <- 3; Mode <- 0.75
34 system.time(T <- triaInverse(u,Min,Max,Mode))
35 hist(T)
```

All variants could be improved. The command pmax(x,y), for instance, could be replaced by

$$\frac{x+y}{2} + \left|\frac{x-y}{2}\right|$$

which is often faster. Likewise, the result of ifelse can often be obtained faster by directly evaluating the logical expression. Such ideas, of course, provide speed at the cost of obscuring the code. The next program creates triangular variates with a Spearman rank correlation of 0.7.

Listing 7.17. C-ModelingDependencies/R/tria.R

```
38 # correlation
39 N <- 1000; p <- 4
40 rho <- 0.7; rho <- 2 * sin(rho * pi / 6) # spearman
41 X <- array(rnorm(N * p), dim = c(N, p))
42 C <- matrix(rho, nrow = p, ncol = p);
43 diag(C) <- 1; C <- chol(C)
44
45 X <- X %*% C
46 cor(X, method = "spearman")
47
48 U <- pnorm(X)
49 T <- triaInverse(U,Min,Max,Mode)
50
51 # graphic (see ?pairs)
52 panel.hist <- function(x) {
```

```
53  usr <- par("usr"); on.exit(par(usr))
54  par(usr = c(usr[1:2], 0, 1.5) )
55  h <- hist(x, plot = FALSE)
56  breaks <- h$breaks; nB <- length(breaks)
57  y <- h$counts; y <- y/max(y)
58  rect(breaks[-nB], 0, breaks[-1], y, col=grey(.5))
59 }
60 par(las = 1, mar = c(2,2,0.5,0.5), ps = 10, tck = 0.01,
61     mgp = c(3, 0.2, 0), pch = '.')
62 pairs(T, diag.panel = panel.hist,gap=0)
```

In case we ever need it, we could also create uniforms with a given linear correlation as specified in a matrix Σ. In the population (or in large samples),

$$\rho^{S}_{Y,Z} = \rho^{\text{linear}}\big(F_Y(Y),F_Z(Z)\big), \qquad (7.4)$$

for two random variables Y and Z. That is, the linear correlation between the uniforms obtained from transforming the original variates equals the Spearman correlation between the original variates. We set up the desired linear correlation matrix Σ; next we need to generate Gaussian Y and Z with Spearman correlation Σ^{rank}. By Eq. (7.4), this will be the linear correlation for the uniforms.

The following Matlab script create 1000 realizations of four correlated random variates, where the first two variates have a Gaussian distribution and the other two are uniformly distributed.

Listing 7.18. C-ModelingDependencies/M/exUniforms.m

```
1  % exUniforms.m -- version 2011-01-07
2  % generate normals, check correlations
3  X = randn(1000,4);
4  corrcoef(X)
5
6  % desired linear correlation
7  M =[1.0  0.7  0.6  0.6;
8      0.7  1.0  0.6  0.6;
9      0.6  0.6  1.0  0.8;
10     0.6  0.6  0.8  1.0];
11
12 % adjust correlations for uniforms
13 M = 2 * sin(pi/6 .* M);
14
15 % induce correlation, check correlations
16 C = chol(M);
17 Xc = X * C;
18 corrcoef(Xc)
19
20 % create uniforms, check correlations
21 Xc(:,3:4) = normcdf(Xc(:,3:4));
22 corrcoef(Xc)
23
24 % plot results (marginals)
```

```
25  for i=1:4
26      subplot(2,2,i);
27      hist(Xc(:,i))
28      title(['X ', int2str(i)])
29  end
```

As a final example, assume we have samples of returns of two assets, collected in vectors Y_1 and Y_2, but assume they are not synchronous; they could even be of different length. We still can induce rank correlation between these empirical distributions and sample from them.

Listing 7.19. C-ModelingDependencies/M/exEmpCor.m

```
1   % exEmpCor.m -- version 2011-01-04
2   NO = 200; % empirical number of obs
3   Y1 = randn(NO,1);
4   Y2 = randn(NO,1); Y2(Y2<0.3) = -0.5; % make Y2 non-Gaussian
5
6   % create CDFs
7   sortedY1 = sort(Y1);
8   sortedY2 = sort(Y2);
9
10  % resample
11  N = 1000; % (re)sample size
12  Z = randn(N,2); rho = 0.9;
13  M = [1 rho; rho 1]; Z = Z*chol(M);
14  U = normcdf(Z); U = ceil(NO*U);
15
16  %check
17  corrcoef(Y1,Y2)
18  corrcoef(sortedY1(U(:,1)),sortedY2(U(:,2)))
19
20  % histograms and scatter of original Y1 and Y2
21  subplot(231), hist(Y1)
22  subplot(232), hist(Y2)
23  subplot(233),scatter(Y1(U(:,1)),Y2(U(:,2)))
24
25  % histograms and scatter of resampled/correlated Y1 and Y2
26  subplot(234), hist(Y1(U(:,1)))
27  subplot(235), hist(Y2(U(:,2)))
28  subplot(236),scatter(sortedY1(U(:,1)),sortedY2(U(:,2)))
```

The plots show that the marginal distributions stay the same, but the joint distribution now shows strong comovement. In the following sections we will discuss methods that give us more control over the joint distribution of random variables.

7.2. Markov chains

7.2.1. Concepts

In a Markov chain, the probability for the next state or value of a variate depends on the current state. This approach is particularly useful for time series with conditional probabilities, and Markov Chain Monte Carlo (MCMC) plays a very prominent role in financial simulations.

In its simplest version, there is only a limited set of alternatives, and the probabilities for the next state of a variable only depend on its current state. For example, consider a bond that can be rated either "investment grade" (*IG* state 1) or "high yield" (*HY* state 2). With a low probability, the rating will change, but most likely, it will remain the same. In other words, the rating in the next period highly depends on its current rating, because upgrading or downgrading usually happens only with a low probability. For example, $\text{prob}(x_{i+1} = IG | x_i = IG) > \text{prob}(x_{i+1} = IG | x_i = HY)$. The conditional probabilities can be collected in a transition matrix Π:

$$\Pi = [p_{x_{i+1}|x_i}] = \begin{bmatrix} p_{IG|IG} & p_{HY|IG} \\ p_{IG|HY} & p_{HY|HY} \end{bmatrix}.$$

Given the transition matrix, sampling is rather straightforward. The rows in the transition matrix provide the conditional probabilities for a given current state x_i; for example, $\Pi = \begin{bmatrix} 0.9 & 0.1 \\ 0.1 & 0.9 \end{bmatrix}$ means that, for either state, there is a 90% chance that the next state will be the same and a 10% chance that the process will switch. Sampling the subsequent state x_{i+1} can then be done with a roulette wheel principle (see Section 6.5.2).

Listing 7.20. C-ModelingDependencies/M/DiscreteMC.m

```
1  function x = DiscreteMC(prob,N,x_0)
2  % DiscreteMC.m  -- version 2011-01-06
3  %    discrete Markov Chain with N samples
4  %    prob: transition variables
5  if nargin < 3
6      uc_prob = prob^50;
7      x_0 = RouletteWheel(uc_prob(1,:),1);
8  end
9  x = zeros(N+1,1);
10 x(1) = x_0;
11 for i = 1:N
12     x(i+1) = RouletteWheel(prob(x(i),:),1);
13 end
14 x(1) = [];
```

If there are n_x different states and $p_{x_{i+1}|x_i} = 1/n_x$, there will be no serial dependence. This changes, however, if the probabilities are state dependent. For $\Pi = \begin{bmatrix} 0.9 & 0.1 \\ 0.0 & 1.0 \end{bmatrix}$, state 1 is likely to be followed by state 1; once state 2 has been sampled, the process will never return to state 1. In this case, state 2 is called an "absorbing state." Alternatively, a transition matrix $\Pi = \begin{bmatrix} 0.01 & 0.99 \\ 0.90 & 0.10 \end{bmatrix}$ will produce heavy oscillation between states, though, again, there is a higher chance that the system is in state 2. To get the conditional probabilities for the state for the period after the next, the transition matrix must be multiplied by itself, $p_{x_{i+2}|x_i} = \Pi^2$; for the tth future period, $p_{x_{i+t}|x_i} = \Pi^t$.

Note that the larger t becomes, the closer these probabilities get to the unconditional probabilities for the different states. Note that Π must be a square $n_x \times n_x$ matrix, and the rows must add up to 1.

This principle can be generalized for joint densities p_{xy} with conditional distributions $p_{x|y}$ and $p_{y|x}$. The simulation procedure is just a variant of the univariate case. An important prerequisite here is that at least one of the variates depends on the lagged value. If, say, x_{i+1} depends on y_i, but y_{i+1} is conditioned on x_{i+1}, one has to bear in mind the sequence for drawing the samples. Also, if x and y can assume a different number of states, n_x and n_y, respectively, then the dimensions for Π_x and Π_y must be $n_y \times n_x$ and $n_x \times n_y$, respectively.

Listing 7.21. C-ModelingDependencies/M/DiscreteMC2.m

```
1  function x = DiscreteMC2(prob_1,prob_2,N,x_0)
2  % DiscreteMC2.m  -- version 2011-01-06
3  %    discrete Markov Chain with N samples
4  %    prob: transition variables
5  if nargin < 4
6      uc_prob_1 = ( prob_2 * prob_1 )^50;
7      uc_prob_2 = ( prob_1 * prob_2 )^50;
8      x_0(1)    = RouletteWheel(uc_prob_1(1,:),1);
9      x_0(2)    = RouletteWheel(uc_prob_2(1,:),1);
10 end;
11
12 x = zeros(N+1,2);
13 x(1,:) = x_0;
14 for i = 1:N
15     x(i+1,1) = RouletteWheel(prob_1(x(i,2),:),1);
16     x(i+1,2) = RouletteWheel(prob_2(x(i,1),:),1);
17 end
18 x(1,:) = [];
```

Markov chains can also be generalized to continuous distributions;[4] the geometric Brownian motion, often used to model stock price processes, would be one example for this: the new price depends on the (realized) previous price plus a (random) price change (see Section 8.3).

7.2.2. The Metropolis algorithm

Metropolis, Rosenbluth, Rosenbluth, Teller, and Teller (1953) suggest a Monte Carlo method to simulate states for a Boltzmann distribution in molecular and atomic systems. Assume the current state (or position) is x_i and the energy function is $E(x_i)$. Then, a random new position is generated within the neighborhood of x_i, $y = x_i + u_i s$, where u_i is vector of uniform samples $u_i \in [-1, +1]$ (same dimensions as x_i), and s is a scalar. This new

---

[4] When speaking about Markov chains, one usually has the discrete version in mind; this, however, is just one special case.

position is accepted for certain if it has lower energy than x_i. But also a higher energy state is accepted with a certain probability $\exp(-\Delta_E / (kT))$, where $\Delta_E = E(y) - E(x_i)$, T is the temperature, and k is the Boltzmann constant. If kT is large (in proportion to Δ_E), chances of acceptance, $x_{i+1} := y$, are high, otherwise they are low.[5]

In terms of the acceptance–rejection method, the idea was to generate a candidate new solution, set the density $f(x_{new})$ in proportion to the majorizing density, and use this proportion as an acceptance probability. The twist here is that the reference point is the current point's density: the new solution is accepted with probability $p = \min(1, f(x_{new})/f(x_i))$. If the new point has a higher density than the current one, it is accepted; if its density is lower in proportion to the current one, the chance of acceptance is also lower. For a d-dimensional variate x, the pseudocode is given in Algorithm 23.

Algorithm 23 Metropolis algorithm.

1: initialize x_1, n, and s
2: **for** $i = 1 : (n - 1)$ **do**
3:    **while** x_{i+1} not assigned **do**
4:       draw $z \in [0,1]$ and $u_i \in [-1,1]^d$
5:       $x_{new} = x_i + u_i \cdot s$
6:       **if** $f(x_{new})/f(x_i) \geq z$ **then** $x_{i+1} = x_{new}$
7:    **end while**
8: **end for**

This algorithm produces a vector of n variates, and the stationary distribution of the x_is will be (proportional to) f. The parameter s governs the maximum step size in any direction. In principle, one is rather free in picking a value for s, though there are some general principles. When s is small, the current and the suggested value will be very similar—and so will be their densities. Hence, the acceptance ratio will be close to 1, and it should not take many attempts to get a new solution. But because of the similarity in values, there will be strong serial dependence between the x_is, and there can be clusters in some parts of the probability space while no samples from other relevant areas exist. Choosing a large s has the exact opposite effect: there will be less serial dependence in the x_is, but it will take more attempts to generate a new variate. Also, increasing the number of dimensions while keeping s fixed, the size of neighborhood will grow, and the overall step size in terms of the Euclidean distance between current and new points will increase. Reducing s with the square root of dimensions will counteract

---

[5] As it turned out later, this concept is also useful in optimization; the Simulated Annealing heuristic is based on this algorithm; see Algorithm 45.

this effect.[6] If serial dependence is a problem and independent variates are required, shuffling can help (see Section 6.5.3). In either case, one must ensure that all new candidates are valid solutions and remain within the support. Finally, to avoid problems with unfortunate starting points, it is advisable to allow the process to burn in and discard initial samples.

Like the acceptance–rejection method, the Metropolis algorithm can readily be applied to multivariate distributions with known joint density. For an illustration, consider the bivariate normal distribution.

Listing 7.22. C-ModelingDependencies/M/MetropolisMVNormal.m

```
1  function x = MetropolisMVNormal(n,d,s,rho)
2  % MetropolisMVNormal.m  -- version 2011-01-06
3  %     generate n standard normal variates
4  %     n .... number of sample
5  %     d .... number of dimensions
6  %     s .... step size for new variate
7  %     rho .. correlation matrix; if scalar all have same corr.)
8
9  if isscalar(rho)
10     R = eye(d)*(1-rho) + ones(d)*rho;
11 else
12     R = rho;
13 end
14 mu = zeros(1,d);
15 x = nan(n,d);
16 x(1,:) = randn(1,d);
17 f_i = mvnpdf(x(1,:),mu,R);
18 for i = 1:(n-1)
19     while isnan(x(i+1,:))
20         x_new = x(i,:) + 2*(rand(1,d)-.5)*s;
21         f_new = mvnpdf(x_new,mu,R);
22         if rand < f_new / f_i
23             x(i+1,:) = x_new;
24             f_i  = f_new;
25         end
26     end
27 end
```

Fig. 7.2 depicts the 2000 samples generated for a required correlation of 0.75. The left panel uses a step size of $s = 0.2$, the right one of 1. To show the movements during the process, the x_1 is depicted in black, and subsequent points are increasingly brighter. As can be seen, larger d scatters the points more evenly over the probability space, yet it requires more run time.

A generalized version of this is the Metropolis–Hastings algorithm (see Hastings, 1970). The idea is to simulate x by again drawing candidate solutions and accepting them according to probabilistic criterion, yet by using a majorizing distribution. Algorithm 24 provides some details.

---

[6] See also the remark on calibrating heuristics in footnote 4 on page 499.

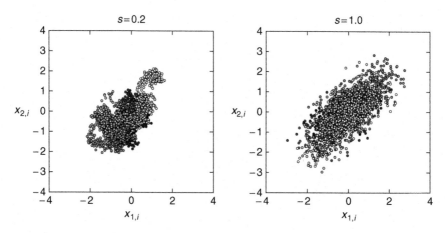

Figure 7.2 Bivariate normal samples, generated with the Metropolis algorithm.
Left panel: `metropolisMVNormal(2000,2,0.2,0.75)` ($s = 0.2$). Right panel:
`metropolisMVNormal(2000,2,1.0,0.75)` ($s = 1.0$).

Algorithm 24 Metropolis–Hastings.

1: initialize x_1 and n
2: **for** $i = 2 : n$ **do**
3:     $x_i = x_{i-1}$
4:     draw y from density $g_{y_{i+1}|y_i}(y|x_i)$
5:     compute Hastings ratio $r = \dfrac{p_x(y)}{p_x(x_i)} \dfrac{g_{y_{i+1}|y_i}(x_i|y)}{g_{y_{i+1}|y_i}(y|x_i)}$
6:     draw u from $(0,1)$ uniform distribution
7:     **if** $r > u$ **then** $x_{i+1} = y$
8: **end for**

Hastings (1970) generalized this approach further. Again, a majorizing
or candidate-generating density g is required, whereas the actual target
density is p. As for the previous example, let x_i be the current solution
and y be a new sample in its proximity. The probability of acceptance
depends on the Hastings ratio, $r = \dfrac{p_x(y)}{p_x(x_i)} \dfrac{g_{y_{i+1}|y_i}(x_i|y)}{g_{y_{i+1}|y_i}(y|x_i)}$. The main advantage
of the Metropolis–Hastings algorithm is that the shape of the target does
not need to be known. If the conditional distribution is known but not the
joint, the Gibbs sampler can be used (see Geman and Geman, 1984).

7.3. Copula models

7.3.1. Concepts

The advantage of covariances and linear correlations as measures of dependence is that they are well understood and readily accessible. In many

financial applications, however, covariances can—at best—only approximate the dependencies between two variables. Apart from the problems with linear correlation discussed in Section 7.1.1, the dispersion of the individual variables (e.g., returns) is rarely described by variance alone, and the marginal distributions (i.e., an individual variable's distribution independent of another variable's state) is rarely a Gaussian.

A more general approach to model dependencies—either between variates or over time—is the use of copulas. Copulas are functions that relate (univariate) marginal CDFs into a joint multivariate CDF. The most common type is bivariate copulas; according to Sklar's theorem, the joint bivariate CDF can then be expressed as a function (i.e., the copula, $C(\cdot,\cdot)$) of the two marginals:

$$F_{XY}(x,y) = C\big(F_X(x), F_Y(y)\big).$$

This implies that the conditional distribution of Y can be expressed as

$$F_{Y|X}(y|x) = \left.\frac{\partial C(x,y)}{\partial x}\right|_x.$$

As discussed in Section 6.2, if x has a CDF F_X, then $u = F_X(x)$ will be uniformly distributed; and with F^{-1} being the inverse of F, x can be "reconstructed" if u is known:

$$F_X(x) = u \iff F_X^{-1}(u) = x, \text{ where } u \sim U(0,1).$$

This means that it is enough to have copulas that accept uniform marginals, $C(u_1, u_2)$. For any other marginal, the variates can be transformed accordingly. Therefore, the copula can also be seen as the joint density of quantiles.

The simplest and, well, most trivial case is the independence copula:

$$C_I(u,v) = uv,$$

where u and v are independent uniform variates. Though not the most relevant example (after all, copulas are supposed to model dependence and not independence), it illustrates several important features: copulas model joint probabilities, and they are, therefore, defined within the unit square—or m-dimensional unit cube if an m-dimensional copula is considered. Already closer to financial applications are Gaussian distributions. If the two marginals are normal, then a Gaussian copula links them into a bivariate normal distribution:

$$C_{N_\rho}(u,v) = \int_{-\infty}^{\Phi^{-1}(u)} \int_{-\infty}^{\Phi^{-1}(v)} \phi_\rho(t_1, t_2) \mathrm{d}t_2 \mathrm{d}t_1 = \Phi_\rho\big(\Phi^{-1}(u), \Phi^{-1}(v)\big),$$

where $\phi_\rho(t_1, t_2)$ is the standard bivariate normal PDF with mean 0, standard deviation 1, and correlation ρ; Φ_ρ is the corresponding multivariate CDF; and Φ^{-1} is the inverse of the univariate standard normal CDF. But this is just one case, and there exist many alternatives. For financial applications, asymmetric variants are of particular interest since they can capture real-world tail dependencies: stocks tend to crash simultaneously, but extreme positive jumps rarely happen at the same time.

The empirical copula, on the other hand, requires no parametric assumption at all. Using the frequency function for a sample of n observations, it can be computed for quantiles $u_1 = i/n$ and $u_2 = j/n$ as the number of pairs not exceeding the corresponding order statistics $x_{(i)}$ and $y_{(j)}$, respectively:

$$C\left(\frac{i}{n}, \frac{j}{n}\right) = \frac{\sharp\{(x,y)|(x \leq x_{(i)}) \wedge (y \leq y_{(j)})\}}{n}.$$

A special (and very important) class is Archimedean copulas. The main ingredient here is the *Archimedean copula generator* which is a decreasing, convex function $\phi(u)$ from the unit interval $u \in [0, 1]$ and produces positive values in $\mathbb{R}^+$. Archimedean copulas can be written as

$$C(u, v) = \phi^{[-1]}\big(\phi(u) + \phi(v)\big).$$

Here, $\phi^{[-1]}(z)$ is the pseudoinverse defined by

$$\phi^{[-1]}(z) = \begin{cases} \phi^{-1}(z) & \text{if } 0 < z \leq \phi(0) \\ 0 & \text{if } z \geq \phi(0), \end{cases}$$

which accepts any positive value z and returns values within the range $[0, 1]$. For $\phi(0) = \infty$, it is equivalent to the "ordinary" inverse, $\phi^{-1}(z)$. A useful feature of Archimedean copulas is that they can easily be expanded to the multivariate case:

$$C(u_1, u_2, \cdots, u_m) = \phi^{[-1]}\big(\phi(u_1) + \phi(u_2) + \cdots + \phi(u_m)\big).$$

Also, Archimedean copulas are symmetric since, obviously, $C(u_1, u_2) = C(u_2, u_1)$.

To calibrate a copula model from empirical data, the canonical maximum likelihood (CML) method can be used. Assume a bivariate sample (x, y) of n observations. The joint distribution can then be represented by

$$F(x, y, \theta) = C\big(\hat{F}(x), \hat{F}(y), \theta\big)$$

where θ is the (set of) parameter(s) for the specific copula. $\hat{F}(x)$ and $\hat{F}(y)$ are the empirical marginals of x and y that are computed using their frequencies,

$$\hat{F}(z) = \frac{1}{N} \sum_{i=1}^{n} 1_{z_{(i)} \leq z}.$$

The copula parameter(s) can be estimated by maximizing the likelihood function

$$\hat{\theta} = \arg\max L(\theta)$$

with the likelihood function

$$L = \sum_{i=1}^{n} \log\left(c\left(\hat{F}(x), \hat{F}(y), \theta\right)\right),$$

where c is the copula's density. As Genest, Ghoudi, and Rivest (1995) showed, this estimator is consistent and asymptotically normally distributed. To assess the goodness of fit, the log-likelihood values and related information criteria, such as Akaike's (AIC) or the Schwarz–Bayesian (SBC), will briefly be addressed on page 202. For those interested in the details, Embrechts, Lindskog, and McNeil (2003) and Cherubini, Luciano, and Vecchiato (2004) provide good introductions to the subject with a focus on financial applications.

7.3.2. Simulation using copulas

Like the estimation process, the simulation process also comprises two main steps: first, the quantiles with the copula dependence are generated, and second, these quantiles are translated into samples according to the marginal distributions. The latter step is usually done with the inversion method. For sampling the quantiles, different approaches exist.

Metropolis sampling
When the density of a copula is available, samples can be drawn by using the acceptance–rejection method. However, one limitation here is that it is not always easy to find a suitable majorizing distribution to generate samples. The Metropolis algorithm would still work in that situation. Remember that in its original incarnation, a new candidate is generated by adding some uniform noise to the current value x_i. Here, however, the support is limited to [0, 1], so the new solution can be generated as pure noise. This helps reduce the serial dependence of the samples (though there will be some left since the density of x_i is used). The downside of lower acceptance rates will often be compensated by the shorter burn-in times.

The following Matlab code produces a matrix of n two-dimensional samples, based on the Gumbel, Frank, Clayton, or Gaussian copula.

Listing 7.23. C-ModelingDependencies/M/CopulaSim.m

```
1  function [u,x,Finv,c] = CopulaSim(n,copula,p)
2  % CopulaSim.m  -- version 2011-01-06
3  %   n ....... number of samples
4  %   copula .. name of copula (Frank,Clayton,Gumbel or Gaussian)
```

```
5  %    p ....... parameter of the copula
6
7  % marginal
8  Finv = @(u) norminv(u);
9  % densities
10 switch upper(copula)
11    case 'FRANK'            % parameter: p<>0
12      c = @(u,v,p) p*(1-exp(-p)).*exp(-p*(u+v)) ./ ...
13          (exp(-p*(u+v)) - exp(-p*u) - exp(-p*v) + exp(-p)).^2;
14    case 'CLAYTON'          % parameter: p>= -1; p~=0
15      c = @(u,v,p) (1+p) ./ ((u.*v).^(1+p) .*(u.^(-p) + ...
16                                     v.^(-p)-1).^(2+1/p) );
17    case 'GUMBEL'           % parameter: p >= 1
18      c = @(u,v,p) ( (-log(u)).^(p-1) .* (-log(v)).^(p-1) .* ...
19          ((-log(u)).^p + (-log(v)).^p).^(1/p-2)) ./ ...
20          (u.*v.*exp( ((-log(u)).^p + (-log(v)).^p).^(1/p)));
21    otherwise % Gaussian % parameter: -1 < p < 1
22      c = @(u,v,p) 1/sqrt(1-p^2) * exp((norminv(u).^2 + ...
23          norminv(v).^2)/(2) + (2*p*norminv(u).*norminv(v) - ...
24          norminv(u).^2-norminv(v).^2) / (2*(1-p^2)));
25 end
26 % Metropolis
27 u = NaN(n,2);
28 u(1,:) = rand(1,2);
29 f_i = c(u(1,1),u(1,2),p);
30 for i = 2:n;
31    while isnan(u(i,:))
32        u_new = rand(1,2);
33        f_new = c(u_new(1),u_new(2),p);
34        if rand < f_new/f_i
35            u(i,:) = u_new;
36            f_i = f_new;
37        end
38    end
39 end
40 x = Finv(u);
```

To illustrate the different properties, Fig. 7.3 depicts contour plots of the copulas' densities and samples drawn from them. To see how this transforms into the distribution of the actual variates, we assume standard normal marginal distributions. The graphs in the right column of each panel show the resulting joint densities and samples. As can be seen, under a Gumbel copula, there is stronger dependence on the positive end of the distribution, whereas for the Clayton, it is on the negative side. This last property coincides with stylized facts for empirical returns: assets tend to move in the same direction when markets crash but are less dependent in boom times. This makes the Clayton a popular choice for empirical applications.

Copula models can be constructed in a "mix-and-match" fashion: any copula can be combined with any marginal. The Gaussian copula, for example, comes with one parameter that corresponds to linear correlation if marginals are normal, and its parameter is well understood. Combining the

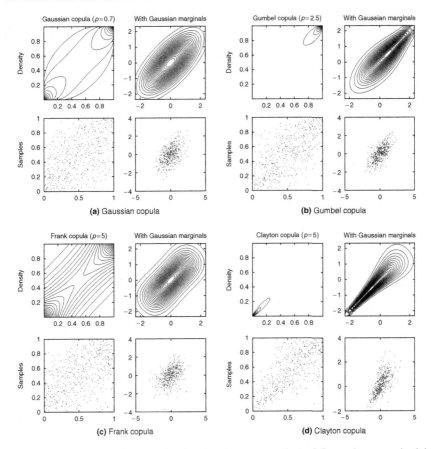

Figure 7.3 Densities for u and x (under the assumption of Gaussian marginals) and 500 samples.

Gaussian copula with Gaussian marginals gives a fancy way of expressing multivariate normals. However, the Gaussian copula can also be combined with other marginals, and Gaussian marginals can be linked via any copula—or combinations of copulas (weighted combinations or nested ones). Also, there exist copulas with more than two dimensions, making it possible to link one variate to the simultaneous states of several others. This flexibility is probably the greatest virtue of this approach—but, in empirical applications, can also lead to overfitting.

Direct sampling

Another approach would be to draw the first variate, v, from the unconditional $(0,1)$ uniform distribution and the second variate from the conditional one. For this, we require the partial derivative of the copula. Let $C_u \left. \frac{\partial C(u,v)}{\partial u} \right|_u$ be the partial derivative of $C(u,v)$ with respect to u and

C_u^{-1} its inverse. Then two samples x and y with marginals F_X and F_Y, respectively, can be generated as outlined in Algorithm 25. For more details on this, including some examples, see, e.g., Fusai and Roncoroni (2008).

Algorithm 25 Direct sampling.

1: draw two independent uniform samples $u_1, u_2 \sim U(0,1)$
2: impose dependence $u_2^* = C_u^{-1}(u_2)$
3: map dependent uniform samples according to marginals $x = F_X^{-1}(u_1), y = F_Y^{-1}(u_2^*)$

## CHAPTER EIGHT

A gentle introduction to financial simulation

8.1. Setting the stage

Simulation can be generally defined as experiments using models. In finance, there are many areas that use simulation techniques. These include the generation of artificial data when there are not enough real observations; the generation of scenarios; and the testing of assumptions, concepts, or strategies when real-world experiments are not advisable; to name just a few. Also, simulation can be useful when analytical solutions are not feasible; pricing and risk estimation problems are the usual suspects in this group. Finally, simulations can be used to get a better understanding of the behavior and properties of systems, and to spot the need for adjustments and extensions.

Traditionally, financial models come as econometric or mathematical sets of equations, describing deterministic and stochastic elements and how they relate. More recently, agent-based models for complex dynamic systems have gained importance; these focus on microstructures and investigate how things behave on an aggregate level (e.g., prices). In particular in complex systems, parts of these structures can change: agents can interact and influence each other's behavior, or their environment changes. Section 8.8 provides an example of this.

In the main part of this chapter, though, we follow the more traditional route: relationships, dependencies, and developments can be captured by a quantitative model, the structure of which is known and does not change over time. Sometimes, all the ingredients are readily available: checking how the price of a bond reacts to an increase in the discount rate would be an example for this. In other situations, some of the variables come from historical or Monte Carlo simulation. Again, we have to limit ourselves, and it is the latter we will mainly address here.

8.2. Single-period simulations

8.2.1. Terminal asset prices

One of the many uses of Monte Carlo simulation is to develop an idea and intuitive understanding for how financial models work and what outcomes to actually expect.

Consider the humble stock. One of the simplest—and most popular—assumptions is that prices are lognormally, and returns therefore normally, distributed. A nice feature of the normal distribution is that it only requires two parameters, mean and variance. The standard deviation (i.e., square root of the variance, or, in finance talk, the volatility) gives us an indication of how likely deviations from the expected value are: two standard deviations around the mean should cover about 19 out of 20 cases, i.e., approximately 95%. The exact probabilities for a confidence interval of c standard deviations around the mean can be computed by prob($X \in \mu \pm c\sigma$) = $N(c) - N(-c) = 2N(c) - 1$. In R, this can be done by

```
2 * pnorm(c) - 1
```

for any prespecified value c. The Matlab equivalent would be

```
2 * normcdf(c) - 1
```

To get a flavor of what this means in practice, let us assume that the yearly volatility of a stock is 20% and the drift of the stock is 5%; hence, $r \sim N(0.05, 0.2^2)$. To get an idea of what the stock could be worth at the end of the year, we can simulate 1000 sample returns

```
r = randn(1000,1) * 0.2 + 0.05
```

and compute the corresponding stock prices

```
S_T = S_0 * exp(r)
```

for given initial stock price S_0. For a sufficiently large sample (or by averaging repeated Monte Carlo simulations), one should find that the mean sample return converges to μ and the volatility actually does converge to σ. Histograms of the returns and terminal stock prices should exhibit the symmetry and positive skewness of the normal and lognormal distribution, respectively. The latter also causes the expected stock price to be above its median: since the normal distribution is symmetric, half of the returns should be above μ, and the other half below; this corresponds to a stock price of $S_0 \exp(\mu)$. In the stock prices, however, the positive deviations will be bigger than the negative ones; this is a straightforward consequence of taking the $\exp(\cdot)$. Consequently, the mean will be shifted to the right, and the average of the simulated terminal stock prices will converge to their expected value $E(S_T) = S_0 \exp(\mu + \sigma^2/2)$. SimulateStk.m provides a short simulation of this case.

Listing 8.1. C-FinancialSimulations/M/SimulateStk.m

```
 1  function SimStk = SimulateStk(mu,sigma,N_samples)
 2  % SimulateStk.m  -- version 2011-01-10
 3  % mu, sigma ....: drift and volatility
 4  % N ...........: number of samples
 5  SimStk.mu = mu;
 6  SimStk.sigma = sigma;
 7  SimStk.r = randn(N_samples,1)*sigma + mu;
 8  SimStk.S = exp(SimStk.r);
 9  SimStk.meanr = mean(SimStk.r);
10  SimStk.stdr  = std(SimStk.r);
11  SimStk.meanS = mean(SimStk.S);
12  SimStk.muS   = exp(mu+sigma^2/2);
13  SimStk.medS  = median(SimStk.S);
14
15  r = SimStk.r; S_T = SimStk.S;
16  % display results
17  fprintf('       mean: %4.2f (mu   = %4.2f)\n',SimStk.meanr,mu);
18  fprintf('  volatility: %4.2f (E(r) = %4.2f)\n',SimStk.stdr,sigma
       );
19  fprintf('  exp. price: %4.2f (E(S) = %4.2f)\n',SimStk.meanS,exp(
       mu+sigma^2/2));
20  fprintf('median price: %4.2f (M(S) = %4.2f)\n',SimStk.medS,exp(
       mu));
```

The asymmetric confidence intervals become also apparent in the graphical output (Fig. 8.1 is an example): what is symmetric in the return histogram becomes asymmetric in the price histogram. Hovering above the median are the mean values. As can be seen, these are (typically) equal to the median for the returns, but shifted to the right for the prices.

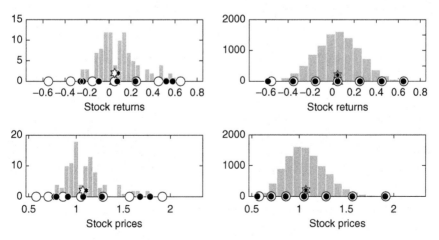

Figure 8.1 Simulated returns and stock prices for 100 (left) and 10,000 samples (right). White circles are theoretical quantiles and black ones are their empirical counterparts. Theoretical and empirical means are white and black stars, respectively.

The distribution of the samples will vary, so every run will produce slightly different sample mean returns and standard deviations. With increasing sample sizes, however, the Monte Carlo noise should be reduced.

8.2.2. 1-over-N portfolios

If one takes this example one step further and is interested in a portfolio of assets rather than individual stocks, one basically has two alternatives:

1. Analytically derive the properties of the portfolio, consider it as a special type of asset, and simulate it in the same fashion as any individual asset. The advantage of this direct simulation approach is that it keeps the number of variables down to a bare minimum. On the downside, it requires that a reliable formal description of the portfolio's properties is possible.

2. Simulate the individual stocks and combine the samples, like empirical data, into a portfolio. The advantage here is that this works even if the properties of the overall portfolio cannot be derived (or are too cumbersome to get) as long as one can get simulations of the constituents. This is particularly true when, for example, individual assets follow nonstandard distributions, have contingent payments, or are linked in a nonlinear fashion. Consider a portfolio that combines stocks, bonds, and derivatives in different currencies. The downside here is that each asset has to be simulated individually, which increases runtime and system requirements.

For the sake of simplicity, we stick with stocks that have normally distributed returns, which all have the same drift μ and volatility σ, and they all have the same pairwise linear correlation of ρ. The latter implies that they all have the same variances σ^2 and the same pairwise covariances $\sigma_{ij} = \rho_{ij}\sigma_i\sigma_j = \rho\sigma^2 \ \forall i \neq j$. The covariance matrix therefore has σ^2 along the diagonal and every off-diagonal element is $\sigma^2\rho$.

If we combine different assets into portfolios, then some of the individual variations will cancel out, and the portfolios' variances should be below the average of individuals assets. A portfolio's variance is the weighted sum of the covariances of all its constituents. To make things even simpler, assume that all of the N assets in the portfolio have the same weight $w_i = 1/N$ because the investor follows a "1-over-N" strategy. The portfolio's statistics for increasingly many different assets should converge as follows:

$$\lim_{N\to\infty} \mu_p = \sum_{i=1}^{N} \underbrace{w_i}_{1/N} \underbrace{\mu_i}_{\mu} = N\frac{1}{N}\mu = \mu$$

$$\lim_{N\to\infty} \sigma_p^2 = \sum_{i=1}^{N}\sum_{j=1}^{N} \underbrace{w_i}_{1/N} \underbrace{w_j}_{1/N} \sigma_{ij} = \underbrace{\frac{1}{N}\bar{\sigma}^2}_{\uparrow 0} + \underbrace{\left(1-\frac{1}{N^2}\right)\bar{\sigma}_{ij}}_{\downarrow 1} = \bar{\sigma}_{ij}$$

where $\bar{\sigma}$ and $\bar{\sigma}_{ij}$ are the average standard deviation and covariance, respectively.

In this case, the direct simulation approach would be straightforward. The mean and volatilities of the portfolio returns are given as part of the above derivation of the limits, and the simulation would be like for a single stock with unchanged drift ($\mu_p(N) = \mu$), yet lowered volatility ($\sigma_p(N) = \sigma\sqrt{1/N + (1 - 1/N^2)\rho}$).

The code `Simulate1overN.m` illustrates the indirect simulation approach. First, the individual assets are simulated and then combined into a portfolio. The larger the number of different assets the closer the portfolio's signatures will be to their theoretical values, and this convergence process will be smoother when more samples are used for this simulation. In the case of the mean portfolio return, this will show also in the changing scale of the y-axis—which, at first glance, might lead to the optical illusion that there isn't a lot of change. The boxplots give a better overall impression: increasing the number of different assets, N, reduces the portfolio's variance (ultimately) to the average covariance, and the bandwidth of portfolio returns becomes smaller.

Listing 8.2. C-FinancialSimulations/M/simulate1overN.m

```
 1 function r_Pf = Simulate1overN(mu,sigma,rho,N_samples,N_stocks)
 2 % Simulate1overN.m   -- version 2011-01-06
 3 %    mu, sigma ...: drift and volatility (same for all stocks)
 4 %    rho ........: linear correlation
 5 %    N_samples ...: number of samples
 6 %    N_stocks ....: maximum number of stocks
 7
 8 CovMat  = eye(N_stocks) * sigma^2 + (ones(N_stocks) - eye(
        N_stocks)) * sigma^2 * rho;
 9 e       = randn(N_samples,N_stocks)* chol(CovMat);
10 r       = mu + e;
11
12 % compute mean return for equally weighted portfolio
13 % of first 1 ... N_stocks stocks
14 r_Pf    = NaN(N_samples,N_stocks);
15 for i = 1:N_stocks
16     w = ones(i,1)/i;
17     r_Pf(:,i) = r(:,1:i) * w;
18 end
```

The results for the 1-over-N portfolios also highlight another point (Fig. 8.2): despite diversification, realized values can differ substantially from the expected ones. What is plainly obvious from a statistician's point of view is sometimes neglected in portfolio evaluation. Volatility is a measure of likely deviations from the expected values. If an asset has normally distributed returns with an expected value of μ and a volatility of σ, then there's roughly a two-thirds chance that the realized (out of sample) return

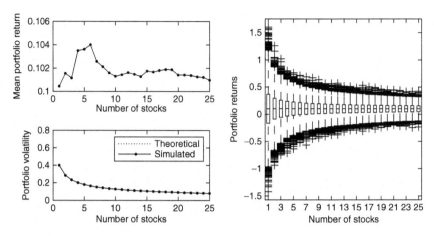

Figure 8.2 Returns for portfolios consisting of N equally weighted assets ("1-over-N").

will be within the range of $\mu \pm \sigma$ and a 95% chance that it will be within $\mu \pm 2\sigma$ (see footnote 10 on page 208). In other words, in one out of three cases, the actual return will deviate by more than the volatility; in one out of 20 cases, it will deviate by more than twice the volatility from what was expected. Likewise, the realized volatility can differ from what was expected, just by chance.

In financial management, this has two main consequences: first, evaluating the performance of a portfolio ex post is difficult because unsuitable portfolio compositions and unlucky market events are hard to distinguish, as is luck from skill. Second, estimations based on past observations are subject to sampling errors, even when the processes are stationary. We will revisit this problem in Chapter 13.

8.2.3. European options

On several occasions in this book, European style options are used as simple examples for derivatives. Call (put) options allow the writer of the option to buy (sell) the underlying asset at the exercise or strike price X. Obviously, the buyer will exercise only if the option has a positive inner value, that is, if the strike is below the underlying's price for a call or above for the put. If the option is European style, this right can be exercised at one specific date only (exercise day or maturity, T), whereas American style options can be exercised anytime until maturity.

Landmark models for option and derivative pricing are the ones suggested by Black and Scholes (1973) and Merton (1973). Their framework assumes, among other things, that the underlying's price follows a geometric

Brownian motion with constant volatility and drift, does not pay dividends,[1] that continuous and frictionless trading is possible, and that trading will not affect prices. Their main idea is that underlying and derivative can be combined such that the combination is risk free, hence a suitable portfolio should earn exactly the safe return—nothing more, nothing less. In other words, it is enough to consider a risk-neutral investor since any risk can be diversified away. In this book, we use the Black–Scholes–Merton framework as a simple setting to demonstrate different numerical methods (see, e.g., Sections 4.3 and 15.1). Here, we will try to use Monte Carlo simulation to demonstrate the basic workings. For convenience, we repeat the main Black–Scholes pricing formula for a European call:

$$c_0 = \underbrace{S_0 \, \mathrm{N}(d_1)}_{①} - \underbrace{X \mathrm{e}^{-r_{\mathrm{f}} T} \, \mathrm{N}(d_2)}_{②} \tag{8.1}$$

with current price of the underlying S_0 and $\mathrm{N}(\cdot)$ being the CDF of the standard normal distribution and parameters

$$d_1 = \frac{\log\left(\frac{S_0}{X}\right) + \left(r_{\mathrm{f}} + \frac{\sigma^2}{2}\right) T}{\sigma\sqrt{T}} \text{ and } d_2 = d_1 - \sigma\sqrt{T}.$$

The inner value of a European call at maturity is

$$c_T = \max(S_T - X, 0),$$

where S_T is the price of the underlying at maturity T and X is the strike. In a risk-neutral world, both the underlying and the option can be assumed to earn the safe return; the present value of the option can then be found by discounting the expected payoff with the risk-free return, r_{f}, while the underlying can be simulated such that the expected price is the present price plus safe interest:[2]

$$\mathrm{E}^{\mathrm{f}}(S_T) = S_0 \exp(r_{\mathrm{f}} T) \qquad \log(S_T / S_0) \sim \mathrm{N}\left(\left(r_{\mathrm{f}} - \frac{\sigma^2}{2}\right) T, \sigma^2 T\right)$$

$$\mathrm{E}^{\mathrm{f}}(c_T) = \mathrm{E}^{\mathrm{f}}(\max(S_T - X, 0)) \qquad c_0 = \mathrm{E}^{\mathrm{f}}(c_T) \exp(-r_{\mathrm{f}} T),$$

where σ is the underlying's volatility. To ease presentation, we drop the reference to risk-neutral settings and assumptions in the following discussion.

The main steps for Monte Carlo pricing of a European call option are collected in Algorithm 26.

---

[1] Subsequent models include discrete dividend payments or continuous dividend yields; Hull (2008) provides a comprehensive survey of pricing models.

[2] In a more realistic, risk-averse world, the risk-adjusted interest rates had to be used; yet under the assumed perfect risk diversification, risk premia ought to cancel each other out, and the investor is left with the risk-free return.

Algorithm 26 Monte Carlo simulation for a European call option.

1: simulate underlying's returns r_T with volatility $\sigma\sqrt{T}$ and mean $(r_f - \sigma^2/2)\sqrt{T}$;
2: compute underlying's price samples, $S_T = S_0 \exp(r_T)$
3: compute call's (inner) values at maturity, $c_T = \max(S_T - X, 0)$
4: compute present value of average call value, $c_0 = \mathsf{E}(c_T)\exp(-r_f T)$

Term ① in the Black–Scholes solution (8.1) relates to the expected value of the underlying, and term ② relates to the expected payments of the strike. Either term can be found in the Monte Carlo simulation.

- The inner value of the option is positive (i.e., the option is exercised) whenever $S_T > X$. The likelihood of the option being exercised is therefore the number of samples with positive inner value in relation to the overall number of samples. In Matlab, a logical check provides a Boolean value coded as 0 (`false`) or 1 (`true`); it is therefore enough to simply take the average of the vector of Booleans: if `ST` is the vector with the underlying's price samples and `X` is the strike, then `ex = ST>X` is a vector of Booleans about exercise yes/no, and `mean(ex)` provides the probability of exercising for the sample. In the Black–Scholes model, this likelihood is $\mathsf{N}(d_2)$ and, with a sufficiently large sample, the Monte Carlo simulation should come close to this theoretical value. X is the strike being payed in case the option is exercised; $X\,\mathsf{N}(d_2)$ is, therefore, the expected payment, and $X e^{-r_f T}\,\mathsf{N}(d_2)$ is its present value—which is term ② in Eq. (8.1).

- If `ex` is the vector with Booleans of exercising, then `ST(ex)` filters the sample prices above the strike, and `mean(ST(ex))` is the conditional price of the underlying in the case of exercise; as we already know, the likelihood for this case is `mean(ex)`. If the option is not exercised, the buyer does not get the underlying, and this position is worth zero. (But then, he or she does not have to pay the strike either.) All in all, the expected future value of this position is, therefore, `mean(ST(ex)) * mean(ex)`. Discounting with the risk-free return provides the present value: `mean (ST(ex)) * mean(ex) * exp(-rF*T)`. This corresponds to term ① in Eq. (8.1).

The following Matlab code provides an implementation; the output contrasts theoretical to simulated values. Section 9.3 presents further Monte Carlo techniques for option pricing.

Listing 8.3. C-FinancialSimulations/M/EuropeanOptionSimulation.m

```
1  % EuropeanOptionSimulation.m  -- version 2011-01-06
2
3  % parameters
4  S0  = 100;
5  X   = 100;
6  rf  = .05;
```

```
 7  sigma = .2;
 8  T     = .25;
 9  ns    = 100000; % number of Monte Carlo samples
10
11  % Black-Scholes price for European call
12  d1    = (log(S0/X)+(rf+sigma^2/2)*T) / (sigma * sqrt(T));
13  d2    = d1 - sigma*sqrt(T);
14  cOBS  = S0*normcdf(d1) - X*exp(-rf*T) * normcdf(d2);
15
16  % MC Simulation
17  rs    = randn(ns,1)*sigma*sqrt(T) + (rf - sigma^2/2)*T;
18  STs   = S0*exp(rs);
19  cTs   = max(STs-X,0);
20  cOMC  = mean(cTs)*exp(-rf*T);
21
22  % "ingredients"
23  ex    = STs>X;      % Boolean: exercise yes/no
24
25  fprintf('Simulation Results: \n=====================\n');
26  fprintf('E(stock price): %8.4f (theor.: %8.3f)\n', ...
27      [mean(STs) S0*exp(rf*T)]);
28  fprintf('prob. exercise: %8.4f (theor.: %8.3f)\n', ...
29      [mean(ex) normcdf(d2)]);
30  fprintf('PV(E(paymt X)): %8.4f (theor.: %8.3f)\n', ...
31      [mean(ex)*X*exp(-rf*T) X*exp(-rf*T) * normcdf(d2)]);
32  fprintf('PV(E(paymt S)): %8.4f (theor.: %8.3f)\n', ...
33      [mean(ex)*mean(STs(ex))*exp(-rf*T) S0*normcdf(d1)]);
34  fprintf('=====================\ncall price:      %8.4f (theor.:
        %8.3f)\n', ...
35      [cOMC cOBS]);
```

8.2.4. VaR of a covered put portfolio

As mentioned, simulating and aggregating a portfolio's constituents is particularly useful when analytical aggregation is challenging. To illustrate this, let's again assume an asset with normally distributed returns, but now it is combined with a put option. Again to keep things simple, we assume that it is a European put and that no intermediate trading is going on. If the strike for the put is X, then the put will be exercised if and only if the underlying's price is lower than the strike ($S_T < X$); in this case, the investor gets a price that is ($X - S_T$) above the stock's then market price. If the stock price exceeds the strike ($S_T > X$), selling the stock directly will provide a higher price, and the put expires without exercise. What happens in the unlikely event of $S_T = X$ does not make a difference; it seems reasonable to let the put expire: exercising does not yield a price higher than the market price but causes extra effort. In the presence of market frictions such as transaction costs, pin risk,[3] and opportunity costs of actually having to act,

---

[3] If there is a temporal gap between receiving the underlier and earliest time to sell it (e.g., if delivered on Friday evening, it cannot be sold before Monday morning), there is a residual risk. When the option is only slightly in the money, the buyer could then opt not to exercise.

the limits between exercising or not could be shifted. In short, the value of the put at maturity is piecewise linear, $\max(X - S_T, 0)$. Clearly, the put's payoff at maturity will not be lognormally distributed like the asset. Hence, simulating the value of a portfolio consisting of stocks and puts directly could be cumbersome. This is even more true for any point in time before maturity, $\tau < T$, where the put's value is a nonlinear convex function with respect to the underlying's price S_τ. In this case, it is much simpler to first simulate the individual constituents and then combine them according to the portfolio's composition.

To illustrate this, assume an investor owns a stock but wants protection against losses at some point T in the future. To do this, he or she buys one European put option per stock and an exercise price equal to the current stock price. The portfolio will be perfectly protected against losses at time T, but not in the intermediate time: at any point $\tau < T$, the absolute Delta of the put is always less than one, $-1 < \Delta_{p_{T-\tau}} < 0$. In plain English, this means that a \$1 drop in the stock price will increase the put price, but by less than \$1.[4] Intuitively, this is because immediate exercise at time τ is not possible, but there is a chance the stock price will recover again until maturity.

Let us assume that the stock has an initial price $S_0 = 100$ and the annual log return is normally distributed with $r \sim N(0.1, 0.2^2)$, whereas the annual safe return is $r_f = 0.05$. The put has time to maturity of $T = 0.5$ and strike $X = S_0 = 100$, and, for simplicity, the Black–Scholes model provides a fair price for it. To simulate the portfolio wealth at $0 \leq \tau \leq T$, one needs to first simulate the stock prices at time τ. The log returns until then are normally distributed with $r_\tau \sim N(0.1/\tau, (0.2/\sqrt{\tau})^2)$.

At time τ, the remaining time to maturity for the put is $T - \tau$. Note that the option is priced under risk neutrality and continuous trading; the Black–Scholes model therefore requires the safe return, not the stock's drift.

Listing 8.4. C-FinancialSimulations/M/SimulateStauPtau.m

```
 1  function [PF_tau,S_tau,p_tau] = SimulateStauPtau(S_0,drift,vol,X
       ,rSafe,T,tau,NSample)
 2  % SimulateStauPtau.m  -- version 2011-01-06
 3  %    simulate portfolio with  1 stock and 1 put at time tau
 4  %    S_0        initial stock price with return ~ N(drift,vol^2)
 5  %    X          strike of put
 6  %    rSafe      riskfree rate of return
 7  %    T          time to maturity of put
 8  %    tau        point of valuation; if not provided: tau = T
 9  %    NSample    number of samples for the simulation
10  if nargin < 7, tau = T;  else tau = min(T,tau); end
11  if nargin < 8, NSample = 10000; end;
12  % -- simulate stock prices at tau
```

---

[4] The Greeks are discussed in more detail in Sections 5.5 and 9.3.3.

```
13  r = randn(NSample,1)*(vol*sqrt(tau)) + drift * tau;
14  S_tau = S_0 * exp(r);
15  % -- compute put prices at tau; time left to maturity (T-tau)
16  T_left = T - tau;
17  p_tau = BSput(S_tau,X,rSafe,0,T_left,vol);
18  % -- value of portfolio at time tau
19  PF_tau  = S_tau + p_tau;
```

`SimulateStauPtau.m` performs exactly this simulation.[5] It also produces histograms of the simulated stock prices and portfolio wealth for the selected time τ. When experimenting with different τs, it becomes apparent that in the beginning (τ close to 0) the portfolio wealth is more or less the stock's distribution, shifted to the right by the price of the option. The closer τ gets to T, however, the more the portfolio's distribution converges to a truncated version of the stock's with extra density at X. This spike represents all the cases where the put is exercised. Fig. 8.3 gives examples for various values of τ.

Under given assumptions, the value of the put at time $t = 0$ is $p_0 = 4.42$; the combination of 1 stock plus 1 put is therefore initially worth $P_0 = S_0 + p_0 = 104.42$. Over time, the portfolio value P_τ will diffuse. At maturity, its lowest possible value will be $P_T = X$. For the time in between, however, the portfolio value is $P_\tau = S_\tau + p_\tau(S_\tau)$ that can be below X. The Value at Risk, $VaR_{\alpha,\tau}$, is the loss at time τ exceeded only with probability α.[6]

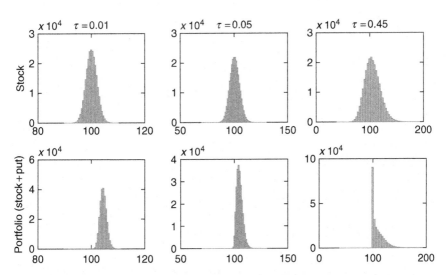

Figure 8.3 Histograms for the value of a stock (top panel) and a portfolio consisting of the stock plus one European put (bottom panel) at times τ.

---

[5] The function BSput was introduced in Chapter 4 and computes the Black–Scholes price for a put.
[6] Sometimes, α denotes the probability that the VaR threshold is *not* exceeded; the shortfall probability is then, obviously, $1 - \alpha$.

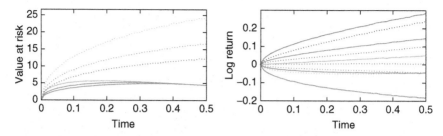

Figure 8.4 Left panel: Value at Risk for stock (dotted lines) and portfolio (solid line) for 1%, 5%, and 10% quantiles (light to dark). Right panel: 5%, 25%, 50%, 75%, and 95% percentiles of log returns for stock (dotted) and portfolio (solid line).

For our purposes, it can be computed by taking the $(1 - \alpha)$ quantile of the simulated portfolio wealth and subtracting it from the initial value of the portfolio. As can be seen from Fig. 8.4, the portfolio's VaR is substantially lower than that of the unprotected stock. But then so is the portfolio's return: the portfolio's median log returns are less than the stock's, and confidence bands are narrower around this lower median as well.

8.3. Simple price processes

When making assumptions about financial price processes, the term "random walk" usually comes up very quickly. The argument behind this is actually quite simple and intuitively appealing: in a perfect world, all publicly available information should be reflected in the current price; hence any price change should be unpredictable or, in other words, random. If this were not the case and price movements were, at least to some extent, predictable, then this could allow for arbitrage or at least statistical arbitrage.[7] With sufficiently many informed investors participating, this should not be possible, and their activities should cause markets to become semi-efficient.

From a modeling perspective, the price process can then be split into a deterministic and a stochastic part. From a theoretical point of view, martingales are the simplest building block for efficient markets:

- If today's price is the best estimate for tomorrow's, then we speak of a martingale. Let Ω_t denote the information available at time t. Then, for log prices $s_t = \log(S_t)$,

$$E_t(s_{t+1}|\Omega_t) = s_t .$$

---

[7] In short, arbitrage exists if a self-financing position can produce a positive net payoff, but will never require a negative net cash flow. In statistical arbitrage, the probabilities for positive and negative net payments should converge to one and zero, respectively.

In particular for short time steps, this is often a convenient and sufficiently accurate assumption.

- If the expected values increase (decrease) over time, they are a sub-martingale (super-martingale):

$$E_t(s_{t+1}|\Omega_t) \geq (\leq)s_t.$$

- When log prices are a martingale, then any price change comes as a surprise, and nonoverlapping price changes are uncorrelated at all leads and lags. In other words, the changes in the log prices (i.e., the log returns) are a fair game:

$$E_t(\Delta s_{t+1}|\Omega_t) = E_t(r_{t+1}|\Omega_t) = 0.$$

- Finally, all market participants p are assumed to use the same information and probability density function:

$$f^p(r_{t+1}|\Omega_t^p) = f(r_{t+1}|\Omega_t).$$

In particular when only short periods of time are considered, martingales are often a convenient working assumption. For longer periods, however, investors want to earn some risk premium, and the above considerations hold for excess returns. The Brownian motion assumes that the new log price is the previous plus a (deterministic) drift, μ, plus a (stochastic) residual, ε_t:

$$s_{t+1} = s_t + \underbrace{\mu + \varepsilon_t}_{=r_t}, \text{ where } \varepsilon_t \sim N(0,\sigma^2).$$

For the residuals, the previous assumption should hold. In particular, there should be no serial correlation at any lead or lag, and their expected values should be zero. By definition, the stock price itself then follows a geometric Brownian motion (GBM). For steps of arbitrary length τ, this reads as

$$S_{t+\tau} = S_t \exp(r_t) \text{ with } r_t \sim N(\mu\tau, \sigma^2\tau).$$

A convenient way of separating the stochastic and deterministic part of this process is to introduce a Wiener process, $\{z_t\}$. This is a (continuous) Brownian motion with $z_0 = 0$ and $z_{t+1} - z_t \sim N(0,1)$. In the discretized version, the model for the prices is therefore

$$\log(S_{t+\Delta t}) = \log(S_t) + \mu\Delta t + \sigma\sqrt{\Delta t}z_t$$

$$S_{t+\Delta t} = S_t \exp\left(\mu\Delta t + \sigma\sqrt{\Delta t}z_t\right).$$

When calibrating and testing this model for a given data set, one estimates the parameters μ and σ and tests whether z_t really is white noise. When simulating data, one takes exactly the opposite route: one simulates the noise with the desired properties and plugs it into the parameterized model.

So for the GBM, the estimation and simulation procedures for a time series $\{S_t\}_{t=0}^{T}$ and unit time steps are as follows:

Model:	Simulation:

```
s     = log(S);                    z = randn(T,1);
r     = diff(s);                   r = z * sigma + mu;
mu    = mean(r);                   s = cumsum([log(S_0); r]);
sigma = std(r);                    S = exp(s);
z     = (r-mu)/sigma;
```

For all remaining models in this chapter, the workings will be similar: generate the residuals by drawing random samples from a specified distribution, and plug them into the model (together with realizations of explanatory variables, where applicable).

Similar to the general principles in Section 6.6.4, variance reduction techniques can be employed to reduce the Monte Carlo noise and promote fast convergence. Section 9.3 will provide examples as well as caveats.

8.4. Processes with memory in the levels of returns

8.4.1. Efficient versus adaptive markets

The efficient market hypothesis states that new information is (i) immediately, and (ii) completely absorbed. A fundamental consequence of this is that returns should not exhibit serial dependencies. In other words, knowing yesterday's return should not allow superior predictions.

In the real world, however, this might not be the case. In this section, we will distinguish three different scenarios:

- New information will impact not only today's, but also the subsequent days' returns. In other words, the return today will be affected not only by new information, but also by information that arrived previously. As a consequence, a (strong) piece of information will affect the performance over a sequence of days. This property can be modeled with *moving average* (MA) models and will be presented in Section 8.4.2.
- When investors consider previous returns as valuable information, then previous returns will directly influence today's performance. In this case, the return will depend on new information and on preceding returns. This can be captured with autoregressive (AR) models where lagged realizations of the dependent variable become explanatory variables. Section 8.4.3 discusses the basic principle for this type of model, and Section 8.4.4 links it to moving average models.
- Finally, adaptive and changing beliefs can be the reason that one (main) signal can have an impact over a longer stretch of time. This property can be captured in learning models, and some further examples will be presented in Section 8.6, dealing with adaptive markets where new information is absorbed only gradually.

In either of these cases, the returns will no longer be normally i.i.d. (n.i.i.d.) even when the arriving information is. The symptoms can be quite diverse: returns can start exhibiting temporal patterns, and their means seem to move over time; autocorrelation can emerge; and volatility can become time varying.

8.4.2. Moving averages

When a market shock (i.e., the residual) has a noticeable "echo" in the subsequent period, this can be modeled by

$$r_t = \mu + \theta_1 e_{t-1} + e_t.$$

If a previous positive shock, e_{t-1}, has a positive effect today, $\theta_1 > 0$, then the expected value for r_t will go up; negative shocks will have the adverse effect. In real markets, this could be due to some trend following market participants. A negative θ_1 will lower expectations at t after a positive shock; the real-life situation could be a correction to a previous overreaction. In either case, any shock will have an instant and a delayed effect, causing the average of r_t to move. More generally, a qth order moving average (MA) model, MA(q) can be denoted as

$$r_t = \mu + \sum_{\ell=1}^{q} \theta_\ell e_{t-\ell} + e_t.$$

Creating a vector of MA(q) returns, $\{r_t\}_{t=1}^{T}$, involves simulating the $T + q$ shocks and then combining them into returns. Note that q additional residuals are required to generate r_1.

Listing 8.5. C-FinancialSimulations/M/MAsim.m

```
 1 function [r,e] = MAsim(T,sigma,theta);
 2 % MAsim.m  -- version 2011-01-06
 3 %    simulation of MA(q) process
 4 q = length(theta);
 5 e = randn(T+q,1) * sigma;
 6 r = zeros(T+q,1);
 7 for t = q+(1:T)
 8     r(t) = mu + e(t-(0:q))' * [1; theta(:)];
 9 end
10 r(1:q)  = [];
11 e(1:q)  = [];
```

Some important properties of this model are as follows:
- The expected value of r_t is μ since all the e_{t-i}s have expected value 0. In the long run, the short-time shifts of averages should vanish since positive and negative effects will outbalance each other (remember that $E(e_t) = 0$).

- If the residuals are n.i.i.d. with variance σ_e^2, then the variance of r_t will be

$$\sigma_r^2 = \sigma_e^2 + \theta_1^2 \sigma_e^2 + \theta_2^2 \sigma_e^2 + \cdots + \theta_e^2 \sigma_e^2 = \left(1 + \sum_{\ell=1}^{q} \theta_\ell^2\right) \sigma_e^2.$$

This implies that the returns will have higher volatility than the individual shocks. Intuitively, this is because any return is influenced by the current innovation as well as the previous ones.

- The returns are autocorrelated. Any shock will have a linear impact on the current and the subsequent q observations. Hence, the covariance between current and lagged returns will be

$$\text{Cov}(r_t, r_{t-b}) = (\theta_0 \theta_b + \theta_1 \theta_{b+1} + \cdots + \theta_{q-b} \theta_q) \sigma_e^2.$$

Obviously, current returns are only correlated to returns that are at most q periods old; any returns that are further apart will be uncorrelated.

8.4.3. Autoregressive models

Moving average models exhibit autocorrelation. However, current values do not depend on shocks older than q, and when there is long memory, then this would require many θ_ℓs to be calibrated. Alternatively, one could simplify matters by stating an autoregressive (AR) model where the current return is linked directly to the previous one (which, after all, contains, e_{t-1}):

$$r_t = \mu + \phi_1 r_{t-1} + e_t.$$

More generally, if the previous p returns are directly affecting the current one, then this is denoted as AR(p) process,

$$r_t = \mu + \phi_1 r_{t-i} + \cdots + \phi_p r_{t-p} + e_t$$

$$= \mu + \sum_{\ell=1}^{p} \phi_\ell r_{t-\ell} + e_t.$$

To see the relationship between AR and MA models, take the simple case of an AR(1) model. Repeated substitution of $r_{t-\tau}$ yields

$$r_t = \mu + \phi_1 \underbrace{(r_{t-1})} + e_t \tag{8.2}$$

$$= \mu + \phi_1 \overbrace{(\mu + \phi_1 \underbrace{(r_{t-2})} + e_{t-1})} + e_t$$

$$= \mu + \phi_1 (\mu + \phi_1 \overbrace{(\mu + \phi_1 \underbrace{(r_{t-3})} + e_{t-2})} + e_{t-1}) + e_t$$

$$\cdots$$

$$= \sum_{\ell=0}^{\infty} \mu \phi_1^\ell + \sum_{\ell=0}^{\infty} e_{t-\ell} \phi_1^\ell.$$

This exercise can be performed for any AR(p) model with more than 1 lag; the equations become slightly more messy, but the basic result is the same: (weighted) drifts are piled up, and so are all of the previous residuals. This has some substantial consequences:

- The former implies that the unconditional expected return of r_t will not be μ, but

$$\mathsf{E}(r_t) = \mu / \left(1 - \phi_1 - \phi_2 \cdots - \phi_p\right).$$

  Note that for reasonable processes, the sum of the ϕ_ℓs should add up to some nonnegative number that is smaller than one.

- As in the MA model, any current and previous returns will be linked. There are some fundamental differences, however. In the MA(q) model, no residual older than q periods is affecting today's return. In the AR model, *all* previous residuals are affecting the current return, either directly or indirectly. Consider the AR(1) model from Eq. (8.2). Today's residual, e_t, is directly affecting today's return. The residual from the day before, e_{t-1}, does not explicitly show up in this equation, but it has an indirect effect because it is contained in r_{t-1}. And because r_{t-1} contains r_{t-2}, e_{t-2} will also have an indirect effect. Consequently, any AR(p) model can be viewed as a special case of an MA(∞) model. Admittedly, the echo of older observations will be increasingly faint (and, in practice, unnoticeable), but if the shock in the price is large enough, it will have a very long impact.

- As in MA models, the returns will also have higher volatility than the individual shocks: every return contains many (weighted) individual residuals, and the (unconditional) variance will be increased. Therefore, the variance of an AR(1) process, for example, is $\sigma_r^2 = \sigma_e^2/(1 - \phi_1^2)$.

- For the same reason, returns will also be autocorrelated. Again considering the AR(1) model, the autocorrelation at lag b is ϕ_1^b. Because of the previously indirect effects, shocks older than the maximum lag in the AR model can have an impact.

Due to its longer memory, it is necessary to allow the system to burn in and the first sample already has some history. The following Matlab code therefore produces twice the amount of samples necessary, but it discards the first half and reports only the second half.

Listing 8.6. C-FinancialSimulations/M/ARsim.m

```
1 function [r,e] = ARsim(T,sigma,phi)
2 % ARsim.m  -- version 2011-01-06
3 %    simulation of AR(p) process
4
5 p = length(phi);
6 e = randn(2*T+p,1) * sigma;
7 r = ones(2*T+p,1) * mu /(1-sum(phi(:)));
```

```
 8   for t = p+(1:(2*T))
 9       r(t) = mu + r(t-(1:p))' * phi(:) + e(t);
10   end
11   r(1:(p+T)) = [];
12   e(1:(p+T)) = [];
```

8.4.4. Autoregressive moving average (ARMA) models

Moving average models capture the fact that returns depend not only on current information, but also on signals that have arrived over a previous stretch of time. This could happen if new information is only gradually absorbed or reaches market participants at different points in time. As a consequence, any new signal has not only an immediate, but also a delayed, effect.

Autoregressive models assume that there is a linear relationship between current returns and their own history. This type of model can be used when (some) investors base their decisions on recent price movements: in a bull market, profits attract more buyers who will drive up the price even further; and falling prices are seen as a sell signal that will prolong the downward movement.

These two concepts can be combined; not surprisingly, the resulting model is then called autoregressive moving average model, ARMA(p, q):

$$r_t = \mu + \sum_{\ell=1}^{p} \phi_\ell r_{t-\ell} + \sum_{\ell=1}^{q} \theta_\ell e_{t-\ell} + e_t. \qquad (8.3)$$

Obviously, this model nests the two individual ones: setting $p = 0$ (or $\phi_\ell = 0 \,\forall \ell$) reduces it to the moving average model MA(q), whereas $q = 0$ (or $\theta_\ell = 0 \,\forall \ell$) blanks out the MA part and leaves an AR(p) model.

In econometric analysis, applying the ARMA model typically starts with the identification, that is, determining p and q. The estimation of the parameters can be done by minimizing the squares of residuals, by maximizing the likelihood, or by using an information criterion. The latter considers not only the residual sum of squares but also the number of parameters used in the model and the number of available observations; by doing so, it can guide identification. Two popular choices are Akaike's information criterion (AIC; Akaike, 1974),

$$AIC = \log(\hat{\sigma}_e) + k\frac{2}{T},$$

and the Schwarz's Bayesian information criterion (SBC; Schwarz, 1978),

$$SBC = \log(\hat{\sigma}_e) + k\frac{\log(T)}{T},$$

where $k = 1 + p + q$ is the number of parameters included in the model. Both information criteria have their respective merits and disadvantages:

AIC is not consistent but usually efficient and tends to prefer larger models, whereas SBC is consistent but inefficient.[8]

8.4.5. Simulating ARMA models

To simulate a moving average process, one can follow the reverse engineering procedure introduced in Section 8.3: first, generate the independent noisy bits, then modify them according to the model specification, and combine them with all dependence structures from the model.

1. Generate the n.i.i.d. residuals $\{e_t\}_{t=1-q}^{T}$ with standard deviation σ_e.
2. To get the returns, add up the drift, the current residuals, the weighted lagged residuals, and the weighted lagged returns.
3. Convert the return series into a price series by adding the returns (which, by definition, are the differences of the log prices) and take the exponentials.

For the Matlab implementation, one has to bear in mind that only positive indices are allowed. Also, because the AR process assumes the existence of previous returns, it is not uncommon to initialize the system, where necessary, with the unconditional expected values and generate more residuals and longer time series than required. The idea is to allow the system to burn in but only use the last T observations.

Listing 8.7. C-FinancialSimulations/M/ARMAsim.m

```
 1 function [S,r,e] = ARMAsim(mu,phi,theta,sigma,T,Tb)
 2 % ARMAsim.m  -- version 2011-01-06
 3
 4 % -- prepare parameters
 5 if nargin < 6, Tb = 0; end
 6 phi = phi(:);          theta = theta(:);
 7 p   = length(phi);   q     = length(theta);
 8 T_compl = T + Tb + max(p,q);
 9 lag_p = 1:p;
10 lag_q = 1:q;
11
12 % -- initialise vectors
13 r = ones(T_compl,1)  * mu;
14 e = randn(T_compl,1) * sigma;
15
16 % -- simulate returns
17 for t = (max(p,q)+1) : T_compl
18    r(t) = mu + r(t-lag_p)' * phi + e(t-lag_q)' * theta + e(t);
19 end
20
21 % -- discard initial values & compute prices
22 e(1:(T_compl-T)) = [];
23 r(1:(T_compl-T)) = [];
24 S = exp(cumsum(r));
```

---

[8] For more details, see Greene (2008).

Experimenting with different parameters for ϕ_ℓ and θ_ℓ can help to get a feeling for the behavior of ARMA processes. Trying rather extreme values can underline the particularities. Fig. 8.5 provides the returns and corresponding prices for simulations in the case where $e_t \sim N(0, 0.01^2)$ and $\mu = 0$, but different values for ϕ_1 and θ_1. Note that the seed was fixed for each situation, so all variants use the same series of e_ts:

```
randn('state',100);
[S,r,e] = ARMAsim(mu,phi,theta,sigma,T,Tb);
```

The graph in the center represents a plain vanilla random walk with (geometric) Brownian motion since $\phi_1 = \theta_1 = 0$; the center column are all MA models, whereas the center row contains AR models. Large negative

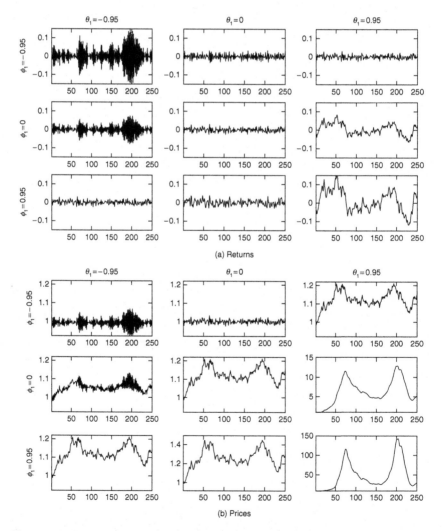

Figure 8.5 Returns and prices for different AR, MA, and ARMA models.

ϕ_1 (left columns) increases negative autocorrelation in the returns, and returns and prices will oscillate. Large positive ϕ_1 (rightmost column) will smooth the price process. θ has similar effects: negative values encourage oscillation, whereas positive values produce trends and smoother behavior. When θ_1 has the same sign as ϕ_1, these effects will be enhanced; opposite signs reduce the effects. Note, however, that ϕ has a much stronger impact. Also, note how volatility clustering can emerge, in particular, when both parameters have equal signs: when negative (top left), the magnitude of (absolute) returns seems to build up and slowly decrease again. Likewise, when both parameters are positive (bottom right), returns move gradually away from the mean (i.e., become more extreme) and only slowly move back to mean values (also, note different scales of the y-axis for some prices). In the former case, the signs of the returns change excessively often, whereas in the latter, sign changes are much less frequent than in the GBM case (center).

For an illustration, the values for ϕ_1 and θ_1 are chosen at rather extreme levels. They would be rather unusual for real-world time series, in particular the ones with negative signs. In stock returns, they are very unusual: large values for ϕ_1 and/or θ_1 produce high autocorrelation, meaning that future returns would be strongly determined by what can already be seen in the market, making profits and losses predictable. And this is clearly not what one can see in efficient markets. Nonetheless, significant ARMA parameters can often be found in empirical data, in particular in interest rates. For Monte Carlo simulations that are used for pricing or stress testing, the usual approach would be a data-driven calibration, in which the parameters are fitted to existing historical time series and then (potentially with variants) used for simulations.

8.4.6. Models with long-term memory

A crucial assumption in financial econometrics is stationarity: in a stationary system, any shock will die away eventually; in nonstationary systems, it will persist. Unlike returns, prices are usually nonstationary:

$$S_t = S_{t-1} \exp(r_t) = \left(S_{t-2} \exp(r_{t-1}) \right) \exp(r_t) = \cdots$$

$$= S_0 \prod_{\tau=1}^{t} \exp(r_\tau) = S_0 \exp\left(\sum_{\tau=1}^{t} r_\tau \right)$$

or, even more obviously, when the log prices are considered,

$$s_t = s_0 + r_1 + r_2 + \cdots + r_t.$$

The impact of r_1 on the price at t might be superposed by the subsequent returns; nonetheless, it is still there. When mean returns are positive, stock prices are, therefore, expected to grow, too, and so will their mean over time. Stock prices then follow a *nonstationary* process, and the random walk model with a drift in Eq. (8.4) is a very simple example of that:

$$s_t = s_{t-1} + \underbrace{\mu + e_t}_{=r_t} \tag{8.4}$$

$$= s_0 + \underbrace{\mu + e_1}_{=r_1} + \underbrace{\mu + e_2}_{=r_2} + \cdots + \underbrace{\mu + e_t}_{=r_t}$$

$$= s_0 + t\mu + \sum_{\tau=1}^{t} e_\tau. \tag{8.5}$$

Equation (8.5) can be made stationary by detrending it; this case is called trend-stationary.

The random walk with drift (Eq. (8.4)) can actually be generalized to

$$s_t = \phi_1 s_{t-1} + \mu + e_t, \tag{8.6}$$

which is just another case of AR(1) model. If $\phi_1 = 1$, then this process has a unit root; $|\phi| > 1$ makes it explosive, whereas $0 < |\phi| < 1$ makes it stationary.[9] In passing, note that $\phi_1 < 0$ should actually never occur for any real-world prices. Further note that the use of nonstationary data can lead to spurious correlations and regressions.

8.5. Time-varying volatility

8.5.1. The concepts

Basic statistics teaches us that a normally distributed variable, X, can be converted into a standard normal one, Z, by first de-meaning it by subtracting the mean and then scaling it:

$$X \sim N(\mu, \sigma^2) \Longrightarrow Z = \frac{X - \mu}{\sigma} \sim N(0, 1). \tag{8.7}$$

This relationship holds both ways: given a standard normal variable Z, rearranging Eq. (8.7) tells us how to convert it into one with prespecified mean, μ, and variance, σ^2. In fact, the relationship

$$X = \mu + Z\sigma \quad \text{where } Z \sim N(0, 1) \text{ and } X \sim N(\mu, \sigma^2) \tag{8.8}$$

was already used for the generation of returns in Section 8.3. The assumption then was that all returns are n.i.i.d. Introducing moving average and autoregressive models still left the residuals n.i.i.d., though the returns were not.

In real financial time series, we often find volatility clustering: large residuals are followed by large residuals, and small residuals by small ones.

---

[9] The classical test for a unit root is provided by Dickey and Fuller (1979); for more details on this, econometrics textbooks such as Greene (2008) are recommended.

In other words, one can distinguish phases of large and small volatility, and the idea of *homoscedasticity* (equal variance) should be replaced with *heteroscedasticity* (different variances). To capture this in our models, all one needs to do is add a time index to the variance parameter, and then even Eq. (8.7) still holds:

$$x_t \sim N(\mu, \sigma_t^2) \Longrightarrow z_t = \frac{x_t - \mu}{\sigma_t} \sim N(0,1) \qquad (8.7^*)$$

And so does relationship (8.8):

$$x_t = \mu + z_t \sigma_t \text{ where } z_t \sim N(0,1) \text{ and } x_t \sim N(\mu, \sigma_t^2) \qquad (8.8^*)$$

This rather inconspicuous extension is actually an extremely powerful approach. Variance, by definition, is the expected squared deviation from the mean. Large variance implies that large deviations are likely, small variance that observations will be close to their expected value. If the magnitude of these deviations varies with time, then this can also be captured by a process that is combined with white noise.

To demonstrate this, let's assume some extreme examples, which, admittedly, are not typically seen in financial time series. If standard deviation grows linearly over time, then $\sigma_t = \beta t$. On the other hand, $\sigma_t = \sin(t/\alpha)$ describes a cyclical pattern in volatility. Fig. 8.6 depicts these relationships: the top panel shows white noise, $\{z_t\} \sim N(0,1)$; the center and bottom panels show scaled versions of it. The dark gray lines indicate one standard deviation above and below the expected value, which remains invariably at zero. The noisy ingredient is normally distributed, so roughly one-third of

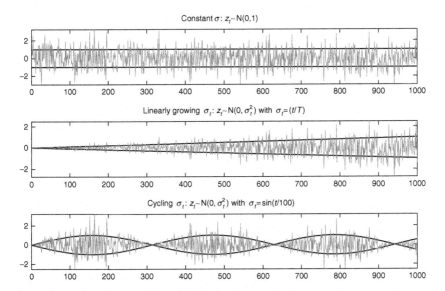

Figure 8.6 Scaled white noise; dark lines indicate $\pm \sigma_t$.

the observations should be within the $\pm\sigma$ confidence interval.[10] This is true regardless of scaling: consider the first panel to be printed on a rubber canvas that, in the other panels, is stretched and squeezed vertically. The levels change, but not the relative positions to the respective standard deviations.

8.5.2. Autocorrelated time-varying volatility

To bring this idea closer to financial problems, let's try to model some stylized facts: in daily returns, high (low) volatility tends to be followed by rather high (low) volatility. Volatility is the square root of variance; and variance, as mentioned, is the expected squared deviation from the mean, that, the expected squared residual, $\sigma_t^2 = \mathsf{E}(e_t^2)$. The current variance could, therefore, be estimated as a weighted sum of recent realizations of squared residuals:

$$r_t = \mu + e_t \quad \text{where} \quad e_t = z_t\sigma_t \sim N(0,\sigma_t^2) \quad \text{and} \quad z_t \sim N(0,1)$$

$$\sigma_t^2 = \alpha_0 + \sum_{\ell=1}^{q} \alpha_\ell e_{t-\ell}^2. \tag{8.9}$$

This approach was suggested by Engle (1982) under the name autoregressive conditional heteroscedasticity (ARCH(q)) model. In this model, the new estimate for variance, σ_t^2, is reacting to its most recent realization, e_{t-1}^2. If memory is longer, then an ARMA model for the variances might be suitable:

$$\sigma_t^2 = \alpha_0 + \alpha_1 e_{t-1}^2 + \beta_1 \sigma_{t-1}^2.$$

A bit of calculus shows that the inclusion of the lagged variance on the right-hand side of the equation introduces the previous error terms: σ_{t-1}^2 contains both e_{t-2}^2 and σ_{t-2}^2; σ_{t-2}^2 contains the values from $t-3$; and so on. It can, therefore, be seen as a generalized version of the ARCH model Eq. (8.9), and in addition to q lagged squared residuals, one could include p lagged variance estimates. Not surprisingly, the inventor of this extended model, therefore, called it Generalized ARCH (GARCH(p,q)) model (see Bollerslev, 1986):

$$\sigma_t^2 = \alpha_0 + \sum_{\ell=1}^{q} \alpha_\ell e_{t-\ell}^2 + \sum_{\ell=1}^{p} \beta_\ell \sigma_{t-\ell}^2. \tag{8.10}$$

---

[10] For a sufficiently large normally distributed sample, approximately 68% of the observations should be within one standard deviation; 95.5% within two standard deviations; and 99.7% within three standard deviations around the mean.

In either case, the parameters for Eqs. (8.9) and (8.10) are estimated by maximizing the log-likelihood function[11]

$$L = -\frac{T}{2}\log(2\pi) - \frac{1}{2}\sum_{t=1}^{T}\left(\log(\sigma_t^2) + \frac{e_t^2}{\sigma_t^2}\right).$$

Similar to other ARMA processes, certain restrictions and properties apply to the parameter values: First, the sum of all α_ℓs and β_ℓs must not exceed 1, otherwise the process becomes explosive and the variance estimate converges to infinity. Second, all αs and βs should be positive, otherwise the estimate for variance could become negative—and the volatility an imaginary number. Third, $z_t = e_t/\sigma_t$ is normally distributed, but e_t is not. In fact, it will have kurtosis of $\frac{3(1+\alpha_1+\beta_1)(1-\alpha_1-\beta_1)}{1-\beta_1^2-2\alpha_1\beta_1-3\alpha_1^2}$. Its unconditional variance, by the way, is $\alpha_0 / (1 - \sum_\ell \alpha_\ell - \sum_\ell \beta_\ell)$.

The α_ℓs govern the short-term impacts of shocks, the β_ℓs model longer persistence. To see the effects of different parameter values, compare the plots in Fig. 8.7. To make the effects of different parameter settings more comparable, all processes use the same simulated sequence of z_ts; also, they all have the same unconditional variance. The higher α_1, the more a shock

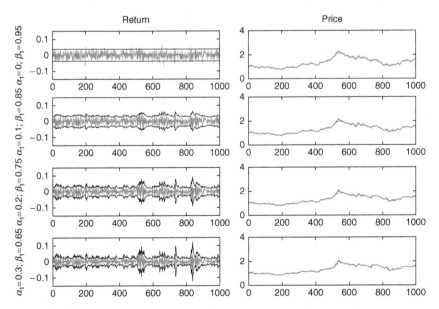

Figure 8.7 Daily returns (gray lines) and $\mu \pm 2\sigma_t$ confidence bands (dark lines) (left panel) for different combinations of $\alpha_1 + \beta_1 = 0.95$ and prices (right panel) for GARCH(1, 1) processes.

[11] Maximizing this log-likelihood function is not as smooth and well behaved as often assumed; the use of heuristics is therefore highly recommended. Maringer (2005b) and Winker and Maringer (2009) provide more on this.

on day t will drive up next day's volatility. However, a lower β_1 will make this shock short lived. Alternatively, if β_1 is high (and α_1 is low), it needs some rather large shocks to noticeably affect the next day's volatility, but if it does, it takes longer to decay. Hence, larger αs make the volatility process more spiky and ragged, favoring rapid changes in the volatility; more emphasis on the βs, on the other hand, smoothes the volatility process and produces longer swings. The extreme case here would be $\alpha_\ell = 0$, where innovations never enter the volatility process and variance becomes constant over time (top panel).

Keeping β_1 fixed while varying α_1 or vice versa will have different effects. The reader is encouraged to use the Matlab code provided below to perform their own experiments. Also, be sure that none of the underlying assumptions is violated ($\alpha_1 + \beta_1 \leq 1$, etc.), otherwise you might be in for a surprise.

For stock returns, $\alpha_1 + \beta_1$ is typically ≥ 0.9. Also, the main emphasis is usually on the long-term GARCH parameter, β_1 with typical values of 0.85 and above. In times of massive turmoil in the market, α_1 can exceed 0.1, but more often than not, it is below that value. In practical applications, however, one often finds that the parameters are not stable over time. This is not unusual for any time-series model; and most of the time, the parameters vary within "reasonable" limits. Consider, for example, the FTSE returns, which have seen some dramatic periods recently.[12] For the three years spanning July 1, 2004 to June 30, 2007, the Matlab `garchfit` toolbox fits the daily log returns with

$$r_t = \underset{(0.00023^*)}{0.00065} + e_t, \quad e_t \sim N(0, h_t)$$

$$h_t = \underset{(1.08e-6^*)}{3.0e-6} + \underset{(0.023^*)}{0.09} e_{t-1}^2 + \underset{(0.04^*)}{0.84} h_{t-1},$$

whereas for the subsequent three years from July 1, 2007 to June 30, 2010, the estimates are

$$r_t = \underset{(0.00051)}{0.00037} + e_t, \quad e_t \sim N(0, h_t)$$

$$h_t = \underset{(2.2e-6^*)}{5.1e-6} + \underset{(0.021^*)}{0.12} e_{t-1}^2 + \underset{(0.022^*)}{0.87} h_{t-1}.$$

For the entire 6 years, however, the fitted model is

$$r_t = \underset{(0.00021^*)}{0.00059} + e_t, \quad e_t \sim N(0, h_t)$$

$$h_t = \underset{(32.18e-6^*)}{91.1e-6} + \underset{(0.013^*)}{0.11} e_{t-1}^2 + \underset{(0.012^*)}{0.89} h_{t-1}.$$

---

[12] The following results are based on adjusted prices as downloaded from finance.yahoo.com. The symbol for the FTSE is ^FTSE, and the one for the S&P 500 used later, is ^GSPC.

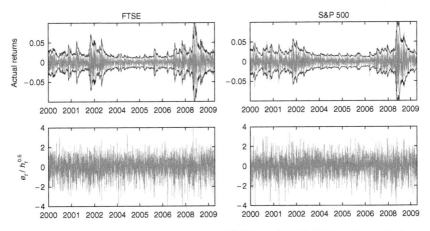

Figure 8.8 Actual daily log returns for the FTSE and S&P 500 for the period Jan 2000 to Dec 2009 and $\pm 2\sqrt{h_t}$ (top panel), and innovations standardized using time-varying volatility, $\sqrt{h_t}$, as fitted with a GARCH$(1,1)$ (bottom panel).

(Values underneath parameters are standard deviations; * indicates significance at the usual 5%.) As can be seen, the parameters α_1 and β_1 do not change dramatically.[13]

If the assumption of a GARCH process holds, the standardized innovations, $z_t = e_t / \sqrt{h_t}$, ought to be standard normally distributed. Fig. 8.8 plots the actual returns and the standardized residuals for the FTSE data set introduced above, as well as for S&P 500 returns. In either case, most of the volatility clustering can be filtered out (bottom panel). Running a Kolmogorow–Smirnov test shows, that for the FTSE data, the z_ts actually can be regarded as normally distributed (p value 0.076), whereas for the S&P 500, this must be rejected (p value 0.001). Neither series passes the Jarque–Berra test for normality.

Also, all the parameters in the variance process are significant, suggesting that they do capture autocorrelation patterns in the variance process. However, this does not mean that these models capture everything that's going on in the data. To illustrate what is left out, again a simulation can help where first the model is fitted to an empirical data set, and then simulations are performed based on it.

8.5.3. Simulating GARCH processes

To generate a sample path that follows a GARCH process, one can again follow the "reverse engineering" principle: the main ingredient of a GARCH model is the variance process h_t; dividing the residuals of the returns e_t by

---

[13] Things look slightly different, though, when shorter time windows are used. Fitting the model to individual years 2000, 2001, ... , 2009 yields β_1s in the range of 0.75 to 0.95, and apart from a few exceptions, $\alpha_1 + \beta_1$ adds up to something in the range of 0.95 to 1.

its square root, $\sqrt{h_t}$, is equivalent to standardizing them, and $z_t = e_t/\sqrt{h_t}$ should follow a standard normal distribution. The simulation works its way in the opposite direction: for any period t along the sample path, one needs to compute the current variance based on the previous variance and realized innovation, $h_t = \alpha_0 + \alpha_1 e_{t-1}^2 + \beta_1 h_{t-1}$, and draw a sample, $z_t \sim N(0,1)$. One then can compute the current innovation, $e_t = z_t\sqrt{h_t}$. These new values for h_t and e_t can then be used to compute h_{t+1}, which, combined with a new sample z_{t+1}, gives the next innovation, e_{t+1}, and so on. With the innovations ready, adding the drift μ provides the return series $r_t = \mu + e_t$.

To get the ball rolling, however, initial values for the first period's variance and innovation need to be provided. There are three approaches that are commonly used:

1. Starting values are the unconditional statistics and values. For GARCH models, one can use the unconditional variance for $h_1 = \alpha_0/(1 - (\alpha_1 + \beta_1))$ with which one can generate e_1.

2. The downside of this is that the first draws from repeated experiments will look rather similar; this can be avoided, though. After initializations, a sequence of blank observations are generated to allow the system to swing in. For example, in order to simulate a path of $T = 1000$ observations, one generates a total of $T_b + T$ periods, but reports only the last T periods. The idea is that over the first T_b samples, the processes have diverged sufficiently. Imagine it as starting the simulation in the past at $t = -(T_b + 1)$. This approach can also be used as an *ad hoc* solution in the absence of reasonable starting solutions. Starting with arbitrary initial values and discarding the early values again is often a good enough approach.

3. If one wants to generate future scenarios for an existing price process, one can use the current values for the respective variables. For example, if one wants to simulate what could happen over the next month, this approach would fit the parameters onto recent observations; estimate the current variance and use this value as the value for h_1; even better, when e_0 is already available, it computes h_1 according to definition by using real data for h_0 and e_0.

The following Matlab code produces a vector of returns of length T. By default, it starts with the unconditional variance. If one wants the system to swing in first, one can provide as a sixth argument the number of additional blank samples; these will not be returned. The sample price process can then be computed via the relationship $S_t = S_{t-1} \exp(r_t)$.

Listing 8.8. C-FinancialSimulations/M/GARCHsim.m

```
1  function [r,e,h] = GARCHsim(mu,a0,a1,b1,T,Tb)
2  % GARCHsim.m  -- version 2011-01-06
3  if nargin < 6, Tb = 0; end  % no "before" periods to swing in
```

```
4  % -- initialize variables
5  z = randn(T+Tb,1);
6  e = zeros(T+Tb,1);
7  h = zeros(T+Tb,1);
8  h(1) = a0/(1-(a1+b1));
9  e(1) = z(1) * sqrt(h(1));
10 % -- generate sample variances and innovations
11 for t = 2:(T+Tb)
12     h(t) = a0 + a1 * e(t-1)^2 + b1 * h(t-1);
13     e(t) = z(t) * sqrt(h(t));
14 end
15 % -- remove excess observations from initialization phase
16 e(1:Tb,:) = [];
17 h(1:Tb,:) = [];
18 % -- compute returns
19 r = e + mu;
```

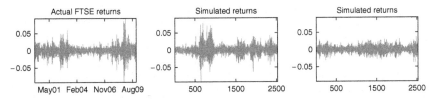

Figure 8.9 Actual FTSE daily log returns for July 2004 to June 2010 (left) and two simulations based on a GARCH model fitted on actual data (center and right; 2525 observations each; seeds fixed with `randn('seed',10)` and `randn('seed',50)`, respectively).

Continuing our example for the FTSE, let's consider the previous results for the entire data set of six years. Fig. 8.9 depicts the actual return process and two simulations. Both actual and simulated returns show volatility clustering, yet at different times. By design, high volatility periods can build up as a consequence of large shocks; since the trigger for such a period occurs randomly, one cannot expect that real and simulated returns have their high-risk episodes synchronized. What is more important, however, is that the simulated returns sometimes lack the extreme spikes. The latter happens even more often, when α_1 is rather low; values of 0.05 can occur for real stock and index prices; having simulations without excessively turbulent periods are then the rule rather than the exception. Running some experiments can help illustrate this.

This underlines another important issue. The more sophisticated the model, the more diverse the outcome from independent experiments can be. It is, therefore, of paramount importance to run many replications in order to see the overall picture. For GARCH simulations, this diversity usually shows in the presence or absence of fat tails; the (unconditional) kurtosis of the e_ts can (and usually will) deviate from its theoretical value

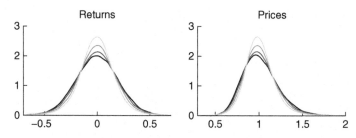

Figure 8.10 Kernel densities for cumulated returns (250 days; left panel) and prices (right panel) where daily returns follow a GARCH$(1,1)$ process with $\alpha_1 \in \{0.05, 0.20.35 0.95\}$ and $\beta_1 = 0.95 - \alpha_1$ (darker lines indicate lower α_1).

$\frac{E(e_t^4)}{E(e_t^2)^2} = \frac{3(1-\alpha_1^2)}{1-3\alpha_1^2}$; the same is true for the (unconditional) variance of the e_ts that, theoretically, ought to be $E(e_t^2) = \frac{\alpha_0}{1-(\alpha_1+\beta_1)}$. Since the numbers of draws per experiment is usually predetermined by the length of the sample path, it is important to have a sufficiently large number of experiments to cater to these issues.

As mentioned on several occasions, returns following a GARCH process will have excess kurtosis: not only per period, but also the cumulated returns, that is, the relative price change over the entire sample period, are also likely to be nonnormal.

Fig. 8.10 illustrates this. Based on 50,000 simulations per parameter constellation, the left panel shows the distribution of cumulated log returns that are equal to the log return over the entire period:

$$\sum_t r_t = \sum_{t=1}^{T} \log(S_t/S_{t-1}) = \sum_{t=1}^{T} \log(S_t) - \log(S_{t-1}) = \log(S_T/S_0).$$

As was the case when we analyzed the distribution over time of a single path (Fig. 8.7), setting $\alpha_1 = 0$ blanks out any impact innovations have on the volatility process, and the normally distributed innovations will translate into normally distributed returns. Increasing α_1 while keeping $\alpha_1 + \beta_1$ constant will increase kurtosis and make not only the distribution of daily returns leptokurtic but also the cumulated returns. Likewise, the distribution of terminal stock prices will move away from a lognormal distribution (Fig. 8.10, right panel).

8.5.4. Selected further autoregressive volatility models

The GARCH model was a major extension to the original ARCH model, and for most practical purposes, the GARCH$(1, 1)$ seems to fit reasonably well (see, e.g., Lunde and Hansen, 2005). However, this has not stopped academics from creating variants that capture other stylized facts or the particularities of certain assets. For a very broad (but still far from exhaustive) survey, Engle (2002) is highly recommended. Also, some textbooks on (financial) econometrics cover the most prominent approaches; see, for example, Brooks (2008).

Additional explanatory variables for returns

In the basic GARCH version, the best guess for the next realization of the dependent variable (usually the return) is its mean: $E(r_t) = E(\mu + z_t h_t) = \mu$. In many cases, however, returns will be driven by—or at least correlate with—other factors f; the usual suspects are market returns, regional developments, industry sector performance, etc. In that case (and under the assumption of linear dependencies), the returns could be modeled as

$$r_t = \phi_0 + \sum_i f_{i,t}\phi_i + e_t, \quad \text{where} \quad e_t \sim N(0,h_t).$$

When using this model for simulations, one can distinguish two situations: either the realizations for the $f_{i,t}$s are given, or they have to be simulated as well. The former would be the case if, for example, one wants to test different scenarios for one asset while controlling for the circumstances. When these factors have been generated with some other simulation (including parametric models and bootstraps), the process of simulating r_t would be extended by generating the $f_{i,t}$s first.

As a special case in this class, one can consider processes where the returns follow an ARMA process.

I-GARCH

Quite often, the parameters dealing with the persistence of shocks add up to something (almost) equal to one. The Integrated GARCH model introduces this as a condition: $\sum_\ell \alpha_\ell + \sum_\ell \beta_\ell \overset{!}{=} 1$. In the I-GARCH(1,1) incarnation, this means that, by default, $\beta_1 = 1 - \alpha_1$. As a consequence, there's one parameter less to estimate (and to provide when simulating). At the same time, the variance process now is integrated and has a unit root.

For simulation purposes, function GARCHsim.m can be modified by setting Statement 12 to

```
h(t) = a0 + a1 * e(t-1)^2 + (1 - a1) * h(t-1);
```

GARCH-M

Empirical evidence suggests that, in riskier times, assets also pay higher returns. In this case, the levels of returns should be directly linked to the level of risk:

$$r_t = \mu + \lambda\sqrt{h_t} + e_t, \quad \text{where} \quad e_t \sim N(0,h_t),$$

where h_t follows a GARCH or ARCH process. Note that alternative versions use the variance h_t instead of standard deviation $\sqrt{h_t}$ as an explanatory variable. Also, it is not uncommon to have additional explanatory variables included in the model state, much in the sense of the version on page 215.

```
function [r,e,h] = GARCHMsim(mu,lambda,a0,a1,b1,T,Tb)
...
for t = 2:(T+Tb)
   h(t) = a0 + a1 * e(t-1)^2 + b1 * h(t-1);
   e(t) = z(t) * sqrt(h(t));
end
% -- compute returns
r = mu + lambda * sqrt(h) * e;
```

GJR-GARCH

A stylized fact for asset returns is that market participants are usually more receptive to bad news than to good. A negative innovation, $e_t < 0$, will have a bigger impact on the next period's volatility than a positive innovation. In other words, the sign of e_t matters. Glosten, Jagannathan, and Runkle (1993) suggested an asymmetric version modeling exactly that:

$$h_t = \alpha_0 + \beta h_{t-1} + \begin{cases} \alpha_1 e_{t-1}^2 & \text{if } e_{t-1} \geq 0 \\ (\alpha_1 + \phi_1) e_{t-1}^2 & \text{if } e_{t-1} < 0 \end{cases}$$

$$= \alpha_0 + \beta h_{t-1} + (\alpha_1 + \phi_1 I_{e_{t-1}<0}) e_{t-1}^2,$$

where $I_{e_{t-1}<0}$ is the indicator function, returning 1 if $e_{t-1} < 0$, and 0 otherwise. ϕ_1 increases with the strength of these asymmetries.

```
function [r,e,h] = GJRGARCHsim(mu,a0,a1,phi1,b1,T,Tb)
...
for t = 2:(T+Tb)
   h(t) = a0 + (a1 + phi1*(e(t-1)<0))* e(t-1)^2 + b1 * h(t-1);
   e(t) = z(t) * sqrt(h(t));
end
...
```

T-GARCH

The Threshold GARCH model works along similar lines: positive shocks will have a different impact than negative ones. The main twist here is that it models the standard deviation rather than the variance:

$$\sqrt{h_t} = \alpha_0 + (\alpha_1^+ + \alpha_1^- I_{e_{t-1}<0}) |e_{t-1}| + \delta_1 \sqrt{h_{t-1}}.$$

Here (and for most other asymmetric models), valid parameters must ensure that the new estimate for the standard deviation, $\sqrt{h_t}$ (or, later, for the variance, h_t), does not become negative.

```
function [r,e,h] = TGARCHsim(mu,a0,a1p,a1m,d1,T,Tb)
...
sh = zeros(T+Tb,1);
```

```
sh(1) = sqrt(a0/(1 - (alp + 0.5*alm + b1)));
for t = 2:(T+Tb)
    sh(t) = abs(a0 + (alp + alm*(e(t-1)<0))* abs(e(t-1)^2) + ...
            d1 * sh(t-1));
    e(t) = z(t) * sh(t);
end
...
```

E-GARCH

In the original version, the updated variance is linearly dependent on its previous value. If volatility is already high, this might be too strong. Nelson (1991), therefore, suggests an Exponential GARCH model to use the logs of the variances rather than their actual levels. In addition, it also caters to asymmetric effects similar to the GJR-GARCH. The original E-GARCH model uses a generalized error distribution; another incarnation (cf., e.g., Brooks, 2008, p. 406), reads

$$\log(h_t) = \alpha_0 + \beta_1 h_{t-1} + \alpha_1 \underbrace{\frac{e_{t-1}}{\sqrt{h_{t-1}}}}_{=z_{t-1}} + \gamma \left(\frac{|e_{t-1}|}{\sqrt{h_{t-1}}} - \sqrt{2/\pi} \right).$$

If negative innovations now increase the variance stronger than positive ones, γ will be negative. Also, in a passing note, there are fewer restrictions on the parameters: in previous variants, parameters must be chosen such that they ensure only positive values of h_t. The E-GARCH models the logs of the variances; negative values will then be simply translated into small variances.

```
function [r,e,h] = EGARCHsim(mu,a0,a1,gamma,b1,T,Tb)
...
lnh = zeros(T+Tb,1);
lnh(1) = sqrt(a0/(1 - ( alp + 0.5*alm + b1)));
...
for t = 2:(T+Tb)
    lnh(t) = a0 + b1 * exp(h(t-1)) + a1 * z(t-1) + ...
            gamma(abs(e(t-1))/lnh(t-1) - sqrt(2/pi)) ;
    e(t) = z(t) * sqrt(exp(h(t)));
end
...
```

N-GARCH

Another way of modeling the relationship between innovation and impact on the new variance estimate was introduced by Engle and Ng (1993). This Nonlinear-GARCH does not (necessarily) check the sign of the recent shock but puts it in relation to the volatility at that point in time:

$$h_t = \alpha_0 + \alpha_1 \left(e_{t-1} + \gamma \sqrt{h_{t-1}} \right)^2 + \beta_1 h_{t-1}.$$

If the parameter γ is equal to 0, then this model collapses into a GARCH(1, 1) model; if $\gamma > 0$, however, negative innovations will have a larger impact. In theory, negative values for γ could also occur; yet it is rare in real markets that price increases increase the volatility more than comparable losses.

```
function [r,e,h] = NGARCHsim(mu,a0,a1,gamma,b1,T,Tb)
...
for t = 2:(T+Tb)
    h(t) = a0  + a1 * (e(t-1) + gamma * sqrt(h(t-1)))^2 + ...
           b1 * h(t-1);
    e(t) = z(t) * sqrt(exp(h(t)));
end
...
```

Further extensions

In addition to the GARCH variants discussed above, numerous further contributions exist. Typically, they cater to different stylized facts observed for empirical data. More recent additions, for example, allow for nonnormal distributions in the innovations or make also the higher moments conditional and time-varying. Most of them do have their merits; however, other variants have also been counted in the class of YA-GARCH models—"yet another GARCH." As already discussed in the above examples, the new extensions come with additional parameters. Sometimes, these new models nest previous ones, and choosing particular parameter values turns them into one of their cousins or predecessors, as was the case with N-GARCH. Some models, such as Augmented GARCH (see Bera, Higgins, and Sangkyu, 1992) are constructed to nest many different variants. Discussing them here, however, would exceed the purpose of this section, and the interested reader is kindly referred to the literature. Creating simulations based on these models is in most cases straightforward and follows the same general principles as the examples provided above.

8.6. Adaptive expectations and patterns in price processes

8.6.1. Price–earnings models

One of the central concepts in asset pricing is that the current fundamental value ought to represent the discounted value of all future payments. In the case of stocks, future payments can occur either as dividends (including other issued rights) or as proceeds from selling on the stock itself. Based on expectations at time t for the next period, the fundamental relationship

$$S_t = \mathsf{E}_t\left(\frac{D_{t+1} + S_{t+1}}{1 + r_1}\right)$$

should hold, where D_{t+1} and S_{t+1} are the future dividend payment and the stock price, respectively, and r_t is the current discount rate for period t.

Obviously, the same argument should hold for S_{t+1} and all subsequent prices. Shifting the time indices and substituting them one after the next one into the fundamental relationship, one gets

$$S_t = \mathsf{E}_t\left(\sum_{\tau=1}^{\infty} \frac{D_{t+\tau}}{(1+r_\tau)^\tau}\right).$$

Admittedly, it would be very brave to claim one can predict a stock's dividend until eternity. For reasonable discount factors, however, it is mainly the first dividends that contribute the most to the present value. Also, for a rough guess, it is often good enough to assume that the discount rate is constant, $r_\tau = r$, and that the dividends either remain constant or grow following a simple process. Gordon (1962) famously suggested a variant where dividends grow at a constant rate, $D_t = gD_{t-1}$. Assuming a constant discount factor r, the fundamental value for a stock would then be

$$S_t = \sum_{\tau=1}^{\infty} \frac{D_t g^\tau}{(1+r)^\tau} = D_t \frac{g}{1+r-g} = \frac{D_{t+1}}{1+r-g}.$$

In his honor, this model is named the Gordon growth model. Note that this and other models based on the price–earnings ratio assume that companies pay out all their profits. If earnings are retained and no dividend is payed, a rational bubble could result. In Eq. (8.6), this would come with $\phi_1 > 1$.

A straightforward implication of this model is that the price–dividend ratio should equal $S_t/D_{t+1} = 1/(r-(g-1))$. Hence, if the price–dividend ratio is, say, 20 (implying that the discount factor exceeds the growth factor by $1+r-g = 5\%$), the current price should be $S_t = 20D_{t+1}$. Assuming average discount rates and growth factors are constant over time is equivalent to saying that the long-run average price–dividend ratio is constant. In that case, variability in the prices should be down to variability in the dividends only. In particular, a 1% change in the dividend should lead to a 1% change in the stock price.

Empirical tests, however, show that this does not hold in the real world. Barsky and DeLong (1993) found for S&P 500 stocks that there is excess volatility in the stock prices: for the period 1949–1969, for example, they found that dividends, on average, grew by 0.72%, whereas stock prices went up by 1.6%. Their explanation for this phenomenon is that market participants have adaptive expectations: investors do have assumptions about the growth rate, but they update it gradually if the recent change in log dividends deviates from their expectations. Replacing the constant growth rate in the original Gordon growth model with a time-varying one that reflects this behavior produces price processes with excess volatility.

8.6.2. Models with learning

At the same time, Timmermann (1993) published a model with a slightly different approach. His assumption is that changes in the log dividends are normally distributed

$$\log(D_t/D_{t-1}) = \Delta \log(D_t) = \mu + \epsilon_t \text{ where } \epsilon_t \sim N(0, \sigma^2).$$

The problem in real life is that investors cannot observe the true parameters μ and σ^2. What they can do is estimate them using the previous n empirical observations. As time progresses, new observations emerge, and adaptive learning will take place where the updated estimates are a weighted combination of previous estimates and realized values:

$$\hat{\mu}_t = \frac{n-1}{n} \hat{\mu}_{t-1} + \frac{1}{n} \Delta \log(D_t)$$

$$\hat{\sigma}_t^2 = \frac{n-1}{n} \hat{\sigma}_{t-1}^2 + \frac{1}{n} \left(\frac{n-1}{n} (\Delta \log(D_t) - \hat{\mu}_{t-1})^2 \right).$$

The expected growth, the next dividend, and the fundamental price, respectively, are then given by

$$\hat{g}_t = \exp\left(\hat{\mu}_t + \frac{\hat{\sigma}_t^2}{2} \right)$$

$$E_t(D_{t+1}) = D_t \hat{g}_t = D_t \exp(\hat{\mu}_t + \hat{\sigma}_t^2/2)$$

$$P_t = D_t \left(\frac{\hat{g}_t}{1 + r - \hat{g}_t} \right).$$

As for the Gordon growth model, the growth factor has to be less than the discount factor, $\hat{g}_t < 1 + r$.

Listing 8.9. C-FinancialSimulations/M/Timmermann.m

```
1  function [S_RE,Div,g_est,S_FT] = Timmermann(T,r,mu,sigma,n)
2  % Timmermann.m  -- version 2011-01-06
3  g_true = mu + randn(T+n,1) * sigma;
4  mu_hat = zeros(T+n,1);    var_hat = zeros(T+n,1);
5  mu_hat(n+1,1)  = mean(g_true(1:n));
6  var_hat(n+1,1) = var(g_true(1:n));
7  log_div(n+1,1) = 0;
8  weight = (n-1)/n;
9  for t = (n+2):(T+n);
10     mu_hat(t)  = weight * mu_hat(t-1)  + (1/n) * g_true(t);
11     var_hat(t) = weight * var_hat(t-1) + (1/n) * ( weight * ...
12                  ( g_true(t)-mu_hat(t-1))^2);
13     log_div(t) = log_div(t-1) + g_true(t);
14 end;
15 % -- discard first n observation (preceeding observations)
16 mu_hat(1:n)  = [];    var_hat(1:n)  = [];   log_div(1:n) = [];
17 % -- compute prices
18 Div    = exp(log_div);
```

```
19 g_est = exp(mu_hat + var_hat/2);
20 g_est = min(g_est,(1 + r -.0001));
21 % -- price under rational expectations
22 S_RE = Div .* (g_est ./ (1+r-g_est));
23 % -- fundamental price under known true parameters
24 S_FT = Div .* (exp(mu + sigma^2/2)/(1+r-exp(mu+sigma^2/2)));
```

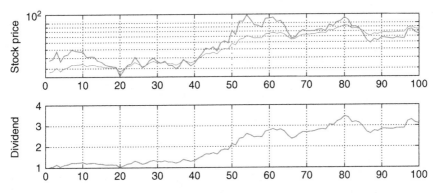

Figure 8.11 Stock prices under rational expectations from the Timmermann (1993) model ($n = 25$, $\mu = 0.01$, $\sigma = 0.05$). Rational expectation prices (thin gray line) and fundamental prices with known parameters (thick gray line).

Again, the factor D_t is multiplied with can be read as the price–dividend ratio (PDR). When estimations are based on a small number of observations, $\hat{g}_t$ will be volatile. A positive shock in the dividend will then have an enhanced effect: not only will the current dividend go up substantially, but investors will also be fast to adapt their $\hat{g}_t$. In other words, their expectations about PDR will go up, and they will be overly optimistic. Negative shocks will have the opposite effect. Fig. 8.11 illustrates this. In the long run, low n will lead to overreactions compared with the fundamental price if parameters were known. If n is large, on the other hand, then the same jump in the dividend will not be followed by a sharp change in $\hat{g}_t$, and the expected PDR will react rather sluggishly. The volatility of the stock prices will then reflect the changes in the dividend, but there should be little excess volatility in the stock price compared with fundamental prices under known parameters. Timmermann also performs a series of Monte Carlo simulations for different parameter settings. The results confirm that shorter lookback periods increase volatility in the stock returns.

This model has inspired a large community and has been the main ingredient in a series of subsequent models. Most notably, Timmermann (1996) suggested a model where dividends are trend-stationary:

$$D_t = \rho D_{t-1} + \mu + \gamma t + \epsilon_t \quad \text{where} \quad \epsilon_t \sim \mathrm{N}(0, \sigma^2).$$

Lewellen and Shanken (2002) extend this approach to an equilibrium model. They confirm that patterns emerge in simulated data; however, they also find that these patterns are an *ex post* phenomenon but do not allow out-of-sample predictions.

8.7. Historical simulation

8.7.1. Backtesting

When a new strategy is evaluated by using historical data to find out how well it would have done, then this is a typical example for backtesting. The underlying assumption is that the available data are representative and independent of what is to be tested. This *ceteris paribus* assumption is particularly relevant when, for example, investment strategies are evaluated, but the orders had a noticeable impact on prices—which, for algo-traders in high-frequency markets, is a serious issue. The general procedure is to split the data in two subsamples where one is used for calibration (if necessary) and the remaining data for validation.

Backtesting is heavily used for risk measurement and reporting. In the presence of a sufficiently large number of representative observations, the reported risk figures are then simply based on what the risk of the given positions would have been in the past. For the case of Value at Risk (a quantile risk measure required by the Basel II and Basel III accords), one usually computes what the value in the past would have been given the current composition of portfolios, and then reports the corresponding quantile of the empirical distribution.

Another common application of backtesting is index tracking. The purpose of this approach is to hold a portfolio that behaves exactly like the benchmark index. If perfect replication is impossible or undesirable, the tracking portfolio can be constructed such that it mimics the benchmark as well as possible. The quality is measured by the tracking error, usually the mean squared deviation between the portfolio's and the benchmark's returns.[14] Mostly, index tracking does not take parametric estimations of asset and benchmark returns but uses past observations directly. The optimal portfolio weights are then found by comparing the past benchmark realizations and how the tracking portfolio would have performed under the chosen weights. To lower transaction costs and monitoring requirements, it is common to limit the number of different assets (see Maringer and Oyewumi, 2007). When the number of assets to choose from is large relative to the number of available (and useable!) data, overfitting issues could arise.

---

[14] For a general survey of index tracking approaches and how to approach them with heuristic optimization, see di Tollo and Maringer (2009).

One way of overcoming this is the introduction of additional limits on the portfolio weights (see Zhang and Maringer, 2009).

A main advantage of backtesting is that it does not require parametric distributions and can therefore use actual observations directly. This, however, can also be one of its main shortfalls. If there are not enough historical samples, one can supplement them with MC-simulated ones. Depending on the problem (and data) at hand, there are several approaches that can be used:

- The further back the observations date, the higher the chance that fundamentals have changed and the observations are less representative for current situations. Transforming and "correcting" for the change can then help; examples for this are scaling to include changes in the volatility (see page 238) or asset-specific shifts such as accrued coupons or shifts in interest rates.

- If there are no data for the asset itself, but sufficient observations for the factors it depends on, historical samples can be constructed. For example, bond prices can be reconstructed if the yield to maturity time is known. Likewise, in the presence of reliable pricing models and data, prices for futures and other options can be simulated. In fact, there are situations where such constructed samples are superior to actual ones. Just think of bonds: to estimate the Value at Risk of an option, one is well advised not to use raw historical observations, but prices simulated under current market conditions. This approach leans toward bootstrapping, which will be discussed in Section 8.7.2.

- Making (semi)parametric assumptions about the underlying processes and fitting suitable models to available data can deliver data-generating processes from which random samples are drawn. Section 8.5.2 provides examples for this. Note, however, that the generated data will be only as good as the models are. In particular, subtleties in the dependence structures across many assets can be lost.

8.7.2. Bootstrap

Bootstrapping is a method to simulate new observations based on an existing sample. A key assumption is that the data are stationary, and this is clearly not true for price series. If a stock price follows a geometric Brownian motion, however, it will be first-order stationary since the log differences will be i.i.d. The bootstrap should then focus on the (stationary) price changes, which then can be translated into a new price process. The Matlab code `bootstrapprice.m` performs this task. Fig. 8.12 shows the original prices and returns for the FTSE for Jan 2007 to Sep 2010 (947 days) and the bootstrap samples for different block lengths. As expected, low values for b break up the volatility-clustering properties; on the other hand, higher values of b maintain it but produce noticeable stretches of identical behavior.

Listing 8.10. C-FinancialSimulations/M/bootstrapPrice.m

```
1  function [S_bs,r_bs] = bootstrapPrice(S,n,b,S_0)
2  % bootstrapPrice.m  -- version 2011-01-06
3  %         returns one bootstrap price path
4  %    S ..... original price series
5  %    n ..... length of bootstrap sample x
6  %    b ..... block length
7  %    S_0 ... initial price for simulation (S(T) if not provided)
8  if nargin < 4, S_0 = S(end,:); end
9
10 r    = diff(log(S));            % log returns
11 r_bs = bootstrap(r,n,b);
12 r_bs_c = cumsum([log(S_0); r_bs]);
13 S_bs = exp(r_bs_c);
```

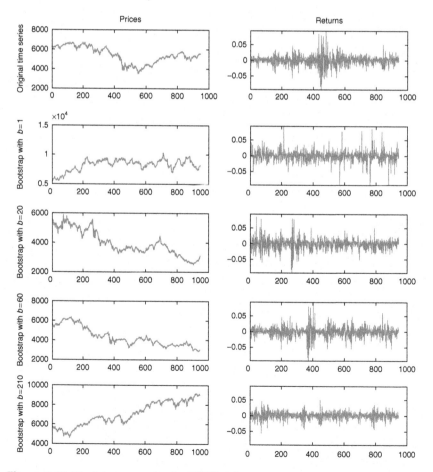

Figure 8.12 Bootstrap samples for FTSE data.

If the return process also is nonstationary but has some memory, one can first compute the changes in the returns, use these bootstrapped data to simulate the returns, and then finally compute the asset prices. A typical application for this would be bond prices that often are second-order stationary. The yield to maturity (YTM) is usually not stationary, but the changes in the YTM are. On the downside, it quickly increases the computational load and other effects could be lost. If the memory in the return series is not very strong, then a block bootstrap can be an efficient and good enough way to capture these time dependencies. This is the approach often chosen for stock prices. As already discussed in Section 6.7.2, there is no clear guidance on how to choose the block length. If there is little or no memory, short block lengths should do; with stronger memory, longer block lengths might be necessary, yet at the risk of having rather identical new samples coming from overlapping blocks. Alternatively, a data-driven, parametric bootstrap can be performed where an (econometric) model for the (assumed) temporal patterns is built and calibrated on the data, and the new samples are then drawn using this model (with the residuals coming either from a parametric distribution or from the empirical distribution of the original residuals). In either case, it is important to consider dividends, stock splits, etc., and to work either with adjusted returns or with adjusted prices.

As mentioned earlier, bootstraps can preserve some of the cross-temporal as well as cross-sectional dependencies without relying on parametric or semiparametric models. This can be useful when, for example, one is interested in the properties of portfolios. Consider the case of an investor who is particularly concerned with high kurtosis and negative skewness—a combination hinting at potentially large negative events. The bootstrap procedure for a bundle of assets is a straightforward extension from the single asset case: after randomly picking a past date, instead of taking just one asset's return, we take all assets' returns on that day, likewise for the block bootstrap. In fact, the bootstrap algorithm suggested above already does that.

To illustrate the basic workings, assume that one is interested in three of the major European stock market indices: FTSE (UK), DAX (Germany), and EuroStoxx50 (Europe). For the sake of simplicity, we assume the observations from August 2005 to July 2010 form a representative sample and that we have a total of 1251 days, where prices for all three indices are available.[15] When looking at daily log returns, the

---

[15] Data have been downloaded from finance.yahoo.com.

investor can compute the first four moments for the indices and find the following:

	Mean	Volatility	Skewness	Kurtosis
FTSE	−0.05e-4	0.0146	−0.092	10.35
DAX	1.83e-4	0.0156	0.162	10.56
STOXX	−1.53e-4	0.0163	0.199	10.76
Portfolio	0.20e-4	0.0149	−0.165	8.91

Not uncommon for stocks and stock indices is excess kurtosis (if returns were normally distributed, we would expect kurtosis to be 3). Also, the volatility of the stocks is lower than the linear combination of volatilities: there is diversification despite the high correlation between the indices (linear correlations between log returns are all around 0.9). What might be surprising, though, is that the skewness of the portfolio is lower than that of the constituents. If negative shocks tend to come simultaneously while positive shocks are not, then losses will not be diversified as nicely as profits.

All these statistics are on daily basis. If investors have a horizon of more than one day in mind, then they need to know the statistics of cumulated returns. For example, when large negative shocks tend to be outbalanced by large positive ones, then over longer horizons, the skewness will go to zero, and so on. To compute such statistics, bootstraps can be performed. Assume that investors have \$1 to invest and are interested in an equally weighted portfolio and considers a buy-and-hold strategy for investment horizons of 1 day, 5 days (i.e., one week), 21 days (approx. one month), and 62 days (approx. one quarter), respectively. For an equally weighted unit portfolio, they split their initial endowment of 1 into individual investments of $E = [1/3 \ 1/3 \ 1/3]$. Using recently introduced functions, one bootstrap simulation for a horizon of T with block length b can be performed with

```
bootstrapPrice(S,T,b,E);
```

where S is the vector with historic prices. The function returns a vector with the simulated values of the three constituents of the portfolio. To get an idea about the distribution, N such simulations have to be performed:

```
for sim = 1:N
    I_bs(sim,:) = bootstrapPrice(S,T,b,E);
end
```

The terminal value of the portfolio is the sum of its constituents' terminal prices. Once all N simulations have been performed,

```
P = I_bs * ones(3,1);
```

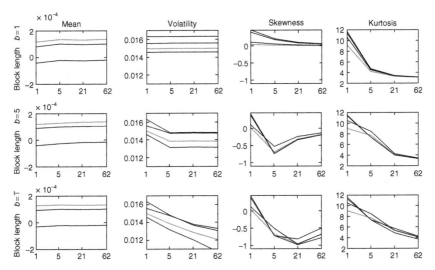

Figure 8.13 Moments of a buy and hold portfolio (thick gray lines) and its constituents (thin black lines; FTSE, DAX, and EuroStoxx) over different lengths of investment horizons (x-axis: $T = 1, 5, 21, 62$ days; corresponding to 1 day, 1 week, 1 month, 1 quarter); based on original data August 2005 to July 2010 and 1,000,000 bootstraps. Top panel, block length $b = 1$; center panel, block length $b = 5$; and bottom panel, block length $b = T$.

computes exactly that. With a total initial investment of 1, the return is simply the log of the terminal price: $r = \log(P_T/P_0) = \log(P_T/1)$:

```
rP = log(P);
```

These returns can then be finally investigated.

Based on 1,000,000 bootstraps, Fig. 8.13 depicts how the volatility, skewness, and kurtosis of the three indices and an equally weighted portfolio of these three develop (returns and volatilities scaled to per-day levels). In the top panel of Fig. 8.13, the block length is just 1 day, implying that there are no dependencies over time. As expected, investments over longer stretches of time have less kurtosis: while a single-day investment has a kurtosis of around 9; the kurtosis of weekly returns (5 days) comes down to about 4, and for a monthly (approx. 21 days) and quarterly (approx. 62 days) returns exhibit almost no excess kurtosis. When averaging returns over longer periods, the skewness of individual indices also converges to that of a Gaussian distribution, whereas portfolio returns are symmetrically distributed even on a daily basis.

Using longer block lengths preserves some of the time-series properties. The center panel uses a block length of 5 days (or 1 day for single-day investments). In the bottom panel, block length corresponds to the investment horizon. Excess kurtosis still diminishes with longer block lengths, yet at a slower pace. Skewness, however, plunges below zero. In fact, the typical monthly investment had a skewness of approximately -1, which is far from a normal distribution.This should be worrying since, according to usual assumptions in utility analysis, investors do not like negative shocks.[16] At the same time, longer investments have lower volatility, implying that there are certain serial dependencies. Note that the mean return is hardly affected. Results in the bottom panel can be read as typical historical outcomes for an investment over the specified investment horizon. Compared with the outcomes with shorter block length, it is apparent that ignoring these time-series properties can lead to substantial errors of judgment.

Similar to higher-order stationary price processes, the time series for option prices can have rather challenging properties: the first-order differences will be nonstationary (in-the-money options behave differently than out-of-the-money ones), and the time to maturity will play an important role. In the presence of a reliable option pricing model, the standard approach here would be to bootstrap the underlying and compute the derivative prices according to the model. One could even stretch this concept and introduce empirical aspects such as the volatility smile that is often a function of the option's moneyness. When interested only in the derivative's price at maturity, things become slightly easier: simulating the underlying at maturity and then computing the option's inner value is sufficient. Note, however, that this does allow estimating the density of the derivative at maturity, but it is not useful for pricing the derivative, in particular if premature exercise is possible.

8.8. Agent-based models and complexity

To understand the behavior of asset prices, it can be useful to understand how market participants tick. Market microstructure models try to do exactly that. Here, starting points are models for the individual buyers and sellers, for the environment within which they operate, and for how things are executed over time. Very much like in the real world, the prices are then the aggregate result. These models can exhibit complex behavior: they are (pseudo)random since their behavior is not (readily) predictable; they are adaptive because heterogeneous agents are connected and can change their behavior; there are patterns on an aggregate level that are not readily visible on the microlevel;[17] they tend to be self-organizing and remarkably robust, even when extreme events occur.[18] In that sense, financial markets are complex: participants interact and adapt, prices can exhibit time-series

---

[16] In fact, investors considering higher moments will even be happy to accept slightly higher volatility if this helps reduce high kurtosis and/or increasing skewness; see Maringer (2008b).

[17] The phenomenon that the whole is more than the sum of its parts is called *emergence*.

[18] Miller and Page (2007) offer a good introduction to complex social systems, which also includes economic systems.

properties that cannot be traced back to any single individual or fundamental source, and even the worst stock market crash has not wiped out the financial system as such.[19]

It is surprising how simple models can often provide realistic price processes. One of the first examples is presented in Kim and Markowitz (1989) in which portfolio insurance strategies[20] have the potential to reinforce positive and negative trends and eventually can lead to market crashes like the one in 1987. Subsequent models have become more and more sophisticated, including, for example, learning agents, realistic market regulations, or real-life information feeds. Similar to flight simulators, these models can be used for testing, experimenting, and training whenever real-life experiments are too costly or infeasible. For more on this, Tesfatsion and Judd (2006) offer a comprehensive introduction.

To illustrate the basic workings, let's consider a simple foreign-exchange market[21] with N participants where each one is either a chartist or a fundamentalist. A chartist, C, expects that the current trend in prices will continue, while a fundamentalist, F, expects the price to return to some fundamental value $\bar{p}$:

$$\mathsf{E}^C(\Delta p_{t+1}) = g\Delta p_t \text{ and } \mathsf{E}^F(\Delta p_{t+1}) = v(\bar{p} - p_t),$$

where $g, v \le 1$ are positive scaling factors. For our purpose, it is sufficient to assume that the fundamental price is constant; in a foreign-exchange market, this could be the long-term equilibrium exchange rate. The actual price change is then the aggregate market opinion plus some noise, that is,

$$p_{t+1} = p_t + \left(w_{t,f}\mathsf{E}^F(\Delta p_{t+1}) + (1 - w_{t,f})\mathsf{E}^C(\Delta p_{t+1}) \right) + \varepsilon_t, \qquad (8.11)$$

where $w_{t,f}$ is the (perceived) current fraction of fundamentalists in the market and $\varepsilon_t \sim \mathsf{N}(0, \sigma_p^2)$.

Agents do not invariably belong to one of the two groups but can change their type. On the one hand, they can be converted: when two agents interact, with a probability δ, the first agent will adopt the second's position. Also, with a small probability ϵ, an agent will randomly change her type. The former mechanism produces a positive feedback loop (the larger group is likely to recruit the remaining minority and generate herding), whereas the

---

[19] In a passing note, there are subtle differences between *complex* and *chaotic* systems. In (deterministic) chaotic systems, the main relationships are usually well known and stationary, but even the smallest of variations in initial conditions or imprecisions can lead to unpredictable behavior. In the well-known example of the butterfly effect by Edward Lorenz, the flap of a butterfly wing can trigger an unpredictable (chaotic) sequence of events, but it will not change the natural laws, nor will laws suddenly appear or disappear. In complex systems, "laws" can change: in a financial system, regulations can be modified, investors change their behavior, and new types of market participants (e.g., algo-traders) can enter the stage.

[20] See Section 9.1.

[21] The following example is heavily inspired by Kirman (1991, 1993), yet with several simplifications.

latter ensures that the market does get stuck in a single-type situation. Given suitable parameters, the combination of these two adaptation rules ensures that in the long run, majorities will swing.

When simulating such a market, it is common to assume that there is a certain (maximum) number of interactions per period, but to report only the end-of-period prices. Algorithm 27 provides the main steps; a Matlab code is given below. Fig. 8.14 depicts a typical simulation result. As can be seen, volatility in the price changes (top panel) goes up when the number of fundamentalists is low. This effect will be stronger when herding is more pronounced (i.e., δ increases), and/or individual opinion changes become rare (i.e., ϵ decreases).

Listing 8.11. C-FinancialSimulations/M/FXagents.m

```
1  % FXagents.m  -- version 2011-01-06
2  % -- parameters
3  N_agents = 50;    % number of agents
4  N_days   = 500;   % number of days
5  N_IPD    = 20;    % number of interactions per day
6
7  P_fund   = 100;   % fundamental price
8  sigma_p  = 0.1;   % additional price volatility
9
10 g        = 1;     % adj. speed chartists; 0 < g <=1
11 nu       = .01;   % adj. speed fundamentalisits;  0 < nu <= 1
12 delta    = .25;   % probbility convincing
13 epsilon  = .01;   % random type change
14
15 % -- initial setting
16 N_I    = N_days * N_IPD;  % total number of interactions
17 isFund = rand(N_agents,1)<.5; % type of investor
18 P      = nan(N_I,1);      % intra period prices; initial values
19 P(1:2) = P_fund + randn(2,1)*sigma_p;
20 w = nan(N_I,1);           % perceived fraction of
        fundamentalists
21
22 % -- emergence over time
23 for i = 3:N_I
24     a = randperm(N_agents);
25     if rand < delta ,  % recruitment
26         isFund(a(2)) = isFund(a(1));
27     end
28
29     if rand < epsilon, % individual change of opinion
30         isFund(a(3)) = ~isFund(a(3));
31     end;
32
33     w(i) = mean(isFund);  % perceived fraction of
        fundamentalists
34
35     % expected price changes and new price
36     E_change_F(i) = (P_fund - P(i-1)) * nu;
37     E_change_C(i) = (P(i-1)-P(i-2)) * g;
38     change = w(i) * E_change_F(i)  + (1-w(i)) * E_change_C(i);
```

```
39      P(i) = abs((P(i-1) + change) +  randn*sigma_p);
40 end;
41
42 % -- extract end of period prices
43 t = N_IPD:N_IPD:N_I;
44 S = P(t);
```

Algorithm 27 Agent-based simulation of prices in a market with chartists and fundamentalists.

1: initialize all parameters;
2: **for** $t = 1$: (number of periods × interactions per period) **do**
3: 　　with probability δ, choose two random agents and recruit
4: 　　with probability ϵ, switch type of one randomly chosen agent
5: 　　for each group, compute expected changes $E^C(\Delta p_{t+1})$ and $E^F(\Delta p_{t+1})$
6: 　　compute new price according to Equation (8.11)
7: **end for**
8: report end-of-period prices

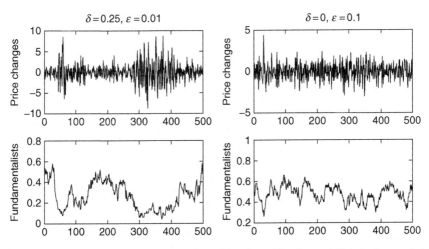

Figure 8.14 Price changes (top panel) and fraction of fundamentalists in the market (bottom panel) from an agent-based simulation (Algorithm 27).

The model offers itself for numerous extensions. To name just a few: for other asset markets, the constant fundamental price can be replaced with some random process (or even a real-life time series). If market participants cannot observe the market composition directly, a noisy signal can be added to the fraction of fundamentalists. Furthermore, if participants tend to adapt their behavior to the (assumed) majority, regardless of his or her own opinion, a logistic transformation of actual to perceived weights, $\tilde{w}_t = 1/(1 + \exp(-\gamma w_t))$, with $\gamma > 0$, can be used.

A general guideline for modeling is Occam's razor: Whenever two models work equally well, pick the simpler one. This is particularly true for agent-based models. Making the model larger by introducing more parameters might bring it closer to reality—however, it can also bring it closer to artifacts: because of calibration issues, unmanageable complexity and the peril of over-fitting make the results hard to interpret. Also, unlike many econometric or "traditional" financial models, agent-based models are not designed for short-term predictions or point estimations. Their strengths lie in dealing with highly dynamic and complex situations and uncovering driving forces behind phenomena on an aggregate level. When applied, it is highly recommended to run many simulations and analyze typical patterns. This can then help to assess likelihoods for certain events and how the system as a whole reacts to variations in the ingredients. In that respect, they could be a suitable answer to Lucas' critique[22] of traditional econometric models.

---

[22] In essence, econometrician Robert Lucas famously criticized that predictions based on historical data leave out fundamental changes and that the outcome will not be independent of the actions taken. For financial markets, traditional approaches are, therefore, of limited use when it comes to extreme market situations (with very few, if any, historical *ceteris paribus* observations) and interventions (which, in a complex fashion, will alter the course of events). The recent financial turmoils can be seen as examples for this.

## CHAPTER NINE

Financial simulation at work: some case studies

9.1. Constant proportion portfolio insurance (CPPI)

9.1.1. Basic concepts

Constant proportion portfolio insurance (CPPI) is a dynamic asset allocation strategy that aims at providing a guaranteed minimum level of wealth
G at maturity T while allowing some participation in market profits.[1] In
its simplest incarnation, products with a guaranteed payback can be considered as a portfolio: the present value of the guaranteed value, the floor
$F_t = Ge^{-r(T-t)}$, is invested in a risk-free asset, whereas the remainder of its
current value V_t, the cushion $C_t = V_t - F_t$, is invested into a risky asset. This
risky asset can be an option, and the product would be called option-based
portfolio insurance (OBPI; see Leland and Rubinstein, 1976). Alternatively,
a stock or an index could be used; however, since the cushion is usually
rather small in proportion to the total value, the actual return of such a
combination will mainly be driven by the risk-free asset's yield. The CPPI
strategy, therefore, suggests to invest a multiple m of the cushion in the
risky asset (exposure, $E_t = mC_t$) and hold less than the floor in the safe
asset, $B_t = V_t - E_t = V_t - mC_t$. If the risky asset goes up, so will the cushion,
and the exposure will be increased; if it goes down, the lower cushion will
trigger a reduction in the exposure. The mechanism is such that V_t never
falls below the floor. Note that in bullish markets, the (theoretical) exposure
could exceed V_t. We assume that the investor may not (or does not want
to) go short in the safe asset and, therefore, introduce a ceiling value on
E_t. Real-life products can differ: some do allow (limited) short selling of
bonds, whereas others increase the guarantee according to prespecified rules
("ratcheting").

---

[1] See Perold (1986) and Black and Jones (1987).

Numerical Methods and Optimization in Finance

In the absence of transaction costs, the entire model reads as follows:

$$V_t = F_t + C_t \qquad\qquad \text{total value}$$

$$F_t = G\exp(-r(T - t)) \qquad \text{floor}$$

$$E_t = \min(mC_t, V_t) \qquad\quad \text{exposure}$$

$$B_t = V_t - E_t \qquad\qquad\quad \text{safe assets}$$

where r denotes the constant safe return of the bond per period, also used as the discount factor for the floor. The Matlab function CPPIgap.m is a simple implementation for this model for a given price process. Fig. 9.1 illustrates this behavior for two different price processes. If $m = 1$, the CPPI is a simple buy-and-hold portfolio mainly consisting of the safe asset. If $m > 1$, additional exposure is built up whenever the risky asset goes up, and vice versa. For the rightmost column, the positions are readjusted only with a low frequency, leading to overexposure when the price of the risky asset drops; ultimately, this could result in violating the floor constraint.

Listing 9.1. C-CaseStudies/M/CPPIgap.m

```
 1 function [V C B F E] = CPPIgap(S, m, G, r_c, gap)
 2 % CPPIgap.m  version -- 2010-12-22
 3 % S   .. stock price series t = 0 .. T
 4 % G   .. guarantueed payback amount
 5 % m   .. multiplier
 6 % r_c .. cumulated save return over entire horizon
 7 % gap .. readjustment frequency; if blank: 1 = always
 8 if nargin < 5, gap = 1;  end;
 9
10 % --initial setting
11 T = length(S)-1;
12 t = 0:T;
13
14 V     = zeros(T+1,1);
15 V(1) = G;
16
17 F = G*exp(-r_c*((T-t)/T))';
18
19 C = zeros(T+1,1);
20 B = zeros(T+1,1);
21 n = zeros(T+1,1);  % number of risky assets
22
23 % --development over time
24 for tau=1:T     % tau = t+1
25     C(tau)    = V(tau)-F(tau);
26
27     if mod(tau-1,gap)==0  % re-adjust now
28         E(tau)    = min(m * C(tau), V(tau));
29         n(tau)    = E(tau) / S(tau);
30         B(tau)    = V(tau) - E(tau);
31     else
32         n(tau)    = n(tau-1);
```

```
33       E(tau)    = V(tau) - B(tau);
34    end;
35
36    B(tau+1) = B(tau)*exp(r_c/T);
37    V(tau+1) = n(tau)*S(tau+1) + B(tau+1);
38 end
```

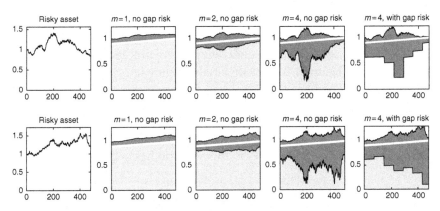

Figure 9.1 CPPI composition for two sample price processes and different multipliers time to maturity of 2 years and daily readjustment ("no gap risk") and quarterly readjustment (rightmost; "with gap risk"). Light gray: safe asset, B_t; dark gray: exposure, E_t; white line: floor, F_t.

The conceptual beauty of this strategy is hampered by real-life limitations. The risky assets are often hedge funds or other investment funds that are only traded at low intervals or might be sensitive to large volumes. The former can lead to gap risk: if the price drops substantially between adjustments, the floor constraint can be violated and the shortfalls are possible.[2] The latter can, in extreme cases, lead to domino effects when price drops trigger sales, which lead to further price drops.[3]

When the risky asset's distribution does not follow a well-behaved geometrical Brownian motion or whenever frictionless trading is not possible, the CPPI's terminal distribution cannot be assessed analytically. In that case, Monte Carlo simulations can help. First, price processes are generated; next, the corresponding CPPIs are simulated; and finally, the simulated CPPI processes are analyzed.

9.1.2. Bootstrap

To illustrate the workings of this strategy, assume the example of a CPPI with multiplier $m = 4$ and a maturity of 1 year (250 days). The risky asset is

---

[2] For a (simulation-based) analysis of gap risk, see Khuman, Maringer, and Constantinou (2008); remedies are suggested in Maringer and Ramtohul (2011).

[3] Kim and Markowitz (1989) show in a simulation study how this leads to market crashes like the one in 1987; see also Section 8.8.

the FTSE, and the safe return is 3%. The following simulations are based on the FTSE prices for the period January 4, 2005 to September 29, 2010 downloaded from finance.yahoo.com and comprising 1491 daily prices. The vector with the prices will be called S. Finally, assume that the guarantee is for $G = 1000$. The price of the risky asset at $t = 0$ is assumed to be equal to the last one in the historical time series. Note, however, that this does not matter; the number of stocks held would change, but not the exposure.

To see how the CPPI behaves over time, one can simulate its prices depending on a scenario for the underlying's price process. For this purpose, a bootstrap can be used. To capture serial dependencies in returns, a block length of 20 days is chosen. Using previously introduced functions, this can be done by

```
S_bs = bootstrap_price(S, 250, 20);
```

Next, the price path for the CPPI in this scenario has to be computed:

```
CPPI_bs = CPPIgap(S_bs, m, G, 0.03, gap);
```

where m and G are the multiplier and guarantee, respectively. gap is the readjustment frequency; 1 means daily readjustment; 5, 20, and 60 represent once per week, once every fourth week, and once per quarter, respectively.

If one repeats these steps several times, one can already get some idea about the CPPI's behavior over time. Fig. 9.2 depicts the original time series of the FTSE (left panel). The second panel contains 15 sample trajectories for a 250-day horizon, generated with a block bootstrap with block length $b = 20$. The two panels on the right exhibit the corresponding CPPI trajectories with daily (gap = 1) and quarterly (gap = 60) readjustments. The floor is given by the dashed line. Note that before maturity, the value of the CPPI can fall below the guarantee but should not fall underneath the floor (dashed line).

After increasing the number of samples further, one can analyze the CPPI's payoff distribution. The graphs in Fig. 9.3 are based on 5000 simulations. They show scatterplots for the prices of the risky asset and the CPPI at maturity. As can be seen, the payoff relationship is similar to that of a call option plus a safe investment (i.e., the option-based portfolio

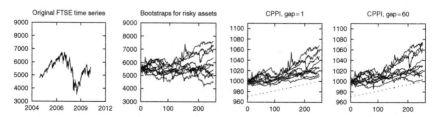

Figure 9.2 FTSE time series, 10-block bootstraps for risky asset and trajectories for CPPI.

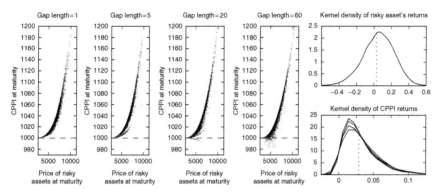

Figure 9.3 Terminal value of CPPI with FTSE as $T = 1$ year, multiplier $m = 4$, and different gap lengths, simulated with block bootstrap (right).

insurance, OBPI). Ideally, the risky asset follows a continuous price process, and continuous readjustment is possible. Then, the value of the CPPI at maturity should be above the guarantee and pay at least some return; and even if the risky asset defaults, the investor should still receive the guarantee. Moving away from the ideal situation undermines the properties. In particular, if the readjustment cycles get longer, there are occasions where the value of the CPPI falls short of the guaranteed amount G (dashed horizontal line in Fig. 9.3). Also, when looking at the results for gap lengths 5 and 20, one can spot scatter points close to the guarantee that appear arranged on curves. What seems like artifacts is in fact an illustration of the gap risk: if a big price drop in the risky asset occurs close to a readjustment point, the CPPI will encounter gap risk. When the time gap until readjustment gets bigger, too many losses will have been accrued, and the CPPI will never fully recover.

The panel on the right-hand side of Fig. 9.3 provides the kernel densities for the log returns of the risky asset and the CPPIs for different gaps. Obviously, the CPPI never encounters such massive losses as the buy-and-hold investor for the risky asset, but it also has lower profits. The dotted vertical lines indicate safe return. Note that the CPPI strategy has a mode below the safe return, but positive skewness. The means are, therefore, higher in these simulations, ranging from 2.9% to 3.15%.

9.2. VaR estimation with Extreme Value Theory

9.2.1. Basic concepts

Value at Risk (VaR) is the maximum loss that one will not exceed with a certain probability α within a given time horizon. VaR has gained considerable importance as a main risk measure. One main reason for its popularity is that it is very intuitive, and its numerical values are easier to interpret than other risk measures such as variance or the omega. Another reason is that it is sanctioned by regulators in the Basel II and Basel III accords.

Although conceptually rather simple, estimating the VaR is often challenging. This risk measure focuses on rare events and, by definition, there are only few historical observations to calibrate models on. At the same time, parametric distributions often seem to work reasonably well for the mass of the distribution, but not so well for the tails. Consider the usual assumption of a normal distribution: 6.4 standard deviations below the mean represent a "one day since the big bang" quantile; the FTSE knows five such days in the 25-year horizon of October 1985 to September 2010 alone.

9.2.2. Scaling the data

Time-varying volatility can also be a major problem for estimating the value at risk properly. One solution to this problem is to fit a suitable econometric model onto the data and then derive the theoretical VaR for this model. Hull and White (1998) suggest a similar approach. Their idea is to correct the returns r_t for the time-varying volatility s_t and scale them such that they all have the same (typically, the current) volatility, s_T:

$$\tilde{r}_t = \frac{s_T}{s_t} r_t.$$

The volatility s_t can be estimated using, for example, a GARCH or any other suitable process.[4] Using Matlab's GARCH toolbox, this can be done as follows:

```
[Coeff,Errors,LLF,Innovations,Sigmas,Summary] = garchfit(r);
[SigmaForecast,MeanForecast] = garchpred(Coeff,r);
r_tilde = SigmaForecast * r./Sigmas;
```

Correcting for the time-varying volatility brings the data closer to being identically distributed, which is one of the assumptions when using Extreme Value Theory. Time-varying volatility can account for changes in the higher moments as well. If skewness and/or kurtosis are time varying, too, extended filtering techniques can be used.[5]

9.2.3. Using Extreme Value Theory

The Hill estimator

The simplest approach for analyzing the tail of a distribution is to assume a certain functional form and estimate the parameters such that it fits the

---

[4] See also the example on page 211 in which real returns are transformed into something close to white noise.

[5] See Maringer and Pliota (2008a), in which time-varying threshold and filtering techniques for higher moments are presented in the context of VaR estimation.

data the best. For exponential decay, it is done via the Hill estimator,[6]

$$\hat{\xi}_{\text{Hill}} = \frac{1}{m} \sum_{i=1}^{m} \log\left(r_{(i)}/r_{(m+1)}\right) = \frac{1}{m} \sum_{i=1}^{m} \log(r_{(i)}) - \log(r_{(m+1)}),$$

where $r_{(i)}$ is the ith order statistic of the returns, that is, the ith smallest return. The VaR estimate for the α quantile can then be estimated by

$$\text{VaR}_{\alpha}^{\text{Hill}} = r_{(m+1)} \left(\frac{m/N}{\alpha}\right)^{\hat{\xi}_{\text{Hill}}}.$$

Though widely used in practice and heavily endorsed by authorities, VaR has received its fair share of criticism because it has some undesirable properties.[7] The conditional Value at Risk, cVaR, is the expected loss encountered in case there is a shortfall, and has some theoretical advantages over VaR. When using the Hill estimator, it can readily be computed by

$$\text{cVaR}_{\alpha}^{\text{Hill}} = \frac{\text{VaR}_{\alpha}^{\text{Hill}}}{1 - \hat{\xi}_{\text{Hill}}}.$$

Listing 9.2. C-CaseStudies/M/VaRHill.m

```
1  function [VaR ES ksi] = VaRHill(r,m,a);
2  % VaRHill.m  -- version 2011-01-06
3  %   r ... historical returns
4  %   m ... number of largest losses used
5  %   a ... probability VaR is exceeded
6
7  % --adjust parameters where necessary
8  if m <  1;   m = ceil(m*length(r)); end;
9  if a >  1;   a = a/100; end
10 if a > .5;   a = 1-a;   end
11
12 % --compute Hill estimator
13 r_order = sort(r);
14 ksi = sum(log(r_order(1:m)/r_order(m+1))) / m;
15
16 % --compute the VaR and ES
17 VaR = r_order(m+1) * ( (m/length(r)) ./ a ) .^ksi;
18 ES  = VaR ./ ( 1-ksi);
```

---

[6] See, for example, Christoffersen (2003).

[7] Most importantly, it is not a coherent risk measure see Artzner, Delbaen, Eber, and Heath (1999), implying that risk diversification is not measured satisfactorily and that, in an optimization framework, it is prone to overfitting and unstable portfolios; see Maringer (2005a) for stock portfolios and Winker and Maringer (2007a) for bond portfolios.

Further Extreme Value Theory approaches

Apart from the Hill estimator, other popular extreme value[8] approaches include the generalized Pareto distribution (GPD) for the block maxima approach[9] and the generalized extreme value approach (GEV) for the peaks over threshold[10] case. In either of these cases, a crucial question is to separate the extreme events from the regular ones: the larger the blocks and the larger the threshold, the fewer events will be considered. In particular for the GPD and the GEV, the convergence results assume an arbitrarily large threshold. This, however, hampers real-world applications: with a limited number of observations, a strict threshold leaves very few observations for model calibration, and arbitrarily increasing the sample length by looking further into the past increases the peril of including irrelevant observations or, even worse, observations from different regimes.[11] Modifying the threshold (or block length or critical return $r_{(m+1)}$, respectively) such that more observations make it into the analysis shifts the focus from the tail to the mass of the distribution, defeating the main purpose of EVT in the first place.

Threshold choice

To get a first idea about threshold choice, a Monte Carlo simulation can help. Let's assume the case that we know the underlying distribution, and we want to find out, for a given sample length N, what might be a good threshold—or, for the Hill estimator, what fraction m/N of the available N observations ought to be used. To illustrate this idea, we distinguish three cases: (i) returns are normally distributed (without loss of generality, we will assume $r \sim N(0, 1)$); and (ii) returns follow a Student t distribution with $v = 5$ degrees of freedom and have, therefore, a slightly heavy tail; and (iii) data are generated via the Cornish–Fisher expansion with $S = -0.3$. The procedure is then to repeatedly draw samples from the specified distributions and estimate the VaR at different confidence levels α and using different thresholds $\tau = r_{(m+1)}$. In either of these cases, the sample length is 1250, corresponding to 5 years' worth of daily data.

For each of these simulations, the estimated VaR is compared with the corresponding theoretical quantile of the distribution. If $VaR^{Hill}/VaR^{theo} = 1$, then the estimates are correct; values above one indicate that the Hill estimator gives too conservative estimates, whereas values less than one imply that the VaR is underestimated.

---

[8] For a general introduction to Extreme Value Theory in finance, see, for example, Embrechts, Lindskog, and McNeil (2003).

[9] In the block maxima approach, the entire sample is split into k blocks of equal length and the "worst" (i.e., lowest) observation is considered.

[10] In the peaks over threshold approach, a critical value, the threshold, is introduced and the exceedances of this threshold are then analyzed.

[11] Maringer and Pliota (2008b) discuss empirical aspects of sample length choice for VaR estimation with EVT.

Listing 9.3. C-CaseStudies/M/exVarThreshold.m

```
1  % exVaRThreshold.m  -- version 2011-01-10
2  N     = 1250;
3  Nruns = 1000;
4  alpha = logspace(0,1,18).^2 / 1e3; % [.001 .005 .01 .025 .05
       .075 .1];
5  mOverNSet    = [ .01 .025 .05 .1];
6  sizemOverNSet = length(mOverNSet)+1;
7  mSet = ceil(mOverNSet*N);
8
9  %% ..... normal distribution
10 VaR_normal   = nan(Nruns,length(alpha),length(mSet)+1);
11 for run = 1:Nruns
12     r = randn(N,1);
13     for j = 1:length(mSet)
14         m = mSet(j);
15         VaR_normal(run,:,j) = VaRHill(r,m,alpha);
16     end;
17     VaR_normal(run,:,end) = quantile(r,alpha);
18 end;
19
20 %% ..... student t distribution
21 VaR_student = nan(Nruns,length(alpha),length(mSet)+1);
22 for run = 1:Nruns
23     r = tinv(rand(N,1),5);
24     for j = 1:length(mSet)
25         m = mSet(j);
26         VaR_student(run,:,j) = VaRHill(r,m,alpha);
27     end;
28     VaR_student(run,:,end) = quantile(r,alpha);
29 end;
30
31 %% ..... via Cornish Fisher approximation
32 VaR_CF       = nan(Nruns,length(alpha),length(mSet)+1);
33 for run = 1:Nruns
34     r = CornishFisherSimulation(0,1,-.3,3,N);
35     for j = 1:length(mSet)
36         m = mSet(j);
37         VaR_CF(run,:,j) = VaRHill(r,m,alpha);
38     end;
39     VaR_CF(run,:,end) = quantile(r,alpha);
40 end;
```

Repeating this experiment 1000 times shows that the Hill estimator's assumption of an exponential decay can lead to unreliable VaR estimates if the fraction of data used, m/N, differs noticeably from the aspired VaR confidence level α; see Fig. 9.4. For other common distributions as well as other EVT approaches, results appear similar.[12]

_____

[12] Here, we demonstrate the procedures only for the Hill estimator. Maringer and Pliota (2008c), on whose findings this section builds, extend their analysis to GPD and to cVaR, both for artificial data from a parametric distribution and from a kernel density estimation fitted to real stock returns.

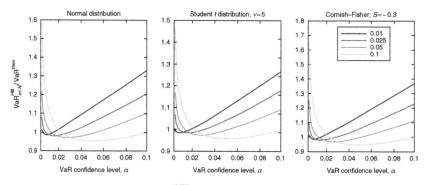

Figure 9.4 Median of ratios VaR^{Hill}/VaR^{theo} for different underlying distributions (panels) and different fractions of data used, m/N (lines).

9.3. Option pricing

The fair value of an option (in fact, of any asset) can be written such:

$$\text{fair value} = \text{discount factor} \times \text{expected payoff}.$$

Let the payoff φ be a deterministic function of a vector Y of state variables. This is the typical case for options; Y could, for instance, be a stock price. So we get

$$\mathsf{E}(\varphi) = \int_{-\infty}^{+\infty} \varphi(Y)\, \mathrm{d}F(Y), \tag{9.1}$$

with F the distribution of Y. To make this approach operational, we need to decide on a model for the distribution F of the underlying state variables, and we need to choose the discount factor. Then, we need to evaluate the integral. The $\pm\infty$ is not a problem: we could either use quadrature schemes that change the variable, or simply cut off the integral at reasonable levels. For a short-term option, if Y is a stock price that is initially at 100, it suffices to integrate from 50 to 200, say.

Now, suppose we could somehow obtain a sample $y_1, y_2, \ldots, y_N$ of Y. Then we could replace Eq. (9.1) by

$$\text{estimator of } \mathsf{E}(\varphi) = \frac{1}{N} \sum_{i=1}^{N} \varphi(y_i).$$

This is the essence of the Monte Carlo (MC) approach to option pricing. In the remainder of this chapter, we will always use the risk-free rate r to discount the expected payoff. Thus, we only need to think about the dynamics of Y, that is, how we can produce the sample.

9.3.1. Modeling prices

In mathematical finance, the evolution of quantities like prices over time is almost always described by stochastic differential equations (SDEs). Then, a process S (a stock price for instance) is typically characterized by

$$dS_t = \underbrace{g_1(S_t, t)dt}_{\text{deterministic drift}} + \underbrace{g_2(S_t, t)dz_t}_{\text{random shock}}. \tag{9.2}$$

The change in S in a small time interval is the sum of a deterministic drift, and a random component. For the applications here, always think of S as a stock price; g_1 and g_2 are functions of S and time t; and z is a Wiener process:

- z_0 is zero,
- the expected change of z is zero: $\mathsf{E}(z_{t_2} - z_{t_1}) = 0$ for $t_2 \geq t_1$,
- the quantity $z_{t_2} - z_{t_1}$ is normally distributed with variance equal to the size if the time step, that is, $\mathsf{Var}(z_{t_2} - z_{t_1}) = t_2 - t_1$.

We will always work with a discretized version of this equation:

$$S_{t+\Delta_t} - S_t = g_1(S_t, t)\,\Delta_t + g_2(S_t, t)(z_{t+\Delta_t} - z_t). \tag{9.3}$$

The second and third property of the Wiener process indicate that to simulate dz we can draw a standard Gaussian variate $Y \sim \mathrm{N}(0, 1)$, and multiply it with the square root of the time step Δ_t. Since we always discretize with a time step greater than zero, we write $\sqrt{\Delta_t}Y$ instead of dz_t.

Discretizing an SDE in general leads to discretization error (a type of truncation error). Thus, to obtain the actual solution of the SDE, the time step would need to go to zero, which is not possible on a computer. There are higher order schemes that reduce this discretization error. But we need to remember what our goals are. The SDE itself is only a model; modeling prices in continuous time is mathematically more convenient, but it is in itself an approximation of reality since prices do not change continuously. So, we will always work with this simple discretization scheme, called Euler scheme. If you want to go deeper into the numerical solution of SDEs, see Kloeden and Platen (1999). Iacus (2008) discusses simulation of SDEs in R.

Example 9.1: Barrier options

Suppose we wanted to price barrier options in a Black–Scholes world. For concreteness, assume a down-and-out call with European exercise. So if the underlier, modeled by a Brownian motion, penetrates the barrier from above, the option expires worthless. For this type of option, a closed-form solution is known. It is easy to see that if we price the option with a discretized version of the SDE, we will always overestimate the price when compared with the analytical model price: we only sample the SDE at given points, and even if the price does not go through the barrier at these points, it could do so between the points. We could reduce this bias by making the time step smaller and smaller. But the bias is there only when compared with the analytic solution of a model which is not true anyway; the actual price does not follow a Brownian motion.

Option prices are functions of the underlying assets, or—in the model—functions of the SDEs. Since we assume that the underlier follows an SDE, so must the option price. Since the option payoff is a deterministic function of the underlier's price, the stochastic process that drives the underlier is the same one that drives the option. Thus, Black, Scholes, and Merton came up with the ingenious idea to not look at the option itself, but at a portfolio of the underlier and the option. This portfolio is chosen such that the stochastic driver just cancels out and, hence, we are left with a deterministic (partial) differential equation. Solving such equations is discussed in Chapter 4. Here we take a different approach: we simulate a large number of paths of the underlier, that is, we simulate the SDE; for each path, we compute the option payoff. Averaging over these payoffs, we get the option price.

As a numerical technique, MC is not very efficient as the sampling error only decreases with the square root of the number of samples. So to get one additional digit in numerical precision, we need to increase N a hundredfold. Then why would we use this approach?

- First, computing power is getting cheaper by the day. At the same time, MC is simple, and most flexible. Even for models with an analytic solution, MC is an ideal candidate to test implementations (e.g., to check prices computed from a complicated analytical solution).
- The expected error of MC methods does not depend on the dimensionality of the problem. A typical application in which this is relevant are path-dependent options: here any point along the time path represents one dimension, so modeling a one-year option with 250 time steps means that we have 250 dimensions (but see the discussion of effective dimension, page 267). For problems in higher dimensions, MC is often the only feasible strategy.
- MC can easily benefit from distributed computing. MC is a prime example for computations that are—as Cleve Moler once called them—"embarrassingly parallel."

Next we will discuss some examples of processes. We will always work in the risk-neutral world, so r will be the risk-free interest rate, and q will be the continuous payout of the asset (the dividend). Current time, t_0, is zero; the option expires at τ.

Arithmetic Brownian motion

Arithmetic Brownian motion was suggested by Bachelier (1900). We set $g_1 = r - q$ and $g_2 = \sqrt{v}$, so over a time step the stock price changes by a deterministic drift term $r - q$ and a random shock with constant variance v.

$$dS_t = (r - q)dt + \sqrt{v}dz_t = (r - q)dt + \sqrt{v}\sqrt{\Delta_t}Y. \qquad (9.4)$$

If we model S with such an equation, the stock price itself will be normally distributed. Thus, S can become negative, and variance is constant in units of S. This SDE has an explicit solution:

$$S_\tau = S_0 + (r - q)\tau + \sqrt{v}z_\tau = S_0 + (r - q)\,\Delta_\tau + \sqrt{v}\sqrt{\Delta_\tau}Y. \qquad (9.5)$$

Such a solution is convenient if we just need the terminal level of S: we can now "jump" to the end in one time step; we need only one Y. Unfortunately, such solutions do not exist for all types of SDEs; an example that we see later on is the Heston model. And sometimes we really want the path, for instance, for path-dependent options.

Geometric Brownian motion

Alternatively we can assume that the returns are normally distributed, so we get:

$$dS_t = (r - q)S_t dt + \sqrt{v}S_t dz_t = (r - q)S_t dt + \sqrt{v}S_t\sqrt{\Delta_t}Y. \qquad (9.6)$$

All that has changed is that we have added S_t into the drift and shock term. Again we have an analytic solution:

$$S_\tau = S_0 \exp\left((r - q - v/2)\tau + \sqrt{v}z_\tau\right) = S_0 \exp\left((r - q - v/2)\tau + \sqrt{\Delta_\tau}Y\right). \qquad (9.7)$$

We see that it is often more convenient to work with the logarithm of S, $s \equiv \log(S)$:

$$s_\tau = s_0 + (r - q - v/2)\,\Delta_\tau + \sqrt{\Delta_\tau}Y. \qquad (9.8)$$

If we want the path, there exist actually different ways in which we can simulate this equation. The most straightforward is "time stepping" where we divide the interval $[0, \tau]$ into $M = \frac{\tau}{\Delta_t}$ subintervals. The function pricepaths creates paths of geometric Brownian motion (GBM); see Fig. 9.5.

Listing 9.4. C-CaseStudies/M/pricepaths.m

```
 1  function paths = pricepaths(S,tau,r,q,v,M,N)
 2  % pricepaths.m -- version 2010-12-08
 3  %    S   = spot
 4  %    tau = time to mat
 5  %    r   = riskfree rate
 6  %    q   = dividend yield
 7  %    v   = volatility^2
 8  %    M   = time steps
 9  %    N   = number of paths
10  dt = tau/M;
```

```
11 g1 = (r - q - v/2)*dt; g2 = sqrt(v * dt);
12 aux = cumsum([log(S)*ones(1,N); g1 + g2 * randn(M,N)],1);
13 paths = exp(aux);
```

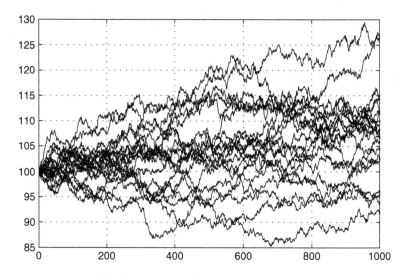

Figure 9.5 20 paths of geometric Brownian motion.

In fact, we are not forced to construct the paths of GBM in chronological order. We could, for instance, first jump to the end (or some other prespecified time) and then construct the remaining points conditionally on this point. This technique is called a (geometric) Brownian bridge (Iacus, 2008).

A Brownian bridge can also be generated vectorized; see the following code. The function generates a standardized GBM that starts at z_0 at time t_0 and ends at z_T at time t_T. Figure 9.6 gives examples. Note that with this approach, the random numbers that are used to construct the bridge are taken sequentially. In other words, the first random variate generates the first time step, the second variate generates the second time step, and so on. When we use so-called low-discrepancy sequences (discussed later), we may not wish to generate random steps sequentially, but recursively.

Listing 9.5. C-CaseStudies/M/bridge.m

```
1 function b = bridge(t0,ttau,z0,ztau,M)
2 % bridge.m -- version 2010-12-08
3 dt = (ttau-t0)/M; vt = linspace(t0,ttau,M+1)';
4 vz = [0; cumsum(randn(M,1) * sqrt(dt))];
5 b = z0 + vz - (vt - t0)/(ttau - t0) .* (vz(M + 1) - ztau + z0);
```

9.3.2. Pricing models

Now we give some concrete examples of option pricing models.

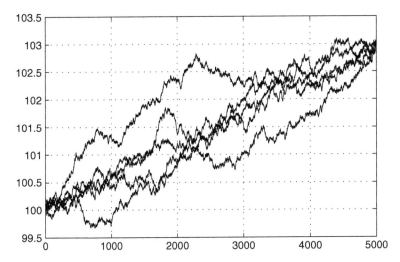

Figure 9.6 Five paths of a geometric Brownian bridge, starting at 100 and ending at 103.

Black–Scholes

Black and Scholes (1973) model the stock price S under the risk-neutral measure via geometric Brownian motion, that is,

$$dS_t = (r - q)S_t dt + \sqrt{v} S_t dz_t. \tag{9.9}$$

The volatility $\sqrt{v}$ is constant. Of course, we would not need to use MC for this model; but it serves as a benchmark. The function `callBSM` implements the analytic solution. Note that we write the price here in terms of variance (volatility squared).

Listing 9.6. C-CaseStudies/M/callBSM.m

```
 1 function call = callBSM(S,X,tau,r,q,v)
 2 % callBSM.m -- version 2010-12-08
 3 % S    = spot
 4 % X    = strike
 5 % tau  = time to mat
 6 % r    = riskfree rate
 7 % q    = dividend yield
 8 % v    = volatility^2
 9 d1 = ( log(S/X) + (r - q + v/2)*tau ) / (sqrt(v*tau));
10 d2 = d1 - sqrt(v*tau);
11 call = S*exp(-q*tau)*normcdf(d1) - X*exp(-r*tau)*normcdf(d2);
```

The MC function `callBSMMC` uses the function `pricepaths` defined before.

Listing 9.7. C-CaseStudies/M/callBSMMC.m

```
 1 function [call,payoff] = callBSMMC(S,X,tau,r,q,v,M,N)
 2 % callBSMMC.m -- version 2010-12-10
 3 % S   = spot
 4 % X   = strike
 5 % tau = time to maturity
 6 % r   = riskfree rate
 7 % q   = dividend yield
 8 % v   = volatility^2
 9 % M   = time steps
10 % N   = number of paths
11 S = pricepaths(S,tau,r,q,v,M,N);
12 payoff = max((S(end,:)-X),0);
13 payoff = exp(-r*tau) * payoff;
14 call = mean(payoff);
```

We return the call price, but also the vector of payoffs associated with the N paths we have generated. This allows us to construct confidence intervals. Recall that a confidence interval is our estimate plus and minus a multiple of the standard error, that is, the sampling error of the quantity we just estimated. We computed the mean payoff, the standard error is then the standard deviation of this payoff across all paths, divided by the square root of the number of paths. The numerator of this ratio is distributed as a Gaussian (by the Central Limit Theorem); the sample variance in the denominator follows as χ^2 distribution. Hence, the ratio has a t-distribution. Practically, we can always work with the Gaussian: N will rarely be small. So, to obtain a 95% confidence interval, we just use $\pm$ two standard errors about our estimate. The width of this confidence interval is determined by the sample variance of the payoff, and N. Hence to get more precise estimates, we can either reduce the variance or increase N (or both).

We should not care too much about precise confidence intervals. Their main use is to compare the variability of two different estimators. This shows whether one method gives more reliable results than another, that is, which one has smaller confidence intervals. In fact, to meaningfully interpret confidence intervals, we would need to establish that our estimator is actually unbiased.

Example code follows. We have set M to 1, since we can directly jump to the end of the time path.

Listing 9.8. C-CaseStudies/M/exBSM.m

```
 1 % exBMS.m -- version 2010-12-08
 2 S      = 100;
 3 X      = 100;
 4 tau    = 1/2;
 5 r      = 0.03;
 6 q      = 0.05; ·
```

```
 7│ v       = 0.2^2;
 8│
 9│ % MC parameters
10│ M = 1;
11│ N = 100000;
12│
13│ %% analytic solution
14│ tic, call = callBSM(S,X,tau,r,q,v); t=toc;
15│ fprintf('The analytic solution.\ncall price %6.2f.   It took
   │     %6.2f seconds.\n', call,t)
16│
17│ %% MC
18│ tic, [call, payoff] = callBSMMC(S,X,tau,r,q,v,M,N); t=toc;
19│ SE = std(payoff)/sqrt(N);
```

We should obtain something like the following:

```
The analytic solution.
call price   5.05.   It took   0.00 seconds.

MC 1 (vectorized).
call price   5.06.   lower band   5.01.   upper band   5.12.
width of CI  0.11.   It took   0.03 seconds.
```

For a not-path-dependent model as Black–Scholes, there is much in the function `pricepaths` that we actually do not need (and, hence, should not do). `pricepaths` computes and stores a matrix of size (M+1) × N; each of the N columns is one price path with M steps (plus the initial price). This is fast in Matlab (or R), faster than looping through the columns and rows, but will not work for larger N and M since the matrix will not fit into memory. An efficient way would be to split N into smaller pieces that fit into memory, or run every path. In any case, there is no need to use `exp()` on any price along the paths; the terminal price suffices.

The function `callBSMMC2` is a second example. It does not use matrices but creates a single path at a time. It is not much slower than `callBSMMC`, but allows much larger N. It is in fact faster than `callBSMMC` for larger M (M > 100, say).

Listing 9.9. C-CaseStudies/M/callBSMMC2.m

```
 1│ function [call,Q]= callBSMMC2(S,X,tau,r,q,v,M,N)
 2│ % callBSMMC2.m -- version 2010-12-10
 3│ % S    = spot
 4│ % X    = strike
 5│ % tau  = time to maturity
 6│ % r    = riskfree rate
 7│ % q    = dividend yield
 8│ % v    = volatility^2
 9│ % M    = time steps
10│ % N    = number of paths
11│ dt = tau/M;
12│ g1 = (r - q - v/2)*dt; g2 = sqrt(v*dt);
```

```
13  sumPayoff = 0; T = 0; Q = 0;
14  s = log(S);
15  for n = 1:N
16      z = g1 + g2*randn(M,1);
17      z = cumsum(z)+s;
18      Send = exp(z(end));
19      payoff = max(Send-X,0);
20      sumPayoff = payoff + sumPayoff;
21      %compute variance
22      if n>1
23          T = T + payoff;
24          Q = Q + (1/(n*(n-1))) * (n*payoff - T)^2;
25      else
26          T = payoff;
27      end
28  end
29  call = exp(-r*tau) * (sumPayoff/N);
```

One-pass algorithms for variance

The function callBSMMC2 computes the variance iteratively with a one-pass algorithm. The sample variance of a vector Y can be computed as follows:

$$\mathrm{Var}(Y) = \frac{1}{N} \sum_{i=1}^{N} (Y_i - m_Y)^2.$$

This formula requires the mean of Y, computed as

$$m_Y = \frac{1}{N} \sum_{i=1}^{N} Y_i,$$

hence, we need to pass twice through the data. We use a one-pass algorithm; see Algorithm 28 (Chan, Golub, and LeVeque, 1983; Youngs and Cramer, 1971).

The advantages are that we do not need to store the results of all single paths and we could stop the algorithm once the standard error has reached a specified size. Then the variance needs to be computed in the loop; see Statement 7 in Algorithm 28.

Algorithm 28 One-pass algorithm for computing the variance.

1: set $Q = 0$ # Q is the sum of squares of $Y - m_Y$
2: set $T = Y_1$ # T is the sum of Y
3: **for** $i = 2$ to N **do**
4:     compute $T = T + Y_i$
5:     compute $Q = Q + \frac{1}{i(i-1)}(iY_i - T)^2$
6: **end for**
7: compute variance Q/N

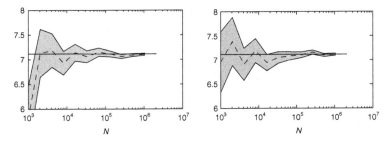

Figure 9.7 Speed of convergence for Monte Carlo pricing. $S_0 = 50$, $X = 50$, $r = 0.05$, $\sqrt{v} = 0.30$, and $\tau = 1$. The true Black–Scholes price is 7.12.

Figure 9.7 gives examples for the convergence of the price. The settings were $S_0 = 50$, $X = 50$, $r = 0.05$, $\sqrt{v} = 0.30$, and $\tau = 1$. We plot the obtained price (the dashed line), the true Black–Scholes price (7.12; the solid line), and a 95% confidence interval. We require a large N to get accurate numbers with respect to the numerical benchmark. For $N = 100,000$, the confidence interval has a width of about 15 cents, or 2% of the option price; with 1,000,000 steps, it shrinks to 5 cents, less than 1% of the option price. To gain intuition about these magnitudes, we can perturb the input parameters. With an interest rate of 0.052 instead of 0.05, the call price under Black–Scholes would have been about 5 cents higher; with a volatility of 0.31 instead of 0.30, the price would increase by about 20 cents.

Variance reduction 1: antithetic variates
The standard error of the mean estimate of some quantity is the standard deviation of the sampled quantity over the square root of the number of samples N. So, to decrease the error in MC methods, we can either increase N, or decrease the variance of the quantities that we compute from our sample. This latter strategy goes by the name of variance reduction (see also page 143). Variance reduction can often help to make simulations more efficient, though it also makes the procedures more complicated and slower, and more vulnerable to (possibly subtle) errors.

For two random variables Y_1 and Y_2 with the same variance, the following holds:

$$\mathsf{Var}\left(\frac{Y_1 + Y_2}{2}\right) = \frac{1}{4}\left(\mathsf{Var}(Y_1) + \mathsf{Var}(Y_2) + 2\mathsf{Cov}(Y_1, Y_2)\right).$$

So we can reduce the variance if Y_1 and Y_2 are negatively correlated. A simple and extreme example is uniform variates. If U is distributed uniformly between 0 and 1, so is $1 - U$, but the linear correlation between the two variates is -1. Imagine we want to compute the mean, which is 0.5, of a sample of such uniforms. We could sample N numbers, and compute $1/N \sum U$. Or we sample $N/2$ numbers, and increase the sample to size N by computing $1 - U$ for all U. So we have pairs $[U, 1 - U]$, and the mean of each pair is exactly $(U + 1 - U)/2 = 0.5$.

To benefit from antithetic (i.e., negatively correlated) variates, we need to make sure that this "anti-correlation" propagates into the things we actually compute with the random numbers. If we use the uniforms to generate nonuniforms, we need be to careful which method we use: the inverse is monotone, so (at least rank) correlation remains. But with acceptance–rejection methods or transformations this is not guaranteed. The contrary, actually: specific algorithms require explicitly uniforms that are independent. So a safer method—if possible—is to induce negative correlation at a higher level. If we use Gaussian variates Y, we can use $-Y$ (which would have been just as likely).

Consider a portfolio of two identical options on underliers $S^{(1)}$ and $S^{(2)}$. Suppose these S satisfy the same SDE, but we switch the signs of the random variates used to simulate them.

$$dS^{(1)} = r S^{(1)}dt + \sqrt{v} S^{(1)}dz$$
$$dS^{(2)} = r S^{(2)}dt - \sqrt{v} S^{(2)}dz$$

The options should have the same price (the same drift and variance term in the SDEs). But $S^{(1)}$ and $S^{(2)}$ are negatively correlated, hence the sampling variance of S is reduced, and consequently the variance of the mean of the two options is smaller than through computing the option price from just one equation.

The following functions callBSMMC3 and callBSMMC4 show implementations of antithetic variates (version 3 uses loops, version 4 is vectorized).

Listing 9.10. C-CaseStudies/M/callBSMMC3.m

```
 1 function [call,Q] = callBSMMC3(S,X,tau,r,q,v,M,N)
 2 % callBSMMC3.m -- version 2010-12-08
 3 % S   = spot
 4 % X   = strike
 5 % tau = time to maturity
 6 % r   = riskfree rate
 7 % q   = dividend yield
 8 % v   = volatility^2
 9 % M   = time steps
10 % N   = number of paths
11 dt = tau/M;
12 g1 = (r - q - v/2)*dt; g2 = sqrt(v*dt);
13 sumPayoff = 0; T = 0; Q = 0;
14 s = log(S);
15 for n = 1:N
16     ee = g2* randn(M,1);
17     z = g1 + ee;
18     z = cumsum(z)+s;
```

```
19   Send = exp(z(end));
20   payoff = max(Send-X,0);
21   z = g1 - ee;
22   z = cumsum(z)+s;
23   Send = exp(z(end));
24   payoff = payoff + max(Send-X,0);
25   payoff = payoff/2;
26   sumPayoff = payoff + sumPayoff;
27   %compute variance
28   if n>1
29       T = T + payoff;
30       Q = Q + (1/(n*(n-1))) * (n*payoff - T)^2;
31   else
32       T = payoff;
33   end
34 end
35 call = exp(-r*tau) * (sumPayoff/N);
```

Listing 9.11. C-CaseStudies/M/callBSMMC4.m

```
1 function [call,payoff] = callBSMMC4(S,X,tau,r,q,v,M,N)
2 % callBSMMC4.m -- version 2010-12-08
3 % S    = spot
4 % X    = strike
5 % tau  = time to maturity
6 % r    = riskfree rate
7 % q    = dividend yield
8 % v    = volatility^2
9 % M    = time steps
10 % N    = number of paths
11 dt = tau/M;
12 g1 = (r - q - v/2)*dt; g2 = sqrt(v*dt);
13 s = log(S);
14 ee = g2 * randn(M,N);
15 z = cumsum(g1+ee,1)+s;  % cumsum(...,1) in case of M=1!
16 S = exp(z(end,:));
17 payoff = max(S-X,0);
18 z = cumsum(g1-ee,1)+s;  % cumsum(...,1) in case of M=1!
19 S = exp(z(end,:));
20 payoff = payoff + max(S-X,0);
21 payoff = payoff/2;
22 payoff = exp(-r*tau) * payoff;
23 call = mean(payoff);
```

The example is not entirely fair since we use two times the number of paths; while we save the generation of the random numbers, they do not account for most of the running time. In general, antithetic variates do not always help much, but they are cheap.

Variance reduction 2: control variates

To price a vanilla call with the MC approach, we simulate paths of the underlier; for each path Y_i, we get a payoff; we average the payoffs and get

our estimate of the price. More formally, we are interested in $\zeta = \mathsf{E}(\varphi(Y))$.
Suppose we have another variable, $c(Y)$, and

(i) $\varphi(Y_i)$ and $c(Y_i)$ are correlated, and

(ii) we know $\mathsf{E}(c(Y)) = \bar{c}(Y)$. Note that $\bar{c}(Y)$ will still be a function of the
      distribution of Y, but we will write $\bar{c}$.

In our example of a vanilla call, c could simply be the underlier's price. When
the stock's terminal price is high, so is the call payoff, and vice versa; so there
exists correlation. Under the lognormal distribution of Black–Scholes, we
know the expected terminal price of the underlier. For a given path, we now
compute

$$\varphi^*(Y_i) = \varphi(Y_i) + \beta\big(c(Y_i) - \bar{c}\big)$$

for a β to be determined. The expectation of φ^* is ζ since the added term is
centered about its mean. To ensure $\mathsf{Var}(\varphi^*) < \mathsf{Var}(\varphi)$, we need to choose β
appropriately. The variance-minimizing value is

$$-\frac{\mathsf{Cov}\big(\varphi(Y_i), c(Y_i)\big)}{\mathsf{Var}(c(Y_i))}.$$

This expression should be familiar: it is the formula for the slope coefficient
in a linear regression (with a constant), yet with a minus in front of it. The
function callBSMMC5 implements an example.

Listing 9.12. C-CaseStudies/M/callBSMMC5.m

```
 1 function [call,Q]= callBSMMC5(S,X,tau,r,q,v,M,N)
 2 % callBSMMC5.m -- version 2010-12-10
 3 % S   = spot
 4 % X   = strike
 5 % tau = time to maturity
 6 % r   = riskfree rate
 7 % q   = dividend yield
 8 % v   = volatility^2
 9 % M   = time steps
10 % N   = number of paths
11 dt = tau/M;
12 g1 = (r - q - v/2)*dt; g2 = sqrt(v*dt);
13 sumPayoff = 0; T = 0; Q = 0;
14 s = log(S);
15 % determine beta
16 nT = 2000;
17 sampleS = S*exp(g1*tau + sqrt(v*tau) * randn(nT,1));
18 sampleO = exp(-r*tau) * max(sampleS - X, 0);
19 aux     = [ones(nT,1) sampleS]\sampleO;
20 beta    = -aux(2);
21 expS    = S*exp((r-q)*tau); % expected stock price
22 % run paths
23 for n = 1:N
24     z = g1 + g2*randn(M,1);
25     z = cumsum(z)+s;
26     Send  = exp(z(end));
27     payoff = max(Send-X,0) + beta*(Send-expS);
```

```
28      sumPayoff = payoff + sumPayoff;
29      %compute variance
30      if n>1
31          T = T + payoff;
32          Q = Q + (1/(n*(n-1))) * (n*payoff - T)^2;
33      else
34          T = payoff;
35      end
36  end
37  call = exp(-r*tau) * (sumPayoff/N);
```

Example calls for all functions.

Listing 9.13. C-CaseStudies/M/exBSM.m

```
1  % exBMS.m -- version 2010-12-08
2  S     = 100;
3  X     = 100;
4  tau   = 1/2;
5  r     = 0.03;
6  q     = 0.05;
7  v     = 0.2^2;
8
9  % MC parameters
10 M = 1;
11 N = 100000;
12
13 %% analytic solution
14 tic, call = callBSM(S,X,tau,r,q,v); t=toc;
15 fprintf('The analytic solution.\ncall price %6.2f.   It took
       %6.2f seconds.\n', call,t)
16
17 %% MC
18 tic, [call, payoff] = callBSMMC(S,X,tau,r,q,v,M,N); t=toc;
19 SE = std(payoff)/sqrt(N);
20 fprintf('\nMC 1 (vectorized).\ncall price %6.2f.   lower band
       %6.2f.   upper band %6.2f.   width of CI %6.2f.   It took
       %6.2f seconds.\n',...
21     call, -2*SE+call, 2*SE+call, 4*SE, t)
22
23
24 %% pathwise
25 tic, [call, Q] = callBSMMC2(S,X,tau,r,q,v,M,N); t=toc;
26 SE = sqrt(Q/N)/sqrt(N);
27 fprintf('\nMC 2 (loop).\ncall price %6.2f.   lower band %6.2f.
         upper band %6.2f.   width of CI %6.2f.   It took %6.2f
         seconds.\n',...
28     call, -2*SE+call, 2*SE+call, 4*SE, t)
29
30
31 %% variance reduction: antithetic
32 tic, [call, Q] = callBSMMC3(S,X,tau,r,q,v,M,N); t=toc;
33 SE = sqrt(Q/N)/sqrt(N);
34 fprintf('\nMC 3 (loop), antithetic variates.\ncall price %6.2f.
         lower band %6.2f.   upper band %6.2f.   width of CI %6.2f.
          It took %6.2f seconds.\n',...
35     call, -2*SE+call, 2*SE+call, 4*SE, t)
```

```
36
37
38 %% variance reduction: antithetic
39 tic, [call, payoff] = callBSMMC4(S,X,tau,r,q,v,M,N); t=toc;
40 SE = std(payoff)/sqrt(N);
41 fprintf('\nMC 4 (vectorized), antithetic variates.\ncall price
       %6.2f.   lower band %6.2f.   upper band %6.2f.   width of CI
         %6.2f.   It took %6.2f seconds.\n',...
42     call, -2*SE+call, 2*SE+call, 4*SE, t)
43
44
45 %% variance reduction: control variate
46 tic, [call, Q] = callBSMMC5(S,X,tau,r,q,v,M,N); t=toc;
47 SE = sqrt(Q/N)/sqrt(N);
48 fprintf('\nMC 5 (loop), control variate.\ncall price %6.2f.
       lower band %6.2f.   upper band %6.2f.   width of CI %6.2f.
         It took %6.2f seconds.\n',...
49     call, -2*SE+call, 2*SE+call, 4*SE, t)
```

We see that with antithetic and control variates, the standard errors are smaller, hence the confidence intervals are tighter. But at the same time the functions are also slower, and take more time to implement.

```
The analytic solution.
call price   5.05.   It took   0.00 seconds.

MC 1 (vectorized).
call price   5.05.   lower band   5.00.   upper band   5.10.
width of CI   0.11.   It took   0.04 seconds.

MC 2 (loop).
call price   5.07.   lower band   5.01.   upper band   5.12.
width of CI   0.11.   It took   0.19 seconds.

MC 3 (loop), antithetic variates.
call price   5.08.   lower band   5.05.   upper band   5.11.
width of CI   0.06.   It took   0.35 seconds.

MC 4 (vectorized), antithetic variates.
call price   5.06.   lower band   5.03.   upper band   5.09.
width of CI   0.06.   It took   0.02 seconds.

MC 5 (loop), control variate.
call price   5.05.   lower band   5.03.   upper band   5.08.
width of CI   0.05.   It took   0.22 seconds.
```

The Heston model

Heston (1993) modeled the stock price S and its variance v by the following two equations:

$$dS_t = (r - q)S_t dt + \sqrt{v_t}S_t dz_t^{(1)} \tag{9.10}$$

$$dv_t = \kappa(\theta - v_t)dt + \sigma\sqrt{v_t}dz_t^{(2)}. \tag{9.11}$$

In this model we now have two SDEs, but they still belong to the general class of equations described in (9.2): for the price equation we have $g_1(S,t) = (r-q)S_t$ and $g_2(S,t) = \sqrt{v_t}S_t$, for the variance equation we have $g_1(v,t) = \kappa(\theta - v_t)$ and $g_2(v,t) = \sigma\sqrt{v_t}$. The Wiener processes $z^{(\cdot)}$ have correlation ρ. The long-run variance is θ, and current variance v_0 reverts back to this mean value with speed κ; σ is the volatility of volatility. For $\sigma \to 0$, the Heston dynamics approach those of Black–Scholes. We will come back to the Heston model in Chapter 15. For this model we cannot (at least not easily) jump to the final time, since the volatility at each step depends on the current S; it is state dependent. So we need the path. The function callHestonMC prices a call under the Heston model.

Listing 9.14. C-CaseStudies/M/callHestonMC.m

```
 1 function [call,Q] = callHestonMC(S,X,tau,r,q,v0,vT,rho,k,sigma,M
     ,N)
 2 % callHestonMC.m -- version 2011-01-08
 3 % S      = spot
 4 % X      = strike
 5 % tau    = time to maturity
 6 % r      = riskfree rate
 7 % q      = dividend yield
 8 % v0     = initial variance
 9 % vT     = long run variance (theta in Heston's paper)
10 % rho    = correlation
11 % k      = speed of mean reversion (kappa in Heston's paper)
12 % sigma  = vol of vol
13 % M      = time steps
14 % N      = number of paths
15 dt = tau/M; sumPayoff = 0;
16 C = [1 rho;rho 1]; C = chol(C);
17 T = 0; Q = 0;
18 for n = 1:N
19     ee = randn(M,2);
20     ee = ee * C;
21     vS = log(S); vV = v0;
22     for t = 1:M
23         % --update stock price
24         dS = (r - q - vV/2)*dt + sqrt(vV)*ee(t,1)*sqrt(dt);
25         vS = vS + dS;
26         % --update squared vol
27         aux = ee(t,2);
28         % --Euler scheme
29         dV = k*(vT-vV)*dt + sigma*sqrt(vV)*aux*sqrt(dt);
30         % --absorbing condition
31         if vV + dV < 0
32             vV = 0;
33         else
34             vV = vV + dV;
35         end
36         % --zero variance: some alternatives
37         %if vV + dV < 0, dV = k*(vT-vV)*dt;end;vV = vV + dV;
38         %if vV + dV <= 0, dV = k*(vT)*dt;end;vV = vV + dV;
39     end
```

```
40   Send = exp(vS);
41   payoff = max(Send-X,0);
42   sumPayoff = payoff + sumPayoff;
43   %compute variance
44   if n>1
45       T = T + payoff;
46       Q = Q + (1/(n*(n-1))) * (n*payoff - T)^2;
47   else
48       T = payoff;
49   end
50 end
51 call = exp(-r*tau) * (sumPayoff/N);
```

The discretized version of the SDE for the variance may well lead to negative variance, in particular if volatility of volatility σ is high, and mean
reversion κ is small. Unfortunately, these are exactly the properties we need
to reproduce the volatility smile (see Chapter 15). One simple method to
simulate the model is to repair the volatility SDE if it becomes negative,
for instance, by setting it to zero (the so-called absorbing condition), or
reflecting it, that is, switching the sign of the last variate. An example call to
the function is given in the next Matlab script.

Listing 9.15. C-CaseStudies/M/exHeston.m

```
1  % exampleHeston.m -- version 2011-01-16
2  S     = 100;      % spot price
3  q     = 0.02;     % dividend yield
4  r     = 0.03;     % risk-free rate
5  X     = 110;      % strike
6  tau   = 0.2;      % time to maturity
7  k     = 1;        % mean reversion speed (kappa in paper)
8  sigma = 0.6;      % vol of vol
9  rho   = -0.7;     % correlation
10 v0    = 0.2^2;    % current variance
11 vT    = 0.2^2;    % long-run variance (theta in paper)
12
13 % --solution by integration (taken from Chapter 15)
14 call = callHestoncf(S,X,tau,r,q,v0,vT,rho,k,sigma)
15
16 M = 200; N = 200000;
17 [call,Q ]= callHestonMC(S,X,tau,r,q,v0,vT,rho,k,sigma,M,N);
18 SE = sqrt(Q/N)/sqrt(N);
19 [-2*SE+call call 2*SE+call 4*SE]
```

9.3.3. Greeks

A straightforward idea to estimate Greeks is to use a finite difference scheme.
Let f_x be the partial derivative of a function f with respect to x, then we

could, for instance, use the finite difference schemes (see also page 78)

$$f_x(x, \cdot) \simeq \frac{f(x+h, \cdot) - f(x, \cdot)}{h}, \qquad (9.12)$$

$$f_x(x, \cdot) \simeq \frac{f(x, \cdot) - f(x-h, \cdot)}{h} \quad \text{or} \qquad (9.13)$$

$$f_x(x, \cdot) \simeq \frac{f(x+h, \cdot) - f(x-h, \cdot)}{2h}. \qquad (9.14)$$

In Chapter 2, we showed that while mathematically h should be as small as possible, with finite numerical precision there is a limit to how small h can become. But that discussion was about deterministic functions. Now, f is the outcome of an MC experiment, and will thus vary substantially compared with round-off and truncation error. Suppose the task was to compute a call option's Delta by running two MC simulations; for the second run we slightly increase spot, that is, we use $S + h$ as the current price. Taking the difference between the obtained option prices and dividing it by h gives the forward approximation of the option's Delta. Now, if h is very small compared with S (e.g., $S = 100$ and $h = 0.01$), it can easily happen that in the second run, the call gets a lower price, hence we have a negative Delta.

Let us run an example. We stay in the Black–Scholes world since here we can evaluate the Greeks analytically, and so have a benchmark. We use $S = 100$, $X = 100$, $\tau = 1$, $r = 0.03$, $q = 0$, and $\sqrt{v} = 0.2$. The analytic Delta for these parameters is 0.60. We compute the Delta via a forward difference. We simulate $N = 100{,}000$ paths with $S = 100$, and $N = 100{,}000$ paths with $S = 100 + h$ with $h \in \{0.01, 0.1, 0.2, 0.5, 1, 2\}$. From the two option values that we get, we compute the Delta. We repeat this whole procedure 100 times. Figure 9.8 gives boxplots of the estimated Delta values. The solid horizontal line is the true Delta, the dotted lines give Delta ± 0.05. The obtained values are mostly completely off the mark, but the results become reasonable for large values of h.

But, actually, we have violated a basic rule in experimental design. Whenever we want to figure out the effect that one variable has, we should not change several variables at the same time. But we have: in the second run, we have used new random numbers. So, next, we repeat the experiment, but we reuse the random variates (this is often called using common random numbers). So, we create one path that starts from $S = 100$, and then create a path that starts from $S = 100 + h$ that uses the same random numbers. And indeed the estimates are very different once we use common random numbers. Results are shown in Fig. 9.9. Note also that while a greater h induces bias, this bias is still not terribly large. The bias disappears for smaller h.

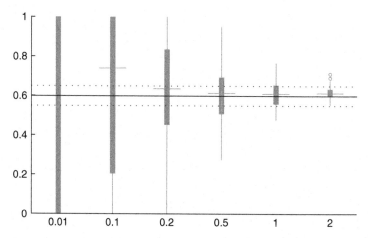

Figure 9.8 Forward difference for Greeks: Boxplots for Delta estimates with $M = 1$ and $N = 100,000$ for different values of h (y-axis). Parameters are $S = 100$, $X = 100$, $\tau = 1$, $r = 0.03$, $q = 0$, and $\sigma = 0.2$. The solid horizontal line is the true BS Delta of 0.60; the dotted lines give Delta ± 0.05.

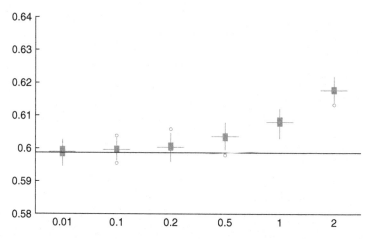

Figure 9.9 Forward difference for Greeks: Boxplots for Delta estimates with $M = 1$ and $N = 100,000$ for different values of h (y-axis), but using common random variates. Parameters are $S = 100$, $X = 100$, $\tau = 1$, $r = 0.03$, $q = 0$, and $\sigma = 0.2$. The solid horizontal line is the true BS Delta of 0.60; the dotted lines give Delta ± 0.05.

A straightforward way to reuse random numbers is to (re)set the seed before each MC run. But we can essentially reuse the paths, so that we do not really need two or three simulations (two for forward or backward differences, three for central differences). There are many clever ideas on how to compute Greeks other than by finite differences; see, for instance, Glasserman (2004, Chapter 7). In any case, the finite difference approach has the advantage that it is very simple, and still relatively cheap if we reuse the random numbers.

9.3.4. Quasi-Monte Carlo

As pointed out at the beginning of this section, when we estimate an option price by MC we are actually computing an expectation, that is, we have to evaluate an integral. In lower dimensions (say, dimension one), deterministic integration schemes are much more efficient to evaluate integrals, that is, it is very likely that a deterministic quadrature rule needs fewer function evaluations than an MC approach to obtain the same error. In fact, one desirable property of random numbers is equidistribution, so random numbers drawn from a certain range should cover the whole range as uniformly as possible. But then, why do we not use a grid? There are two disadvantages: first, in higher dimensions we generally cannot use a grid since the number of grid points grows exponentially with the number of dimensions (but generally, two or three is not higher dimensions). Furthermore, an advantage of MC is that we do not have to compute the number of grid points in advance, but could stop if some convergence criterion is satisfied (e.g., the width of a confidence interval) which we cannot do with a grid since there is no probabilistic interpretation.

Nevertheless, the idea to enforce more grid-style equidistribution is the basis of so-called quasi-Monte Carlo (see also Section 6.6.2). This is quite a misnomer, for as we pointed out in Chapter 6, MC methods are not really random either. Anyway, it is the name by which these methods are handled. A very readable introduction to quasi-Monte Carlo methods in option pricing is the paper by Boyle and Tan (1997). For a more formal treatment, see Niederreiter (1992).

The essence of quasi-Monte Carlo methods is to replace the usual random numbers by so-called low discrepancy (LD) sequences.

Discrepancy

Intuitively, the idea of discrepancy is the following: assume a sample of N points from some "area" $\mathbb{Q}$ (which could be of any dimension). Let vol($\mathbb{Q}$) be the "size" (volume) of this area. Next, pick any subarea from $\mathbb{Q}$, and call it $\mathbb{S}$. If our N points were uniformly distributed on $\mathbb{Q}$, we would expect that

$$\frac{\text{vol}(\mathbb{S})}{\text{vol}(\mathbb{Q})} \simeq \frac{\text{number of points in } \mathbb{S}}{N};$$

that is, the number of points in $\mathbb{S}$ should be proportional to the volume of $\mathbb{S}$. There are actually different formal definitions of discrepancy. Often used is the so-called star discrepancy, which is defined as follows. Start with a hypercube of dimension p, and define a subcube $\mathbb{S}$ that contains the origin and has volume vol($\mathbb{S}$). Now,

$$\text{star discrepancy} = \sup_{\mathbb{S} \in [0,1)^p} \left| \frac{\text{number of points in } \mathbb{S}}{N} - \text{vol}(\mathbb{S}) \right|.$$

This discrepancy should be as small as possible; so the aim is to find sequences that are uniform on the hypercube, that is, sequences with low discrepancy (LD).

A really random sequence has expected discrepancy

$$\mathcal{O}\left(\frac{\log\left(\log(N)\right)}{\sqrt{N}}\right).$$

Important is the $\sqrt{N}$ term, and the fact that there is no p: the dimension is not relevant. LD sequences on the other hand are characterized by an asymptotic discrepancy of

$$\mathcal{O}\left(\frac{\log(N)^p}{N}\right).$$

So, now p appears (which is bad), but in the denominator we have N instead of $\sqrt{N}$ (which is good).

Practically, there are a number of problems with such measures: they hold only asymptotically, and it is difficult to compute discrepancy for a given sequence of points. That means that the best way to see if a given method really improves over standard MC techniques is often experimentation.

Van der Corput sequences

We only look into the simplest type of LD sequences, those named after Johannes van der Corput. In more than one dimension, van der Corput (VDC) sequences are called Halton sequences.

Say we wish to construct the kth number (an integer) in a VDC sequence. We first represent k in a basis b:

$$k = (d_m \cdots d_3 d_2 d_1 d_0)_b \quad \text{with} \quad d \in \{0, 1, \ldots, b-1\}.$$

The d are the digits; m is the number of digits that we need to represent k in base b, computed as

$$m = 1 + \lfloor \log_b(k) \rfloor.$$

In Matlab, we cannot set the base of the logarithm; but we can use the fact that $\log_b(k) = \log(k)/\log(b)$. In R, the log function has an optional argument base.

Next, we flip the order of the digits from left to right and add a radix point[13] such that the resulting number lies in $(0, 1)$; thus we obtain the kth VDC number $H_k(b)$ in basis b,

$$H_k(b) = (0.d_0 d_1 d_2 d_3 \cdots d_m)_b.$$

---

[13] Radix point is the formal name for the symbol that delimits the integer part of a number from its fractional part.

Converting back to basis 10, we have our "quasi-random number."

More compactly, we can write, for any integer $k \geq 1$,

$$k = \sum_{j=0}^{m} d_j b^j \qquad (9.15)$$

and

$$H_k(b) = \sum_{j=0}^{m} d_j \frac{1}{b^{j+1}} \qquad (9.16)$$

where b is the integer base, and the digits d are functions of k and b.

We need an example. Let us compute the 169th VDC number in basis 3 (i.e., $k = 169$ and $b = 3$):

$$k = 169 = (20021)_3$$

$$H_k(3) = (0.12002)_3$$

$$= 1 \times 3^{-1} + 2 \times 3^{-2} + 0 \times 3^{-3} + 0 \times 3^{-4} + 2 \times 3^{-5}$$

$$= 0.33333 + 0.22222 + 0 + 0 + 0.00823$$

$$= 0.56378.$$

Or, using Eqs. (9.15) and (9.16):

$$k = 2 \times 3^4 + 0 \times 3^3 + 0 \times 3^2 + 2 \times 3^1 + 1 \times 3^0$$

$$H_{169}(3) = 2 \times 3^{-5} + 0 \times 3^{-4} + 0 \times 3^{-3} + 2 \times 3^{-2} + 1 \times 3^{-1}.$$

As a check: Matlab provides the function dec2base that converts an integer into a character string that holds the digits in a given base. So the command

```
dec2base(169,3)
```

returns

```
ans =
    20021
```

The following function digits does the same, but returns the digits as a vector, which is more helpful for our purposes.

Listing 9.16. C-CaseStudies/M/digits.m

```
1  function dd = digits(k,b)
2  % digits.m -- version 2010-12-08
3  nD = 1 + floor(log(max(k))/log(b)); % required digits
4  dd = zeros(length(k),nD);
5  for i = nD:-1:1
6      dd(:,i) = mod(k,b);
7      if i>1; k = fix(k/b); end
8  end
```

Let us use the example a last time: the following table demonstrates step-by-step how `digits` works. We first calculate the number of digits that we need (five in this case), and then work backward through the digits: we divide by b, set the digit equal to the remainder, and set $k = \texttt{floor(k/b)}$. (To build intuition, try the trivial example `digits(169,10)`.)

j	k	remainder after division by b
0	169	1 % the last bit
1	56	2
2	18	0
3	6	0
4	2	2

Checking Eq. (9.15), the following command should give 169:

```
digits(169,3) * (b.^(4:-1:0))'  % taking the scalar product
```

It is now only a short step to a VDC number; see Eq. (9.16). Entering

```
sum(digits(169,3) ./ b.^(5:-1:1) )
```

gives the VDC number mapped into $(0,1)$. The function VDC does just that.

Listing 9.17. C-CaseStudies/M/VDC.m

```
 1  function vv = VDC(k,b)
 2  % VDC.m -- version 2010-12-08
 3  nD = 1 + floor(log(max(k))/log(b)); % required digits
 4  nN = length(k);                     % number of VDC numbers
 5  vv = zeros(nN,nD);
 6  for i = nD:-1:1
 7      vv(:,i) = mod(k,b);
 8      if i>1; k = fix(k/b); end
 9  end
10  ex = b .^ (nD:-1:1);
11  vv = vv ./ (ones(nN,1)*ex);
12  vv = sum(vv,2);
```

The argument `k` of this function can be a vector:

```
VDC(1:100,7)    % generates first 100 VDC numbers in base 7
VDC(1:2:100,7)  % generates VDC numbers 1, 3, 5 ... in base 7
```

Table 9.1 gives the first ten VDC numbers in base 2.

There are ingenious approaches to accelerate these computations by updating from the last number (since they require loops, they need not be faster in Matlab, though they will usually be memory saving); the VDC sequence can in fact be updated without explicitly computing the base b expansion in every iteration. See Glasserman (2004) for examples and references.

If we want VDC sequences in more dimensions (Halton sequences), we just generate sequences with different bases b that are coprime (i.e., have no common divisor except 1). Thus, a natural choice is to pick prime numbers as bases. Table 9.2 lists some prime numbers, just in case.

Smaller bases are generally preferred since for a fixed number of steps the VDC numbers are more uniform; in a higher base we need more numbers to really "fill" our range. An example: the VDC numbers 1 to 20 in base 59 lie in the range $(0.017, 0.339)$ and not in $(0, 1)$. Figure 9.10 gives some examples. This example points to a property of VDC numbers: they consist

Table 9.1 The first 10 VDC numbers in base 2.

#	in base 2	mapped to $(0, 1)$	
1	$(0001)_2$	0.5000	
2	$(0010)_2$	0.2500	
3	$(0011)_2$	0.7500	
4	$(0100)_2$	0.1250	
5	$(0101)_2$	0.6250	
6	$(0110)_2$	0.3750	
7	$(0111)_2$	0.8750	
8	$(1000)_2$	0.0625	
9	$(1001)_2$	0.5625	
10	$(1010)_2$	0.3125	

0   1

Table 9.2 Prime numbers smaller than 1000.

2	3	5	7	11	13	17	19	23	29	31	37	41	43
47	53	59	61	67	71	73	79	83	89	97	101	103	107
109	113	127	131	137	139	149	151	157	163	167	173	179	181
191	193	197	199	211	223	227	229	233	239	241	251	257	263
269	271	277	281	283	293	307	311	313	317	331	337	347	349
353	359	367	373	379	383	389	397	401	409	419	421	431	433
439	443	449	457	461	463	467	479	487	491	499	503	509	521
523	541	547	557	563	569	571	577	587	593	599	601	607	613
617	619	631	641	643	647	653	659	661	673	677	683	691	701
709	719	727	733	739	743	751	757	761	769	773	787	797	809
811	821	823	827	829	839	853	857	859	863	877	881	883	887
907	911	919	929	937	941	947	953	967	971	977	983	991	997

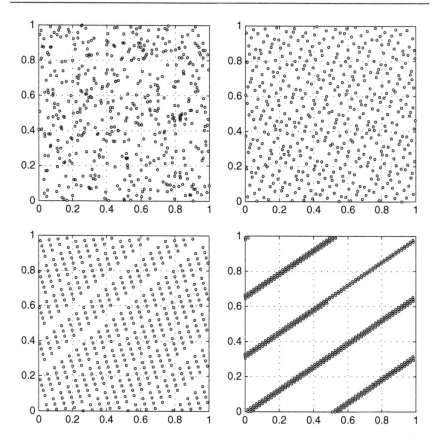

Figure 9.10 Top left: scatter of 500 against 500 points generated with Matlab's `rand`. Top right: scatter of 500 against 500 generated with Halton sequences (bases 2 and 7). Bottom left: scatter of 500 against 500 generated with Halton sequences (bases 23 and 29). Bottom right: scatter of 500 against 500 generated with Halton sequences (bases 59 and 89).

of monotone subsequences of length b (Glasserman, 2004, p. 294). For instance, in base 59, any sequence 1,2,… will consist of 59 increasing points.

We can use a VDC sequence to price a BS call. We create uniforms with the function VDC and transform these into Gaussian variates with the inverse (we use Matlab's `norminv` function). Convergence is shown in Fig. 9.11 (cf. Fig. 9.7).

Listing 9.18. C-CaseStudies/M/callBSMQMC.m

```
1 function call = callBSMQMC(S,K,tau,r,q,v,N)
2 % callBSMQMC.m -- version 2010-12-08
3 % S   = spot
4 % X   = strike
5 % tau = time to mat
6 % r   = riskfree rate
7 % q   = dividend yield
```

```
 8 % v   = volatility^2
 9 g1 = (r - q - v/2)*tau; g2 = sqrt(v*tau);
10 U  = VDC(1:N,7);
11 ee = g2 * norminv(U);
12 z  = log(S) + g1 + ee;
13 S  = exp(z);
14 payoff = exp(-r*tau)  * max(S-K,0);
15 call = sum(payoff)/N;
```

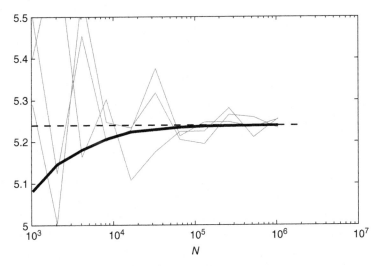

Figure 9.11 Convergence of price with quasi-MC (function `callBSMQMC`). The light gray lines show the convergence with standard MC approach.

Dimensionality

In the example, we priced the European option by just sampling S_T; the dimensionality is one. If we price an option whose payoff depends on the terminal prices of p underliers, the dimensionality is p. Now, suppose we create paths for one stock S with M time steps. We have a dimension of M because we sample from S_1, S_2, and so on. We cannot use a sequence in a single base to generate a path. This is easy to "prove": recall that a VDC in base b consists of monotonously increasing subsequences of length b. Suppose we transform the uniforms with the inverse of the Gaussian which preserves monotonicity. The commands

```
plot(cumprod(1+norminv(VDC(1:1000,3))/100),'k'), hold on
plot(cumprod(1+norminv(VDC(1:1000,13))/100),'k')
plot(cumprod(1+norminv(VDC(1:1000,31))/100),'k')
```

result in Fig. 9.12.

However, there is the notion of "effective dimension." In the case in which we have p terminal prices, but all prices are highly correlated, the effective dimension is smaller than p (Tan and Boyle, 1997). Likewise, for

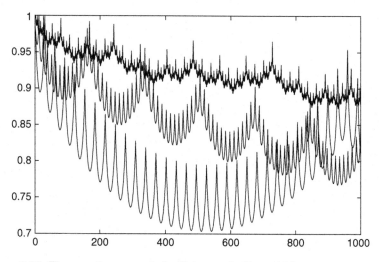

Figure 9.12 Three paths generated with bases 3, 13, and 31.

a sampled path the effective dimensionality is not M. Assume we have sampled a path up to step $M - 1$, and suppose M is large. Then, clearly, the final step makes little difference. In other words, the early random variates will be more important. Every stock price after time step 1 will contain the shock of step 1; but the final variate will have influence only in the last step. Therefore, several authors have suggested using few, large time steps generated with LD sequences, that is, creating a "coarse" time path, and then building the remaining points by a Brownian bridge. For an implementation, see Brandimarte (2006, Chapter 8). Note that for the coarse time path we could not use the function `bridge` given earlier in this section since it uses random numbers sequentially.

In conclusion, LD sequences are a way to speed up convergence; at the same time they offer scope for subtle errors (i.e., where outcomes look reasonable but are faulty). In Fig. 9.12 the error was easy to spot—once we had plotted the paths. It may not always be so obvious. Thus, extensive testing is required. One of the advantages of MC methods was their simplicity; this feature is not necessarily shared by quasi-Monte Carlo methods.

## PART THREE

Optimization

## CHAPTER TEN

Optimization problems in finance

Optimization is essentially a practical tool and one principally used by
non-mathematicians; in contrast, most research papers in optimization
are written in a style that is only intelligible to a mathematician.

(Murray, 1972, p. vii)

In this chapter, we discuss financial optimization models in general: we
discuss how models are set up, how they are solved, and how obtained
solutions are evaluated. The chapter is concluded by several examples of
financial optimization models; some of these examples will be revisited in
later chapters. Following William Murray's statement, all descriptions will
be rather informal.

10.1. What to optimize?

An optimization model consists of an objective function (also called optimization criterion or goal function) and constraints. For all the applications
discussed in later chapters, the objective function is scalar valued; it takes
as arguments a vector x of decision variables, and the data. So our basic
problem is

$$\underset{x}{\text{minimize}}\, f(x, \text{data}),$$

subject to constraints. "Minimize" is not restrictive: if we wanted to maximize, we would minimize $-f$. The model specification will be determined
by considering and balancing different aspects:

financial The straightforward part. We define goals and the means to
achieve them; and we make these notions precise. For an asset allocation
model, for instance, we may need to decide how to define risk—for
example, variability of returns, average losses, probability of failing to
meet an obligation—or how to measure portfolio turnover.

empirical In finance, we are rarely interested in the past. (Even though
we should be. Reading Charles Kindleberger or John Kenneth Galbraith

shows why.) All models deal with future—and hence unknown—quantities. So we need to forecast, estimate, simulate, or approximate these quantities. Building the model (the finance part) must not be separated from the empirical part; we may only deal with quantities that we can forecast to a sufficient degree. This is a strong, yet unavoidable, constraint on formulating the model.

computational There is a second constraint: the model must be solvable. Computational aspects of such models are the topic of this part of the book. We will argue that they are much less of a constraint than is sometimes thought.

We can think of model building as a meta-optimization in which we try to obtain the best possible results (or more realistically, good results; results that improve the current status) for our financial goals under the restrictions that the model remains empirically meaningful and can be solved.

We will briefly discuss the ingredients of a model here. The objective function is often given by the problem at hand. In asset allocation, for instance, we may want a high return and low risk; when we calibrate a model, we want to choose parameter values so that the output of the model is "close" to observed quantities. Of course, these descriptions need to be made more precise. There are many ways to define what "close" means. We have to select, say, a specific norm of absolute or relative differences. In fact, many problems can be spelled out in different ways. When we estimate interest rate models, we may look at interest rates, but also at bond prices. When we look at options, we may work with prices, but also with implied volatilities. Bond prices are functions of interest rates; there is a bijective relationship between option prices and Black–Scholes-implied volatilities. Conceptually, different model formulations may be equivalent; numerically and, especially, empirically they are often not. Specific choices can make a difference, and they often do.

We can phrase this more to the point: can we directly optimize the quantities that we are interested in? The answer is No; at least, Not Always. A well-known example comes from portfolio selection. If we wanted to maximize return, we should not write it without safeguards into our objective function. The reason is that (i) we cannot predict future returns, and (ii) there is a cost involved in failing to correctly predict: the chosen portfolio performs poorly. Theory may help, but determining a good objective function—one that serves our financial goals—ultimately is an empirical task.

Most realistic problems have constraints. Constrained optimization is generally more difficult than the unconstrained case. Constraints may, like the objective function, be given by the problem at hand. In asset allocation we may have legal or regulatory restrictions on how to invest. Empirically, restrictions often have another purpose. They act as safeguards against optimization results that follow more from our specific data, rather than from the data-generating process. This can concern out-of-sample performance: in portfolio selection, there is much evidence that imposing maximum position sizes helps to improve performance. But constraints can also help to make estimated parameters interpretable. For example, variances cannot be negative, and probabilities must lie in the range [0, 1]. Yet when such quantities are the outputs of a numerical procedure, we are not guaranteed that these restrictions are observed, and so we need to make sure that our algorithms yield meaningful results.

10.2. Solving the model

10.2.1. Problems

The focus of this book is neither on financial nor empirical aspects of optimization models, but on their numerical solution. In the coming chapters we describe a number of optimization models that cannot be solved with standard methods, that is, models that pose difficult optimization problems. This is not meant presumptuously; it simply reflects the fact that many problems in finance are difficult to solve. Heuristic methods which we will describe below can help to obtain good solutions, as will be demonstrated in the following chapters. A clarification is needed here: in optimization theory, the solution of a model is the optimum; it is not necessary to speak of "optimal solutions." But that is not the case in practical applications. A solution here is rather the result obtained from a computer program. The quality of this solution will depend on the interplay between the problem and the chosen method (and chance).

From a practical perspective, difficulty in solving a problem can be measured by the amount of computational resources required to compute a (good) solution. In computer science, there are the fields of complexity theory and analysis of algorithms that deal with the difficulty of problems, but results are often of limited use in applications. The practical efficiency of algorithms depends on their implementation; sometimes minor details can make huge differences. Often the only way to obtain results is to run computational experiments, which is exactly what we will do in later chapters.

But what makes an optimization problem difficult? For combinatorial problems, it is the problem size. Such problems have an exact solution method—just write down all possible solutions and pick the best one—but this approach is almost never feasible for realistic problem sizes. For continuous problems, difficulties arise when:

- The objective function is not smooth (e.g., has discontinuities) or is noisy. In either case, relying on the gradient to determine search directions may fail. An example is a function that needs to be evaluated for given arguments by a stochastic simulation or by another numerical procedure (e.g., a quadrature or a finite-difference scheme).

• The objective function has many local optima.

Practically, even in the continuous case we could apply complete enumeration. We could discretize the domain of the objective function and run a so-called grid search. But it is easy to see that this approach, just like for combinatorial problems, is not feasible in practice once the dimensionality of the model grows.

Let us look at some stylized examples of objective functions to make these problems clearer. First, we picture the nice case.

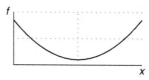

We only have one optimum, the function is smooth, and it is convex. But now imagine we have functions like this.

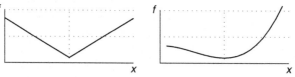

The left figure shows a kink in the objective function, so we cannot use an analytical derivative. The figure on the right has an inflection point, so the objective function is not convex. Newton's method for instance relies on f being globally convex as it will approximate f by a quadratic function, and then solve for the minimum of this function (see Figure 11.9 on page 310). Already such apparently innocuous properties may cause trouble for standard optimization methods.

The functions pictured so far had one minimum, but what if the function looks like this:

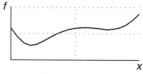

We have two local minima, and one is clearly better than the other. Yet traditional methods will easily get trapped in such local (but suboptimal) minima.

As a final example, we may not be able to evaluate our objective function precisely, but only subject to noise.

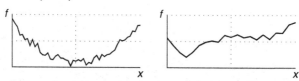

These functions were stylized, but these problems really occur. Several real examples are presented below.

10.2.2. Classical methods and heuristics

To solve optimization models, many researchers and practitioners rely on what we call here standard or classical techniques. (You may have noticed that we have referred to "standard" methods several times before.) Classical methods are, for the purpose of this book, defined as methods that require convexity or at least well behaved objective functions since these techniques are often based on exploiting the derivatives of the objective function. Classical methods are mathematically well founded; numerically, there are powerful solvers available which can efficiently solve even large-scale instances of given problems. Methods that belong to this approach are, for instance, linear and quadratic programming. The efficiency and elegance of these methods comes at a cost, though, since considerable constraints are put on the problem formulation, that is, the functional form of the optimization criterion and the constraints. We often have to shape the problem such that it can be solved by these methods. Thus, the answer that the final model provides is a precise one, but often only to an approximative question.

An alternative approach that we will describe in this book is the use of heuristic optimization techniques. Heuristics are a relatively new development in optimization theory. Even though early examples date back to the 1950s or so, these methods have become practically relevant only in recent decades with the enormous growth in computing power. Heuristics aim at providing good and fast approximations to optimal solutions; the underlying theme of heuristics may thus be described as seeking approximative answers to exact questions. Heuristics have been shown to work well for problems that are completely infeasible for classical approaches (Michalewicz and Fogel, 2004). Conceptually, they are often simple; implementing them rarely requires high levels of mathematical sophistication or programming skills. Heuristics are flexible: we can easily add, remove, or change constraints, or modify the objective function. These advantages come at a cost as well, as the obtained solution is only a stochastic approximation, a random variable. However, such a stochastic solution may still be better than a poor deterministic one (which, even worse, we may not even recognize as such) or no solution at all when classical methods cannot be applied. In fact, for many practical purposes, the goal of optimization is far more modest than to find the truly best solution. Rather, any good solution, where good means an improvement of the status quo, is appreciated. And practically, we often get *very* good solutions. We give examples in later chapters.

Heuristics are not better optimization techniques than classical methods; the question is rather when to use what kind of method. If classical techniques can be applied, heuristic methods will practically always be less efficient. When, however, given problems do not fulfill the requirements of classical methods (and the number of such problems seems large), we suggest not to tailor the problem to the available optimization technique, but to choose an alternative—heuristic—technique for optimization.

We will briefly discuss classical methods in Chapter 11. In Chapter 12, we then give a selective overview of heuristic techniques; the remaining chapters of Part 3 detail the implementation of these methods.

10.3. Evaluating solutions

Modeling is approximation. As described in Chapter 1, whenever we approximate we commit errors. Hence, a solution to our model will inherit these errors. In Chapter 1, we suggested to divide errors into two broad categories: model errors (i.e., empirical errors), and numerical errors. This book is mainly about the second type. In finance, however, the first type is much more important. And evaluating it is much more difficult. A practical approach is to compare different models of which some are "more accurate" than others. Accurate means that a model cannot only be solved with sufficient numerical precision, but that it is also economically meaningful. When a model is more accurate than another model, it has a lower empirical error, at least regarding some aspect of the original problem. Suppose we have two models that serve the same purpose. One model can be solved precisely, but is less accurate than a second model that can be only solved approximatively. We still can empirically test whether an only moderately good solution to the more accurate model provides a better answer to our real problem than the precise solution to the less accurate model. Again, an example from portfolio selection can illustrate this point. Markowitz (1959, Chapter 9) compares two risk measures, variance and semi-variance, along the dimensions cost, convenience, familiarity, and desirability; he concludes that variance is superior in terms of cost, convenience, and familiarity. For variance we can compute exact solutions to the portfolio selection problem; for semi-variance we can only approximate the solution. Today, we can empirically test whether, even with an inexact solution for semi-variance, the gains in desirability outweigh the increased effort.

Even if we accept a model as true, the quality of the model's solution will be limited by the quality of the model's inputs, that is, data or parameter estimates. Appreciating these limits helps to decide how precise a solution we actually need. This decision is relevant for many problems in computational finance since we generally face a trade-off between the precision of a solution and the effort required (most visibly, computing time). Surely, the numerical precision with which we solve a model is important; we need reliable methods. Yet, empirically, there must be a sufficient precision for any given problem. Any improvement beyond this level cannot translate into gains regarding the actual problem any more; only in costs (increased computing time or development costs). Given the rather low empirical accuracy of many financial models, this required precision cannot be high. More specifically, when it comes to optimization we can decide whether we actually need an exact solution as promised by the application of classical methods, or whether a good solution provided by a heuristic is enough.

In principle, of course, there would seem to be little cost in computing precise solutions. Yet there is. First, highly precise or "exact" solutions will give us a sense of certainty that can never be justified by a model. Second, getting more-precise solutions will require more resources. This does not just mean more computing time, but also more time to develop a particular method. Grinold and Kahn (2008, pp. 284–285) give an example; they describe the implementation of algorithms for an asset selection problem— finding the portfolio with cardinality 50 that best tracks the S&P 500. This is a combinatorial problem for which an exact solution could never be computed (there are about 10^{70} possible portfolios), hence we need an approximation. A specialized algorithm took six months to be developed, but then delivered an approximative solution within seconds. As an alternative, a heuristic technique, a Genetic Algorithm, was tested. Implementation took two days; the algorithm found similar results, but also needed two days of computing time. A remark is in order: the example is from the 1990s. Today, the computing time of a Genetic Algorithm for such a problem would on a standard PC be of the order of minutes, perhaps seconds. Researchers may have become cleverer since the 1990s, that is, they may also develop models faster today; but it is unlikely that their performance improvement matches that of computer technology.

A final consideration of the quality of a solution is the distinction between in-sample and out-of-sample. For financial models, this distinction is far more relevant than any numerical issue. More precise solutions will by definition appear better in-sample, but we need to test if this superiority is preserved out-of-sample. Given the difficulty we have in predicting or estimating financial quantities, it seems unlikely that highly precise solutions are necessary in financial models once we compare out-of-sample results. Again, we can set up an empirical test here. Suppose we have a model for which we can compute solutions with varying degrees of precision. Each such solution can be evaluated by its in-sample objective function value (its in-sample fit), but each solution also maps into a certain out-of-sample quality. We can now sort our solutions by in-sample precision, and then see if out-of-sample quality is a roughly monotonous function of this precision, and if the slope of this function is economically meaningful.

To sum up this discussion: the numerical precision with which we solve a model matters, and in-sample tests can show whether our optimization routines work properly. But the more relevant question is to what extent this precision translates into economically meaningful solutions to our actual problems.

In the remaining part of this chapter, several examples for optimization problems that cannot be solved with classical methods will be given. This is not a survey, but a selection of problems to illustrate and motivate the use of heuristic methods in finance. Some of these problems will be revisited in later chapters. For more detailed studies, see for example Maringer (2005b). Many references to specific applications can be found in Schlottmann and Seese (2004) or Gilli, Maringer, and Winker (2008).

10.4. Examples

Portfolio optimization with alternative risk measures

In the framework of modern portfolio optimization (Markowitz, 1952, 1959), a portfolio of assets is often characterized by a desired property, the reward, and something undesirable, the risk. Markowitz identified these two properties with the expectation and the variance of returns, respectively, hence the expression mean–variance optimization. By now, there exists a large body of evidence that financial asset returns are not normally distributed (see, for instance, Cont, 2001), thus, describing a portfolio by only its first two moments is often regarded as insufficient. Alternatives to mean–variance optimization have been proposed, in particular, replacing variance as the risk measure.

Assume an investor has wealth v_0 and wishes to invest for a fixed period of time. A given portfolio, as it comprises risky assets, maps into a distribution of wealth v_T at the end of the period. The optimization problem can be stated as follows

$$\min_x f\bigl(v_T(x)\bigr)$$
$$x_j^{\text{inf}} \le x_j \le x_j^{\text{sup}} \qquad j \in J$$
$$K_{\text{inf}} \le \#\{J\} \le K_{\text{sup}}$$

$$\dots \text{and other constraints}.$$

The objective function $f(\cdot)$ could be a risk measure or a combination of multiple objectives to be minimized. Candidates include the portfolio's drawdown, partial moments, or whatever we wish to optimize. The vector x stores the weights or the units (integer numbers) of assets held. x_j^{inf} and x_j^{sup} are vectors of minimum and maximum holding sizes, respectively, for those assets included in the portfolio (i.e., those in the set J). If short sales are allowed, this constraint could be modified to $x_j^{\mathrm{inf}} \leq |x_j| \leq x_j^{\mathrm{sup}}$. K_{inf} and K_{sup} are cardinality constraints which set a minimum and maximum number of assets to be in J. There may be restrictions on transaction costs (in any functional form) or turnover, lot size constraints (i.e., restrictions on the multiples of assets that can be traded), and exposure limits. We may also add constraints that, under certain market conditions, the portfolio needs to behave in a certain way (usually give a required minimum return).

Similar to this framework are index-tracking problems. Here investors try to replicate a predefined benchmark; see, for example, Gilli and Këllezi (2002). This benchmark need not be a passive equity index. In the last few years, for instance, there have been attempts to replicate the returns of hedge funds; see Lo (2008).

Applying alternative risk measures generally necessitates using the empirical distribution of returns. (There is little advantage in minimizing kurtosis when stock returns are modeled by a Brownian motion.) The resulting optimization problem cannot be solved with classical methods (except for special cases like mean–variance optimization). To give an example, Fig. 10.1 shows the search space, that is, the values of the objective function that particular solutions map into, for a problem where f is the portfolio's Value-at-Risk. The resulting surface is not convex and not smooth. Any search that requires a globally convex model, like a gradient-based method, will stop at the first local minimum encountered, if it arrives there at all.

For some objective functions, the optimization problem can be reformulated to be solved with classical methods; examples are Gaivoronski and Pflug (2005) or Rockafellar and Uryasev (2000); Chekhlov, Uryasev, and Zabarankin (2005). But such solutions are problem specific and do not

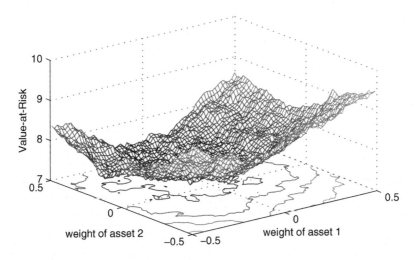

Figure 10.1 Objective function for Value-at-Risk.

accommodate changes in the model formulation. How to use heuristics for portfolio selection will be discussed more thoroughly in Chapter 13.

Model selection

Linear regression is a widely used technique in finance. A common application are factor models where the returns of single assets are described as functions of other variables. Then

$$r = \begin{bmatrix} F_1 & \cdots & F_k \end{bmatrix} \begin{bmatrix} \beta_1 \\ \vdots \\ \beta_k \end{bmatrix} + \epsilon \tag{10.1}$$

with r being a vector of returns for a given asset, F_i are the vectors of factor realizations, β are the factor loadings, and ϵ captures the remaining variation. Such models are widely applied for instance to construct variance–covariance matrices or in attempts to forecast future returns. The factors F may be macroeconomic quantities or firm specific characteristics; alternatively, the analyst may use statistical factors, for instance extracted by principal component analysis. In practice, observable factors are often preferred since they are easier to interpret and to explain to clients. Given the vast amounts of financial data available, these factors may have to be picked from hundreds or thousands of available variables, in particular, since we may also consider lagged variables (Maringer, 2004). Model selection becomes a critical issue, as we often wish to use only a small number k of regressors from K possible ones, with $K \gg k$. We could use an information criterion, which penalizes additional regressors, as the objective function; alternatively, techniques like cross-validation can be applied or the problem can be formulated as an in-sample fit maximization under the restriction that k is not greater than a (small) fixed number.

Robust/resistant regression

Empirical evidence over the last decades has shown that the Capital Asset Pricing Model (CAPM) explains asset returns in the cross-section rather badly (Fama and French, 1993, 2004). However, when we re-interpret the CAPM as a one-factor model (Luenberger, 1998, Chapter 8), the β estimates become useful measures of a stock's general correlation with the market, which may be used to construct variance–covariance matrices (Chan, Karceski, and Lakonishok, 1999).

The standard method to obtain parameter estimates in a linear regression is Least Squares. Least Squares has appealing theoretical and practical (numerical) properties, but obtained estimates are often unstable in the presence of extreme observations which are common in financial time series

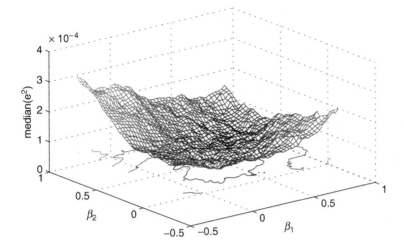

Figure 10.2 LMS objective function.

(Chan and Lakonishok, 1992; Knez and Ready, 1997; Genton and Ronchetti, 2008). Some earlier contributions in the finance literature suggested some form of shrinkage of extreme β estimates towards more reasonable levels, with different theoretical justifications (see for example Blume, 1971, or Vasicek, 1973). Alternatively, the use of robust or resistant estimation methods to obtain the regression parameters has been proposed (Chan and Lakonishok, 1992; Martin and Simin, 2003). Among possible regression criteria, high breakdown point estimators are often regarded as desirable. The breakdown point of an estimator is the smallest percentage of outliers that may cause the estimator to be affected by a bias. The Least Median of Squares (LMS) estimator, suggested by Rousseeuw (1984), ranks highly in this regard, as its breakdown point is 50%. (Note that Least Squares may equivalently be called Least Mean of Squares.)

Unfortunately, LMS regression leads to nonconvex optimization models, a particular search space for the simple model $y = \beta_1 + \beta_2 x + \epsilon$ is shown in Fig. 10.2. Estimation will be discussed in Chapter 14.

Agent-based models

Agent-based models (ABM) abandon the attempt to model markets and financial decisions with one representative agent (Kirman, 1992). This results in models that quickly become analytically intractable, hence researchers rely on computer simulations to obtain results. ABM are capable of producing many of the "stylized facts" actually observed in financial markets like volatility clustering, jumps or fat tails. For overviews on ABM in finance, see, for example, LeBaron (2000, 2006); see also Section 8.8.

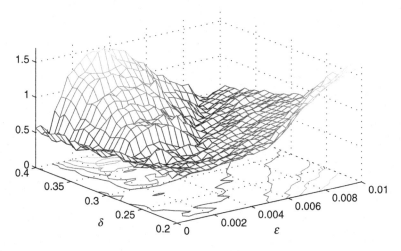

Figure 10.3 Simulated objective function for Kirman's model for two parameters.

Unfortunately, the conclusion of many studies stops at asserting that these models can in principle produce realistic market behavior when parameters (like preferences of agents) are specified appropriately. This leads to the question what appropriate values should be like, and how different models compare with one another when it comes to explaining market facts.

Gilli and Winker (2003) suggest estimating the parameters of such models by indirect inference. This requires an auxiliary model that can easily be estimated, which in their case is simply a combination of several moments of the actual price data. A given set of parameters for the ABM is evaluated by measuring the distance between the average realized moments of the simulated series and the moments obtained from real data. This distance is then to be minimized by adjusting the parameters of the ABM. Winker, Gilli, and Jeleskovic (2007) provide a more detailed analysis of objective functions for such problems.

Fig. 10.3 shows the resulting search space for a particular ABM (see Kirman, 1993). The objective function does not seem too irregular at all, but since the function was evaluated by a stochastic simulation of the model, it is noisy and does not allow for the application of classical methods.

Calibration of option-pricing models

Prices of options and other derivatives are modeled as functions of the underlying securities' characteristics (Madan, 2001). Parameter values for such models are often obtained by solving inverse problems, that is, we try to obtain parameter values for which the model gives prices that are close to actual market prices. In case of the Black–Scholes model, only one parameter, volatility, needs to be specified, which can be done efficiently with Newton's method (Manaster and Koehler, 1982). More recent option-pricing models (see, for instance, Bakshi, Cao, and Chen, 1997, or Bates, 2003) aim to generate prices that are consistent with the empirically observed implied volatility surface (Cont and da Fonseca, 2002). Calibrating these models requires setting more parameters, which leads to more difficult optimization problems.

One particular pricing model is that of Heston (1993); it is popular since it gives closed-form solutions. "Closed-form" is somewhat deceiving: pricing still requires numerical integration of a complex-valued function. Under the Heston model, the stock price (S) and variance (v) dynamics are described by

$$dS_t = rS_t dt + \sqrt{v_t} S_t dW_t^1$$

$$dv_t = \kappa(\theta - v_t)dt + \sigma\sqrt{v_t}dW_t^2$$

where the two Brownian motion processes are correlated, that is, $dW_t^1 dW_t^2 = \rho dt$. As can be seen from the second equation, volatility is mean-reverting to its long-run level θ with speed κ in the Heston model. In total, the model requires (under the risk-neutral measure) the specification of five parameters (Mikhailov and Nögel, 2003). Even though some of these parameters could be estimated from the time series of the underlying, the general approach to fit the model is to minimize the differences between the theoretical and observed prices. A possible objective function is, hence,

$$\min \sum_{n=1}^{N} w_n (C_n^H - C_n^M)^2$$

where N is the number of option quotes available, C^H and C^M are the theoretical and actual option prices, respectively, and w are weights (Hamida and Cont, 2005). Sometimes the optimization model also includes parameter restrictions, for example to enforce the parameters to be such that the volatility cannot become negative.

Fig. 10.4 shows the resulting objective function values for two parameters (volatility of volatility and mean-reversion speed) with the remaining parameters fixed. As can be seen, in certain parts of the parameter domain the resulting objective function is not too well behaved, hence standard methods may not find the global minimum. The Heston model is discussed in Chapter 15.

Calibration of yield structure models

The model of Nelson and Siegel (1987) and its extended version, introduced by Svensson (1994), are widely used to approximate the term structure of interest rates. Many central banks use the models to represent the spot

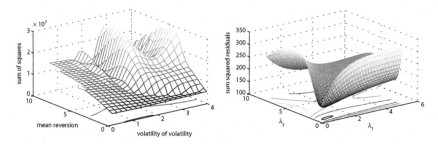

Figure 10.4 Left panel: Heston model objective function. Right panel: Nelson–Siegel–Svensson model objective function.

and forward rates as functions of time to maturity; in several studies (e.g., Diebold and Li, 2006) the models have also been used for forecasting interest rates.

Let $y_t(\tau)$ be the yield of a zero-coupon bond with maturity τ at time t, then the Nelson–Siegel model describes the zero rates as

$$y_t(\tau) = \beta_{1,t} + \beta_{2,t}\left[\frac{1 - \exp(-\gamma_t)}{\gamma_t}\right] + \beta_{3,t}\left[\frac{1 - \exp(-\gamma_t)}{\gamma_t} - \exp(-\gamma_t)\right]$$
$$(10.2)$$

where $\gamma_t = \tau/\lambda_t$. The Svensson version is given by

$$y_t(\tau) = \beta_{1,t} + \beta_{2,t}\left[\frac{1 - \exp(-\gamma_{1,t})}{\gamma_{1,t}}\right] + \qquad\qquad (10.3)$$

$$\beta_{3,t}\left[\frac{1 - \exp(-\gamma_{1,t})}{\gamma_{1,t}} - \exp(-\gamma_{1,t})\right] + \beta_{4,t}\left[\frac{1 - \exp(-\gamma_{2,t})}{\gamma_{2,t}} - \exp(-\gamma_{2,t})\right]$$

where $\gamma_{1,t} = \tau/\lambda_{1,t}$ and $\gamma_{2,t} = \tau/\lambda_{2,t}$. The parameters of the models (β and λ) can be estimated by minimizing the difference between the model rates y_t and observed rates y_t^M where the superscript stands for "market." An optimization problem could be stated as

$$\min_{\beta,\lambda} \sum \left(y_t - y_t^M\right)^2$$

subject to constraints. We need to estimate four parameters for model (10.2), and six for model (10.3). Again, this optimization problem is not convex; an example for a search space is given in Fig. 10.4. The calibration of the Nelson–Siegel model and Svensson's extension is discussed in more detail in Chapter 14.

10.5. Summary

In this chapter, we have tried to motivate the application of optimization models in finance. The coming chapters will demonstrate how to solve such models. In Chapter 11, we will discuss classical methods: methods for zero-finding and gradient-based methods. In Chapter 12, we will give a brief introduction to heuristic methods. The emphasis of that chapter will be on principles, not on details. Later chapters will then discuss the process of solving particular problems with heuristics.

## CHAPTER ELEVEN

Basic methods

This chapter is about classic methods for unconstrained optimization, including the special case of nonlinear Least Squares. Optimization is also related to finding the zeros of a function; thus, the solution of nonlinear systems of equations is also part of this chapter. A variety of approaches is considered, depending on whether we are in a one-dimensional setting or we solve problems in higher dimensions. To enhance the clarity of the presentation, Fig. 11.1 shows a diagram that might help to structure the problems discussed in this chapter. Among the general unconstrained optimization problems, we distinguish the one-dimensional case (1-D) and the n-dimensional case (n-D), and within each category, we distinguish between gradient-based and direct search methods. In Fig. 11.1, the solution of a linear system $Ax = b$, presented in Chapter 3, is connected by dotted arrows to the methods where it constitutes a building block.

In order to gain insight and understanding of the workings of the methods presented, most algorithms have been coded and executed to solve illustrative examples. These codes are not meant to be state of the art. We indicate the corresponding functions provided in Matlab and briefly illustrate their use by solving some of the problems presented in the illustrations.

11.1. Finding the roots of $f(x) = 0$

11.1.1. A naïve approach

The problem consists in finding the value of x satisfying the equation

$$f(x) = 0.$$

The solution is called a zero of the function. Several solutions may exist.

A function like $1 - e^{-x} = 0.5$ can be put into the form $f(x) = 0$ by simply moving all terms to the left of the equality sign

$$1 - e^{-x} - 0.5 = 0.$$

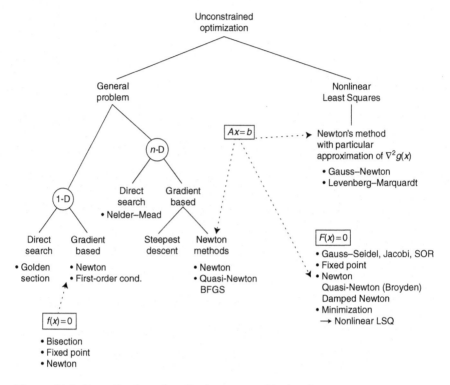

Figure 11.1 Synoptic view of methods presented in the chapter.

For this particular case, it is easy to find the (analytical) solution

$$x = -\log(0.5).$$

However, in practice, an analytical solution does not always exist or may be expensive to get. In these cases, we resort to numerical solutions. In the following, we discuss with a number of examples several numerical methods for finding the zeros of a function.

Graphical solution

Let us consider the expression $\left(1 + \frac{1}{n-1}\right)^x = x^n$ defined for $n > 1$. We want to find the zeros in the interval $x \in [x_L, x_U]$ by inspection of the plot of the function. This is done with the following Matlab code:

```
f = inline('(1 + 1/(P1-1)).^x - x.^P1',1);
xL = -2; xU = 5;
x = linspace(xL,xU);
plot(x,f(x,2));
```

In the function `inline`, P1 corresponds to the parameter n which has been set to 2. Note that f is coded using element-wise operations so that a vector can be used as an argument. From the plot, we can read that in the interval $[-2, 5]$ the function takes the value of zero for $x \approx -0.75$, $x \approx 2$, and $x \approx 4$.

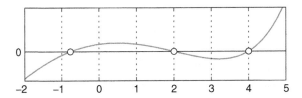

Random search

We randomly generate values for x and compute the corresponding value of $f(x)$. Given X, the set of generated values, the solution x^{sol}, is defined as

$$x^{\text{sol}} = \underset{x \in X}{\operatorname{argmin}} |f(x)|.$$

For the generation of the x we use the Matlab function rand, which generates uniform random variables in the interval $[0, 1]$. For given values of x_L, x_U, and a realization of the uniform random variable u, we generate x as

$$x = x_L + (x_U - x_L) u.$$

Evaluating the function $f(x)$ of the previous example for $R = 100,000$ randomly generated values of x in the interval $[-2, 5]$ we obtain the following results with a Matlab implementation for four executions:[1]

```
f = inline('(1+(1/(P1-1))).^x - x.^P1',1);
xL = -2; xU = 5; n = 2; R = 1e5;
rand('twister', 123456);
for k = 1:4
    x = xL + (xU - xL)*rand(R,1);   z = f(x,n);
    [sol,i] = min(abs(z));
    fprintf(' f(%9.6f) = %8.6f\n',x(i),sol);
end

 f(-0.766673) = 0.000015
 f( 3.999999) = 0.000002
 f( 2.000028) = 0.000035
 f(-0.766670) = 0.000009
```

11.1.2. Bracketing

With this technique, we try to construct intervals likely to contain zeros. Later, the search can be refined for a given interval. We divide a given domain $[x_L, x_U]$ into regular intervals and examine whether the function crosses the

---

[1] The Matlab random generator has been initialized so that the same results can be reproduced. The option twister refers to the Mersenne Twister algorithm by Matsumoto and Nishimura (1998).

abscissa by checking the sign of the function evaluated at the borders of the interval. Algorithm 29 details the procedure.

Algorithm 29 Bracketing.

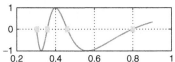

```
 1: initialize x_L, x_U and n
 2: Δ = (x_U − x_L)/n
 3: a = x_L
 4: for i = 1 : n do
 5:     b = a + Δ
 6:     if sign f(a) ≠ sign f(b) then
 7:         # may contain a zero, save [a,b]
 8:     end if
 9:     a = b
10: end for
```

The Matlab implementation is given hereafter.

Listing 11.1. C-BasicMethods/M/Bracketing.m

```
 1 function I = Bracketing(f,xL,xU,n)
 2 % Bracketing.m   version 2010-03-27
 3 delta = (xU - xL)/n;
 4 a   = xL;   k = 0; I = [];
 5 fa = feval(f,a);
 6 for i = 1:n
 7     b   = a + delta;
 8     fb  = feval(f,b);
 9     if sign(fa)~=sign(fb)
10         k = k + 1;
11         I(k,:) = [a b];
12     end
13     a   = b;   fa = fb;
14 end
```

Example for bracketing zeros of the function $g(x) = \cos(1/x^2)$ in the domain $x \in [0.3, 0.9]$ with $n = 25$ intervals.

```
f = inline('cos(1./x.^2)');
I = Bracketing(f,0.3,0.9,25)
I =
    0.3000    0.3240
    0.3480    0.3720
    0.4440    0.4680
    0.7800    0.8040
```

11.1.3. Bisection

The method of bisection seeks the zero of a function in a given interval $[a, b]$ by halving the interval and identifying the semi-interval containing the zero. The procedure is reiterated until a sufficiently small interval is reached (see Algorithm 30).

Algorithm 30 Bisection.

```
 1: define error tolerance η
 2: if sign f(a) = sign f(b) then stop
 3: while |a − b| > η do
 4:     c = a + (b − a)/2
 5:     if sign f(a) ≠ sign f(b) then
 6:         b = c        # (z left of c)
 7:     else
 8:         a = c        # (z right of c)
 9:     end if
10: end while
```

In Statement 4 the center of the interval is computed as $a + (b − a)/2$. This is numerically more stable than computing $(a + b)/2$ for large values of a and b. The Matlab implementation follows.

Listing 11.2. C-BasicMethods/M/Bisection.m

```
 1 function c = Bisection(f,a,b,tol)
 2 % Bisection.m  -- version 2005-05-25
 3 % Zero finding with bisection method
 4 if nargin == 3, tol = 1e-8; end
 5 fa = feval(f,a); fb = feval(f,b);
 6 if sign(fa) == sign(fb)
 7     error('sign f(a) is not opposite of sign f(b)');
 8 end
 9 done = 0;
10 while abs(b-a) > 2*tol & ~done
11     c = a + (b - a) / 2;
12     fc = feval(f,c);
13     if sign(fa) ~= sign(fc)
14         b  = c;
15         fb = fc;
16     elseif sign(fc) ~= sign(fb)
17         a  = c;
18         fa = fc;
19     else          % center and zero coincide
20         done = 1;
21     end
22 end
```

Hereafter, we use the bisection method to compute the zeros for the intervals identified previously with the bracketing method.

```
f = inline('cos(1./x.^2)');
I = Bracketing(f,0.3,0.9,25);
for i = 1:size(I,1)
    z(i) = Bisection(f,I(i,1),I(i,2));
end

z =
    0.3016    0.3568    0.4607    0.7979
```

11.1.4. Fixed point method

Given $f(x) = 0$, we reorganize the expression of the function in the following way

$$x = g(x), \qquad (11.1)$$

where g is called the iteration function. Inserting a starting value x^{old} in g we can compute a new value $x^{\text{new}} = g(x^{\text{old}})$. Repeating the procedure generates a sequence $\{x^{(k)}\}_{k=0,1,...}$. This defines the fixed point iteration which is formalized in Algorithm 31.

Algorithm 31 Fixed point iteration.

1: initialize starting value $x^{(0)}$
2: **for** $k = 1, 2, \ldots$ until convergence **do**
3:     $x^{(k)} = g(x^{(k-1)})$
4: **end for**

Before discussing the convergence in more detail a few remarks: The complete sequence of values of x needs not to be stored, as only two successive elements are used in the algorithm.

---

initialize starting value $x0$
while not converged **do**
    $x1 = g(x0)$
    $x0 = x1$
end while

The solution satisfies the iteration function $x^{\text{sol}} = g(x^{\text{sol}})$ and is, therefore, also called a fixed point as the sequence remains constant from that point on. The choice of the iteration function $g(x)$ determines the convergence of the method. An implementation with Matlab is given hereafter, and we discuss the method by solving two problems.

Listing 11.3. C-BasicMethods/M/FPI.m

```
 1 function x1 = FPI(f,x1,tol)
 2 % FPI.m  -- version 2008-05-08
 3 % FPI(f,x0)  Fixed point iteration
 4 if nargin == 2, tol = 1e-6; end
 5 it = 0; itmax = 200; x0 = realmax;
 6 while ~converged(x0,x1,tol)
 7     x0 = x1;
 8     x1 = feval(f,x0);
 9     it = it + 1;
10     if it > itmax, error('Maxit in FPI'); end
11 end
```

We consider the function $x - x^{7/5} + 1/5 = 0$ and the corresponding two iteration functions

$$g_1(x) = x^{7/5} - 1/5 \qquad g_2(x) = (x + 1/5)^{5/7}.$$

We first use iteration function g_1 with starting value $x0 = 1.2$ and observe that the solution does not converge, and then we use g_2 with starting value $x0 = 0.2$ for which we get a solution.

```
g1 = inline('x.^(7/5)-1/5');
z = FPI(g1,1.2)

??? Error using ==> FPI at 11
Maxit in FPI

z  = FPI(g1,1.6)

??? Error using ==> FPI at 11
Maxit in FPI

g2 = inline('(x+1/5).^(5/7)');
z = FPI(g2,0.2)
z =
    1.3972

z = FPI(g2,2.4)
z =
    1.3972
```

Figure 11.2 plots the iteration functions, g_1 in the left panel and g_2 in the right panel. For g_1, the divergence is also observed for a starting value of 1.6, whereas g_2 converges also for a starting value of 2.4. From this graph we already see, what will be formalized below, that convergence is linked to the slope of the iteration function. For g_1, this slope is greater than 1, and for g_2, it is smaller than 1 (the slope of the bisectrix is 1).

Now, we consider another function $x - 2x^{3/5} + 2/3 = 0$ and the iteration functions

$$g_3(x) = 2x^{3/5} - 2/3 \qquad g_4(x) = \left(\frac{x + 2/3}{2}\right)^{5/3}.$$

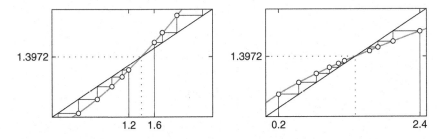

Figure 11.2 Left panel: iteration function g_1. Right panel: iteration function g_2.

First, we explore the function values for the interval $x \in [0,8]$ with our bracketing algorithm and, then, we apply the fixed point method.

```
f = inline('x-2*(x).^(3/5)+2/3');
I = Bracketing(f,0,8,10)
I =
          0     0.8000
     3.2000     4.0000

g3 = inline('2*x.^(3/5)-2/3');
z = FPI(g3,0.6)
z =
     3.7623

z = FPI(g3,4.8)
z =
     3.7623

z = FPI(g4,0)
z =
     3.7623

z = FPI(g4,3)
z =
     3.7623
```

The two solutions can be seen in Fig. 11.3, in which, for the iteration function g_3 and a starting value of 0.6, we diverge from the solution to the left (0.2952) because the slope is greater than 1 and evolve toward the second solution (3.7623). For g_4 when starting from 3, we move away from the nearest solution and evolve toward 0.2952. We see how this behavior depends on the local value of the slope of the iteration functions.

Convergence

A necessary condition for a fixed point method to converge for $x \in [a,b]$ is that the interval contains a zero and that the derivative of the iteration function satisfies

$$|g'(x)| < 1 \quad \text{for} \quad x \in [a,b].$$

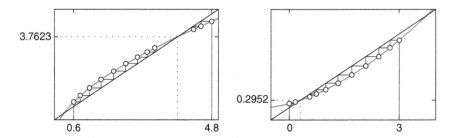

Figure 11.3 Left panel: iteration function g_3. Right panel: iteration function g_4.

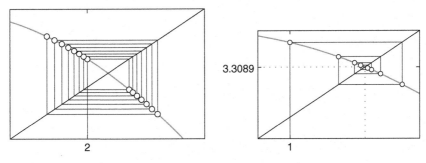

Figure 11.4 Left panel: iteration function satisfies $g'(x) < -1$. Right panel: iteration function satisfies $-1 < g'(x) < 0$.

As already pointed out before, Fig. 11.2 gives a graphical illustration of this condition: in the left panel, we observe that g_1 is steeper than the bisectrix and the iterations diverge, whereas in the right panel, the slope of g_2 is less than 1 and the iterations converge.

The convergence condition is necessary for local convergence. Nevertheless, starting from a point not satisfying the convergence condition the iterations can move into a region where convergence takes place. This is illustrated in Fig. 11.3 where, starting from $x = 0.6$ in the left panel and $x = 3$ in the right panel, values for which $g'(x) > 1$, we converge. In both cases we first diverge from the nearest solution and then move to another solution located in a region of convergence.

Finally, in Fig. 11.4, we see that for $g'(x) < 0$, the iterations oscillate, they converge for $-1 < g'(x) < 0$ (right panel), and diverge for $g'(x) < -1$ (left panel).

We see that according to the value of the derivative, an iteration function may, for a specific interval, converge or diverge.

Example 11.1

The S-estimator is among the solutions proposed in high breakdown point regression estimation.[2] Its estimation involves finding the zero of a nonlinear function.[3] The fixed point method is quite appropriate to solve this problem, and we illustrate an implementation with Matlab.

Consider the linear regression model

$$y_i = \begin{bmatrix} x_{i1} & \cdots & x_{ip} \end{bmatrix} \begin{bmatrix} \theta_1 \\ \vdots \\ \theta_p \end{bmatrix} + u_i \qquad i = 1, \ldots, n,$$

---

[2] Examples with the LMS and LTS estimator are discussed in Section 14.2.
[3] See Marazzi (1992) and Ruppert (1992).

where $\theta \in \mathbb{R}^p$ are the parameters to be estimated and $u \sim N(0, \sigma^2 I)$ is white noise. The residuals are $r_i = y_i - x_{i,\bullet} \theta$ and the S-estimator is defined as

$$\hat{\theta}_S = \underset{\theta}{\arg\min}\, S(\theta), \tag{11.2}$$

where $S(\theta)$ is the solution of

$$\frac{1}{n-p} \sum_{i=1}^{n} \rho\left(\frac{r_i}{S}\right) = \beta. \tag{11.3}$$

ρ is a weighting function, with $k = 1.58$ a given constant, and is defined as

$$\rho_k(s) = \begin{cases} 3\,(s/k)^2 - 3\,(s/k)^4 + (s/k)^6 & \text{if } |s| \le k \\ 1 & \text{if } |s| > k \end{cases},$$

and β is a constant computed as

$$\beta = \int_{-\infty}^{\infty} \rho_k(s)\, \mathrm{d}\phi(s)$$

with $\phi(s)$ being the standard normal distribution. The left panel in Fig. 11.5 shows the shape of the function ρ_k, and we see that the constant k determines the limits beyond which the weights are equal to 1. The vector ρ_k is computed with the function Rho.m. Note that k is set in the code, and the way the powers of s/k are computed is about six times faster than coding exponents. This is important as the function will be called many times as the fixed point algorithm is nested in the optimization procedure that successively evaluates $S(\theta)$ in the search for $\hat{\theta}_S$.

Listing 11.4. C-BasicMethods/M/Rho.m

```
 1  function F = Rho(s)
 2  % Rho.m  -- version 2010-11-12
 3  k = 1.58;
 4  F = ones(length(s),1);
 5  I = (abs(s) <= k);
 6  temp1 = s(I)/k;
 7  temp2 = temp1 .* temp1;
 8  temp4 = temp2 .* temp2;
 9  temp6 = temp4 .* temp2;
10  F(I) = 3*temp2 - 3*temp4 + temp6;
```

To compute β, we have to evaluate the integral of the product of ρ_k times the standard normal density. As this density rapidly tends to zero, it is sufficient to integrate from -5 to 5. This can also be verified in Fig. 11.5 in which the right panel shows the graph of $\rho_k(s)\,\phi(s)$. We computed $\beta = 0.4919$ using the Matlab function quad for the integration.

```
b = quad('RhoN',-5,5)

b =
    0.4919
```

Listing 11.5. C-BasicMethods/M/RhoN.m

```
 1  function F = RhoN(s)
 2  % RhoN.m  -- version 2010-11-12
 3  d = exp(-0.5 * s.^2) ./ sqrt(2*pi);
 4  F = Rho(s) .* d';
```

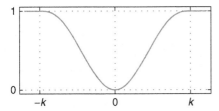 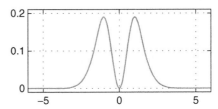

Figure 11.5 Shape of function ρ_k (left panel) and shape of function $\rho_k(s)\phi(s)$ (right panel).

The iteration function is then derived by dividing Eq. (11.3) by β

$$\frac{1}{(n-p)\beta} \sum_{i=1}^{n} \rho\left(\frac{r_i}{S}\right) = 1,$$

multiplying the result by S^2,

$$\frac{S^2}{(n-p)\beta} \sum_{i=1}^{n} \rho\left(\frac{r_i}{S}\right) = S^2,$$

and taking the square root,

$$S = \sqrt{\frac{S^2}{(n-p)\beta} \sum_{i=1}^{n} \rho\left(\frac{r_i}{S}\right)}. \tag{11.4}$$

The solution method is now tested on a small data set taken from Brown and Hollander (1977). First, we only seek S that solves Eq. (11.3) for one given residual vector r.

```
load BrHo.dat % read Brown and Hollander (1977) data

[n,p] = size(BrHo);
y = BrHo(:,2); X = [ones(n,1) BrHo(:,1)];
theta0 = X \ y;   % compute OLS estimate
r = y - X*theta0;
b = 0.4919; c = (n - p) * b;
S0 = median(abs(r)) / b;   % starting value
S1 = FPIS(S0,r,c)


S1 =
   13.6782
```

To complete the exercise, we can think of solving the optimization problem defined in Eq. (11.2). For simplicity, we chose the Nelder–Mead direct search method[4] explained in Section 11.4.4. The Matlab code below calls the fminsearch function which performs the Nelder–Mead search. We note the improvement of the value of S with respect to the initial value obtained before.

```
load BrHo.dat % read Brown Hollander (1977) data
[n,p] = size(BrHo);
y = BrHo(:,2); X = [ones(n,1) BrHo(:,1)];
```

---

[4] There exist specific methods to solve this problem efficiently, see Marazzi (1992) and Salibian-Barrera and Yohai (2006).

```
options = optimset('fminsearch');
theta0 = X \ y ; b = 0.4919; p = size(X,2); c = (n - p) * b;
[theta, S, flag] = fminsearch('OF',theta0,options,y,X,b,c)


theta =
    81.8138
    28.5164
S =
    12.5412
flag =
     1
```

Listing 11.6. C-BasicMethods/M/OF.m

```
1 function F = OF(theta,y,X,b,c)
2 % OF.m  -- version 2010-11-11
3 r  = y - X*theta;
4 S0 = median(abs(r)) / b;
5 F  = FPIS(S0,r,c);
```

11.1.5. Newton's method

Newton's method is derived from the Taylor expansion of a function f in the neighborhood of x,

$$f(x + \triangle_x) = f(x) + \triangle_x f'(x) + R(x).$$

Ignoring the remainder $R(x)$, we seek the step $\triangle_x$ for which we have $f(x + \triangle_x) = 0$

$$f(\underbrace{x_{k+1}}_{x+\triangle_x}) \approx f(x_k) + \underbrace{(x_{k+1} - x_k)}_{\triangle_x} f'(x) = 0$$

from which we can compute the step s from x_k to x_{k+1}, improving the approximation of the zero of f (Algorithm 32):

$$x_{k+1} = x_k - \underbrace{\frac{f(x_k)}{f'(x_k)}}_{s}.$$

Algorithm 32 Newton's method for zero finding.

1: initialize starting value x_0

2: **for** $k = 0,1,2,\ldots$ until convergence **do**

3:   compute $f(x_k)$ and $f'(x_k)$

4:   $s = -\frac{f(x_k)}{f'(x_k)}$

5:   $x_{k+1} = x_k + s$

6: **end for**

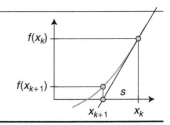

In the following, we give an implementation with Matlab in which the derivative is approximated numerically.

Listing 11.7. C-BasicMethods/M/Newton0.m

```
1  function x1 = Newton0(f,x1,tol)
2  % Newton0.m  -- version  2010-03-30
3  % Newton method with numerical derivation
4  if nargin == 2, tol = 1e-8; end
5  it = 0; itmax = 10; x0 = realmax; h = 1e-8;
6  while ~converged(x0,x1,tol)
7      x0 = x1;
8      f0 = feval(f,x0);
9      f1 = feval(f,x0 + h);
10     df = (f1 - f0) / h;
11     x1 = x0 - f0/df;
12     it = it + 1;
13     if it > itmax, error('Maxit in Newton0'); end
14 end
```

The working of Newton's method is illustrated in Fig. 11.6 in which we seek zeros for the function $f(x) = e^{-x}\log(x) - x^2 + x^3/3 + 1$ for different starting values $x0 = 2.750, 0.805, 0.863,$ and 1.915. Note that using a numerical approximation instead of the analytical derivative will have little influence on our results.

```
f = inline('exp(-x).*log(x)-x.^2+x.^3/3+1');
z1 = Newton0(f,2.750)
z1 =
    2.4712
```

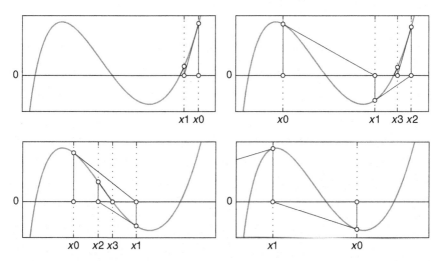

Figure 11.6 Behavior of the Newton method for different starting values. Upper left: $x0 = 2.750$ and $x^{\text{sol}} = 2.4712$. Upper right: $x0 = 0.805$ and $x^{\text{sol}} = 2.4712$. Lower left: $x0 = 0.863$ and $x^{\text{sol}} = 1.4512$. Lower right: $x0 = 1.915$ and algorithm diverges.

```
z2 = Newton0(f,0.805)
z2 =
    2.4712
z3 = Newton0(f,0.863)
z3 =
    1.4512
z4 = Newton0(f,1.915)

??? Error using ==> Newton0 at 13
Maxit in Newton0
```

Comments

The choice of a particular method may depend on the application. For instance, the method of bisection needs an interval and may, therefore, be considered more robust. For the fixed point and Newton's method the convergence depends on the starting value, and a value close to a zero does not necessarily drive the algorithm to this solution (e.g., see Fig. 11.3 where in the left panel, $x0 = 0.6$ goes to $x^{sol} = 3.7623$ and not to the closer solution 0.2952).

Note that for finding the roots of a polynomial, there exist specific algorithms which resort to the computation of the eigenvalues of the so-called companion matrix.

In Matlab, the function dedicated to finding the zeros of a function is fzero. Below we compute the zeros of the function for the illustration of Newton's method and use the same starting values we did before. We observe that the algorithm produces the same result only for the first starting value and converges to different solutions for the remaining ones. The default options for fzero are initialized with the function optimset.

```
f = inline('exp(-x).*log(x)-x.^2+x.^3/3+1');
options = optimset('fzero');
z1 = fzero(f,2.750);
z2 = fzero(f,0.805);
z3 = fzero(f,0.863);
z4 = fzero(f,1.915);
disp([z1 z2 z3 z4])

    2.4712    0.2907    0.2907    1.4512
```

These default options can be overwritten with the function optimset. Below we modify the tolerance for the convergence and display the complete list of output arguments computed by fzero.

```
options = optimset(options,'TolFun',1e-3);
[x,fval,exitflag,output] = fzero(f,2.750,options)

x =
    2.4712
fval =
   -8.8818e-016
```

```
exitflag =
     1
output =
     intervaliterations: 5
              iterations: 6
               funcCount: 16
               algorithm: 'bisection, interpolation'
                 message: [1x42 char]
```

11.2. Classical unconstrained optimization

We consider the (mathematical) problem of finding for a function $f : \mathbb{R}^n \rightarrow \mathbb{R}$ of several variables the argument that corresponds to a minimal function value

$$x^* = \underset{x \in \mathbb{R}^n}{\operatorname{argmin}} f(x).$$

The function f is called the objective function, and x^* is the solution (minimizer). The function f is assumed to be twice-continuously differentiable. The solution $x^* \in X$ is a global minimizer of f if $f(x^*) \le f(x) \; \forall x \in X$, where X is the feasible region or constraint set. If $\exists \delta > 0 \,|\, f(x^*) \le f(x) \, \forall x \in X \cap \mathbb{B}(x^*, \delta)$, x^* is called a local minimizer. In this latter case, the function is minimal within a region $\mathbb{B}$ as defined. Local and global minimizers as well as a saddle point are illustrated in the following figure.

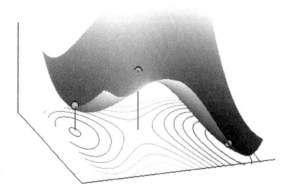

Typically, an optimization problem is unconstrained if $X = \mathbb{R}^n$ and constrained if X is described by a set of equality (E) and inequality (I) constraints:

$$X = \left\{ x \in \mathbb{R}^n \mid c_i(x) = 0 \text{ for } i \in E \quad \text{and} \quad c_i(x) \ge 0 \text{ for } i \in I \right\}.$$

A maximization problem can easily be reformulated into a minimization problem by changing the sign of the objective function.

Optimization problems come in many different flavors, and the following criteria could be used for classification: number of variables, number of constraints, properties of the objective function (linear, quadratic, nonlinear, convex, ...), and properties of the feasibility region or constraints (convex, only linear or inequality constraints, linear or nonlinear constraints, ...).

For optimization problems with a particular structure, specific algorithms have been developed taking advantage of this structure. Below is a short list of optimization problems with special structure.

- Linear programming: $f(x)$ and $c_i(x)$ are linear.
- Quadratic programming: $f(x)$ is quadratic and $c_i(x)$ are linear.
- Convex programming: $f(x)$ is convex and the set X is convex.
- Nonlinear Least Squares: $f(x) = \frac{1}{2}\sum_{j=1}^{n} f_j^2(x)$ and $X = \mathbb{R}^n$.
- Bound-constrained optimization: $\ell_i \le x_i \le u_i$.
- Network optimization: objective function and constraints have a special structure arising from a graph.

In the following, the gradient $\nabla f(x)$ of $f(x)$, $x \in \mathbb{R}^n$, and the Hessian matrix $\{\nabla^2 f(x)\}_{ij} = \frac{\partial^2 f(x)}{\partial x_i \partial x_j}$ is denoted, respectively:

$$
\nabla f(x) = \begin{bmatrix} \frac{\partial f}{\partial x_1} \\ \vdots \\ \frac{\partial f}{\partial x_n} \end{bmatrix} \quad \text{and} \quad \nabla^2 f(x) = \begin{bmatrix} \frac{\partial^2 f(x)}{\partial x_1^2} & \frac{\partial^2 f(x)}{\partial x_1 \partial x_2} & \cdots & \frac{\partial^2 f(x)}{\partial x_1 \partial x_n} \\ \frac{\partial^2 f(x)}{\partial x_2 \partial x_1} & \frac{\partial^2 f(x)}{\partial x_2^2} & \cdots & \frac{\partial^2 f(x)}{\partial x_2 \partial x_n} \\ \vdots & \vdots & \ddots & \vdots \\ \frac{\partial^2 f(x)}{\partial x_n \partial x_1} & \frac{\partial^2 f(x)}{\partial x_n \partial x_2} & \cdots & \frac{\partial^2 f(x)}{\partial x_n^2} \end{bmatrix}.
$$

Convergence

The algorithms in the following presentation are iterative procedures, and the speed with which they approach the solution is expressed as the convergence rate defined by the magnitude of the exponent r in the expression,

$$
\lim_{k \to \infty} \frac{\|e^{(k+1)}\|}{\|e^{(k)}\|^r} = c,
$$

where $e^{(k)}$ is the error at iteration k and c is a finite constant. The following situations are distinguished:

- $r = 1$ and $c < 1$, linear convergence
- $r > 1$, superlinear convergence
- $r = 2$, quadratic convergence

In practice, this corresponds to a gain in precision per iteration that is a constant number of digits for linear convergence; the increment of precise digits increases from iteration to iteration for the superlinear convergence and, in the case of quadratic convergence, the precision doubles with every iteration.

Conditions for local minimizer

The Taylor expansion at a local minimizer x^* is

$$f(\underbrace{x^* + z}_{x}) = f(x^*) + \underbrace{\nabla f(x^*)' z}_{C1} + \frac{1}{2} \underbrace{z' \nabla^2 f(x^* + \xi) z}_{C2}$$

with $\xi \in [0, 1]$. The sufficient conditions for a local minimizer are then given by the first-order conditions (C1)

$$\nabla f(x^*) = 0,$$

that is, the gradient has to be zero, and the second-order conditions (C2)

$$z' \nabla^2 f(x^*) z \geq 0 \qquad \forall z \in \mathbb{R}^n,$$

that is, the Hessian matrix must be positive-definite. If the latter is not the case, x^* is a saddle point. The problem is closely related to solving nonlinear equations $F(x) = 0$, where $F(x)$ corresponds to $\nabla f(x)$.

Classification of methods

We distinguish two categories of methods for solving the unconstrained optimization problems:
- Gradient-based methods
  - Steepest descent
  - Newton's method
- Direct search methods
  - Golden section method (one dimension)
  - Simplex method (Nelder–Mead)

Direct search can be defined as follows:
- The method uses only objective function evaluations to determine a search direction.
- The method does not model the objective function or its derivatives to derive a search direction or a step size; in particular, it does not use finite differences.

This definition loosely follows Wright (1996).

11.3. Unconstrained optimization in one dimension

Steepest descent has no meaning in one dimension.

11.3.1. Newton's method

For a given value of x, Newton's method approximates the function by a local model which is a quadratic function. The local model is derived from the truncated second-order Taylor series expansion of the objective function

$$\underbrace{f(x+h) \approx f(x) + f'(x)\,h + \frac{1}{2}f''(x)\,h^2.}_{\text{local model}}$$

We then establish the first-order conditions $\partial f(x+h)/\partial h = 0$ for the minimum of the local model

$$f'(x) + h\,f''(x) = 0$$

from which we derive that h has its minimum for $h = -\frac{f'(x)}{f''(x)}$, suggesting the iteration scheme[5]

$$x^{(k+1)} = x^{(k)} - \frac{f'(x)}{f''(x)}.$$

Algorithm 33 resumes Newton's method for unconstrained optimization of a function in one dimension.

Algorithm 33 Newton's method for unconstrained optimization.

1: initialize $x^{(0)}$ (close to the minimum)
2: **for** $k = 0,1,2,\dots$ until convergence **do**
3:     compute $f'(x^{(k)})$ and $f''(x^{(k)})$
4:     $x^{(k+1)} = x^{(k)} - \frac{f'(x)}{f''(x)}$
5: **end for**

As an example, we consider the function

$$f(x) = 1 - \log(x)\,e^{-x^2},$$

where the first- and second-order derivatives, respectively, are

$$f'(x) = -(e^{-x^2}/x) + 2\log(x)\,x\,e^{-x^2},$$

$$f''(x) = (e^{-x^2}/x^2) + 4e^{-x^2} + 2\log(x)\,e^{-x^2} - 4\log(x)\,x^2 e^{-x^2}.$$

In order to draw the local model (only for illustration purposes)

$$f(x^{(0)} + h) = f(x^{(0)}) + f'(x^{(0)})\,h + \frac{1}{2}f''(x^{(0)})\,h^2,$$

we have to replace the expressions for the first- and second-order derivatives and the value for $x^{(0)}$, the point where the local model is constructed. This leads to a rather lengthy expression not reproduced here. In practice, the length h of the step to the minimum is easy to compute. In the following figures, we draw the local model (thin dark line) for two successive steps $x^{(0)}$ and $x^{(1)}$.

---

[5] We recognize that this corresponds to Newton's method for finding the zero of the function $f'(x) = 0$.

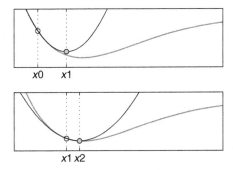

A starting point $x^{(0)}$ in a nonconvex region leads to a nonconvex local model and the computed step h goes to a maximum at $x^{(1)}$ instead of a minimum.

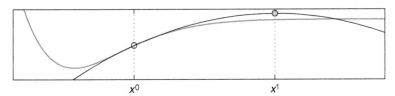

11.3.2. Golden section search

The method applies to a unimodal function $f(x)$ in the interval $x \in [a,b]$,

$$f(x) > f(x^*) \begin{cases} \text{if} & x < x^* \\ \text{if} & x > x^* \end{cases},$$

and searches the minimum by reducing the interval containing the minimum by a constant ratio[6] $\tau = \frac{\sqrt{5}-1}{2}$. Algorithm 34 details the procedure.

Algorithm 34   Golden section search.

1:   compute $x_1 = a + (1-\tau)(b-a)$ and $f_1 = f(x_1)$
2:   compute $x_2 = a + \tau(b-a)$ and $f_2 = f(x_2)$
3:   **while** $(b-a) > \eta$ **do**
4:     **if** $f_1 < f_2$ **then**
5:       $b = x_2$
6:       $x_2 = x_1$
7:       $f_2 = f_1$
8:       $x_1 = a + (1-\tau)(b-a)$
9:       $f_1 = f(x_1)$
10:     **else**
11:       $a = x_1$
12:       $x_1 = x_2$
13:       $f_1 = f_2$
14:       $x_2 = a + \tau(b-a)$
15:       $f_2 = f(x_2)$
16:     **end if**
17:   **end while**

---

[6] The procedure is similar to the bisection algorithm in which this reduction is 1/2.

The graphic illustrates the first three steps when minimizing the function given in the example for Newton's method.

Listing 11.8. C-BasicMethods/M/GSS.m

```
 1 function c = GSS(f,a,b,tol)
 2 % GSS.m  -- version 2006-05-26
 3 % Golden Section Search
 4 if nargin == 3, tol = 1e-8; end
 5 tau = (sqrt(5) - 1)/2;
 6 x1 = a + (1-tau)*(b-a); f1 = feval(f,x1);
 7 x2 = a +    tau *(b-a); f2 = feval(f,x2);
 8 while (b-a) > tol
 9     if f1 < f2
10         b  = x2;
11         x2 = x1;   f2 = f1;
12         x1 = a + (1-tau)*(b-a); f1 = feval(f,x1);
13     else
14         a  = x1;
15         x1 = x2;   f1 = f2;
16         x2 = a +    tau *(b-a); f2 = feval(f,x2);
17     end
18 end
19 c = a + (b-a)/2;
```

```
a = 1; b = 2;
f = inline('1-log(x).*exp(-x.^2)');
z = GSS(f,a,b)
z =
    1.3279
```

For unconstrained optimization, Matlab provides the two functions fminunc and fminbnb. Examples for their use are given in Section 11.4.5.

11.4. Unconstrained optimization in multiple dimensions

11.4.1. Steepest descent method

The negative gradient $-\nabla f(x)$ is locally the direction of steepest descent, that is, the function f decreases more rapidly along the direction of the negative gradient than along any other direction. Starting from an initial point $x^{(0)}$, the successive approximations of the solution are given by

$$x^{(k+1)} = x^{(k)} - \alpha \nabla f(x^{(k)}),$$

where α is the solution of the one-dimensional minimization problem

$$\min_{\alpha} f\left(x^{(k)} - \alpha \nabla f(x^{(k)})\right).$$

The steepest descent method is formalized in Algorithm 35.

Below we find a simple implementation of the steepest descent method with Matlab. The gradient is computed numerically with the function numG,

---

Algorithm 35 Steepest descent method.

1: initialize $x^{(0)}$
2: **for** $k = 0, 1, 2, \ldots$ until convergence **do**
3:     compute $\nabla f(x^{(k)})$
4:     compute $\alpha^* = \mathrm{argmin}_\alpha f\left(x^{(k)} - \alpha \nabla f(x^{(k)}) \right)$
5:     $x^{(k+1)} = x^{(k)} - \alpha^* \nabla f(x^{(k)})$
6: **end for**

---

and the one-dimensional minimization is performed with `lineSearch`. The optimal α is simply determined by moving forward with constant steps along the direction of the negative gradient until f starts to increase.

Listing 11.9. C-BasicMethods/M/SteepestD.m

```
1  function x1 = SteepestD(f,x1,tol,ls)
2  % SteepestD.m  -- version2010-08-31
3  if nargin == 2, tol = 1e-4; ls = 0.1; end
4  x1 = x1(:); x0 = -x1;  k = 1;
5  while ~converged(x0,x1,tol)
6      x0 = x1;
7      g  = numG(f,x1);
8      as = lineSearch(f,x0,-g,ls);
9      x1 = x0 - as * g;
10     k = k + 1; if k > 300, error('Maxit in SteepestD'); end
11 end
```

Listing 11.10. C-BasicMethods/M/numG.m

```
1  function g = numG(f,x)
2  % numG.m  -- version 2010-08-31
3  n = numel(x); g = zeros(n,1); x = x(:);
4  Delta = diag(max(sqrt(eps) * abs(x),sqrt(eps)));
5  F0 = feval(f,x);
6  for i = 1:n
7      F1   = feval(f,x + Delta(:,i));
8      g(i) = (F1 - F0) / Delta(i,i); % forward difference
9  end
```

Listing 11.11. C-BasicMethods/M/lineSearch.m

```
1  function a1 = lineSearch(f,x,s,d)
2  % lineSearch.m  -- version 2010-09-13
3  if nargin == 3, d = 0.1; end
4  done = 0; a1 = 0; k = 0;
5  f1 = feval(f,x);
6  while ~done
7      a0 = a1;   a1 = a0 + d;
8      f0 = f1;   f1 = feval(f,x+a1*s);
9      if f1 > f0, done = 1; end
10     k = k + 1;
11     if k > 100, fprintf('Early stop in lineSearch'); break, end
12 end
```

Example 11.2

We illustrate the steepest descent method by searching the minimum of the function

$$f(x_1, x_2) = \exp\left(0.1(x_2 - x_1^2)^2 + 0.05(1 - x_1)^2\right).$$

Using as starting point $x^{(0)} = [-0.3\ 0.8]$ and the default tolerance for the convergence test, we obtain the solution $x^{sol} = [0.9983\ 0.9961]$. If we want to get closer to the minimum $[1\ 1]$, we have to use a lower value for the tolerance, for example, 10^{-6}.

```
f = inline('exp(0.1*(x(2)-x(1).^2)^2 + 0.05*(1-x(1))^2)');
x0 = [-0.3 0.8];
xs = SteepestD(f,x0)


xs =
    0.9983
    0.9961
```

Figure 11.7 reproduces the first 30 steps of the algorithm. We observe the slow (linear) convergence of the algorithm when reaching the flat region near the minimum. The solution $x^{sol} = [0.9983\ 0.9961]$ is reached after 137 steps.

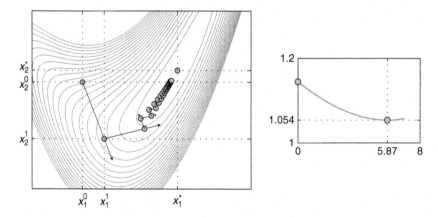

Figure 11.7 Minimization of $f(x_1, x_2) = \exp\left(0.1(x_2 - x_1^2)^2 + 0.05(1 - x_1)^2\right)$ with the steepest descent method. Right panel: minimization of α for the first step ($\alpha^* = 5.87$).

11.4.2. Newton's method

Newton's method presented for the one-dimensional optimization in Section 11.3.1 can be generalized to the n-dimensional problem. We consider a local quadratic approximation for the function $f(x)$ at $x \in \mathbb{R}^n$ using the truncated Taylor series expansion

$$f(x + h) \approx \underbrace{f(x) + \nabla f(x) h + \frac{1}{2} h' \nabla^2 f(x) h.}_{\text{quadratic model}}$$

The first-order condition for the minimum of the quadratic model is

$$\nabla f(x) + \nabla^2 f(x) h = 0,$$

and the step h that minimizes the local model is then the solution of the linear system

$$\nabla^2 f(x) h = -\nabla f(x).$$

Algorithm 36 Newton's method for unconstrained optimization in n dimensions.

1: initialize $x^{(0)}$
2: **for** $k = 0, 1, 2, \ldots$ until convergence **do**
3:    compute $\nabla f(x^{(k)})$ and $\nabla^2 f(x^{(k)})$
4:    solve $\nabla^2 f(x^{(k)}) s^{(k)} = -\nabla f(x^{(k)})$
5:    $x^{(k+1)} = x^{(k)} + s^{(k)}$
6: **end for**

The Matlab script below is a very simple implementation of Algorithm 36 to solve the two-dimensional minimization of the function given in Example 11.2. The symbolic expressions for the first and second derivatives are computed by Matlab's Symbolic Toolbox. In Fig. 11.8, we observe the fast (quadratic) convergence of Newton's method.

```
syms x1 x2
f = exp(0.1*(x2-x1^2).^2 + 0.05*(1-x1)^2);
dx1 = diff(f,x1);        dx2 = diff(f,x2);
dx1x1 = diff(f,'x1',2); dx1x2 = diff(dx1,x2);
dx2x2 = diff(f,'x2',2);
y1 = [-0.30 0.80]';
%
tol = 1e-4; k = 1; y0 = -y1;
while ~converged(y0,y1,tol)
    y0 = y1;
    x1 = y0(1); x2 = y0(2);
    J = [eval(dx1)   eval(dx2)];
    H = [eval(dx1x1) eval(dx1x2)
         eval(dx1x2) eval(dx2x2)];
    s = -H \ J';
    y1 = y0 + s
    k = k + 1; if k > 10, error('Maxit in NewtonUOnD'); end
end
y1, k


y1 =
    1.0000
    1.0000
k =
    10
```

The quadratic convergence of Newton's method occurs only if the starting point is chosen appropriately. Figure 11.9 illustrates how the method

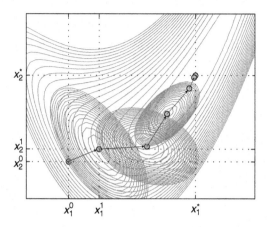

Figure 11.8 Minimization of $f(x_1,x_2) = \exp\left(0.1\,(x_2 - x_1^2)^2 + 0.05\,(1 - x_1)^2\right)$ with Newton's method. Contour plots of the local model for the first three steps.

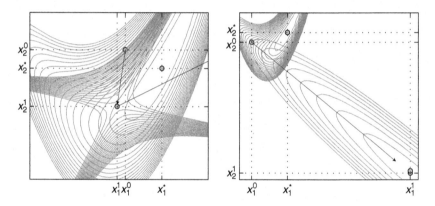

Figure 11.9 Nonconvex local model for starting point (left panel) and convex local model but divergence of the step (right panel).

can diverge if the local model is either nonconvex (left panel), or convex but leads to a large step into a nonappropriate region (right panel).

11.4.3. Quasi-Newton method

The exact computation of the gradient and the Hessian matrix in the Newton algorithm does not guarantee convergence to a solution. Two reasons are in favor of using approximated gradients and Hessian matrices. For one, they may be cheaper to compute and second, more importantly, they may contribute to a more robust behavior of the algorithm. This is, of course, at the cost of a slower convergence.

Algorithm 37 sketches a classical quasi-Newton method with updating of the Hessian matrix. One can take $B_0 = I$, and the way matrix U is computed defines a particular method. In the following, we give an illustration with the popular BFGS method, developed independently by Broyden, Fletcher,

---

Algorithm 37 Quasi-Newton for unconstrained optimization in n dimensions.

1: initialize $x^{(0)}$ and B_0
2: **for** $k = 0, 1, 2, \ldots$ until convergence **do**
3:     solve $B_k p^{(k)} = -\nabla f(x^{(k)})$
4:     $s^{(k)} = \alpha \, p^{(k)}$ # (Line search along $p^{(k)}$)
5:     $x^{(k+1)} = x^{(k)} + s^{(k)}$
6:     $y^{(k)} = \nabla f(x^{(k+1)}) - \nabla f(x^{(k)})$
7:     update $B_{k+1} = B_k + U$
8: **end for**

Goldfarb, and Shanno in the seventies.[7] The gradient $\nabla f(x^{(k)})$ is evaluated numerically with the function numG already given on page 307. The updating matrix U is defined as

$$U = \frac{y^{(k)} y^{(k)\prime}}{y^{(k)\prime} s^{(k)}} - \frac{(B_k s^{(k)}) (B_k s^{(k)})'}{s^{(k)\prime} B_k s^{(k)}}.$$

Listing 11.12. C-BasicMethods/M/BFGS.m

```
1  function x1 = BFGS(f,x1,tol,ls)
2  % BFGS.m  -- version  2010-09-14
3  if nargin == 2, tol = 1e-4; ls = 0.1; end
4  g1 = numG(f,x1);   B1 = eye(numel(x1));
5  x1 = x1(:);  x0 = -x1;   k = 1;
6  while ~converged(x0,x1,tol)
7      x0 = x1; g0 = g1; B0 = B1;
8      p0 = -B0\g0;
9      as = lineSearch(f,x0,p0,ls);
10     s0 = as * p0;
11     z0 = B0 * s0;
12     x1 = x0 + s0;
13     g1 = numG(f,x1);
14     y0 = g1 - g0;
15     B1 = B0 + (y0*y0')/(y0'*s0) - (z0*z0')/(s0'*z0);
16     k = k + 1; if k > 100, error('Maxit in BFGS'); end
17 end
```

Figure 11.10 compares the behavior of the BFGS method and Newton's method for the previously solved problem. We observe that Newton's method takes, in this case, first a wrong direction and then converges very rapidly once it is in an appropriate region. The first step of the BFGS method corresponds to a steepest descent move, and then the steps progress more slowly toward the solution.

11.4.4. Direct search methods

In order to be successful, that is, assuring rapid and global convergence, gradient-based methods require f to be nicely behaved, a situation which in

---

[7] For more details see Nocedal and Wright (2006).

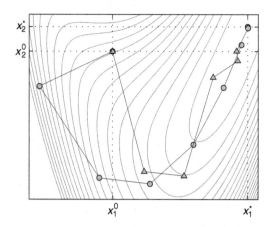

Figure 11.10 Comparison of the first seven Newton iterations (circles) with the first five BFGS iterations (triangles).

practice is not always satisfied and calls for alternative approaches. In particular, we consider problems where the function f to be optimized falls into one of the following categories:

- Derivatives of $f(x)$ are not available, or do not exist.
- Computation of $f(x)$ is very expensive, that is, is obtained by a huge amount of simulations.
- Values of f are inherently inexact or noisy as is the case when they are affected by Monte Carlo variance.
- We are only interested in an improvement of f rather than a fully accurate optimum.

This class of problems is suitable to be approached with direct search methods.

Direct search methods were first suggested in the 1950s and developed until mid-1960s (Hooke and Jeeves (1961), Spendley, Hext, and Himsworth (1962), Nelder and Mead (1965)) and have been considered as part of mainstream optimization techniques. By the 1980s, direct search methods became invisible in the optimization community but remained extremely popular among practitioners, in particular, in chemistry, chemical engineering, medicine, etc. In academia, they regained interest due to the work by Torczon (1989). Current research is undertaken by Torczon (1997), Lagarias et al. (1999), Wright (2000), Frimannslund and Steihaug (2004), etc. Similar algorithms are multidirectional search and pattern search.

The idea of the simplex-based direct search method introduced by Spendley, Hext, and Himsworth (1962) is as follows: the objective function f is evaluated at the vertices of a simplex in the search space. The simplex evolves toward the minimum by constructing a new simplex obtained

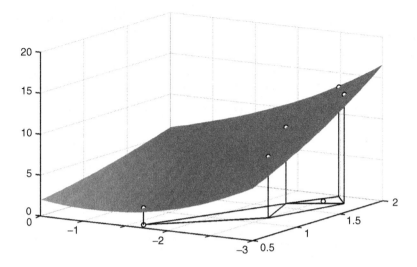

Figure 11.11 Evolution of starting simplex in the Nelder–Mead algorithm.

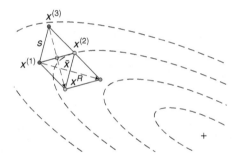

Figure 11.12 Detailed starting simplex and two reflections.

by reflecting the original simplex away from the vertex with the largest value of f. Figure 11.11 gives an intuition on how the starting simplex on the right evolves by reflecting the vertex with the highest function value in the direction of lower values.

The coordinates X of the simplex for an n-dimensional function are defined as

$$\underset{n\times(n+1)}{X} = \begin{bmatrix} 0 & d_1 & d_2 & \cdots & d_2 \\ 0 & d_2 & d_1 & \cdots & d_2 \\ \vdots & \vdots & \vdots & \ddots & \vdots \\ 0 & d_2 & d_2 & \cdots & d_1 \end{bmatrix}, \quad \text{where} \quad \begin{aligned} d_1 &= s(\sqrt{n+1}+n-1)/(n\sqrt{2}) \\ d_2 &= s(\sqrt{n+1}-1)/(n\sqrt{2}) \end{aligned}$$

and s is the length of an edge. In Fig.11.12, we see the starting simplex with the vertices $x^{(1)}$, $x^{(2)}$, and $x^{(3)}$; its reflection $x^{(1)}$, $x^{(2)}$, and x^R; and a further reflection in the direction of descent.

We now detail the rules according to which the simplex evolves toward the minimum. Consider a function depending on n variables. Then, at iteration k, the simplex is defined by the vertices $x^{(i)}$, $i = 1,\ldots,n+1$ (left panel in following figure). These vertices are renamed such that $f(x^{(1)}) \le f(x^{(2)}) \le \cdots \le f(x^{(n+1)})$ (right panel). We then compute the mean over all vertices except the worst (the one with the highest function value):

$$\bar{x} = \frac{1}{n}\sum_{i=1}^{n} x^{(i)} \quad i = 1,\ldots,n.$$

The vertex x_{n+1} with the worst function value is now reflected through the mean $\bar{x}$ of the remaining points. This reflection is computed as

$$x^{(R)} = (1+\rho)\,\bar{x} - \rho\,x^{(n+1)}.$$

If the function value at the reflected vertex satisfies $f(x^{(R)}) < f(x^{(1)})$, that is, is better than all remaining points, we expand the reflection further until $x^{(E)}$, which is computed as

$$x^{(E)} = (1+\rho)\,x^{(R)} - \rho\,\bar{x}.$$

Note that when computing the expansion, we do not check whether the function goes up again.

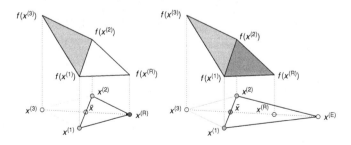

If the reflection point satisfies $f(x^{(R)}) < f(x^{(n+1)})$ but $f(x^{(R)}) \ge f(x^{(n)})$, that is, if the function value goes up again but is not the worst in the new simplex, we compute an out-contraction as

$$x^{(O)} = (1 + \psi\rho)\bar{x} - \psi\rho x^{(n+1)}.$$

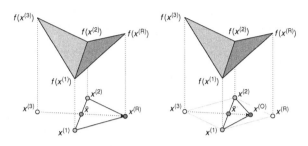

If the function at the reflection point is going up such that $f(x^{(R)}) > f(x^{(n+1)})$, we compute an in-contraction as

$$x^{(I)} = (1 - \psi\rho)\bar{x} + \psi\rho x^{(n+1)}.$$

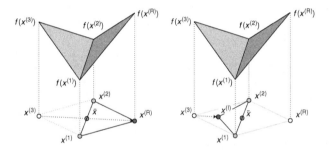

Finally, if outside or inside contraction results in no improvement over $f(x^{(n+1)})$, we shrink the simplex:

$$x^{(i)} = x^{(1)} - \sigma(x^{(i)} - x^{(1)}) \quad i = 2,\ldots,n+1.$$

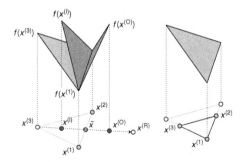

Typical values for the different parameters in the construction mechanism are: $\rho = 1$, $\psi = 1/2$ and $\sigma = 2$. These parameters are very robust and generally one has not to tune them. Algorithm 38 summarizes the

Nelder–Mead simplex direct search method. In order to keep the presentation compact, we do not repeat how the new vertices are computed but simply use their notation.

Algorithm 38 Nelder–Mead simplex direct search.

1: construct vertices $x^{(1)},\ldots,x^{(n+1)}$ of starting simplex
2: **while** stopping criteria not met **do**
3:     rename vertices such that $f(x^{(1)}) \le \cdots \le f(x^{(n+1)})$
4:     **if** $f(x^{(R)}) < f(x^{(1)})$ **then**
5:         **if** $f(x^{(E)}) < f(x^{(R)})$ **then** $x^* = x^{(E)}$ **else** $x^* = x^{(R)}$
6:     **else**
7:         **if** $f(x^{(R)}) < f(x^{(n)})$ **then**
8:             $x^* = x^{(R)}$
9:         **else**
10:            **if** $f(x^{(R)}) < f(x^{(n+1)})$ **then**
11:                **if** $f(x^{(O)}) < f(x^{(n+1)})$ **then** $x^* = x^{(O)}$ **else** shrink
12:            **else**
13:                **if** $f(x^{(I)}) < f(x^{(n+1)})$ **then** $x^* = x^{(I)}$ **else** shrink
14:            **end if**
15:         **end if**
16:     **end if**
17:     **if** not shrink **then** $x^{(n+1)} = x^*$ # Replace worst vertex by x^*
18: **end while**

Matlab function `fminsearch` implements the Nelder–Mead algorithm. Below we illustrate its use by minimizing the function $f(x) = (x_1^2 + x_2 - 11)^2 + (x_1 + x_2^2 - 7)^2$ and choosing $x = [0 \ -2]'$ as the starting point.

```
F = inline('(x(1)^2 + x(2)-11)^2 + (x(1) + x(2)^2 - 7)^2');
x0 = [0 -2];
options = optimset('fminsearch');
[x,f,FLAG,output] = fminsearch(F,x0,options)

x =
    3.5844   -1.8481
f =
  2.0449e-008
FLAG =
     1
output =
    iterations: 64
     funcCount: 124
     algorithm: 'Nelder-Mead simplex direct search'
       message: [1x196 char]
```

If `F` is defined by a function with arguments `a1,a2,...`, then we use a function handle, and the call is

```
fminsearch(@F,x0,options,a1,a2,...)
```

11.4.5. Practical issues with Matlab

Unconstrained optimization in Matlab

In the following, we illustrate how the unconstrained optimization problems of some of the preceding examples can be solved with the Matlab function `fminunc`.[8] We initialize the default options for `fminunc` and call the function without providing the gradient.

```
f = inline('exp(0.1*(x(2)-x(1).^2)^2 + 0.05*(1-x(1))^2)');
x0 = [-0.3 0.8];
options = optimset('fminunc');
xs = fminunc(f,x0,options)

Warning: Gradient must be provided for trust-region method;
    using line-search method instead.
> In fminunc at 281
Optimization terminated: relative infinity-norm of gradient
    less than options.TolFun.
xs =
    1.0000    1.0000
```

To provide the gradient, we use the function `FnG` which has two output arguments, that is, the function value and the gradient. When modifying the options, we have to include the previously set default options (`options`) as input argument in `optimset`.

```
options = optimset(options,'GradObj','on');
[xs,fs] = fminunc(@(x) FnG(x,f),x0,options)

Optimization terminated: relative function value changing by
    less than OPTIONS.TolFun.
xs =
    0.9774    0.9495
fs =
    1.0000
```

Listing 11.13. C-BasicMethods/M/FnG.m

```
1 function [f,g] = FnG(x,func)
2 % FnG.m  -- version 2010-12-21
3 f = func(x);
4 g = numG(func,x);
```

We observe the flat region around the minimum as the function value is reasonably close to its minimum, whereas the function argument is not. To improve the precision of the solution, we further modify the default options of the algorithm.

```
options = optimset(options,'GradObj','on','TolFun',1e-14,'
    MaxFunEvals',300,'TolX',1e-8);
[xs,fs,exflag,output,g] = fminunc(@(x) FnG(x,f),x0,options)
```

[8] Refer to Matlab's help for a complete description of `fminunc`.

```
Optimization terminated: relative function value changing by
    less than OPTIONS.TolFun.
xs =
    1.0000    1.0000
fs =
    1.0000
exflag =
    3
output =
        iterations: 284
        funcCount: 285
      cgiterations: 270
    firstorderopt: 1.6391e-007
         algorithm: 'large-scale: trust-region Newton'
           message: [1x86 char]
g =
  1.0e-006 *
   -0.0447
   -0.1639
```

Solution for nonlinear systems of equations in **Matlab**
The system specified in Example 11.5 can be solved as follows:

```
y0 = [1 5]';
y0 = fsolve('ex2NLeqs',y0)

ys =
   -0.0000
    3.0000
```

11.5. Nonlinear Least Squares

11.5.1. Problem statement and notation

The optimization problem arising in the case of linear Least Squares has already been introduced in Section 3.4. The optimization of nonlinear Least Squares is a special case of unconstrained optimization. We have the same objective function as in the linear case

$$g(x) = \frac{1}{2}r(x)'r(x) = \frac{1}{2}\sum_{i=1}^{m} r_i(x)^2, \qquad (11.5)$$

but the residuals

$$r_i(x) = y_i - f(t_i,x), \qquad i = 1,\ldots,m,$$

are nonlinear as "the model" $f(t_i,x)$ is a nonlinear function with t_i being the independent variables and $x \in \mathbb{R}^n$ the vector of parameters to be estimated.

In order to write the local quadratic approximation (see page 308) for the minimization of Eq. (11.5), we need the first and second derivatives of $g(x)$. The first derivative writes

$$\nabla g(x) = \sum_{i=1}^{m} r_i(x) \cdot \nabla r_i(x) = \nabla r(x)' r(x),$$

where

$$\nabla r(x) = \begin{bmatrix} \frac{\partial r_1(x)}{\partial x_1} & \cdots & \frac{\partial r_1(x)}{\partial x_n} \\ \vdots & & \vdots \\ \frac{\partial r_m(x)}{\partial x_1} & \cdots & \frac{\partial r_m(x)}{\partial x_n} \end{bmatrix}$$

is the Jacobian matrix. The vector

$$\nabla r_i(x) = \begin{bmatrix} \frac{\partial r_i(x)}{\partial x_1} \\ \vdots \\ \frac{\partial r_i(x)}{\partial x_n} \end{bmatrix}$$

corresponds to the ith row of the Jacobian matrix. The second derivative is

$$\nabla^2 g(x) = \sum_{i=1}^{m} \left(\nabla r_i(x) \cdot \nabla r_i(x)' + r_i(x) \cdot \nabla^2 r_i(x) \right)$$

$$= \nabla r(x)' \nabla r(x) + S(x), \tag{11.6}$$

with $S(x) = \sum_{i=1}^{m} r_i(x) \nabla^2 r_i(x)$.

We now consider $m_c(x)$, the quadratic approximation of $g(x)$ in a neighborhood of x_c

$$m_c(x) = g(x_c) + \nabla g(x_c)'(x - x_c) + \frac{1}{2}(x - x_c)' \nabla^2 g(x_c)(x - x_c),$$

and search the point $x_+ = x_c + s_N$ satisfying the first-order condition $\nabla m_c(x_+) = 0$ so that x_+ is the minimum of m_c. We have

$$\nabla m_c(x_+) = \nabla g(x_c) + \nabla^2 g(x_c) \underbrace{(x_+ - x_c)}_{s_N} = 0,$$

where s_N is the Newton step computed by solving the linear system

$$\nabla^2 g(x_c) s_N = -\nabla g(x_c).$$

The minimization of the function defined in Eq. (11.5) could then be done with Newton's method in which the kth iteration is defined as

$$\texttt{Solve} \quad \nabla^2 g(x^{(k)}) s_N^{(k)} = -\nabla g(x^{(k)})$$

$$x^{(k+1)} = x^{(k)} + s_N^{(k)}.$$

However, in practice, we proceed differently as the evaluation of $S(x)$ in Eq. (11.6) can be very difficult or even impossible. This difficulty is circumvented by considering only an approximation of the matrix of second derivatives $\nabla^2 g(x)$. The way this approximation is done defines the particular methods presented in the following sections.

11.5.2. Gauss–Newton method

This method approximates the matrix of second derivatives (Eq. 11.6) by dropping the term $S(x)$. $S(x)$ is composed by a sum of expressions $r_i(x)\nabla^2 r_i(x)$ and, therefore, in situations where the model is close to the observations, we have small residuals leading to a matrix $S(x)$ with relatively small elements. Algorithm 39 summarizes the method.

Algorithm 39 Gauss–Newton method.

1: initialize $x^{(0)}$
2: **for** $k = 0, 1, 2, \ldots$ until convergence **do**
3:     compute $\nabla r(x^{(k)})$
4:     Solve $\left(\nabla r(x^{(k)})'\nabla r(x^{(k)})\right) s_{GN}^{(k)} = -\nabla r(x^{(k)})'r(x^{(k)})$
5:     update $x^{(k+1)} = x^{(k)} + s_{GN}^{(k)}$
6: **end for**

Note that the linear system defining the Gauss–Newton step $s_{GN}^{(k)}$ is a system of normal equations and, therefore, at each iteration, we solve a linear Least Squares problem. According to our earlier suggestion concerning the linear Least Squares problem, we generally prefer to consider this an overidentified system

$$\nabla r(x^{(k)}) s_{GN}^{(k)} \approx -r(x^{(k)}),$$

which is then solved via QR factorization. Of course, convergence is not guaranteed, in particular, for large residuals.

11.5.3. Levenberg–Marquardt method

In case Gauss–Newton does not converge, or the Jacobian matrix does not have full rank, Levenberg–Marquardt suggests approximating the matrix $S(x)$ by a diagonal matrix μI. This leads to Algorithm 40.

Algorithm 40 Levenberg–Marquardt method.

1: initialize $x^{(0)}$
2: **for** $k = 0, 1, 2, \ldots$ until convergence **do**
3:     compute $\nabla r(x^{(k)})$ and μ_k
4:     solve $\left(\nabla r(x^{(k)})'\nabla r(x^{(k)}) + \mu_k I\right) s_{LM}^{(k)} = -\nabla r(x)'r(x)$
5:     update $x^{(k+1)} = x^{(k)} + s_{LM}^{(k)}$
6: **end for**

The step $s_{\mathrm{LM}}^{(k)}$ is the solution of a linear Least Squares problem and is computed by solving the overidentified system

$$\begin{bmatrix} \nabla r(x^{(k)}) \\ \mu_k^{1/2} I \end{bmatrix} s_{\mathrm{LM}}^{(k)} \approx - \begin{bmatrix} r(x^{(k)}) \\ 0 \end{bmatrix},$$

where we resort to QR factorization avoiding the product $\nabla r(x^{(k)})' \nabla r(x^{(k)})$.

In Statement 3, the parameter μ is adjusted at every iteration. However, in practice, a constant $\mu = 10^{-2}$ appears to be a good choice. For $\mu = 0$, we have the special case of Gauss–Newton. With an appropriate choice of μ, the Levenberg–Marquardt method appears very robust in practice and is, therefore, the method of choice in most of the specialized software. Again, as always in nonlinear problems, convergence is not guaranteed and depends on the starting point chosen.

Example 11.3

We introduce a small example to illustrate the methods just presented. Consider the data

t	0.0	1.0	2.0	3.0
y	2.0	0.7	0.3	0.1

where t and y are the independent and dependent variables, respectively. The variable y is assumed to be explained by the model $f(t, x) = x_1 e^{x_2 t}$ where x_1, x_2 are the parameters to be estimated. The vector of residuals is then

$$r(x) = \begin{bmatrix} y_1 - x_1 e^{x_2 t_1} \\ y_2 - x_1 e^{x_2 t_2} \\ y_3 - x_1 e^{x_2 t_3} \\ y_4 - x_1 e^{x_2 t_4} \end{bmatrix}.$$

Figure 11.13 plots the observations and the model for parameter values $x_1 = 2.5$ and $x_2 = 2.5$. The right panel shows the shape of the objective function $g(x)$ which is the sum of squared residuals to be minimized. The function is only locally convex.

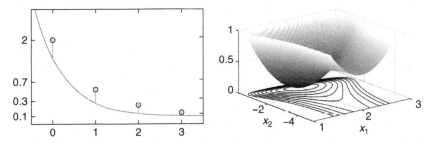

Figure 11.13 Left panel: Plot of observations, model for $x_1 = 2.5$, $x_2 = 2.5$ and residuals. Right panel: plot of sum of squared residuals $g(x)$.

The Jacobian matrix writes

$$
\nabla r(x) =
\begin{bmatrix}
\frac{\partial r_1(x)}{\partial x_1} & \frac{\partial r_1(x)}{\partial x_2} \\[4pt]
\frac{\partial r_2(x)}{\partial x_1} & \frac{\partial r_2(x)}{\partial x_2} \\[4pt]
\frac{\partial r_3(x)}{\partial x_1} & \frac{\partial r_3(x)}{\partial x_2} \\[4pt]
\frac{\partial r_4(x)}{\partial x_1} & \frac{\partial r_4(x)}{\partial x_2}
\end{bmatrix}
=
\begin{bmatrix}
-e^{x_2 t_1} & -x_1 t_1 e^{x_2 t_1} \\[4pt]
-e^{x_2 t_2} & -x_1 t_2 e^{x_2 t_2} \\[4pt]
-e^{x_2 t_3} & -x_1 t_3 e^{x_2 t_3} \\[4pt]
-e^{x_2 t_4} & -x_1 t_4 e^{x_2 t_4}
\end{bmatrix}
$$

and the first derivatives are

$$
\nabla g(x) =
\begin{bmatrix}
\frac{\partial g(x)}{\partial x_1} \\[4pt]
\frac{\partial g(x)}{\partial x_2}
\end{bmatrix}
= \nabla r(x)' r(x) =
\begin{bmatrix}
-\sum_{i=1}^{4} r_i(x) e^{x_2 t_i} \\[4pt]
-\sum_{i=1}^{4} r_i(x) x_1 t_i e^{x_2 t_i}
\end{bmatrix}.
$$

The m matrices forming $S(x)$ are

$$
\nabla^2 r_i(x) =
\begin{bmatrix}
\frac{\partial^2 r_i(x)}{\partial x_1^2} & \frac{\partial^2 r_i(x)}{\partial x_1 \partial x_2} \\[4pt]
\frac{\partial^2 r_i(x)}{\partial x_1 \partial x_2} & \frac{\partial^2 r_i(x)}{\partial x_2^2}
\end{bmatrix}
=
\begin{bmatrix}
0 & -t_i e^{x_2 t_i} \\[4pt]
-t_i e^{x_2 t_i} & -x_1 t_i^2 e^{x_2 t_i}
\end{bmatrix},
$$

and the Hessian matrix of second derivatives of $g(x)$ is

$$
\nabla^2 g(x) =
\begin{bmatrix}
\sum_{i=1}^{4} (e^{x_2 t_i})^2 & \sum_{i=1}^{4} x_1 t_i (e^{x_2 t_i})^2 \\[4pt]
\sum_{i=1}^{4} x_1 (t_i e^{x_2 t_i})^2 & \sum_{i=1}^{4} (x_1 t_i e^{x_2 t_i})^2
\end{bmatrix}
- \sum_{i=1}^{4} r_i(x)
\begin{bmatrix}
0 & t_i e^{x_2 t_i} \\[4pt]
t_i e^{x_2 t_i} & x_1 t_i^2 e^{x_2 t_i}
\end{bmatrix}.
$$

With the Matlab code given below, we compute for the particular starting point $x_c = [1.5 \; -1.7]$ one step for the Newton, Gauss–Newton, and Levenberg–Marquardt method.

```
y = [2   0.7   0.3   0.1]';
t = [0  1.0   2.0   3.0]';
xc = [1.5 -1.7]';  % Staring value
m  = 4; n = 2;      % number of observations and parameters
v = exp( xc(2)*t );
r = y - xc(1)*v;
J = [-v  -xc(1)*t.*v];
nablagxc = J'*r;   P = J'*J;
S = zeros(n,n);
for i=1:m
    S = S + r(i)*v(i) * [ 0  -t(i); -t(i)  -xc(1)*t(i)^2];
end
H = P + S;  % Exact Hessian
% -- Newton step
  sN = - H \ nablagxc;
  xnN = xc + sN;
% -- Gauss-Newton step
  H = P;
  sGN = - H \ nablagxc;
  xnGN = xc + sGN;
% -- Levenberg-Marquardt step
  mu = 2; M = sqrt(mu)*eye(n);
  sLM = [J; M] \ [r' zeros(1,n)]';
  xnLM = xc - sLM;
%
```

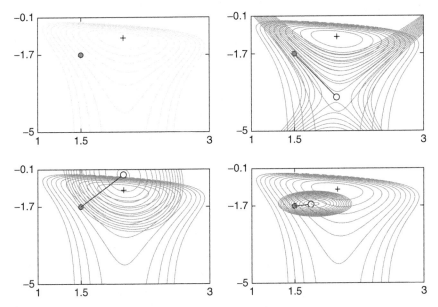

Figure 11.14 Starting point (bullet), one step (circle) and contour plots of local models for Newton (upper right), Gauss–Newton (lower left) and Levenberg–Marquardt (lower right).

```
fprintf('\n              Newton step:  [%6.3f  %6.3f]',xnN);
fprintf('\n       Gauss-Newton step:  [%6.3f  %6.3f]',xnGN);
fprintf('\n Levenberg-Marquardt step:  [%6.3f  %6.3f]\n',xnLM);
```

```
              Newton step:  [ 1.990  -3.568]
       Gauss-Newton step:  [ 1.996  -0.330]
 Levenberg-Marquardt step:  [ 1.692  -1.636]
```

Figure 11.14 shows the starting point (bullet) and the step (circle) for the three methods. We observe in the right upper panel that the local model for the Newton step is not convex and the minimum is a saddle point. In the lower left panel, we have the results for the Gauss–Newton method. The local model is convex, but its minimum falls into a region outside of the domain of definition of $g(x)$. Finally, in the lower right panel, we have the local model for the Levenberg–Marquardt method, which is convex and has its minimum in a position that is appropriate to progress toward the minimum of $g(x)$.

For the particular step given in the illustration, Levenberg–Marquardt is the only method that works. This, of course, is not always the case. We wanted to highlight that using the exact Hessian matrix with Newton's method does not at all guarantee an efficient step.

11.6. Solving systems of nonlinear equations $F(x) = 0$

11.6.1. General considerations

Contrary to the case with linear systems, the solution of nonlinear systems is a delicate matter. Generally, there is no unique solution and no guarantee to converge to the solution, and the computational complexity grows very fast

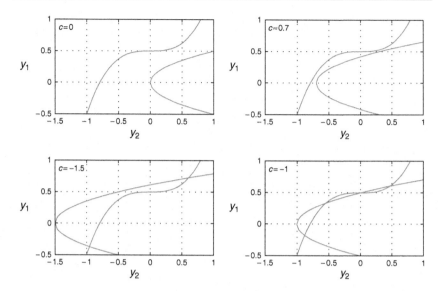

Figure 11.15 Solutions for varying values of parameter c of the systems of two nonlinear equations.

with the size of the system. To illustrate the problem, we consider a system of two equations

$$y_1 - y_2^3 - 1/2 = 0$$
$$4 y_1^2 - y_2 + c = 0.$$

Depending on the value of the parameter c, there are between 0 and 4 solutions in the domain considered. The different situations are illustrated in Fig. 11.15.

A system of n nonlinear equations is generally specified in its implicit form using the notation

$$F(y) = 0 \quad \equiv \quad \begin{cases} f_1(y) = 0 \\ \quad \vdots \\ f_n(y) = 0 \end{cases}, \qquad (11.7)$$

where at least one of the equations f_i, $i = 1, 2, \ldots, n$, must be nonlinear. The equations of such a system, in particular if it is large, may often be rearranged such that the Jacobian matrix

$$\nabla F(y) = \begin{bmatrix} \dfrac{\partial f_1}{\partial y_1} & \cdots & \dfrac{\partial f_1}{\partial y_n} \\ \vdots & \ddots & \vdots \\ \dfrac{\partial f_n}{\partial y_1} & \cdots & \dfrac{\partial f_n}{\partial y_n} \end{bmatrix} \qquad (11.8)$$

can be put into a block triangular form, that is, showing a pattern like

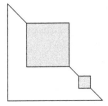

with the matrices on the diagonal being indecomposable. In such a situation, the solution of the system of equations consists in solving a sequence of recursive and interdependent systems.[9] In the following we suppose the system to be interdependent, that is, indecomposable.

In economics, we often find a different notation:

$$h(y, z) = 0,$$

where $y \in \mathbb{R}^n$ are the endogenous variables and $z \in \mathbb{R}^m$ the exogenous variables. In the previous notation, the exogenous variables are not explicit but incorporated into the function F. The Jacobian matrix for this notation is $\partial h / \partial y'$.

A variety of methods may be considered to solve systems of nonlinear equations. The following sections discuss fixed point methods, Newton's methods, and minimization.

11.6.2. Fixed point methods

Jacobi, Gauss–Seidel, and SOR method

The Jacobi, Gauss–Seidel, and SOR methods presented in Section 3.2 can be extended for the solution of nonlinear systems of equations (Algorithm 41). In general, the equations are normalized, that is, they are written in the form

$$y_i = g_i(y_1, \ldots, y_{i-1}, y_{i+1}, \ldots, y_n, z), \qquad i = 1, \ldots, n,$$

where the equations g_i can now also be nonlinear.

For the Jacobi method, the generic iteration writes:

$$y_i^{(k+1)} = g_i(y_1^{(k)}, \ldots, y_{i-1}^{(k)}, y_{i+1}^{(k)}, \ldots, y_n^{(k)}, z), \qquad i = 1, \ldots, n.$$

With the Gauss–Seidel method, the generic iteration i uses the $i - 1$ updated components of $y^{(k+1)}$ as soon as they are available:

$$y_i^{(k+1)} = g_i(y_1^{(k+1)}, \ldots, y_{i-1}^{(k+1)}, y_{i+1}^{(k)}, \ldots, y_n^{(k)}, z), \qquad i = 1, \ldots, n.$$

---

[9] Refer to page 58 for how to compute the block triangular decomposition. If the decomposition is an upper block triangular matrix, the sequence of recursive and interdependent systems is solved from bottom to top.

The stopping criterion is identical to the one used in the linear case, that is, iterations are stopped if the following condition is satisfied

$$\frac{|y_i^{(k+1)} - y_i^{(k)}|}{|y_i^{(k)}| + 1} < \varepsilon, \qquad i = 1, 2, \ldots, n,$$

where ε is a given tolerance.

As explained earlier for the linear case, convergence depends on the spectral radius of the matrix $M^{-1}N$ defined on page 48. In the nonlinear case, the matrices M and N change from iteration to iteration and we cannot predict their quantification at the solution of the system.

The Jacobi method is part of the class of fixed point methods, formalized as

$$y = g(y),$$

Algorithm 41 Jacobi, Gauss–Seidel, and SOR for nonlinear systems.

1: initialize $y^{(1)}$, $y^{(0)}$, ε and maximum number of iterations
2: **while** ~converged $(y^{(0)}, y^{(1)}, \varepsilon)$ **do**
3:     $y^{(0)} = y^{(1)}$ # Store precedent iteration in $y^{(0)}$
4:     compute $y^{(1)}$ with Jacobi, Gauss–Seidel, or SOR
5:     check number of iterations
6: **end while**

---

where g is the iteration function corresponding to a particular normalization, and the fixed point iteration is written

$$y^{(k+1)} = g(y^{(k)}), \qquad k = 0, 1, 2, \ldots,$$

with $y^{(0)}$ being the starting solution. The condition for convergence is

$$\rho\left(\nabla g(y^{\mathrm{sol}})\right) < 1 \qquad \nabla g(y^{\mathrm{sol}}) = \begin{bmatrix} \frac{\partial g_1}{\partial y_1}\Big|_{y_1 = y_1^{\mathrm{sol}}} & \cdots & \frac{\partial g_1}{\partial y_n}\Big|_{y_n = y_n^{\mathrm{sol}}} \\ \vdots & \ddots & \vdots \\ \frac{\partial g_n}{\partial y_1}\Big|_{y_1 = y_1^{\mathrm{sol}}} & \cdots & \frac{\partial g_n}{\partial y_1}\Big|_{y_1 = y_1^{\mathrm{sol}}} \end{bmatrix},$$

which as mentioned earlier is useless in practice as the Jacobian matrix has to be evaluated at the solution y^{sol}.

Example 11.4

We illustrate the fixed point method by solving the following system of nonlinear equations representing a straight line and a circle:

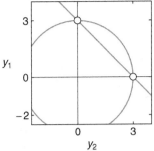

$$F(y) = 0 \Leftrightarrow \begin{cases} f_1(y_1, y_2) : y_1 + y_2 - 3 = 0 \\ f_2(y_1, y_2) : y_1^2 + y_2^2 - 9 = 0 \end{cases}$$

and verifying the two solutions $y = [0\ 3]'$ and $y = [3\ 0]'$. The Matlab code below solves the system with the fixed point method. The iteration functions, that is, the normalized equations, are stored in matrix G in the form of character strings. For larger systems of equations, it would be preferable to evaluate the iteration functions in Statements 7 and 8 in a loop. The sequence of solutions has been saved by means of Statements 4 and 10. These statements are otherwise not necessary.

Listing 11.14. C-BasicMethods/M/FPInD.m

```
1  % FPInD.m  -- version 2010-12-23
2  G = str2mat('-y0(2) + 3','sqrt(-y0(1)^2 + 9)');
3  y1 = [2 0]; y0 = -y1; tol = 1e-2; k = 1; itmax = 10;
4  Y = NaN(itmax,2); Y(1,:) = y1';
5  while ~converged(y0,y1,tol)
6      y0 = y1;
7      y1(1) = eval(G(1,:));
8      y1(2) = eval(G(2,:));
9      k = k + 1;
10     Y(k,:) = y1';
11     if k > itmax, error('Iteration limit reached'); end
12 end
13 y1
```

Figure 11.16 shows how the algorithm evolves during the iterations for the starting solution $y0 = [1\ 5]'$. If we consider a different starting solution $y0 = [2\ 0]'$, the solutions oscillate between $y = [0\ 0]'$ and $y = [3\ 3]'$ without converging. This is illustrated in the Fig. 11.17.

Iter	Solution		Error	
k	$y_1^{(k)}$	$y_2^{(k)}$	$y_1^{(k)} - y_1^{\text{sol}}$	$y_2^{(k)} - y_2^{\text{sol}}$
0	1.000	5.000	1.000	2.000
1	−2.000	2.828	2.000	0.172
2	0.172	2.236	0.172	0.764
3	0.764	2.995	0.764	0.005
4	0.005	2.901	0.005	0.099
5	0.099	3.000	0.099	0.000
6	0.000	2.998	0.000	0.002
7	0.002	3.000	0.002	0.000

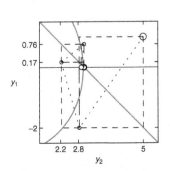

Figure 11.16 Steps of the fixed point algorithm for the starting solution $y0 = [1\ 5]'$.

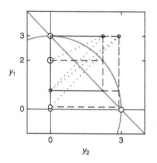

Iter	Solution		Error	
k	$y_1^{(k)}$	$y_2^{(k)}$	$y_1^{(k)} - y_1^{\text{sol}}$	$y_2^{(k)} - y_2^{\text{sol}}$
0	2.000	0.000	2.000	3.000
1	3.000	2.236	3.000	0.764
2	0.764	0.000	0.764	3.000
3	3.000	2.901	3.000	0.099
4	0.099	0.000	0.099	3.000
5	3.000	2.998	3.000	0.002
6	0.002	0.000	0.002	3.000
7	3.000	3.000	3.000	0.000
8	0.000	0.000	0.000	3.000
9	3.000	3.000	3.000	0.000
10	0.000	0.000	0.000	3.000

Figure 11.17 Oscillatory behavior of the fixed point algorithm for the starting solution $y0 = [2\ \ 0]'$.

11.6.3. Newton's method

Newton's method for the solution of a system of nonlinear equations is a generalization of Newton's method for finding the roots of a one-dimensional function presented in Section 11.1.5. The fact that an algorithm for a one-dimensional problem can be efficiently generalized to an n-dimensional problem is an exceptional situation in numerical computation. Newton's method is also often termed Newton–Raphson method.

The solution y^* of a system of nonlinear equations defined in (11.7) is approximated by the sequence $\{y^{(k)}\}_{k=0,1,2,\ldots}$. Given $y^{(k)} \in \mathbb{R}^n$ and an evaluation of the Jacobian matrix

$$\nabla F(y^{(k)}) = \begin{bmatrix} \left.\dfrac{\partial f_1}{\partial y_1}\right|_{y_1=y_1^{(k)}} & \cdots & \left.\dfrac{\partial f_1}{\partial y_n}\right|_{y_n=y_n^{(k)}} \\ \vdots & \ddots & \vdots \\ \left.\dfrac{\partial f_n}{\partial y_1}\right|_{y_1=y_1^{(k)}} & \cdots & \left.\dfrac{\partial f_n}{\partial y_n}\right|_{y_n=y_n^{(k)}} \end{bmatrix}$$

we construct an improved $y^{(k+1)}$ by approximating $F(y)$ in the neighborhood of $y^{(k)}$ with the "local model"

$$F(y) \approx \underbrace{F(y^{(k)}) + \nabla F(y^{(k)})(y - y^{(k)})}_{\text{local model}}.$$

This local model is solved for y to satisfy

$$F(y^{(k)}) + \nabla F(y^{(k)})(y - y^{(k)}) = 0$$

which then results into

$$y = y^{(k)} - \left(\nabla F(y^{(k)})\right)^{-1} F(y^{(k)}).$$

The procedure is repeated for the new value of y. At iteration k, we have

$$y^{(k+1)} = y^{(k)} - \left(\nabla F(y^{(k)})\right)^{-1} F(y^{(k)}),$$

and $y^{(k+1)}$ is the solution of the linear system

$$\underbrace{\nabla F(y^{(k)})}_{J} \underbrace{(y^{(k+1)} - y^{(k)})}_{s} = \underbrace{-F(y^{(k)})}_{b}.$$

Algorithm 42 summarizes Newton's method for the solution of a system of nonlinear equations.

Algorithm 42 Newton's method for nonlinear systems.

1: initialize $y^{(0)}$
2: **for** $k = 0, 1, 2, \ldots$ until convergence **do**
3:     compute $b = -F(y^{(k)})$ and $J = \nabla F(y^{(k)})$
4:     verify condition of J
5:     solve $Js = b$
6:     $y^{(k+1)} = y^{(k)} + s$
7: **end for**

Example 11.5

We illustrate Newton's method by solving the system of equations presented in Example 11.4. The Jacobian matrix is

$$\nabla F(y^{(k)}) = \begin{bmatrix} \frac{\partial f_1}{\partial y_1}\big|_{y_1=y_1^{(k)}} & \frac{\partial f_1}{\partial y_2}\big|_{y_2=y_2^{(k)}} \\ \frac{\partial f_2}{\partial y_1}\big|_{y_1=y_1^{(k)}} & \frac{\partial f_2}{\partial y_2}\big|_{y_2=y_2^{(k)}} \end{bmatrix} = \begin{bmatrix} 1 & 1 \\ 2y_1^{(k)} & 2y_2^{(k)} \end{bmatrix}.$$

Choosing $y^{(0)} = [1\ 5]'$ for the starting solution, we have

$$F(y^{(0)}) = \begin{bmatrix} 3 \\ 17 \end{bmatrix} \quad \text{and} \quad \nabla F(y^{(0)}) = \begin{bmatrix} 1 & 1 \\ 2 & 10 \end{bmatrix}.$$

Solving the linear system

$$\begin{bmatrix} 1 & 1 \\ 2 & 10 \end{bmatrix} s^{(0)} = \begin{bmatrix} -3 \\ -17 \end{bmatrix},$$

we get $s^{(0)} = [-13/8\ -11/8]'$ from where we compute

$$y^{(1)} = y^{(0)} + s^{(0)} = \begin{bmatrix} -5/8 \\ 29/8 \end{bmatrix}$$

and update the function and the Jacobian

$$F(y^{(1)}) = \begin{bmatrix} 0 \\ 145/32 \end{bmatrix}, \quad \nabla F(y^{(1)}) = \begin{bmatrix} 1 & 1 \\ -5/4 & 29/4 \end{bmatrix}.$$

We again consider the linear system

$$\begin{bmatrix} 1 & 1 \\ -5/4 & 29/4 \end{bmatrix} s^{(1)} = \begin{bmatrix} 0 \\ -145/32 \end{bmatrix},$$

the solution of which is $s^{(1)} = [145/272 \ -145/272]'$, and we get the solution for the second iteration

$$y^{(2)} = y^{(1)} + s^{(1)} = \begin{bmatrix} -25/272 \\ 841/272 \end{bmatrix}.$$

The following Matlab code represents a very simple way to solve this particular problem.

```
Feq = str2mat('y0(1) + y0(2) - 3','y0(1)^2 + y0(2)^2 - 9');
y1 = [1 5]'; y0 = -y1; tol = 1e-2; k = 1; itmax = 10;
Y = NaN(itmax,2); Y(1,:) = y1';
while ~converged(y0,y1,tol)
    y0 = y1;
    F(1) = eval(Feq(1,:));
    F(2) = eval(Feq(2,:));
    b = -F'; J = [1 1; 2*y0(1) 2*y0(2)];
    s = J \ b;
    y1 = y0 + s;
    k = k + 1;
    Y(k,:) = y1';
    if k > itmax, error('Iteration limit reached'); end
end
y1


y1 =
    -0.0000
     3.0000
```

Figure 11.18 shows the steps of the algorithm for the starting solution $y0 = [1 \ 5]'$, and we notice the faster convergence. Indeed, the convergence rate of Newton's method is quadratic as we verify $\left| y_i^{(k+1)} - y_i^{sol} \right| < \left| y_i^{(k)} - y_i^{sol} \right|^2$.

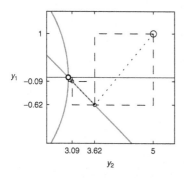

Iter	Solution		Error	
k	$y_1^{(k)}$	$y_2^{(k)}$	$y_1^{(k)} - y_1^{sol}$	$y_2^{(k)} - y_2^{sol}$
0	1.000	5.000	1.000	2.000
1	−0.625	3.625	0.625	0.625
2	−0.092	3.092	0.092	0.092
3	−0.003	3.003	0.003	0.003

Figure 11.18 Steps of the Newton algorithm for starting solution $y0 = [1 \ 5]'$.

A more general code is given with the Matlab function NewtonnD.m where the system to be solved and the starting point are the input arguments. The Jacobian is computed numerically with the function numJ. $F(y)$ of the system to be solved is coded with the function ex2NLeqs.m.

Listing 11.15. C-BasicMethods/M/NewtonnD.m

```
1  function x1 = NewtonnD(f,x1,tol,itmax)
2  % NewtonnD.m  -- version  2010-09-12
3  if nargin < 3, tol = 1e-2; itmax = 10; end
4  x1 = x1(:); x0 = -x1;   k = 0;
5  while ~converged(x0,x1,tol)
6      x0 = x1;
7      F = feval(f,x0);
8      b = -F; J = numJ(f,x0);
9      s = J \ b;
10     x1 = x0 + s;
11     k = k + 1;
12     if k > itmax, error('Maxit in NewtonnD'); end
13 end
```

Listing 11.16. C-BasicMethods/M/ex2NLeqs.m

```
1  function F = ex2NLeqs(x)
2  % ex2NLeqs.m  -- version 2010-12-23
3  F = zeros(numel(x),1);
4  F(1) = x(1) + x(2)  - 3;
5  F(2) = x(1)^2 + x(2)^2 - 9;
```

Listing 11.17. C-BasicMethods/M/numJ.m

```
1  function J = numJ(f,x)
2  % numJ.m  -- version  2010-09-16
3  n = numel(x); J = zeros(n,n); x = x(:);
4  Delta = diag(max(sqrt(eps) * abs(x),sqrt(eps)));
5  F = feval(f,x);
6  for j = 1:n
7      Fd = feval(f,(x + Delta(:,j)));
8      J(:,j) = (Fd - F) / Delta(j,j);
9  end
```

```
y0 = [1 5];
ys = NewtonnD('ex2NLeqs',y0)

ys =
    -0.0000
     3.0000
```

Matlab provides the function fsolve to find the solution of a nonlinear system (see Section 11.4.5).

Convergence

Under certain conditions, Newton's method converges quadratically. In practice, these conditions cannot be checked in advance. We have

$$\| y^{(k+1)} - y^* \| \;\leq\; \beta\gamma \| y^{(k)} - y^* \|^2, \quad k = 0,1,2,\ldots,$$

where β measures the relative nonlinearity $\| \nabla F(y^*)^{-1} \| \leq \beta < 0$ and γ is the Lipschitz constant. Moreover, convergence is only guaranteed if the starting point $y^{(0)}$ lies in a neighborhood of the solution y^*, where the neighborhood has to be defined. In the case of macroeconomic models, the starting point $y^{(0)}$ is naturally defined by the solution of the preceding period, which in general constitutes a good neighborhood.

Computational complexity

The computational complexity of Newton's method is determined by the solution of the linear system. If we compare the fixed point methods with Newton's method, we observe that the difference in the amount of computations comes from the evaluation of the Jacobian matrix and the solution of the linear system. This might appear to be a disadvantage for Newton's method. However, in practice, we observe that if we use a sparse direct method, the complexity of the two methods is comparable as the number of iterations for Newton's method is significantly below the one for the iterative methods.

11.6.4. Quasi-Newton methods

Newton's method necessitates at every iteration the evaluation of the Jacobian matrix, which in the case of a dense system requires the computation of n^2 derivatives, and the solution of a linear system, which is $O(n^3)$. In order to avoid the computation of the Jacobian matrix at every iteration, one might think to replace these computations by an inexpensive update of the Jacobian matrix. This gives rise to a variety of variants for Newton's method called quasi-Newton methods.

Broyden's method

This method updates the Jacobian matrix by means of rank one matrices. Given an approximation $B^{(k)}$ of the Jacobian matrix at iteration k, the approximation for iteration $k+1$ is computed as

$$B^{(k+1)} = B^{(k)} + \frac{(dF^{(k)} - B^{(k)} s^{(k)}) s^{(k)\prime}}{s^{(k)\prime} s^{(k)}},$$

where $dF^{(k)} = F(y^{(k+1)}) - F(y^{(k)})$ and $s^{(k)}$ is the solution to $B^{(k)} s^{(k)} = -F(y^{(k)})$. Broyden's algorithm (Algorithm 43) is formalized hereafter.

Algorithm 43 Broyden's method for nonlinear systems.

1: initialize $y^{(0)}$ and $B^{(0)}$ (an approximation for $\nabla F(y^{(0)})$)
2: **for** $k = 0, 1, 2, \ldots$ `until` convergence **do**
3:      solve $B^{(k)} s^{(k)} = -F(y^{(k)})$
4:      $y^{(k+1)} = y^{(k)} + s^{(k)}$
5:      $dF^{(k)} = F(y^{(k+1)}) - F(y^{(k)})$
6:      $B^{(k+1)} = B^{(k)} + (dF^{(k)} - B^{(k)} s^{(k)}) s^{(k)\prime} / (s^{(k)\prime} s^{(k)})$
7: **end for**

Example 11.6

Again we consider the system of Example 11.4 but use Broyden's method to solve it. First, we start with an identity matrix as approximation for the Jacobian matrix and the algorithm converges in 7 iterations from $y0 = [5/2 \ 1]$ to the solution $y^* = [0 \ 3]$ as can be seen in Fig. 11.19.

Next, we take the Jacobian matrix evaluated at the starting point for our initial $B^{(0)}$ matrix. In this case, the algorithm converges faster, that is, in 5 iterations, but to a different solution which is $y^* = [3 \ 0]$. This is illustrated in Fig. 11.20. The Matlab code for the Broyden algorithm and the call to it is given below.

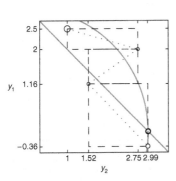

Iter	Solution		Error	
k	$y_1^{(k)}$	$y_2^{(k)}$	$y_1^{(k)} - y_1^{sol}$	$y_2^{(k)} - y_2^{sol}$
0	2.500	1.000	0.500	1.000
1	2.000	2.750	1.000	2.750
2	1.163	1.524	1.837	1.524
3	−0.361	2.995	3.361	2.995
4	0.199	2.808	2.801	2.808
5	0.017	2.986	2.983	2.986
6	−0.001	3.001	3.001	3.001
7	0.000	3.000	3.000	3.000

Figure 11.19 Steps of the Broyden algorithm for starting point $y0 = [5/2 \ 1]$ and identity matrix for $B^{(0)}$.

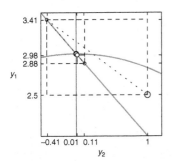

Iter	Solution		Error	
k	$y_1^{(k)}$	$y_2^{(k)}$	$y_1^{(k)} - y_1^{sol}$	$y_2^{(k)} - y_2^{sol}$
0	2.500	1.000	0.500	1.000
1	3.417	−0.417	0.417	0.417
2	2.883	0.117	0.117	0.117
3	2.985	0.015	0.015	0.015
4	3.001	−0.001	0.001	0.001
5	3.000	0.000	0.000	0.000

Figure 11.20 Steps of the Broyden algorithm for starting point $y0 = [5/2 \ 1]'$ and Jacobian matrix evaluated at the starting point for $B^{(0)}$.

Listing 11.18. C-BasicMethods/M/Broyden.m

```
1 function y1 = Broyden(f,y1,B,tol,itmax)
2 % Broyden.m  -- version  2010-08-10
3 n = numel(y1);
4 if nargin < 3, B = eye(n,n); tol = 1e-2; itmax = 10; end
5 y1 = y1(:); y0 = -y1;  k = 0;
6 F1 = feval(f,y1);
7 while ~converged(y0,y1,tol)
8     y0 = y1;
9     F0 = F1;
10    s = B \ -F0;
11    y1 = y0 + s;
12    F1 = feval(f,y1);
13    dF = F1 - F0;
14    B = B + ((dF - B*s)*s')/(s'*s);
15    k = k + 1;
16    if k > itmax, error('Iteration limit reached'); end
17 end
```

```
y0 = [5/2 1];
ys = Broyden('ex2NLeqs',y0)

ys =
     0.0000
     3.0000

B = numJ('ex2NLeqs',y0);
ys = Broyden('ex2NLeqs',y0,B,1e-2,10)

ys =
     3.0000
     0.0000
```

11.6.5. Further approaches

Damped Newton

If the starting point is far from the solution, Newton's method and its variants generally do not converge. This is due to the fact that the direction and, in particular, the length of the step are highly unreliable. In order to construct at iteration k a more conservative step, $y^{(k+1)}$, can be computed as

$$y^{(k+1)} = y^{(k)} + \alpha^{(k)} s^{(k)},$$

where $\alpha^{(k)}$ is a scalar to be determined and $s^{(k)}$ is a regular Newton step. Thus we set $0 < \alpha^{(k)} < 1$ if $y^{(k)}$ is far from the solution and $\alpha^{(k)} = 1$ if we get near the solution. One way to monitor the parameter $\alpha^{(k)}$ is to link its value to the value of $\|F(y^{(k)})\|$. This approach is called damped Newton.

A more sophisticated method to maintain the Newton step in the appropriate direction is the so-called trust region method which essentially consists in estimating the radius of a region within which the Newton step is constrained to stay. For more details, see, for example, Heath (2005).

Solution by minimization

To solve $F(y) = 0$, one can minimize the following objective function

$$g(y) = \| F(y) \|_p,$$

where p can be any norm in $\mathbb{R}^n$. One reason motivating this approach is that it provides a decision criterion about whether $y^{(k+1)}$ constitutes a better approximation to the solution y^* than $y^{(k)}$. As the solution satisfies $F(y^*) = 0$, we may compare the norm of the vectors $F(y^{(k+1)})$ and $F(y^{(k)})$. What we want is

$$\| F(y^{(k+1)}) \|_p < \| F(y^{(k)}) \|_p,$$

which can be achieved by minimizing the objective function

$$\min_y g(y) = \frac{1}{2} F(y)' F(y)$$

if we choose $p = 2$ for the norm. This minimization of a sum of squares can be solved with the Gauss–Newton or Levenberg–Marquardt algorithm presented in Sections 11.5.2 and 11.5.3. Figure 11.21 shows the objective function defined as $\| F(y) \|_2$ of the system of nonlinear equations defined in Example 11.4.

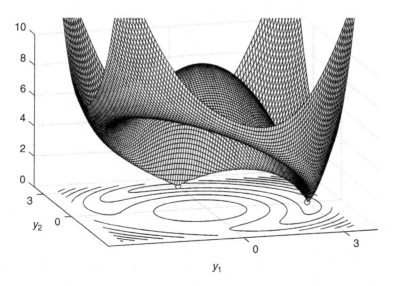

Figure 11.21 Objective function minimizing $\|F(y)\|_2$ for the solution of the system of nonlinear equations defined in Example 11.4.

11.7. Synoptic view of solution methods

The solution of linear systems of equations is a basic component in the methods presented in this chapter. Indeed, when we use a classical optimization technique, solve Least Squares problems, linear or nonlinear systems of equations, we have to find the solution of a linear system or a sequence of linear systems. Several approaches have been presented, and it might be clarifying to give a synthetic view and indicate the possible combinations among these methods. Figure 11.22 attempts to provide this overview. The leaf nodes with the block method indicate that for each block in turn, we have a choice for the solution and, therefore, they link to the nodes $\boxed{L}$ and $\boxed{NL}$, respectively. Similarly for Newton's method, we link to the node $\boxed{L}$ for the solution of the linear system in the successive steps.

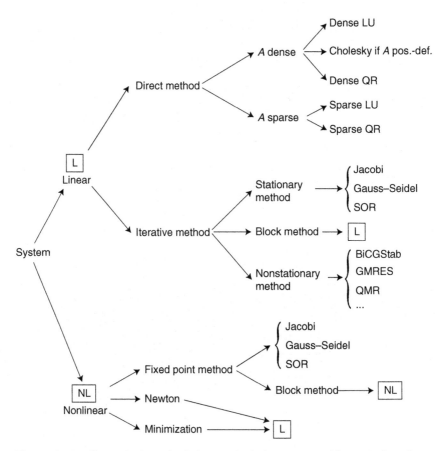

Figure 11.22 Synoptic view of solution methods for systems of linear and nonlinear equations.

## CHAPTER TWELVE

Heuristic methods in a nutshell

In 1957, Herbert Simon famously conjectured that within 10 years, computer chess programs would be written that surpass the best human players (Coles, 1994). It took longer: only in 1997 scored IBM's Deep Blue a tournament victory against then world champion Garry Kasparov (Campbell, A. Joseph Hoane, and Hsu, 2001). What is important here is not that Simon (who was well aware of human limitations in forecasting) underestimated the required time, but the "philosophy" with which Deep Blue approached the problem. The aim for Deep Blue was not to emulate human players, their strategies and decision rules, in particular in pattern recognition. Deep Blue beat Kasparov because with its specialized hardware it could evaluate more than 100 million board positions in a second, which allowed it to do a deep search among possible moves (Campbell, A. Joseph Hoane, and Hsu, 2001; Hsu, 2007); it beat Kasparov by sheer force.

This book is not about chess (though choosing a move in a game is an optimization problem). But the story is instructive nevertheless. It mirrors the start of a paradigm shift that takes place in optimization, away from subtle mathematical theory towards simpler techniques, which in turn require fewer assumptions. The price to pay: much more computing power is needed. But "much more" is a relative term—your desktop PC suffices.

12.1. Heuristics

In this chapter, we will outline the basic principles of heuristic methods and summarize several well-known techniques. These descriptions are not meant as definite references (all the presented techniques exist in countless variations), but they are meant to give the basic rules by which these methods operate. In the following chapters we will discuss the implementation of several techniques.

The term heuristic is used in various scientific fields for different, though often related, purposes. In mathematics, it is used for derivations that are not provable, sometimes even formally false, but lead to correct conclusions nonetheless. The term was made famous in this context by

George Pólya (1957). Psychologists use the word heuristics for simple rules of thumb for decision making. The term acquired a negative connotation through the works of Daniel Kahneman and Amos Tversky in the 1970s, since their heuristics-and-biases program involved a number of experiments that showed the apparent suboptimality of such simple decision rules (Tversky and Kahneman, 1974). More recently, however, an alternative interpretation of these results has been advanced; see, for example, Gigerenzer (2004, 2008). Many studies indicate that while simple rules underperform in stylized settings, they yield surprisingly good results in more realistic situations, in particular, in the presence of noise and uncertainty (e.g., estimation error). Curiously, substantial strands of literature in different disciplines document the good performance of simple methods when it comes to prediction, and judgment and decision making under uncertainty. Points in case are forecasting (see Makridakis, Hibon, and Moser, 1979, Makridakis and Hibon, 2000, Goldstein and Gigerenzer, 2009; see specifically the so-called M-competitions), econometrics (see Armstrong, 1978), psychology and decision analysis (Dawes, 1979, 1994, Lovie and Lovie, 1986). Still, within its respective discipline, each of these strands represents a niche. Such a strand developed in portfolio optimization in the 1970s; see, for instance, Elton and Gruber (1973); Elton, Gruber, and Urich (1978). The idea of these papers was to justify the use of computationally feasible, but simplifying techniques. The problem then was to reduce computational cost, and the authors tried to give empirical justification for these simpler techniques. Today, complicated models are feasible, but they are still not necessarily better.

The term heuristic is also used in computer science; Pearl (1984, p. 3) describes heuristics as methods or rules for decision making that (i) are simple, and (ii) give good results sufficiently often. Among computer scientists, heuristics are often related to research in artificial intelligence; sometimes specific methods like Genetic Algorithms are put on a level with, say, Neural Networks in the sense that both are computational architectures that solve problems. In this book, we will define heuristics in a narrower sense. We will always stay in the framework of optimization models, thus our basic problem will be

$$\underset{x}{\text{minimize}}\, f(x, \text{data})$$

where f is a scalar-valued function and x is a vector of decision variables. (Recall that by switching the sign of f we can make it a maximization problem.) In fact, we have found it helpful not to think in terms of a mathematical description, but rather something like `solutionQuality = function(x,data)`. That is, we only need to be able to write down (to program) a mapping from a solution to its quality, given the data. In most cases, this optimization problem will be constrained. Heuristics, in the sense the term is used in this book, are a class of numerical methods that can solve such problems. Following similar definitions in Zanakis and Evans (1981), Barr et al. (1995), and Winker and Maringer (2007b), we characterize the term optimization heuristic through several criteria:

- The method should give a "good" stochastic approximation of the true optimum; "goodness" can be measured in computing time and solution quality.
- The method should be robust to changes in the given problem's objective function and constraints, and also to changes in the problem size. Furthermore, results should not vary too much with changes in the parameter settings of the heuristic.
- The technique should be easy to implement.
- Implementation and application of the technique should not require subjective elements.

Such a definition is not unambiguous. Even in the optimization literature we find different characterizations of the term heuristic. In operations research, heuristics are often not regarded as stand-alone methods but as workarounds for problems in which "real" techniques like linear programming do not work satisfactorily; see, for instance, Hillier (1983). Or the term is used for ad hoc adjustments to methods that seem to work well but whose advantage cannot be proved mathematically. We will not follow this conception. Heuristics as defined here are general-purpose methods that can, as we will show, handle problems that are sometimes completely infeasible for classical approaches. Still, even though there exists considerable evidence of the good performance of heuristics, they are still not widely applied in research and practice.

In a very broad sense, we can differentiate between two classes of heuristics: constructive methods and iterative search methods. Constructive methods build new solutions in a stepwise procedure. An algorithm starts with an empty solution and adds components iteratively. Thus, the procedure terminates once we have found one complete solution. An example for this approach comes from the Traveling Salesman Problem. Solution methods exist where we start with one city and then add the remaining cities one at a time until a complete tour (i.e., one solution) is created.

For iterative search methods, the algorithm moves from solution to solution, that is, a complete existing solution is changed to obtain a new solution. These new solutions need not always be close to the previous ones, as some methods (e.g., Genetic Algorithms) are discontinuous in their creation of new solutions. Hence, a new solution may be quite different from its predecessor; it will, however, usually share some characteristics with it.

In this book, we will only consider iterative search methods. For such a method, we start with one or several solutions, and then modify these solutions until a stopping criterion is satisfied. To describe such a method, we need to specify:

(i) how we generate new solutions (i.e., how we modify existing solutions),

(ii) when to accept such a new solution, and

(iii) when to stop the search.

These three steps summarize the basic idea of an iterative search method. Clearly, such a description is very broad; it includes even many of the classical techniques discussed in the previous chapter. As an example, think of a steepest descent method (see Section 11.4.1). Suppose we have an initial (current) solution x^c, and we want to find a new solution x^n. Then the rules could be as follows:

(i) We estimate the slope (i.e., the gradient) of f at x^c which gives us the search direction. The new solution x^n is then $x^c - \gamma \nabla f(x^c)$, where γ is a step size.

(ii) If $f(x^n) < f(x^c)$, then we accept x^n, that is, we replace x^c by x^n.

(iii) We stop if no further improvements in f can be found, or if we reach a maximum number of function evaluations.

Problems will mostly occur with rules (i) and (ii). Problems can occur with rule (iii), too. They are mostly caused by round-off error, but can, at least for the applications in this book, be avoided by careful programming; see Chambers, 2008, Chapter 6, for a discussion.

As was noted already in Chapter 10, there are models in which the gradient does not exist, or cannot be computed meaningfully (e.g., when the objective function is not smooth). Hence, we may need other approaches to compute a search direction. The acceptance criterion for classical methods is strict: if there is no improvement, a candidate solution is not accepted. But if the objective function has several minima, this means we will never be able to move away from a local minimum, even if it is not the global optimum.

Iterative search heuristics follow the same basic pattern (i)–(iii), but they have different rules that are better suited for problems with noisy objective functions, multiple minima and other properties that may cause trouble for classical methods. In this sense, heuristics can be traced back to a class of numerical optimization methods that were introduced back in the 1950s, direct search methods. This is not to say that there is a direct historical development from direct search to heuristic methods. Contributions to the development of modern heuristics came from different scientific disciplines. Yet, it is very instructive to study direct search methods: first, they are still widely applied, in particular the Nelder–Mead algorithm (in Matlab implemented in the function fminsearch, in R in the function optim). Second, and more important for us, they share several of the characteristics of heuristic methods: they are simple, easy to implement, and simply work well for many problems.

In the last chapter, we already looked into a direct search technique, Nelder–Mead search. Nelder–Mead search shares one feature with modern heuristics: it does not compute the search direction in a theoretically optimal way; rather, a good search direction is chosen. In fact, many heuristic techniques show an even more remote reliance on good search directions. However, Nelder–Mead still has "classical" features. It has a strict acceptance criterion, that is, a new solution is only accepted if it is better than the current solution; and the method is deterministic, so from a given starting point it will always move to the same solution. If this solution is only a local minimum, Nelder–Mead will get stuck. Most heuristics thus add strategies to overcome local minima; one such strategy is randomness.

In the following sections we will describe several well-known heuristics. To keep the presentation simple we only differentiate between trajectory methods and population-based methods, both terms to be explained below. More detailed classification systems of heuristics can be found in Talbi (2002) and Winker and Gilli (2004).

12.2. Trajectory methods

Trajectory methods evolve a single solution over time. By changing this solution gradually, the algorithm follows a path, a trajectory, through the search space.

12.2.1. Stochastic local search

Assume that we have again a current solution x^c, and wish to obtain a search direction to compute a new solution. But now instead of computing the slope of the objective function or of reflecting a simplex as in Nelder–Mead, we use a much simpler mechanism. We randomly select one element in x^c (e.g., one decision variable), and change it slightly. If this new solution is better than x^c, we keep it; if not, we keep x^c. This is the basic idea of a (stochastic) local search.

The concept of local search is not new, but the technique was not regarded as a complete method in the literature. Rather, it was considered a component within other techniques, for example, as a safeguard against saddle points (Gill, Murray, and Wright, 1986, p. 295). This reluctance is understandable: if gradient-based methods can be applied, local search will be grossly inefficient since it ignores the information that the derivatives of the objective function provide. This inefficiency will always remain—on a relative basis. But absolute computing time for given problems has declined so much in recent decades that local search could become a central building block of various methods.

A typical local search starts with a randomly chosen feasible solution x^c and picks, again randomly, a new solution x^n close to x^c. This new solution x^n is called the neighbor solution. If it is better than x^c, the new solution is accepted and replaces x^c; if not, it is rejected. This procedure is repeated many times over. For a given objective function, a local search is completely described by how it chooses a neighbor solution and its stopping criterion. The latter may simply be a preset number of steps. Algorithm 44 summarizes the procedure. In fact, local search could be called a direct search method, even though it is rarely described as such in the literature. And there are differences: unlike Nelder–Mead, local search does not exploit an accepted search direction; and it is not deterministic.

Algorithm 44 Local search.

1: set n_{steps}
2: randomly generate current solution x^c
3: **for** $i = 1 : n_{steps}$ **do**
4:     generate $x^n \in \mathcal{N}(x^c)$ and compute $\Delta = f(x^n) - f(x^c)$
5:     **if** $\Delta < 0$ **then** $x^c = x^n$
6: **end for**
7: $x^{sol} = x^c$

In a sufficiently well-behaved setting, a local search will, for a suitable neighborhood definition and enough iterations, succeed in finding the global minimum. The compensation for its lack of efficiency is that local search only requires that the objective function be evaluated for a given solution x; there is no need for the objective function to be continuous or differentiable or well-behaved in any other sense. Unfortunately, a local search will, like direct search methods, also stop at the first local optimum it encounters. However, repeatedly restarting the algorithm, even with the same initial solution, will normally produce different results. So there is at least a chance of finding better solutions; there is at least a chance of not getting trapped. We discuss local search in Chapter 13 as a tool for asset selection. Hoos and Stützle (2004) provide a detailed discussion of the technique and its many variants.

Heuristic methods that build on local search employ further strategies to avoid getting trapped in local minima. One common feature is the acceptance of solutions that do not lower (i.e., improve) the objective function, but actually increase it. The heuristics described in the following sections all share this feature.

12.2.2. Simulated Annealing

The probably best-known trajectory method is Simulated Annealing (SA), introduced in Kirkpatrick, Gelatt, and Vecchi (1983). SA was conceived for combinatorial problems, but can easily be used for continuous problems as well. Algorithm 45 gives the pseudocode of the procedure.

Algorithm 45 Simulated Annealing.

1: set $R_{\max}$ and T
2: randomly generate current solution x^c
3: **for** $r = 1$ to $R_{\max}$ **do**
4:     **while** stopping criteria not met **do**
5:         generate $x^n \in \mathcal{N}(x^c)$ (neighbor to current solution)
6:         compute $\Delta = f(x^n) - f(x^c)$ and generate u (uniform random variable)
7:         **if** $(\Delta < 0)$ or $(e^{-\Delta/T} > u)$ **then** $x^c = x^n$
8:     **end while**
9:     reduce T
10: **end for**
11: $x^{\mathrm{sol}} = x^c$

Like the stochastic local search in the previous section, SA starts with a random solution x^c and creates a new solution x^n by adding a small perturbation to x^c. If the new solution is better than the current one ($\Delta < 0$), it is accepted and replaces x^c. In case x^n is worse, SA does not reject it right away, but applies a stochastic acceptance criterion, thus there is still a chance that the new solution will be accepted, albeit only with a certain probability. This probability is a decreasing function of both the order of magnitude of the deterioration and the time the algorithm has already run. This time factor is controlled by the temperature parameter T which is reduced over time; hence, impairments in the objective function become less likely to be accepted and, eventually, SA turns into standard local search. The algorithm stops after a predefined number of iterations $R_{\max}$.

The acceptance criterion can be specified in different ways. In Algorithm 45, we have used the so-called Metropolis function for which the probability of accepting an inferior solution is $\min(1, e^{-\Delta/T})$. Graphically, the probability as a function of Δ is:

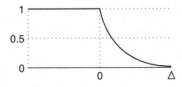

There are alternatives: the Barker criterion $\frac{1}{1+e^{\Delta/T}}$, for instance, completely blurs the distinction between improvement and deterioration of a solution (Schuur, 1997):

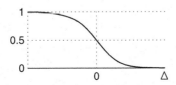

12.2.3. Threshold Accepting

Threshold Accepting (TA) is similar to SA. Algorithm 46 shows that the two methods only differ in their acceptance criterion (Statement 7 in Algorithm 45, Statement 7 in Algorithm 46). Indeed, both SA and TA are sometimes called threshold methods.

Algorithm 46 Threshold Accepting.

1: set n_{rounds} and n_{steps}
2: compute threshold sequence τ_r
3: randomly generate current solution x^c
4: **for** $r = 1 : n_{\text{rounds}}$ **do**
5:      **for** $i = 1 : n_{\text{steps}}$ **do**
6:          generate $x^n \in \mathcal{N}(x^c)$ and compute $\Delta = f(x^n) - f(x^c)$
7:          **if** $\Delta < \tau_r$ **then** $x^c = x^n$
8:      **end for**
9: **end for**
10: $x^{\text{sol}} = x^c$

Whereas in SA solutions that lead to a higher objective function value are accepted stochastically, TA accepts deteriorations unless they are greater than some threshold τ_r. The n_{rounds} thresholds decrease over time, hence like SA the algorithm turns into a local search. Graphically, the probability of accepting a solution as a function of Δ is:

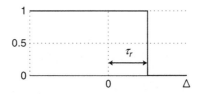

Threshold Accepting was introduced by Dueck and Scheuer (1990); Moscato and Fontanari (1990) suggested the same deterministic updating rule in SA and called it "threshold updating." For an in-depth description of TA, see Winker (2001). We will discuss the implementation of local search and TA for portfolio optimization in Chapter 13.

12.2.4. Tabu Search

Most heuristics differ from classical methods by introducing an element of chance. In methods like SA or TA, for example, we picked neighbor solutions randomly. Tabu Search (TS), at least in its standard form, is an exception. It is deterministic for a given starting value. TS was designed for discrete search spaces; it is described in Glover (1986), Glover and Laguna (1997), and detailed in Algorithm 47. Its strategy to overcome local minima is to keep a memory of recently visited solutions. These are forbidden (tabu) as long as they stay in the algorithm's memory. In this way, a TS can manage to walk away from a local minimum as it is temporarily not allowed to revisit this solution.

Algorithm 47 Tabu Search.

1: initialize tabu list $T = \emptyset$
2: randomly generate current solution x^c
3: **while** stopping criteria not met **do**
4:     compute $V = \{x | x \in \mathcal{N}(x^c)\} \backslash T$
5:     select $x^n = \mathrm{argmin}_{\{x | x \in V\}} f(x)$
6:     $x^c = x^n$ and $T = T \cup x^n$
7:     update memory, update best solution x^{sol}
8: **end while**
9: return x^{sol}

12.3. Population-based methods

For trajectory methods, the key mechanism for escaping local minima is to temporarily allow uphill moves; the methods do not enforce an improvement of the objective function in every iteration. Population-based methods employ the same principle, but they do so by maintaining a whole collection of different solutions at a time, some of which are worse than others. Population-based methods are often better at exploration than trajectory methods, that is, they are often good at identifying favorable regions in the search space.

12.3.1. Genetic Algorithms

The best-known technique in this category are Genetic Algorithms (GA). Genetic Algorithms were described by John Holland in the 1970s (Holland, 1992); pseudocode can be found in Algorithm 48. GA are inspired by evolutionary biology, hence, the procedure appropriately starts with a population of solutions; the objective function becomes a fitness function (to be maximized); iterations become generations. In a standard GA, solutions are coded as binary strings like `0 1 1 1 0 0 0 1`. Such a string may be a binary representation of an integer or real number, but in many discrete problems there is a more natural interpretation: in a selection problem, a `1` may indicate a selected item from an ordered list, a `0` may stand for an item that does not enter the solution. New candidate solutions, called children or offspring, are created by crossover (i.e., mixing existing solutions) and mutation (i.e., randomly changing components of solutions), as illustrated here:

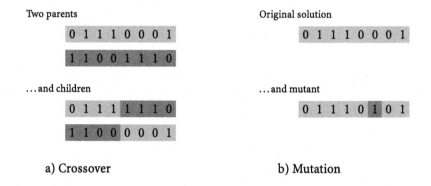

Two parents   Original solution

...and children   ...and mutant

a) Crossover   b) Mutation

To have the population size #{P} remain constant, a selection among parents and children takes place at the end of each generation (Statement 10). Many variations exist; for example, only the #{P} fittest solutions may stay in P, or the survival of a solution may be stochastic with the probability of survival proportional to a solution's fitness. Depending on the selection mechanism (the function survive in Statement 10), the currently best member of the population may become extinct. In such a case, we may want to keep track of the best solution over time.

Algorithm 48 Genetic Algorithms.

1: randomly generate initial population P of solutions
2: **while** stopping criteria not met **do**
3:     select $P' \subset P$ (mating pool), initialize $P'' = \emptyset$ (set of children)
4:     **for** $i = 1$ to n **do**
5:         randomly select individuals x^a and x^b from P'
6:         apply crossover to x^a and x^b to produce x^{child}
7:         randomly mutate produced child x^{child}
8:         $P'' = P'' \cup x^{child}$
9:     **end for**
10:    $P = survive(P', P'')$
11: **end while**
12: return best solution

12.3.2. Differential Evolution

A more recent contribution to population-based methods is Differential Evolution (DE; Storn and Price, 1997). Algorithm 49 gives the pseudocode. DE evolves a population of n_P solutions, stored in real-valued vectors of length d. Thus, solutions are represented in DE in a way that is immediately appropriate for continuous problems. The population P will be handled as a matrix of size $d \times n_P$; each column holds one candidate solution, each row gives the values that one particular decision variable takes on in the population. In every iteration (or generation) k, the algorithm goes through the columns of this matrix and creates a new candidate solution for each existing solution $P_{\cdot,i}^{(0)}$. Such a candidate solution is constructed by taking the difference between two other solutions, weighting this difference by a scalar F, and adding it to a third solution. Then an element-wise crossover takes place between this auxiliary solution $P_{\cdot,i}^{(v)}$ and the existing solution $P_{\cdot,i}^{(0)}$ (see Statement 9; rand represents a random variable that is uniformly distributed between zero and one, the crossover probability is CR). If this final candidate solution $P_{\cdot,i}^{(u)}$ is better than $P_{\cdot,i}^{(0)}$, it replaces it; if not, the old solution $P_{\cdot,i}^{(0)}$ is kept. By construction, the best solution will always be kept in the population. The algorithm stops after n_G generations.

Algorithm 49 Differential Evolution.

1: set n_P, n_G, F and CR
2: randomly generate initial population $P_{j,i}^{(1)}$, $j = 1,\ldots,d$, $i = 1,\ldots,n_P$
3: **for** $k = 1$ to n_G **do**
4:    $P^{(0)} = P^{(1)}$
5:    **for** $i = 1$ to n_P **do**
6:       randomly generate $r_1, r_2, r_3 \in \{1,\ldots,n_P\}$, $r_1 \neq r_2 \neq r_3 \neq i$
7:       compute $P_{\cdot,i}^{(v)} = P_{\cdot,r_1}^{(0)} + F \times (P_{\cdot,r_2}^{(0)} - P_{\cdot,r_3}^{(0)})$
8:       **for** $j = 1$ to d **do**
9:          **if** rand $<$ CR **then** $P_{j,i}^{(u)} = P_{j,i}^{(v)}$ **else** $P_{j,i}^{(u)} = P_{j,i}^{(0)}$
10:       **end for**
11:       **if** $f(P_{\cdot,i}^{(u)}) < f(P_{\cdot,i}^{(0)})$ **then** $P_{\cdot,i}^{(1)} = P_{\cdot,i}^{(u)}$ **else** $P_{\cdot,i}^{(1)} = P_{\cdot,i}^{(0)}$
12:    **end for**
13: **end for**
14: return best solution

In its standard form as described here, DE randomly chooses solutions to be mixed and crossed. This particular chance mechanism also means that in any given generation, potential changes to a given solution come from a finite set of possible moves. Practically, this simply means we need a sufficiently large population (Storn and Price suggest ten times the number of decision variables, that is, $10d$); we may also introduce additional randomness. Many variations of DE are described in Price, Storn, and Lampinen (2005). We will use DE in Chapters 14 and 15.

12.3.3. Particle Swarm Optimization

The metaphor for GA and DE was evolution, but for Particle Swarm Optimization (PSO) it is flocks of birds that search for food (Eberhart and

Kennedy, 1995). Like DE, PSO is directly applicable to continuous problems; the population of n_P solutions is again stored in real-valued vectors. In each iteration, a solution is updated by adding another vector called velocity v_i (see Algorithm 50). We can picture a solution as a position in the search space, and velocity as the direction of movement of this solution. Velocity changes over the course of the optimization. At the start of each generation the directions towards the best solution found by the particular solution, $Pbest_i$, and the best overall solution, $Pbest_{gbest}$, are determined. The sum of these two directions—which are the differences between the respective vectors; see Statement 7—are perturbed by multiplication with a uniform random variable $u_{(.)}$ and a constant $c_{(.)}$. The vector so obtained is added to the previous v_i; the resulting updated velocity is added to the respective solution. The algorithm stops after n_G generations.

Algorithm 50 Particle Swarm Optimization.

1: set n_P, n_G and c_1, c_2
2: randomly generate initial population $P_i^{(0)}$ and velocity $v_i^{(0)}$, $i = 1,\ldots,n_P$
3: evaluate objective function $F_i = f(P_i^{(0)})$, $i = 1,\ldots,n_P$
4: $Pbest = P^{(0)}$, $Fbest = F$, $Gbest = \min_i(F_i)$, $gbest = \operatorname{argmin}_i(F_i)$
5: **for** $k = 1$ to n_G **do**
6:     **for** $i = 1$ to n_P **do**
7:         $\Delta v_i = c_1 u_1 (Pbest_i - P_i^{(k-1)}) + c_2 u_2 (Pbest_{gbest} - P_i^{(k-1)})$
8:         $v_i^{(k)} = v_i^{(k-1)} + \Delta v_i$
9:         $P_i^{(k)} = P_i^{(k-1)} + v_i^{(k)}$
10:    **end for**
11:    evaluate objective function $F_i = f(P_i^{(k)})$, $i = 1,\ldots,n_P$
12:    **for** $i = 1$ to n_P **do**
13:        **if** $F_i < Fbest_i$ **then** $Pbest_i = P_i^{(k)}$ and $Fbest_i = F_i$
14:        **if** $F_i < Gbest$ **then** $Gbest = F_i$ and $gbest = i$
15:    **end for**
16: **end for**
17: return best solution

PSO is used in Chapter 14 for robust regression.

12.3.4. Ant Colony Optimization

Ant Colony Optimization (ACO) was introduced in the early 1990s by Marco Dorigo in his PhD thesis (see Dorigo, Di Caro, and Gambardella, 1999, for an overview); it is inspired by the search behavior of ants (Goss, Aron, Deneubourg, and Pasteels, 1989).

ACO is applicable to combinatorial optimization problems which are coded as graphs. A solution is a particular path through the graph. ACO algorithms start with a population of ants, each of which represents an empty solution (thus, ACO has elements of a constructive method). The ants then traverse the graph, until each ant has constructed a solution. The ants' way is guided by a pheromone trail: at each node, there is a probability to move along a particular edge; this probability is an increasing function of the pheromone (a positive number) that is associated with the specific edge. Initially edges are chosen with equal probability. After each iteration, the quality of the solutions is assessed; edges that belong to good solutions receive more pheromone. In later iterations, such edges are more likely to be chosen by the ants. Algorithm 51 summarizes the procedure.

Algorithm 51 Ant Colony Optimization.

1: set parameters
2: **while** stopping criteria not met **do**
3:     randomly place ants in graph
4:     **for** each ant **do**
5:         construct solution (tour)
6:         evaluate solution
7:     **end for**
8:     save best solution x^{sol}
9:     update trails
10: **end while**
11: return best solution

12.4. Hybrids

The heuristics presented in the previous section can be considered as general procedures applicable to a wide range of problems, but they all have their particular features. Hybrid heuristics are made up by assembling components from different heuristics. The construction of hybrid heuristics can be motivated by the need to achieve a trade-off between the desirable features of specific heuristics. A more general notion of a hybrid heuristic would also allow for combining a heuristic with classical optimization tools such as direct search. Nevertheless our advice is to always start with a "standard" heuristic and switch to a hybrid method only in exceptional situations.

As the components of different heuristics can be combined in numerous ways, it might prove useful to give a structured view about the possibilities of constructing hybrids. We first classify the heuristics according to their main features in a more fine-grained way as done in the previous section and then provide a simple scheme for possible combinations.[1]

---

[1] This presentation builds on Talbi, 2002, Taillard et al., 2000, and Birattari et al., 2001.

Trajectory methods
The current solution is slightly modified by searching within the neighborhood of the current solution. This is typically the case for threshold methods and Tabu Search.

Discontinuous methods
Full solution space is available for the new solution. The discontinuity is induced by genetic operators (crossover, mutation) as is the case for Genetic Algorithms, Differential Evolution, and Particle Swarm Optimization and which corresponds to jumps in the search space.

Single-agent methods
One solution per iteration is processed. This is the case for threshold methods and Tabu Search.

Multi-agent or population-based methods
A population of searching agents contributes to the collective experience. This is the case for Genetic Algorithms, Ant Colonies, Differential Evolution, and Particle Swarm Optimization.

Guided search or search with memory usage
Incorporates some additional rules and hints on where to search. In Genetic Algorithms, Differential Evolution, and Particle Swarm Optimization, the population represents the memory of the recent search experience. In Ant Colony Optimization, the pheromone matrix represents an adaptive memory of previously visited solutions. In Tabu Search, the tabu list provides a short-term memory.

Unguided search or memoryless methods
Relies perfectly on the search heuristic. This is the case for threshold methods.

Talbi (2002) suggests a classification combining a hierarchical scheme and a flat scheme. The hierarchical scheme distinguishes between low-level and high-level hybridization and within each level we distinguish relay and co-evolutionary hybridization. Low-level hybridization replaces a component of a given heuristic by a component from another heuristic. In the case of high-level hybridization, different heuristics are self-contained. Relay hybridization combines different heuristics in a sequence whereas in co-evolutionary hybridization the different heuristics cooperate.

For the flat scheme we distinguish the following hybridizations: (i) homogenous hybrids where the same heuristics are used and heterogeneous hybrids where different heuristics are combined; (ii) global hybrids where all algorithms explore the same solution space and partial hybrids

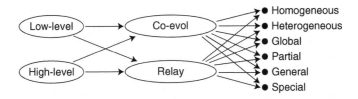

Figure 12.1 Scheme for possible hybridizations.

which work in a partitioned solution space; (iii) specialist hybrids combine heuristics solving different problems whereas in general hybrids the algorithms all solve the same problem. Fig. 12.1 illustrates this hierarchical and flat classification.

A few examples might demonstrate the construction of hybrids following the two-level hierarchical and flat scheme.

Low-level relay hybrid

As an example we could consider a Simulated Annealing where a neighbor x^n is obtained as follows: Select a point x^i in the larger neighborhood of x^c and perform a descent local search. If this point is not accepted (upper panel) we return to x^c (not x^i) and continue (lower panel):

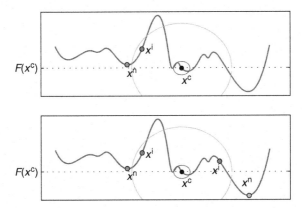

Low-level co-evolutionary hybrid

Population-based algorithms perform well in the exploration of the search space but are weak in the exploitation of the solutions found. Therefore, for instance, a possible hybridization would be to use in a Genetic Algorithm a greedy heuristic[2] for the crossover and a Tabu Search for the mutation as indicated in the following pseudocode.

---

[2] The term greedy optimization is mostly used for constructive methods. A greedy method constructs a solution by, in each iteration, taking the best possible move according to an optimality criterion. Greedy techniques do not look ahead (they are myopic) and, hence, cannot escape local minima.

1: $\cdots$
2: select $P' \subset P$ (mating pool), initialize $P'' = \emptyset$ (children)
3: **for** $i = 1$ to n **do**
4:      select individuals x^a and x^b at random from P'
5:      apply crossover to x^a and x^b to produce x^{child} (greedy algorithm)
6:      randomly mutate produced child x^{child} (Tabu Search (TS))
7:      $P'' = P'' \cup x^{child}$
8: **end for**
9: $\cdots$

High-level relay hybrid

Examples are the use of a greedy heuristic to generate the initial population of a Genetic Algorithm and/or threshold method and Tabu Search to improve the population obtained by the Genetic Algorithm as described below.

1: generate current population P of solutions   (greedy algorithm)
2: compute GA solution
3: improve solution with threshold method (TM)

Another example is the use of a heuristic to optimize another heuristic, that is, find the optimal values for the parameters.

High-level co-evolutionary hybrid

In this scheme, many self-contained algorithms cooperate in a parallel search to find an optimum.

12.5. Constraints

Nothing in the algorithms that we presented above ensures that a constraint on a solution x is observed. But it is often constraints that make models realistic—and difficult. Several strategies exist for including restrictions. Note that in what follows, we do not differentiate between linear, nonlinear, integer constraints, and so on. It rarely matters for heuristics to what class a constraint belongs; computationally, any functional form is possible.

All techniques discussed before are iterative methods, that is, we move from one solution to the next. The simplest approach is to "throw away" infeasible new solutions. Suppose we have a current solution, and we modify it to get a neighbor solution. If this neighbor violates a constraint, we just pick a new neighbor. Clearly, this works only for stochastic choices of neighbor solutions, but almost all heuristics are stochastic. This strategy may appear inefficient, but if our model has only few constraints which are not often hit, it is often a good strategy.

A second approach is to directly use the information of the constraint to create new solutions. An example from portfolio optimization (discussed in more detail in the next chapter) is the budget constraint, that is, we require that all asset weights sum to one. This constraint can be enforced when we compute new solutions by increasing some weights and decreasing others such that the sum of all weight changes is zero.

An older but still used idea is to transform variables. This approach sometimes works for constraints that require that the elements of x lie in certain ranges; see the discussion in Powell (1972). For instance, $\sin(x)$ will map any real x to the range $[-1, 1]$; $\alpha (\sin(x))^2$ will give a mapping to $[0, \alpha]$. But such transformations come with their own problems; see Gill, Murray, and Wright (1986, Section 7.4); in particular it may become difficult to change a problem later on, or to handle multiple constraints.

Fourth, we can repair a solution that does not observe a restriction. We can introduce mechanisms to correct such violations. To stick with our example, if a solution x holds the portfolio weights, then scaling every element j in x as $x_j/\sum x$ will ensure that the weights sum to unity.

Finally, we can penalize infeasible solutions. Whenever a constraint is violated, we add a penalty term to the objective function and so downgrade the quality of the solution. In essence, this changes the problem to an unconstrained one for which we can use the heuristic. The penalty is often made an increasing function of the magnitude of violation. Thus, the algorithm may move through infeasible areas of the search space, but will have guidance to return to feasible areas. The penalty approach is the most generic strategy to include constraints; it is convenient since the computational architecture needs rarely to be changed. Penalties create soft constraints since the algorithm could in principle always override a penalty; practically, we can set the penalty so high that we have hard constraints. The preferred strategy is to start with a low penalty; if the final solution still violates any constraints, the penalty is increased gradually until we get a feasible solution.

So which approach is best? Unfortunately, it depends on the problem. Often, we will use a mixture of these approaches. In fact, we can never know whether we have found the most efficient implementation. But fortunately, we do not need to. Herbert Simon's "satisficing" gives the rule: if we can solve our model to sufficient precision under the given practical constraints (e.g., available time), we can stop searching. So which approach is good? In our experience, a good way to start is with penalties. Penalties are quickly implemented, and they offer other advantages; for instance, they work well if the search space is not convex or even disconnected. See the following picture.

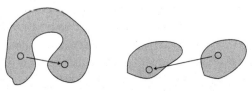

When we need a really fast implementation, repairing or using the constraints directly is likely more efficient. But it is also less flexible—adding further constraints or changing the problem may require changes in the repair mechanism—and simply requires more time for development and testing. Thus, again, for testing purposes and as long as a model is not put into very final form, penalties are a good idea. Needless to say, there are exceptions. We will see some in the coming chapters.

12.6. The stochastics of heuristic search

12.6.1. Stochastic solutions and computational resources

Suppose we wanted to solve an optimization problem with a naïve random sampling approach. We would (i) randomly generate a large number of candidate solutions, (ii) evaluate these solutions, and (iii) pick the best one. If we repeated the whole procedure a second time, our final solution would probably be a different one. Thus, the solution x we obtain from step (iii) is stochastic. The difference between our solution and the actual optimum would be a kind of truncation error since if we sampled more and more, we should in theory come arbitrarily close to the optimum. Importantly, the variability of the solution stems from our numerical technique; it has nothing to do with the error terms that we often have in our models to account for uncertainty. Stochastic solutions may even occur with non-stochastic methods: think of search spaces like those shown in Chapter 10. Even if we used a deterministic method like a gradient search, the many local minima would make sure that repeated runs from different starting points would result in different solutions.

Almost all heuristics are stochastic algorithms. So running the same technique twice, even with the same starting values, will usually result in different solutions. To make the discussion more tangible, we use again the example of portfolio selection (we discuss such models in the next chapter). A solution x is a vector of portfolio weights for which we can compute the objective function value $f(x)$. The objective function could be the variance of the portfolio or another function of the portfolio return. So, if we have two candidate solutions $x^{(1)}$ and $x^{(2)}$, we can easily determine which one is better.

Since our algorithms are stochastic, we can treat the result of our optimization procedures as a random variable with some distribution D. What exactly the "result" of a restart is depends on our setting. In most cases that we discuss later, it is only the objective function value (i.e., the solution quality) that we obtain from a single run of our technique. Alternatively, we may also look at decision variables given by a solution, that is, the portfolio weights. In any case, we collect all the quantities of interest in a vector ϱ. The result ϱ_j of a restart j is a random draw from D.

The trouble is that we do not know what D looks like. But fortunately, there is a simple way to find out for a given problem. We run a reasonably large number of restarts, each time store ϱ_j, and finally compute the empirical distribution function of the ϱ_j, $j = 1, \ldots,$ number of restarts as an estimate for D. For a given problem or problem class, the shape of the distribution D will depend on the chosen method. Some techniques will be more appropriate than others and give less variable and on average better results. And it will often depend on the particular settings of the method, in particular the number of iterations—the search time—that we allow for.

Unlike classical optimization techniques, heuristics can walk away from local minima; they will not necessarily get trapped. Intuitively, then, if we let the algorithm search for longer, we can hope to find better solutions. Thus the shape of D is strongly influenced by the amount of computational resources spent. One way to measure computational resources is the number of objective function evaluations. For minimization problems, when we increase computational resources, the mass of D will move to the left, and the distribution will become less variable. Ideally, when we let the computing time grow ever longer, D should degenerate into a single point, the global minimum. There exist proofs of this convergence to the global minimum for many heuristic methods (e.g., Gelfand and Mitter, 1985, for Simulated Annealing; Rudolph, 1994, for Genetic Algorithms; Gutjahr, 2000, Stützle and Dorigo, 2002, for Ant Colony Optimization; or van den Bergh and Engelbrecht, 2006, for Particle Swarm Optimization). But unfortunately these proofs are not much help for practical applications. First, they often rely on asymptotic arguments, but with an infinity of iterations even random sampling will eventually produce the global optimum. We can always make sure that the global optimum is achievable, we just need to randomly select starting values for our algorithm such that any feasible solution could be chosen. Then, with an infinity of restarts, we are bound to find the global optimum. But random sampling achieves the same theoretical guarantees, so search iterations that a heuristic adds would then not increase our confidence.

Second, many such proofs are nonconstructive (e.g., Althöfer and Koschnick, 1991, for TA). They demonstrate that there exist parameter settings for given methods that lead (asymptotically) to the global optimum. Yet, practically, there is no way of telling whether the chosen parameter setting is correct in this sense; we are never guaranteed that D really degenerates to the global optimum as the number of iterations grows.

Fortunately, we do not need these proofs to make meaningful statements about the performance of specific methods. For a given problem class, we can run experiments. We choose a parameter setting for a method, and we repeatedly solve the given problem. Each run j gives a solution with parameters ϱ_j; from such a sample we can compute an estimate for D. So when we speak of "convergence," we always mean "change in the shape of D." Such experiments also allow investigation of the sensitivity of the solutions with respect to different parameter settings for the heuristic. Experimental results are of course no proof of the general appropriateness of a method, but they are evidence of how a method performs for a given class of problems; often this is all that is needed for practical applications.

12.6.2. An illustrative experiment

Asset allocation in practice

The discussion about stochastic solutions is best illustrated by an example. Before we do so however, we would like to make clear what this example shows, and what it does not show. There is a trade-off between, in general terms, search time (or computing time) and quality of a solution. We search for longer, we find (on average) better solutions. Quality of the solution here refers solely to the numerical solution of our optimization model. We need be careful for there are actually two relationships that we should be interested in: if we search for longer, we should at least on average find better solutions to our model, given our data. That is, for a typical financial application, we find better solutions in-sample. So, we have one trade-off between computing time and quality of the in-sample solution. Then, we would hope, better solutions to the model should result in better solutions to our actual problem (like selecting a portfolio that yields a high risk-adjusted return over the next month). The first relationship (in-sample) seems reasonable, though to be practically useful we need be more concrete; we should run experiments to estimate the speed of convergence. This is what we do in this example. But the second trade-off is not at all clear. There is no reason to assume that there exists a positive relationship between in-sample and out-of-sample quality. This is something that needs to be tested empirically. This could imply that in some cases we might not even want the optimal solution to our model. From an optimization viewpoint this is awkward: our model is misspecified. Thus, we should write down the model such that we are interested in its optimum. Yes, agreed; but how can we know? Only by testing. This point is well understood in applications in which the model itself is chosen by some automatic procedure, for instance, when people train neural networks, or in model selection. It is rarely discussed when it comes to parameter optimization for a chosen model.

Now let us look at a concrete example. We describe the problem informally here; code is given in the next chapter. Suppose we are given a universe of 500 assets (for example, mutual funds), completely described by a given variance–covariance matrix, and we are asked to find an equal-weight portfolio with minimal variance under the constraints that we have only between K_{inf} and K_{sup} assets in the portfolio. Thus, we have a pure selection problem, a discrete problem.

How could we compute a solution to this problem? Here are several possible approaches.

1. Write down all portfolios that fulfill the constraints (i.e., have between K_{inf} and K_{sup} components), compute the variance of each, and pick the one with the lowest variance.
2. Choose k portfolios randomly and keep the one with the lowest variance.
3. Compute the variance of each asset and sort the assets by their variance. Then construct a portfolio with the K_{inf} assets with the lowest variance, then with $K_{inf} + 1$ assets, and so on until a portfolio of the K_{sup} assets with the lowest variance. Of those $K_{sup} - K_{inf} + 1$ portfolios, pick the one with the lowest variance.

Approach (1) is infeasible. Suppose we were to check cardinalities between 30 and 100. For 100 out of 500 alone we have 10^{107} possibilities, and that leaves us 30 out of 500, 31 out of 500, and so on. Even if we could evaluate millions of portfolios in a second it would not help.

Approach (2) has the advantage of being simple, and we can scale computational resources (increase k). That is, we can use the trade-off between available computing time and solution quality. Approach (2) can be thought of as a sample substitute for Approach (1).

In Approach (3), we ignore the covariation of assets (i.e., we only look at the main diagonal of the variance–covariance matrix), but we only have to check $K_{sup} - K_{inf} + 1$ portfolios. There may be cases, however, in which we would wish to include correlation.

To see how Approaches (2) and (3) perform, we set up an experiment. We create an artificial data set of 500 assets, each with a volatility of between 20% and 40%; each pairwise correlation is 0.6. ϱ in our case is the volatility (the square root of the variance) of the portfolio that our algorithm returns. The following figure gives estimates of D, each obtained from 500 restarts.

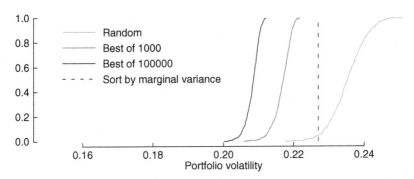

We see that completely random portfolios produce a distribution with a median of about 23½%. What would happen if we drew more portfolios? The shape of D would not change, since we are merely increasing our sample size. Our estimates of the tails would become more precise. We also plot the distribution of a "best-of-1000" and a "best-of-100,000" strategy. With this, we get the median volatility below 21%. We also add the results for the sort algorithm (Approach 3).

Stochastic local search

Now let us use a simple heuristic, a stochastic local search. We start with a random portfolio and compute its volatility. Then we randomly pick any asset of our universe. If it is already in the portfolio, we remove it. If it is not in the portfolio, we put it in. We compute the volatility of this new portfolio. If it is lower than the old portfolio's volatility, we keep the new portfolio; if not, we stick with the old portfolio. We include constraints in the simplest way: if a new portfolio violates a constraint, we never accept it. We run this search for 100 steps, 1000 steps, and 10,000 steps. The picture below shows the results. Again the distributions are computed from 500 restarts.

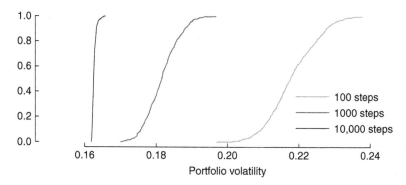

We see that the local search easily finds better portfolios than random search, and in less time. Compare the distribution of the "best-of-100,000" strategy with the distribution of a local search with 10,000 steps. The latter one needs only one-tenth of the number of objective function evaluations.

For the local search, we picked one asset and either put it into the portfolio or removed it. How would the results change if we chose two assets, or five? The following figure shows results with 10,000 steps (note that the x-scale has changed). It appears that changing only one asset at a time works better than changing several assets.

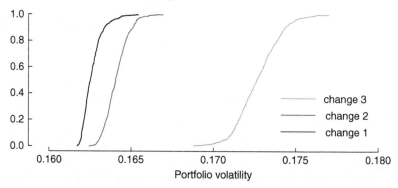

In sum, a simple strategy like local search yielded very good results for a problem whose exact solution could never be computed. The quality of the solution was evidently determined by the chosen method, by the computational resources (how many steps?), and by the particular settings (how many assets to change?). As a rule, computational resources have much more influence on the results than parameter settings.

It will not always be so simple. In later chapters, we will discuss how we can solve more-difficult problems, in particular when we have constraints.

12.7. General considerations

12.7.1. What technique to choose?

It is difficult to give general advice on this question. Different methods may be able to solve a given problem class, so one possibility would be to test which technique is best. We do not suggest pursuing such a strategy; "best" is certainly not required. What we need is a technique that provides sufficiently good solutions. This is, again, the satisficing rule: we define a desired quality for a solution, and once we have found a solution that meets this requirement, we stop searching. Admittedly, this is not too helpful, so here are a few more concrete points.

First, one should start with a method that allows a "natural" representation of the problem. For instance, for a combinatorial problem, a "natural" technique may be a Genetic Algorithm, or perhaps Simulated Annealing; for a continuous problem, Differential Evolution will probably be a promising first candidate. A second suggestion is to start simple and only add features if really required; hybridization in particular is not recommended, at least not at an early stage. Not because hybrids are not useful for certain problems, but because exploring a problem with a simpler method often allows a better understanding of where the difficulties lie.

A final remark, which is valid for different methods: since heuristics are stochastic, repeated runs will differ in their results. Also, varying the parameters of a method will often change its performance, but because of the random nature of the obtained solutions it is difficult to differentiate meaningful differences from noise. It is easy to spend hours and days changing something here or there, but without actually arriving anywhere. In our experience it is better to first spend some time on an efficient implementation of a model, and then to run (small) experiments, with at least 10 or 20 runs with given parameter settings.

12.7.2. Efficient implementations

Heuristics allow us to solve models that do not fulfill the requirements of classical optimization methods. In a sense, they achieve this by giving up mathematical sophistication. For instance, they do not compute optimal search directions like a gradient search, but often choose randomly. We gain a lot with heuristics: we are freed of many of the assumptions and requirements of classical optimization techniques like convexity, but at the price of more computational effort.

Thus, heuristics are computationally intensive. Computational effort of an algorithm can be measured in a platform-independent way by the number of objective function evaluations it takes to provide an acceptable solution. This number is often large when compared with the number of evaluations required by a classical method. But such a comparison would be deceiving if we do not pay attention to solution quality: if classical methods are not appropriate, we obtain a fast solution by giving up solution quality (because we are likely to get stuck in local minima). This is again the trade-off between the time required to obtain a solution, and the (numerical) quality of this solution.

It immediately follows that we should try to implement the components of the model efficiently. We need to think about how we represent the data, and, in particular, we should spend some time on how we compute the objective function. Matlab and R offer several utilities to measure computing time, from simple "stop watches" (`tic` and `toc` in Matlab; `system.time` in R) to tools for profiling code (see `profile` in Matlab; or `Rprof` in R).

Speeding up computation is not a mechanical task; it requires experimentation and testing. We can make a computation faster by exploiting structure in a problem (i.e., already in the model), but also by choosing the right way to compute a quantity. In particular, when we work with high-level languages like Matlab and R, operation count may give hints, but cannot replace experiments. As a concrete example, we look into different possibilities to compute moving averages in R.

Assume we have a time series of observations y_t for $t = 1,\ldots,N$. We define a moving average of order O as

$$M_t = \frac{\sum_{o=1}^{O} y_{t-o+1}}{O}. \tag{12.1}$$

Note that our computation of M at t includes the price at t. The most basic idea is now loop over y, and at each t compute the mean of y_t over the past O observations. This is shown in the script below.

Listing 12.1. C-HeuristicsNutshell/R/fastMA.r

```
1 # fastMA.R -- version 2010-12-11
2 # N = length of times series
3 # O = order of moving average
4 # trials = number of runs for speed test
5 N <- 1000; O <- 50; trials <- 100
6 y <- rnorm(N)
7
8 # variant 1 -- slow
```

```
 9 MA1 <- numeric(N)
10 system.time({
11    for(i in 1:trials) {
12        for(t in O:N) MA1[t] <- mean(y[(t-O+1):t])
13    }
14 })
```

```
user      system    elapsed
3.37      0.00      3.38
```

Curiously, using `sum` and dividing by `O` is already faster:

Listing 12.2. C-HeuristicsNutshell/R/fastMA.r

```
16 # ... continues fastMA.R
17 # variant 2 -- compute mean
18 MA2 <- numeric(N)
19 system.time({
20    for(i in 1:trials) {
21        for(t in O:N) MA2[t] <- sum(y[(t-O+1):t])/O
22    }
23 })
24 all.equal(MA1[-(1:(O-1))],MA2[-(1:(O-1))])
```

```
user      system    elapsed
1.03      0.00      1.03
```

```
[1] TRUE
```

There is actually structure in how we compute a moving average. We have

$$M_t = \frac{y_t}{O} + \frac{y_{t-1}}{O} + \frac{y_{t-2}}{O} \cdots + \frac{y_{t-O+1}}{O}. \tag{12.2}$$

We can shift M_t to $t+1$ and "add a zero" to get

$$M_{t+1} = \frac{y_{t+1}}{O} + \underbrace{\frac{y_t}{O} + \frac{y_{t-1}}{O} + \cdots + \frac{y_{t-O+1}}{O} + \frac{y_{t-O+1}}{O}}_{M_t} - \frac{y_{t-O+1}}{O} \tag{12.3}$$

or

$$M_{t+1} = M_t + \frac{y_{t+1}}{O} - \frac{y_{t-O+1}}{O}. \tag{12.4}$$

So we add one term and we delete one term; there is no need to recompute the whole sum at each time step.[3] In R:

Listing 12.3. C-HeuristicsNutshell/R/fastMA.r

```
26 # ... continues fastMA.R
27 # variant 3 -- updating
28 MA3 <- numeric(N)
```

---

[3] Curiously, a number of authors and operators prefer exponential moving averages because they can be computed by updating; see, for instance, Schwager, 1993, pp. 158–159, or Dacorogna et al., 2001, Chapter 3.

```
29  system.time({
30      for(i in 1:trials) {
31          MA3[O] <- sum(y[1:O])/O
32          for(t in (O+1):N)
33              MA3[t] <- MA3[t-1]+y[t]/O - y[t-O]/O
34      }
35  })
36  all.equal(MA1[-(1:(O-1))],MA3[-(1:(O-1))])
```

```
   user      system     elapsed
   0.82       0.00        0.83
```

```
[1] TRUE
```

These variants still require loops. Two functions come to mind that
would allow a vectorized computation: `filter` from R's `stats` package (a
moving average is a linear filter), and `cumsum`. These functions also require
loops but execute them at a "lower level," usually in C. `cumsum` seems fastest
by far.

Listing 12.4. C-HeuristicsNutshell/R/fastMA.r

```
38  # ... continues fastMA.R
39  ## variant 4 -- use filter
40  MA4 <- numeric(N)
41  system.time({
42      for(i in 1:trials) MA4 <- filter(y, rep(1/O,O), sides=1)
43  })
44  all.equal(MA1[-(1:(O-1))],MA4[-(1:(O-1))])
45
46  # variant 5 -- use cumsum
47  MA5 <- numeric(N)
48  system.time({
49      for(i in 1:trials) {
50          MA5 <- cumsum(y) / O;
51          MA5[O:N] <- MA5[O:N] - c( 0,MA5[1:(N-O)] )
52      }
53  })
54  all.equal(MA1[-(1:(O-1))],MA5[-(1:(O-1))])
```

```
   user      system     elapsed
   0.08       0.00        0.10
```

```
[1] TRUE
```

```
   user      system     elapsed
   0.01       0.00        0.01
```

```
[1] TRUE
```

12.7.3. Parameter settings

Boyd and Vandenberghe (2004, p. 5, emphasis theirs) call a method for
solving a particular problem "a (mature) *technology*, [if it] can be reliably
used by many people who do not know, and do not need to know, the

details." As an example of such a technology, they suggest Least Squares. Heuristics, today, are no such technology.

A difficulty is the number of decisions that we have to take. For trajectory methods, for instance, we need to think about how to choose a neighborhood; for Genetic Algorithms, we need to decide what mutation operators we include, and so on. If heuristics are to become a mature technology, an important question is not which parameter values are optimal for a given problem class (or more often, a single instance of a problem), but how sensitive a method's solutions are to specific choices. To put it the other way around, we would like to know classes of problems for which a given method with a given implementation works robustly across different parameter settings.

12.8. Summary

This chapter has given a brief overview of different heuristic methods. The presentation has not been complete; it could not even include the innumerable variations of the discussed techniques. Different methods can also be combined into hybrid techniques, further increasing the number of available methods. This actually leads to a dilemma. On the one hand, essentially all heuristics build on only a few, often very simple, principles, such as accepting inferior solutions. If we only want to understand how heuristics work, these principles are enough. Our main goal in this chapter has been motivation, so we have tried to keep the discussion simple and did not start with a detailed taxonomy of different methods or insisted that a minor modification of some method is a new technique. It is often difficult to even clearly define when a particular algorithm is considered a method of its own, and not just a variant. Such a distinction is not only driven by the actual characteristics of a technique, but also in a path-dependent way by how well researchers and operators accept a given idea. Threshold Accepting, for instance, changes only one element in Simulated Annealing, the acceptance criterion. Strictly speaking, it does not even change it, but uses a special case. Still, the method has been accepted. Moscato and Fontanari (1990) suggested the same mechanism, but did not consider the technique a new method. Another example is Memetic Algorithms (Moscato, 1989). A Memetic Algorithm develops a population of solutions, but each member of the population also searches individually via a trajectory method. The solutions then cooperate (e.g., by crossover), but also compete (good solutions replace inferior ones). In essence, this is a hybrid of a population-based procedure and a trajectory method; still, the algorithm is accepted as a single technique.

But on the other hand, the principles on which heuristics are built are so general (or vague) that different methods based on the same principles will often perform very differently for given problems. It becomes useful then to define specific techniques more strictly in terms of their characteristics and "stick to the algorithm" in order to establish a common language. For instance, with the definition of direct search given earlier (page 303), all methods discussed in this chapter could be called direct search methods. But the term direct search should be used for methods like Nelder–Mead not because of pedantry, but because it facilitates communication between researchers and practitioners. As pointed out above, how well a method is accepted depends not only on its merits, but also on how knowledge about the method diffuses throughout communities of researchers and practitioners. In order to promote the proliferation of heuristic methods, it should help to have clear algorithms in mind, not just rough principles. Repeated successes of a method to solve problems of a given class (or even several classes) should then provide us with a picture of the strengths and weaknesses of the technique, and also increase the confidence that operators and researchers have into the method and, hence, its acceptance. This book aims to contribute to the acceptance of heuristics in finance by demonstrating their capability to solve optimization problems that are infeasible for classical methods. The appendix to this chapter will show a few examples of how different methods can be implemented with Matlab. The remaining chapters will discuss the implementation of heuristics for specific applications from portfolio selection, option pricing, econometric models, and other fields.

12.A. Implementing heuristic methods with Matlab

The following implementations are simple general translations of the presented algorithms. They may guide the reader in writing his code.[4] The workings of the codes is illustrated with a set of particular functions for which the minimum is known analytically.

Shekel function

For the given matrix A and vector c

$$
A = \begin{bmatrix}
4 & 4 & 4 & 4 \\
1 & 1 & 1 & 1 \\
8 & 8 & 8 & 8 \\
6 & 6 & 6 & 6 \\
3 & 7 & 3 & 7 \\
2 & 9 & 2 & 9 \\
5 & 5 & 3 & 3 \\
8 & 1 & 8 & 1 \\
6 & 2 & 6 & 2 \\
7 & 3.6 & 7 & 3.6
\end{bmatrix}
\qquad
c = \begin{bmatrix}
0.1 \\
0.2 \\
0.2 \\
0.4 \\
0.4 \\
0.6 \\
0.3 \\
0.7 \\
0.5 \\
0.5
\end{bmatrix}
$$

---

[4] An R implementation with more-detailed discussion can be found in Chapter 13.

and for $X = [0, 10]^d$, $1 \le d \le 4$, and $1 \le m \le 10$, the Shekel function

$$f(x) = -\sum_{i=1}^{m} \left(\sum_{j=1}^{d} (x_j - A_{ij})^2 + c_i \right)^{-1} \qquad (12.5)$$

has m local minima. The global minimum is at $x_i = 4$, $i = 1, \ldots, d$, and its value is -11. The function Shekel.m evaluates Eq. (12.5) at the coordinates given in vector x. The function parameters are passed with the second argument Data which is a structure where the mandatory fields are the dimension d and the domain int for the variables. A plot of the function for $d = 2$ and $m = 10$ is shown in Fig. 12.2.

Listing 12.5. C-HeuristicsNutshell/M/Shekel.m

```
1  function F = Shekel(x,Data)
2  % Shekel.m  -- version 2011-01-08
3  d = Data.d;  m = Data.m;
4  if d > 4; error('More than 4 dimensions'); end
5  if nargin==1, m=10; elseif m>10||m<2, error('Wrong m');else end
6  A = [4 4 4 4;  1 1 1 1;  8 8 8 8;  6 6 6 6;  3 7.0 3 7.0;
7       2 9 2 9;  5 5 3 3;  8 1 8 1;  6 2 6 2;  7 3.6 7 3.6];
8  c = [0.1 0.2 0.2 0.4 0.4 0.6 0.3 0.7 0.5 0.5];
9  %
10 F = 0;
11 for i = 1:m
12     for j = 1:d
13         c(i) = c(i) + (x(j) - A(i,j))^2;
14     end
15     F = F - 1 / c(i);
16 end
```

Ackley function

The function is defined for a vector of dimension two and its minimum value is zero for $x_1 = 0$ and $x_2 = 0$. The shape of the function is plotted

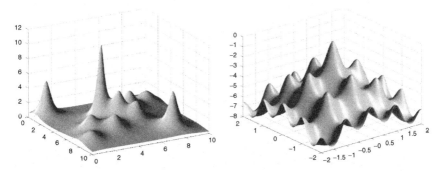

Figure 12.2 Shekel function (left) and Ackley function (right). For better visibility $-f$ has been plotted.

in Fig. 12.2.

$$f(x) = -20\exp\left(-0.2\sqrt{\frac{x_1^2+x_2^2}{2}}\right) - \exp\left(\frac{\cos(2\pi x_1)+\cos(2\pi x_2)}{2}\right) + 20 + \exp(1).$$

(12.6)

The function `Ackley.m` evaluates Eq. (12.6) at the coordinates given in vector x. The second argument of `Ackley.m` is not used but allows us to keep a uniform structure for the objective functions.

Listing 12.6. C-HeuristicsNutshell/M/Ackley.m

```
1  function F = Ackley(x,ignore)
2  % Ackley.m  -- version 2011-01-08
3  F = -20*exp(-0.2*sqrt( (x(1)^2 + x(2)^2 )/2 )) -  ...
4      exp( (cos(2*pi*x(1)) + cos(2*pi*x(2)) )/2 ) + 20 + exp(1);
```

A discrete function

We consider the discrete problem of finding a particular given pattern of bits in a binary string of 52 bits. The nonzero bits of the particular pattern are in the positions 0, 5, 20, 25, and 50 as shown hereafter.

51	50		25		20		5		0
0	0	···	1	···	1	···	1	···	1

Such a string can be considered as the binary representation of the integer $I^* = 2^{50} + 2^{25} + 2^{20} + 2^5 + 2^0 = 1125899941445665$. Imagine this pattern is hidden in the function

$$f(x) = |\text{bin2dec}(x) - I^*|.$$

(12.7)

The function (12.7) will be minimum, that is, zero, for the binary string x that is identical to the hidden pattern. The function bin2dec converts a binary string into a decimal number. The function `BitString.m` evaluates Eq. 12.7 for a given binary vector x.

Listing 12.7. C-HeuristicsNutshell/M/BitString.m

```
1  function F = BitString(x,Data)
2  % BitString.m  -- version 2011-01-08
3  F = abs( bin2dec(x) - Data.X );
```

Next we describe the Threshold Accepting algorithm, the Genetic Algorithm, Differential Evolution, and Particle Swarm Optimization. Below we show the commands that are used to pass the information to the different functions.

```
OF = 'Shekel'; Data = struct('int',[0 10; 0 10],'d',2,'m',10);
OF = 'Ackley'; Data = struct('int',[-2 2; -2 2],'d',2);
NF = 'CNeighbor';

OF = 'BitString'; Data = struct('X',2^50+2^25+2^20+2^5+2^0,...
                                'nc',52);
NF = 'DNeighbor';

OF = 'GAShekel'; Data = struct('int',[0 10;0 10],'m',10,'d',2);
```

The Threshold Accepting algorithm is applicable to all functions. The Genetic Algorithm is mainly designed to solve discrete problems but can also be used for continuous functions. An example is provided with the function GAShekel. Differential Evolution and Particle Swarm Optimization solve continuous problems.

12.A.1. Threshold Accepting

The script goTA declares the function name (OF) of the problem to be optimized together with the corresponding data (Data), the function (NF) to be used for the computation of the neighbor solutions, and the parameters (TA) for the Threshold Accepting algorithm. First a starting solution and the threshold sequence are computed and then the repeated calls (restarts) to TA are executed.

Listing 12.8. C-HeuristicsNutshell/M/goTA.m

```
 1  % goTA.m  -- version 2007-11-12
 2  OF = 'Shekel'; Data = struct('int',[0 10; 0 10],'d',2,'m',10);
 3  NF = 'CNeighbor';
 4  TA = struct('Restarts',9,'Rounds',5,'Steps',4000,...
 5              'ptrim',0.1,'frac',0.2);
 6  TA.Percentiles = linspace(0.9,0,TA.Rounds);
 7
 8  Data = StartingSol(OF,Data);
 9  output = thSequence(TA,OF,NF,Data);
10  TA.th = output.th;
11  for r = 1:TA.Restarts
12      Data = StartingSol(OF,Data);
13      output = TAH(TA,OF,NF,Data);
14      Sol(r) = output.Fbest;
15      X(r,:) = output.xbest;
16      plotTA(TA,output)
17  end
18  [Sbest,i] = min(Sol);
19  fprintf('\n Sol = %6.3f  ',Sbest); disp(X(i,:));
20
21  figure(2), subplot(211)
22  H = cdfplot(Sol);
```

The function plotTA.m serves as a diagnostic tool and visualizes the threshold sequence and objective function values for every restart. Examples

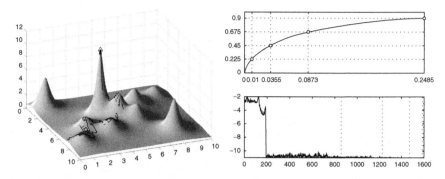

Figure 12.3 Left panel: search path for the TA algorithm (TA searches for minima but for better visibility $-f$ has been plotted). Upper right panel: empirical distribution of distances of neighbor solutions used to compute the threshold sequence. Lower right panel: evolution of objective function value for a particular restart.

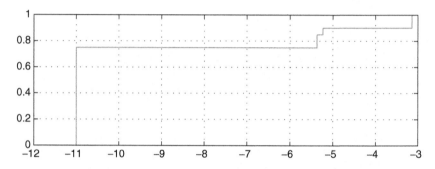

Figure 12.4 Empirical distribution of the objective function values corresponding to the solutions in the successive restarts.

of these graphics are shown in Fig. 12.3. Finally the empirical distribution of the objective function values for the successive restarts is plotted (see Fig. 12.4).

Below we have the function TAH, the functions CNeighbor called by TAH, as well as the functions StartingSol, thSequence, and plotTA.

Listing 12.9. C-HeuristicsNutshell/M/TAH.m

```
 1  function output = TAH(TA,OF,NF,Data)
 2  % TAH.m -- version 2009-11-09
 3  F0 = Data.Fs;   x0 = Data.xs;
 4  output.FF = repmat(NaN,TA.Rounds*TA.Steps,1);
 5  Fbest = F0;     xbest = x0;   output.FF(1) = F0;
 6  iup = 1; tic
 7  wbh = waitbar(0,[int2str(TA.Rounds),' rounds with ',int2str(TA.
        Steps),' steps ...']);
 8  for iround = 1:TA.Rounds
 9      for istep = 1:TA.Steps
10          x1 = feval(NF,x0,Data,TA);
11          F1 = feval(OF,x1,Data);
```

```
12        if F1 <= F0 + TA.th(iround)
13            iup = iup + 1;
14            output.FF(iup) = F1;
15            F0 = F1;
16            x0 = x1;
17            if F1 < Fbest, Fbest = F1; xbest = x1; end
18        end
19    end  % end steps
20    output.uprounds(iround) = iup;
21    waitbar(iround/TA.Rounds,wbh);
22 end, close(wbh), fprintf(' TA done (%i sec)\n', fix(toc));
23 output.Fbest = Fbest;  output.xbest = xbest;  output.iup = iup;
```

A neighbor solution is computed by selecting randomly one variable of
the function; its value is then modified by adding a scaled normal random
variable. The modifications are restricted to the domain of definition of the
function.

Listing 12.10. C-HeuristicsNutshell/M/CNeighbor.m

```
1 function x1 = CNeighbor(x0,Data,TA)
2 % CNeighbor.m  -- version 2011-01-08
3 x1 = x0;
4 j = unidrnd(Data.d);    % Randomly select element of x0
5 x1(j) = x1(j) + randn * TA.frac;
6 % x1(j) = x1(j) + (4*rand - 2) * TA.frac;
7 % Check domain constraints
8 x1(j) = min(Data.int(j,2), max(Data.int(j,1),x1(j)) );
```

Listing 12.11. C-HeuristicsNutshell/M/StartingSol.m

```
1 function Data = StartingSol(OF,Data)
2 % StartingSol.m -- version 2009-12-09
3 for i = 1:Data.d
4    Data.xs(i)=Data.int(i,1)+(Data.int(i,2)-Data.int(i,1))*rand;
5 end
6 Data.Fs = feval(OF,Data.xs,Data);
```

Listing 12.12. C-HeuristicsNutshell/M/thSequence.m

```
1 function output = thSequence(TA,OF,NF,Data)
2 % thSequence.m -- version 2011-05-22
3 F0 = Data.Fs;   x0 = Data.xs;
4 nND = min(TA.Rounds*TA.Steps,5000);
5 ND0 = zeros(1,nND);
6 wbh = waitbar(0,['Exploring ',int2str(nND),' neighbor solutions
      ...']);
7 for s = 1:nND
8     x1 = feval(NF,x0,Data,TA);
9     F1 = feval(OF,x1,Data);
10    ND0(s) = F1 - F0;
```

```
11     F0 = F1;  x0 = x1;
12     if ~rem(s,fix(nND/50)), waitbar(s/nND,wbh); end
13 end, close(wbh);
14 ntrim = max(fix(length(nND)*TA.ptrim),10);
15 ND = sort(ND0);
16 ip = find(ND > 0);
17 output.ND = ND(ip:end-ntrim);
18 output.th = quantile(output.ND,TA.Percentiles);
19 %
20 figure(1), subplot(211)
21 H = cdfplot(output.ND); xlim([0 output.th(1)]);
22 hold on; xlabel(''); ylabel(''); title('');
23 set(H,'Color',.7*[1 1 1],'LineWidth',2), set(gca,'FontSize',10)
24 plot(fliplr(output.th),fliplr(TA.Percentiles),'ko',...
25     'MarkerSize',6);
26 set(gca,'ytick',fliplr(TA.Percentiles));
27 set(gca,'xtick',fliplr(output.th));
```

Listing 12.13. C-HeuristicsNutshell/M/plotTA.m

```
1 function plotTA(TA,output)
2 % plotTA.m  -- version 2011-01-08
3 figure, subplot(212)
4 iup = output.iup;
5 plot(output.FF(100:iup),'k-'), hold on  % title('Obj. func.')
6 ymax = max(output.FF(1:iup)); ymin = min(output.FF(1:iup));
7 for i = 1:length(output.uprounds)
8     x = output.uprounds(i);
9     plot([x x],[ymin ymax],'k:');
10 end
11 ylim([ymin ymax]);
```

If we want to optimize the Ackley function, we simply specify the following in the script goTA.

```
OF = 'Ackley'; Data = struct('int',[-2 2; -2 2],'d',2);
```

To solve the discrete problem BitString, we have to define appropriate functions for the computation of the starting and neighbor solution. Possible ways to do this are:

Listing 12.14. C-HeuristicsNutshell/M/DStartingSol.m

```
1 function Data = DStartingSol(OF,Data)
2 % DStartingSol.m  -- version 2011-01-09
3 Imax = 2^Data.nc - 1 ;
4 k = unidrnd(Imax,1) ;
5 Data.xs = dec2bin(k,Data.nc) ;
6 Data.Fs = feval(OF,Data.xs,Data);
7 end
```

Listing 12.15. C-HeuristicsNutshell/M/DNeighbor.m

```
1 function x1 = DNeighbor(x0,Data,ignore)
2 % DNeighbor.m  -- version  2011-01-09
```

```
 3  x1 = x0;
 4  j = unidrnd(Data.nc); % Select bit
 5  i = unidrnd(Data.nc); % Select bit
 6  u = rand;
 7  if u < 1/3
 8      x1(j) = x0(i); x1(i) = x0(j);
 9  elseif u < 2/3
10      if strcmp(x1(i),'0'), x1(i) = '1'; else x1(i) = '0'; end
11  else
12      if strcmp(x1(j),'0'), x1(j) = '1'; else x1(j) = '0'; end
13  end
```

In this case, the problem, neighbor function, and the call for a starting solution are specified in goTA with the following commands:

```
OF='BitString';Data=struct('X',2^50+2^25+2^20+2^5+2^0,'nc',52);
NF = 'DNeighbor';
Data = DStartingSol(OF,Data);
```

12.A.2. Genetic Algorithm

The script goGA declares the function name (OF) of the problem to be optimized together with the corresponding data (Data). The GA parameters are stored in the structure GA with the fields:

nC	Chromosome length (number of bits)
nP	Population size
nP1	Size of mating pool
nP2	Number of children generated
nG	Number of generations
pM	Probability to undergo mutation

Listing 12.16. C-HeuristicsNutshell/M/goGA.m

```
 1  % goGA.m -- version 2009-11-07
 2  OF = 'BitString';  Data.X = 2^50 + 2^25 +2^20 + 2^5 + 2^0;
 3  GA = struct('nG',500,'pM',0.2,'nC',52,'nP',200,'nP1',100,...
 4              'nP2',200,'Restarts',10);
 5
 6  for r = 1:GA.Restarts
 7      output = GAH(GA,OF,Data);
 8      Sol(r) = output.Fbest;
 9      X{r} = output.xbest;
10      plotGA(GA,output);
11  end
12  [Sbest,i] = min(Sol);
13  fprintf('\n Sol = %6.3f  ',Sbest); disp(X{i});
14
15  figure(2), subplot(211)
16  H = cdfplot(Sol);
```

`plotGA` produces a plot of the best solution over the generations; after completion of the restarts, the corresponding empirical distribution of the solutions is produced.

In the function `GAH`, the information concerning the population (P), the mating pool (P1), and the generated children (P2) is stored in the structures P, P1, and P2 in the fields C (Chromosome string) and F the corresponding fitness.

Listing 12.17. C-HeuristicsNutshell/M/GAH.m

```
1  function output = GAH(GA,OF,Data)
2  % GAH.m -- version 2009-11-07
3  P = StartingPop(GA,OF,Data);
4  S = zeros(GA.nG,1); Fbest = realmax;
5  wbh = waitbar(0,[int2str(GA.nG),' generations ...']); tic
6  for r = 1:GA.nG
7      P1 = MatingPool(GA,P);
8      for i = 1:GA.nP2
9          P2.C{i} = Crossover(GA,P1);
10         P2.C{i} = Mutate(GA,P2.C{i});
11     end
12     P = Survive(GA,P1,P2,OF,Data);
13     S(r) = P.F(1);
14     if P.F(1) < Fbest, Fbest = P.F(1); xbest = P.C(1); end
15     if all(~diff(P.F)), output.ng = r; break, end
16     if ~rem(r,5),waitbar(r/GA.nG,wbh);end
17 end,close(wbh),fprintf(' GA done (%i sec)\n',fix(toc))
18 output.P  = P;  output.S  = S;  output.ng = r;
19 output.Fbest = Fbest; output.xbest = xbest;
```

The five key tasks—generation of starting population, selection of a mating pool, crossover, mutation, and selection of survivors—are coded in separate functions.

Listing 12.18. C-HeuristicsNutshell/M/StartingPop.m

```
1  function P = StartingPop(GA, OF, Data)
2  % StartingPop.m  -- version 2007-02-11
3  Imax = 2^GA.nC - 1 ;
4  Pd = unidrnd(Imax, GA.nP, 1) ;
5  for i = 1:GA.nP
6          P.C{i} = dec2bin(Pd(i), GA.nC) ;
7          P.F(i) = feval(OF, P.C{i}, Data) ; % Compute fitness
8  end
```

Listing 12.19. C-HeuristicsNutshell/M/MatingPool.m

```
1  function P1 = MatingPool(GA,P)
2  % MatingPool.m  -- version 2001-02-11
3  IP1 = unidrnd(GA.nP,1,GA.nP1); % Set of indices defining P1
4  for k = 1:GA.nP1
5          P1.C{k} = P.C{IP1(k)};
6  end
7  P1.F = P.F(IP1);
```

Listing 12.20. C-HeuristicsNutshell/M/Crossover.m

```
1  function C = Crossover(GA,P1)
2  % Crossover.m  -- version 2007-02-12
3  p = unidrnd(GA.nP1,2,1); % Select parents
4  a = p(1);   b = p(2);
5  k = unidrnd(GA.nC - 1) + 1;
6  C = [P1.C{a}(1:k-1),P1.C{b}(k:GA.nC)];
```

Listing 12.21. C-HeuristicsNutshell/M/Mutate.m

```
1  function C = Mutate(GA,C)
2  % Mutate.m  -- version 2007-02-11
3  if rand < GA.pM
4      % Child undergoes mutation
5      j = unidrnd(GA.nC); % Select chromosome
6      if strcmp(C(j),'0')
7          C(j) = '1';
8      else
9          C(j) = '0';
10     end
11 end
```

Listing 12.22. C-HeuristicsNutshell/M/Survive.m

```
1  function P = Survive(GA,P1,P2,OF,Data)
2  % Survive.m  -- version 2007-02-15
3  P2.F = zeros(1,GA.nP2);
4  for i = 1:GA.nP2
5      P2.F(i) = feval(OF,P2.C{i},Data); % Fitness of children
6  end
7  F = [P1.F,P2.F];
8  [ignore,I] = sort(F);
9  for i = 1:GA.nP
10     j = I(i);
11     if j<= GA.nP1
12         P.C{i} = P1.C{j}; % Surviving parents
13         P.F(i) = P1.F(j);
14     else
15         P.C{i} = P2.C{j - GA.nP1}; % Suriving children
16         P.F(i) = P2.F(j - GA.nP1);
17     end
18 end
19 % Dying population
20 k = 0;
21 for i = GA.nP+1:length(F)
22     k = k + 1;
23     j = I(i);
24     if j<= GA.nP1
25         P.DC{k} = P1.C{j}; % Surviving parents
26         P.DF(k) = P1.F(j);
27     else
28         P.DC{k} = P2.C{j - GA.nP1}; % Suriving children
29         P.DF(k) = P2.F(j - GA.nP1);
30     end
31 end
```

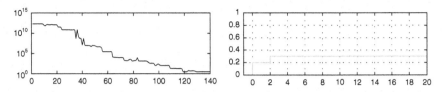

Figure 12.5 Left panel: evolution of objective function values for a particular restart. Right panel: Empirical distribution of objective function values corresponding to the solution of 20 restarts (left tail only).

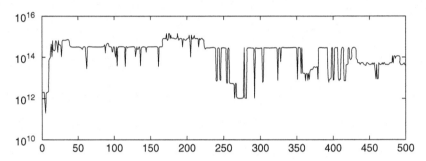

Figure 12.6 Evolution of objective function values for a particular restart and $nP = nP1 + nP2$.

Running the code `goGA` for the discrete problem produces the expected result. Fig. 12.5 illustrates the workings of the algorithm and monitors the execution.

```
Sol = 0  '01000000000000000000000000001000010000000000000000100001'
```

Using the following setting for the population

```
GA.nP  = 200; GA.nP1 = 100; GA.nP2 = 200;
```

would be a bad choice as there will be no selection. The corresponding behavior of the objective function is shown in Fig. 12.6.

The GA can also be used to solve continuous problems. We illustrate this with the Shekel function for $d = 2$. To code the value of the coordinates, we half the chromosome: the first 26 bits represent the first coordinate and the remaining ones the second coordinate. This is done with the function `GAShekel`. In `goGA` we specify:

```
OF = 'GAShekel';  Data = struct('m',10,'d',2);
```

Listing 12.23. C-HeuristicsNutshell/M/GAShekel.m

```
1 function [F,z] = GAShekel(x,Data)
2 % GASheckel.m -- version 2009-11-07
3 d = Data.d;
4 n = length(x);
5 y = zeros(1,d);
6 for i = 1:d
```

```
 7     y(i) = bin2dec(x( 1+(i-1)*n/d : i*n/d ));
 8 end
 9 % written for domain (0,10) for all variables (Data.int !!)
10 y = y*10 /(2^(n/d) - 1);
11 if any(y>10) || any(y<0) ,error('values outside domain'),end
12 F = Shekel(y,Data);
13 if nargout == 2, z = y; end
```

12.A.3. Differential Evolution

The script goDE declares the function name (OF) of the problem to be optimized together with the corresponding data (Data). The DE parameters are stored in the structure DE with the fields:

nP	Size of population
nG	Number of generations
CR	Parameter
F	Parameter
oneElemfromPv	Parameter

Listing 12.24. C-HeuristicsNutshell/M/goDE.m

```
 1 % goDE.m  -- version 2011-01-08
 2 OF = 'Ackley'; Data = struct('int',[-2 2; -2 2],'d',2);
 3
 4 DE = struct('nG',50,'CR',0.8,'F',0.8,'nP',15,...
 5             'oneElemfromPv',1,'Restarts',20);
 6 tic
 7 for r = 1:DE.Restarts
 8     output = DEH(DE,OF,Data);
 9     Sol(r) = output.Fbest;
10     X(r,:) = output.xbest;
11     plotDE(DE,output);
12 end
13 [Sbest,i] = min(Sol);
14 fprintf('\n Sol = %6.3f (%i sec)',Sbest,fix(toc));disp(X(i,:));
15
16 figure(1), subplot(211)
17 H = cdfplot(Sol);
```

plotDE produces a plot of the best solutions along the generations and after completion of all restarts the empirical distribution of the value of the objective function at the solutions is produced.

The function DEH.m implements the Differential Evolution algorithm.

Listing 12.25. C-HeuristicsNutshell/M/DEH.m

```
1 function output = DEH(DE,OF,Data)
2 % DEH.m  -- version 2007-03-09
3 % --Construct starting population
```

```
 4 P1 = zeros(Data.d,DE.nP);
 5 Pu = zeros(Data.d,DE.nP);
 6 for i = 1:Data.d
 7     P1(i,:) = Data.int(i,1) + (Data.int(i,2)-Data.int(i,1))*...
 8                 rand(PS.nP,1);
 9 end
10 Fbv   = NaN(DE.nG,1);
11 Fbest = realmax;
12 F = zeros(DE.nP,1);
13 for i = 1:DE.nP
14     F(i) = feval(OF,P1(:,i)',Data);
15     if F(i) < Fbest
16         Fbest = F(i);   xbest = P1(:,i);
17     end
18 end
19 Col = 1:DE.nP;
20 for k = 1:DE.nG
21     P0 = P1;
22     Io = randperm(DE.nP)';
23     Ic = randperm(4)';
24     I  = circshift(Io,Ic(1));
25     R1 = circshift(Io,Ic(2));
26     R2 = circshift(Io,Ic(3));
27     R3 = circshift(Io,Ic(4));
28     % --Construct mutant vector
29     Pv = P0(:,R1) + DE.F * (P0(:,R2) - P0(:,R3));
30     % --Crossover
31     mPv = rand(Data.d,DE.nP) < DE.CR;
32     if DE.oneElemfromPv
33         Row = unidrnd(Data.d,1,DE.nP);
34         mPv1 = sparse(Row,Col,1,Data.d,DE.nP);
35         mPv = mPv | mPv1;
36     end
37     mP0  = ~mPv;
38     Pu(:,I) = P0(:,I).*mP0 + mPv.*Pv;
39     % --Select vector to enter new generation
40     flag = 0;
41     for i = 1:DE.nP
42         Ftemp = feval(OF,Pu(:,i)',Data);
43         if Ftemp <= F(i)
44             P1(:,i) = Pu(:,i);
45             F(i) = Ftemp;
46             if Ftemp < Fbest
47                 Fbest = Ftemp;  xbest = Pu(:,i);  flag = 1;
48             end
49         else
50             P1(:,i) = P0(:,i);
51         end
52     end
53     if flag, Fbv(k) = Fbest; end
54 end
55 output.Fbest = Fbest;  output.xbest = xbest;  output.Fbv = Fbv;
```

The result for the Ackley function is:

```
Sol =  0.000 (1 sec)   1.0e-004 *
                       0.1515   -0.2059
```

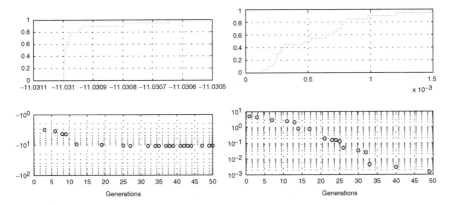

Figure 12.7 Upper row: Empirical distributions of objective function values corresponding to the solution of 20 restarts for the Shekel function (left) and the Ackley function (right). Lower row: Evolution of objective function value over generations for a particular restart.

and for the Shekel function we obtain:

```
Sol = -11.031 (2 sec)    4.0027    4.0021
```

Fig. 12.7 illustrates the workings of the algorithm for the optimization of the Shekel and the Ackley function.

Listing 12.26. C-HeuristicsNutshell/M/plotDE.m

```
1 function plotDE(DE,output)
2 % plotDE.m  -- version 2011-01-08
3 clf(gcf), figure(1), subplot(212)
4 semilogy(1:PS.nG,output.Fbv,'ko','MarkerSize',8,...
5          'MarkerFaceColor',.7*[1 1 1]);
6 set(gca,'FontSize',10); grid on; xlabel('Generations');
```

12.A.4. Particle Swarm Optimization

The script goPS declares the function name (OF) of the problem to be optimized together with the corresponding data (Data). The parameters of the Particle Swarm Optimization algorithm are stored in the structure PS with the fields:

nP	Size of population
nG	Number of generations
c1	Parameter
c2	Parameter
cv	Parameter
cvmax	Parameter
Restarts	Number of restarts

Listing 12.27. C-HeuristicsNutshell/M/goPS.m

```
1  % goDE.m  -- version 2007-01-08
2  OF = 'Ackley'; Data = struct('int',[-2 2; -2 2],'d',2);
3
4  PS = struct('nP',15,'nG',50,'c1',2,'c2',2,'cv',1,'vmax',1,...
5                'Restarts',20);
6  tic
7  for r = 1:PS.Restarts
8      output = PSO(PS,OF,Data);
9      Sol(r) = output.Fbest;
10     X(r,:) = output.xbest;
11     plotPS(PS,output);
12 end
13 [Sbest,i] = min(Sol);
14 fprintf('\n Sol = %6.3f (%i sec)',Sbest,fix(toc));disp(X(i,:));
15
16 figure(1), subplot(211)
17 H = cdfplot(Sol);
```

plotPS produces a plot of the best solution along the generations and after completion of the restarts the empirical distribution of the value of the objective function at the solutions is produced.

The function PSO.m implements the Particle Swarm Optimization algorithm.

Listing 12.28. C-HeuristicsNutshell/M/PSO.m

```
1  function output = PSO(PS,OF,Data)
2  % PSO.m  -- version   2011-01-09
3  nP = PS.nP;   nG = PS.nG;   d = Data.d;   int = Data.int;
4  FF = zeros(nG,1);   F = zeros(nP,1);   P = zeros(nP,d);
5  for i = 1:d
6      P(:,i) = int(i,1) + (int(i,2)-int(i,1)) * rand(nP,1);
7  end
8  v = PS.cv * rand(nP,d);
9  for i = 1:nP
10     F(i) = feval(OF,P(i,:),Data);
11 end
12 Pbest = P;   Fbest = F;
13 [Gbest,gbest] = min(F);
14 for k = 1:nG
15     v = v + PS.c1* rand(nP,d) .* (Pbest      - P) + ...
16             PS.c2* rand(nP,d) .* (ones(nP,1)*Pbest(gbest,:)-P);
17     v = min(v, PS.vmax);
18     v = max(v,-PS.vmax);
19     P = P + v;
20     for i = 1:nP
21         F(i) = feval(OF,P(i,:),Data);
22     end
23     I = find(F < Fbest);
24     if ~isempty(I)
25         Fbest(I)   = F(I);
26         Pbest(I,:) = P(I,:);
27         [Fmin,ib] = min(F(I));
```

```
28          if Fmin < Gbest
29              Gbest = Fmin;  gbest = I(ib);  FF(k) = Gbest;
30          end
31      end
32 end
33 output.xbest = Pbest(gbest,:);
34 output.Fbest = Gbest; output.FF = FF;
```

Listing 12.29. C-HeuristicsNutshell/M/plotPS.m

```
1 function plotPS(PS,output)
2 % plotDE.m  -- version 2011-01-08
3 clf(gcf), figure(1), subplot(212)
4 semilogy(1:PS.nG,output.FF,'ko','MarkerSize',8,...
5          'MarkerFaceColor',.7*[1 1 1]);
6 set(gca,'FontSize',10); grid on; xlabel('Generations');
```

## CHAPTER THIRTEEN

Portfolio optimization

The aim of portfolio selection is to determine combinations of assets like bonds or stocks that are optimal with respect to performance measures based, for instance, on capital gains, volatility, or drawdowns. A portfolio selection model, in other words, is a quantitative decision rule that tells us how to invest. In this chapter, we will discuss how to implement such models.

The workhorse model for portfolio selection is mean–variance optimization (Markowitz, 1952). To a considerable extent, this specification is owed to computational restrictions. Already in the 1950s, Markowitz pondered using downside semi-variance as a measure for risk, but eventually rejected it mainly because it was much more difficult to compute optimal portfolios. However, with heuristics, we can solve portfolio selection models without restrictions on the functional form of the selection criterion or the constraints.

13.1. The investment problem

We are endowed with an initial wealth v_0, and wish to select a portfolio

$$w = [w_1 \ w_2 \ \dots \ w_{n_A}]'$$

of the available n_A assets; w represents portfolio weights. When we talk about quantities, we will call the portfolio u (as in "units"), so, for example,

$$u = [20{,}000 \ \ 100{,}000 \ \dots]$$

means 20,000 units of the first asset, 100,000 units of the second asset, and so on. A subscript to u or w identifies a specific asset (i.e., w_j for $j = 1 \dots, n_A$).

The chosen portfolio is held for one period, from time 0 to time T. End-of-period wealth is given by

$$v_T = u' p_T = v_0 \, w' \underbrace{\left(\frac{p_T}{p_0} \right)}_{\text{elementwise}} = v_0 \, w' \, (1 + r)$$

where the vectors p_0 and p_T hold the prices at time 0 and T, respectively. The vector r holds the returns of the n_A assets for the given period:

$$r = [r_1\ r_2\ \dots\ r_{n_A}]'.$$

Since these returns are not known at the time the portfolio is constructed, v_T will be a random variable to us, following an unknown distribution that depends on w. We will usually rescale v_T into portfolio returns $r^P = v_T/v_0 - 1$.

Our computational problem will be to choose the w according to a selection criterion Φ. This criterion may be a function of final wealth v_T or the path $\{v_t\}_0^T$ that wealth takes over time. In the latter case, we still have a one-period problem since we do not trade between 0 and T. The basic optimization model can be written as

$$\min_{w}\ \Phi(w),\qquad\qquad\qquad (13.1)$$

$$w'\iota = 1.$$

ι is a vector of ones with appropriate length (in Eq. (13.1) it has length n_A). Typical building blocks for Φ may be central moments (e.g., variance), partial or conditional moments, or quantiles. Criteria that depend on the path of wealth are often based on the drawdown, but we can easily think of things like technical indicators to be included in Φ. In principle, Φ can be any function that can be evaluated for a sample of portfolio returns, and possibly the portfolio's time path. In fact, the time path of portfolio wealth itself may contain valuable information that is disregarded by using differences or returns.

In this chapter we will discuss computational methods for solving given models like (13.1). This essentially skips the phase of setting up (13.1), that is, deciding on Φ, on the constraints, on the data that we use. So before we discuss methods to solve this model, we need to stress our actual problem. We are at time 0, and we do not know $\{v_t\}_1^T$ for any portfolio. We need to forecast these values. This is not just a nuisance, it is the necessary step to make our models meaningful. If we do not get these forecasts right, we should not optimize at all. Portfolio optimization is not a risk-free proposition, failing to properly handle the data entails a cost—our portfolio will usually perform worse than simple and cheap portfolio rules like equal weights. In the literature, the problem is often framed as an estimation problem, but it is only an estimation problem if we assume some underlying process for our assets. Such a process may or may not be a good description of reality (or rather a description good enough for our purposes).

This leads to a remark about objective functions: we need to distinguish between what we want, and what we should put into our model. What we want is that v_T or $\{v_t\}_0^T$ have desirable properties, say, low volatility. This does not imply, however, that we should necessarily pick a portfolio that also has these properties in-sample. It is worth reflecting on this idea. Let us give two examples.

First, imagine we wish to minimize the variance of portfolio returns. Empirically, variance is persistent; if we have two portfolios $w^{(1)}$ and $w^{(2)}$, and $w^{(1)}$ is less risky than $w^{(2)}$ in one period, then chances are that $w^{(1)}$ is also less risky than $w^{(2)}$ in the following period. It would make sense to find a portfolio that "looked good" with respect to our objective in the past, and hope it continues to do so in the future. But here is a counterexample. Several authors since De Bondt and Thaler (1985) have argued that mean-reversion occurs in stock markets, hence buying past losers and selling past winners will lead to higher returns. We could include this in our selection criterion, building a portfolio that is maximally oversold, subject to constraints. But it is unlikely that we would wish for persistence in our optimization criterion. In other words, our objective function would include just the opposite of what we actually want.

The only restriction included in Model (13.1) is the budget constraint: all the weights need to sum to one. The solution to this model would not be very relevant in practice, we will need more constraints. We may introduce minimum and maximum holding sizes for the assets included in the portfolios, and also cardinality constraints that set a minimum and maximum number of assets. We can also include other kinds of constraints like exposure limits to specific risk factors, or sector constraints. We may want to represent certain quantities as integers or discretize them in other ways: maybe because in some markets, quantities are traded in specific lot sizes; or maybe just because a trader simply refuses to buy or sell a nominal amount of 12,132,189.09 of government bonds. We can include transaction costs, or turnover constraints (measured with respect to an initial or benchmark portfolio). Not all these constraints will be necessary and meaningful for given problems; but the important point is that we could include them, and then after empirical testing decide whether we need them or not; but we need not exclude them because our computational techniques do not allow for certain features.

In general, then, Model (13.1) cannot be solved with classical methods; hence we will use heuristics. But we start with a specific case that can be solved. It is the classical case: mean–variance optimization.

13.2. The classical case: mean–variance optimization

13.2.1. The model

Mean–variance analysis was introduced in Markowitz (1952) and Roy (1952). The idea is to base Φ not on the complete distribution of portfolio returns, but only their first two moments, expected return and variance. Markowitz's selection rule states to choose a portfolio w that is mean–variance efficient. A corresponding objective function, to be minimized, can be written as

$$\Phi = (1 - \lambda)\mathsf{Var}(r^{\mathrm{P}}) - \lambda\, m^{\mathrm{P}}. \tag{13.2}$$

m^{P} and $\mathsf{Var}(r^{\mathrm{P}})$ are our forecasts for the portfolio return r^{P} and its variance, respectively. The parameter $\lambda \in [0, 1]$ is a measure of risk-aversion. With $\lambda = 1$ we maximize return, with $\lambda = 0$ with minimize variance. This function includes only mean and variance, without regard to the overall shape of the return distribution. Furthermore, it only uses final wealth, not the path that wealth takes between time 0 and T. The function can be computed from the forecast returns, variances, and covariances of the single assets. Recall that r is a vector of n_{A} returns; hence, the return r^{P} of a portfolio w is

$$r^{\mathrm{P}} = r'w.$$

For a vector

$$m = [m_1\, m_2\, \ldots\, m_{n_{\mathrm{A}}}]'$$

of return forecasts, $m'w$ is the portfolio's return forecast. For the variance we have

$$\mathsf{Var}(r^{\mathrm{P}}) = w'\Sigma w.$$

Σ is our forecast of the variance–covariance matrix of the assets' returns (see also Section 13.2.5 below).

Returns and variances can be computed with Matlab or R. Suppose we have a sample of prices of n_{A} assets, with $n_{\mathrm{S}} + 1$ observations. We collect them in a matrix P such that the assets are in the columns; each row holds the prices for a given scenario, for instance, historical observations. Keep in mind that if we use these historical moments as inputs into our model, we make the assumption that the underlying processes are stable enough that we can estimate these parameters.

Matlab and Rcode:

Listing 13.1. C-PortfolioOptimization/M/returns.m

```
1 % returns.m -- version 2010-09-11
2 %% generate artificial price data:
3 % R = returns, P = prices
4 ns = 100;  % number of scenarios
5 na = 10;   % number of assets
6 R  = 1 + randn(ns, na) * 0.01;
7 P  = cumprod( [100 * ones(1, na); R] );
8 plot(P);
9
```

```
10  %% discrete returns
11  % compute returns: rets should be equal to R
12  rets1 = P(2:end,:) ./ P(1:(end-1),:) ;
13  % ... or
14  rets2 = diff(P) ./ P(1:(end-1),:) + 1;
15  max(max(abs(rets1-R)))  % not 'exactly' equal
16  max(max(abs(rets2-R)))  % not 'exactly' equal
17  max(max(abs(rets1-rets1)))  % 'exactly' equal
18
19  %% log-returns
20  rets3 = diff(log(P));
21  % ... almost like discrete returns
22  plot(rets1(:) - rets3(:) - 1)
```

Listing 13.2. C-PortfolioOptimization/R/returns.R

```
1   # returns.R -- version 2010-09-11
2   ## generate artificial price data:
3   #  R = returns, P = prices
4   ns <- 100  # number of scenarios
5   na <- 10   # number of assets
6   R  <- 1 + array(rnorm(ns * na) * 0.01, dim = c(ns, na))
7   P  <- rbind(100,R)
8   P  <- apply(P,2,cumprod)
9   matplot(P, type="l") # ... or ts.plot(P)
10
11  ## discrete returns
12  # compute returns: rets should be equal to R
13  rets1 <- P[2:nrow(P),] / P[1:(nrow(P)-1),]
14  # ... or
15  rets2 <- diff(P) / P[1:(nrow(P)-1),] + 1;
16  max(abs(rets1-R)) # not 'exactly' equal
17  max(abs(rets2-R)) # not 'exactly' equal
18  max(abs(rets1-rets1)) # 'exactly' equal
19
20  ## log-returns
21  rets3 <- diff(log(P));
22  # ... almost like discrete returns
23  plot(as.vector(rets1) - as.vector(rets3) - 1,cex = 0.5)
```

The variance–covariance matrix can be computed from these returns (use the function named `cov` in both Matlab and R).

13.2.2. Solving the model

Model (13.2)—as long as we have only linear constraints—can be solved by quadratic programming (QP). We will not describe QP in detail here; see Gill, Murray, and Wright (1986). A typical QP solver computes solutions to the following problem (details depend on the particular implementation):

$$\min_{w} -c'w + \tfrac{1}{2}w'Qw \tag{13.3}$$

subject to the constraints

$$Aw = a,$$

$$Bw \geq b.$$

Thus, we minimize a quadratic function subject to linear equality and inequality constraints. For our purposes, the matrix Q is symmetric and of size $n_A \times n_A$; the vector c is of length n_A. The $1/2$ in front of $w'Qw$ is there only for convenience: the derivative of $w'Qw$ with respect to w is $(Q + Q')w$ or, since Q is symmetric, $2Qw$ (Petersen and Pedersen, 2008, p. 11). Hence, the $1/2$ cancels out. A is a matrix with as many rows as equality constraints, and n_A columns. B is a matrix with as many rows as inequality constraints, and n_A columns. a and b are vectors with lengths equal to the numbers of rows of A and B.

QP is an iterative method. It starts with an initial guess supplied by the user and then successively changes this portfolio until some convergence criteria are met. In a given iteration, the program evaluates a new portfolio by computing its mean and variance. The variance–covariance matrix Σ (size $n_A \times n_A$) and the return forecast vector m (length n_A) are fixed; hence, computing time will generally increase with the number of assets, but not with the number of observations.

It is the inequality constraints that require a QP-solver. A quadratic model with linear equality constraints can, at least in principle, be solved by computing its first derivatives (which are linear equations), setting them to zero and solving the equations.

13.2.3. Mean–variance models

In this section, we will discuss several classical portfolio selection models that can be formulated as Model (13.3).

Minimum-variance portfolios
We start with the simplest and—when constrained—practically most useful case: minimizing the variance of a portfolio. For now, we include only one restriction, the budget constraint. Formally, our model will be

$$\min_{w} \; w'\Sigma w \tag{13.4}$$

subject to

$$w'\iota = 1.$$

In the formulation of Model (13.3), we have

$$Q = 2\Sigma, \qquad c = \underbrace{[0,0,0,\ldots]'}_{n_A},$$

$$A = \underbrace{[1,1,1,\ldots]'}_{n_A}, \qquad a = 1.$$

We could also set $Q = \Sigma$ for if w minimizes

$$w'\Sigma w,$$

then it also minimizes

$$\text{positive constant} \times w'\Sigma w.$$

An example in R; we use the function `solve.QP` from the `quadprog` package (Turlach and Weingessel, 2007).

Listing 13.3. C-PortfolioOptimization/R/portOpt1.R

```
1  # portOpt1.R -- version 2010-12-11
2  # minimum-variance portfolio with budget constraint
3  require(quadprog)
4
5  # create random returns
6  na    <- 10                  # number of assets
7  ns    <- 60                  # number of observations
8  R     <- array(rnorm(ns*na, mean = 0.005, sd = 0.015),
9                 dim = c(ns,na))
10
11 # minimize variance
12 Q <- 2 * cov(R)
13 A <- rbind(rep(1,10))
14 a <- 1
15 result <- solve.QP(Dmat = Q,
16                    dvec = rep(0,10),
17                    Amat = t(A),
18                    bvec = a,
19                    meq  = 1)
20
21 ## check budget constraint and solution
22 w <- result$solution
23 sum(w)
24 all.equal(as.numeric(var(R %*% w)),result$value)
```

Typically we include minimum and maximum holding sizes, that is,

$$w_j^{\text{inf}} \le w_j \le w_j^{\text{sup}} \quad \text{for all } j.$$

The vectors w^{inf} and w^{sup} hold lower and upper position bounds. Every asset can have specific limits. Let I_{n_A} be the identity matrix of size $n_A \times n_A$, then the constraints can be written such:

$$
B = \begin{bmatrix} -1 & & & & \\ & -1 & & & \\ & & \ddots & & \\ & & & -1 & \\ 1 & & & & \\ & 1 & & & \\ & & \ddots & & \\ & & & & 1 \end{bmatrix} = \begin{bmatrix} -I_{n_A} \\ I_{n_A} \end{bmatrix} \quad \text{and} \quad b = \begin{bmatrix} -w_1^{\text{sup}} \\ -w_2^{\text{sup}} \\ \vdots \\ -w_{n_A}^{\text{sup}} \\ w_1^{\text{inf}} \\ w_2^{\text{inf}} \\ \vdots \\ w_{n_A}^{\text{inf}} \end{bmatrix}.
$$

Example: we have 50 assets, then the matrix B can be constructed with the following commands.

In Matlab: In R:

```
[-eye(50); eye(50)]
```
```
rbind(-diag(50),diag(50))
```

To compute a long-only minimum-variance portfolio with Matlab, we can use the following code.

Listing 13.4. C-PortfolioOptimization/M/minVar.m

```
 1 % minVar.m -- version 2010-12-12
 2
 3 % generate artificial returns data
 4 ns = 60;   % number of scenarios
 5 na = 10;   % number of assets
 6 R = 0.005 + randn(ns, na) * 0.015;
 7 Q = 2 * cov(R);
 8
 9 % set up
10 c = zeros(1,na);
11 A = ones(1,na); a = 1;
12 B = -eye(na); b = zeros(na,1);
13
14 % solution
15 w = quadprog(Q,c,B,b,A,a);
16
17 % check constraints
18 sum(w)
19 all(w>=0)
```

The lower limit w^{inf} need not be zero. We could, for example, have assets selected with weights between 2% and 5%. But this method does not allow us to specify constraints like "either zero weight (not in the portfolio), or a weight between 2% and 5%." Models with such restrictions can be solved with heuristics.

Mean–variance efficient portfolios

Suppose we wish to find a portfolio that has minimal variance for a given required return r_d. We need to solve the following problem:

$$\min_{w} w' \Sigma w \qquad (13.5)$$

subject to

$$w' \iota = 1,$$

$$m' w \geq r_d,$$

$$w \geq w^{\text{inf}},$$

$$-w \geq -w^{\text{sup}} \qquad (\text{i.e., } w \leq w^{\text{sup}}).$$

With a vector m of return forecasts, we get the following formulation:

$$Q = 2\Sigma, \qquad c = [0,0,0,\ldots]',$$

$$A = [1,1,\ldots], \qquad a = 1,$$

$$B = \begin{bmatrix} m' \\ -I_{n_A} \\ I_{n_A} \end{bmatrix}, \qquad b = \begin{bmatrix} r_d \\ -w^{\text{sup}} \\ w^{\text{inf}} \end{bmatrix}.$$

An example with holding size constraints looks as follows in R.

Listing 13.5. C-PortfolioOptimization/R/portOpt2.R

```
1  # portOpt2.R -- version 2010-12-28
2  # mean--variance-efficient portfolio
3  require(quadprog)
4
5  # create random returns
6  na    <- 20                    # number of assets
7  ns    <- 60                    # number of observations
8  R     <- array(rnorm(ns * na, mean = 0.005, sd = 0.015),
9                 dim = c(ns, na))
10 m       <- colMeans(R)         # means
11 rd      <- mean(m)             # desired mean
12 wsup    <- 0.1                 # maximum holding size
13 winf    <- 0.0                 # minimum holding size
14
15 # set up matrices
16 Q <- 2 * cov(R)
17 A <- array( 1, dim = c(1,na))
18 a <- 1
19 B <- array(m, dim = c(1,na))
20 B <- rbind(B,-diag(na),diag(na))
21 b <- rbind(rd, array(-wsup, dim = c(na,1)),
22            array( winf, dim = c(na,1)))
23 result <- solve.QP(Dmat = Q,
24                    dvec = rep(0,na),
25                    Amat = t(rbind(A,B)),
```

```
26|                          bvec = rbind(a,b),
27|                          meq  = 1)
28|
29| w <- result$solution
30| sum(w)              # check budget constraint
31| w %*% m > rd        # check return constraint
32| summary(w)          # check holding size constraint
```

The tangency portfolio

The tangency portfolio is the portfolio that maximizes the ratio of excess return to portfolio volatility (Tobin, 1958), that is, it is obtained from

$$\max_{w} \frac{m'w - r_f}{\sqrt{w'\Sigma w}} \tag{13.6}$$

subject to

$$w'\iota = 1 \tag{13.7}$$

and possibly other constraints. r_f is the risk-free rate (assumed to be a constant). The optimization makes sense only if there exists at least one portfolio for which $m'w$ is larger than r_f. Otherwise excess return is negative and no one would want to hold risky assets.

In the following R code, we provide two further ways to compute the tangency portfolio: the regression formulation of Britten-Jones (1999) and the computation via the first-order conditions.

Listing 13.6. C-PortfolioOptimization/R/portOpt3.R

```
 1| # portOpt3.R -- version 2010-12-11
 2| # tangency portfolio
 3| require(quadprog)
 4|
 5| # create random returns
 6| na   <- 20           # number of assets
 7| ns   <- 60           # number of observations
 8| R    <- array(rnorm(ns*na, mean = 0.005, sd = 0.015),
 9|                 dim = c(ns,na))
10| mu   <- colMeans(R)  # means
11| rf   <- 0.0001       # riskfree rate (about 2.5% pa)
12| mu2 <- mu - rf       # excess means
13|
14| # set up matrices
15| Q <- cov(R)                    # covariance matrix
16| B <- array(mu2, dim = c(1,na))
17| b <- 1
18| result <- solve.QP(Dmat = Q,
19|                      dvec = rep(0,na),
20|                      Amat = t(B),
21|                      bvec = b,
22|                      meq  = 1)
```

```
23
24 # rescale variables to obtain weights
25 w <- as.matrix(result$solution/sum(result$solution))
26
27 # compute sharpe ratio
28 SR     <- t(w) %*% mu2 / sqrt(t(w) %*% Q %*% w)
29 sum(w)                 # check budget constraint
30 t(w) %*% mu > rf       # check return constraint
31
32 # test 1: regression approach from Britten-Jones (1999)
33 R2     <- R - rf
34 ones   <- array(1, dim = c(ns,1))
35 solR   <- lm(ones~-1 + R2)
36 w2 <- coef(solR); w2 <- w2/sum(w2)
37 # ... w2 should be the same as w
38 all.equal(as.numeric(w),as.numeric(w2))
39
40 # test 2: no inequality constraints >> solve FOC
41 w3 <- solve(Q,mu2)
42 w3 <- w3/sum(w3)
43 # ... w3 should be the same as w2 and w
44 all.equal(as.numeric(w2),as.numeric(w3))
```

A tracking portfolio

We may also want to minimize a function of relative returns. Suppose we know a benchmark portfolio w^{bm} and wish to minimize the variance of the difference between the benchmark returns and the returns of our portfolio. The following formulation is possible:

$$\min_{w} \text{Var}(r^{P} - r'w^{bm}) = \text{Var}(r^{P}) + \text{Var}(r'w^{bm}) - 2\text{Cov}(r^{P}, r'w^{bm})$$

The variance of the benchmark portfolio does not depend on the portfolio weights w, so we drop it from the expression and rearrange:

$$-\text{Cov}(r'w^{bm}, r'w) + \tfrac{1}{2}w'\underbrace{\text{Var}(r)}_{\Sigma}w .$$

For a scenario set of asset returns R (size $n_{S} \times n_{A}$), the benchmark returns are Rw^{bm}. Hence:

$$-\underbrace{\text{Cov}(Rw^{bm}, R)}_{c}w + \tfrac{1}{2}w'\underbrace{\text{Var}(R)}_{Q}w .$$

The c term is a vector of the covariances of the benchmark portfolio with the single assets; $\text{Var}(R)$ is the variance–covariance matrix of the columns of R.

Computing the whole frontier

As a final example, we will trace out the complete mean–variance efficient frontier. There are three ways to do so.

1. Minimize variance while varying desired return r_d;
2. maximize return while varying the maximally allowed variance (note that this problem cannot be solved with QP because we have a linear objective function, but quadratic constraints); or
3. directly work with the objective function (13.2). This third representation has two advantages. First, we do not need to fix r_d beforehand—if we had to, we would need to compute the return of the minimum-variance portfolio first, and set r_d greater than this return. Second, we need not care what the highest possible r_d is—with constraints, the maximum achievable return may not be immediately obvious.

We recall our mean–variance problem as

$$\Phi = (1 - \lambda)w'\Sigma w - \lambda w'r .$$

We now vary λ between 0 and 1. Note that we used the expressions for the portfolio return and variance that explicitly rely on the portfolio weights. We set

$$Q = 2(1 - \lambda)\Sigma, \qquad c = \lambda m,$$

$$A = [1,1,1,\dots], \qquad a = 1,$$

$$B = \begin{bmatrix} -I_{n_A} \\ I_{n_A} \end{bmatrix}, \qquad b = \begin{bmatrix} -w^{\text{sup}} \\ w^{\text{inf}} \end{bmatrix}.$$

The following R and Matlab programs illustrate such a computation.

Listing 13.7. C-PortfolioOptimization/R/frontier.R

```
1  # frontier.R -- version 2010-11-24
2  require(quadprog)
3  require(NMOF)
4
5  # get data
6  R <- fundData[1:100,1:50]
7
8  # true values and settings
9  na <- dim(R)[2L]     # number of assets
10 ns <- 50
11 m  <- colMeans(R)
12 Sigma <- cov(R)
13 wsup  <- 1.0         # maximum holding size
14 winf  <- 0.0         # minimum holding size
15
16 # compute frontier
17 nFP        <- 100 # number of frontier points
18 lambdaSeq <- seq(0.001, 0.999, length = nFP)
19 A <- array( 1, dim = c(1,na))
20 B <- rbind(-diag(na),diag(na))
21 a <- 1
22 b <- rbind(array(-wsup, dim = c(na,1)),
23            array( winf, dim = c(na,1)))
24
```

```
25 # matrix for effcient portfolios
26 pMat       <- array(NA, dim=c(na,nFP))
27 for(lambda in lambdaSeq) {
28     result <- solve.QP(Dmat = 2*(1-lambda)*Sigma,
29                        dvec = lambda*m,
30                        Amat = t(rbind(A,B)),
31                        bvec = rbind(a,b),
32                        meq  = 1)
33     pMat[,which(lambda==lambdaSeq)] <- result$solution
34 }
35
36 # plot results
37 barplot(pMat,legend.text = TRUE,space=0)
```

Listing 13.8. C-PortfolioOptimization/M/meanVar.m

```
1  % meanVar.m -- version 2011-05-16
2  %% compute a mean--variance efficient portfolio (long-only)
3  % generate artificial returns data
4  ns = 60;  % number of scenarios
5  na = 10;  % number of assets
6  R = 0.005 + randn(ns, na) * 0.015;
7  Q = 2 * cov(R);
8  m = mean(R);
9  rd = 0.0055; % required return
10
11 c = zeros(1,na);
12 A = ones(1,na);          % equality constraints
13 a = 1;
14 B = [-m; -eye(na)];      % inequality constraints
15 b = [-rd zeros(1,na)]';
16
17 w = quadprog(Q,c,B,b,A,a);
18
19 % check constraints
20 sum(w), all(w>=0), m * w
21
22 %% compute and plot a whole frontier (long-only)
23 npoints = 100;
24 lambda = sqrt(1-linspace(0.99,0.05,npoints).^2);
25 B = -eye(na); b = zeros(1,na)';
26 for i = 1:npoints
27     Q = 2*lambda(i) * cov(R);
28     c = -(1-lambda(i)) * m;
29     w = quadprog(Q,c,B,b,A,a);
30     plot(sqrt(w'*cov(R)*w),m*w,'r.'), hold on
31 end
32 xlabel('Volatility')
33 ylabel('Expected portfolio return')
```

13.2.4. True, estimated, and realized frontiers

Efficient frontiers should not be used as a practical quantitative model. The trouble does not come from the model, but from the data. We do not know the "true" expected returns, variances, and correlations. Not knowing a quantity is not necessarily a problem in itself; after all, statistics is all about inferring unknown quantities from sample data. But here the statistics enter as an ingredient into our decision what portfolio to hold. So, the relevant question is not "How large are our forecast errors?" but rather "Given a typical forecast error, what are the costs of such an error?" It turns out that the costs are high, and the chosen portfolios often perform miserably. For empirical evidence, see for instance the early results of Cohen and Pogue (1967); Frankfurter, Phillips, and Seagle (1971); and, in particular, Jobson and Korkie (1980); Jorion (1985, 1986); Best and Grauer (1991); Chopra, Hensel, and Turner (1993); Board and Sutcliffe (1994); DeMiguel, Garlappi, and Uppal (2009). Brandt (2009) gives a very good overview. Thus, the idea of an efficient frontier is an insightful "instrument of thought," but not a quantitative decision tool.

Unfortunately, the academic literature has mostly treated these problems as an "estimation" problem. But that actually obscures the issue—it is practically much more useful to consider portfolio optimization as a forecasting problem. When we estimate a quantity and then use it as an input to the optimization, we make an (often implicit) assumption about a model for the quantity of interest, or about properties of the model. For example, when we estimate expected returns by historical mean returns, we assume that expected returns are constant. But there is no reason to assume that a quantity like the expected return is constant over time or slow-moving. If we treat the issue really as an estimation problem, we should first make explicit our choice of the model. Very likely then, the problem will be model selection, not estimation.

For the sake of the argument, suppose all the quantities of interest were constant. Even then it would be extremely difficult to estimate them. These difficulties are well studied in the academic literature. Early papers go back to the 1960s and 1970s; a main contribution came from Jobson and Korkie (1980). To demonstrate their basic idea, (i) we fix true expected returns m_* and a true variance–covariance matrix Σ_*, (ii) we simulate data with these parameters, and (iii) we estimate parameters m and Σ from these data and compute optimal portfolio weights w corresponding to the estimates. Since we know the true parameters, we can compute the truly optimal portfolio w_*, and we can judge how close w and w_* are. We compute three different frontiers (Broadie, 1993, and Windcliff and Boyle, 2004):

1. The true frontier $(1 - \lambda)w_*'\Sigma_* w_* - \lambda m_*' w_*$,
2. the estimated ("hoped-for") frontier $(1 - \lambda)w'\Sigma w - \lambda m' w$, and finally
3. the realized frontier $(1 - \lambda)w'\Sigma_* w - \lambda w' m_*$.

We use the data set fundData from the NMOF package. This data set consists of 500 scenarios of weekly returns of 200 mutual funds. These returns are no time series, but they were created by a resampling procedure described in Gilli and Schumann (forthcoming), and Schumann (2010, Chapter 4). The basis for the scenarios were 200 price series of mutual funds that are registered in Germany. All series ran from January 2007 to December 2009; all funds were denominated in euro. The funds were randomly chosen from a larger database with the restriction that volatility was not degenerate (it had to be greater than 1% for weekly returns). A fund's return was modeled by a linear model with just two factors, the German DAX 30 and the REXP index. For each fund, we estimated the factor equation and so obtained coefficients and a vector of residuals. The scenarios were then built by bootstrapping factor returns and residuals. The details of the data set do not matter here; it only serves to test the algorithms (as a matter of fact, we could have set up any arbitrary vector m_* and matrix Σ_*). What is important is that, by construction, the returns in a given column of fundData are i.i.d.

We select the first 25 columns (assets), and 100 rows (scenarios) and compute the sample means and variance–covariance matrix of this subset as the true parameters. Next we create Gaussian random samples with these moments, and compute optimal portfolios for these samples. Finally, we evaluate the portfolios with respect to the true parameters. For every random draw, we obtain one estimated frontier and one realized frontier; the true frontier does not change. Figure 13.1 shows typical results.

Michaud (1989) calls this effect "error maximization." The estimated frontiers are generally above the true frontier; they promise more return for a given level of risk. But we do not get the estimated frontiers, but the realized

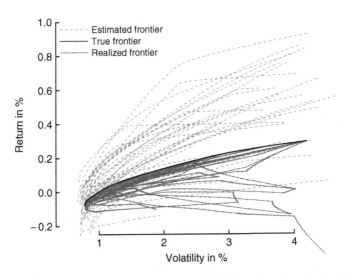

Figure 13.1 True frontier and estimated and realized frontiers (no short sales, n_A is 25, n_S is 100).

ones. A realized frontier cannot be better than the true frontier.[1] There are several lessons to be taken from this picture: first, a portfolio that appears efficient in-sample is often inefficient out-of-sample; second, we should not expect efficient frontiers to slope upwards out-of-sample. Also, even if we are relatively efficient out-of-sample, it is virtually impossible to achieve a desired mean–variance trade-off (see also Broadie, 1993). Importantly, this picture is still far too optimistic: we have assumed a fixed data-generating process for our data, but this is not the case in reality.

Let us make a few qualifications to these results. First, empirically, an exploitable trade-off likely exists across asset classes. For instance high-quality government bonds should over time give lower returns with lower risk. (As indeed they have over the last century; see Dimson, Marsh, and Staunton, 2002. Whether we need a very precise tool to handle this trade-off is another question.) Second, there is some empirical evidence for an intertemporal positive relationship between risk and return within single asset classes (though only over longer horizons); see, for instance, Harrison and Zhang (1999); and Bali, Demirtas, and Levy (2009). We only look at one-period optimization models, so we do not try to incorporate such a relationship.

Note that our point here is not against portfolio optimization but we caution against efficient frontiers. We do not argue that there is no trade-off between risk and reward, but we are skeptical about the idea that we can precisely control reward *and* risk. Empirically, there is substantial evidence that we can control the risk of a portfolio (e.g., Chan, Karceski, and Lakonishok, 1999, among many other studies); for returns, there is no such evidence.

Altogether, portfolio optimization is a valuable tool. But we do advocate not to simply translate the textbook description of portfolio selection into an empirical model. In particular, be wary of efficient frontiers. In fact, the generic portfolio selection model (13.1) did not imply we had to compute efficient frontiers.

13.2.5. Repairing matrices

Correlation and variance–covariance matrices are building blocks of many financial models, not just in portfolio optimization. In this section we discuss cases in which the variance–covariance matrix is not full-rank or is indefinite.

A helpful identity

We have a matrix R of size $n_S \times n_A$ (a sample of n_S observations of a random vector r of length n_A). Define the vector m as the vector of column means

---

[1] This follows from the definition of the realized frontier. We can always be lucky in a single draw.

of R, that is,

$$m = \frac{1}{n_S} R' \iota,$$

then the identity[2]

$$\frac{1}{n_S} R'R = \mathrm{Cov}(R) + mm' \qquad (13.8)$$

holds. The operators Var and Cov map given quantities into their variances and covariances (we use the maximum likelihood estimators, so we divide by n_S).[3] So if the mean vector is zero, the cross product of R equals the variance–covariance matrix up to a scalar. This identity shows how R and $\mathrm{Cov}(R)$ are related: essentially, the variance–covariance matrix is the cross product of R.

The following script tests Eq. (13.8) in R.

Listing 13.9. C-PortfolioOptimization/R/inR.R

```
1 # inR.R -- version 2010-12-24
2 ns <- 100; na <- 10
3 R <- array(rnorm(ns * na), dim = c(ns, ns))
4 R1 <- crossprod(R)/ns
5 R2 <- ((ns-1)/ns)*cov(R) + outer(colMeans(R),colMeans(R))
6 identical(R1,R2); all.equal(R1,R2)
```

Numerically, `R1` and `R2` will not be exactly equal, hence `identical` will give a `FALSE`.

Indefinite matrices

We have n_S return observations of n_A assets, collected in a matrix R (each series is one column). An estimator for the variance–covariance matrix of

---

[2] This is the matrix equivalent to $E(X^2) = \mathrm{Var}(X) + (E(X))^2$.

[3] The sample variance is usually estimated by dividing by $n_S - 1$ because this gives an unbiased estimator for the variance—and we are sure not to try to compute the variance if we only have a single observation. More seriously, dividing by n_S is just as fine for several reasons:

1. It does not matter practically. For small n_S, the obtained values will differ numerically, but there is no telling which value is more appropriate for the application at hand. For larger n_S, the values will be similar.

2. Unbiasedness is certainly a desirable property for an estimator, yet it also matters how large the bias is, and how large the variance of an estimator is. These two properties are combined in the mean squared error of an estimator, which is the sum of variance and bias squared. It turns out that dividing by n_S instead of $n_S - 1$ leads to an estimator with a lower mean squared error. Thus, dividing by n_S results in an estimator that is actually more accurate; see Greene (2008, Appendix C).

3. If we take the degrees-of-freedom issue really seriously, we need to consider the specific application. When we compute a variance–covariance matrix for a portfolio optimization problem, we actually require (analytically) the inverse of this matrix. Having an unbiased estimator for the variance matrix will not assure that the inverse is also unbiased; in fact, it will not be. The correct degrees of freedom are then $n_S - n_A - 2$. See Brandt (2009).

these returns can analytically be written as

$$\Sigma = \frac{1}{n_S} R' \underbrace{\left(I - \frac{1}{n_S} u u'\right)}_{M} R = \frac{1}{n_S} R' M R. \tag{13.9}$$

The matrix M transforms each column of R into deviations from their respective mean. M is idempotent; hence, $R'M'MR = R'MR$. M has rank $n_S - 1$; thus, if R has full column rank, we need at least $n_A + 1$ observations to obtain a full-rank variance–covariance matrix.

The variance–covariance matrix can be rewritten as follows:

$$\Sigma = \underbrace{\begin{bmatrix} \sigma_1 & & & \\ & \sigma_2 & & \\ & & \ddots & \\ & & & \sigma_{n_A} \end{bmatrix}}_{D} \underbrace{\begin{bmatrix} 1 & \rho_{1,2} & \cdots & \rho_{1,n_A} \\ \rho_{2,1} & 1 & \cdots & \rho_{2,n_A} \\ \vdots & \vdots & \ddots & \vdots \\ \rho_{n_A,1} & \rho_{n_A,2} & \cdots & 1 \end{bmatrix}}_{C} \underbrace{\begin{bmatrix} \sigma_1 & & & \\ & \sigma_2 & & \\ & & \ddots & \\ & & & \sigma_{n_A} \end{bmatrix}}_{D}$$

where C is the correlation matrix (the elements $\rho_{i,j}$ are the linear correlations), D is a matrix with the assets' standard deviations (σ_i) as its diagonal elements, and zeros elsewhere. So we need a correlation matrix and the volatilities of the assets.

Example 13.1

Fast computation with diagonal matrices.
The product DCD can be computed considerably faster by computing $\text{diag}(D)\,\text{diag}(D)'$ and then multiplying this rank-one matrix element-wise with the dense matrix C. (Here, diag is an operator that creates a column vector out of a matrix's main diagonal.) This computation requires $3n^2$ operations, while the operation count for the full matrix product is $4n^3$. Of course, for very small matrices, the speedup may be inconsequential. Note also that if C has a particular structure (e.g., is symmetric as in the case of a correlation matrix), even more efficient algorithms may be applied. Example code follows.

Listing 13.10. C-PortfolioOptimization/R/diagonalmult.R

```
 1  ## diagonalmult.R -- version 2010-11-27
 2
 3  # set size of matrix
 4  N <- 1000
 5
 6  # create matrices
 7  D <- diag(runif(N))
 8  C <- array(runif(N * N), dim = c(N, N))
 9
10  # compute product / compare time
11  system.time(Z1 <- D %*% C %*% D)
12  system.time(Z2 <- outer(diag(D), diag(D)) * C)
13
```

```
14  # check difference between matrices
15  max(abs(Z1 - Z2)) # ... or use all.equal(Z1,Z2)
16
17  # ... or with the Matrix package
18  require(Matrix)
19  D2 <- Diagonal(x=diag(D))
20  system.time(Z3 <- D2 %*% C %*% D2)
21  system.time(Z4 <- outer(diag(D2), diag(D2)) * C)
22  all.equal(as.numeric(Z1),as.numeric(Z4))
```

Listing 13.11. C-PortfolioOptimization/M/diagonalmult.M

```
1   % diagonalmult.m -- version 2010-11-27
2
3   % set size of matrix
4   N = 500;
5
6   % create matrices
7   D = diag(rand(N, 1));
8   M = rand(N, N);
9
10  % compute product / compare time
11  tic, Z1 = D * M * D; toc
12  tic, Z2 = diag(D) * diag(D)' .* M; toc
13
14  % check difference between matrices
15  max(max(abs(Z1 - Z2)))
```

The diagonal matrix D is of full rank unless at least one standard deviation is zero (conditional on numerical precision). But this would imply that we have a degenerate asset, with constant return; the correlation between a constant and a random variable is not defined. In any case, D will at least be positive-semidefinite, since the standard deviations cannot be negative. So if the variance–covariance matrix is not positive-semidefinite, then neither is the correlation matrix C. This suggests that it is enough to investigate the correlation matrix.

There are cases in which the correlation matrix is indefinite. The most obvious case occurs if we arbitrarily change entries of the matrix (e.g., for stress tests); it can also happen if the correlations are computed pairwise and some series have missing values. Importantly, the variance–covariance matrix will never be indefinite if we compute it from complete time series, that is, from the product $R'R$. What would be the problem if the matrix were indefinite? A semidefinite matrix Σ ensures that $w'\Sigma w \geq 0$ for all w. This implies that the variance cannot become negative (which makes sense). But we do not have such a guarantee anymore if the matrix is indefinite.

An example: suppose we are to construct a portfolio of three assets, each asset having a volatility of 0.3. We also have the correlation matrix C,

$$C = \begin{bmatrix} 1.0 & 0.9 & 0.9 \\ 0.9 & 1.0 & 0.2 \\ 0.9 & 0.2 & 1.0 \end{bmatrix}.$$

Now, consider the following strategy: sell short 100% of the first asset, buy 100% of the second and the third asset, that is, select a portfolio $w = [-1, 1, 1]'$. The portfolio's variance is -0.018, the standard deviation is $0.13i$, where $i = \sqrt{-1}$.

A simple repair mechanism is based on the spectral decomposition of the correlation matrix. If the correlation matrix is indefinite, then at least one eigenvalue is negative. The eigenvalues of the matrix C are

$$2.38, \quad 0.80, \quad -0.18,$$

so it is indefinite. (Use `eig(C)` in Matlab, `eigen(C)` in R.) To repair it, we replace all negative eigenvalues with zero. Since the resulting matrix will not have a main diagonal of ones anymore (which is required for a correlation matrix), we need to rescale the matrix. Algorithm 52 summarizes the procedure. For more details, see Rebonato and Jäckel (1999).

Algorithm 52 Repair mechanism for correlation matrix.

1: compute eigenvalue decomposition $C = V \Lambda V'$
2: set $\Lambda_c = \max(\Lambda, 0)$
3: compute $C_c = V \Lambda_c V'$
4: rescale C_c to obtain unit main diagonal

The matrix V stores the eigenvectors of C as its columns, and Λ is a diagonal matrix of the eigenvalues. The scaling matrix S is the main diagonal of $V \Lambda_c V'$. The rescaled correlation matrix C is given by $\sqrt{S} V \Lambda V' \sqrt{S}$. The expression $\sqrt{S}$ means to take the square root of the elements of S (which are nonnegative by construction).

With Matlab:

Listing 13.12. C-PortfolioOptimization/M/repair.m

```
1 % repair.m  -- version  2010-12-10
2 % --compute eigenvectors/-values
3 [V,D]   = eig(C);
4
5 % --replace negative eigenvalues by zero
6 D       = max(D, 0);
7
8 % --reconstruct correlation matrix
```

```
 9 CC      = V * D * V';
10
11 % --rescale correlation matrix
12 S       = 1 ./ sqrt(diag(CC));
13 SS      = S * S';
14 C       = CC .* SS;
```

In R (the function is also contained in NMOF):

Listing 13.13. C-PortfolioOptimization/R/repairMatrix.R

```
 1 repairMatrix <- function(C) {
 2         # compute eigenvectors/-values
 3         E    <- eigen(C, symmetric = TRUE)
 4         V    <- E$vectors
 5         D    <- E$values
 6
 7         # replace negative eigenvalues by zero
 8         D    <- pmax(D,0)
 9
10         # reconstruct correlation matrix
11         BB   <- V %*% diag(D) %*% t(V)
12
13         # rescale correlation matrix
14         T    <- 1/sqrt(diag(BB))
15         TT   <- outer(T,T)
16         C    <- BB * TT
17         return(C)
18 }
```

Note that here we discussed indefinite matrices, so we have negative and positive eigenvalues. The same procedure is sometimes suggested to transform positive-semidefinite matrices (i.e., matrices with some zero eigenvalues) into positive-definite matrices (i.e., matrices with only positive eigenvalues). That is, we can turn a rank-deficient matrix into a full-rank matrix by changing step 2 in Algorithm 52 into

$$\text{set } \Lambda_c = \max(\Lambda, \varepsilon)$$

with ε set to a very small number. This may allow us to run certain numerical procedures. For example, the algorithm called by solve.QP in the quadprog package requires a positive-definite matrix Q, which implies full rank. But: we only exchange one "bad" matrix against another one. In other words, we may be able to work with a matrix numerically, but this does not mean that the results need be meaningful empirically. A simple example can illustrate this. Assume we have a linear regression model with just two regressors, z_1 and z_2. Suppose that z_2 is actually $1.5z_1$. Now obviously, we cannot estimate such an equation because we have perfect collinearity. But would we regard this problem as solved if we replaced z_2 with $z_2^* = z_2 + \varepsilon$?

If a matrix R does not have full column rank, then we should call this a numerical property of R, but not a numerical problem in the sense of "if we could solve the numerical issues we would be fine." Rank-deficiency is an empirical problem. In fact, often it is not even a "real" problem. Three examples:

(i) Suppose the correlation matrix of R is a matrix of ones, so each pairwise correlation is unity. Clearly, this matrix has rank one. Is that a problem? Yes and no. Our chosen measure of dependence is correlation, and this correlation matrix tells us that no long-only combination of assets will yield any diversification benefit. So, financially, we do not get diversification. But is it a problem numerically? No, we just pick a portfolio that satisfies our needs best; for example, we pick the asset with the highest Sharpe ratio.

(ii) Suppose R does not have full column rank. Then there are linear combinations of the columns (i.e., portfolios) that behave exactly like other linear combinations (i.e., other portfolios). Potentially, then, our chosen solution is not unique. Such linear combinations are not always feasible (e.g., they may require short sales), so once we include constraints, our solution may become unique. But suppose that even with restrictions we still do not get a unique solution. Then, according to our model, we cannot differentiate between different solutions. Why should that be a numerical problem? We could either pick a portfolio randomly, or (more likely) think about how we should extend our model.

It is also possible that R has full column rank, but $R'R$ does not, as a result of finite-precision arithmetic. This is hardly a concern for finance problems when we work in double precision, and all the points just made still apply.

(iii) If we have fewer observations than assets, a correlation matrix will not have full rank. But again, this is an empirical problem; the matrix still will be nonnegative-definite. Not all implementations will accept such a matrix (a heuristic method could always be used; see the next section). Yet the main problem is that we try to estimate many quantities from too few data points.

To summarize: when we encounter numerical difficulties with variance–covariance matrices, then our problem is almost always empirical. This is in particular true if the difficulties result from finite-precision arithmetic. In other words, when our computer finally complains, we have probably gone too far, anyway. On modern computers, we can still compute solutions to problems when—empirically—we should do so no more. See also the regression/conditioning example on page 29.

13.3. Heuristic optimization of one-period models

In all the examples in the last section, we were constrained in how we could set up the model. The objective could only be linear or quadratic; the constraints had to be linear. To be sure, there are other variants of mathematical programming, but they all put restrictions on the functional form of the objective and the constraints. But what if we wanted to include a straightforward constraint like "every pairwise correlation should be below 0.7"? Or think of the simple asset selection problem we introduced in Chapter 12. We were to pick K out of n_A assets such that these assets optimize a given criterion. Such models can still be solved numerically, but we need other methods. In this section, we now turn to such alternative techniques: heuristics.

13.3.1. Asset selection with local search

We will first go back to the problem introduced in the last chapter.

Aim: select between K_{inf} and K_{sup} out of n_A assets such that an equally-weighted portfolio has the lowest-possible variance.

The formal model is:

$$\min_{w} w'\Sigma w \tag{13.10}$$

subject to the constraints

$$w_j = 1/K \quad \text{for } j \in J,$$

$$K_{inf} \le K \le K_{sup}.$$

The symbol J stands for the set of assets in the portfolio, and $K = \#\{J\}$ is the cardinality of this set, that is, the number of assets in the portfolio.

A simple strategy for this problem was described in the last chapter: local search. We start with a random portfolio and evaluate it. Then we iteratively change (or perturb) this portfolio until some criterion tells us to stop. The strategy is summarized in Algorithm 53; it also shows a shortened version of an R function that implements local search. The symbol x denotes a solution. To run a local search we need

- a method for evaluating a portfolio (the function Φ in Algorithm 53);
- a method for changing a given portfolio (the function $\mathcal{N}$ in Algorithm 53);
- a rule that tells us whether to accept a new solution;
- finally, we need a rule that tells us when to stop our search.

We will now discuss these ingredients in more detail.

Algorithm 53 Local Search for asset selection.

1: set n_{steps}
2: randomly generate current solution x^c
3: **for** $i = 1 : n_{\text{steps}}$ **do**
4:     generate $x^n \in \mathcal{N}(x^c)$ and compute $\Delta = \Phi(x^n) - \Phi(x^c)$
5:     **if** $\Delta < 0$ **then** $x^c = x^n$
6: **end for**
7: $x^{\text{sol}} = x^c$

Listing 13.14. C-PortfolioOptimization/R/LSabbr.R

```
1  # LSabbr.R -- version 2010-12-31
2  function(OF, algo=list(), ...) {
3      # add defaults to algo, do some checks
4      # ...
5      OF1 <- function(x) OF(x,...)
6      N1 <- function(x) algo$neighbour(x,...)
7      Fmat <- array(NA, dim = c(algo$nS,2))
8      xc  <- algo$x0; xcF <- OF1(xc)
9      for (s in 1:algo$nS) {
10         xn <- N1(xc)
11         xnF <- OF1(xn)
12         if (xnF <= xcF) {
13             xc  <- xn
14             xcF <- xnF
15         }
16         Fmat[s,1] <- xnF
17         Fmat[s,2] <- xcF
18     }
19     return( list(xbest = xc, OFvalue = xcF, Fmat = Fmat) )
20 }
```

The function LSopt, contained in the NMOF package, implements the skeleton of a local search. LSopt is called with three arguments.

```
LSopt(OF, algo = list(), ...)
```

The ... enables us to pass other objects into the algorithm; all such objects will be passed on into the objective function and the neighborhood function. We will collect all such variables in a list data, hence we call LSopt with the arguments OF, algo, and data.

OF is the objective function.

algo is a list that holds the settings of the local search. There are only few: an initial solution x0, a neighborhood definition, and the number of steps nS.

data is a list that holds the pieces of data necessary to evaluate the objective function.

In each step, the algorithm calls the neighborhood function, and evaluates the new solution through a call of OF. In the code, we use the notation xc for the current solution, and xn for the neighbor solution. LSopt returns a list with three components.

xbest is the solution.

OFvalue is the objective function value associated with xbest.

Fmat is a matrix with two columns. The first column contains the solution quality of the new solution for every step. The second contains the value of the current (i.e., accepted) solution. This must also be the best solution overall.

Let us go through the given problem step by step; all the code is contained in the R script exampleLS.R.

Coding and evaluating a portfolio

Conceptually, a portfolio is a vector. Since we look for an equal-weight portfolio, a solution x can be coded as a vector of zeros and ones. The L is a shorthand for telling R that the 1 is to be treated as an integer.

Listing 13.15. C-PortfolioOptimization/R/exampleLS.R

```
1 # random solution
2 card0 <- sample(data$Kinf:data$Ksup, 1L, replace = FALSE)
3 assets <- sample.int(na, card0, replace = FALSE)
4 x0 <- numeric(na)
5 x0[assets] <- 1L
```

We obtain weights by dividing each element of the vector by sum(x). Such a portfolio w is evaluated as stated in Model (13.10), that is, given the variance–covariance matrix Σ and w, we compute the portfolio variance $w'\Sigma w$.

Listing 13.16. C-PortfolioOptimization/R/exampleLS.R

```
1 # objective function
2 OF <- function(x, data) {
3     xx <- as.logical(x)
4     w <- x/sum(x)
5     res <- crossprod(w[xx],data$Sigma[xx,xx])
6     res <- tcrossprod(w[xx],res)
7     return(res)
8 }
```

We call the objective function with two arguments: a solution, and the list data. The list data contains the objects we need to evaluate a solution; in the example, this is just Sigma. We use the functions crossprod and tcrossprod to compute the variance, since these functions are usually more efficient than the %*% operator. Note also that we do not use the full vector w, but only those elements that are greater than zero.[4] Our solution x is a numeric vector like 0 1 0 0 1 ... so before we use this vector to subset w and the variance–covariance matrix, we make it a logical vector with as.logical. This is important in R since indexing a vector by 0 returns a vector of the same mode as the original vector but with length zero. Typing

```
(1:4)[0]
array(1:4, dim=c(2,2))[0,0]
```

we should get

```
integer(0)
<0 x 0 matrix>
```

This can lead to errors that are not easily detected.

Changing a portfolio—the neighborhood

Now we come to the most important part of local search, the neighborhood $\mathcal{N}$. The neighborhood defines what a solution "close to" another solution means. Formally, the neighborhood of a given solution is a subset of the solution space such that a given distance criterion is met. In the extreme, the neighborhood of a portfolio could contain all other possible portfolios, but then we would actually do a random search because from any portfolio we could step to any other feasible portfolio. In general we will choose the neighborhood such that the objective function exhibits "local behavior." This means that $\Phi(\mathcal{N}(x))$ should, at least on average, be close to $\Phi(x)$, for instance, when compared with randomly chosen solutions.

For our problem, as a measure for the distance between two portfolios, we can use the number of different positions, the so-called Hamming distance. A portfolio is a vector x of length n_A, so if x[j] is 1, then asset j is in the portfolio; if x[j] is 0, it is not included. A neighborhood can be defined by the number of different bits.

When we speak of a neighborhood function when it comes to the code, this will always mean a mapping from a given portfolio to one specific other portfolio. That is, we call the function with a current solution xc and obtain

---

[4] An even simpler objective function which only works for equal weights is given in the following code:

Listing 13.17. C-PortfolioOptimization/R/exampleLS.R

```
60 # a simpler objective function
61 OF2 <- function(x, data) {
62     xx <- as.logical(x); w <- 1/sum(x)
63     res <- sum(w * w * data$Sigma[xx,xx])
64     return(res)
65 }
```

one neighbor solution xn. With our encoding it is straightforward to generate neighbors: randomly pick a j, and change x[j]. This is summarized in Algorithm 54; R code follows.

Algorithm 54 Neighborhood (asset selection).

1: randomly select $j \in 1,\ldots,n_A$
2: **if** $x_j = 1$
3:    set $x_j = 0$
4: **else**
5:    set $x_j = 1$
6: **end if**

Listing 13.18. C-PortfolioOptimization/R/exampleLS.R

```
1  # neighborhood function
2  neighbour <- function(xc, data) {
3      xn <- xc
4      p <- sample.int(data$na, data$nn, replace = FALSE)
5      xn[p] <- abs(xn[p]-1L)
6      # reject infeasible solution
7      if( (sum(xn)>data$Ksup) || (sum(xn)<data$Kinf) ) {
8          return(xc)} else return(xn)
9  }
```

We pass a variable nn with data which gives the number of bits that are changed. Note also that we handle the constraints in this neighborhood definition: if the new solution violates a constraint, we reject it, and return the old solution.

So, we are almost done already; we have

- a method for evaluating a portfolio: the function OF, and
- a method for changing a portfolio: the function neighbour.
- We need an acceptance rule: In a classic local search we accept a new solution if it is better (at least not worse) than the previous solution.
- We stop the search after a predefined number of steps ns.

Let us run the example. We start with creating random data. We set a number of assets, construct a correlation matrix with constant pairwise correlation, and draw volatilities for our assets from the range 0.2 to 0.4.

Listing 13.19. C-PortfolioOptimization/R/exampleLS.R

```
1  # create random data
2  na <- 500L
3  C <- array(0.6, dim = c(na,na)); diag(C) <- 1
4  minVol <- 0.20; maxVol <- 0.40
5  Vols <- (maxVol - minVol) * runif(na) + minVol
6  Sigma <- outer(Vols,Vols) * C
```

We obtain `Sigma`, the variance–covariance matrix for `na` = 500 assets. We want to select a portfolio of between 30 and 60 assets. We collect all information in the list `data`.

Listing 13.20. C-PortfolioOptimization/R/exampleLS.R

```
1 # data
2 data <- list(Sigma = Sigma,
3              Kinf = 30L,
4              Ksup = 60L,
5                na = na,
6                nn = 1L)
```

Now we need an initial solution which we choose randomly. We use the R function `sample`. Note that we assume that `data$Kinf` is smaller than `data$Ksup`.

Listing 13.21. C-PortfolioOptimization/R/exampleLS.R

```
1 # random solution
2 card0 <- sample(data$Kinf:data$Ksup, 1L, replace = FALSE)
3 assets <- sample.int(na, card0, replace = FALSE)
4 x0 <- numeric(na)
5 x0[assets] <- 1L
```

Our settings—the initial solution `x0`, the `neighbour` function, and number of steps `nS`—go into the list `algo`.

Listing 13.22. C-PortfolioOptimization/R/exampleLS.R

```
1 # settings
2 algo <- list(x0 = x0,
3        neighbour = neighbour,
4               nS = 5000L)
```

Finally, we can run the algorithm.

Listing 13.23. C-PortfolioOptimization/R/exampleLS.R

```
 1 system.time(sol1 <- LSopt(OF, algo, data))
 2 # result
 3 sqrt(sol1$OFvalue)
 4 # plot best solution over time
 5 par(ylog=TRUE); plot(sqrt(sol1$Fmat[,2]),type="l")
 6
 7 # run more trials
 8 trials <- 100L
 9 allRes <- restartOpt(LSopt, n=trials, OF, algo = algo, data =
      data)
10 allResOF <- numeric(trials)
11 for (i in 1:trials) allResOF[i] <- sqrt(allRes[[i]]$OFvalue)
```

With 5000 steps and 500 assets, one run takes less than a second.

```
user     system    elapsed
0.56      0.00       0.57
```

We let the algorithm run not just once, but 100 times. We can use the function `restartOpt` for that.

```
restartOpt <- function (fun, n, OF, algo = NULL, ...) {
    n <- as.integer(n)
    stopifnot(n > 0L)
    allResults <- vector('list', n)
    for (i in 1L:n) allResults[[i]] <- fun(OF, algo, ...)
    allResults
}
```

This function takes an optimization algorithm `fun` (here, `LSopt`), a number `n` of restarts, and the arguments for `fun`. It is a simple wrapper for a loop in which `fun` is called `n` times. `restartOpt` uses the same initial solution for each restart. The function returns a list `allResults`. With this, we can reproduce the results presented in the last chapter.

Local search is simple and yet powerful enough to produce good solutions to the problem here. A disadvantage is that it might get stuck in local minima. The following figure shows objective functions of several restarts over the 5000 steps. (These values are stored in the matrix `Fmat` that is returned when `LSopt` is called.) If we were really concerned with the fact the solutions do not converge on a single point, we could make sure by using the method we outline next; or we could use several restarts. Practically, for this case, this does not seem necessary. But note that it is not necessarily the case that local search alone works so well.

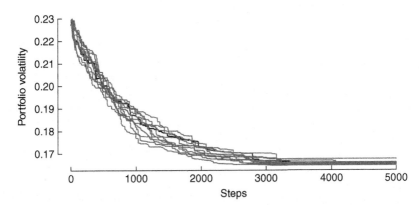

13.3.2. Scenario optimization with Threshold Accepting

In this section, we discuss generic portfolio optimization models with Threshold Accepting (TA). TA was introduced in Dueck and Scheuer (1990) and Moscato and Fontanari (1990). It was actually the first heuristic applied to portfolio selection problems (Dueck and Winker, 1992); see also Gilli and Schumann (2010f). We start by describing the general approach—scenario optimization—and then move to several examples.

Ingredient 1: handling scenarios

Recall that in the standard mean–variance model, we work with the properties of single assets—means, variances, and correlations—independently of specific portfolio weights. All information is condensed into an expected-return vector of length n_A, and a variance–covariance matrix of size $n_A \times n_A$. Computing time will increase with the number of selectable assets but not with the number of observations. Importantly, we capture the relevant information about the distribution of assets independently of the specific portfolio chosen. This is very convenient—it is the reason for the success of mean–variance optimization—but it rarely generalizes to other specifications, or only in ways that are computationally very expensive. (See, for instance, Jondeau, Poon, and Rockinger (2007, Chapter 9) for how to set up skewness or kurtosis "matrices." In fact, for skewness we actually have a cube, that is, a three-dimensional array; for kurtosis we have a four-dimensional array. See also Konno, Shirakawa, and Yamazaki (1993); Konno and Suzuki (1995).)

There is a much more flexible approach: scenario optimization. For scenario optimization, we assume that we can obtain a return sample $r^P = [r_1^P \; r_2^P \; \dots \; r_{n_S}^P]'$, that is, a sample for a specific portfolio. Given such a sample we can easily evaluate any objective function, for instance compute partial moments, and, hence, evaluate the portfolio. In essence, scenario optimization is equivalent to working with the empirical distribution function of the portfolio returns, but this is not restrictive: if we preferred a parametric approach, we would consider the historical observations as scenarios, and estimate the necessary parameters from these scenarios.

Let us go through the idea in a bit more detail. Suppose we have n_A assets, and n_S return scenarios. For now, think that the latter are simply historical returns. We collect all data in a matrix R of size $n_S \times n_A$. One row of R thus stores the returns for one state of nature. We can equivalently work with price scenarios, computed as

$$P = (1 + R) \times \text{diag}(p_0)$$

where 1 is a matrix of ones of size $n_S \times n_A$, $\text{diag}(\cdot)$ is an operator that transforms a vector into a diagonal matrix, and p_0 is the vector of initial prices. Note that the columns of P need not be time series. In any case, if you think, for instance, of mean–variance optimization, they need not be treated as such. Rather, every row of P holds the prices for one possible future scenario that might occur, given initial prices of p_0. In fact, for many objective functions (e.g., moments) it is not relevant whether the scenarios are sorted in time, since such criteria only capture the cross-section of returns.

A portfolio is either described by u (the holdings), or w (the weights). The portfolio values in the scenarios can then be obtained by $v = Pu$; equivalently, we can compute returns $r^P = Rw$. For selection criteria that need a path of portfolio wealth (for instance drawdowns), we need to work with time series. For simplicity, assume again that we work with historical data, and arrange the prices in a matrix P^{path} of size $(T + 1) \times n_A$, where each column holds the historical prices of one asset. The portfolio values over time are still computed by $v = P^{path}u$. But now, v is no longer a sample of portfolio returns across the scenarios, but a time series of portfolio wealth.

To stress the difference between Pu and $P^{path}u$: Pu gives a sample of portfolio values over the cross-section of scenarios, while $P^{path}u$ gives one path of the portfolio value from time 0 to time T. For both scenarios and paths, we transform the prices or returns of the single assets into one vector v of portfolio values. Given v, any objective function can easily be computed. Thus, we can easily evaluate a given portfolio u. So we start with an initial guess u for a portfolio and then change it iteratively until we like the resulting vector v. This is the essence of scenario optimization; all the rest is detail (Dembo, 1991; Maringer, 2008b; Maringer and Parpas, 2009).

A disadvantage of scenario optimization is that the computation Pu needs to be performed in every iteration of an algorithm; so potentially tens or hundreds of thousands of times. Since the matrix R is of size $n_S \times n_A$, the computing time will increase with the number of assets, but also with the number of scenarios. The matrix R may be large and so the multiplication is expensive. Later on we will discuss how to speed up this computation.

Before we go on, a final remark on scenarios. Setting up scenarios is a crucial part of the optimization. The simplest (and probably most widely used) way is to use historical data. We can also resample. Resampling is possible for time series, too: we could, for instance, estimate a model that captures serial dependencies (like a GARCH model) and then resample from its residuals; or we may use a block bootstrap method. See Section 6.7 for possibilities. In the following examples we use the relatively small data set `fundData` that comes with NMOF; see page 394.

Ingredient 2: building blocks for selection criteria

Suppose we have a scenario set, then next we need a selection criterion Φ. In essence, anything is possible (though not everything is a good idea), so we rather discuss building blocks for alternative reward and risk functions, that is, building blocks for Φ.

We can combine several ideas; for instance, in ratios. Ratios are easy to communicate and interpret (Stoyanov, Rachev, and Fabozzi, 2007); when associated with an optimized portfolio, they always have a certain optimality feature, like "the maximum reward for a unit of risk," or the "minimum risk for a unit of reward." With ratios, we always need to safeguard our objective functions for cases where numerator or denominator could switch signs while moving through the search space. Ratios that use the mean return for reward, for instance, are not directly interpretable anymore if mean returns are negative. Also, we need to think about what happens when either the numerator or denominator become zero.

If we do not like ratios we can use linear combinations like

$$\Phi(u) = \omega_1 \Phi_1 + \omega_2 \Phi_2 \ldots$$

in which the Φ_i are different criteria and the ω_i are weights. Actually, any combination (nonlinear ones as well) is possible; but it is often more convenient to keep Φ simple.

Moments

Moments are a natural way to condense sample information into a single number. A moment can be defined as

$$\text{average}\left((r^P - \text{threshold})^k\right)$$

with threshold and k being scalars. Most often, the expectation is taken for average, but we may as well use the median. The kth moment is the expectation of a random variable raised to a power k, which need not be an integer.

For a sample, computing expectations reduces to summing returns. We have already used the mean and variance; higher moments like skewness and kurtosis are possible as well. Moments with $k > 1$ are usually centered around their mean. Practically, when the mean is very small (e.g., for daily returns), it does not matter much whether it is subtracted or not. Not including it may even be more appropriate sometimes; the famous example is the stock price that rises 1% per day, every day. If we define the stock's variability as deviation around the average return, then there is no variability. But apparently this is not how traders understand volatility.

Partial moments

Partial moments are a convenient way to distinguish between returns above and below a desired return threshold r_d, and to capture potential asymmetry around this threshold. For a sample of n_S return observations, partial moments $\text{PM}_\gamma(r_d)$ can be computed as

$$\text{PM}_\gamma^+(r_d) = \frac{1}{n_S} \sum_{r^P > r_d} \left(r^P - r_d\right)^\gamma, \tag{13.11a}$$

$$\text{PM}_\gamma^-(r_d) = \frac{1}{n_S} \sum_{r^P < r_d} \left(r_d - r^P\right)^\gamma. \tag{13.11b}$$

The superscripts $+$ and $-$ indicate the tail (i.e., upside or downside). Partial moments take two more parameters, an exponent γ and the threshold r_d. The expression "$r^P > r_d$" indicates to sum only over those returns that are greater than r_d.

A well-known partial moment is the semi-variance $PM_2^-(m^P)$, or more generally $PM_2^-(r_d)$. The square root of this expression, sometimes called downside deviation, is used as the risk function in several performance measures like the Sortino and the Upside Potential ratio (Sortino, van der Meer, and Plantinga, 1999). The Sortino ratio, to be maximized, is defined as

$$\frac{m^P - r_d}{\sqrt{PM_2^-(r_d)}}$$

for a fixed r_d. The Upside Potential ratio, also to be maximized, is defined as

$$\frac{\sqrt{PM_1^+(r_d)}}{\sqrt{PM_2^-(r_d)}}.$$

When we minimize, we turn the ratios upside down.

Conditional moments

Conditional moments can be calculated as

$$CM_\gamma^+(r_d) = \frac{1}{\#\{r^P > r_d\}} \sum_{r^P > r_d} \left(r^P - r_d\right)^\gamma, \qquad (13.12a)$$

$$CM_\gamma^-(r_d) = \frac{1}{\#\{r^P < r_d\}} \sum_{r^P < r_d} \left(r_d - r^P\right)^\gamma. \qquad (13.12b)$$

Again $+$ and $-$ indicate the tail, and "$\#\{r^P > r_d\}$" is a counter for the number of returns greater than r_d.

We could also recombine such moments: suppose we wish to minimize variability, but we would like to penalize the upside less than the downside. Then we could use something like the following:

$$\frac{1}{\#\{r^P < r_d\}} \sum_{r^P < r_d} \left(r_d - r^P\right)^{\gamma^-} + \frac{1}{\#\{r^P > r_d\}} \sum_{r^P > r_d} \left(r^P - r_d\right)^{\gamma^+}.$$

Conditional and partial moments are closely related. For a threshold r_d, the lower partial moment of order γ equals the lower tail's conditional moment of the same order times the lower partial moment of order zero. That is,

$$PM_\gamma^+(r_d) = CM_\gamma^+(r_d)\, PM_0^+(r_d),$$

$$PM_\gamma^-(r_d) = CM_\gamma^-(r_d)\, PM_0^-(r_d).$$

The partial moment of order zero is simply the probability of obtaining a return beyond r_d. So, in words, conditional moments measure the magnitude of returns around r_d, while partial moments also take into account the probability of such returns. For a fixed r_d, conditional and partial moments convey different information because both the probability and the conditional moment need to be estimated from the data to obtain a partial moment.

Listing 13.24. C-PortfolioOptimization/R/pmcm.R

```
1  # pmcm.R -- version 2010-12-05
2
3  x <- rnorm(20)
4
5  # mean and probability of loss
6  theta      <- 0.1 # ... or mean(x)
7  prob.loss <- ecdf(x)(theta)
8  exponent   <- 2
9
10 # conditional moment (CM)
11 (cm <- mean((x[x < theta] - theta)^exponent))
12
13 # partial moment (PM)
14 xx <- x - theta; xx[xx > 0] <- 0
15 (pm <- mean(xx^exponent))
16
17 # relationship between PM and CM
18 all.equal(cm * prob.loss, pm)
```

Partial and conditional moments, in our definitions, are centered around r_d. If r_d is fixed, we can directly work with Eq. (13.11) and (13.12). To give an example, Fig. 13.2 (left panel) pictures the return distributions of two portfolios. If we aim to find a portfolio that minimizes a function of the returns below r_d, there should be little debate which portfolio to choose.

Indeed, it is intuitive to fix r_d at a specific level; for example, $r_d = 0$. Alternatively, we could use quantiles to determine r_d, for instance, the loss (negative return) that is only exceeded with a given probability. This convention is often found with conditional moments. In that case, we cannot use Eq. (13.12), since fixing a quantile says nothing about the location of the return distribution that the algorithm selects. This is illustrated below

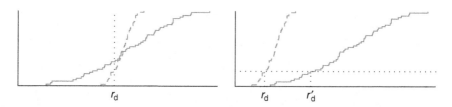

Figure 13.2 Portfolio return distributions: the influence of r_d.

in Fig. 13.2 (right panel): in that picture we would certainly prefer the more variable distribution but a decision rule based on a moment centered around the quantile would choose the dominated one on the left.

The simplest remedy is not to center around r_d, but to set

$$\text{CM}_\gamma^+(r_d) = \frac{1}{\#\{r^P > r_d\}} \sum_{r^P > r_d} (r^P)^\gamma, \tag{13.13a}$$

$$\text{CM}_\gamma^-(r_d) = \frac{1}{\#\{r^P < r_d\}} \sum_{r^P < r_d} (r^P)^\gamma. \tag{13.13b}$$

Without centering, we have no more guarantee for the sign of r^P. Hence, for $\gamma \neq 1$, we replace r^P with $\max(r^P, 0)$ in Eq. (13.13a), and by $\min(r^P, 0)$ in Eq. (13.13b).

Quantiles

A quantile of a sample $r^P = [r_1^P \, r_2^P \, \ldots \, r_{n_S}^P]'$ is defined as

$$Q_q = \text{CDF}^{-1}(q) = \min\{r^P \mid \text{CDF}(r^P) \geq q\},$$

where CDF is the cumulative distribution function and q may range from 0% to 100% (we leave out the percent sign in subscripts). Thus, the qth quantile is a number Q_q such that q of the observations are smaller, and $(100\% - q)$ larger than Q_q. For a given sample, we will usually have several numbers that satisfy this definition (Hyndman and Fan, 1996). The simplest approach is to use the order statistics of the portfolio returns $[r_{(1)}^P \, r_{(2)}^P \, \ldots \, r_{(n_S)}^P]'$, that is, a step function. If ℓ is the smallest integer not smaller than $q \times n_S$, then the qth quantile is the $\max(\ell, 1)$th order statistic. This is consistent with the convention in many implementations that Q_0 is the minimum of the sample (an estimator for the worst-case return), and Q_{100} is the maximum. Importantly, when we are interested in the tails of the distribution, we can only work with order statistics when we have a large enough sample. Imagine, for instance, we have only 20 observations; estimating Q_5 via an order statistic would not make much sense. In fact, using a parametric approximation like setting the quantile equal to some multiple of volatility would be much preferred in such a case.

The most famous quantile in finance is Value-at-Risk (VaR). VaR is the loss only to be exceeded with a given, usually small, probability at the end of a defined horizon. Thus, VaR is a quantile of the return distribution.

Quantiles can also be used as reward measures; we could maximize a higher quantile (e.g., the 90th). We need to be careful when we construct ratios here, since ideally we would want to maximize all quantiles (i.e., move the return distribution to the right). One way to build a ratio is to consider deviations from a quantile in the middle of the distribution (the median being the natural candidate). If we use quantiles far in the tails, we can form ratios of the form $-Q_{lo}/Q_{hi}$ and assume (and check numerically) that Q_{lo} is below zero, and Q_{hi} is above.

Drawdown

The functions described so far are applied to the distribution of final wealth. We may as well observe the evolution of a portfolio over time. A useful function of the portfolio's time path is the drawdown. Let v be a time series of portfolio values, with observations at $t = 0, 1, 2 \dots T$. Then the drawdown DD of this series at time t is defined as

$$DD_t = v_t^{\max} - v_t \qquad (13.14)$$

where $v_t^{\max}$ is the running maximum, that is, $v_t^{\max} = \max\{v_{t'} \mid t' \in [0, t]\}$.

DD is a whole vector of length $T + 1$, a subscript indicates a scalar value, for instance, the drawdown's mean, its maximum or its standard deviation, or the drawdown at a particular point in time. Other functions may be computed to capture the information in the drawdown vector, for example, the mean time underwater (i.e., the average time elapsed between two consecutive values in DD that are sufficiently close to zero), or the correlation between a portfolio's drawdown and the drawdown of an alternative asset, like an index. The definition in Eq. (13.14) gives DD in currency terms. A percentage drawdown is often preferred, obtained by using the logarithm of v, or by dividing Eq. (13.14) by $v_t^{\max}$.

In R, the drawdown can be computed with the function `cummax`. We demonstrate this for an artificial time series:

```
v <- rnorm(100, mean = 0.01, sd = 0.03)
v <- c(1, cumprod(1 + v))
plot(v,type = 'l')
```

Then we only need to compute:

```
absD <- cummax(v) - v
```

`absD` is the absolute DD of the series. To compute the maximum drawdown, for instance, just find the maximum of this vector.

We often want the relative drawdown, or drawdown in percentage points. There are several equivalent possibilities to compute it. We could take the logarithm of the time series.

```
logv  <- log(v)
d     <- logv - cummax(logv)
relD1 <- 1 - exp(d)
```

The last line converts the continuous returns back into discrete ones. A much simpler (and faster) way is to compute

```
cv    <- cummax(v)
relD2 <- (cv - v) / cv
```

`relD2`, up to numerical precision, equals `relD1`.

Matlab does not have a `cummax` function; we need a loop. We update the current maximum of v when going through the observations.

```
v = randn(1,100)*0.03 + 0.01;
v = cumprod([1 1+v]);
plot(v)

tmax = v(1);
nO   = length(v);
D = NaN(nO,1);
for i = 2:nO
    tmax = max(tmax,v(i));
    D(i) = (tmax - v(i))/tmax; % or D(i) = tmax - v(i)
end
```

It would be much slower (by orders of magnitude) if we used

```
tmax = max(v(1:i))
```

within the loop, that is, if we did not update the maximum.

Ingredient 3: Threshold Accepting

Threshold Accepting builds on local search. The algorithm has already been described in Chapter 12; we repeat the pseudocode in Algorithm 55. We use the symbol x generically for a solution.

Compared with local search, there is only a small difference: we do not require new solutions to be better than the current solution. They can be worse, but only up to a threshold. For intuition, suppose the thresholds were very large; then, our optimization algorithm would become a random walk and any new portfolio would be accepted. On the other hand, if the thresholds were too small, the algorithm would be too restrictive, and become stuck in local minima; for zero thresholds, we get exactly a local search. So the thresholds need to be connected to the step size for the algorithm, which is defined by the neighborhood.

Algorithm 55 uses two nested loops. The outer loop controls the size of the threshold, and the inner loop runs a number of steps for each threshold.

Algorithm 55 Threshold Accepting.

1: set n_{rounds} (number of thresholds) and n_{steps} (number of steps)
2: compute threshold sequence τ_r
3: randomly generate current solution x^c
4: **for** $t = 1 : n_{\text{rounds}}$ **do**
5:     **for** $s = 1 : n_{\text{steps}}$ **do**
6:         generate $x^n \in \mathcal{N}(x^c)$ and compute $\Delta = \Phi(x^n) - \Phi(x^c)$
7:         **if** $\Delta < \tau_t$ **then** $x^c = x^n$
8:     **end for**
9: **end for**
10: $x^{\text{sol}} = x^c$

(We could also use only one loop and change τ as a function of the iteration.) We use the word step when we explicitly refer to one step of the inner loop; we use iteration for the product $n_{rounds} \times n_{steps}$.

A basic implementation of TA, called `TAopt`, is contained in the NMOF package. Like `LSopt` before, the function is called with three arguments:

```
TAopt(OF, algo = list(), ...)
```

Again, we collect all information other than `algo` in a list `data`. In our experience, directly passing all arguments in one list makes for a clearer structure, and is less error prone.

OF is the objective function.

algo is a list that holds the settings of the TA algorithm (discussed below).

data is a list that holds the pieces of data necessary to evaluate the objective function.

`TAopt` runs for a fixed number of iterations, then it returns a list with four components:

xbest is the solution.

OFvalue is the objective function value associated with the solution.

Fmat is a matrix with two columns. The first column contains the solution quality of the new solution x^n in any iteration. The second contains the objective function value of the current (i.e., accepted) solution. Other than in `LSopt`, this does not necessarily coincide with the best solution overall. The best solution can be found by computing `cummin(Fmat[,2])`.

vT are the thresholds (discussed below).

Like with `LSopt`, we operate on solutions through functions that we define beforehand. Hence x need not just be a vector, but can be a list or another data structure. For instance, with many available assets and a small portfolio, it may be more advantageous to only store the weights of the included assets. To use TA for a specific problem, we need to decide about several settings and parameters, quite similar to local search before.

Initial solution Provide a random guess. We could even let R draw a random solution. Unfortunately, getting a feasible solution may not be trivial for a constrained problem. If we use penalties, this is less problematic—as long as there exist feasible solutions—since the algorithm will be enticed to find a way back to a feasible solution. In any case, if TA (or any other heuristic) works correctly, the solution should not depend on the initial guess in a predictable way, so there should be no need for "good starting values" (Gilli and Schumann, 2010c).

Neighborhood The key ingredient of local search and also of TA. The neighborhood function defines how we move from one solution to the next. In principle, it is very simple because for portfolio selection problems we have a natural way to create neighbor solutions: we pick one asset in the portfolio randomly, "sell" a small quantity of this asset, and "invest" the amount received into another asset. If short positions are allowed, the chosen asset to be sold does not have to be in the portfolio. The "small quantity" could be a random variate (e.g., a uniform over 0% to 0.5%), or a small fixed fraction (e.g., 0.2%). In our experience, using a fixed fraction is often somewhat more efficient, even though, for practical purposes, both methods give similar results. The neighborhood gives us a lot of flexibility (unlike, for instance, in methods like Differential Evolution, where the rules for how to change solutions essentially define the method). But it also requires some time to come up with good neighborhoods.

Thresholds The thresholds are another important element of TA. In principle, it is clear what we need: the threshold sequence is an ordered vector of positive numbers that decrease to zero or at least become very small. (In fact, thresholds need not be monotonous, but can increase as well.) We need to decide how many thresholds, and how exactly to set them. Thresholds are closely connected to the neighborhood definition. Larger neighborhoods, which imply larger changes from one candidate portfolio compared with the next, need be accompanied by larger initial threshold values, and the other way around. Fortunately, once we have settled on a neighborhood, there exist procedures to compute the thresholds from the neighborhood. Below we will describe such algorithms; thus, we only need to decide how many thresholds we want.

Iterations The number of iterations (number of thresholds × number of steps per threshold).

Stopping criterion We use a simple stopping criterion: a fixed number of function evaluations, given by the product number of thresholds × number of steps per threshold. We can often reduce computing time by adding a break if, for instance, there was no change in the best solution over a number of iterations.

Constraints TA is very flexible when it comes to enforcing constraints. All the strategies discussed in Section 12.5 can be applied: we can repair solutions, transform them, or penalize them. By choosing an appropriate neighborhood function, we can also create solutions such that they conform with the constraints.

So to get started we need an objective function, a neighborhood function, possibly some functions for constraint handling, and thresholds. We begin with the last ingredient, the thresholds, because the method of computing them will stay the same for all examples. Winker and Fang (1997) suggested the following method to obtain thresholds: generate a large number of random solutions, and select a neighbor for every solution. All these solutions are then evaluated according to the objective function, so for every pair (random solution|neighbor solution), we obtain a difference in the objective function value. The thresholds are then a number of decreasing quantiles of these changes. The procedure is summarized in Algorithm 56.

Algorithm 56 Computing the threshold sequence—Variant 1.

1: set n_{rounds} (# of thresholds), n_{deltas} (# of random solutions)
2: **for** $i = 1$ to n_{deltas} **do**
3:     randomly generate feasible current solution x^c
4:     generate $x^n \in \mathcal{N}(x^c)$
5:     compute $\Delta_i = |\Phi(x^n) - \Phi(x^c)|$
6: **end for**
7: sort $\Delta_1 \leq \Delta_2 \leq \cdots \leq \Delta_{n_{\text{deltas}}}$
8: set $\tau = \Delta_{n_{\text{rounds}}}, \ldots, \Delta_1$

The number of thresholds n_{rounds} with this approach is usually large; hence, the number of steps n_{steps} per threshold (in the inner loop of Algorithm 55) can be low; often it is only one step per threshold.

A variation of this method, described in Gilli, Këllezi, and Hysi (2006) and summarized in Algorithm 57, is to take a random walk through the data with steps made according to the neighborhood definition.[5] At every iteration, the changes in the objective function value are recorded. The thresholds are then a number of decreasing quantiles of these changes. We will use this second variant.

Algorithm 57 Computing the threshold sequence—Variant 2.

1: set n_{rounds} (# of thresholds), n_{deltas} (# of random steps)
2: randomly generate feasible current solution x^c
3: **for** $i = 1 : n_{\text{deltas}}$ **do**
4:     generate $x^n \in \mathcal{N}(x^c)$ and compute $\Delta_i = |\Phi(x^n) - \Phi(x^c)|$
5:     $x^c = x^n$
6: **end for**
7: compute empirical distribution CDF of Δ_i, $i = 1, \ldots, n_{\text{deltas}}$
8: compute threshold sequence $\tau_k = \text{CDF}^{-1}\left(\dfrac{n_{\text{rounds}} - k}{n_{\text{rounds}}}\right)$, $k = 1, \ldots, n_{\text{rounds}}$

Many variations are possible. For example, Algorithm 57 uses equidistant quantiles, so for $n_{\text{rounds}} = 5$, the 80th, 60th, 40th, 20th, and zeroth quantile are used. The convention in Matlab or R is to set the zeroth quantile equal to the minimum of the sample; hence, the last threshold is not necessarily zero. There is some evidence that the efficiency of the algorithm can be increased by starting with a lower quantile (e.g., the 50th), but TA is robust to different settings of these parameters. Algorithm 57 is

---

[5] This procedure is also used in Matlab's Genetic Algorithm and Direct Search toolbox.

advantageous if feasible solutions are difficult to find because we need just one feasible initial solution.[6] For this second variant, Gilli and Schumann (2010b) study the quality of solutions obtained in portfolio optimization problems for different numbers of thresholds for a fixed $n_{\text{rounds}} \times n_{\text{steps}}$. They find that the performance of the algorithm deteriorates for very small numbers of thresholds (e.g., 2 or 3), but stays roughly the same for more than 10 thresholds.

13.3.3. Examples

In this section we discuss two simple examples. These examples are not meant as "ready to go" applications but they may give guidance how to approach given problems.

Minimizing squared returns

It is advisable to run a newly implemented algorithm on problems that can be solved by other, reliable techniques. This helps to find errors in the implementation, and it builds intuition about the randomness of the solutions. The prime candidate for such a benchmark is a mean–variance problem with only few restrictions (budget constraint, long positions only with maximum holding sizes). For such a problem, an exact solution can be found with quadratic programming (QP). We use `solve.QP` from the `quadprog` package.

Aim: to find a long-only portfolio w that minimizes squared returns across all scenarios.

We want to solve the following problem:

$$\min_{w} \Phi \tag{13.15}$$

$$w'\iota = 1,$$

$$0 \le w_j \le w_j^{\text{sup}} \quad \text{for } j = 1,2,\ldots,n_{\text{A}}.$$

We set w_j^{sup} to 5% for all assets. Φ is the squared return of the portfolio, $w'R'Rw$, which is similar to the portfolio return's variance. We have

$$\frac{1}{n_{\text{S}}}R'R = \text{Cov}(R) + mm'$$

with Cov being the variance–covariance matrix operator that maps the columns of R into their variance–covariance matrix; m is a column vector that holds the column means of R, that is, $m' = 1/n_{\text{S}}\iota'R$ (see also

---

[6] If we use penalties, and scale the penalty function with the current objective function values, we need be cautious since the random walk can make the objective function explode.

Section 13.2.5). For short time horizons, the mean of a column is small compared with the average squared return of the column. Hence we ignore the matrix mm', and variance and squared returns become equivalent.

The objective function will be proportional to the inner product $w'R'Rw$, so we can save much time by computing $R'R$ beforehand. But, in general, this is not possible with other objective functions; we rather need to compute Rw in every iteration to evaluate Φ. As the scenario set we use fundData, which consists of 500 return scenarios for 200 funds.

Example 13.2

Computing sums of squares.

In many objective functions, a final step is to compute a sum of squares, that is, for some vector ϵ of length n we need to compute

$$\sum_{i}^{n} \epsilon_i^2.$$

With Matlab and R, matrix computations are often more efficient than directly squaring the elements. Hence, replacing the explicit sum by $\epsilon'\epsilon$, we get the same result (up to numerical precision), but generally the computation is faster for large vectors.

Listing 13.25. C-PortfolioOptimization/R/sumSquares.R

```
1 trials <- 1000; n <- 20000; ee <- rnorm(n)
2 system.time(for (i in 1:trials) z1 <- sum(ee^2))
3 system.time(for (i in 1:trials) z2 <- ee %*% ee)
4 system.time(for (i in 1:trials) z3 <- crossprod(ee))
```

The function crossprod is fastest.

Listing 13.26. C-PortfolioOptimization/M/sumSquares.M

```
1 % sumSquares.m  -- version  2010-12-23
2 trials = 1000; n = 50000; ee = randn(n,1);
3 tic, for i = 1:trials, z1 = sum(ee .^ 2); end, toc
4 tic, for i = 1:trials, z2 = ee' * ee; end, toc
5 tic, for i = 1:trials, z3 = dot(ee,ee); end, toc
```

The function dot (which is not a built-in function) is slowest.

Algorithm 58 Neighborhood (budget constraint).

1: set ϵ
2: randomly select asset i
3: set $w_i = w_i - \epsilon$
4: randomly select asset i
5: set $w_i = w_i + \epsilon$

The basic mechanism of the neighborhood is given in Algorithm 58. In each iteration, the value of ϵ is determined by a draw of a random variate that is uniformly distributed over the range $[0, 0.5\%]$. Practically, ϵ should not be too small. We work with portfolio weights, but the same principle could be used with actual position sizes.

The neighborhood automatically enforces the budget constraint, but the holding size constraints are not observed, not even the long-only constraint. (We may also select the same asset twice, leading to a no-change step. But such an occurrence is unlikely and leads to negligible inefficiencies.) The simplest way to enforce the constraints would be through a penalty function.[7] For this relatively simple constraint, it is easier and more efficient to incorporate the constraint directly into the neighborhood; see Algorithm 59. This algorithm requires that we start with a feasible solution (which may not be so simple in more complicated problems) with respect to holding size constraints. A general remark: there is always an infinity of possible implementations of the neighborhood, so we never know whether we found an optimal or close-to-optimal specification. But a rule in financial optimization (not just for heuristics) is that we can always stop searching if our solution is good enough. So if we have found a neighborhood that works sufficiently well, we can stop searching for a better implementation.

Algorithm 59 Neighborhood (holding sizes).

1: randomly select $i \in \{$assets with weight $> w^{\text{inf}}\}$
2: randomly select $j \in \{$assets with weight $< w^{\text{sup}}\}$
3: set ϵ
4: $w_i = w_i - \epsilon$
5: $w_j = w_j + \epsilon$

So let us go through this example step-by-step. We start by attaching the package and preparing the data. All necessary information is collected in the list `data`. In particular, we put in the actual data (the matrix R), but also, to demonstrate the possible speedup, the cross product RR. Note that we transpose R because we will compute Rw with `crossprod`.

---

[7] Minimizing squared returns is essentially minimizing variance. Suppose we combine two assets into a portfolio with weights w_1 and w_2, then the portfolio variance is going to be

$$w_1^2 \text{Var(asset 1)} + w_2^2 \text{Var(asset 2)} + 2w_1 w_2 \text{Cov(asset 1, asset 2)}.$$

If there is positive correlation (and, hence, covariance), the algorithm will always like to short one of the assets. Which is not so bad if short sales are allowed, but not in a long-only portfolio. The average correlation between the funds in the data set is about 0.5. A penalty may thus not be very efficient, that is, it would require more iterations than a repair mechanism. The same effect would occur if we wanted to incorporate the budget constraint through a penalty term: a zero vector has zero variance; hence, it will require some "tinkering" until the constraint is observed.

Listing 13.27. C-PortfolioOptimization/R/exampleSquaredRets.R

```
2   require(NMOF)
3   resample <- function(x, ...) x[sample.int(length(x), ...)]
4
5   na <- dim(fundData)[2L]
6   ns <- dim(fundData)[1L]
7   winf <- 0.0
8   wsup <- 0.05
9   data <- list(R = t(fundData),
10                RR = crossprod(fundData),
11                na = dim(fundData)[2L],
12                ns = dim(fundData)[1L],
13                eps = 0.5/100,
14                winf = winf,
15                wsup = wsup)
```

A neighborhood, following Algorithm 59, looks as follows. The logical vectors `toSell` and `toBuy` are transformed into indices with `which`. The function `which` is clearer and usually faster than the equivalent `(1:na)[toSell]`.

Listing 13.28. C-PortfolioOptimization/R/exampleSquaredRets.R

```
17  neighbour <- function(w, data){
18      eps <- runif(1) * data$eps
19      toSell <- w > data$winf
20      toBuy  <- w < data$wsup
21      i <- resample(which(toSell), size = 1L)
22      j <- resample(which(toBuy), size = 1L)
23      eps <- min(w[i] - data$winf, data$wsup - w[j], eps)
24      w[i] <- w[i] - eps
25      w[j] <- w[j] + eps
26      w
27  }
```

If we use `sample`, we need to test the length of `which(toSell)` and `which(toBuy)`. Suppose `which(toSell)` evaluates to a single integer, then `sample` will return a sample from `1:which(toSell)`. The documentation of `sample` suggests as an elegant solution the function `resample`.

```
resample <- function(x, ...) x[sample.int(length(x), ...)]
```

Objective functions: `OF1` uses the general scenario approach, so it computes Rw in every step. `OF2` uses the cross product $R'R$.

Listing 13.29. C-PortfolioOptimization/R/exampleSquaredRets.R

```
29  OF1 <- function(w, data) {
30      Rw <- crossprod(data$R,w)
31      crossprod(Rw)
32  }
```

```
33 OF2 <- function(w, data) {
34     aux <- crossprod(data$RR,w)
35     crossprod(w,aux)
36 }
```

Now we create a random weight vector `w0`, collect all settings in `algo`, and call `TAopt`.

Listing 13.30. C-PortfolioOptimization/R/exampleSquaredRets.R

```
38 # random solution
39 w0 <- runif(na); w0 <- w0/sum(w0)
40
41 algo <- list(x0 = w0,
42         neighbour = neighbour,
43               nS = 2000L,
44               nT = 10L,
45               nD = 5000L,
46               q = 0.20)
47 system.time(res <- TAopt(OF1,algo,data))
48 100*sqrt(crossprod(fundData %*% res$xbest)/ns)
49 system.time(res <- TAopt(OF2,algo,data))
50 100*sqrt(crossprod(fundData %*% res$xbest)/ns)
```

Finally, we compare our results with the exact solution.

Listing 13.31. C-PortfolioOptimization/R/exampleSquaredRets.R

```
52 # benchmark
53 require(quadprog)
54 covMatrix <- crossprod(fundData)
55 A <- rep(1, na); a <- 1
56 B <- rbind(-diag(na),
57              diag(na))
58 b <- rbind(array(-data$wsup, dim = c(na,1)),
59              array( data$winf, dim = c(na,1)))
60 system.time({
61     result <- solve.QP(Dmat = covMatrix,
62                        dvec = rep(0,na),
63                        Amat = t(rbind(A,B)),
64                        bvec = rbind(a,b),
65                         meq = 1)
66 })
67 wqp <- result$solution
68 # compare results
69 100 * sqrt( crossprod(fundData %*% wqp)/ns )
70 100 * sqrt( crossprod(fundData %*% res$xbest)/ns )
71 # check constraints
72 min(res$xbest); max(res$xbest); sum(res$xbest) # TA
73 min(wqp); max(wqp); sum(wqp) # QP
```

We scale the returned solution, that is, we average, take the square root, and multiply by 100.

```
100 * sqrt( crossprod(fundData %*% wqp)/ns )
```

Hence, the exact solution, provided by QP, corresponds to a weekly return of 0.34%.

```
        [,1]
[1,]  0.3361227
```

TA provides us with essentially the same solution, but it needs more time to compute it. The time difference between OF1 and OF2 will increase when we increase the number of scenarios. A typical TA result may look like this:

```
        [,1]
[1,]  0.3365394
```

How precise should we be?

When we run the example, we will get an objective function that is close to the exact solution, but it will not be the same. When we increase the number of iterations, we will get closer and closer to the optimum as found by QP. When is enough? To look into this question, we use again the data set fundData. Recall that the returns were created with a resampling procedure; thus, they are by construction i.i.d. returns. We randomly select 400 of the 500 scenarios and compute an optimal portfolio with QP, and also with TA. Then we compare both obtained solutions with respect to the 400 selected scenarios ("in-sample"), and also with respect to the remaining 100 scenarios ("out-of-sample"). We repeat this procedure 5000 times, each time we increase the number of steps. The procedure is summarized here:

1: **for** $i = 1 : 5000$ **do**
2:      sample 400 scenarios without replacement
3:      compute optimal portfolio with QP
4:      set $n_{steps} = i$
5:      compute portfolio with TA, compute in-sample difference between QP and TA
6:      compute out-of-sample difference for QP and TA on remaining 100 scenarios
7: **end for**

We compute the difference between QP and TA as

objective function value of QP − objective function value of TA;

hence, a negative number means that QP was better (had a lower objective function; we again scale the values into weekly returns). In-sample, differences could at most be zero, since QP computes the exact solution. Out-of-sample, positive differences are possible.

The main objective of this experiment is to see how these differences change when we increase the iterations of TA. We use 10 thresholds, so we test 10 to 50,000 iterations. Actually, the procedure confounds two effects, the randomness from the resampled scenarios, and the randomness of the algorithm. Alternatively, we could have used two loops: resample, then run TA with 1 to 5000 steps. But the results are clear enough; see Fig. 13.3.

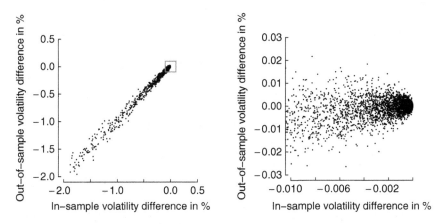

Figure 13.3 In-sample versus out-of-sample differences.

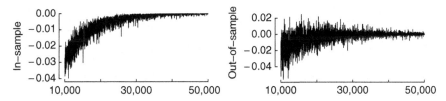

Figure 13.4 In-sample versus out-of-sample difference depending on the number of iterations.

On the left of Fig. 13.3, we plot the in-sample difference of a solution pair (QP minus TA) against the associated out-of-sample difference. If a difference is negative, QP is better (has a smaller risk). Not unexpectedly, there is indeed a positive relationship between the size of the in-sample difference and the out-of-sample difference. On the right, we zoom in on the small rectangle (actually the rectangle would need to be much smaller, so small that it could barely be recognized); more specifically, we select all portfolios for which the in-sample difference is less than one basis point. With this criterion, of the 5000 portfolios, more than 3000 are within the right picture, so more than 3000 portfolios have an in-sample disadvantage of less than one basis point. The mean absolute out-of-sample difference across these more than 3000 solutions is less than one-tenth of one basis point—less than 0.001%.

Practically, we cannot directly measure the in-sample error since we typically do not know the global optimum. But we can use the fact that the in-sample error is correlated with computational resources; see Fig. 13.4. (We drop the first 1000 solution pairs, that is, those TA runs with only 10 to 10,000 iterations.)

On the left of Fig. 13.4, the in-sample difference (in absolute terms) decreases slowly as there are more iterations. Clearly, the difference can never become positive. Fortunately, we are rather interested in the out-of-sample differences, plotted on the right; these quickly center around zero.

Updating scenarios

Like many other heuristics, TA is computationally intensive, with the main part of running time spent on evaluating the objective function. In our case, the objective function requires two steps: compute Rw (or Pu), then evaluate the resulting vector. We can often reduce computing time by carefully analyzing and profiling (and then rewriting) the objective function.

The matrix R is often large, storing thousands of scenarios for hundreds or thousands of assets. Without structure inherent in R, it may seem unlikely that we can speed up this multiplication. But structure actually exists in the way the optimization method proceeds from one solution to the next. With our neighborhood function, we will only change the portfolio weights of two assets in one iteration—then we can update the multiplication as follows: Let w^Δ be the vector of portfolio changes, then

$$w^n = w^c + w^\Delta$$

$$Rw^n = R(w^c + w^\Delta) = \underbrace{Rw^c}_{\text{known}} + Rw^\Delta.$$

Let R_* denote the submatrix of changed columns (size $n_S \times 2$) and w_*^Δ the vector of position changes (size 2×1), then we can replace Rw^Δ with $R_* w_*^\Delta$. This makes the matrix multiplication practically independent of the number of assets. The procedure is summarized in Algorithm 60.

Algorithm 60 Threshold Accepting—scenario updating.

1: ...
2: randomly generate current solution w^c
3: compute $r^P = Rw^c$
4: **for** $t = 1 : n_{\text{rounds}}$ **do**
5:     **for** $s = 1 : n_{\text{steps}}$ **do**
6:         generate $w^n \in \mathcal{N}(w^c)$, and compute R_*, w_*^Δ
7:         $r_*^P = r^P + R_* w_*^\Delta$
8:         compute $\Delta = \Phi(w^n, r_*^P) - \Phi(w^c, r^P)$
9:         **if** $\Delta < \tau_t$ **then** $w^c = w^n$, $r^P = r_*^P$
10:    **end for**
11: **end for**
12: ...

When we implement this updating, we could specify our neighborhood $\mathcal{N}$ such that it returns not just the new solution, but also the weights that have changed so that we can set up P_* and w_*^Δ. We have explicitly written

$\Phi(w, r^{\mathrm{P}})$ to emphasize the objective function's dependence on both the portfolio and data. In principle, this approach could also be applied to other methods; but we need to make sure that only a few asset weights are changed in every iteration. We can, for instance, no longer repair the budget constraint by simple rescaling. We mentioned above that TAopt works on solutions through functions, so a solution can be more than just a vector of weights. In fact, the product Rw is always associated with a given weight vector, so it need not be computed in the objective function, but can be part of the neighborhood. Such we can implement the updating mechanism without changing the function TAopt.

Let us look now at a numerical example. We start with a random solution. Such a solution is now a list with weights w and a vector Rw.

Listing 13.32. C-PortfolioOptimization/R/exampleSquaredRets2.R

```
30 # random solution
31 w0 <- runif(data$na); w0 <- w0/sum(w0)
32 x0 <- list(w = w0, Rw = fundData %*% w0)
```

The neighborhood function then looks as follows (U stands for Updating).

Listing 13.33. C-PortfolioOptimization/R/exampleSquaredRets2.R

```
4  neighbourU <- function(sol, data){
5      wn <- sol$w
6      toSell <- wn > data$winf
7      toBuy  <- wn < data$wsup
8      i <- resample(which(toSell), size = 1L)
9      j <- resample(which(toBuy), size = 1L)
10     eps <- runif(1) * data$eps
11     eps <- min(wn[i] - data$winf, data$wsup - wn[j], eps)
12     wn[i] <- wn[i] - eps
13     wn[j] <- wn[j] + eps
14     Rw <- sol$Rw + data$R[,c(i,j)] %*% c(-eps,eps)
15     return(list(w = wn, Rw = Rw))
16 }
```

The complete example is given in the following code.

Listing 13.34. C-PortfolioOptimization/R/exampleSquaredRets2.R

```
18 OF <- function(sol, data) crossprod(sol$Rw)
19
20 # prepare data
21 na <- dim(fundData)[2L]; ns <- dim(fundData)[1L]
22 winf <- 0.0; wsup <- 0.05
23 data <- list(R = fundData,
24              na = na,
25              ns = ns,
26              eps = 0.5/100,
```

```
27                 winf = winf,
28                 wsup = wsup)
29
30 # random solution
31 w0 <- runif(data$na); w0 <- w0/sum(w0)
32 x0 <- list(w = w0, Rw = fundData %*% w0)
33 algo <- list(x0 = x0,
34          neighbour = neighbourU,
35                 nS = 2000L,
36                 nT = 10L,
37                 nD = 5000L,
38                  q = 0.20)
39 system.time(res2 <- TAopt(OF,algo,data))
40 100*sqrt(crossprod(fundData %*% res2$xbest$w)/ns)
```

As a final remark, for this kind of problem we could actually speed up convergence. The best heuristic algorithm will be the one that resembles a gradient search as closely as possible. For instance, if we set all thresholds for TA to zero, the solution quality improves faster. But we will not do that. The aim of this problem was to see if our implementations worked reliably, not if TA could compete with QP on such a problem—which TA cannot. Heuristic methods deliberately employ strategies like randomness, or the acceptance of inferior solutions, which make heuristics inefficient for well-behaved problems like here when compared with classical methods. But these strategies are necessary to move away from local minima. In fact, changing model (13.15) only slightly already renders classic methods infeasible. To such a problem we go next.

Minimizing a risk–reward ratio

Aim: to find a long-only portfolio w of between K_{inf} and K_{sup} assets that minimizes a risk–reward ratio across a scenario set.

More formally, our model is the following:

$$\min_{w} \Phi$$

$$w'\iota = 1,$$

$$0 \le w_j \le w_j^{sup} \quad \text{for } j = 1,2,\ldots,n_A.$$

$$K_{inf} \le K \le K_{sup}.$$

We set w_j^{sup} to 10% for all assets, hence K_{inf} cannot be smaller than 10. The cardinality constraints are included to enforce a small portfolio (say, between 10 and 30 assets).[8]

---

[8] If they were to (meaningfully) enforce greater cardinality, we would need to include minimum holding sizes greater than zero for the assets in the portfolios.

As the objective function we choose the ratio of two conditional moments, so

$$\Phi = \frac{CM_{\gamma-}^-}{CM_{\gamma+}^+}. \qquad (13.16)$$

This ratio has also been called the Generalized Rachev ratio (Biglova et al., 2004). We do not normalize the conditional moments; out-of-sample comparisons showed that there is little difference between CM_γ and $CM_\gamma^{1/\gamma}$ (Gilli and Schumann, forthcoming). Computing this objective function is more expensive than computing squared returns as we did in the previous example, in particular for non-integer exponents. There are different ways to compute powers of returns Rw (recall that $r^P = Rw$). If the exponent is two, we can compute inner products. R's function crossprod is often even more efficient than %*%, but altogether the differences are less pronounced; only for larger vectors do we get sizable speedups. In Matlab the differences are greater. The computation $\sum_i (r_i^P)^2$ should always be carried out as Rw' * Rw. When such a scalar product is not possible but the exponent is an integer like in $\sum_i (r_i^P)^3$, it is faster to compute the element-wise product Rw .* Rw .* Rw, and then sum. The following code example compares different ways of computation.

Listing 13.35. C-PortfolioOptimization/M/condMoment.m

```
1  % condMoment.m -- version 2010-12-31
2  rp = randn(10000,1); trials = 1000;
3
4  %% squared
5  tic, for i = 1:trials, a = rp' * rp;       end, toc
6  tic, for i = 1:trials, b = sum(rp .^ 2); end, toc
7  max(abs(a-b))
8
9  %% other exponent
10 e = 4;
11 tic
12 for i=1:trials
13     r = rp;
14     for j = 2:e, r = r .* rp; end
15     a = sum(r);
16 end
17 toc
18 tic, for i=1:trials, b = sum(rp .^ e); end, toc
19 max(abs(a-b))
```

Minimizing this risk–reward ratio is more demanding than minimizing squared returns not just because it is more expensive to evaluate a solution.[9]

---

[9] If instead we minimized a ratio of partial instead of conditional moments, the computation would be slightly cheaper since we would not have to count the positive and negative scenarios. Also, the objective function is usually smoother with partial moments than with conditional moments.

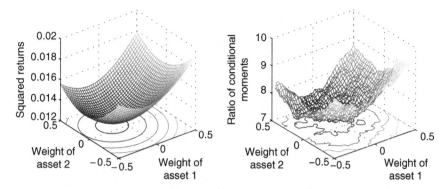

Figure 13.5 Squared returns (left panel) and ratio of conditional moments (right panel) for different portfolio weights.

Suppose we have to solve a three-asset problem with only the budget constraint. Figure 13.5 shows the objective functions of two different choices for Φ: on the left, we minimize squared returns (minimizing variance would result in a similar picture), on the right we minimize the ratio described above. The pictures show the objective function values for different asset weights (the third weight is fixed by the budget constraint). For the risk–reward ratio, the direct mapping from solutions into the objective function leads to a very rough surface. The problem gets more complicated because it actually combines two tasks: a combinatorial one (find the correct assets), and a continuous one (find the correct weights).

The new feature in this example is the explicit cardinality constraint. We can modify our last neighborhood (Algorithm 59) as described in Algorithm 61 which leads to the function `neighborUK` (UK stands for Updating and Kardinalty.)

Algorithm 61 Neighborhood (budget constraint, cardinality constraints).

1: set ϵ
2: **if** $K_{\inf} < K < K_{\sup}$ **then**
3:     randomly select $i \in \{$ assets with weight $> 0\}$
4:     randomly select $j \in \{$ assets with weight $< w^{\sup}\}$
5: **else if** $K = K_{\inf}$ **then**
6:     randomly select $i \in \{$assets with weight $> \epsilon\}$
7:     randomly select $j \in \{$assets with weight $< w^{\sup}\}$
8: **else**
9:     randomly select $i \in \{$assets with weight $> 0\}$
10:     randomly select $j \in \{$assets with weight > 0 and $< w^{\sup}\}$
11: **end if**
12: adjust ϵ
13: $w_i = w_i - \epsilon$
14: $w_j = w_j + \epsilon$

Listing 13.36. C-PortfolioOptimization/R/exampleRatio.R

```
16 neighbourUK <- function(sol, data){
17     wn <- sol$w
18     J <- wn > 0; K <- sum(J)
19     eps <- data$eps * runif(1)
20     if (K > data$Kinf && K < data$Ksup) {
21         toSell <- wn > 0
22         toBuy  <- wn < data$wsup
23     } else {
24         if (K == data$Ksup) {
25             toSell <- wn > 0
26             toBuy  <- J & (wn < data$wsup)
27         } else {
28             toSell <- wn > eps
29             toBuy  <- wn < data$wsup
30         }
31     }
32     i <- resample(which(toSell),1)
33     j <- resample(which(toBuy),1)
34     eps <- min(wn[i], data$wsup - wn[j], eps)
35     wn[i] <- wn[i] - eps
36     wn[j] <- wn[j] + eps
37     Rw <- sol$Rw + data$R[,c(i,j)] %*% c(-eps,eps)
38     return(list(w = wn, Rw = Rw))
39 }
```

A straightforward objective function looks as follows. We pass the exponents γ with the list `data`. In the example we use $\gamma = 2$ for both gains and losses.

Listing 13.37. C-PortfolioOptimization/R/exampleRatio.R

```
 4 # objective function
 5 OFcmR <- function(sol,data) {
 6     Rw <- sol$Rw
 7     losses <- Rw - abs(Rw)
 8     gains <- Rw + abs(Rw)
 9     nL <- sum(losses < 0)
10     nG <- sum(gains  > 0)
11     vG <- sum(gains^data$eG)
12     vL <- sum(abs(losses)^data$eL)
13     (vL/nL) / (vG/nG)
14 }
```

We could include control structures to change the computation depending on the exponents (e.g., use `crossprod` if exponents are 2). The simplest way is to explicitly pass an instruction with `data` that details if the exponent is 2, not 2 but an integer, and so on.

A complete example follows.

Listing 13.38. C-PortfolioOptimization/R/exampleRatio.R

```
41 # prepare data
42 na <- dim(fundData)[2L]
43 ns <- dim(fundData)[1L]
44
45 data <- list(R = fundData,
46              na = na, ns = ns,
47              eps = 0.5/100,
48              wsup = 0.1,
49              eG = 2, eL = 2,
50              Kinf = 10L, Ksup = 50L)
51
52 # initial solution
53 card0 <- sample(data$Kinf:data$Ksup, 1)
54 assets <- sample.int(data$na, card0, replace = FALSE)
55 w0 <- numeric(data$na); w0[assets] <- 1/card0
56 sol0 <- list(w = w0, Rw = fundData %*% w0)
57
58 algo <- list(x0 = sol0, neighbour = neighbourUK,
59              nS = 1000L, nT = 10L,
60              nD = 10000L, q = 0.9)
61 system.time(res <- TAopt(OFcmR,algo,data))
62 plot(res$Fmat[,1], type = 'l')
63 res$OFvalue; sum(res$xbest$w <= 1e-8); sum(res$xbest$w > 1e-8)
```

It is much more difficult to evaluate the quality of the solution since it is difficult to give an economic meaning to such a ratio. Some possible benchmarks could be:

- Choose feasible random portfolios and compare them with the solution obtained with TA. Random portfolios should be easy to beat (in-sample), they rather serve as a check of the implementation. Here we sample 10 million equal-weight portfolios with feasible cardinalities and plot the best 10,000 of these.
- Compute the objective function for each single asset, sort them, and compare portfolios built from the best assets.
- Solve a similar but simpler problem; for instance, try to find the best equal-weight portfolio of fixed cardinality.
- Solve the problem with another heuristic.

The simplest diagnostic is to run the algorithm several times and increase the number of iterations. The following picture shows the results. We leave the number of thresholds at 10, and restart TA 100 times with 2000, 5000, and 15,000 steps per threshold, respectively.

The distribution slowly moves to the left, but so far there is no telling whether we are near the global optimum. We could now increase the iterations further but there is also another way. As we said before, the optimization problem here can be seen from two perspectives: as a continuous problem (find good weights), or as a discrete one (find good assets). Our neighborhood function emphasizes weights; there is no explicit mechanism to change the cardinality.

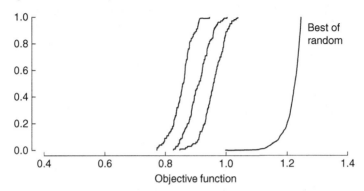

There are good reasons for choosing such a neighborhood specification. We would like the changes in the objective function, for a specified neighborhood definition, to be similar all over the solution space. This is important in Threshold Accepting, for suppose that for a given neighborhood the changes can either be very large or very small. It will then become more difficult to set up effective threshold sequences: with large thresholds, essentially all changes that lead to small changes in the objective function will be accepted; with small thresholds, we cannot escape local minima that require large changes in the objective function. You may now (rightfully) argue that the small changes in the objective function are by definition less important than the large changes, so if we do not like this behavior, we have either misspecified our model (i.e., we need to rewrite our objective function), or we should realize where our priorities are. Something similar is the case here.

Increasing the cardinality with the neighborhood as specified above means to pick an asset with zero weight, and increase this weight slightly. So an asset can be quickly added to the portfolio, but suppose its weight should be 10%, then it will possibly need a large number of iterations to arrive there. Conversely, if an asset does not belong into the portfolio it will have its weight decreased until, finally, the weight drops to zero. In that way, the impact on the objective function value of a given portfolio will be small when an asset is added or removed, no matter how good or bad this particular asset appears. This is fine if we need a precise solution.

When we pick a small number of assets from a large universe of different assets, the asset selection—which assets to put into the portfolio—becomes often more important than computing weights (in particular, if the weights cannot become very large, as is the case here). We have defined the neighbors of a portfolio x^c as those portfolios that differ only by a small fraction of the weights from x^c. If asset selection is more important, a reasonable alternative definition of a neighborhood would be portfolios that differ by no more than a fixed number of selected assets. (We used such a neighborhood definition in Section 13.3.1.) We do not need to rewrite our code to test this strategy. We only change two details: first, we use fixed weight changes, so in the neighborhood function instead of

```
eps <- data$eps * runif(1)
```

we use

```
eps <- data$eps
```

We also use a larger step size, for instance 2%, hence

```
data$eps <- 2/100
```

The following figure shows results with 3000, 10,000, 50,000, 100,000 and 200,000 steps per threshold (in increasingly darker gray). We have left the results obtained with the "small" neighborhood. We obtain lower objective function values in less time when compared with a weight-based neighborhood definition.

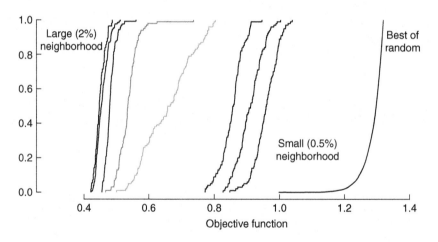

This example demonstrates that the neighborhood has a large impact on the performance of TA. The example also allows us to demonstrate the advantage of TA when compared with a local search. We use the same neighborhood and the same number of iterations, but once we include thresholds (TA) and once we use zero thresholds (i.e., local search). The following figures show objective function values over the course of the optimization.

In the left panel, we plot the best solutions found by the algorithms. The light gray lines are the results obtained with Local Search, the dark ones come from TA. In the right panel, we plot, for a single run of TA, the objective function values of the best solution and also the accepted solution. Since TA accepts inferior solutions, the function values do not

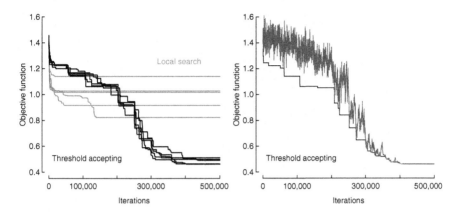

decline monotonously. Initially, with larger thresholds, the algorithm often moves to portfolios with a higher objective function value. Over time, as the thresholds become smaller, the objective function descends more smoothly.

13.3.4. Diagnostics

In this section, we discuss potential problems that may occur when implementing portfolio selection models and some "rules of thumb" that we found helpful in spotting trouble. It is difficult to clearly characterize where TA works well, and where it does not. Generally, TA may run into trouble if the objective function is very noisy, or very "flat" overall.

Benchmarking the algorithm

When we implement the algorithm afresh, it is a good idea to start with a well-known problem, one which can also be solved with another method. The obvious candidate is a mean–variance optimization with a quadratic programming solver as we did above. This does not only help to spot errors in the implementation, but also gives an intuition of how closely TA approximates the exact solution. If, for a convex problem like mean–variance, the solutions from TA differ widely across different optimization runs, this indicates insufficient computational resources (i.e., too few iterations).

The neighborhood and the thresholds

It is helpful to gain some intuition into the local structure of the objective function during the search. For low-dimensional problems, we can plot the objective function as in Fig. 13.5. With more dimensions, we can take random walks through the data (like in Algorithm 57). Thus we start with a random portfolio and move through the search space according to our neighborhood function, accepting any new portfolio. The changes in the objective function accompanying every step should be visually inspected; for instance, with histograms or CDF plots. A large number of zero changes indicates a flat surface: in such regions of the search space the algorithm will get no guidance from the objective function. Another sign of potential trouble is the clustering of changes, that is, if we have a large number of very small changes and a large number of very large changes, which may indicate a bad scaling of the problem.

The observed changes should be of a roughly similar magnitude as the thresholds, which is why such random walks are often used to inform the threshold setting, as was described in Algorithms 56 and 57. If the thresholds are too large compared with average changes, our optimization algorithm will become a random search, since any new portfolio will be accepted. If the thresholds are too small, the algorithm will be too restrictive, and become stuck in local minima.

During the actual optimization run, it is good practice to store the accepted changes in the objective function values (i.e., the accepted Δ-values in Algorithm 55). In TAopt, we do this in the matrix Fmat. As a rule of thumb, the standard deviation of these accepted changes should be of the same order of magnitude as the standard deviation of the changes in the objective function values recorded from the random walk (i.e., the Δ_i-values in Algorithms 56 or 57).

In any case, the path that a solution has taken through the search path should be studied. As a measure of performance, we can store the amount of improvement from an initial (random) solution to the final solution.

Testing the neighborhood function
The neighborhoods discussed above have all been simple. As a start, simple is good. Simple makes it easier to find mistakes (or make fewer in the first place), and it also allows us to enhance the model later on, for instance, by adding more constraints. We can later always add more features to the algorithm, and better judge how they perform. There is a trade-off: more-complex neighborhoods may be more error prone and less flexible—but they are often more efficient. Remarks:

- Use inequalities or tolerance levels instead of exact equality if comparisons are important in a neighborhood function.
- When testing a neighborhood, start with extreme portfolios (like all weights at upper boundary, initial cardinality of portfolio equal to K_{inf}, and so on).
- If cardinality constraints are important, then check how cardinality changes over time.

Arbitrage opportunities
A serious empirical problem with scenario optimization are arbitrage opportunities in the scenario set. This is a problem of the setup, not of the

optimization, so it is relevant for any optimization technique, not just for TA. There exist formal tests to detect arbitrage (described, for instance, in Ingersoll, 1987, Chapter 2), but they do not really help to remove them. Furthermore, these tests will not find spurious "good deals" in the data. The resulting overfit is particularly pronounced if short positions are allowed, because then the algorithm will finance seemingly advantageous positions by short-selling less-attractive assets. This becomes most obvious if we consider portfolios that also include options. If some stock never drops more than 10% in our scenarios, the algorithm will suggest writing a put on this stock at 90% of the current price. In fact, an unconstrained algorithm will sell an infinity of options. Such problems are not limited to long–short portfolios, long-only portfolios also overfit in such cases, even though the effect is less pronounced (Gilli, Schumann, di Tollo, and Cabej, 2011).

A practical solution for the equity-only case is to increase the number of observations in relation to the number of assets. When working with historical data, we may either use a longer historical time horizon, or reduce the number of selectable assets. If we work with resampled scenarios, we can simply increase the number of replications.

Including restrictions like maximum holding sizes is always advisable, even though it just reflects the fact that we cannot model asset prices properly. Such constraints may not just limit position sizes, but if applicable we can also include constraints on aggregate Greeks like Delta or Gamma, or a minimum required performance in added artificial crash scenarios.

Degenerate objective functions

Numerically, ratios have some unfavorable properties when compared with linear combinations. If the numerator becomes zero, the ratio becomes zero and the search becomes unguided; if the denominator is zero, we get an error (Inf). If the sign of the numerator or denominator changes over the course of the search, the ratio often becomes uninterpretable; an example is the Sharpe ratio for negative mean excess return.

So we generally need safeguards. To avoid sign problems, we can use centered quantities. Lower partial moments, for example, are computed as $r_d - r$ for returns lower than r_d; thus, the numbers will always be nonnegative. An alternative is to use operations like $\max(\cdot, 0)$ or $\min(\cdot, 0)$ to assure the sign of some quantity.

But there is also a valuable aspect in these instabilities, for they are not only of a numerical nature. In fact, problems when computing a ratio may indicate problems with the model or the data, which would go unnoticed with a linear combination. For instance, if a risk–reward ratio turns zero, this means we have found a portfolio with no risk at all—which, unfortunately, is more often an indication of a data problem rather than a really excellent portfolio.

13.A. More implementation issues in R

In this appendix we discuss several points about how to implement the objective function. This discussion is general and is, thus, relevant for all R functions discussed (DEopt, LSopt, PSopt, TAopt).

13.A.1. Scoping rules in R and objective functions

Scoping rules detail how a symbol (e.g., "x") is associated with a particular value. R's scoping rules are described in Gentleman and Ihaka (2000).

The intuitive idea of a function is that of a script that takes input, and returns an output. Concretely, an objective function takes the parameters of the model, and also data and perhaps other pieces of information; it then returns a real number that characterizes the quality of our solution. In R we could actually create a function such that it already includes the data and only takes the model's parameters as inputs. What is special about R (compared with Matlab) is that such a function could be created as the output of another function. An example: we create random data for a linear regression; the matrix X has nC columns, and nR rows.

Listing 13.39. C-PortfolioOptimization/R/exampleOF.R

```
1  # exampleOF.R -- version 2010-12-28
2  nR <- 100; nC <- 5
3  X <- array(rnorm(nR*nC),dim=c(nR,nC)); y <- rnorm(nC)
```

Say we want to minimize the residuals of $X\beta = y$ not with Least Squares, but we wish to minimize the maximum absolute residual. An objective function would need a vector param (the coefficients), the matrix X, and the vector y.

Listing 13.40. C-PortfolioOptimization/R/exampleOF.R

```
5  OF1 <- function(param,X,y)  max(abs(y - X %*% param))
```

We could also proceed as follows:

Listing 13.41. C-PortfolioOptimization/R/exampleOF.R

```
7   createF <- function(X,y) {
8       newFun <- function(param) max(abs(y - X %*% param))
9       newFun
10  }
11  OF2 <- createF(X,y)
```

The function `createF` takes our data (`X` and `y`), but then it defines a new function `newFun`. `newFun` takes only `param` as arguments, but not `X` and `y`. These objects are now in the environment of `newFun`.

```
> OF1
function(param,X,y)  max(abs(y - X %*% param))
> OF2
function(param) max(abs(y - X %*% param))
<environment: 01eb0194>
```

We can test both functions.

Listing 13.42. C-PortfolioOptimization/R/exampleOF.R

```
13 param <- rnorm(nC)
14 OF1(param,X,y)
15 OF2(param)
```

The results are the same. This could be a "trap." When R evaluates a function call and finds that an object does not exist in the current environment, it will search the enclosing environments until it either finds an object of that name, or reaches the global environment (where R gives us an error). We can even remove `X` and `y` from the global environment.

Listing 13.43. C-PortfolioOptimization/R/exampleOF.R

```
17 remove(list=c("X","y"), envir = .GlobalEnv); ls()
18 OF1(param,X,y)
19 OF2(param)
20
21 environment(OF2)
22 whereToLook <- environment(OF2)
```

We suggest being careful with R's scoping rules; if possible, pass all required objects directly into the function. In our experience, this is more reliable.

13.A.2. Vectorized objective functions

Local Search and Threshold Accepting are trajectory methods; they develop a single solution at a time. The basic structure of the objective function is clear: pass a solution, and receive a number. When we use population-based heuristics, we need to decide how we implement the objective function: we can either write the function for a single solution (i.e., one column of the population matrix), or pass the whole population into the function and only then evaluate the single solutions.

A function for a single solution is more user-friendly and allows for easier reuse of code; internally the optimization procedure could then call a function of the `apply` family and evaluate the objective function for the columns of the population matrix. But if we go for speed (and we often should with heuristic methods), we should better directly pass the whole population into the objective function, which then returns a vector of numbers. This makes it slightly more complicated for users to write alternative objective functions since now they have to handle the evaluation of the whole population themselves. But the advantage is that in some cases truly vectorized evaluation is possible. (`apply` functions are still loops, see Chambers, 2008, Chapter 6.) In our particular application, this includes the question when and how to compute the product Rw (or Pu).

An example can illustrate this. Suppose we wish to minimize a ratio of partial moments of order one, the so-called Omega ratio (Keating and Shadwick, 2002). For a given sample of portfolio returns $r^P = Rw$, this can be computed as

$$\frac{\sum \max(\theta - r^P, 0)}{\sum \max(r^P - \theta, 0)}$$

where θ is a threshold, the watershed between losses and gains. An R function could look like

Listing 13.44. C-PortfolioOptimization/R/exampleApply.R

```
2 # objective function
3 omega <- function(r,theta) {
4     rr <- r - theta
5     omega <- -sum(rr - abs(rr)) / sum(rr + abs(rr))
6     omega
7 }
```

where we have used the fact that for some vector `rr`, computing `pmax(rr,0)` gives the same result as `(rr + abs(rr))/2`. This is generally faster than using a logical expression like

```
omega <- -sum( rr[rr < 0] ) / sum( rr[rr > 0] )
```

or directly using `pmax` and `pmin`.

It is then straightforward to evaluate a single portfolio. We create an artificial data set R, a random portfolio w, and compute its Omega ratio.

Listing 13.45. C-PortfolioOptimization/R/exampleApply.R

```
9  # create artifical data
10 # ...ns = number of scenarios
11 # ...na = number of assets
12 ns <- 200
13 na <- 100
14 R   <- array(rnorm(ns*na)*0.05, dim = c(ns,na) )
15
16 # set up a random portfolio
17 w   <- runif(na)
18 w   <- w / sum(w)
19
```

```
20 # compute returns
21 rp <- R %*% w
22
23 # compute omega
24 omega(rp, theta = 0.001)
```

Now, we have a whole matrix P of solutions. We can compute Omega for this whole matrix like follows.

Listing 13.46. C-PortfolioOptimization/R/exampleApply.R

```
26 # objective function, alternative
27 omega2 <- function(r,theta) {
28     rr <- r - theta
29     omega2 <- -colSums(rr - abs(rr)) / colSums(rr + abs(rr))
30     omega2
31 }
32
33 # check: compute omega
34 omega2(rp, theta = 0.001)
```

We can test several evaluation strategies.

Listing 13.47. C-PortfolioOptimization/R/exampleApply.R

```
36 # set up a random population
37 # ...nP = population size
38 nP <- 200
39 P   <- array(runif(na*nP), dim = c(na,nP))
40 P   <- P / outer(numeric(na)+1,colSums(P)) # budget constraint
41
42 # evaluate population
43 # ...variant 1
44 rp <- R %*% P
45 system.time({
46     for (r in 1:100){
47         for(i in 1:nP) a1 <- omega(rp[,i],theta=0.001)
48     }
49 })
50
51 # ...variant 2
52 rp <- R %*% P
53 system.time({
54     for (r in 1:100)
55         a2 <- apply(rp,2,omega,theta=0.001)
56 })
57
58 # ...variant 3
59 rp <- R %*% P
60 system.time({
61     for (r in 1:100)
62         a3 <- omega2(rp,theta=0.001)
63 })
```

Each time, we evaluate the columns of the matrix P. (We repeat this 1000 times to get a more reliable time measurement.) The first variant is the most straightforward. We loop over the columns, and pass each solution into the objective function. In fact, there is little performance difference between this approach and using `apply`, as demonstrated in variant 2. However, the most efficient implementation is the third, which in our runs led to a speedup of two when compared with the other variants. In all timing tests, we excluded the matrix product Rw. This can be justified, since it needs to be computed for all variants.

## CHAPTER FOURTEEN

Econometric models

14.1. Term structure models

14.1.1. Yield curves

Whenever we read about the yield curve or the term structure of interest rates, chances are that there is a diagram that shows the interest rate as a smooth function of time. Such a function is actually not observable, it must be estimated or constructed somehow from what is available: deposits, coupon bonds, swaps, and a vast number of other interest rate products. Sometimes these products are quoted in terms of price, like a bond, or in terms of an interest rate, like a deposit. The existence of such a smooth curve can be justified by arbitrage. If there were two products with similar properties like default risk or liquidity, but different prices (which are functions of the interest rate), operators would exchange one product for the other.

Bond prices and yields

In this section we will explain methods to calibrate a yield curve model. For an introduction to the algebra of bonds, yields, and related concepts (and many other things), see Luenberger (1998). Here we just recall those notions that we later need. Notation: a bond with current price b_0 receives future cash flows c. Subscripts indicate time; times to payment are called $\tau_1, \ldots, \tau_m$, all measured in years. $\tau_0 = 0$ is today. (We could have simplified notation by assuming that all the τ are integers. But in practice, they will be fractions of years, and for portfolios they will not be equidistant.)

A bond is, for our purposes, a list of payments with associated payment dates. The theoretical price b_0 of the bond today is its present value,

$$b_0 = d_{\tau_1} c_{\tau_1} + d_{\tau_2} c_{\tau_2} + d_{\tau_3} c_{\tau_3} + \cdots = \sum_i d_{\tau_i} c_{\tau_i} \qquad (14.1)$$

where the $d_{\tau_i} \leq 1$ are discount factors. These discount factors can be defined as

$$d_{\tau_i} \equiv \left(\frac{1}{1+r} \right)^{\tau_i}$$

with r an interest rate (e.g., 0.05). For convenience, define also $d_* \equiv \left(\frac{1}{1+r}\right)$. The d_* are constant, independent of payment date. We have

$$0 = -b_0 + d_{\tau_1} c_{\tau_1} + d_{\tau_2} c_{\tau_2} + d_{\tau_3} c_{\tau_3} + \cdots \tag{14.2}$$

$$= \underbrace{-b_0 + d_*^{\tau_1} c_{\tau_1} + d_*^{\tau_2} c_{\tau_2} + d_*^{\tau_3} c_{\tau_3} + \cdots}_{g(d_*)} \tag{14.3}$$

$$= -b_0 + \left(\frac{1}{1+r}\right)^{\tau_1} c_{\tau_1} + \left(\frac{1}{1+r}\right)^{\tau_2} c_{\tau_2} + \cdots . \tag{14.4}$$

The r that solves (14.4) is called yield-to-maturity, or internal interest rate; the corresponding d_* must be a zero of the polynomial (14.3). If we know the price and the cash flows of the bond, we can compute this zero with one of the techniques discussed in Chapter 11. If all c are greater than zero, there is a nice graphical intuition that there is a unique zero, pictured below. Let $g(d_*)$ be the right-hand side of (14.3) as a function of d_*.

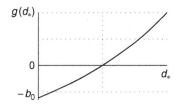

For a d_* of zero (i.e., r very large), g is $-b_0$. But as d_* grows, the present value of the future cash flows increases, until at some point it equals the price of the bond b_0, and, hence, $g(d_*) = 0$.

Let us use Newton's method to compute this yield-to-maturity. The first derivative g' of the polynomial is

$$\tau_1 d_*^{\tau_1 - 1} c_{\tau_1} + \tau_2 d_*^{\tau_2 - 1} c_{\tau_2} + \tau_3 d_*^{\tau_3 - 1} c_{\tau_3} + \cdots$$

and an updating rule is

$$d_*^{(k+1)} = d_*^{(k)} - \frac{g\left(d_*^{(k)}\right)}{g'\left(d_*^{(k)}\right)} .$$

In the following R script we define a 6-year coupon bond with a yield to maturity of 4.6%. Note that we have not taken the trouble to provide the analytic derivative but rather computed it by a forward difference.

Listing 14.1. C-EconometricModels/R/newton.R

```
1 # newton.R -- version 2010-12-29
2 cf <- c(5,5,5,5,5,105)  # cashflows
3 tm <- 1:6               # maturities
4 ytm <- 0.046            # the 'true' yield
5 b0 <- sum(cf/((1+ytm)^tm))
```

```
 6 cf <- c(-b0,cf); tm <- c(0,tm)
 7
 8 r <- 0.1    # initial value for r
 9 h <- 1e-6   # fin-diff step
10 dr <- 1     # change in r
11 while(abs(dr) > 1e-5) {
12     g <- sum(cf/((1+r)^tm))
13     dg <- ( sum(cf/((1+r+h)^tm)) - g ) / h
14     dr <- g/dg
15     print(r <- r - dr)
16 }
```

The initial guess is 10%; already after a few iterations we obtain the true yield-to-maturity of 4.6%.

```
[1] 0.03588320
[1] 0.04567604
[1] 0.04599966
[1] 0.046
```

Practically we will rarely work with a constant r, but assume different rates y_τ for different maturities. We will later often write $y(\tau)$ to stress that y is a function of τ. We obtain

$$b_0 = \left(\frac{1}{1+r}\right)^{\tau_1} c_{\tau_1} + \left(\frac{1}{1+r}\right)^{\tau_2} c_{\tau_2} + \cdots$$

$$= \left(\frac{1}{1+y_{\tau_1}}\right)^{\tau_1} c_{\tau_1} + \left(\frac{1}{1+y_{\tau_2}}\right)^{\tau_2} c_{\tau_2} + \cdots.$$

We define forward rates f

$$1 + y_{\tau_i} = (1 + f_{\tau_0,\tau_1})(1 + f_{\tau_1,\tau_2}) \cdots (1 + f_{\tau_{i-1},\tau_i}).$$

The subscripts to f indicate the start and the end of the period. All the quantities discussed can also be expressed in continuous time. Let

$$f' \equiv \log(1+f), \quad r' \equiv \log(1+r), \quad y' \equiv \log(1+y);$$

then we have

$$d_\tau \equiv \exp(-\tau r')$$

and so on. When manipulating equations, continuous time expressions are often easier to handle.

Constructing yield curves

When we speak of yield curves in the remainder of this chapter, we mean zero rates y, or their associated discount factors or forward rates. (Knowing either quantity for all maturities allows us to determine both others.) There are essentially two ways to move from discrete data points to a yield curve, that is, a function $y(\tau)$ which specifies a y for all τ. We can interpolate the available data, or we can approximate. When we interpolate, we obtain a function

Figure 14.1 Interpolation and approximation. The panels show a set of market rates. Left: we interpolate the points. Right: we approximate the points.

$y(\tau)$ which exactly prices the instruments that were used to construct the function. When we approximate, then $y(\tau)$ prices the instruments only approximately; see Fig. 14.1. In this chapter, we will deal with the second approach; still, we will outline the essence of the first approach since it is widely applied in practice, and both methods can also be combined.

Interpolation is based on bootstrapping (which has nothing to do with the resampling technique that goes by the same name). The textbook version of bootstrapping goes like this: we have m bonds with time to maturity $\tau_i = 1, 2, \ldots, m$; each bond pays a fixed coupon at the end of each period. Our aim is now to find discount factors d such that

$$b_0^{(j)} = \sum_i d_{\tau_i} c_{\tau_i}^{(j)}$$

for all bonds $j = 1, \ldots, m$. It is helpful to put this problem (and many other problems, too) into matrix form. We can rely on intuition and results from linear algebra; and sometimes we can directly implement the model in matrix form and so make use of fast available algorithms. In the textbook version of bootstrapping, we obtain the system of equations

$$
\underbrace{
\begin{bmatrix}
c_1^{(1)} & & & & \\
c_1^{(2)} & c_2^{(2)} & & & \\
c_1^{(3)} & c_2^{(3)} & c_3^{(3)} & & \\
\vdots & \vdots & \vdots & \ddots & \\
c_1^{(m)} & c_2^{(m)} & c_3^{(m)} & \cdots & c_m^{(m)}
\end{bmatrix}}_{C}
\underbrace{
\begin{bmatrix}
d_1 \\
d_2 \\
d_3 \\
\vdots \\
d_m
\end{bmatrix}}_{d}
=
\underbrace{
\begin{bmatrix}
b_0^{(1)} \\
b_0^{(2)} \\
b_0^{(3)} \\
\vdots \\
b_0^{(m)}
\end{bmatrix}}_{b}
\qquad (14.5)
$$

which we can solve by forward substitution (see Chapter 3). The jth row in the matrix C corresponds to the cash flows of the jth bond with price $b_0^{(j)}$. The computed discount factors (i.e., the vector d that solves the equations) will "interpolate" the bond prices; thus, the model prices will exactly equal the market prices.

But in practice we never have this nice case. C will not be square: we may have more dates than bonds (more columns than rows), and hence, potentially, an infinity of solutions. Or we may have more bonds than dates (more rows than columns); then in general no solution exists. So, C will not have a nice triangular structure. As an example, Table 14.1 shows a

Table 14.1 A sample data set of German government bonds. Prices as of 31 May 2010.

ISIN	coupon	maturity	dirty price
DE0001135150	5.25	2010-07-04	105.225
DE0001141471	2.5	2010-10-08	102.448
DE0001135168	5.25	2011-01-04	105.173
DE0001141489	3.5	2011-04-08	103.282
DE0001135184	5	2011-07-04	109.642
DE0001141497	3.5	2011-10-14	106.555
DE0001135192	5	2012-01-04	109.396
DE0001141505	4	2012-04-13	107.248
DE0001135200	5	2012-07-04	113.852
DE0001141513	4.25	2012-10-12	111.383
DE0001135218	4.5	2013-01-04	111.627
DE0001141521	3.5	2013-04-12	108.469
DE0001135234	3.75	2013-07-04	112.241
DE0001141539	4	2013-10-11	112.864
DE0001135242	4.25	2014-01-04	112.945
DE0001141547	2.25	2014-04-11	104.821
DE0001135259	4.25	2014-07-04	115.747
DE0001141554	2.5	2014-10-10	106.672
DE0001135267	3.75	2015-01-04	111.571
DE0001141562	2.5	2015-02-27	105.405
DE0001141570	2.25	2015-04-10	103.547
DE0001135283	3.25	2015-07-04	110.815
DE0001135291	3.5	2016-01-04	110.589
DE0001134468	6	2016-06-20	128.904
DE0001135309	4	2016-07-04	115.669
DE0001134492	5.625	2016-09-20	125.13
DE0001135317	3.75	2017-01-04	112.071
DE0001135333	4.25	2017-07-04	117.547
DE0001135341	4	2018-01-04	113.343
DE0001135358	4.25	2018-07-04	117.377
DE0001135374	3.75	2019-01-04	111.231
DE0001135382	3.5	2019-07-04	111.235
DE0001135390	3.25	2020-01-04	107.140
DE0001135408	3	2020-07-04	103.161
DE0001134922	6.25	2024-01-04	138.951
DE0001135044	6.5	2027-07-04	148.880
DE0001135069	5.625	2028-01-04	133.666
DE0001135085	4.75	2028-07-04	124.534
DE0001135143	6.25	2030-01-04	144.801
DE0001135176	5.5	2031-01-04	133.995
DE0001135226	4.75	2034-07-04	126.884
DE0001135275	4	2037-01-04	112.663
DE0001135325	4.25	2039-07-04	120.167
DE0001135366	4.75	2040-07-04	130.134

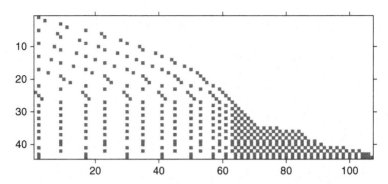

Figure 14.2 The matrix C for the cash flows of the 44 bonds in `bundData`, each square represents a nonzero entry. Each row gives the cash flows of one bond, each column is associated with one payment date.

list of German government bonds as of end of May 2010. These bonds are included in `NMOF` as the data set `bundData`.

Putting the cash flows of these bonds into a matrix results in the plot shown in Fig. 14.2. The plot was created with the `Matrix` package (Bates and Maechler, 2010). Try:

```
require(Matrix)
(M <- Matrix(c(1,0,0,0,0,1), 3, 2))
image(M)
```

The first command results in the output below; the second in a plot like in Fig. 14.2.

```
3 x 2 sparse Matrix of class "dgCMatrix"

[1,] 1 .
[2,] . .
[3,] . 1
```

Such plotting devices are helpful to recognize structure in a matrix.

The data set has more payment dates than bonds, that is, there are more columns than rows. This form of C is the more practically relevant case (at least for Germany; see Jaschke, Stehle, and Wernicke, 2000).

From the purely numerical point of view, we need to solve

$$Cd = b \qquad (14.6)$$

for d, under the constraints

$$1 \geq d_{\tau_m} \geq \cdots \geq d_{\tau_2} \geq d_{\tau_1} \geq 0.$$

Since a solution may not exist, we may have to settle for

$$\operatorname*{argmin}_{d} \ \|Cd - b\| \qquad (14.7)$$

where $\|$ is a specified norm. There are several ways to obtain d. We could try a purely numerical approach, that is, minimizing the residuals. If a solution exists for an underidentified system as we have here, it will not be unique, so we may need to add further constraints (typically, procedures to solve the system will also minimize a norm of the solution). In practice, with an underidentified system, people often prefer to add identifying assumptions that are economically motivated. For example, suppose there are two bonds that pay coupons annually. The first bond expires in 0.5 years, the second in 1.25 years. So we have two prices $b_0^{(1)}$ and $b_0^{(2)}$, but three payment dates: 0.25, 0.5, and 1.25 years. We could assume now that the very short end of the curve is flat below our shortest zero bond, that is, we assume that the rates for 0.25 and 0.5 years are the same. Now we are left with only two unknowns.

With an overidentified system (more bonds than payment dates), we can accept an approximate solution for which we minimize the residuals of Eq. (14.6), or we could "throw away" rows, that is, use a subset of the available instruments.

No matter how we decide to solve this problem, we will end up with a discrete set of discount factors (those in the vector d) for specified maturities. To price cash flows at other dates, we may now again interpolate these zero rates, or fit an approximating function through our data points. This is the approach we describe in the next sections. We will discuss a widely used model, that of Nelson and Siegel (1987).

14.1.2. The Nelson–Siegel model

The model of Nelson and Siegel (1987) and its extension by Svensson (1994) are used by many operators, in particular at central banks, as a model for the term structure of interest rates (Bank for International Settlements (BIS), 2005). Unfortunately, model calibration, that is, obtaining parameter values such that model yields accord with market yields, is difficult; different authors have reported "numerical difficulties" when working with the model (for instance, Bolder and Stréliski, 1999; Cairns, 1998; Gurkaynak, Sack, and Wright, 2006; and De Pooter, 2007). In this section, we analyze the calibration of the model in more detail. We show that the problem is twofold: first, the optimization problem is not convex and has multiple local optima. Hence methods that are readily available in statistical packages—in particular, methods based on derivatives of the objective function—are not appropriate to obtain parameter values. We will use an optimization heuristic, Differential Evolution, to obtain parameters. Second, in certain ranges of the parameters, the model is badly conditioned, thus estimated parameters are unstable given small perturbations of the data. We discuss to what extent these difficulties affect applications of the model.

Nelson and Siegel (1987) suggested modeling the yield curve at a point in time as follows: let $y(\tau)$ be the zero rate for maturity τ, then

$$y(\tau) = \beta_1 + \beta_2 \left[\frac{1 - \exp(-\tau/\lambda_1)}{\tau/\lambda_1} \right] + \beta_3 \left[\frac{1 - \exp(-\tau/\lambda_1)}{\tau/\lambda_1} - \exp(-\tau/\lambda_1) \right].$$

(14.8)

Thus, for a given cross-section of yields, we need to fix four parameters: β_1, β_2, β_3, and λ_1. We do not assume that the model's parameters are constant; they can change over time. But in this chapter we are only interested in the cross-section; hence, to simplify notation, we do not add subscripts for the time period.

In the Nelson–Siegel (NS) model, the yield y for a particular maturity is, hence, the sum of several components. β_1 is independent of time to maturity, and so it is often interpreted as the long-run yield level. β_2 is weighted by a function of time to maturity. This function is unity for $\tau = 0$ and exponentially decays to zero as τ grows; hence, the influence of β_2 is only felt at the short end of the curve. β_3 is also weighted by a function of τ, but this function is zero for $\tau = 0$, increases, and then falls back to zero as τ grows. It thus adds a hump to the curve. The parameter λ_1 affects the weight functions for β_2 and β_3; in particular it determines the position of the hump. An example is shown in Figs. 14.3–14.5.

The parameters of the model thus have, to some extent, a direct (observable) interpretation, which brings about the constraints $\beta_1 > 0$ (long-term rate needs to be positive), and $\beta_1 + \beta_2 > 0$ (short-term rate needs to be positive). We also require that $\lambda_1 > 0$. Two conventions: first, we define parameters in units of percentage points, so $\beta_1 = 2$ means 2%; second, we measure all maturities in years.

The Nelson–Siegel–Svensson (NSS) model adds a second hump term (see Fig. 14.5) to the NS model. Let $y(\tau)$ be the zero rate for maturity τ

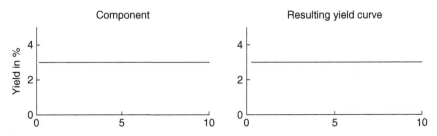

Figure 14.3 Level. The left panel shows $y(\tau) = \beta_1 = 3$. The right panel shows the corresponding yield curve, in this case also $y(\tau) = \beta_1 = 3$. The influence of β_1 is constant for all τ.

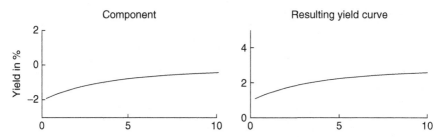

Figure 14.4 Short-end shift. The left panel shows $y(\tau) = \beta_2 \left[\frac{1-\exp(-\tau/\lambda_1)}{\tau/\lambda_1}\right]$ for $\beta_2 = -2$. The right panel shows the yield curve resulting from the effects of β_1 and β_2, that is, $y(\tau) = \beta_1 + \beta_2 \left[\frac{1-\exp(-\tau/\lambda_1)}{\tau/\lambda_1}\right]$ for $\beta_1 = 3$, $\beta_2 = -2$. The short end is shifted down by 2%, but then the curve grows back to the long-run level of 3%.

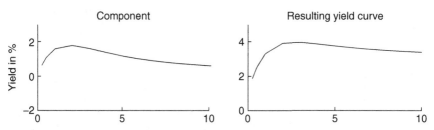

Figure 14.5 Hump. The left panel shows $\beta_3 \left[\frac{1-\exp(-\tau/\lambda_1)}{\tau/\lambda_1} - \exp(-\tau/\lambda_1)\right]$ for $\beta_3 = 6$. The right panel shows the yield curve resulting from all three components. In all panels, λ_1 is 2.

again, then

$$y(\tau) = \beta_1 + \beta_2 \left[\frac{1 - \exp(-\tau/\lambda_1)}{\tau/\lambda_1}\right] + \beta_3 \left[\frac{1 - \exp(-\tau/\lambda_1)}{\tau/\lambda_1} - \exp(-\tau/\lambda_1)\right]$$

$$+ \beta_4 \left[\frac{1 - \exp(-\tau/\lambda_2)}{\tau/\lambda_2} - \exp(-\tau/\lambda_2)\right].$$

$$(14.9)$$

Here we need to estimate six parameters: β_1, β_2, β_3, β_4, λ_1, and λ_2. The constraints remain the same, we also have $\lambda_2 > 0$. Given a set of parameters, the forward rates in the NS model are given by

$$f(\tau) = \beta_1 + \beta_2 \exp\left(-\frac{\tau}{\lambda}\right) + \beta_3 \frac{\tau}{\lambda} \exp\left(-\frac{\tau}{\lambda}\right)$$

and for the NSS case we get

$$f(\tau) = \beta_1 + \beta_2 \exp\left(-\frac{\tau}{\lambda_1}\right) + \beta_3 \frac{\tau}{\lambda_1} \exp\left(-\frac{\iota}{\lambda_1}\right) + \beta_4 \frac{\tau}{\lambda_2} \exp\left(-\frac{\tau}{\lambda_2}\right).$$

There exist many variants of this model (De Pooter, 2007); the simplest idea is to add more humps. But depending on our purpose for using the model, this may not be a good idea, as we show next.

Collinearity

A first step after having implemented a model (i.e., Eqs. (14.8) and (14.9)), is to "play around" with it. This has at least two benefits: we gain intuition about the model and—since we only just implemented it—we may spot errors in our code. In fact, we can investigate one unfortunate property of the Nelson–Siegel model (and its variants) without any data.

Suppose we have obtained zero yields y^M for m different maturities $\tau_1, \ldots, \tau_m$. The superscript M in y^M indicates that these are market rates. Now we wish to calibrate an NS model to these yields. Fixing the λ_1-value, we have m linear equations from which to estimate three parameters:

$$\begin{bmatrix} 1 & \frac{1-\exp(-\tau_1/\lambda_1)}{\tau_1/\lambda_1} & \frac{1-\exp(-\tau_1/\lambda_1)}{\tau_1/\lambda_1} - \exp(-\tau_1/\lambda_1) \\ 1 & \frac{1-\exp(-\tau_2/\lambda_1)}{\tau_2/\lambda_1} & \frac{1-\exp(-\tau_2/\lambda_1)}{\tau_2/\lambda_1} - \exp(-\tau_2/\lambda_1) \\ 1 & \frac{1-\exp(-\tau_3/\lambda_1)}{\tau_3/\lambda_1} & \frac{1-\exp(-\tau_3/\lambda_1)}{\tau_3/\lambda_1} - \exp(-\tau_3/\lambda_1) \\ \vdots & \vdots & \vdots \\ 1 & \frac{1-\exp(-\tau_m/\lambda_1)}{\tau_m/\lambda_1} & \frac{1-\exp(-\tau_m/\lambda_1)}{\tau_m/\lambda_1} - \exp(-\tau_m/\lambda_1) \end{bmatrix} \begin{bmatrix} \beta_1 \\ \beta_2 \\ \beta_3 \end{bmatrix} = \begin{bmatrix} y^M(\tau_1) \\ y^M(\tau_2) \\ y^M(\tau_3) \\ \vdots \\ \vdots \\ y^M(\tau_m) \end{bmatrix}$$

$$(14.10)$$

We need to solve these equations for β.

We can interpret the NSS model analogously, just now we have to fix two parameters, λ_1 and λ_2. Then we have a fourth regressor

$$\left[\ldots \frac{1-\exp(-\tau_i/\lambda_2)}{\tau_i/\lambda_2} - \exp(-\tau_i/\lambda_2) \right]',$$

and can proceed as before. This system of equations is overidentified for the practical case $m > 3$ (or $m > 4$ for NSS), so we need to minimize a norm of the residuals. Below we will discuss the Least-Squares case, that is, we use the 2-norm. But here we do not stress a specific solution technique, but are interested in the conditioning of the regressor matrix.

We can compute the regressors of this linear model with the functions NSf and NSSf, given in the following script.

Listing 14.2. C-EconometricModels/R/NSf.R

```
1  # NSf.R -- version 2010-12-29
2  NSf <- function(lambda,tm) {
3      aux <- tm / lambda
4      ll <- length(tm)
5      Y <- array(1, dim = c(ll,3))
6      Y[,2] <- ((1 - exp(-aux)) / aux)
7      Y[,3] <- (((1 - exp(-aux)) / aux) - exp(-aux))
8      Y
9  }
10 NSSf <- function(lambda1,lambda2,tm) {
11     aux1 <- tm / lambda1
```

```
12    aux2 <- tm / lambda2
13    l1 <- length(tm)
14    Y <- array(1, dim = c(l1,4))
15    Y[,2] <- ((1 - exp(-aux1)) / aux1)
16    Y[,3] <- (((1 - exp(-aux1)) / aux1) - exp(-aux1))
17    Y[,4] <- (((1 - exp(-aux2)) / aux2) - exp(-aux2))
18    return(Y)
19 }
```

Note that the resulting matrix will not depend on the observed rates y^M, only on the maturities that we use and the values for λ_1. Some authors suggest linking λ_1 to the longest time to maturity in the sample (i.e., it should not be larger than the longest maturity; see Bolder and Stréliski, 1999, p. 49, Manousopoulos and Michalopoulos, 2009, p. 596, Wets and Bianchi, 2006, p. 57). Now suppose that we have bonds with a maturity up to ten years, and we fix λ_1 at 6. Then the call

```
cor(NSf(lambda = 6, tm = 1:10))
```

reveals a correlation of −0.97 between the second and the third regressor. If we use the NSS model, then the call

```
cor(NSSf(lambda1 = 1, lambda2 = 5, tm = 1:10))
```

gives the output

```
        [,1]        [,2]        [,3]        [,4]
[1,]     1          NA          NA          NA
[2,]    NA    1.0000000   0.8453944  -0.9959025
[3,]    NA    0.8453944   1.0000000  -0.8710049
[4,]    NA   -0.9959025  -0.8710049   1.0000000
```

(A correlation between a constant and a varying quantity is not defined; hence the NA values.) Figure 14.6 shows the correlations for different values of λ_1 and λ_2. Over wide ranges of the λ-parameters the correlations are either −1 or 1.

Practically we may have 20 to 40 maturities, so 20 to 40 equations. We should feel uncomfortable whenever we estimate a linear regression model

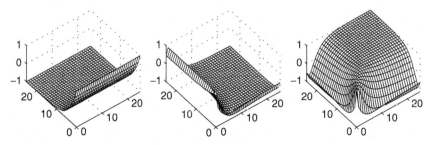

Figure 14.6 The three panels show the correlation between the second and the third, the second and the fourth, and the third and the fourth regressors for different λ-values (the x- and y-axes show λ_1 and λ_2 between 0 and 25).

with 20 to 40 observations when the regressors are so highly correlated. The result of such correlation is an identification problem: we cannot accurately compute the regressors any more. But a bad conditioning of the regressor matrix does not imply large residuals (see Section 2.5). In other words, we may well fit our model to market rates and so have small residuals; but the parameters themselves are not reliable. We show an example of the effects of collinearity in the next section, when we discuss the calibration of the model.

14.1.3. Calibration strategies

In this section we discuss numerical approaches to obtain parameter estimates for the NS/NSS model.

Case 1: Linear regression with bootstrapped zero rates
   Aim: to find β-parameters for the NS/NSS model such that $y(\tau_i)$ is close to $y^M(\tau_i)$ for all i, given fixed λ-values.

Suppose we have obtained a set of zero rates from a bootstrapping procedure, and now wish to find the NS or NSS parameters that approximate this set of rates. There is a simple strategy to obtain parameters for both the NS and NSS model: fix the λ-parameters, and then estimate the β-values with Least Squares (Nelson and Siegel, 1987, p. 478); see Eq. (14.10). This estimation approach is easily implemented. In the following code we set up a true yield curve and then estimate the parameters with R's lm function. The fixed λ_1 in the regression does not equal the true λ_1, yet the errors seem small. (The functions NS and NSS are included in the NMOF package.)

Listing 14.3. C-EconometricModels/R/exampleLS.R

```
1  # exampleLS.R -- version 2010-12-18
2  # set up artificial yield curve and plot it
3  tm <- 1:10; paramTRUE <- c(4,-2,2,1)
4  yM <- NS(paramTRUE,tm)
5  plot(tm, yM, xlab = "maturities in years",
6               ylab = "yields in %-points")
7
8  # fix lambda and run regression
9  lambda <- 1.5
10 result <- lm(yM ~ -1 + NSf(lambda,tm))
11
12 # compare results
13 plot(yM - result$fitted.values, xlab = "maturities in years",
14                          ylab = "errors in %-points")
```

This approach has a number of disadvantages, though. We need to use the Least-Squares criterion to measure goodness-of-fit, inequality constraints are more difficult to add, and we still have to do a line search (NS) or a grid search (NSS) for good λ-values. But the Least-Squares approach allows us to demonstrate the effect of collinearity in a context of estimating a linear regression.

We first define true NS parameters, namely `c(4,-2,2)` for the β, and 1 for λ_1, as before. With these we compute y^M from Eq. (14.8). Then we use `lm` to estimate the parameters; unsurprisingly, we get exactly the true parameters. Next, we add a bit of random noise, order of magnitude 1 bp, to the y^M, and then redo our estimation. We repeat this 1000 times, as shown in the next script. Note that here we have not used the function `lm` but `qr.solve`, which is much faster.

Listing 14.4. C-EconometricModels/R/exampleLS2.R

```
1  # exampleLS2.R -- version 2011-01-11
2  trials <- 1000
3
4  lambda <- 1; betaTRUE <- c(4,-2,2,lambda)
5  allResults <- array(NA, dim=c(trials,3))
6  for (t in 1:trials) {
7      yM <- NS(betaTRUE,tm)+rnorm(length(tm), mean = 0, sd = 0.01)
8      allResults[t,] <- qr.solve(NSf(lambda,tm), yM)
9  }
10
11 # compare results
12 par( mfrow=c(1,3) )
13 for (i in 1:3) plot( ecdf( allResults[,i]) )
```

Finally, we repeat the whole procedure a second time, but now with a λ_1 of 10. Figure 14.7 shows estimates for the parameters when λ_1 is fixed at 1 (the gray lines), and 10 (the black lines).

While the magnitude of the noise was the same in both cases (about 1 bp), we see massive differences in the distributions of the parameters. For a λ_1 of 1, we are always close to the true parameters; for a λ_1 of 10, we are sometimes way off. (Check the correlations between the regressors.) This

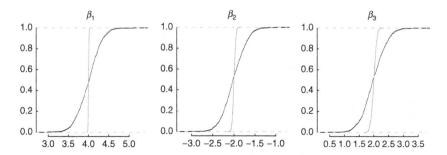

Figure 14.7 Estimated parameters. The true parameters are 4, −2, and 2.

is not necessarily a problem if we want to fit the curve, that is, if we want $\|y^M - y\|_2$ or another norm to be small. But it is a problem if we want to work with the parameters (e.g., for forecasts, or to interpret them). Do not expect these errors to be smaller in the NSS model, or in more-complex variants. We need to stress that these large errors did not result from an inappropriate method—they solely followed from our choice of λ. The only remedy is that if we want to identify the parameters, we need to constrain the λ-values such that the resulting correlations remain reasonable. This also applies to the cases that we discuss next.

Case 2: Fitting bootstrapped zero rates with Differential Evolution

Aim: to find parameters for the NS/NSS model such that $y(\tau_i)$ is close to $y^M(\tau_i)$ for all i.

For Least Squares we had to fix a λ, now we want to determine all parameters in one run. For this, we need another optimization technique, a heuristic. Why would we not use the Least-Squares approach? Finding a good λ requires a grid search, but Least Squares is so fast that this is not really a hindrance. (Some variants of NSS require more parameters, however.) The advantage of a heuristic is that it is much more flexible. First, we can write down any objective function, not just a sum of squares. And we can add further constraints. Let us give an example. We require that $\beta_1 > 0$, and $\beta_1 + \beta_2 > 0$ to have nonnegative interest rates. Yet, even with these constraints not violated we may have negative interest rates. Here is an example.

```
tm <- seq(1, 10, length.out = 100) # 1 to 10 years
paramTRUE <- c(3,-2,-8,1.5)         # 'true' parameters
yM <- NS(paramTRUE, tm)
plot(tm, yM, xlab = "maturities in years",
            ylab = "yields in percent")
abline(h = 0)
```

So, the constraints are not violated, yet the parameters imply negative interest rates. (Conversely, for a finite set of maturities, we may find positive interest rates even though the β parameters violate their constraints.) A more direct way would be to require that $y(\tau) > 0$ for all $\tau > 0$. This is a nonlinear constraint (not that this matters much for a heuristic). Some testing showed that it is usually not necessary to include such a constraint. But importantly, if we decide to leave it out, it is because we deem it not necessary—not because our optimization technique cannot handle it.

The formal optimization model to solve is:

$$\min_{\beta,\lambda} \|y - y^M\|$$

subject to

$$y(\tau) = \beta_1 + \beta_2 \left[\frac{1 - \exp(-\tau/\lambda_1)}{\tau/\lambda_1} \right] + \cdots \quad \begin{cases} \text{Eq. (14.8) for NS,} \\ \text{Eq. (14.9) for NSS} \end{cases}$$

$$\beta_1 > 0$$

$$\beta_1 + \beta_2 > 0$$

$$\lambda_i > 0 \quad (i = 1 \text{ for NS, } i = 1,2 \text{ for NSS}).$$

Note that $\|y - y^M\|$ could be any norm (not necessarily the 2-norm) or distance function. To solve this model, we turn to a heuristic method, Differential Evolution (DE). The basic algorithm for DE was given on page 347; we repeat it for convenience in Algorithm 62.

Algorithm 62 Differential Evolution for yield curve models.

1: set n_P, n_G, F and CR
2: randomly generate initial population $P_{j,i}^{(1)}$, $j = 1,\ldots,p$, $i = 1,\ldots,n_P$
3: **for** $k = 1$ to n_G **do**
4:    $P^{(0)} = P^{(1)}$
5:    **for** $i = 1$ to n_P **do**
6:       randomly generate $\ell_1, \ell_2, \ell_3 \in \{1,\ldots,n_P\}$, $\ell_1 \neq \ell_2 \neq \ell_3 \neq i$
7:       compute $P_{\cdot,i}^{(v)} = P_{\cdot,\ell_1}^{(0)} + \text{F} \times (P_{\cdot,\ell_2}^{(0)} - P_{\cdot,\ell_3}^{(0)})$
8:       **for** $j = 1$ to p **do**
9:          **if** rand $<$ CR **then** $P_{j,i}^{(u)} = P_{j,i}^{(v)}$ **else** $P_{j,i}^{(u)} = P_{j,i}^{(0)}$
10:       **end for**
11:       **if** $f(P_{\cdot,i}^{(u)}) < f(P_{\cdot,i}^{(0)})$ **then** $P_{\cdot,i}^{(1)} = P_{\cdot,i}^{(u)}$ **else** $P_{\cdot,i}^{(1)} = P_{\cdot,i}^{(0)}$
12:    **end for**
13: **end for**
14: return best solution

Listing 14.5. C-EconometricModels/R/DEabbr.R

```
1  # DEabbr.R -- version 2010-12-30
2  function (OF, algo = list(), ...) {
3      # add defaults to algo, do a few sanity checks
4      # ...
5      mRU <- function(m, n) array(runif(m * n), dim = c(m, n))
6      mRN <- function(m, n) array(rnorm(m * n), dim = c(m, n))
7      shift <- function(x) c(x[length(x)], x[1:(length(x) - 1)])
8      d   <- length(algo$max)
9      vF <- numeric(algo$nP)
10     vF[] <- NA; vFv <- vF
11     mP <- algo$min +
12         diag(algo$max - algo$min) %*% mRU(d, algo$nP)
13     for (s in 1:algo$nP) vF[s] <- OF(mP[, s], data = data)
14     for (g in 1:algo$nG) {
15         vI <- sample(1:algo$nP, algo$nP)
16         R1 <- shift(vI); R2 <- shift(R1); R3 <- shift(R2)
```

```
17    mPv <- mP[, R1] + algo$F * (mP[, R2] - mP[, R3])
18    mI <- mRU(d, algo$nP) > algo$CR
19    mPv[mI] <- mP[mI]
20    for (s in 1:algo$nP) vFv[s] <- OF(mPv[,s], data = data)
21    logik <- vFv < vF
22    mP[, logik] <- mPv[, logik]
23    vF[logik] <- vFv[logik]
24    Fmat[g, ] <- vF
25  }
26  sGbest <- min(vF); sgbest <- which.min(vF)[1]
27  return(list(vPar = mP[, sgbest], OFvalue = sGbest))
28 }
```

The function DEopt is a (relatively) straightforward translation of the given pseudocode. To see the complete function, attach package NMOF, and type DEopt.

The function DEopt is called with three arguments:

```
DEopt(OF, algo, ...)
```

The ... allow to pass several variables, but we will always collect all additional variables in a single list data. Doing so makes for a clearer structure, and is less error prone in our experience. Thus we need three objects: OF, algo, and data.

```
DEopt(OF, algo, data)
```

OF is the objective function.

algo is a list that holds the settings of the DE algorithm (discussed below).

data is a list that holds the pieces of data necessary to evaluate the objective function.

Eventually, DEopt will return a list of four elements:

xbest is the solution; the parameter vector with the lowest objective function value,

OFvalue is the objective function value associated with xbest,

popF is the vector with the final objective function values of all population members (i.e., OFvalue equals min(popF)), and

Fmat is a matrix of size of size $n_G \times n_P$. It holds the objective function values of all solutions over time.

Implementing an optimization technique always requires decisions on various parameters and settings. If we use optim in R or fminunc in Matlab, we may not be aware that these parameters are there, but they are. They have been set, but not necessarily ideally for all problems. This is not a case of a flawed implementation. Optimization always requires testing, evaluation, and checking. For this, the analyst should have an idea of what certain parameters do. So specifically for DE, we need to think about the following settings, most of which are passed with the list algo.

Initial population The initial solutions are drawn from a uniform distribution over specified ranges.

```
mP <- algo$min +
        diag(algo$max - algo$min) %*% mRU(d, algo$nP)
```

These ranges need to be fixed through the vectors `algo$min` and `algo$max`. The ranges serve only two purposes: they tell the algorithm how many elements a given solution has (`length(algo$min)`), and over what range to initialize the population. They are no constraints. Not specifying `algo$min` and `algo$max` will produce an error.

F The step size. Recall that DE computes a new solution by adding a weighted difference between two existing solutions to a third one. F is the weight, normally set between 0 and 1. Smaller values mean that a given vector is changed by smaller increments; hence, we make smaller steps when we move through the solution space.

CR The probability of crossover; hence, between 0 and 1. A high value means that a new solution is changed along many dimensions; a low value indicates that a change affects only few elements of a solution.

n_G (**nG**) The number of generations.

n_P (**nP**) The number of solutions (population size).

Stopping criterion We use a simple stopping criterion: a fixed number of function evaluations, given by the product $n_G \times n_P$. We can often reduce computing time by adding a break if the population has converged, that is, if all solutions are similar (in terms of parameters, or objective function value).

We also need to think how to implement the constraints. But before we do so, let us discuss the algorithm so far.

Algorithm 62 contains three nested loops. In both inner loops, however, iteration `i+1` does not depend on iteration `i`; hence, the two inner loops can in principle be vectorized. This is intuitive: in these loops we create new solutions and evaluate them, but there is no need to do this in a specific order. For very expensive objective functions, we could even distribute the evaluation.

According to Statement 7 in Algorithm 62, we have to compute auxiliary solutions $P^{(v)}$ as follows:

$$
P^{(v)}_{\cdot,i} = F \left[P^{(0)}_{\cdot,\ell_2} - P^{(0)}_{\cdot,\ell_3} \right] + P^{(0)}_{\cdot,\ell_1}
$$

This vector addition/subtraction is executed for all n_P solutions in the population. Let π be a random permutation of the numbers from 1 to n_P, and π_i be the ith number in this vector. Let π' and π'' be two further permutations such that $\pi_i \neq \pi'_i$, $\pi'_i \neq \pi''_i$, and $\pi_i \neq \pi''_i$ for all i. This is easily implemented by randomly drawing one permutation π and then shifting the elements in the vector, for instance, $\pi'_i = \pi_{i-1}$ with $\pi_0 \equiv \pi_{n_P}$. In Matlab the function circshift does just that; in R we can write our own function.

```
shift <- function(x) c(x[length(x)], x[1:(length(x)-1)])
```

A more general function shift is available in the magic package (Hankin, 2005), available from CRAN. Now we can write the instruction from Statement 7 as:

$$
\begin{bmatrix} P^{(v)}_{\cdot,1} & P^{(v)}_{\cdot,2} & \cdots \end{bmatrix} = F \begin{bmatrix} \begin{bmatrix} P^{(0)}_{\cdot,\pi_1} & P^{(0)}_{\cdot,\pi_2} & \cdots \end{bmatrix} - \begin{bmatrix} P^{(0)}_{\cdot,\pi'_1} & P^{(0)}_{\cdot,\pi'_2} & \cdots \end{bmatrix} + \begin{bmatrix} P^{(0)}_{\cdot,\pi''_1} & P^{(0)}_{\cdot,\pi''_2} & \cdots \end{bmatrix} \end{bmatrix}
$$

So we compute all auxiliary solutions in one step by adding/subtracting matrices instead of vectors. This is much faster than looping through the columns of P. The crossover in Statement 9 of the pseudocode can also be vectorized, if not for speed, then for clarity.

Now that we have new solutions, we need to evaluate them. In a given iteration, the clearest approach is to loop over the solutions, and to compute the objective function for each solution:

```
for (s in 1:algo$nP) vFnew[s] <- OF(mPnew[ ,s], data)
```

Alternatively, we could have done this with

```
vFnew <- apply(mPnew, 2, OF, data)
```

but this rarely makes the code faster, since it essentially still loops over the solutions; see Chambers (2008). We can often accelerate the computation by truly evaluating the whole population in one step, that is, by truly evaluating it in a "vectorized way." While the code becomes faster it also becomes often less straightforward—and in any case, it is not always possible to vectorize. But if it can be done, it is often worth the effort because the computing time can be substantially reduced. In the complete code of DEopt, we find the following structure:

```
if (algo$loopOF==TRUE) {
    for (s in 1:algo$nP) vF[s] <- OF(mPnew[ ,s], data = data)
} else {
    vF <- OF(mPnew, data = data)
}
```

Thus, the parameter `algo$loopOF` determines whether R loops over the columns of `mPnew`, or whether we pass the whole population to the objective function. In this latter case, we need to write `OF` differently. Normally, we would call the objective function as

```
OF(solution, data)
```

where `solution` is a vector, that is, a single solution. By convention, we always pass the list `data`. `OF` would then return a scalar, the objective function value of `solution`. If we can vectorize the evaluation, we need to write the functions such that `solution` is the whole matrix P of solutions. The function then returns a vector whose elements belong to the columns of P. For our problem here, we will do this only for the constraints, discussed below. For examples of vectorized objective functions, see page 441 and page 489.

Let us look at the actual objective function. It takes two arguments, a solution `param` (a vector of parameters) and further information collected in data. The list `data` comprises, among other things, the times-to-payment (`tm`) and the market rates (`yM`), both numeric vectors; and the `model` (e.g., `NS`) which is a function.

Listing 14.6. C-EconometricModels/R/example1.R

```
1  data <- list(yM = yM,
2               tm = tm,
3               model = NS,
4               ww = 0.1,
5               min = c( 0,-15,-30, 0),
6               max = c(15, 30, 30,10))
```

Now we can evaluate `param`.

Listing 14.7. C-EconometricModels/R/example1.R

```
1  OF <- function(param,data) {
2      y   <- data$model(param,data$tm)
3      aux <- y - data$yM
4      aux <- max(abs(aux))
5      return(aux)
6  }
```

We compute model rates `y` for the given `tm` and parameters `param`, and return the maximum absolute difference between `y` and `yM`.

Finally we want to enforce constraints. Constraints can be incorporated in `DEopt` either through repair mechanisms, or through penalties. In this section, we choose the latter option. The most straightforward way is to compute the penalty directly in the objective function, possibly required parameters can be passed with `data`. Suppose for instance we wanted to include the constraint $y > 0$.

Listing 14.8. C-EconometricModels/R/example1b.R

```
1 OF <- function(param,data) {
2     y   <- data$model(param,data$tm)
3     aux <- y - data$yM
4     res <- max(abs(aux))
5     # compute the penalty
6     aux <- y - abs(y) # ... aux == zero for nonnegative y
7     aux <- -sum(aux) * data$ww
8     return(res + aux)
9 }
```

data$ww is a weight. DEopt also offers a separate call to a penalty function (and a repair function, too). This is helpful, again, in cases when we can vectorize only a particular computation (e.g., only the penalty evaluation, but not the objective function).

To use this separate call, algo holds two functions, repair and penalty (both default to NULL). These functions, like the objective function, are called as

```
fun(solution, data)
```

The repair function (if specified) is applied in every generation to new solutions before the objective function is computed. It returns a repaired-solution. penalty is applied after the objective function was called; it returns zero if no constraint is violated, or a positive number in case the particular solution violates a restriction. This penalty is added to the objective function value.

As with the objective function, if these computations can be vectorized, they will usually be faster. Thus, as the default both functions take as arguments one solution (a vector), and they always have passed the list data. repair will then return a single repaired solution; penalty will return a scalar. Yet if we set

```
algo$loopRepair <- FALSE
algo$loopPen    <- FALSE
```

then, as with the objective function, we pass the whole population. repair then needs to return the repaired population, and penalty needs to return a vector. The penalty function serves as an example. We can compute the penalties in one step for the whole population.

Listing 14.9. C-EconometricModels/R/example1.R

```
1 penalty <- function(mP,data) {
2     minV <- data$min
3     maxV <- data$max
4     ww <- data$ww
5     # if larger than maxV, element in A is positiv
6     A <- mP - as.vector(maxV); A <- A + abs(A)
7     # if smaller than minV, element in B is positiv
```

```
 8    B <- as.vector(minV) - mP; B <- B + abs(B)
 9    # beta 1 + beta2 > 0
10    C <- ww*((mP[1,]+mP[2,])-abs(mP[1,]+mP[2,]))
11    A <- ww * colSums(A + B) - C
12    return(A)
13 }
```

This function evaluates the minimum and maximum constraints, and the constraint that $\beta_1 + \beta_2 \geq 0$.[1] The penalty function is passed with the `algo` list, along with the setting `algo$loopPen=FALSE`. A weight parameter `ww` is added to `data`.

A complete example is given in Listing 14.10. Listing 14.11 shows that almost the same code can be used for the NSS model. Both examples are included in a vignette in `NMOF`.

Listing 14.10. C-EconometricModels/R/example1.R

```
 1 # set up yield curve (here: artificial data), and plot it
 2 tm <- c(c(1,3,6,9)/12,1:10)
 3 betaTRUE <- c(6,3,8,1)
 4 yM    <- NS(betaTRUE,tm)
 5 plot(tm, yM, xlab = "maturities in years",
 6               ylab = "yields in %")
 7
 8 # collect everything in data
 9 data <- list(yM = yM,
10              tm = tm,
11              model = NS,
12              ww = 0.1,
13              min = c( 0,-15,-30, 0),
14              max = c(15, 30, 30,10))
15
16 # initialize algo settings
17 algo <- list(nP = 200,
18              nG = 600,
19              F = 0.50,
20              CR = 0.99,
21              min = c( 0,-15,-30, 0),
22              max = c(15, 30, 30,10),
23              pen = penalty,
24           repair = NULL,
25           loopOF = TRUE,
26          loopPen = FALSE,
27       loopRepair = TRUE)
28
29 system.time(sol <- DEopt(OF = OF, algo = algo, data=data))
30 # max. error and objective function value: should be the same
31 max(abs(data$model(sol$xbest,tm)-data$model(betaTRUE,tm)))
32 sol$OFvalue
33 lines(tm,data$model(sol$xbest,tm), col="blue")
34
```

---

[1] It can be helpful to scale the penalty to the magnitude of the objective function. This should be intuitive: a penalty of 0.02 will not help much if our objective function is of a magnitude of 15,000.

```
35 s0 <- algo$min + (algo$max-algo$min) * runif(length(algo$min))
36 system.time(sol2 <- nlminb(s0, OF, data = data,
37                            lower = data$min,
38                            upper = data$max,
39                            control = list(eval.max = 50000,
40                                           iter.max = 50000)))
41 # max. error and objective function value: should be the same
42 max(abs(data$model(sol2$par,tm)-data$model(betaTRUE,tm)))
43 sol2$objective
44 lines(tm,data$model(sol2$par,tm), col="green", lty=2)
45 legend(x = "bottom", legend = c("true yields","DE","nlminb"),
```

Listing 14.11. C-EconometricModels/R/example2.R

```
 1 # ... continues example1.R
 2
 3 # set up yield curve (here: artificial data), and plot it
 4 tm <- c(c(1,3,6,9)/12,1:10)
 5 betaTRUE <- c(5,-2,5,-5,1,6)
 6 yM <- NSS(betaTRUE,tm)
 7 plot(tm, yM, xlab = "maturities in years",
 8                ylab = "yields in %")
 9
10 # collect everything in data
11 data <- list(yM = yM,
12              tm = tm,
13              model = NSS,
14              min = c( 0,-15,-30,-30,  0,5),
15              max = c(15, 30, 30, 30,  5, 10),
16              ww = 1)
17
18 algo <- list(nP = 200,
19              nG = 600,
20              F = 0.50,
21              CR = 0.99,
22              min = c( 0,-15,-30,-30,  0,5),
23              max = c(15, 30, 30, 30,  5, 10),
24              pen = penalty,
25              repair = NULL,
26              loopOF = TRUE,
27              loopPen = FALSE,
28              loopRepair = TRUE)
29
30 system.time(sol <- DEopt(OF = OF, algo = algo, data = data) )
31 # max. error and objective function value: should be the same
32 max(abs(data$model(sol$xbest,tm)-data$model(betaTRUE,tm)))
33 sol$OFvalue
34 lines(tm,data$model(sol$xbest,tm), col="blue")
35
36 s0 <- algo$min + (algo$max-algo$min) * runif(length(algo$min))
37 system.time(sol2 <- nlminb(s0,OF,data = data,
38                            lower = data$min,
39                            upper = data$max,
40                            control = list(eval.max = 50000,
41                                           iter.max = 50000)))
42 # max. error and objective function value: should be the same
43 max(abs(data$model(sol2$par,tm)-data$model(betaTRUE,tm)))
```

```
44  sol2$objective
45  lines(tm,data$model(sol2$par,tm), col="green", lty=2)
46
47  legend(x   = "bottom", legend = c("true yields","DE","nlminb"),
48               col = c("black","blue","green"),
49               pch = c(1,NA,NA), lty=c(0,1,2))
```

Case 3: Fitting prices with Differential Evolution

In the two previous examples, we assumed that we already had a vector of zero rates (e.g., obtained from a bootstrapping procedure). Now we shall calibrate the model parameters directly to a vector b^M of bond prices. As in y^M, the superscript stands for "market."

Aim: to find parameters for the NS/NSS models such that theoretical bond prices b, computed from $y(\tau)$, are close to observed prices b^M. The path from a set of parameters of the NS/NSS model to theoretical bond prices is straightforward:

1: compute yield curve from NS/NSS model,
2: compute theoretical bond prices,
3: compute discrepancy between theoretical bond prices and observed bond prices.

So our problem is

$$\min_{\beta,\lambda} \| b - b^M \|$$

subject to

$$b = \left(\frac{1}{1 + y(\tau_1)} \right)^{\tau_1} c_{\tau_1} + \left(\frac{1}{1 + y(\tau_2)} \right)^{\tau_2} c_{\tau_2} + \cdots$$

$$y(\tau) = \beta_1 + \beta_2 \left[\frac{1 - \exp(-\tau/\lambda_1)}{\tau/\lambda} \right] + \cdots \quad \begin{cases} \text{Eq. (14.8) for NS,} \\ \text{Eq. (14.9) for NSS} \end{cases}$$

$$\beta_1 > 0$$

$$\beta_1 + \beta_2 > 0$$

$$\lambda_i > 0 \quad (i = 1 \text{ for NS}, i = 1,2 \text{ for NSS}).$$

As noted before, a bond is a collection of dates and associated payments. So, in R a bond comprises a vector `cf` of payments, like $[4.25, 4.25, 104.25]$, and a vector `tm` of times-to-payment, like $[1, 2, 3]$. Using actual dates, we have something like

```
cf <- c(4.25, 4.25, 104.25)
mats <- c("2010-10-12", "2011-10-12", "2012-10-12")
# compute time to maturity in years
today <- as.Date("2010-05-31")
tm <- as.numeric((as.Date(mats) - today))/365
```

For given zero rates y for the payment dates, we can price the bond by computing a vector of discount factors, and then computing the inner product of this vector and the cash flow vector. This we will have to do for all bonds in our data set, and many times over. Let us first organize our data.

The package NMOF includes a data set bundData, which contains information on 44 German government bonds. bundData is a list with three components:

cfList is a list of length 44 with cash flow vectors for the bonds. Each element of the list is a numeric vector.

tmList is a list of length 44 with payment dates associated with cfList. These are the contractual payment dates. If such a date is a weekend or a holiday, the payment will usually be made on the next business day. Hence, cash flows may occur later than stated, which makes such a bond slightly less attractive than when evaluated at contractual payment dates. In practice, people often correct for non business days. Each element of the list is a character vector. (So the dates are not of class Date but are formatted according to ISO 8601 as YYYY-MM-DD; thus we can easily coerce them to the Date class with as.Date.)

bM is a vector of market prices as of 31 May 2010. These are dirty prices, so they already include accrued interest.

It is convenient to store all cash flows in a single matrix, as in Eq. (14.5).

```
cfList <- bundData$cfList
tmList <- bundData$tmList
mats   <- unlist(tmList, use.names = FALSE)
mats   <- sort(unique(mats))
ISIN   <- names(bundData$cfList)

# set up cash flow matrix
nR <- length(mats); nC <- length(cfList)
cfMatrix <- array( 0, dim = c(nR, nC) )
for (j in seq(nC))
    cfMatrix[mats %in% tmList[[j]], j] <- cfList[[j]]
rownames(cfMatrix) <- mats
colnames(cfMatrix) <- ISIN
```

The matrix cfMatrix should look as follows:

```
            DE0001135150 DE0001141471 DE0001135168 #....
2010-06-20         0.00          0.0         0.00
2010-07-04       105.25          0.0         0.00
2010-09-20         0.00          0.0         0.00
2010-10-08         0.00        102.5         0.00
2010-10-10         0.00          0.0         0.00
2010-10-11         0.00          0.0         0.00
2010-10-12         0.00          0.0         0.00
2010-10-14         0.00          0.0         0.00
2011-01-04         0.00          0.0       105.25
2011-02-27         0.00          0.0         0.00
#....
```

cfMatrix corresponds to C'; every column of cfMatrix stores the cash
flows of one bond, the rownames of cfMatrix give the time of payment.
For a given set of NS/NSS parameters, we compute a vector of zero rates y
for the payment dates, then this vector can be transformed into discount
factors diFa with

```
diFa <- 1 / ((1 + y)^tm)
```

from which we can compute bond prices with

```
b <- diFa %*% cfMatrix
```

So we compute all the bond prices in one step. Finally, we can compare
these prices b with the market prices bM. OF2 is an example for a complete
objective function in which we compute the maximum absolute difference
between theoretical and observed prices.

Listing 14.12. C-EconometricModels/R/example3data.R

```
1 # objective function
2 OF2 <- function(param,data) {
3     tm  <- data$tm; bM  <- data$bM; model <- data$model
4     cfMatrix <- data$cfMatrix
5     diFa <- 1 / ( (1 + model(param,tm)/100)^tm )
6     b <- diFa %*% cfMatrix
7     aux <- b-bM; aux <- max(abs(aux))
8     return(aux)
9 }
```

The complete example:

Listing 14.13. C-EconometricModels/R/example3data.R

```
1  # reprice bonds with known yield curve
2  today <- as.Date("2010-05-31")
3  tm <- as.numeric((as.Date(mats) - today))/365
4  betaTRUE <- c(5,-2,1,10,1,5); yM <- NSS(betaTRUE,tm)
5  diFa <- 1 / ((1 + yM/100)^tm)
6  bM <- diFa %*% cfMatrix
7  #bM <- bundData$bM
8
9  plot(tm,yM,xlab="maturities in years",ylab="yields in %")
10
11 # collect all in dataList
12 data <- list(bM = bM, tm = tm, cfMatrix = cfMatrix,
13             model = NSS, ww=1,
14             min = c( 0,-15,-30,-30,0  ,3),
15             max = c(15, 30, 30, 30,2.3,6  ))
16
17 # set parameters for de
18 algo <- list(
19         nP  = 50, nG = 500, F = 0.5, CR = 0.9,
20         min    = c( 0,-15,-30,-30,0,3),
21         max    = c(15, 30, 30, 30,3,6),
```

```
22           pen = penalty, repair = NULL,
23           loopOF = TRUE, loopPen = FALSE, loopRepair = FALSE)
24
25  system.time(sol <- DEopt(OF = OF2, algo = algo, data = data))
26  # maximum yield error
27  max(abs(data$model(sol$xbest,tm) - data$model(betaTRUE,tm)))
28  # max. abs. price error and obj. function: should be the same
29  diFa <- 1 / ((1 + NSS(sol$xbest,tm)/100)^tm)
30  b <- diFa %*% cfMatrix
31  max(abs(b - bM)); sol$OFvalue
32  lines(tm,data$model(sol$xbest,tm), col="blue")
33
34  s0 <- algo$min + (algo$max-algo$min) * runif(length(algo$min))
35  system.time(sol2 <- nlminb(s0, OF2, data = data,
36                             lower = data$min,
37                             upper = data$max,
38                     control = list(eval.max = 50000,
39                                    iter.max = 50000)))
40  # maximum yield error
41  max(abs(data$model(sol2$par,tm)-data$model(betaTRUE,tm)))
42  # max. abs. price error and obj. function: should be the same
43  diFa <- 1 / ((1 + NSS(sol2$par,tm)/100)^tm)
44  b <- diFa %*% cfMatrix
45  max(abs(b - bM))
46  sol2$objective
47  lines(tm,data$model(sol2$par,tm), col="green", lty=2)
48
49  legend(x = "bottom", legend = c("true yields","DE","nlminb"),
50         col = c("black","blue","green"),
51         pch = c(1,NA,NA), lty=c(0,1,2))
```

Note that we have actually not used the bM that are contained in bundData, but have repriced the bonds with a known term structure. This allows us to see if the algorithm works.

We may sometimes find that there are still relatively large remaining errors in the short-term zero rates. For instance, for the example given above, we can plot the errors in the interest rates and prices with the following code example.

```
# plot rate error against ttm of payment
plot(tm, NSS(sol$xbest, tm) - NSS(betaTRUE, tm))
# plot price error against tm of bond
plot(as.numeric((as.Date(unlist(lapply(tmList, max))) - today)
/365), as.vector(b - bM))
```

There are two reasons for these larger errors. First, we did not ask the algorithm to minimize differences in rates, but prices. And the price differences are numerically small (typically smaller than 10^{-4} in the given example). Which is economically small given that we measure prices in percentage points; the errors are less than one-hundredth of a basis point.

There is a second reason. For short-dated bonds, any reasonable interest rate gives a good approximation of the price. Short bonds have a low duration; hence, changes in the interest rate have little impact on prices.

Reversing this argument, a small change in the bond price may bring about a large change in the interest rate. For our sample of bond prices, this is just an artifact; if we use the obtained yield curve to price the bonds, the computed prices will be fine. But if you need the rates to price other instruments, this may cause problems (or at least discomfort). To overcome this problem, we can weight the different bonds (e.g., by the inverse of time to maturity, or by inverse duration). We can also calibrate our parameters to yields-to-maturity. This latter approach is used by several central bank (e.g., Switzerland's SNB; see Müller, 2002). In the next section we see how to solve such a problem.

Case 4: Fitting yields-to-maturity with Differential Evolution
　　Aim: to find parameters for the NS/NSS models such that the yields-to-maturity r of theoretical bond prices, computed from $y(\tau)$, are close to observed yield-to-maturity r^M.

Compared with the last example, we now need one further step to move from a given set of NS/NSS parameters to an objective function value:

1: compute yield curve from NS/NSS model,
2: compute theoretical bond prices,
3: compute theoretical yields-to-maturity for every bond,
4: compute discrepancy between theoretical yields-to-maturity and observed yields-to-maturity.

More formally, our problem now becomes

$$\min_{\beta,\lambda}\|r - r^M\|$$

subject to

$$r = \mathrm{argmin}_r \left| -b + \left(\frac{1}{1+r}\right)^{\tau_1} c_{\tau_1} + \left(\frac{1}{1+r}\right)^{\tau_2} c_{\tau_2} + \cdots \right|$$

$$b = \left(\frac{1}{1+y(\tau_1)}\right)^{\tau_1} c_{\tau_1} + \left(\frac{1}{1+y(\tau_2)}\right)^{\tau_2} c_{\tau_2} + \cdots$$

$$y(\tau) = \beta_1 + \beta_2 \left[\frac{1 - \exp(-\tau/\lambda_1)}{\tau/\lambda}\right] + \cdots \quad \begin{cases} \text{Eq. (14.8) for NS,} \\ \text{Eq. (14.9) for NSS} \end{cases}$$

$$\beta_1 > 0$$

$$\beta_1 + \beta_2 > 0$$

$$\lambda_i > 0 \quad (i = 1 \text{ for NS, } i = 1,2 \text{ for NSS}).$$

The downside of this approach is that it is more expensive than directly fitting the bond prices. In every iteration we now need to compute the internal rate of return (see page 446) for every bond. With 20 to 50 bonds, an optimization can then easily take several minutes, compared with less than a minute before.

We first write a function to compute yields.

Listing 14.14. C-EconometricModels/R/example4data.R

```
 1 # ... continues example1.R
 2
 3 compYield <- function(cf,tm,guess=NULL) {
 4     fy <- function(ytm,cf,tm) sum(cf/((1+ytm)^tm))
 5     logik <- cf!=0; cf <- cf[logik]; tm <- tm[logik]
 6     if(is.null(guess)){ytm <- 0.05} else {ytm <- guess}
 7     h <- 1e-8; dF <- 1; ci <- 0
 8     while (abs(dF) > 1e-5) {
 9         ci <- ci + 1; if(ci>5) break
10         FF <- fy(ytm,cf,tm)
11         dFF <- (fy(ytm+h,cf,tm)-FF) / h
12         dF <- FF / dFF
13         ytm <- ytm - dF
14     }
15     return(ytm)
16 }
```

We use Newton's method, as above; again we do not use analytic derivatives. We exit the algorithm's `while` structure if Newton has not converged after 5 steps. Converged means that the difference between two consecutive guesses is smaller than 0.00005.

The objective function:

Listing 14.15. C-EconometricModels/R/example4data.R

```
 1 OF3 <- function(param,data) {
 2     tm <- data$tm; rM <- data$rM; model <- data$model
 3     cfMatrix<- data$cfMatrix;  nB <- dim(cfMatrix)[2L]
 4     zrates <- model(param,tm)
 5     aux <- 1e8
 6     diFa    <- 1/((1 + zrates/100)^tm)
 7     b <- diFa %*% cfMatrix
 8     r <- numeric(nB)
 9     if( all( !is.na(b), diFa<1, diFa>0, b>1 ) ) {
10         # compute theoretical yields
11         for(bb in 1:nB) {
12             if(bb==1) guess <- 0.05 else guess <- r[bb-1]
13             r[bb] <- compYield(c(-b[bb],cfMatrix[,bb]),c(0,tm),
                    guess)
14         }
15         aux <- abs(r - rM)
16         aux <- sum(aux)
17     }
18     return(aux)
19 }
```

Newton's method is sensitive to "strange" parameter values, thus we have added several checks: if a price is smaller than 1 for instance, we just set the objective function to a large number.

The following listing shows the complete example.

Listing 14.16. C-EconometricModels/R/example4data.R

```
 1  for(j in seq(nC))
 2      cfMatrix[mats %in% tmList[[j]], j] <- cfList[[j]]
 3  rownames(cfMatrix) <- mats
 4  colnames(cfMatrix) <- ISIN
 5
 6  # compute artificial market prices
 7  today <- as.Date("2010-05-31")
 8  tm <- as.numeric((as.Date(mats) - today))/365
 9  betaTRUE <- c(5,-2,1,10,1,3); yM <- NSS(betaTRUE,tm)
10  diFa <- 1 / ((1 + yM/100)^tm)
11  bM <- diFa %*% cfMatrix
12  rM <- apply(rbind(-bM, cfMatrix), 2, compYield, c(0,tm))
13  plot(tm, yM, xlab = "maturities in years",
14               ylab = "yields in %")
15
16  # collect all in dataList
17  data <- list(rM = rM, tm = tm, cfMatrix = cfMatrix,model = NSS,
18  min = c( 0,-15,-30,-30,0 ,2.5),
19  max = c(15, 30, 30, 30,2.5,5  ), ww = 0.1)
20
21  # set parameters for de
22  algo <- list(nP = 50, nG = 300,
23               F = 0.50, CR = 0.99,
24               min = c( 0,-15,-30,-30,0  ,2.5),
25               max = c(15, 30, 30, 30,2.5,5  ),
26               pen = penalty, repair = NULL,
27               loopOF = TRUE, loopPen = FALSE,
28               loopRepair = FALSE, printDetail = TRUE)
29
30  system.time(sol <- DEopt(OF = OF3, algo = algo, data = data))
31
32  # maximum error
33  max(abs(data$model(sol$xbest,tm) - data$model(betaTRUE,tm)))
34  # maximum abs. yield error and objective function
35  diFa <- 1 / ((1 + NSS(sol$xbest,tm)/100)^tm)
36  b <- diFa %*% cfMatrix
37  r <- apply(rbind(-b, cfMatrix), 2, compYield,c(0, tm))
38  sum(abs(r - rM))
39  sol$OFvalue
40  lines(tm,data$model(sol$xbest,tm), col="blue")
41
42  s0 <- algo$min + (algo$max - algo$min)*runif(length(algo$min))
43  system.time(sol2 <- nlminb(s0, OF3, data = data,
44                       lower = algo$min,
45                       upper = algo$max,
46                   control = list(eval.max = 50000,
47                                  iter.max = 50000)))
48  # maximum error
49  max(abs(data$model(sol2$par,tm) - data$model(betaTRUE,tm)))
```

```
50 # maximum abs. yield error and objective function
51 diFa <- 1 / ((1 + NSS(sol2$par,tm)/100)^tm)
52 b <- diFa %*% cfMatrix
53 r <- apply(rbind(-b, cfMatrix), 2,compYield,c(0, tm))
54 sum(abs(r - rM))
55 sol2$objective
56 lines(tm,data$model(sol2$par,tm), col = "green", lty=2)
57
58 legend(x  = "bottom", legend = c("true yields","DE","nlminb"),
59                col = c("black","blue","green"),
60                pch = c(1,NA,NA), lty=c(0,1,2))
```

14.1.4. Experiments

In the examples above, we always used artificial data. Because we knew the true parameters, we also knew how well or badly the algorithms worked. In this section we describe several experiments in such settings. These are not meant as once-and-for-all references, but they should give ideas on how to test implementations, and how to do diagnostic checking.

The objective function

We fix parameters for the NS/NSS model and a vector of payment dates. From these, we compute a vector yM. Then we run DEopt and try to find parameters such that $\max(\text{abs}(y-yM))$ (or some other function) is minimized. We know that ideally, the objective function should reach zero.

More specifically we set

```
tm <- c(1,3,6,9,12,15,18,21,24,30,36,48,60,72,84,96,108,120)/12
```

and we draw parameters uniformly from the following ranges (if they lead to negative interest rates we discard them and draw afresh).

parameter	minimum	maximum	parameter	minimum	maximum
β_1	0.1	10	λ_1	0	10
β_2	$-\beta_1 + 0.1$	10	λ_2	0	10
β_3	-10	10			
β_4	-10	10			

We are not interested in parameter identification here, only in fitting the model yields to the true yields. We draw 1000 parameter sets. For each parameter vector, we compute the corresponding yM, and pass this vector to the DEopt function. Each time, we record the maximum absolute error $\max(\text{abs}(y - yM))$ (e.g., 0.2 means we have an error of 0.2 percentage points).

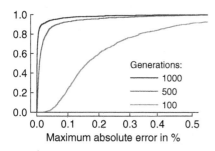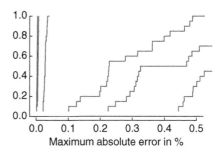

Maximum absolute error in %   Maximum absolute error in %

Figure 14.8 Left: convergence of solutions (i.e., best population members). Right: convergence of population (i.e., objective function values across members at the end of DE run).

As an example, we fix the parameters of DE as follows: F is set to 0.8, CR is set to 0.8. We use a population size of 20, and run DE for 100 generations. (If you know DE, you will at once object to these settings; but they serve to make a point.) Since we have 1000 parameter sets, we get 1000 solutions. Figure 14.8, in its left panel, shows the distribution function of the absolute errors. We also add the distributions obtained after 500 generations, and after 1000.

For only 100 generations, the results are bad. The median error is about 0.2% with a maximum error of sometimes a whole percentage point; essentially no run reaches a zero error. But for the runs with more generations, we get much better results. There are a few outliers, but apart from that the distribution really converges on zero.

The solution from a DE run is the best member of the population. What about the other members? In the right panel of the figure, we have plotted a first indication of why we obtained bad results with 100 generations. The panel shows not solutions, but the final distribution of objective function values across the population. The light gray distributions are those from 100 generation runs; the darker ones (the steeper ones) come from 500 generations. After 500 generations, the population has converged much more. This is typical for DE: the members of the population all move to the best point found. In other words, if the objective function values across members are vastly different, this indicates too few generations. The following test can be used: do 100 runs of DE, for each extract not only the best member, but also the standard deviation (or range) of population members. Then look at the correlation between the objective function value of the best member and the standard deviation of the populations. If algo$printDetails is set to TRUE (the default) for DEopt, the function will print the standard deviation of the final population's objective function values.

In our example here, with 1000 generations, the populations converge for all practical purposes. We have about 90% of all solutions with an error smaller than one basis point. But importantly: while non convergence is often a sign that the number of generations is too small, convergence does not guarantee that we have found the global optimum, usually just a local minimum. Of course, in our setting we know that the true optimum if zero, so we know that we have found the global optimum.

We could increase n_G further, but there is often a better approach: we can try to find more-appropriate values of F and CR, and n_P. If we need to repeatedly solve a specific optimization problem, we should try to find good values for the parameters of a method. This is again an optimization problem, and not an easy one since the objective function is noisy. But we do not need the best possible parameters—remember that the robustness of the method with respect to parameter settings was one defining criterion for a heuristic. Rather, we can run experiments to find "good" parameter values. Instead of a (pointless) "F should be 0.62," we look for answers like "F should be around 0.7–0.9."

The trouble is that to test all possibilities, the number of experiments we would like to run grows exponentially in the number of parameters of the heuristic. For DE, we need to set F and CR; it also matters how we distribute the function evaluations between n_P and n_G. Practically, this is rarely a problem since, as said before, we do not really want to optimize, we only want to make sure we choose reasonable parameters. And in many applications, even inferior parameter settings can often be cured by just letting the algorithm search longer (i.e., by choosing a bigger population and more generations). The computing time lost is often only a fraction of the time one can spend on testing alternative settings.

Let us run some experiments to find reasonable parameter values. We fix the number of function evaluations, and run the algorithm with different parameters. Possible value for CR are $\{0.3, 0.5, 0.7, 0.9\}$. Lower values, say 0.1, would not make much sense for this problem. Recall that in the NSS model, we have six parameters to estimate. With a CR of 0.1, the probability that a given solution stays unchanged would be $0.9^6 \approx 53\%$. F can be $\{0.1, 0.3, 0.5, 0.7, 0.9\}$.

To save space, we do not plot the empirical distributions but use quartile plots. Quartile plots can be thought of as "reduced-form" boxplots (Tufte, 2001). They only print the median (the dot in the middle) and the whiskers of the boxplot. The following figure illustrates their construction.

Q_q stands for the qth quantile, the interquartile range IQR is $Q_{75} - Q_{25}$. As in the standard boxplot, the limits of the whiskers are $Q_{25} - 1.5 \times$ IQR (or, if it is greater, the smallest observed value), and $Q_{75} + 1.5 \times$ IQR (or, if it is smaller, the greatest observed value). Quartile plots are described in Tufte (2001, Chapter 6). The package NMOF contains the function qTable that helps to generate the table (but generally needs some hand-formatting). qTable uses the picture environment in LaTeX, so no further LaTeX packages are required.

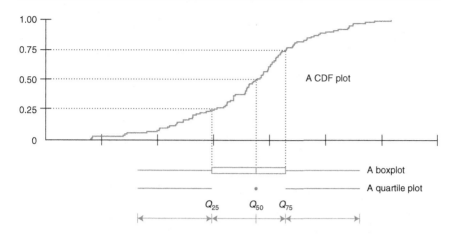

Table 14.2 gives a an impression of how the parameters affect the solution quality. The parameter F should be rather small, CR should be high. A good combination is a high CR (say, 0.9), and a small to medium F (say, 0.3–0.5). Another useful check is to look at the population over time. A solution returned from DEopt contains a matrix Fmat that stores the objective function values of all members of the population over all generations, thus the matrix is of size $n_G \times n_P$. It is useful to plot the results, for instance with

```
plot( apply(sol$Fmat, 1, median), type = "l")
lines(apply(sol$Fmat, 1, min), type = "l", lty = 3)
lines(apply(sol$Fmat, 1, max), type = "l", lty = 3)
```

Figure 14.9 shows an example. The objective here was to minimize the absolute price difference between bonds; hence, the objective function is measured in percentage points. Both plots show the average (median), best, and worst solution for the same data set; but with different parameter settings. Left, we have F = 0.5, CR = 0.99; right, F = 0.9, CR = 0.5. We see that the parameter settings can have a large influence on the speed of convergence.

Constraints

We should also check if the penalties did their job. For a particular run, we can just look at the final solution and see if the returned parameters are feasible (or the penalty function evaluates to zero). But this is not really a test.

A simple way to test a restriction is to set true parameters outside the feasible ranges, and then see if the algorithm halts at the parameter boundaries. This is advisable for any method we might use since it helps us to spot "unexpected behavior" (possibly caused by errors in the code). For penalties, it is important because it helps us to find sufficient weights for the penalties.

An example: the true parameters for the NSS model are c(5,-2, 1,10,1,5). We are mainly interested in β_1, the long-run rate is at 5%.

Table 14.2 Errors in % for NSS model for different parameters of DE. Each block corresponds to $F \in \{0.1, 0.3, 0.5, 0.7, 0.9\}$ for a given F. FE stands for objective function evaluations.

CR	F	1000 FE ($n_P = 20$, $n_G = 50$)			10,000 FE ($n_P = 50$, $n_G = 200$)			120,000 FE ($n_P = 200$, $n_G = 600$)		
		Med.	Min	Max	Med.	Min	Max	Med.	Min	Max
0.3	0.1	0.30	0.02	1.81	0.07	0.01	1.01	0.02	0.00	0.47
	0.3	0.35	0.02	1.81	0.09	0.01	0.93	0.03	0.00	0.50
	0.5	0.41	0.03	1.87	0.11	0.00	0.81	0.03	0.00	0.46
	0.7	0.48	0.04	1.86	0.13	0.01	1.15	0.04	0.00	0.51
	0.9	0.58	0.04	2.17	0.16	0.01	0.85	0.05	0.01	0.48
0.5	0.1	0.17	0.01	1.85	0.03	0.00	0.76	0.01	0.00	0.57
	0.3	0.23	0.02	1.51	0.05	0.00	0.80	0.01	0.00	0.57
	0.5	0.30	0.02	1.88	0.07	0.00	1.03	0.03	0.00	0.53
	0.7	0.43	0.03	2.05	0.10	0.02	0.94	0.03	0.00	0.56
	0.9	0.58	0.08	1.99	0.14	0.02	1.16	0.05	0.00	0.58
0.7	0.1	0.10	0.01	1.87	0.02	0.00	1.19	0.00	0.00	0.57
	0.3	0.11	0.01	1.69	0.01	0.00	0.74	0.00	0.00	0.57
	0.5	0.20	0.02	1.54	0.03	0.00	0.78	0.00	0.00	0.57
	0.7	0.35	0.04	1.74	0.07	0.01	1.21	0.02	0.00	0.57
	0.9	0.59	0.05	2.37	0.12	0.01	1.11	0.04	0.00	0.59
0.9	0.1	0.23	0.00	2.26	0.06	0.00	1.78	0.01	0.00	0.58
	0.3	0.04	0.00	1.37	0.00	0.00	1.03	0.00	0.00	0.57
	0.5	0.07	0.01	1.37	0.00	0.00	0.98	0.00	0.00	0.57
	0.7	0.21	0.02	1.75	0.02	0.00	0.72	0.00	0.00	0.57
	0.9	0.52	0.09	2.24	0.07	0.01	1.24	0.01	0.00	0.53

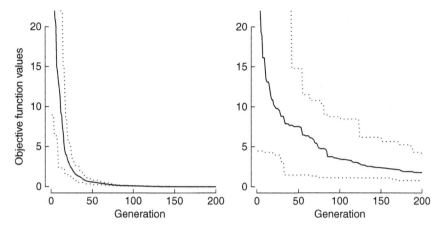

Figure 14.9 OF over time. The left panel shows F=0.5, CR=0.99. For the same problem, the right panel shows F=0.9, CR=0.5.

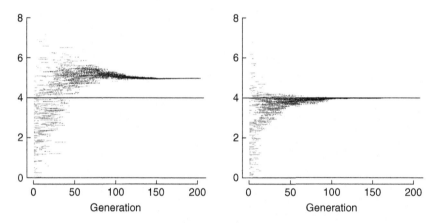

Figure 14.10 The true value of β_1 is 5. Left: without constraint (penalty weight is zero). Right: with constraint $\beta_1 \leq 4$.

Assume we have a very strong view that this rate should be positive but below 4%, so, $4 > \beta_1 > 0$. We run DE once without constraints, and once with a penalty; the population size is 50 and we run for 200 generations.

Figure 14.10 shows on the y-axis the values of β_1 for the members of the population, the x-axis gives the generation (we included a bit of jittering).

Adding the penalty clearly forces the parameter value inside the feasible boundaries. There is another remarkable observation: in both cases, we initialized the population within the feasible ranges, so initial β_1-values were all between 0 and 4. But in the unconstrained case, DE had little trouble moving the population outside this band and finding the correct values.

14.2. Robust and resistant regression

Linear regression is a widely used tool in finance. It is, for instance, common practice to model asset returns as a linear combination of the returns of various types of factors. Such regressions can then be used to explain past returns, or in attempts to forecast future returns. In financial economics, such factor models are the primary tools in asset pricing; they are used routinely to calibrate the Capital Asset Pricing Model (CAPM) or the Arbitrage Pricing Theory (APT). Even if these models—as equilibrium models—may not hold in reality, such regressions are still valuable. A main area of application is risk management where the regression estimates can be used to construct variance–covariance matrices. There is considerable evidence of the usefulness of such models in this context (Chan, Karceski, and Lakonishok, 1999).

Regression models may not only be used to inform financial decisions by analyzing assets, but may be explicitly used when constructing portfolios. For instance, a possible approach to replicate a portfolio or an index is to find investable assets whose returns "explain" the chosen regressand (e.g., the index); see, for instance, Rudolf, Wolter, and Zimmermann (1999). We could also solve other portfolio problems with a regression: assume we have p assets, and let the symbol x_i stand for the return of asset i at some point in time; we use x_i^* for the excess return over a constant risk-free rate. If a risk-free asset exists, mean–variance portfolio optimization reduces to finding the portfolio with the maximum ratio of excess return to portfolio volatility. This optimization problem can be rewritten as

$$1 = \theta_1 x_1^* + \theta_2 x_2^* + \cdots + \theta_p x_p^* + \epsilon$$

where θ_i are the coefficients to be estimated and ϵ holds the errors. Estimating the θ_i with Least Squares and rescaling them to conform with the budget constraint is equivalent to solving a mean–variance problem for the tangency portfolio weights; see Britten-Jones (1999). The approach is outlined in the Appendix.

The following R-script tests this approach.

Listing 14.17. C-EconometricModels/R/portReg.R

```
1  # portReg.R -- version 2011-01-06
2  # create artifical data ('daily returns')
3  n   <- 100     # number of observations
4  p   <- 10      # number of assets
5  X   <- array(rnorm(n * p, mean = 0.001, sd = 0.01),
6              dim = c(n, p))
7  rf <- 0.0001   # riskfree rate (2.5% pa)
8  m   <- apply(X, 2, mean)   # means
9  m2   <- m - rf             # excess means
10
11 ## (1) solve the problem with qp
```

```
12 require(quadprog)
13 aMat  <- as.matrix(m2); bVec  <- 1
14 zeros <- array(0, dim = c(p,1))
15 solQP <- solve.QP(cov(X), zeros, aMat, bVec, meq = 1)
16 # rescale variables to obtain weights
17 w       <- solQP$solution/sum(solQP$solution)
18 # compute sharpe ratio
19 SR      <- t(w) %*% m2 / sqrt(t(w) %*% cov(X) %*% w)
20
21 ## (2) solve with regression
22 X2       <- X - rf # excess returns
23 ones    <- array(1, dim = c(n,1))
24 # run regression
25 solR  <- lm(ones~-1 + X2)
26 # rescale variables to obtain weights
27 w2       <- coef(solR)
28 w2       <- w2/sum(w2)
29
30 ## (3) solve first-order conditions
31 w3 <- solve(cov(X),m2)
32 # rescale
33 w3 <- w3/sum(w3)
34
35 ## check they are the same
36 all.equal(as.vector(w),as.vector(w2))
37 all.equal(as.vector(w),as.vector(w3))
38 all.equal(as.vector(w2),as.vector(w3))
```

We can also find the global minimum-variance portfolio by running a regression (Kempf and Memmel, 2006). We write the portfolio return as the sum of its expectation μ and an error ϵ, hence,

$$\mu + \epsilon = \theta_1 x_1 + \theta_2 x_2 + \cdots + \theta_p x_p.$$

Imposing the budget constraint $\sum \theta = 1$ and rearranging we get

$$x_p = \mu + \theta_1 (x_p - x_1) + \theta_2 (x_p - x_2) + \cdots + \theta_{p-1}(x_p - x_{p-1}) + \epsilon.$$

We can directly read off the portfolio weights from the regression; the weight of the pth position is determined via the budget constraint.

Listing 14.18. C-EconometricModels/R/portRegMV.R

```
1 # portRegMV.R -- version 2011-01-06
2 # create artificial data with mean 0 and sd 5%
3 n <- 100 # number of observations
4 p <- 10  # number of assets
5 X <- array(rnorm(n * p, mean = 0, sd = 0.05),
6             dim = c(n, p))
7
8 ## (1) solve with qp
9 require(quadprog)
10 aMat   <- array(1, dim = c(1, p)); bVec   <- 1
11 zeros <- array(0, dim = c(p, 1))
12 solQP <- solve.QP(cov(X), zeros, t(aMat), bVec, meq = 1)
13 # ... and check solution
```

```
14 all.equal(as.numeric(var(X %*% solQP$solution)),
15          as.numeric(2 * solQP$value))
16
17 ## (2) regression
18 y  <- X[,1]               # choose 1st asset as regressand
19 X2 <- X[,1] - X[,2:p]     # choose 1st asset as regressand
20 solR <- lm(y~X2)
21 ## compare results of regression with qp
22 # weights from qp
23 as.vector(solQP$solution)
24 # weights from regression
25 as.vector(c(1-sum(coef(solR)[-1]), coef(solR)[-1]))
26 # variance of portfolio
27 all.equal(as.numeric(var(X %*% solQP$solution)), var(
       solR$residuals))
28
29
30 ## (3) solve first-order conditons
31 x <- solve(cov(X), numeric(p)+1) # or any other constant != 0
32 # rescale
33 x <- x / sum(x)
34 all.equal(solQP$solution, x)
```

Running a portfolio optimization as a regression is an instructive exercise, but it is normally not the most convenient tool to really compute portfolios. It becomes more difficult to include constraints, and the real problems (like getting the data right) remain; see Chapter 13. The main insight comes from the fact that if a problem can be written as a regression, it will inherit the characteristics (in particular, the weaknesses) of a regression.[2]

Linear models are also used to evaluate the ex post performance of investment managers. Since Sharpe (1992), "style analysis" has become a building block in performance measurement and evaluation. The regression coefficients are then interpreted as portfolio weights and the residuals as managerial skill (or luck).

The standard method to obtain parameter estimates for a linear regression model is Least Squares (LS). LS has appealing theoretical and numerical properties, but the resulting estimates are often unstable if there exist extreme observations—and these are common in financial time series (Chan and Lakonishok, 1992; Knez and Ready, 1997; Genton and Ronchetti, 2008). A few or even a single extreme data point can heavily influence the resulting estimates. Figure 14.11 presents a concrete example of what can happen with data errors. A much-studied example is the estimation of β-coefficients for the CAPM, where small changes in the data (resulting, for instance, from a moving-window scheme) often lead to large changes in the estimated

---

[2] As an example, it is well known that with multi-collinearity it becomes difficult to identify regressors. Since a portfolio selection problem can be written as a regression, it will suffer from the same problem. With high correlation between the assets—which is the normal case—it becomes more difficult to "identify" (i.e., compute accurately) weights.

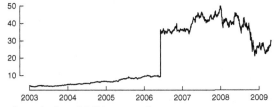

(a) The adjusted price of Adidas according to finance.yahoo.com.

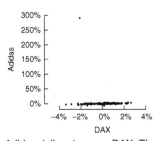

(b) Adidas daily returns vs DAX. The "split return" is recognizable in the upper left corner. This is clearly a data error since the price series was not correctly adjusted.

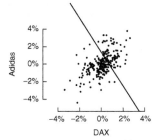

(c) Adidas daily returns vs DAX, but rescaled. We add an LS regression. The single outlier forces the slope to be negative.

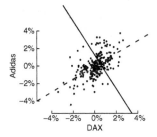

(d) We keep the LS regression, but add another line (dashed) for which we removed the outlier. The result looks more reasonable.

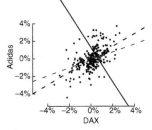

(e) Finally, we add an LMS regression line (also dashed). It was estimated with data including the outlier.

Figure 14.11 The effects of a single outlier. On 6 June 2006, Adidas split 4-for-1. The data was obtained from www.yahoo.com in April 2009. According to www.yahoo.com the series in the upper panel is split adjusted. (Curiously enough, that's even true; but it was adjusted twice.)

β-values. Earlier contributions in the finance literature suggested some form of shrinkage of extreme coefficients towards more reasonable levels, with different theoretical justifications (see, for example, Blume, 1971; Vasicek, 1973; Klemkosky and Martin, 1975). An alternative approach, which we will deal with in this chapter, is the application of robust or resistant estimation methods (Chan and Lakonishok, 1992; Martin and Simin, 2003).

To make the point clear: we do not suggest ignoring known errors in the data. The question is whether we always find the errors.

There is, of course, a conceptual question: what exactly is an extreme observation or outlier in a financial time series? Extreme returns may occur rather regularly, and completely disregarding such returns by removing or winsorizing them could mean ignoring information. Errors in the data, though, for example stock splits that have not been accounted for, are clearly outliers (as in Fig. 14.11). Such data errors occur on a wide scale, even with commercial data providers (Ince and Porter, 2006). In particular if data are processed automatically, alternative techniques like robust estimation methods may be advisable.

In this section, we will discuss the application of robust estimators. Such estimators were specially designed not to be influenced too heavily by outliers, even though this characteristic often comes at the price of low efficiency if the data actually contain no outliers. (Efficiency here means sampling efficiency, that is, an estimator is more efficient than another one if it has lower sampling variance.) Robust estimators are often characterized by their breakdown value. In words, the breakdown point is the smallest percentage of contaminated (outlying) data that may cause the estimator to be affected by an arbitrary bias (Rousseeuw, 1997). While LS has a breakdown point of 0%, other estimators have breakdown points of up to 50%. Unfortunately, the estimation becomes much more difficult, and for many models only approximative solutions exist. We will describe the application of a heuristic, Particle Swarm Optimization, to such problems.

14.2.1. The regression model

We consider the linear regression model

$$y = \begin{bmatrix} x_1 & \cdots & x_p \end{bmatrix} \begin{bmatrix} \theta_1 \\ \vdots \\ \theta_p \end{bmatrix} + \epsilon.$$

Here, y is a vector of n observations of the independent variable; there are p regressors whose observations are stored in the column vectors x_j. We will usually collect the regressors in a matrix $X = \begin{bmatrix} x_1 & \cdots & x_p \end{bmatrix}$, and write θ for the vector of all coefficients. The jth coefficient is denoted θ_j. We will normally include a constant as a regressor; hence, x_1 will be a vector of ones.

The residuals e (i.e., the estimates for the ϵ), are computed as

$$e = y - X\hat{\theta}$$

where $\hat{\theta}$ is an estimate for θ. Least Squares (LS) requires minimizing the sum or, equivalently, the mean of the squared residuals; hence, the estimator is defined as

$$\hat{\theta}_{LS} = \underset{\theta}{\operatorname{argmin}} \frac{1}{n} \sum_{i=1}^{n} e_i^2.$$

The advantage of this estimator is its computational tractability; the LS solution is found by solving the system of normal equations

$$(X'X)\theta = X'y$$

for θ.[3]

Rousseeuw (1984) suggested replacing the mean of the squared residuals with their median. The resulting Least Median of Squares (LMS) estimator can be shown to be less sensitive to outliers than LS; in fact, LMS's breakdown point is almost 50%. More formally, LMS is defined as

$$\hat{\theta}_{\text{LMS}} = \underset{\theta}{\operatorname{argmin}} \operatorname{median}\left(e^2\right).$$

LMS can be generalized to the Least Quantile of Squares (LQS) estimator. Let Q_q be the qth quantile of the squared residuals, that is

$$Q_q = \text{CDF}^{-1}(q) = \min\{e_i^2 \mid \text{CDF}\left(e_i^2\right) \geq q\}, \qquad (14.11)$$

where q may range from 0% to 100% (we drop the percent sign in subscripts). Hence the LMS estimator becomes

$$\hat{\theta}_{\text{LMS}} = \underset{\theta}{\operatorname{argmin}} Q_{50}\left(e^2\right),$$

and more generally we have

$$\hat{\theta}_{\text{LQS}} = \underset{\theta}{\operatorname{argmin}} Q_q\left(e^2\right).$$

For a given sample, several numbers satisfy definition (14.11); see Hyndman and Fan (1996). A convenient approach is to work directly with the order statistics $\left[e_{(1)}^2 \, e_{(2)}^2 \, \dots \, e_{(n)}^2\right]'$. For LMS, for instance, the maximum breakdown point is achieved not by minimizing $Q_{50}\left(e^2\right)$, but by defining

$$h = \left\lfloor \frac{n}{2} \right\rfloor + \left\lfloor \frac{p+1}{2} \right\rfloor \qquad (14.12)$$

and minimizing $e_{(h)}^2$ (Rousseeuw, 1984, p. 873).

The Least Trimmed Squares (LTS) estimator requires minimizing the order statistics of e^2 up to some maximum order k. Formally,

$$\hat{\theta}_{\text{LTS}} = \underset{\theta}{\operatorname{argmin}} \frac{1}{k} \sum_{i=1}^{k} e_{(i)}^2.$$

To achieve a high breakdown value, the number k is set to roughly $\lfloor 1/2(n + p + 1) \rfloor$, or the order statistic defined in Eq. (14.12).

LQS and LTS estimators are sometimes called "resistant" estimators, since they do not just reduce the weighting of outlying points, but essentially

---

[3] More often we directly solve the Least Squares problem $X\theta = y$ without explicitly forming $X'X$; see Chapter 3.

ignore them. This property in turn results in a low efficiency if there are no outliers. However, we can sometimes exploit this characteristic when we implement specific estimators.

14.2.2. Estimation

Robust estimation is computationally more difficult than LS estimation. A straightforward estimation strategy is to directly map the coefficients of a model into the objective function values, and then to evolve the coefficients according to a given optimization method until a "good" solution is found. For LMS, for instance, we may start with a guess for the parameters θ and then change θ iteratively until the median squared residual cannot be reduced any further. The difficulty with this approach arises from the many local minima that the objective function exhibits. Heuristic methods deploy different strategies to overcome such local minima. We will show how to use Particle Swarm Optimization for this problem (and compare it with another heuristic, Differential Evolution).

Since many resistant estimators essentially fit models on only a subset of the data, we may also associate such subsets with particular objective function values—hence transform the estimation into a combinatorial problem. An intuitive example is the LTS estimator. Since the objective is to minimize the sum of the k smallest squared residuals, we could also, for every subset of size k, estimate LS coefficients. The subset with the minimum objective function will give us the exact solution to the problem. But such a complete enumeration strategy is infeasible for even moderately sized data sets, so we need again a heuristic. The subset approach is discussed in Gilli and Schumann (2010g).

Implementing Particle Swarm Optimization

Particle Swarm Optimization (PSO) was described in Chapter 12. For convenience, we repeat the pseudocode in Algorithm 63. A straightforward implementation in R follows.

Listing 14.19. C-EconometricModels/R/PSabbr.R

```
1 # PSabbr.R -- version 2010-12-30
2 function (OF, algo = list(), ...) {
3     # add defaults to algo, do a few sanity checks
4     # ...
5     mRU <- function(m,n) array(runif(m * n), dim = c(m, n))
6     mRN <- function(m,n) array(rnorm(m * n), dim = c(m, n))
7     d <- length(algo$max); vF <- numeric(algo$nP); vF[] <- NA
8     mP <- algo$min + diag(algo$max-algo$min) %*% mRU(d,algo$nP)
9     mV <- algo$initV * mRN(d,algo$nP)
10    for (s in 1:algo$nP) vF[s] <- OF(mP[, s], ...)
11    mPbest <- mP; vFbest <- vF
12    sGbest <- min(vFbest); sgbest <- which.min(vFbest)[1]
```

```
13│    for (g in 1:algo$nG) {
14│        mDV <- algo$c1*mRU(d,algo$nP) * (mPbest - mP) +
15│                algo$c2*mRU(d,algo$nP) * (mPbest[,sgbest] - mP)
16│        mV <- algo$iner * mV + mDV
17│        logik <- mV > 0
18│        mV[logik] <- pmin(mV, algo$maxV)[logik]
19│        logik <- mV < 0
20│        mV[logik] <- pmax(mV, -algo$maxV)[logik]
21│        mP <- mP + mV
22│        for (s in 1:algo$nP) vF[s] <- OF(mP[, s], ...)
23│        logik <- vF < vFbest
24│        mPbest[, logik] <- mP[, logik]
25│        vFbest[logik] <- vF[logik]
26│        if (min(vF) < sGbest) {
27│            sGbest <- min(vF); sgbest <- which.min(vF)[1]
28│        }
29│    }
30│    return(list(vPar = mPbest[,sgbest],
31│                OFvalue = sGbest, popF = vFbest))
32│ }
```

Algorithm 63 Particle Swarm Optimization for robust regression.

1: set n_P, n_G and c_1, c_2
2: randomly generate initial population $P_i^{(0)}$ and velocity $v_i^{(0)}$, $i = 1,\ldots,n_P$
3: evaluate objective function $F_i = f(P_i^{(0)})$, $i = 1,\ldots,n_P$
4: $Pbest = P^{(0)}$, $Fbest = F$, $Gbest = \min_i(F_i)$, $gbest = \operatorname{argmin}_i(F_i)$
5: **for** $k = 1$ to n_G **do**
6:   **for** $i = 1$ to n_P **do**
7:     $\Delta v_i = c_1 u_1 (Pbest_i - P_i^{(k-1)}) + c_2 u_2 (Pbest_{gbest} - P_i^{(k-1)})$
8:     $v_i^{(k)} = v_i^{(k-1)} + \Delta v_i$
9:     $P_i^{(k)} = P_i^{(k-1)} + v_i^{(k)}$
10:   **end for**
11:   evaluate objective function $F_i = f(P_i^{(k)})$, $i = 1,\ldots,n_P$
12:   **for** $i = 1$ to n_P **do**
13:     **if** $F_i < Fbest_i$ **then** $Pbest_i = P_i^{(k)}$ and $Fbest_i = F_i$
14:     **if** $F_i < Gbest$ **then** $Gbest = F_i$ and $gbest = i$
15:   **end for**
16: **end for**
17: return best solution

The PSO algorithm is implemented as a function that is called with three arguments:

```
PSopt(OF, algo = list(), ...)
```

(Note that the implementation is very similar to that of Differential Evolution.) We will collect all objects to be passed with the ... in a list data and always call

```
PSopt(OF, algo, data)
```

OF is the objective function.

algo is a list that holds the settings of the PSO algorithm (discussed below).

data is a list that holds the pieces of data necessary to evaluate the objective function. For a regression model, **data** will typically contain the matrix X and the vector y.

The pseudocode for PSO shows two nested loops, but we can vectorize the inner loop. The variables P, *Pbest*, and v in the pseudocode are matrices; the iterator i in the inner loop in Algorithm 63 subsets the ith column of such a matrix, that is, it points to the ith solution. We can compute all instructions in one step by adding the weighted matrices. The variable *gbest* indicates the best solution of *Pbest*, so the vector *Pbest$_{gbest}$* has to be expanded to make it compatible with $P^{(k-1)}$. We do not have to do this explicitly in R because we can use the so-called recycling rule; see Venables and Ripley (2000, p. 17).

Example 14.1: Recycling vectors in R

If A is a matrix and a is a scalar, then in linear algebra an operation like $A + a$ is not defined. Rather, we need to multiply a by a matrix of ones that has the same size as A. But in Matlab and R (and other vector-oriented languages), the command $A + a$ is accepted and executed. In R, this idea of making matrices automatically compatible goes even further. Assume A is of size $m \times n$ and b is a vector of length m. Then R will consider $A + b$ as equivalent to $A + b\iota'$, where ι is a vector of ones of length n. As an illustration, the script

```
m <- 20; n <- 10
A <- array(0, dim = c(m, n)); b <- 1:m
A - b
```

results in

```
        [,1]  [,2]  [,3]  [,4]  [,5]  [,6]  [,7]  [,8]  [,9]  [,10]
 [1,]    -1    -1    -1    -1    -1    -1    -1    -1    -1     -1
 [2,]    -2    -2    -2    -2    -2    -2    -2    -2    -2     -2
 [3,]    -3    -3    -3    -3    -3    -3    -3    -3    -3     -3
 #....
[18,]   -18   -18   -18   -18   -18   -18   -18   -18   -18    -18
[19,]   -19   -19   -19   -19   -19   -19   -19   -19   -19    -19
[20,]   -20   -20   -20   -20   -20   -20   -20   -20   -20    -20
```

`PSopt` will return a list with four elements:

xbest is the solution; the parameter vector with the lowest objective function value,

OFvalue is the objective function value associated with **xbest**,

popF is the vector with the final objective function values of the population members (i.e., **OFvalue** equals `min(popF)`), and

Fmat is a matrix of size $n_G \times n_P$. It holds the objective function values of all solutions over time.

Running PSO requires several ingredients:

Initial population The initial solutions are drawn from a uniform distribution over given ranges. These ranges need to be specified through the vectors `algo$min` and `algo$max`. These ranges serve two purposes: to tell the algorithm how many elements a given solution has (by computing `length(algo$min)`), and over what range to initialize the population. The ranges are not constraints. If we want to use them in restrictions, we should pass them as `data$min` and `data$max`.

Initial velocity (initV) After we have initialized the population, we need to initialize the velocities. The parameter `initV` serves as a factor to randomly set the velocities (computed as `initV × mRU(d,nP)`). In many cases, this parameter can be set to 0.

Weights c_1 and c_2 (c1 and c2) The weights.

Inertia δ (iner) Inertia systematically reduces the velocity in each generation.

Population size n_P (nP) The number of solutions (population size).

Stopping criterion We use a simple stopping criterion: a fixed number of generations, given by the product n_G. Altogether, we will have nP × nG objective function evaluations.

These parameters are collected in the list `algo` and then passed to the function `PSopt`.

When we discussed Differential Evolution in Section 14.1, we argued that sometimes it is possible to evaluate the whole population at once (which is generally faster than looping over the single solutions). Let us give a concrete example for the objective function (the same holds for a `penalty` or `repair` function). Assume we have a regressor matrix X of size $n \times p$, and a population matrix P of size $p \times n_P$ (each column of P is one solution). A straightforward computation of the residuals for each solution would then be the following loop:

1: **for** $i = 1$ to n_P **do**
2:     compute residuals $y - XP_i$
3:     evaluate f for residuals
4: **end for**

Alternatively, we can compute XP in one step, and so obtain a matrix of residuals of size $n \times n_P$. See the next script.

Listing 14.20. C-EconometricModels/R/exampleLoop.R

```
1 # exampleLoop.R -- version 2010-12-30
2 # set up X matrix with n rows and p columns
3 n <- 100; p <- 5
```

```
 4  X <- array(rnorm(n*p), dim = c(n,p))
 5  # set up population
 6  nP <- 100
 7  mP <- array(rnorm(p*nP),dim=c(p,nP))
 8
 9  Y <- array(0, dim = c(n,nP)); Z <- Y
10
11  system.time({
12      for(r in 1:1000) {for(i in 1:nP) Y[,i] <- X%*%mP[,i]}
13  })
14  system.time({
15      for(r in 1:1000){Z <- X%*%mP}
16  })
17  all.equal(Y,Z)   # ... should be TRUE
```

Now since we have an unconstrained problem, all we need is an objective function. For LQS, this could look like the following:

Listing 14.21. C-EconometricModels/R/comparisonLMS.R

```
14  OF <- function(param, data) {
15      X <- data$X
16      y <- data$y
17      # as.vector(y) for recycling; param is a matrix
18      aux <- as.vector(y) - X %*% param
19      aux <- aux * aux
20      aux <- apply(aux, 2, sort, partial = data$h)
21      return(aux[data$h,]) # LQS
22  }
```

The function takes two arguments: candidate solutions `param`, and the list `data`. The latter contains three pieces of information, the actual data X and y, and the target residual h. For LTS the formulation is almost identical, we only need to change one line in the code.

Listing 14.22. C-EconometricModels/R/comparisonLMS.R

```
12      return(colSums(aux[1:data$h,])) # LTS
```

If `param` is a single solution, that is, vector of length p, `OF` will return a vector of length one. But `param` can also be a matrix of size $p \times n_P$. In this case, the function will return a vector of length n_P. To see the difference in performance, we just need to set `algo$loopOF` to TRUE (see the code of the complete example).

The most time-consuming part of the whole computation will be the sorting of the residuals. For both LQS and LTS, we do not need to sort all the residuals, but can make use of the `partial` argument of R's sort function.

```
x <- rnorm(101)
xp <- sort(x, partial = 51)
plot(xp)
middle <- xp[51]
abline(h = middle, v = 51)
```

14.2.3. An example

We will run an LQS regression as an example. For a benchmark we use the function lqs in the MASS package (Venables and Ripley, 2002).

We start with creating some random data.

Listing 14.23. C-EconometricModels/R/comparisonLMS.R

```
1  createData <- function(n, p, constant = TRUE,
2      sigma = 2, oFrac = 0.1) {
3      X <- array(rnorm(n*p), dim = c(n,p))
4      if (constant) X[,1] <- 1
5      b <- rnorm(p)
6      y <- X %*% b + rnorm(n)*0.5
7      nO <- ceiling(oFrac*n)
8      when <- sample.int(n,nO)
9      X[when,-1] <- X[when,-1] + rnorm(nO, sd = sigma)
10     return(list(X = X, y = y))
11 }
12
13 n <- 100  # number of observations
14 p <- 10   # number of regressors
15 constant <- TRUE; sigma <- 5; oFrac <- 0.15
16 h <- 70   # ...or use something like floor((n+1)/2)
17
18 aux <- createData(n,p,constant,sigma,oFrac)
19 X <- aux$X; y <- aux$y
```

We put X and y into data, also the residual h that we wish to minimize.

Listing 14.24. C-EconometricModels/R/comparisonLMS.R

```
1  data <- list(y = y, X = X, h = h)
```

The settings for PSO and DE.

Listing 14.25. C-EconometricModels/R/comparisonLMS.R

```
1  popsize <- 100; generations <- 400
2  ps <- list(min = rep(-10,p),
3             max = rep(10,p),
4             c1 = 1.0,
```

```
 5                c2 = 2.0,
 6              iner = 0.8,
 7             initV = 0.0,
 8                nP = popsize,
 9                nG = generations,
10              maxV = 3,
11            loopOF = FALSE)
12 de <- list(min = rep(-10,p),
13            max = rep(10,p),
14             nP = popsize,
15             nG = generations,
16              F = 0.2,
17             CR = 0.5,
18         loopOF = FALSE)
19
20 system.time(solPS <- PSopt(OF = OF,algo = ps, data = data))
21 system.time(solDE <- DEopt(OF = OF,algo = de, data = data))
22
23 system.time(test1 <- lqs(y ~ X[,-1], adjust = TRUE,
24              nsamp = 100000, method = "lqs", quantile = h))
25 res1 <- sort((y - X %*% as.matrix(coef(test1)))^2)[h]
26 res2 <- sort((y - X %*% as.matrix(solPS$xbest))^2)[h]
27 res3 <- sort((y - X %*% as.matrix(solDE$xbest))^2)[h]
28 cat("lqs:   ",res1,"\n",
29     "PSopt: ",res2,"\n",
30     "DEopt: ",res3,"\n", sep = "")
```

Finally, we can run the three methods. Note that we have set the number nsamp of samples in lqs relatively high so that the functions have roughly similar computing time.

There are two points that we would like to emphasize. First, many algorithms that have been suggested for robust estimators are based on sampling; hence, these algorithms also are stochastic. The algorithm behind lqs is a point in case. Thus, the results obtained with such algorithms should be analyzed just like heuristics as discussed in Chapter 12. (See also Zeileis and Kleiber, 2009.) When we change the number of samples for lqs, we can improve the solution. Thus, we also have a trade-off between solution quality and computing time. The following code provides an example. Results are shown in Fig. 14.12.

Listing 14.26. C-EconometricModels/R/exampleRobust.R

```
 1 # exampleRobust.R -- version 2010-12-29
 2 n <- 100  # number of observations
 3 p <- 10   # number of regressors
 4 constant <- TRUE; sigma <- 5; oFrac  <- 0.15
 5 h <- 70   # ... or use something like floor((n+1)/2)
 6 aux <- createData(n,p,constant,sigma,oFrac)
 7 X <- aux$X; y <- aux$y
 8
 9 trials <- 100
10 res1 <- numeric(trials)
```

```
11  for (t in 1:trials) {
12      mod1 <- lqs(y ~ X[,-1], adjust = TRUE,
13          nsamp = 'best', method = 'lqs', quantile = h)
14      res1[t] <- sort((y - X %*% as.matrix(coef(mod1)))^2)[h]
15  }
16  #
17  res2 <- numeric(trials)
18  for (t in 1:trials) {
19      mod1 <- lqs(y ~ X[,-1], adjust = TRUE,
20          nsamp = 10000, method = 'lqs', quantile = h)
21      res2[t] <- sort((y - X %*% as.matrix(coef(mod1)))^2)[h]
22  }
23  #
24  res3 <- numeric(trials)
25  for (t in 1:trials) {
26      mod1 <- lqs(y ~ X[,-1], adjust = TRUE,
27          nsamp = 100000, method = 'lqs', quantile = h)
28      res3[t] <- sort((y - X %*% as.matrix(coef(mod1)))^2)[h]
29  }
30  xx <- pretty(res1,res2,res3)
31  Y <- sort(res1); N <- trials
32  plot( c(Y[1] ,Y), (0:N)/N, type = 's', col=grey(0.6),
33      xlim = c(min(xx),max(xx)))
34  Y <- sort(res2); N <- trials
35  lines(c(Y[1] ,Y), (0:N)/N, type = 's', col=grey(0.2))
36  Y <- sort(res3); N <- trials
37  lines(c(Y[1] ,Y), (0:N)/N, type = 's', col=grey(0.0))
```

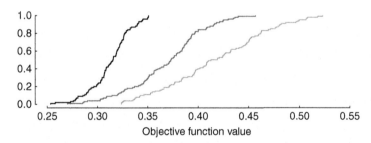

Figure 14.12 Objective function values obtained with `lqs` with increasing number of samples (see code example).

Second, in line with the theme of the book, before you let PSO and DE run with ever more generations, think about why you use LMS or another estimator. LMS is useful to find data errors (recall Fig. 14.11). But for that, we often do not need a very precise solution. In particular, for LTS there exists a simple algorithm called fastLTS that is practically extremely powerful (Rousseeuw and Van Driessen, 2005). So why use heuristics? The advantage of heuristics comes when we want to the change the standard setup. For example, when we have constraints. Or, though we have chosen a linear model, the heuristics could just as well be used with nonlinear models—we just need to write another objective function.

14.2.4. Numerical experiments

As we discussed in Chapter 12, almost all heuristics are stochastic algorithms. PSO is no exception, so restarting the algorithm several times for the same data set will result in different solutions. We characterize a solution θ by its associated objective function value, and treat such a solution obtained from one optimization run as the realization of a random variable with an unknown distribution D. For a given data set and a model to estimate (LMS in our case), the shape of D will depend on the particular optimization technique and its parameter settings, and, in particular, on the amount of computational resources spent on an optimization run. Heuristic methods are specially designed such that they can move away from local optima, so if we allow more iterations, we would expect the method to produce better results on average. In fact, for an ever increasing number of iterations, we would finally expect D to degenerate to a single point, the global minimum. In practice, we cannot let an algorithm run forever, hence we are interested in the convergence of specific algorithms for finite amounts of computational resources. "Convergence" thus means the change in the shape of D when we increase the number of iterations. To analyze D, we fix the settings for a method (data, parameters, numbers of iterations) and repeatedly restart the algorithm. Thus we obtain a sample of draws from D, from which we can compute an empirical distribution function as an estimate for D.

In the following section, we will describe experiments conducted in Gilli and Schumann (2010g). We will compare two different heuristics, DE and PSO, for LMS regression. We define computational resources as the number of objective function evaluations. For DE and PSO, this is equal to the number of generations times the population size. This is justified for LMS regression since the overhead incurred from evolving solutions is small compared with the time necessary to compute the median of the squared residuals (which requires at least a partial sorting of the squared residuals). Fixing the number of function evaluations has the advantage of allowing us to compare the performance of different methods for a given amount of computational resources.

We use the experimental setting described in Salibian-Barrera and Yohai (2006). They consider the regression model

$$y = X\theta + \epsilon, \tag{14.13}$$

where X is of size $n \times p$, θ is the p-vector of coefficients, and ϵ is Gaussian noise, that is, $\epsilon \sim N(0, 1)$. We always include a constant, so the first column of X is a vector of ones. The remaining elements of X and y are normally distributed with a mean of zero and a variance of one. Accordingly, the true θ-values are all zero, and the estimated values should be close to zero. We replace, however, about 10% of the observations with outliers. More precisely, if a row in $[y \; X]$ is contaminated with an outlier, it is replaced by

$$[M \; 1 \; 100 \; 0 \; ... \; 0]$$

where M is a value between 90 and 200. This setting results in a region of local minima in the search space where θ_2 will be approximately $M/100$. The function genData can be used to create data sets.

Listing 14.27. C-EconometricModels/R/genData.R

```
 1 # genData.R -- version 2010-12-29
 2 genData <- function(nP,nO,ol,dy) {
 3     # create data file [Salibian-Barrera & Yohai 2006]
 4     # nP = 36  % regressors
 5     # nO = 400 % number of obs
 6     # ol = 40  % number of outliers
 7     # dy = 110 % outlier size ('M' in S-B&Y 2006): 90 to 200
 8     y <- mRN(nO,1)
 9     X <- cbind(as.matrix(numeric(nO)+1),mRN(nO,nP-1))
10     zz <- sample(nO)
11     z <- cbind(1,100, array(0, dim = c(1,nP-2)))
12     for (i in 1:ol){
13         X[zz[i],] <- z
14         y[zz[i]]  <- dy
15     }
16     return(list(X = X, y = y))
17 }
```

Results

All the methods employed require us to set a number of parameters. When we start with some problem, we will normally use "typical" parameter values. But all our results are conditional on the chosen values for the method's parameters. An important part of implementing heuristics is, hence, the tuning of the algorithm, that is, finding good parameter values. This search is again an optimization problem: find those parameter values that lead to optimal (or, following our theme, good enough) results in every restart. In other words, we want parameter values that lead to a "good" D. Since all methods need several parameters to be set, this optimization problem is not trivial, in particular, since the objective function has to be evaluated from simulation and thus will be noisy. Though this problem can be handled as an optimization problem, for our purposes here, we do not need such an optimization—in fact, it will be the opposite actually. Parameter setting is sometimes portrayed as an advantage, for it allows us to adapt methods to different problems. True. But at the same time it requires the analyst who wishes to apply the method to have a much deeper understanding of the respective method. In other words, the analyst will have to be a specialist in optimization, rather than in finance or econometrics. So what we would be much more interested in is to see if a method completely breaks down for certain parameters.

To illustrate this point, we look at the model with $p = 20$ regressors, and solve it with different settings for the parameters. We set M to 150, and the number of observations n is fixed at 400. The number of function evaluations was set to 30,000. For every parameter setting we conducted 1000 restarts. The results shown below are based on the same instance of the problem; thus, the results in the following tables are directly comparable for different methods.

Table 14.3 shows the results when we vary F and CR. We include the median, best, and worst value of the obtained solutions. Furthermore we include quartile plots (Tufte, 2001) of the distributions (see page 476).

The solutions returned by DE improve drastically when we set F to untypically low values while different choices for CR have less influence. With small F, we evolve the solutions by adding small changes at several dimensions of the solution. In a sense, then, we have a population of local searches, or at least of slowly moving individuals.

Tables 14.4–14.7 give the result for PSO; here the picture is different. While there are differences in the results for different settings of the parameters, the results are quite stable when we vary δ, c_1, and c_2. Each table gives results for different values of c_1 and c_2, with δ fixed for the whole table. The

Table 14.3 Parameter sensitivity DE.

CR	F	median	best	worst	0 0.5 1.0 1.5 2.0
0.2	0.2	0.47	0.424	0.507	--
	0.4	0.53	0.464	0.575	--
	0.6	0.75	0.56	0.962	—·—
	0.8	1.54	0.988	2.08	——— · ———
0.4	0.2	0.44	0.399	0.472	--
	0.4	0.49	0.437	0.558	--
	0.6	0.91	0.631	1.19	——— · ——
	0.8	2.81	1.66	4.03	not pictured
0.6	0.2	0.41	0.356	0.443	--
	0.4	0.48	0.41	0.512	--
	0.6	1.39	0.848	1.88	——— · ———
	0.8	5.36	2.35	7.73	not pictured
0.8	0.2	0.38	0.338	0.432	--
	0.4	0.48	0.409	0.523	--
	0.6	2.29	1.20	3.64	not pictured
	0.8	9.05	3.36	12.77	not pictured
					0% 0.5 1.0 1.5 2.0

Table 14.4 Parameter sensitivity PSO for $\delta = 1$.

c_2	c_1	median	best	worst				
					0	0.5	1.0	1.5	2.0
0.5	0.5	0.46	0.384	0.921	–·–			
	1.0	0.45	0.376	0.944	–·–			
	1.5	0.45	0.394	0.985	–·–			
	2.0	0.45	0.399	0.938	–·-			
1.0	0.5	0.47	0.404	0.872	–·–			
	1.0	0.46	0.391	0.91	–·–			
	1.5	0.45	0.371	0.936	–·–			
	2.0	0.45	0.402	1.03	–·–			
1.5	0.5	0.46	0.406	0.96	–·–			
	1.0	0.46	0.395	0.89	–·–			
	1.5	0.45	0.399	0.926	–·–			
	2.0	0.45	0.402	0.829	–·–			
2.0	0.5	0.46	0.402	1.12	–·–			
	1.0	0.46	0.39	1.01	–·–			
	1.5	0.45	0.401	0.85	–·–			
	2.0	0.45	0.392	0.833	–·–			
					0%	0.5	1.0	1.5	2.0

Table 14.5 Parameter sensitivity PSO for $\delta = 0.5$.

c_2	c_1	median	best	worst				
					0	0.5	1.0	1.5	2.0
0.5	0.5	0.61	0.416	1.23	— · —			
	1.0	0.59	0.409	1.01	— · —			
	1.5	0.59	0.419	0.935	— · —			
	2.0	0.58	0.401	0.962	— · —			
1.0	0.5	0.57	0.385	1.09	— · —			
	1.0	0.55	0.372	1.04	— · —			
	1.5	0.54	0.366	0.854	— · —			
	2.0	0.52	0.343	0.89	— · —			
1.5	0.5	0.53	0.353	1.03	— · —			
	1.0	0.53	0.361	1.05	— · —			
	1.5	0.50	0.36	0.924	— · —			
	2.0	0.48	0.339	1.07	— · —			
2.0	0.5	0.50	0.348	0.933	— · —			
	1.0	0.49	0.337	0.90	— · —			
	1.5	0.46	0.331	0.867	— · —			
	2.0	0.44	0.33	0.835	— · —			
					0%	0.5	1.0	1.5	2.0

Table 14.6 Parameter sensitivity PSO for $\delta = 0.75$.

c_2	c_1	median	best	worst	0	0.5	1.0	1.5	2.0
0.5	0.5	0.47	0.348	0.89		—·—			
	1.0	0.46	0.339	0.923		—·—			
	1.5	0.45	0.339	0.797		—·—			
	2.0	0.43	0.327	0.806		—·—			
1.0	0.5	0.46	0.333	0.881		—·—			
	1.0	0.44	0.324	0.822		—·—			
	1.5	0.43	0.326	0.81		—·—			
	2.0	0.41	0.327	0.80		—·—			
1.5	0.5	0.43	0.328	0.834		—·—			
	1.0	0.43	0.316	0.818		—·—			
	1.5	0.42	0.316	0.84		—·—			
	2.0	0.42	0.338	0.847		—·—			
2.0	0.5	0.42	0.332	0.818		—·—			
	1.0	0.42	0.337	0.878		—·—			
	1.5	0.43	0.327	0.774		—·—			
	2.0	0.44	0.358	0.873		—·—			

0%   0.5   1.0   1.5   2.0

Table 14.7 Parameter sensitivity PSO for $\delta = 0.9$.

c_2	c_1	median	best	worst	0	0.5	1.0	1.5	2.0
0.5	0.5	0.41	0.330	0.879		—·—			
	1.0	0.41	0.328	0.82		—·—			
	1.5	0.41	0.335	0.776		—·—			
	2.0	0.42	0.348	0.766		—·—			
1.0	0.5	0.42	0.335	0.913		—·—			
	1.0	0.42	0.332	0.884		—·—			
	1.5	0.42	0.356	0.845		—·—			
	2.0	0.43	0.365	0.758		—·—			
1.5	0.5	0.44	0.366	0.882		—·—			
	1.0	0.44	0.361	0.83		—·—			
	1.5	0.44	0.367	0.781		—·—			
	2.0	0.44	0.377	0.832		—·—			
2.0	0.5	0.45	0.375	0.79		—·—			
	1.0	0.45	0.386	0.858		—·—			
	1.5	0.44	0.38	0.922		—·—			
	2.0	0.44	0.364	0.891		—·—			

0%   0.5   1.0   1.5   2.0

most salient result is that velocity should not be reduced too fast; hence, δ should be below but close to one.

In sum, for this problem, PSO worked robustly for all kinds of parameter settings. DE on the other hand worked fine only if properly tuned. In particular, for typical values of F (in the range of 0.7–0.9, say) the method did not return good results.[4] Rather we had to use small values, and ideally also for CR.

What is a good solution?

In their paper Salibian-Barrera and Yohai (2006) analyze how often a given estimator converges to the wrong solution, that is, a biased θ_2. Such an analysis, however, confounds two issues: the ability of a given estimator to identify the outliers on the one hand, and the numerical optimization on the other. Since we are interested in the optimization, we have not compared coefficients, but have looked at the value of the objective function.

Let us dwell on this point for a moment. The aim of robust regression methods—to be outlier resistant—cannot be directly pursued: we cannot maximize the probability of identifying outliers, or minimize the probability of converging on a biased parameter value. Instead, estimators are evaluated theoretically by general characteristics like the breakdown value (Rousseeuw, 1997) or the influence function (Hampel, Ronchetti, Rousseeuw, and Stahel, 1986). Such properties are almost always of an asymptotic nature and offer little guarantee in finite samples. Hence, when we compare different estimators with one another in applications, there are two aspects that we should investigate: (i) what is the quality of the estimator when it comes to its actually desired function, namely to spot outliers, or to converge to correct parameter values?, and (ii) what is the quality of the optimization and how is finding a good numerical solution related to question (i)?

These two notions of a good solution are not always distinguished in the literature. Rousseeuw and Van Driessen (2005, p. 35), for instance, refer to the "global optimum" as a subset of data that contains no outliers. In optimization, a global optimum would be the parameter values that give the objective function its minimum value (beyond Monte Carlo settings, Rousseeuw and Van Driessen's definition could never be checked). If an estimator fails to identify outliers, we need to investigate whether it is not just due to a poor optimization. On the other hand, even if the estimator does as expected (which, of course, is only testable in experiments), we need to know how relevant a good fit is. Assume our criterion of fit is a function (a norm) of the residual vector, and our aim is to identify outliers in a sample.

---

[4] See, however, Maringer (2008a) where a calibration study with a different test problem is reported and where typical values for F worked well. It is possible that the parameter F needs to be linked to the dimensionality of the problem, akin to the situation for the Metropolis algorithm; see footnote 6 on page 177.

Then ideally we would like to have a monotonous, or "threshold" behavior in the optimization: once we have found a solution better than a certain threshold, the model always identifies the outlying points. Unfortunately, it is not clear whether this is the case for specific estimators; here comes an example in which we do not have threshold behavior.

We stay with the data-generating process of Salibian-Barrera and Yohai (2006), that is, Eq. (14.13), and look at a univariate regression ($p = 2$), so we only have a constant θ_1 and a slope θ_2 to estimate. We set M to 90, so the true θ_2 should be around zero, and the wrong value will be 0.9. The following figure shows the objective function for different values of θ_1 and θ_2. Where the slope has a value of 0.9, we see a sharp "valley" in the surface, seen more clearly in the right panel.

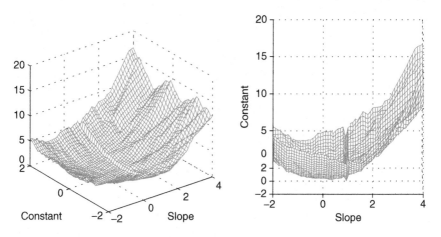

The trouble is that this optimum is actually lower than the region associated with the true parameters.

This can be seen in Fig. 14.13. The graphs show the result of 500 runs of LMS and LTS for the univariate regression, but with varying computational resources. Thus, the solutions differ widely in their realized objective function values. In the left panels, we plot all solutions against the estimate θ_2; in the right panel, we "zoom in" on the 100 best solutions. Clearly, getting better in terms of the objective function does not necessarily help in finding the correct parameter value. In Fig. 14.14, we repeat the whole procedure but with $M = 150$. Hence, the correct θ_2 is still zero, the wrong value is 1.5. We see a more satisfactory behavior: with a lower objective function, we essentially always find the correct parameter value.

14.2.5. Final remarks

In this section we have described how optimization heuristics can be used for robust regression, in particular, LMS regression. Both PSO and DE seem capable of giving "good" solutions to the LMS problem, even though the

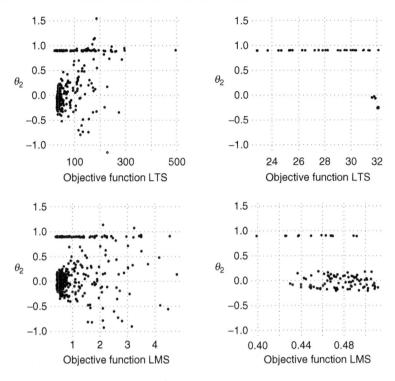

Figure 14.13 True θ_2 is zero. The outliers lead to a biased value of 0.9.

computational resources (i.e., number of function evaluations) would have to be increased drastically to make the distribution of outcomes collapse to a very narrow support. In other words, there always remains randomness in the solutions. It is difficult to judge the importance of this remaining randomness without a particular application.

DE performed well for small models, but the obtained results were sensitive to the specific parameter settings once we estimated models with more coefficients, that is, once we went into higher dimensions.[5] PSO showed a more robust performance. Given this robustness, we may prefer PSO for this particular problem. But there are several points to be kept in mind. First, all results are conditional on the chosen setup. Artificial settings as here are helpful to check algorithms since we know the true solution and we can also easily scale the size of problems. Yet if a model works well on artificial data, this may not be much proof that it works with real data (of course, if a technique fails in such experiments, we have a clear indication about its quality).

---

[5] Properly tuned, DE often found very good solutions, also for larger models. But that does not change the fact that results were sensitive to "improper" parameter settings.

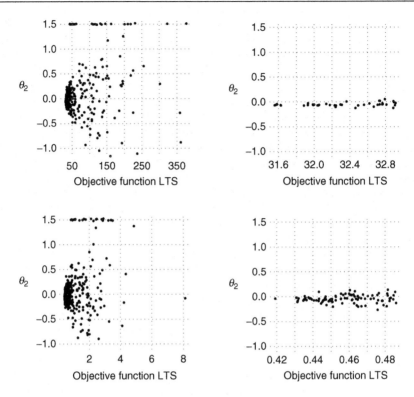

Figure 14.14 True θ_2 is zero. The outliers lead to a biased value of 1.5.

Furthermore, while PSO performed well on average, some restarts returned low-quality solutions. It is difficult to judge the relevance of such outcomes: the errors that may occur from the optimization have to be weighted in light of the actual application, for example, a portfolio construction process. A suggestion for actual implementations is thus to "diversify," that is, to implement several methods for a given problem, at least as benchmarks or test cases. At the very least, the algorithm should be restarted several times.

14.A. Maximizing the Sharpe ratio

Assume there are p assets, with expected excess returns (over the risk-free rate) collected in a vector $\bar{x}$. The variance–covariance matrix of the assets' returns is Ω. Maximizing the ratio of excess return to portfolio volatility can be formalized as

$$\max_{\theta} \frac{\theta'\bar{x}}{\sqrt{\theta'\Omega\theta}}.$$

The first-order conditions of this problem lead to the system of linear equations

$$\bar{x} = \Omega\theta\,;$$

see, for instance, Cuthbertson and Nitzsche (2005, Chapter 6). Solving the system and rescaling θ to sum to unity gives the optimal weights.

Assume now that we have n observations; we define $\bar{x}$ to be the sample mean, and collect the p return series in a matrix X of size $n \times p$. For the regression representation as proposed in Britten-Jones (1999), we need to solve

$$\iota = X\theta^*$$

(which is an LS problem), where ι is the unit vector and the superscript $*$ only serves to differentiate between θ and θ^*.

This can be rewritten as

$$\frac{1}{n}X'\iota = \frac{1}{n}X'X\theta^*,$$

$$\bar{x} = \frac{1}{n}X'X\theta^*,$$

$$\bar{x} = \frac{1}{n}(\Omega + \bar{x}\bar{x}')\theta^*.$$

Applying the Sherman–Morrison formula (Golub and Van Loan, 1989, Chapter 2) allows us to show that θ^* will be proportional to θ, and hence after rescaling we have $\theta^* = \theta$.

## CHAPTER FIFTEEN

Calibrating option pricing models

Option pricing models represent the price of the option as a function of the underlier; this underlier is then modeled usually via stochastic differential equations. Such differential equations require fixing certain parameters, for instance, the volatility of the underlier. Choosing such parameters is usually called calibration. There exist different strategies to calibrate a model:

- We are given observed quantities, and try to find model parameters such that model output equals these quantities. This is the problem we will deal with in this chapter. This is useful when we use models to interpolate (and extrapolate) market prices: we start with a set of observed market prices and then set the parameters such that the model prices are close to these actual prices.

- There are other strategies: the idea in option pricing is to model the underlier; then the option price is a function of this underlier. Thus calibration as described before means to "reverse-engineer" the market's implied view about the underlier, forced into the dynamics (or just the language) of the model. But even if this model were a useful approximation of the world, we may find that option prices in the market do not reflect our own view of the world. Thus, we may also calibrate option prices to the actual time series of the underlier, or a model of this underlier.

Example 15.1

The forward price F of an asset that does not pay any dividends is related to the spot price S by

$$F = Se^{r\tau}.$$

r is the discount rate, and τ the time to maturity of the contract. Assume the asset is an equity index that does not incorporate dividends (like the S&P 500, the EuroStoxx 50, or the Nikkei 225). Then we often assume that the dividend is paid continuously with rate q, thus we get $F = Se^{(r-q)\tau}$. Suppose we can observe S and a future price F, we know τ, and assume we have a reasonable idea about r. Hence q, the implied yield, should be

$$\frac{\log(S) - \log(F) + r\tau}{\tau}.$$

For futures on the same underlier, but different times to expiration, the implied yield q need not be the same. For instance, the EuroStoxx 50 is a basket of 50 underliers, and many of them pay dividends in the second quarter of the year. So we usually find a higher (annualized) dividend yield for contracts that cover that period.

Example 15.2

Assume we have prices of a European put and a European call option for a given strike X and a given time to maturity τ. Let the underlier pay one or several dividends during the lifetime of these options, and let the present value of the dividends be D. Then put–call parity links these together as

$$\text{Call} + e^{-r\tau} X = \text{Put} + S - D. \tag{15.1}$$

If we model dividends as a rate q, put–call parity becomes

$$\text{Call} + e^{-r\tau} X = \text{Put} + e^{-q\tau} S. \tag{15.2}$$

We can solve for D or q and so obtain dividends/dividend yields. The trouble is that with bid–ask spreads a range of dividends is feasible.

15.1. Implied volatility with Black–Scholes

In a Black–Scholes (BS) world, the stock price S_t under the risk-neutral measure follows

$$dS_t = (r - q)S_t dt + \sqrt{v} S_t dz_t \tag{15.3}$$

where z is a Wiener process (Black and Scholes, 1973). Note that we use the subscript t to denote a point in time (usually current time). The volatility $\sqrt{v}$ does not have a subscript; it is constant. The well-known pricing formula for the call under this model is given by

$$C_t = e^{-q\tau} S_t \, N(d_1) - X e^{-r\tau} N(d_2) \tag{15.4}$$

with

$$d_1 = \frac{1}{\sqrt{v\tau}} \left(\log\left(\frac{S_t}{X}\right) + \left(r - q + \frac{v}{2}\right)\tau \right) \tag{15.5a}$$

$$d_2 = \frac{1}{\sqrt{v\tau}} \left(\log\left(\frac{S_t}{X}\right) + \left(r - q - \frac{v}{2}\right)\tau \right) = d_1 - \sqrt{v\tau} \tag{15.5b}$$

and $N(\cdot)$ the Gaussian distribution function. For the put, we can "flip around" Eq. (15.4), that is, we multiply by -1, and replace $d_{1,2}$ by $-d_{1,2}$.

We can also use put–call parity, see Eqs. (15.1) and (15.2). The latter approach is convenient because it holds for any European call option, no matter how we computed the price. So we only need to price the call. The BS model is quickly coded with Matlab (an R implementation should be sufficiently similar, the function pnorm is the equivalent to Matlab's normcdf).

Listing 15.1. C-OptionCalibration/M/callBSM.m

```
 1  function C0 = callBSM(S,X,tau,r,q,v)
 2  % callBSM.m -- version 2010-10-26
 3  %   S    = spot
 4  %   X    = strike
 5  %   tau  = time to mat
 6  %   r    = riskfree rate
 7  %   q    = dividend yield
 8  %   v    = variance (vol squared)
 9  d1 = (log(S./X) + (r - q + v / 2) .* tau) ./ (sqrt(v * tau));
10  d2 = d1 - sqrt(v*tau);
11  C0 = S.*exp(-q.*tau).*normcdf(d1,0,1) - ...
12        X.*exp(-r.*tau).*normcdf(d2,0,1);
```

The BS pricing function is also implemented in a number of R packages. We have always liked RQuantLib (Eddelbuettel and Nguyen, 2010); see ?EuropeanOption after attaching the package.

Note that we have already given a pricing function for BS in Chapter 4; here we write the models in terms of variance v (not volatility). This is a convention chosen to be consistent with models that we describe later.

Suppose we fix all arguments $(S, r, \dots)$ except the volatility, so let us write $C(\sqrt{v})$ for the price of a plain vanilla call. Under BS, this price is a monotonously increasing function of volatility; the same holds for the put. Thus, letting C_{market} be the observed price of the call, the difference

$$C(\sqrt{v}) - C_{\text{market}} \tag{15.6}$$

will have exactly one zero. (This is not generally true for other types of options, notably not for barrier options.)

We can use any of the zero-finding methods described in Chapter 11 to locate the zero of the difference (15.6). Newton's method seems particularly attractive. There is a saddle point where the option's vega is maximized; see Manaster and Koehler (1982):

$$\sqrt{\frac{2}{\tau} \left| \log\left(\frac{S}{X}\right) + (r - q)\tau \right|}; \tag{15.7}$$

this point can be used as a starting value for Newton's method. We can directly use the function Newton0 given in Chapter 11.

Listing 15.2. C-OptionCalibration/M/computeIV.m

```
1 function iv = computeIV(S,X,tau,r,q,start,C)
2 % computeIV.m -- version 2010-10-24
3 % x is volatility; start is x0
4 diffF = @(x) callBSM(S,X,tau,r,q,x^2)-C;
5 iv = Newton0(diffF,start);
```

A test: we fix a volatility, price an option with it, and then try to recover this implied volatility.

Listing 15.3. C-OptionCalibration/M/exampleIV.m

```
 1 % exampleIV.m -- version 2010-10-26
 2 S = 110;  % spot
 3 X = 80;   % strike
 4 r = 0.09; % interest rate
 5 q = 0.00; % dividend
 6 tau = 1;  % time to maturity
 7
 8 % compute a market price
 9 trueVol = 0.3;
10 C = callBSM(S,X,tau,r,q,trueVol^2);
11
12 % ... and try to get trueVol back
13 start = sqrt(abs(log(S/X)+(r-q)*tau)*2/tau);
14 computeIV(S,X,tau,r,q,start,C)
```

The result is as expected.

```
ans =
    0.3000
```

A few remarks:
- Newton's method is usually very fast; we should be suspicious if it takes more than, say, 10 steps to converge. This may happen, however, for deep in-the-money or out-of-the money options, also for options with a long time until expiry.
- There is no restriction on how to compute the price. We may use analytical formulæ, but other methods will work as well, for instance, a binomial tree.
- The same holds for the derivative: we have used a finite difference to compute the vega, but we can use the analytic expression as well. Likewise, we could have used another method to find the zero, like bisection (to do so, exchange the function Newton0 in the code above with another function). Approximating the derivative is accurate enough, and in most cases Newton's method is going to be faster than bisection. Of course, if we price by MC, we need to make allowances for randomness; see the discussion on Greeks, page 258.
- The procedure is the same for European and American options.

The smile

BS is the standard option pricing model. Practitioners may not use it as it was intended, but it has become their language of choice. No other model will achieve this. In some products (for instance currencies), option prices are actually quoted in implied volatility. The success of the BS model stems not so much from its empirical quality, but from its simplicity and—important for us—its computational convenience. This convenience comes in two flavors. First, we have closed-form pricing equations. True, the Gaussian distribution function is not available analytically, but fast and precise approximations exist. Second, calibrating the model requires only one parameter to be determined, the volatility. We have seen that this can be readily computed from market prices with Newton's method or another zero-finding technique. So what is the trouble with BS?

It turns out that implied volatilities obtained by inverting the BS model vary systematically with strike and maturity. This relationship is called the volatility surface. For a given maturity, we generally have a curved shape: the smile. Figure 15.1 shows the implied volatilities of options as of the end of October 2010. Different strategies are possible for incorporating this surface into a model. We can accept that volatility is not constant across strikes and maturities, and directly model the volatility surface and its evolution. This is what most people in practice do. This assumes that a single underlier has different volatilities which does not make an internally consistent model. Nevertheless, model consistency is only a desirable byproduct, never the goal.

An alternative is to model the option prices such that the BS volatility surface is obtained, for instance by including locally varying volatility (Derman and Kani, 1994; Dupire, 1994), jumps, or by making volatility stochastic. In this chapter, we look into models that follow the latter two approaches, namely the models of Heston (1993) and Bates (1996). We first discuss how

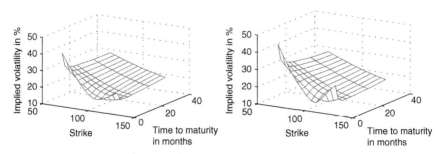

Figure 15.1 Implied volatilities for options on the S&P 500 (left) and DAX (right) as of 28 October 2010.

to price options under these models. For this, we describe how to implement an alternative pricing technique based on the characteristic function of the stock return. Then, we look into calibrating the models. Fast pricing routines are important since the heuristics that we use are computationally intensive; hence, to obtain calibration results in a reasonable period of time, we need to be able to evaluate the objective function (which requires pricing) speedily. Finally, we describe a computational experiment (from Gilli and Schumann, 2011) and its results.

15.2. Pricing with the characteristic function

There are several generic approaches to price options. The essence of BS is a no-arbitrage argument; it leads to a partial differential equation that can be solved numerically or, in particular cases, even analytically. In this section, we will discuss another pricing technique based on the characteristic function of the logarithm of the stock price. We will be brief on the background of this method. In fact, there exist variations of this kind of pricing formula; see Carr and Madan (1999), Duffie, Pan, and Singleton (2000), Lewis (2000), Chourdakis (2005), Fang and Oosterlee (2008). We have chosen the formulation of Bakshi and Madan (2000) because it is straightforward, and sufficiently fast. A good description of this pricing approach is given in the book by Schoutens (2003).

15.2.1. A pricing equation

European options can be priced by the following equation (Bakshi and Madan, 2000; Schoutens, 2003):

$$C_0 = e^{-q\tau} S_0 \Pi_1 - e^{-r\tau} X \Pi_2 \qquad (15.8)$$

where C_0 is the call price today (time $t = 0$), S_0 is the spot price of the underlier, and X is the strike price; r and q are the risk-free rate and dividend yield; time to expiration is denoted τ. The Π_j are calculated as

$$\Pi_1 = \frac{1}{2} + \frac{1}{\pi} \int_0^\infty \mathrm{Re}\left(\frac{e^{-i\omega \log(X)} \phi(\omega - i)}{i\omega \phi(-i)} \right) d\omega, \qquad (15.9a)$$

$$\Pi_2 = \frac{1}{2} + \frac{1}{\pi} \int_0^\infty \mathrm{Re}\left(\frac{e^{-i\omega \log(X)} \phi(\omega)}{i\omega} \right) d\omega. \qquad (15.9b)$$

We define $\Pi_j^* \equiv \pi(\Pi_j - 1/2)$ for the integrals in these equations. The symbol ϕ stands for the characteristic function of the log stock price; the function $\mathrm{Re}(\cdot)$ returns the real part of a complex number. For a given ϕ we can compute Π_1 and Π_2 by numerical integration and, hence, obtain prices for the call from Eq. (15.8). For the put, we can use put–call parity.

The Black–Scholes model

Given the dynamics of S, the log price $s_\tau = \log(S_\tau)$ follows a Gaussian distribution with $s_\tau \sim N\left(s_0 + \tau(r - q - \frac{1}{2}v), \tau v\right)$, where s_0 is the natural logarithm of the current spot price. The characteristic function of s_τ is given by

$$\phi_{BS}(\omega) = E(e^{i\omega s_\tau})$$

$$= \exp\left(i\omega s_0 + i\omega\tau\left(r - q - \frac{1}{2}v\right) + \frac{1}{2}i^2\omega^2 v\tau\right)$$

$$= \exp\left(i\omega s_0 + i\omega\tau(r - q) - \frac{1}{2}\left(i\omega + \omega^2\right)\tau v\right). \tag{15.10}$$

Note that the characteristic function is sometimes given for the log-return $\log(S_\tau/S_0)$, sometimes for the log price $s_\tau = \log S_\tau$. Since

$$\log\left(\frac{S_\tau}{S_0}\right) = s_\tau - s_0$$

we have

$$E\left(e^{i\omega(s_\tau - s_0)}\right) = e^{i\omega s_0} E\left(e^{i\omega s_\tau}\right).$$

Inserting (15.10) into Eq. (15.8) should, up to numerical precision, give the same result as Eq. (15.4). With Matlab, code for the characteristic function looks as follows.

Listing 15.4. C-OptionCalibration/M/cfBSMGeneric.m

```
1 function cf = cfBSMGeneric(om,S,tau,r,q,param)
2 % cfBSMGeneric.m -- version 2010-10-24
3 vT = param(1);
4 cf = exp(1i * om * log(S) + 1i * tau * (r - q) * ...
5        om - 0.5 * tau * vT * (1i * om + om .^ 2));
```

Note that we directly pass ω (om), S, τ, r, and q, and collect all other parameters (in this case, just the variance v) into a vector param. Also, it is good practice to use 1i when we want to use the imaginary unit i. The variable i (and also j) is defined as $0 + 1.0000i$ when we start Matlab, but it is also a prime candidate for a loop counter variable and may often be overwritten.

Merton's jump–diffusion model

Merton (1976) suggested modeling the underlier's movements as a diffusion with occasional jumps; thus we have

$$dS_t = (r - q - \lambda\mu_J)S_t dt + \sqrt{v}S_t dz_t + J_t S_t dN_t. \tag{15.11}$$

N_t is a Poisson counting process, with intensity λ; the J_t is the random jump size (given that a jump occurred). In Merton's model the log-jumps are distributed as

$$\log(1 + J_t) \sim \mathrm{N}\left(\log(1 + \mu_J) - \frac{v_J^2}{2}, v_J^2\right).$$

The pricing formula is the following (Merton, 1976, p. 135):

$$C_0 = \sum_{n=0}^{\infty} \frac{e^{-\lambda'\tau}(\lambda'\tau)^n}{n!} C_0'(r_n, \sqrt{v_n}) \tag{15.12}$$

where $\lambda' = \lambda(1 + \mu_J)$ and C_0' is the BS formula (15.4), but the prime indicates that C_0' is evaluated at adjusted values of r and v:

$$v_n = v + \frac{n v_J}{\tau}$$

$$r_n = r - \lambda \mu_J + \frac{n \log(1 + \mu_J)}{\tau}.$$

The factorial in Eq. (15.12) may easily lead to an overflow (`Inf`), but it is benign for two reasons. First, we do not need large numbers for n, a value of about 20 is well sufficient. Second (if we insist on large n), Matlab or R will evaluate `1/Inf` as zero; hence, the summing will add zeros for large n. Numerical analysts may also prefer to replace $n!$ by $\exp(\sum_{i=1}^n \log i)$ since this leads to better accuracy for large n. This will not cost us much, but again, for Merton's model it is not really needed.

Depending on the implementation, working with large values for n may lead to a warning or an error, and so interrupt a computation. In R, for instance, the handling of such a warning will depend on the options setting:

```
> options()$warn
[1] 0
```

This is the standard setting. Computing the factorial for a large number will result in a warning; the computation continues.

```
> factorial(200)
[1] Inf
Warning message:
In factorial(200) : value out of range in 'gammafn'
```

But with `warn` set to 2, any warning will be transformed into an error. Thus,

```
> options(warn=2)
> factorial(200)
Error in factorial(200) :
    (converted from warning) value out of range in 'gammafn'
```

and our computation breaks. We may want to safeguard against such possible errors. We can, for instance, replace the function call `factorial(n)` by its actual calculation which produces:

```
> options(warn=2)
> exp( sum(log(1:200)) )
[1] Inf
> prod(1:200)
[1] Inf
```

Or even simpler, as in Matlab's implementation of `factorial`, we can check the given value of n; if it is too large, we have it replaced with a more reasonable value.

The characteristic function of Merton's model is given by

$$\phi_{\text{Merton}} = e^{A+B} \tag{15.13}$$

where

$$A = i\omega s_0 + i\omega\tau\left(r - q - \frac{1}{2}v - \mu_J\right) + \frac{1}{2}i^2\omega^2 v\tau$$

$$B = \lambda\tau\left(\exp\left(i\omega\log(1+\mu_J) - \frac{1}{2}i\omega v_J^2 - \omega^2 v_J^2\right) - 1\right);$$

see Gatheral (2006, Chapter 5). The A-term in ϕ_{Merton} corresponds to the BS dynamics with a drift adjustment to account for the jumps; the B-term adds the jump component. Like in the BS case, we can compare the results from Eq. (15.8) with those obtained from Eq. (15.12).

The function `cfMertonGeneric` codes the characteristic function with Matlab. Note that the arguments are the same as for BS; `param` collects the four parameters necessary to specify the process.

Listing 15.5. C-OptionCalibration/M/cfMertonGeneric.m

```
 1 function cf = cfMertonGeneric(om,S,tau,r,q,param)
 2 % cfMertonGeneric.m -- version 2010-10-24
 3 % S      = spot
 4 % tau    = time to mat
 5 % r      = riskfree rate
 6 % q      = dividend yield
 7 % v      = variance (volatility squared)
 8 % -- jumps --
 9 % lambda = intensity;
10 % muJ    = mean of jumps;
11 % vJ     = variance of jumps;
12 v        = param(1);
13 lambda   = param(2);
14 muJ      = param(3);
15 vJ       = param(4);
16 A = 1i*om*log(S) + 1i*om*tau*(r-q-0.5*v-lambda*muJ) ...
17      - 0.5*(om.^2)*v*tau;
18 B = lambda*tau*(exp(1i*om*log(1+muJ) ...
19      -0.5*1i*om*vJ-0.5*vJ*om.^2) - 1);
20 cf = exp(A + B);
```

The Heston model

Under the Heston (1993) model, the stock price S and its variance v are described by

$$dS_t = rS_t dt + \sqrt{v_t} S_t dz_t^{(1)} \tag{15.14a}$$

$$dv_t = \kappa(\theta - v_t)dt + \sigma\sqrt{v_t} dz_t^{(2)}. \tag{15.14b}$$

The long-run variance is denoted by θ, mean reversion speed is κ, and σ is the volatility-of-volatility. The Wiener processes $z^{(\cdot)}$ have correlation ρ. For $\sigma \to 0$, the Heston dynamics approach those of BS. A thorough discussion of the model can be found in Gatheral (2006). The characteristic function of the log price in the Heston model looks as follows; see Albrecher, Mayer, Schoutens, and Tistaert (2007).

$$\phi_{\text{Heston}} = e^{A+B+C} \tag{15.15}$$

where

$$A = i\omega s_0 + i\omega(r - q)\tau$$

$$B = \frac{\theta\kappa}{\sigma^2}\left((\kappa - \rho\sigma i\omega - d)\tau - 2\log\left(\frac{1 - ge^{-d\tau}}{1 - g}\right)\right)$$

$$C = \frac{\frac{v_0}{\sigma^2}\left(\kappa - \rho\sigma i\omega - d\right)\left(1 - e^{-d\tau}\right)}{1 - ge^{-d\tau}}$$

$$d = \sqrt{(\rho\sigma i\omega - \kappa)^2 + \sigma^2(i\omega + \omega^2)}$$

$$g = \frac{\kappa - \rho\sigma i\omega - d}{\kappa - \rho\sigma i\omega + d}.$$

Listing 15.6. C-OptionCalibration/M/cfHestonGeneric.m

```
1  function cf = cfHestonGeneric(om,S,tau,r,q,param)
2  % cfHestonGeneric.m -- version 2010-10-04
3  % S     = spot
4  % tau   = time to mat
5  % r     = riskfree rate
6  % q     = dividend yield
7  % v0    = initial variance
8  % vT    = long run variance (theta in Heston's paper)
9  % rho   = correlation
10 % k     = speed of mean reversion (kappa in Heston's paper)
11 % sigma = vol of vol
12
13 v0    = param(1);
14 vT    = param(2);
15 rho   = param(3);
16 k     = param(4);
```

```
17 sigma = param(5);
18
19 d = sqrt( (rho * sigma * 1i*om - k).^2 + sigma^2 * ...
20           (1i*om + om .^ 2) );
21 g = (k - rho*sigma*1i*om - d) ./ (k - rho*sigma*1i*om + d);
22 cf1 = 1i*om .* (log(S) + (r - q) * tau);
23 cf2 = vT * k / (sigma^2) * ((k - rho*sigma*1i*om - d) * ...
24       tau - 2 * log((1 - g .* exp(-d * tau)) ./ (1 - g)));
25 cf3 = v0/sigma^2 * (k - rho*sigma*1i*om - d) .* ...
26       (1 - exp(-d*tau)) ./ (1 - g .* exp(-d * tau));
27 cf  = exp(cf1 + cf2 + cf3);
```

The Bates model

This model, described in Bates (1996), adds jumps to the dynamics of the Heston model. The stock price S and its variance v are described by

$$dS_t = (r - q - \lambda \mu_J) S_t dt + \sqrt{v_t} S_t dz_t^{(1)} + J_t S_t dN_t$$

$$dv_t = \kappa(\theta - v_t)dt + \sigma\sqrt{v_t}dz^{(2)}.$$

N_t is a Poisson count process with intensity λ; hence the probability to have a jump of size one is λdt. As in Merton's model, the logarithm of the jump size J_t is distributed as a Gaussian, that is,

$$\log(1 + J_t) = N\left(\log(1 + \mu_J) - \frac{v_J^2}{2}, v_J\right).$$

The characteristic function becomes (Schoutens, Simons, and Tistaert, 2004):

$$\phi_{\text{Bates}} = e^{A+B+C+D} \tag{15.16}$$

with

$$A = i\omega s_0 + i\omega(r - q)\tau$$

$$B = \frac{\theta\kappa}{\sigma^2}\left((\kappa - \rho\sigma i\omega - d)\tau - 2\log\left(\frac{1 - ge^{-d\tau}}{1 - g}\right)\right)$$

$$C = \frac{\frac{v_0}{\sigma^2}\left(\kappa - \rho\sigma i\omega - d\right)\left(1 - e^{-d\tau}\right)}{1 - ge^{-d\tau}}$$

$$D = -\lambda\mu_J i\omega\tau + \lambda\tau\left((1 + \mu_J)^{i\omega}e^{\frac{1}{2}v_J^2 i\omega(i\omega - 1)} - 1\right)$$

$$d = \sqrt{(\rho\sigma i\omega - \kappa)^2 + \sigma^2(i\omega + \omega^2)}$$

$$g = \frac{\kappa - \rho\sigma i\omega - d}{\kappa - \rho\sigma i\omega + d}.$$

Since the jumps are assumed independent, the characteristic function is the product of ϕ_{Heston} and the function for the jump part (D). We will see below (see Fig. 15.3 on page 526) that adding jumps makes it easier to introduce curvature into the volatility surface, at least for short maturities.

Listing 15.7. C-OptionCalibration/M/cfBatesGeneric.m

```
 1 function cf = cfBatesGeneric(om,S,tau,r,q,param)
 2 % cfBatesGeneric.m -- version 2010-10-24
 3 % S      = spot
 4 % tau    = time to mat
 5 % r      = riskfree rate
 6 % q      = dividend yield
 7 % v0     = initial variance
 8 % vT     = long run variance (theta in Heston's paper)
 9 % rho    = correlation
10 % k      = speed of mean reversion (kappa in Heston's paper)
11 % sigma  = vol of vol
12 % -- jumps --
13 % lambda = intensity;
14 % muJ    = mean of jumps;
15 % vJ     = variance of jumps;
16 %
17 v0    = param(1);
18 vT    = param(2);
19 rho   = param(3);
20 k     = param(4);
21 sigma = param(5);
22 %
23 lambda= param(6);
24 muJ   = param(7);
25 vJ    = param(8);
26
27 d = sqrt( (rho * sigma * 1i*om - k).^2 + ...
28            sigma^2 * (1i*om + om .^ 2) );
29 g = (k - rho*sigma*1i*om - d) ./ (k - rho*sigma*1i*om + d);
30 cf1 = 1i*om .* (log(S) + (r - q) * tau);
31 cf2 = vT*k / (sigma^2) * ((k - rho*sigma*1i*om - d) * tau - ...
32       2 * log((1 - g .* exp(-d * tau)) ./ (1 - g)));
33 cf3 = v0/sigma^2*(k-rho*sigma*1i*om-d).*(1-exp(-d*tau)) ./ ...
34        (1-g.*exp(-d*tau));
35 % jump
36 cf4 = -lambda*muJ*1i*tau*om + lambda*tau* ...
37        ((1+muJ).^(1i*om) .* exp( vJ*(1i*om/2) .* (1i*om-1) )-1);
38 cf  = exp(cf1 + cf2 + cf3 + cf4);
```

15.2.2. Numerical integration

Pricing with Matlab's quad

Let us start with a straightforward implementation of Eq. (15.8). To compute the integrals, we use Matlab's quad function. This function uses an adaptive quadrature algorithm with Simpson's rule (this quadrature rule is described below). For a pedagogical description of `quad`, see Moler (2004, Chapter 6). For more details on `quad`, see Gander and Gautschi (2000).

Black–Scholes

The classic formula was given above. With the characteristic function:

Listing 15.8. C-OptionCalibration/M/callBSMcf.m

```
 1 function call = callBSMcf(S,X,tau,r,q,vT)
 2 % callBSMcf.m -- version 2010-10-24
 3 % S     = spot
 4 % X     = strike
 5 % tau   = time to mat
 6 % r     = riskfree rate
 7 % q     = dividend yield
 8 % vT    = variance (volatility squared)
 9 vP1 = 0.5 + 1/pi * quad(@P1,0,200,1e-14,[],S,X,tau,r,q,vT);
10 vP2 = 0.5 + 1/pi * quad(@P2,0,200,1e-14,[],S,X,tau,r,q,vT);
11 call = exp(-q * tau) * S * vP1 - exp(-r * tau) * X * vP2;
12 end
13 %
14 function p = P1(om,S,X,tau,r,q,vT)
15 p = real(exp(-1i*log(X)*om) .* cfBSM(om-1i,S,tau,r,q,vT) ./ ...
16     (1i * om * S * exp((r-q) * tau)));
17 end
18 %
19 function p = P2(om,S,X,tau,r,q,vT)
20 p = real(exp(-1i*log(X)*om) .* cfBSM(om  ,S,tau,r,q,vT) ./ ...
21     (1i * om));
22 end
23 %
24 function cf = cfBSM(om,S,tau,r,q,vT)
25 cf = exp(1i * om * log(S) + 1i * tau * (r - q) * om - ...
26     0.5 * tau * vT * (1i * om + om .^ 2));
27 end
```

Merton

The classic formula can be implemented as follows.

Listing 15.9. C-OptionCalibration/M/callMerton.m

```
 1 function call = callMerton(S,X,tau,r,q,v,lambda,muJ,vJ,N)
 2 % callMerton.m -- version 2010-10-24
 3 % S      = spot
 4 % X      = strike
 5 % tau    = time to mat
 6 % r      = riskfree rate
 7 % q      = dividend yield
 8 % v      = variance (volatility squared)
 9 % lambda = intensity of poisson process
10 % muJ    = mean jump size
11 % vJ     = variance of jump process
12 % N      = number of jumps to be included in sum
```

```
13 lambda2  = lambda*(1+muJ); call = 0;
14 for n=0:N
15     v_n = v + n*vJ/tau;
16     r_n = r - lambda*muJ+ n*log(1+muJ)/tau;
17     call = call + ( exp(-lambda2*tau) * (lambda2*tau)^n ) * ...
18         callBSM(S,X,tau,r_n,q,v_n)/ exp( sum(log(1:n)) );
19 end
```

With the characteristic function:

Listing 15.10. C-OptionCalibration/M/callMertoncf.m

```
1  % callMertoncf.m -- version 2010-11-13
2  function call = callMertoncf(S,X,tau,r,q,v,lambda,muJ,vJ)
3  % S     = spot
4  % X     = strike
5  % tau   = time to mat
6  % r     = riskfree rate
7  % q     = dividend yield
8  % v     = variance (volatility squared)
9  % lambda= intensity of poisson process
10 % muJ   = mean jump size
11 % vJ    = variance of jump process
12 vP1 = 0.5 + 1/pi * ...
13     quad(@P1,0,200,1e-14,[],S,X,tau,r,q,v,lambda,muJ,vJ);
14 vP2 = 0.5 + 1/pi * ...
15     quad(@P2,0,200,1e-14,[],S,X,tau,r,q,v,lambda,muJ,vJ);
16 call = exp(-q * tau) * S * vP1 - exp(-r * tau) * X * vP2;
17 end
18 %
19 function p = P1(om,S,X,tau,r,q,v,lambda,muJ,vJ)
20 p = real(exp(-1i*log(X)*om) .* ...
21     cfMerton(om-1i,S,tau,r,q,v,lambda,muJ,vJ) ./ ...
22         (1i * om * S * exp((r-q) * tau)));
23 end
24 %
25 function p = P2(om,S,X,tau,r,q,v,lambda,muJ,vJ)
26 p = real(exp(-1i*log(X)*om) .* ...
27     cfMerton(om  ,S,tau,r,q,v,lambda,muJ,vJ) ./ (1i * om));
28 end
29 %
30 function cf = cfMerton(om,S,tau,r,q,v,lambda,muJ,vJ)
31 A = 1i*om*log(S) + 1i*om*tau*(r-q-0.5*v-lambda*muJ) - ...
32     0.5*(om.^2)*v*tau;
33 B = lambda*tau*(exp(1i*om*log(1+muJ)-0.5*1i*om*vJ - ...
34     0.5*vJ*om.^2) -1);
35 cf = exp(A + B);
36 end
```

Heston

With Matlab, we can price call options under the Heston model with the following function.

Listing 15.11. C-OptionCalibration/M/callHestoncf.m

```
 1 function call = callHestoncf(S,X,tau,r,q,v0,vT,rho,k,sigma)
 2 % callHestoncf.m -- version 2010-10-25
 3 % callHestoncf Pricing function for European calls
 4 % callprice = callHestoncf(S,X,tau,r,q,v0,vT,rho,k,sigma)
 5 % ---
 6 % S    = spot
 7 % X    = strike
 8 % tau  = time to mat
 9 % r    = riskfree rate
10 % q    = dividend yield
11 % v0   = initial variance
12 % vT   = long run variance (theta in Heston's paper)
13 % rho  = correlation
14 % k    = speed of mean reversion (kappa in Heston's paper)
15 % sigma = vol of vol
16 vP1 = 0.5 + 1/pi * ...
17        quadl(@P1,0,200,[],[],S,X,tau,r,q,v0,vT,rho,k,sigma);
18 vP2 = 0.5 + 1/pi * ...
19        quadl(@P2,0,200,[],[],S,X,tau,r,q,v0,vT,rho,k,sigma);
20 call = exp(-q * tau) * S * vP1 - exp(-r * tau) * X * vP2;
21 end
22 %
23 function p = P1(om,S,X,tau,r,q,v0,vT,rho,k,sigma)
24 i=1i;
25 p = real(exp(-i*log(X)*om) .* ...
26            cfHeston(om-i,S,tau,r,q,v0,vT,rho,k,sigma) ./ ...
27            (i * om * S * exp((r-q) * tau)));
28 end
29 %
30 function p = P2(om,S,X,tau,r,q,v0,vT,rho,k,sigma)
31 i=1i;
32 p = real(exp(-i*log(X)*om) .* ...
33            cfHeston(om,S,tau,r,q,v0,vT,rho,k,sigma) ./ (i * om));
34 end
35 %
36 function cf = cfHeston(om,S,tau,r,q,v0,vT,rho,k,sigma)
37 d = sqrt((rho * sigma * 1i*om - k).^2 + sigma^2 * ...
38            (1i*om + om .^ 2));
39 g2  = (k - rho*sigma*1i*om - d) ./ (k - rho*sigma*1i*om + d);
40 cf1 = 1i*om .* (log(S) + (r - q) * tau);
41 cf2 = vT * k / (sigma^2) * ((k - rho*sigma*1i*om - d) * ...
42        tau - 2 * log((1 - g2 .* exp(-d * tau)) ./ (1 - g2)));
43 cf3 = v0 / sigma^2 * (k - rho*sigma*1i*om - d) .* ...
44        (1 - exp(-d * tau)) ./ (1 - g2 .* exp(-d * tau));
45 cf  = exp(cf1 + cf2 + cf3);
46 end
```

We can translate this function into R. The main ingredient, the `quad` function, is replaced by a call to `integrate` from the `stats` package (which is part of any standard installation of R).

Listing 15.12. C-OptionCalibration/R/callHestoncf.R

```
 1 callHestoncf <- function(S,X,tau,r,q,v0,vT,rho,k,sigma,
 2          implVol = FALSE) {
 3 # callHestoncf.R -- version 2010-01-16
 4 # S     = spot
 5 # X     = strike
 6 # tau   = time to mat
 7 # r     = riskfree rate
 8 # q     = dividend yield
 9 # v0    = initial variance
10 # vT    = long run variance (theta in Heston's paper)
11 # rho   = correlation
12 # k     = speed of mean reversion (kappa in Heston's paper)
13 # sigma = vol of vol
14 # implVol = compute equivalent BSM volatility?
15
16 # -- functions --
17 P1 <- function(om,S,X,tau,r,q,v0,vT,rho,k,sigma) {
18     i <- 1i
19     p <- Re(exp(-i*log(X)*om) *
20             cfHeston(om-i,S,tau,r,q,v0,vT,rho,k,sigma) /
21                 (i * om * S * exp((r-q) * tau)))
22     return(p)
23     }
24 P2 <- function(om,S,X,tau,r,q,v0,vT,rho,k,sigma) {
25     i <- 1i
26     p <- Re(exp(-i*log(X)*om) *
27             cfHeston(om  ,S,tau,r,q,v0,vT,rho,k,sigma) /
28                 (i * om))
29     return(p)
30     }
31 cfHeston <- function(om,S,tau,r,q,v0,vT,rho,k,sigma) {
32     d <- sqrt((rho * sigma * 1i * om - k)^2 + sigma^2 *
33             (1i * om + om ^ 2))
34     g2 <- (k - rho * sigma * 1i * om - d) /
35             (k - rho * sigma * 1i * om + d)
36     cf1 <- 1i * om * (log(S) + (r - q) * tau)
37     cf2 <- vT*k/(sigma^2)*((k - rho * sigma * 1i * om - d) *
38             tau - 2 * log((1 - g2 * exp(-d * tau)) / (1 - g2)))
39     cf3 <- v0 / sigma^2 * (k - rho * sigma * 1i * om - d) *
40             (1 - exp(-d * tau)) / (1 - g2 * exp(-d * tau))
41     cf  <- exp(cf1 + cf2 + cf3)
42     return(cf)
43     }
44 # -- pricing --
45 vP1 <- 0.5 + 1/pi * integrate(P1,lower = 0,upper = 200,
46                     S,X,tau,r,q,v0,vT,rho,k,sigma)$value
47 vP2 <- 0.5 + 1/pi * integrate(P2,lower = 0,upper = 200,
48                     S,X,tau,r,q,v0,vT,rho,k,sigma)$value
49 result <- exp(-q * tau) * S * vP1 - exp(-r * tau) * X * vP2;
50
51 # -- implied BSM vol --
52 if (implVol) {
53     diffPrice <- function(vol,call,S,X,tau,r,q){
54         d1 <- (log(S/X)+(r - q + vol^2/2)*tau)/(vol*sqrt(tau))
55         d2 <- d1 - vol*sqrt(tau)
56         callBSM <- S * exp(-q * tau) * pnorm(d1) -
```

```
57       X * exp(-r * tau) * pnorm(d2)
58       return(call - callBSM)
59     }
60     impliedVol <- uniroot(diffPrice, interval = c(0,2),
61                   call = result, S = S, X = X,
62                   tau = tau, r = r, q = q)[[1]]
63     result <- list(callPrice = result,impliedVol = impliedVol)
64   }
65   return(result)
66 }
```

Note that the function also has an argument implVol that defaults to FALSE. If set to TRUE, the function returns a list with the callPrice and the volatility that would give the same price with the BS model. Here we have used the function uniroot.

Bates
With Matlab:

Listing 15.13. C-OptionCalibration/M/callBatescf.m

```
1 function call = callBatescf(S,X,tau,r,q,v0,vT,rho,k,sigma,
     lambda,muJ,vJ)
2 % callBatescf.m -- version 2011-01-07
3 % S    = spot
4 % X    = strike
5 % tau  = time to mat
6 % r    = riskfree rate
7 % q    = dividend yield
8 % v0   = initial variance
9 % vT   = long run variance (theta in Heston's paper)
10 % rho  = correlation
11 % k    = speed of mean reversion (kappa in Heston's paper)
12 % sigma = vol of vol
13 % lambda= intensity of jumps;
14 % muJ  = mean of jumps;
15 % vJ   = variance of jumps;
16 vP1 = 0.5 + 1/pi * quadl(@P1,0,200,[],[],S,X,tau,r,q,v0,vT,...
17                     rho,k,sigma,lambda,muJ,vJ);
18 vP2 = 0.5 + 1/pi * quadl(@P2,0,200,[],[],S,X,tau,r,q,v0,vT,...
19                     rho,k,sigma,lambda,muJ,vJ);
20 call = exp(-q * tau) * S * vP1 - exp(-r * tau) * X * vP2;
21 end
22 %
23 function p = P1(om,S,X,tau,r,q,v0,vT,rho,k,sigma,lambda,muJ,vJ)
24 i=1i;
25 p = real(exp(-i*log(X)*om) .* cfBates(om-i,S,tau,r,q,v0,vT,...
26     rho,k,sigma,lambda,muJ,vJ)./(i * om * S * exp((r-q)*tau)));
27 end
28 %
29 function p = P2(om,S,X,tau,r,q,v0,vT,rho,k,sigma,lambda,muJ,vJ)
30 i=1i;
31 p = real(exp(-i*log(X)*om) .* cfBates(om ,S,tau,r,q,v0,vT,...
32         rho,k,sigma,lambda,muJ,vJ) ./ (i * om));
33 end
```

```
34 %
35 function cf = cfBates(om,S,tau,r,q,v0,vT,rho,k,sigma,lambda,muJ,
      vJ)
36 d = sqrt((rho * sigma * 1i*om - k).^2 + sigma^2 * ...
37       (1i*om + om .^ 2));
38 %
39 g2 = (k - rho*sigma*1i*om - d) ./ (k - rho*sigma*1i*om + d);
40 %
41 cf1 = 1i*om .* (log(S) + (r - q) * tau);
42 cf2 = vT * k / (sigma^2) * ((k - rho*sigma*1i*om - d) * ...
43       tau - 2 * log((1 - g2 .* exp(-d * tau)) ./ (1 - g2)));
44 cf3 = v0 / sigma^2 * (k - rho*sigma*1i*om - d) .* ...
45       (1 - exp(-d * tau)) ./ (1 - g2 .* exp(-d * tau));
46 % jump
47 cf4 = -lambda * muJ * 1i * tau * om + lambda*tau*...
48       ((1+muJ).^(1i*om) .* exp( vJ*(1i*om/2) .* (1i*om-1) )-1);
49 cf  = exp(cf1 + cf2 + cf3 + cf4);
50 end
```

The following example shows how to call the functions. We have wrapped all function calls in `tic`, `toc` calls to give an idea of the time required to compute a price. For an actual performance comparison, we should always run the functions many times and then look at the average elapsed time.

Listing 15.14. C-OptionCalibration/M/example.m

```
1 % example.m -- version 2010-10-24
2 %% example BSM
3 S       = 100;       % spot price
4 q       = 0.08;      % dividend yield (eg, 0.03)
5 r       = 0.02;      % interest rate (eg, 0.03)
6 X       = 100;       % strike
7 tau     = 1;         % time to maturity
8 v       = 0.2^2;     % variance
9 clc
10 tic, call = callBSMcf(S,X,tau,r,q,v); t=toc;
11 fprintf('BSM\nwith CF:         %6.3f, required time: %4.3f
      seconds\n',call,t)
12
13 tic, call = callBSM(S,X,tau,r,q,v);t=toc;
14 fprintf('classic formula: %6.3f, required time: %4.3f seconds\n-
      --\n\n',call,t)
15
16 %% example Heston
17 S       = 100;
18 q       = 0.08;
19 r       = 0.02;
20 X       = 100;
21 tau     = 1;
22 k       = 1.0;        % mean reversion speed (kappa in paper)
23 sigma   = 0.00001;      % vol of vol
24 rho     = -0.7;       % correlation
25 v0      = 0.2^2;      % current variances
```

```
26 vT       = 0.2^2;    % long-run variance (theta in paper)
27
28 tic, call = callHestoncf(S,X,tau,r,q,v0,vT,rho,k,sigma); t=toc;
29 fprintf('Heston\nwith CF:         %6.3f, required time: %4.3f
         seconds\n---\n\n',call,t)
30
31 %% example Bates
32 S       = 100;
33 q       = 0.08;
34 r       = 0.02;
35 X       = 100;
36 tau     = 1;
37 k       = 1.0;      % mean reversion speed (kappa in paper)
38 sigma   = 0.00001;  % vol of vol
39 rho     = -0.3;     % correlation
40 v0      = 0.2^2;    % current variances
41 vT      = 0.2^2;    % long-run variance (theta in paper)
42 lambda  = 0.0;      % intensity of jumps;
43 muJ     = -0.0;     % mean of jumps;
44 vJ      = 0.00001^2;  % variance of jumps;
45
46 tic, call = callBatescf(S,X,tau,r,q,v0,vT, ...
47                        rho,k,sigma,lambda,muJ,vJ); t=toc;
48 fprintf('Bates\nwith CF:         %6.3f, required time: %4.3f
         seconds\n---\n\n',call,t)
49
50 %% example Merton jump--diffusion
51 S       = 100;
52 q       = 0.08;
53 r       = 0.02;
54 X       = 100;
55 tau     = 1;
56 v       = 0.2^2;    % variance (volatility squared)
57 lambda  = 0.2;      % intensity of jumps;
58 muJ     = -0.1;     % mean of jumps;
59 vJ      = 0.2^2;    % variance of jumps;
60 N       = 20;       % number of jumps for classic formula
61
62 tic, call = callMertoncf(S,X,tau,r,q,v,lambda,muJ,vJ); t = toc;
63 fprintf('Merton jump-diffusion\nwith CF:        %6.3f, required
         time: %4.3f seconds\n',call,t)
64
65 tic, call = callMerton(S,X,tau,r,q,v,lambda,muJ,vJ,N); t = toc;
66 fprintf('classic formula: %6.3f, required time: %4.3f seconds\n
         ',call,t)
```

Running this code should result in the following output.

```
BSM
with CF:          5.064, required time: 0.004 seconds
classic formula:  5.064, required time: 0.000 seconds
---


Heston
with CF:          5.064, required time: 0.008 seconds
---
```

```
Bates
with CF:         5.064, required time: 0.008 seconds
---

Merton jump-diffusion
with CF:         5.702, required time: 0.004 seconds
classic formula: 5.702, required time: 0.002 seconds
```

The smile, again: comparing the models

To get some intuition about these models, we now (i) choose a model and fix parameter values, (ii) price a matrix of options (different strikes, different maturities) under this model, and (iii) compute the implied volatilities under BS. Figures 15.2–15.4 show examples. On the left, we always plot the implied volatilities for a given time to maturity (one month and three years) but different strikes. On the right, we plot term structure of implied volatility, that is, the implied volatility of at-the-money options for times to maturity up to three years.

The Bates model nests BS, Heston and Merton; therefore, the implied volatilities of those models can all be reproduced with this model.

A primer on numerical integration

Matlab's `quad` is reliable but slow. The pricing can be accelerated by pre-computing a fixed number of nodes and weights under the given quadrature scheme. We start with a brief overview of how numerical integration works. For a textbook exposition, see, for instance, Heath (2005, Chapter 8). Davis and Rabinowitz (2007) is a comprehensive reference. A highly recommended paper is Trefethen (2008a); it is one of the rare occasions where actual convergence—as opposed to theoretical optimality—is discussed for specific rules.

The essence of numerical integration, or quadrature, is to replace an integral

$$\int_a^b f(x)\mathrm{d}x$$

by the sum

$$\sum_{i=1}^{n} w_i f(x_i). \tag{15.17}$$

The x_i are called the nodes or abscissas, the w_i are weights. We either assume there are n nodes, or that the interval $[a, b]$ is subdivided into m partitions. Quadrature rules detail how to choose these nodes and weights. A rule is called closed if it requires evaluating the endpoints a and b; otherwise, the rule is called open.

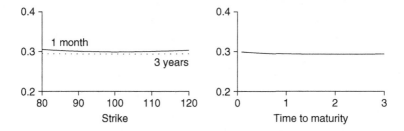

(a) The base case: $S = 100$, $r = 2\%$, $q = 2\%$, $\sqrt{v_0} = 30\%$, $\sqrt{\theta} = 30\%$, $\rho = 0$, $\kappa = 1$, $\sigma = 30\%$.

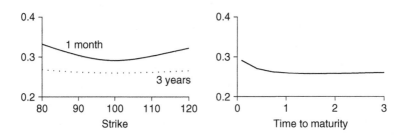

(b) $\sigma = 90\%$: short-term smile (the position of the kink is controlled by ρ); often we need substantial volatility-of-volatility to induce a smile.

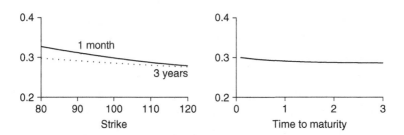

(c) $\rho = -0.5$: skew (a positive correlation induces positive slope).

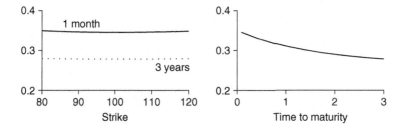

(d) $v_0 = 35\%$, $\theta = 25\%$: term structure is determined by the difference between current and long-run variance, and κ.

Figure 15.2 Heston model: re-creating the implied volatility surface. The graphics show the BS-implied volatilities obtained from prices under the Heston model. The panels on the right show the implied volatility of ATM options.

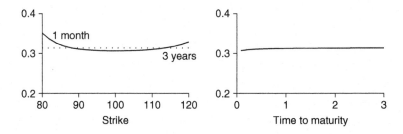

(a) The base case: $S = 100$, $r = 2\%$, $q = 2\%$, $\sqrt{v_0} = 30\%$, $\sqrt{\theta} = 30\%$, $\rho = 0$, $\kappa = 1$, $\sigma = 0.0\%$, $\lambda = 0.1$, $\mu_J = 0$, $v_J = 30\%$. Volatility-of-volatility is zero, as is the jump mean.

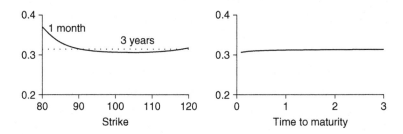

(b) $\mu_J = -10\%$: more asymmetry

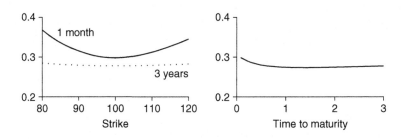

(c) $\sigma = 90\%$: stochastic volatility included.

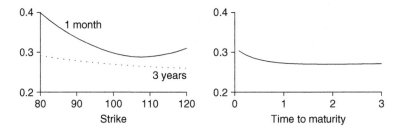

(d) $\mu_J = -10\%$, $\sigma = 70\%$, $\rho = -0.3$.

Figure 15.3 Bates model: re-creating the implied volatility surface. The graphics show the BS-implied volatilities obtained from prices under the Bates model. The panels on the right show the implied volatility of ATM options.

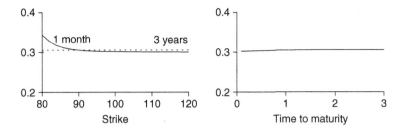

(a) $S = 100, r = 2\%, q = 2\%, \sqrt{v} = 30\%, \lambda = 0.01, \mu_J = -50\%, v_J = 30\%$.

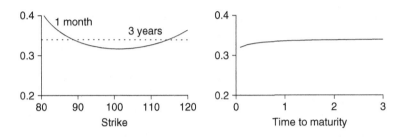

(b) $S = 100, r = 2\%, q = 2\%, \sqrt{v} = 30\%, \lambda = 0.30, \mu_J = -2\%, v_J = 30\%$.

Figure 15.4 Merton model: re-creating the implied volatility surface. The graphics show the BS-implied volatilities obtained from prices under the Merton model. The panels on the right show the implied volatility of ATM options. Importantly, jumps need to be volatile to get a smile (i.e., $v_J \geq 30\%$).

An intuitive approach is to follow Riemann's original idea and replace the integral (15.17) by the sum of the area of m rectangles. Such a Riemann sum is defined as follows. Assume

$$a = x_1 < x_2 < \cdots < x_m < x_{m+1} = b,$$

then any collection of nodes $v_k \in [x_k, x_{k+1}]$, for $k = 1, \ldots, m$, defines a Riemann sum

$$\sum_{k=1}^{m} (x_{k+1} - x_k) f(v_k). \tag{15.18}$$

We define $h \equiv (b-a)/m$; then some possible quadrature rules based on Riemann sums are:

Rectangular rule $h \sum_{k=0}^{m-1} f(a + kh)$ (evaluation on the left side), or

$h \sum_{k=1}^{m} f(a + kh)$ (evaluation on the right side).

Midpoint rule   We evaluate the rectangle in the middle, hence

$$h\sum_{k=0}^{m} f\left(a + \left[k + \tfrac{1}{2}\right] h\right).$$

Trapezoidal rule $h\left(\sum_{k=1}^{m-1} f(a+kh) + \frac{f(a)}{2} + \frac{f(b)}{2}\right)$ for $m \geq 2$; or

$h\left(\frac{f(a)+f(b)}{2}\right)$ for $m = 1$.

The following code shows how to implement such rules with Matlab. We include a call to Matlab's quad function as a comparison.

Listing 15.15. C-OptionCalibration/M/exampleQuad1.m

```
1  % exampleQuad1.m -- version 2010-10-24
2  %% Riemann sums - example
3  Fun1 = @(x)(exp(-x));
4  m = 5; a = 0; b = 5; h = (b-a)/m;
5
6  % rectangular rule -- left
7  w = h; k = 0:(m-1); x = a + k * h;
8  fprintf('rectangular (left)  with %i rectangles:\t %f\n',m,sum(w
       * Fun1(x)))
9
10 % rectangular rule -- right
11 w = h; k = 1:m; x = a + k * h;
12 fprintf('rectangular (right) with %i rectangles:\t %f\n',m,sum(w
       * Fun1(x)))
13
14 %midpoint rule
15 w = h; k = 0:(m-1); x = a + (k + 0.5)*h;
16 fprintf('midpoint            with %i rectangles:\t %f\n',m,sum(w
       * Fun1(x)))
17
18 %trapezoidal rule
19 w = h; k = 1:(m-1); x = [a a + k*h b];
20 aux = w * Fun1(x); aux([1 end]) = aux([1 end])/2;
21 fprintf('trapezoidal         with %i rectangles:\t %f\n',m,sum(
       aux))
22
23 %adaptive Simpson
24 fprintf('Adaptive Simpson (Matlab):\t\t\t\t %f\n',quad(Fun1,a,b)
       )
```

```
rectangular (left)  with 5 rectangles:   1.571317
rectangular (right) with 5 rectangles:   0.578055
midpoint            with 5 rectangles:   0.953052
trapezoidal         with 5 rectangles:   1.074686
Adaptive Simpson (Matlab):               0.993262
```

Interpolatory rules

The three rules stated above partition the interval $[a,b]$ into equal-sized subintervals and approximate the integrand in each subinterval by a rectangle or a trapezoid. The accuracy of this approach improves as the number of subintervals increases. But rectangles or trapezoids may not be natural candidates to approximate a function; if the function is smooth, we can do better. Given $n+1$ nodes, we can fit a polynomial of order n that interpolates the function values at these nodes. This polynomial can then be integrated exactly as an approximation of the true integral. We do not actually have to fit and integrate a polynomial in each case; it turns out that the approach is equivalent to setting the weights w such that the monomials $x^0, x^1, \ldots, x^n$ are integrated exactly; see Davis and Rabinowitz (2007, Chapter 2) for a proof. For equidistant nodes, the resulting quadrature schemes are called Newton–Cotes rules.

Assume we wish to determine a k-point Newton–Cotes rule: we fix x_1, $x_2, \ldots, x_k$, then choose the $w_1, w_2, \ldots, w_k$ such that the resulting rule integrates the polynomials $x^0 = 1, x^1, \ldots, x^{k-1}$ exactly on the interval $[a, b]$. We obtain

$$w_1 x_1^0 + w_2 x_2^0 + w_3 x_3^0 + \cdots + w_k x_k^0 = \int_a^b 1 \, dx = b - a \qquad (15.19)$$

$$w_1 x_1 + w_2 x_2 + w_3 x_3 + \cdots + w_k x_k = \int_a^b x \, dx = \frac{1}{2}(b - a)^2$$

$$w_1 x_1^2 + w_2 x_2^2 + w_3 x_3^2 + \cdots + w_k x_k^2 = \int_a^b x^2 \, dx = \frac{1}{3}(b - a)^3$$

$$\vdots$$

$$w_1 x_1^{k-1} + w_2 x_2^{k-1} + w_3 x_3^{k-1} + \cdots + w_k x_k^{k-1} = \int_a^b x^{k-1} \, dx = \frac{1}{k}(b - a)^k.$$

This can be rewritten conveniently as

$$\begin{bmatrix} 1 & 1 & 1 & \ldots & 1 \\ x_1 & x_2 & x_3 & \ldots & x_k \\ \vdots & \vdots & \vdots & \ddots & \vdots \\ x_1^{k-1} & x_2^{k-1} & x_3^{k-1} & \ldots & x_k^{k-1} \end{bmatrix} \begin{pmatrix} w_1 \\ w_2 \\ \vdots \\ w_k \end{pmatrix} = \begin{pmatrix} b - a \\ \frac{1}{2}(b-a)^2 \\ \vdots \\ \frac{1}{k}(b-a)^k \end{pmatrix} \qquad (15.20)$$

and then solved for w. (Compare this with the rules based on Riemann sums: for equidistant nodes, all function values were equally weighted there.)

With $h \equiv (b-a)/m = (b-a)/(n-1)$, we have the following closed rules:

n	Name	x	w
2	Trapezoidal rule	a, b	$\frac{1}{2}h, \frac{1}{2}h$
3	Simpson's rule	$a, a+h, b$	$\frac{1}{3}h, \frac{4}{3}h, \frac{1}{3}h$
4	Simpson's 3/8-rule	$a, a+h, a+2h, b$	$\frac{3}{8}h, \frac{9}{8}h, \frac{9}{8}h, \frac{3}{8}h$
5	Boole's rule	$a, a+h, a+2h, a+3h, b$	$\frac{14}{45}h, \frac{64}{45}h, \frac{24}{45}h, \frac{64}{8}h, \frac{14}{45}h$

Newton–Cotes rules of very high order are rarely used, though, since convergence is not guaranteed for $n \to \infty$, and (see Eq. (15.20)) become ever more badly conditioned as n increases. Instead, the interval of integration is subdivided into smaller subintervals, and to each a low-order rule is applied. Such an implementation is called a composite (or compound) rule.

The reasoning of Eq. (15.19) can be taken one step further by also freely choosing the x_i. This will leave us $2n$ variables, the w and the x. Choosing them such that they integrate $x^0, x^1, x^2, \ldots, x^{2n-1}$ exactly leads to Gauss rules. In principle, we could use the approach of Eq. (15.19), but this leads to nonlinear equations that are much harder to solve. Fortunately, nodes and weights can also be computed in alternative ways; for instance, as the zeros of certain polynomials. We outline next how to compute the nodes and weights as suggested by Golub and Welsch (1969).

Finding the nodes for Gauss rules

Let $\varphi_0, \varphi_1, \varphi_2, \ldots, \varphi_n$ be a sequence of orthogonal polynomials, that is,

$$\int_a^b \varphi_i(x)\varphi_j(x)\omega(x)\mathrm{d}x = 0, \quad \text{for all } i \neq j.$$

The subscripts of the φ indicates the order of the polynomial. Orthogonality holds with respect to a weight function ω, and for an interval $[a,b]$. The zeros of $\varphi_n(x)$, that is, the x that satisfy $\varphi_n(x) = 0$, are the nodes of an n-point Gauss rule for the interval $[a,b]$. If the sequence is also normalized, so that we have

$$\int_a^b \varphi_i(x)\varphi_i(x)\omega(x)\mathrm{d}x = 1, \quad \text{for all } i,$$

we call the polynomials orthonormal.

For orthogonal polynomials, the following three-term recurrence relation holds:

$$\varphi_n(x) = (\alpha_n x + \beta_n)\varphi_{n-1}(x) - \gamma_n \varphi_{n-2}(x), \quad n \geq 1 \quad (15.21)$$

and $\phi_{-1} \equiv 0$ and $\phi_0 \equiv 1$. The numbers α_n, β_n, and γ_n are functions of the coefficients of the polynomials. We can rearrange (15.21) into

$$x\varphi_{n-1}(x) = \frac{1}{\alpha_n}\varphi_n(x) + \underbrace{\left(-\frac{\beta_n}{\alpha_n}\right)}_{\delta_n}\varphi_{n-1}(x) + \frac{\gamma_n}{\alpha_n}\varphi_{n-2}(x). \qquad (15.22)$$

For normalized polynomials, γ_n is equal to α_n/α_{n-1}, so the relation becomes even simpler. In such a case, the coefficient of $\varphi_{n-2}(x)$ becomes $\frac{1}{\alpha_{n-1}}$. (This is a way to check if the polynomials are normalized: reduce n in the coefficient of $\varphi_n(x)$ by -1, then the coefficient of $\varphi_{n-2}(x)$ must result.)

We can put Eq. (15.22) into matrix notation (Wilf, 1978), with $\varphi_n(x) \equiv 0$ for $n < 0$:

$$x\underbrace{\begin{bmatrix} \varphi_0(x) \\ \varphi_1(x) \\ \varphi_2(x) \\ \vdots \\ \varphi_{n-1}(x) \end{bmatrix}}_{\Phi(x)} = \underbrace{\begin{bmatrix} \delta_1 & \frac{1}{\alpha_1} & & & \\ \frac{\gamma_2}{\alpha_2} & \delta_2 & \frac{1}{\alpha_2} & & \\ & \frac{\gamma_3}{\alpha_3} & \delta_3 & \ddots & \\ & & \ddots & \ddots & \frac{1}{\alpha_{n-1}} \\ & & & \frac{\gamma_n}{\alpha_n} & \delta_n \end{bmatrix}}_{A}\underbrace{\begin{bmatrix} \varphi_0(x) \\ \varphi_1(x) \\ \varphi_2(x) \\ \vdots \\ \varphi_{n-1}(x) \end{bmatrix}}_{\Phi(x)} + \begin{bmatrix} 0 \\ \vdots \\ \vdots \\ 0 \\ \frac{1}{\alpha_n}\varphi_n(x) \end{bmatrix}$$

$$(15.23)$$

Now assume we insert x^* into Eq. (15.23), and x^* is a zero of φ_n. Then the last term in (15.23) vanishes, and we are left with

$$x^*\Phi(x^*) = A\Phi(x^*).$$

This equation can only hold if x^* is an eigenvalue of A, hence the zeros of φ_n, and thus the nodes of an n-point Gauss rule, are the eigenvalues of A. This matrix can be made to have even more structure: if the polynomials are normalized, A will be symmetric. If A is not symmetric, we can perform a diagonal similarity transformation (i.e., make A symmetric while not changing its eigenvalues). For this, we define

$$\eta_n = \sqrt{\frac{\gamma_{n+1}}{\alpha_n\alpha_{n+1}}}$$

and replace the matrix A by

$$B = \begin{bmatrix} \delta_1 & \eta_1 & & & \\ \eta_1 & \delta_2 & \eta_2 & & \\ & \eta_2 & \delta_3 & \ddots & \\ & & \ddots & \ddots & \eta_{n-1} \\ & & & \eta_{n-1} & \delta_n \end{bmatrix}.$$

The matrix B has the same eigenvalues as A, that is, it returns the same Gauss nodes. But since it is symmetric, there are more-efficient algorithms to compute the eigenvalues. Matlab's `eig` will exploit symmetry but not the fact that B is tridiagonal. Since the eigenvalues of a symmetric matrix are all real, we also have a proof that the Gauss nodes are real.

Having computed the nodes, we could compute weights with Eqs. (15.19) and (15.20); but the weights can also be obtained from the eigenvectors of B. More specifically, the weight corresponding to an eigenvalue/node is given by

$$\epsilon_1^2 \int_a^b \omega(x)\mathrm{d}x$$

where ϵ_1 is the first element of the eigenvector that belongs to the particular eigenvalue.

For many polynomials, the α, β, and γ from Eq. (15.21) are known, and hence A (and its symmetric counterpart) can be set up. We will later on use the Legendre polynomials φ_n^{L}. They have weight function $\omega(x) \equiv 1$ and are defined on the interval $[-1, 1]$. Abramowitz and Stegun (1965) tell us that

$$(n+1)\varphi_{n+1}^{\mathrm{L}} = (2n+1)x\varphi_n^{\mathrm{L}} - n\varphi_{n-1}^{\mathrm{L}},$$

or

$$\varphi_n^{\mathrm{L}} = \underbrace{\frac{2n-1}{n}}_{\alpha_n} x\varphi_{n-1}^{\mathrm{L}} - \underbrace{\frac{n-1}{n}}_{\gamma_n} \varphi_{n-2}^{\mathrm{L}}$$

with $\beta_n = 0$. Note that these polynomials are not normalized. So we set up A and use the above expressions, arriving at $\delta_n = 0$, and

$$\eta_n = \sqrt{\frac{1}{4 - 1/n^2}}.$$

With Matlab:

Listing 15.16. C-OptionCalibration/M/GLnodesweights.m

```
1  function [x,w] = GLnodesweights(n)
2  % GLnodesweights  -- version 2010-10-24
3  % (G_auss L_egendre...)
4  eta = 1 ./ sqrt(4-(1:(n-1)).^(-2));
5  A = diag(eta,1) + diag(eta,-1);
6  [V,D] = eig(A);
7  x = diag(D);
8  % Matlab does not guaranty sorted eigenvalues
9  [x,i] = sort(x);
10 % weights: for Legendre w(x)=1; integral from -1 to 1 = 2
11 w = 2 * V(1,i) .^ 2;
```

A Gauss rule for an interval $[a_0, b_0]$ can be transferred to an interval $[a\ b]$ as follows (Heath, 2005, pp. 352–353):

$$x' = \frac{(b-a)x + ab_0 - ba_0}{b_0 - a_0}$$

$$w' = \frac{b-a}{b_0 - a_0} w.$$

It is convenient to put this transformation into a function.

Listing 15.17. C-OptionCalibration/M/changeInterval.m

```
1 % changeInterval.m -- version 2010-10-24
2 function [x,w] = changeInterval(x, w, aFrom, bFrom, aTo, bTo)
3 a0 = aFrom; b0 = bFrom;           % interval for Gauss rule
4 a = aTo; b = bTo;
5 x = ((b-a)*x + a*b0-b*a0)/(b0-a0);   % new nodes
6 w = w * (b-a)/(b0-a0);               % new weights
```

Listing 15.18. C-OptionCalibration/M/exampleQuad2.m

```
1 % exampleQuad2.m -- version 2010-10-24
2 % ... continues exampleQuad1.m
3
4 % compute nodes/weights
5 [x,w] = GLnodesweights(m);
6 % change interval of integration
7 [x,w] = changeInterval(x, w, -1, 1, 0, 5);
8 fprintf('Gauss-Legendre:\t %f\n', w * Fun1(x))
```

```
Gauss-Legendre:   0.993260
```

Example 15.3

The distribution function of a Gaussian random variable is given by

$$N(b) = \frac{1}{\sqrt{2\pi}} \int_{-\infty}^{b} e^{-u^2/2} du.$$

This integral cannot be computed analytically. We try a Gauss rule. But how do we integrate from $-\infty$? If a non-periodic function from or to infinity is to have an integral, it needs to be at zero most of the time. For the integrand here, the Gauss density, we know that it is essentially zero when—let us be conservative—its argument is smaller than -10 or greater than 10. So:

Listing 15.19. C-OptionCalibration/M/integrateGauss.m

```
1 % integrateGauss.m -- version 2010-10-24
2 % goal: to compute N(b)
3 b = 2;
```

```
 4
 5 % number of nodes
 6 n = 25;
 7 % replace minus infinity by ...
 8 lowerLim = -10;
 9 % compute nodes/weights
10 [x,w] = GLnodesweights(n);
11 % change interval of integration
12 [x,w] = changeInterval(x, w, -1, 1, lowerLim, b);
13
14 % result of integration
15 ourResult = w*GaussF(x)
16 % result of normcdf from Statistics Toolbox
17 MatlabResult = normcdf(b)
18
19 abs(ourResult-MatlabResult)
```

The absolute error against Matlab's `normcdf` is

```
ans =
    5.9397e-014
```

A remark: integration rules like Gauss–Legendre (or others, e.g.,
Clenshaw–Curtis) prescribe to sample the integrand at points that cluster around the endpoints of the interval. This happens because essentially a
Gauss rule approximates the function to be integrated by a polynomial, and
then integrates this polynomial exactly. Gauss rules are even optimal in the
sense that for a given number of nodes, they integrate exactly a polynomial
of the highest order possible. For an oscillating function, however, we may
need a very-high-order polynomial to obtain a good approximation, and,
therefore, alternative rules may be more efficient for such functions (Hale
and Trefethen, 2008).

Suppose we want to approximate the following functions by polynomials
(the third function is taken from Gander and Gautschi, 2000).

(i) $x = e^{-t}$ for $t \in [0,10]$

(ii) $x = \sin(t)$ for $t \in [0,10\pi]$

(iii) $x = \begin{cases} t+1 & \text{if } t < 1 \\ 3-t & \text{if } 1 \le t \le 3 \\ 2 & \text{if } t > 3 \end{cases}$

The following figures show the function (in gray) and the approximation by
a polynomial of order 5 (in dashed black). We can barely distinguish function (i) from its polynomial approximation anymore, but for function (ii)
and (iii) we need very-high-order polynomials, even though the functions
are not necessarily difficult, in particular, function (iii).

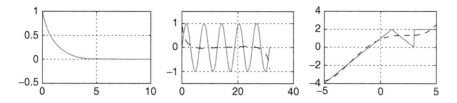

Here is the code to fit the polynomials:

Listing 15.20. C-OptionCalibration/M/exPolynomial.m

```
1 % nice example
2 Fun1 = @(x)(exp(-x));
3 a = 0; b = 10; points = 200;
4 t = linspace(a,b,points);
5 x = Fun1(t);
6 plot(t,x);ylim([-0.5 1]);grid on, hold on
7 %
8 p = polyfit(t,x,5);f = polyval(p,t);
9 plot(t,f,'k--')
```

Listing 15.21. C-OptionCalibration/M/exPolynomial.m

```
1 % not so nice example 1
2 a = 0; b = 10*pi; points = 200;
3 t = linspace(a,b,points);
4 x = sin(t);
5 plot(t,x);ylim([-1.5 1.5]);grid on, hold on
6 %
7 p = polyfit(t,x,5);f = polyval(p,t);
8 plot(t,f,'k--');
```

Listing 15.22. C-OptionCalibration/M/exPolynomial.m

```
1 % not so nice example 2
2 a = -5; b = 5; points = 200;
3 t = linspace(a,b,points);
4 x = testFun(t)';
5 plot(t,x);ylim([-4 4]);grid on; hold on
6 %
7 p = polyfit(t,x,5);f = polyval(p,t);
8 plot(t,f,'k--');
```

Note that we have used the Matlab function `polyfit` to find the coefficients of the polynomial. We could have computed them ourselves with the following regression.

Listing 15.23. C-OptionCalibration/M/exPolynomial.m

```
1 % ... fit polynomial
2 p2 = [t'.^0 t'.^1 t'.^2 t'.^3 t'.^4 t'.^5]\x';
```

Matlab will do some rescaling of the Vandermonde matrix $[t^0\ t^1\ t^2\ ...]$. The function testFun is given by

Listing 15.24. C-OptionCalibration/M/testFun.m

```
1 % testFun.m -- version 2010-10-30
2 function z = testFun(x)
3 ind = NaN(length(x),1);
4 ind(x<=3 & x>=1)=0;ind(x<1)=-1;ind(x>3) = 1;
5 %
6 z(ind==0)  = 3-x(ind==0);
7 z(ind==-1) = x(ind==-1)+1;
8 z(ind==1)  = 2;
9 z=z';
```

Pricing tests

In this section and the final part of this chapter, we present some results from Gilli and Schumann (2011). There we used a Gauss–Legendre rule. We experimented with alternatives like Gauss–Lobatto as well, but no integration scheme was clearly dominant over another, given the required precision of our problem (there is no need to compute option prices to eight decimals).

To test the pricing algorithms, we first investigate the BS model and Merton's jump–diffusion model. For these models, we can compare the solutions obtained from the classic formulas with those from integration. Furthermore, we can investigate several polar cases: for Heston with zero volatility-of-volatility, we should get BS prices; for Bates with zero volatility-of-volatility, we should obtain prices as under Merton's jump diffusion (and, of course, Bates with zero volatility-of-volatility and no jumps should again give BS prices).

When we calibrate models, then we price not just one option, but a whole array of different strikes and different maturities. But for a given set of parameters that describe the underlying process of the model, the characteristic function ϕ only depends on the time to maturity, not on the strike price. This makes sense because ϕ is a transform of the stock density. This density is not influenced by the option's strike.

This suggests that speed improvements can be achieved by preprocessing those terms of ϕ that are constant for a given maturity, and then compute the prices for all strikes for this maturity. See Kilin (2007) for a discussion and Algorithm 64 for a summary.

Speed

First, we compare the performance of direct integration with the performance of quad. Example code for the Bates model follows; we start by fixing parameters.

Algorithm 64 Computing the prices for a given surface.

1: set parameters, set maturities $\{\tau\}$, set strikes $\{X\}$
2: **for** $\tau \in \{\tau\}$ **do**
3:     compute characteristic function ϕ
4:     **for** $X \in \{X\}$ **do**
5:         compute price for strike X, maturity τ
6:     **end for**
7: **end for**
8: compute objective function

Listing 15.25. C-OptionCalibration/M/examplePricing.m

```
1  % examplePricing.m -- version 2011-01-02
2  %% price matrix of options
3  S = 100; q = 0.02; r = 0.02;
4  XX = 70:5:130;                    % strikes
5  TT = [1/12 3/12 6/12 9/12 1 2 3]; % time to maturity in years
6  nS = length(XX); nT = length(TT);
7  % example parameters Bates
8  v0     = 0.2^2;   % current variances
9  vT     = 0.2^2;   % long-run variance (theta in paper)
10 rho    = -0.7;    % correlation
11 k      = 1.0;     % mean reversion speed (kappa in paper)
12 sigma  = 0.3;     % vol of vol
13 lambda = 0.1;     % intensity of jumps;
14 muJ    = -0.2;    % mean of jumps;
15 vJ     = 0.1^2;   % variance of jumps;
16 runs   = 100;     % for tic/toc
```

The first strategy is to loop over the strikes and maturities, and each time price the option with `callBatescf`.

Listing 15.26. C-OptionCalibration/M/examplePricing.m

```
19 prices1 = NaN(nS,nT);
20 tic
21 for rr = 1:runs
22     for kk = 1:nS
23         for tt = 1:nT
24             prices1(kk,tt) = callBatescf(S,XX(kk),TT(tt), ...
25                         r,q,v0,vT,rho,k,sigma,lambda,muJ,vJ);
26         end
27     end
28 end
29 t1 = toc;
```

Next we test the integration approach with fixed nodes and weights. We get a speedup of about 200.

Listing 15.27. C-OptionCalibration/M/examplePricing.m

```
32  cfGeneric = @cfBatesGeneric;
33  param(1) = v0;
34  param(2) = vT;
35  param(3) = rho;
36  param(4) = k;
37  param(5) = sigma;
38  param(6) = lambda;
39  param(7) = muJ;
40  param(8) = vJ;
41  prices2 = NaN(nS,nT);   % matrix of model prices
42
43  from = 0; to = 200; N = 50;
44  [x,w]  = GLnodesweights(N);
45  [x,w]  = changeInterval(x, w, -1, 1, from, to);
46  auxX   = NaN(nS,N);     %
47
48  tic
49  for rr = 1:runs
50      ix = 1i * x;
51      for tt = 1:nT
52          tau = TT(tt);
53          % evaluate CF at nodes
54          CFi = S * exp((r-q) * tau);
55          CF1 = cfGeneric(x - 1i,S,tau,r,q,param) ./ (ix * CFi);
56          CF2 = cfGeneric(x     ,S,tau,r,q,param) ./  ix;
57          for kk = 1:nS
58              X = XX(kk);
59              if tt == 1  % store for later maturities
60                  auxX(kk,:) = exp(-ix*log(X))';
61              end
62              P1 = 0.5 + w * real(auxX(kk,:)' .* CF1) / pi;
63              P2 = 0.5 + w * real(auxX(kk,:)' .* CF2) / pi;
64              prices2(kk,tt) = exp(-q * tau) * S * P1 - ...
65                               exp(-r * tau) * X * P2;
66          end
67      end
68  end
69  t2 = toc;  % compute speedup: t1/t2
```

Note that there is room for many small improvements: the ubiquitous $e^{-r\tau}$ terms can be precomputed; more importantly, in the characteristic function many terms can be stored. For instance, the terms d and g are independent of τ, and could be computed once for the whole matrix.

Accuracy

We also need to check the numerical accuracy[1] of our pricing methods. The BS model is an ideal candidate to compare prices computed via integration with the analytical solution; see the Matlab script compareAccuracy.m.

---

[1] Accuracy here refers to the size of numerical errors compared with the trustworthy numerical benchmark.

It presents three ways to compute the BS prices: with the classical formula (variant 1), through integration with fixed nodes and weights (variant 2), and through integration with quad (variant 3).

Listing 15.28. C-OptionCalibration/M/compareAccuracy.m

```
1  % compareAccuracy.m -- version 2010-11-05
2  %% price matrix of options
3  S = 100; q = 0.02; r = 0.02;
4  XX = 70:5:130;                        % strikes
5  TT = [1/12 3/12 6/12 9/12 1 2 3];  % time to maturity in years
6  nS = length(XX); nT = length(TT);
7  v  = 0.2^2;     % BS parameter (vol squared)
8
9  %% variant 1
10 prices1 = NaN(nS,nT);
11 for kk = 1:nS
12     for tt = 1:nT
13         prices1(kk,tt) = callBSM(S,XX(kk),TT(tt),r,q,v);
14     end
15 end
16
17 %% variant 2
18 cfGeneric = @cfBSMGeneric;
19 param(1) = v;
20 from = 0; to = 200; N = 50;
21 [x,w] = GLnodesweights(N);
22 [x,w] = changeInterval(x, w, -1, 1, from, to);
23 prices2 = NaN(nS,nT);  % matrix of model prices
24 auxX    = NaN(nS,N); ix = 1i * x;
25 for tt = 1:nT
26     tau = TT(tt);
27     % evaluate CF at nodes
28     CFi = S * exp((r-q) * tau);
29     CF1 = cfGeneric(x - 1i,S,tau,r,q,param) ./ (ix * CFi);
30     CF2 = cfGeneric(x     ,S,tau,r,q,param) ./  ix;
31     for kk = 1:nS
32         X = XX(kk);
33         if tt == 1  % store for later maturities
34             auxX(kk,:) = exp(-ix*log(X))';
35         end
36         P1 = 0.5 + w * real(auxX(kk,:)' .* CF1) / pi;
37         P2 = 0.5 + w * real(auxX(kk,:)' .* CF2) / pi;
38         prices2(kk,tt) = exp(-q * tau) * S * P1 - ...
39                          exp(-r * tau) * X * P2;
40     end
41 end
42
43 %% variant 3
44 prices3 = NaN(nS,nT);
45 for kk = 1:nS
46     for tt = 1:nT
47         prices3(kk,tt) = callBSMcf(S,XX(kk),TT(tt),r,q,v);
48     end
49 end
50
```

```
51 %% compare
52 max(max(abs(100*(prices2-prices1))))
53 max(max(abs(100*(prices3-prices1))))
54 surf(prices2./prices1-1)
```

Figures 15.5 and 15.6 show the numerical differences. We see that it is important to look at both absolute and relative errors (see also Section 2.2 on page 21). With 25 nodes, there is one substantial relative pricing error of more than 100%. But the price of this option is 0.00. We can increase the precision by using more nodes. With 50 nodes, we get the errors in Fig. 15.6

The accuracy when integrating "by hand" is even higher than with `quad`. If (repeat: if) we wanted the same numerical accuracy, we could change the function `callBSMcf` as follows:

```
% ...
vP1 = 0.5 + 1/pi * quad(@P1,0,200,1.0e-12,[],S,X,tau,r,q,vT);
vP2 = 0.5 + 1/pi * quad(@P2,0,200,1.0e-12,[],S,X,tau,r,q,vT);
% ...
```

That is, we enforce a lower tolerance than the default which is 10^{-6}.

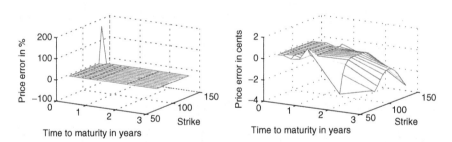

Figure 15.5 Relative (left) and absolute (right; in cents) price errors for BS with direct integration with 25 nodes (compared with analytical solution).

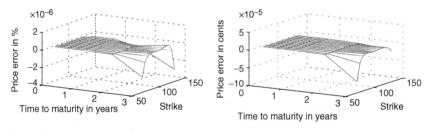

Figure 15.6 Relative (left) and absolute (right; in cents) price errors for BS with direct integration with 50 nodes (compared with analytical solution).

15.3. Calibration

As we pointed out at the start of the chapter, our calibration problem will be to find parameters such that the model's prices are consistent with market prices. This can be written as an optimization problem of the form

$$\min \sum_{i=1}^{M} \frac{\left| C_i^{\text{model}} - C_i^{\text{market}} \right|}{C_i^{\text{market}}} \tag{15.24}$$

where M is the number of market prices. Alternatively, we could specify absolute price differences, use squares instead of absolute values, or introduce weighting schemes. The choice of the objective function depends on the application; in the end, it is an empirical task to determine a good objective function. Since here we are interested in numerical aspects, we will use specification (15.24).

It turns out that this problem, like many others in finance, is not easy to solve, and gradient-based methods will likely fail to do the job. Thus, we use heuristics. The results described in this section are based on Gilli and Schumann (2011).

15.3.1. Techniques

We apply Differential Evolution (DE) and Particle Swarm Optimization (PSO). These methods have been described in Chapter 12, so we will not repeat the algorithms here. We will use a Matlab implementation; the code is given below.

Population-based methods like PSO and DE are often effective in exploration. They can quickly identify promising areas of the search space; but then these methods converge only slowly. In the literature we thus often find combinations of population-based search with local search (in the sense of a trajectory method that evolves only a single solution). An example of such a combination are Memetic Algorithms (Moscato, 1989). So we also test a simple hybrid based on this idea; it combines DE and PSO with a direct search component. In the classification systems of Talbi (2002) or Winker and Gilli (2004), this is a high-level relay hybrid (see also the brief discussion in Chapter 12, page 349).

Preliminary tests suggested that the objective function is often flat, thus different parameter values give similar objective function values. This indicates that (i) our problem may be sensitive to small changes in the data when we are interested in precise parameter estimates; and that (ii) if we insist on precisely computing parameters, we may need either many iterations, or an algorithm with a large step size. Thus, as a local search strategy, we use the direct search method of Nelder and Mead (1965) as implemented in Matlab's `fminsearch`. This algorithm can change its step size; it is also robust in case of noisy objective functions (e.g., functions evaluated by numerical techniques that may introduce truncation error, as could be the case here). The hybrid is summarized in Algorithm 65.

Algorithm 65 Hybrid search.

1: set parameters for population-based method
2: **for** $k = 1$ to n_G **do**
3:     do population-based search
4:     **if** local search **then**
5:         select n_S solutions as starting values for local search
6:         **for** each selected solution **do**
7:             perform direct search
8:         **end for**
9:     **end if**
10: **end for**
11: return best solution

For an implementation, we need to decide how often we start the direct search, how many solutions we select, and how we select them. With just one generation and n_S equal to the population size, we would have a simple restart strategy for the direct search method.

Nelder–Mead direct search was described in Section 11.4.4; Fig. 15.7 recalls its operations. Let us give a few more details on how the method operates. When we call the function fminsearch, Matlab will transform

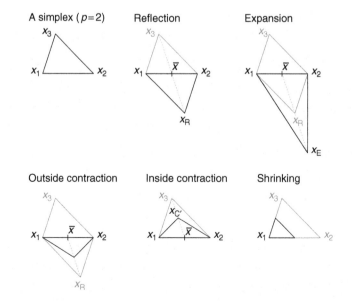

Figure 15.7 Operations of Nelder–Mead.

our initial guess x into

$$
\begin{matrix}
x^{(1)} & x^{(1)}+\varepsilon x^{(1)} & x^{(1)} & x^{(1)} & \cdots & x^{(1)} \\
x^{(2)} & x^{(2)} & x^{(2)}+\varepsilon x^{(2)} & x^{(2)} & \cdots & x^{(2)} \\
x^{(3)} & x^{(3)} & x^{(3)} & x^{(1)}+\varepsilon x^{(3)} & \cdots & x^{(3)} \\
\vdots & \vdots & \vdots & \vdots & \ddots & \vdots \\
x^{(p)} & x^{(p)} & x^{(p)} & x^{(p)} & \cdots & x^{(p)}+\varepsilon x^{(p)}
\end{matrix}
\tag{15.25}
$$

where the superscript $^{(i)}$ denotes the ith element of x. In the implementation used here (`Matlab 2008a`), ε is 0.05. If $x^{(i)}$ is zero, then $\varepsilon x^{(i)}$ is set to 0.00025.

The simplex adjusts to the contours of the objective function (i.e., it can stretch itself) and so can make larger steps into favorable directions. But this flexibility can also be a disadvantage. Try to visualize a narrow valley along which a long-stretched simplex ⟨⎯⎯⎯⎯⎯⟩ advances. If this valley were to take a turn, the simplex could not easily adapt (see Wright, 1996 for a discussion of this behavior). Some testing showed that this phenomenon occurs in our problem. When we initialize the simplex, the maximum of a parameter value is 5% greater than its minimum, and this is true for all parameters by construction; see Eq. (15.25). Thus, the stretch in relative terms along any dimension is the same. When we run a search and compare this initial with the final simplex, we often find that the stretch along some dimensions is 200 times greater than along other dimensions; the condition number of a simplex often increases from 10^3 or so to 10^{12} and well beyond. This is a warning sign, and indeed it turns out that restarting the algorithm, that is, re-initializing the simplex several times, leads to much better solutions. (A remark: for practical applications, restarting Nelder–Mead by re-initializing the simplex is often a cheap and thus helpful way to improve solution quality. We are not aware of any implementation that does this automatically.)

Constraints
We constrain all heuristics to favor interpretable values: we want nonnegative variances, correlation between -1 and 1, and parameters like κ, σ, and λ also nonnegative. There are various ways how these constraints could be implemented. Straightforward is a penalty term: for any violation a positive number proportional to the violation is added to the objective function. Here we use a repair function, described below.

Note that we are actually cheating a bit: for the hybrid, we do not adapt Nelder–Mead to include the constraints. This would not be necessary if we were using penalties; adding a penalty actually changes the problem into an unconstrained problem and, hence, we need not adapt Nelder–Mead.

We could modify Nelder–Mead so that it takes care of constraints (e.g., by rejecting operations that lead to infeasible candidate solutions), but we found that this is not necessary here. The problem is, practically, only mildly constrained, since we only want to enforce that our parameters remain meaningful; the constraints are not part of the financial model.

15.3.2. Organizing the problem and implementation

We implement both DE and PSO with Matlab. The functions follow in a straightforward way from the algorithms given in Chapter 12 (see, in particular, the appendix of that chapter). Note that, unlike in R, we need not put too much emphasis on vectorization; loops are for the most part comparable in speed to vectorized computations with Matlab.

We start with a matrix of given prices, named `prices0`. This matrix has in its rows the different strikes, and in its columns the different times to maturity. The strikes are stored in a vector `XX` and time to maturity in years is a vector `TT`. We collect all such pieces of information in a structure `Data`. When we later call the objective function, we shall pass as arguments a particular solution and the structure `Data`.

`Data.model`	a string (`heston`, `bates`, `merton`, or `bsm`)
`Data.S`	the stock price
`Data.q`	the dividend yield
`Data.r`	the interest rate
`Data.prices0`	the market prices (a matrix of size `nS` × `nT`)
`Data.XX`	a vector of strikes
`Data.TT`	a vector of times to maturity
`Data.x`	integration nodes
`Data.w`	integration weights
`Data.Dc`	`[minP maxP]`, matrix with min and max for parameters
`Data.d`	`length(minP)`

The functions `DE` and `PSO` are later called with three arguments: an objective function `OF`, a structure `Data`, and a structure `P`. The objective function is a function called with two arguments: a particular solution (a vector), and the structure `Data`. The structure `P` holds all settings of the optimization procedure.

The script `calibOF.m` gives an implementation of the objective function.

Listing 15.29. C-OptionCalibration/M/calibOf.m

```
1 function [res, me] = calibOF(param,Data)
2 % calibOF.m -- version 2011-01-16
3 model = Data.model;
4 S = Data.S; q = Data.q; r = Data.r;
```

```
 5  XX = Data.XX; TT = Data.TT;
 6  prices0 = Data.prices0;
 7  x = Data.x; w = Data.w;
 8
 9  if strcmp(model,'heston')
10      cfGeneric = @cfHestonGeneric;
11  elseif strcmp(model,'bates')
12      cfGeneric = @cfBatesGeneric;
13  elseif strcmp(model,'bsm')
14      cfGeneric = @cfBSMGeneric;
15  elseif strcmp(model,'merton')
16      cfGeneric = @cfMertonGeneric;
17  else
18      error('model not specified')
19  end
20
21  % initialize structures
22  nS      = length(XX);  % number of strikes
23  nT      = length(TT);  % number of expiries
24  N       = length(x);   % number of nodes
25  Prices  = NaN(nS,nT);  % matrix of model prices
26  auxX    = NaN(nS,N);   %
27
28  % evaluate surface
29  ix = 1i * x;
30  for tt = 1:nT  % loop over times to maturity
31      tau = TT(tt);
32      % evaluate CF at nodes
33      CFi = S * exp((r-q) * tau);
34      CF1 = cfGeneric(x - 1i,S,tau,r,q,param) ./ (ix * CFi);
35      CF2 = cfGeneric(x    ,S,tau,r,q,param) ./  ix;
36      for kk = 1:nS  % loop over strikes
37          if ~isnan(prices0(kk,tt))
38              X = XX(kk);
39              if tt == 1 % store for later maturities
40                  auxX(kk,:) = exp(-ix*log(X))';
41              end
42              P1 = 0.5 + w * real(auxX(kk,:)' .* CF1) / pi;
43              P2 = 0.5 + w * real(auxX(kk,:)' .* CF2) / pi;
44              Price = exp(-q * tau) * S * P1 - exp(-r*tau)*X*P2;
45              Prices(kk,tt) = max(Price,0);
46          end
47      end
48  end
49  % replace missing values by zero
50  prices0(isnan(prices0)) = 0; Prices(isnan(Prices)) = 0;
51  % compute distance between Prices and prices0
52  aux = abs(Prices(:) - prices0(:));
53  res = mean(aux ./ prices0(:));
54  me  = max(aux);
```

As pointed out before, the functions could be accelerated by precomputing more quantities. In `calibOF`, the term `ix = 1i * x` is fixed for all parameter values. We could (and should) thus compute it outside the objective function. But here we have tried to reduce such precomputations to make the code clearer.

The following script shows the function DE.

Listing 15.30. C-OptionCalibration/M/DE.m

```
1  function [xbest,Fbest,Fbv] = DE(OF,Data,P)
2  % DE.m -- version 2011-01-07
3  % settings for direct search
4  if P.NM > 0
5      optionsA = optimset('Display','off','MaxIter',P.NMiter,...
6                          'MaxFunEvals',P.NMiter);
7      z = @(param)calibOF(param,Data);
8  end
9
10 % initialize matrices
11 Fbv   = NaN(P.nG,1);     % best F-value over generations
12 Fbest = realmax;         % best solution value
13 F = zeros(P.nP,1);       %vector of F-values of members of population
14
15 % construct starting population
16 hi_lo = Data.Dc(:,2)-Data.Dc(:,1);
17 P1 = diag(hi_lo) * rand(Data.d,P.nP);
18 for i = 1:Data.d, P1(i,:) = P1(i,:) + Data.Dc(i,1); end
19
20 % ... and evaluate it
21 for i = 1:P.nP
22     F(i) = feval(OF,P1(:,i),Data);
23     if isnan(F(i)), F(i) = 1e7; end   % just in case...
24     if F(i) < Fbest
25         Fbest = F(i);
26         xbest = P1(:,i);
27     end
28 end
29
30 % start generations
31 for k = 1:P.nG
32     P0 = P1;
33     Io = randperm(P.nP)'; Ic = randperm(4)';
34     R1 = circshift(Io,Ic(1));
35     R2 = circshift(Io,Ic(2));
36     R3 = circshift(Io,Ic(3));
37     Pv = P0(:,R1) + P.F * (P0(:,R2) - P0(:,R3));% new solutions
38     mPv = rand(Data.d,P.nP) < P.CR;             % crossover
39     Pu = P0; Pu(mPv) = Pv(mPv);
40     for i = 1:P.nP
41         Pu(:,i) = repair(Pu(:,i),Data);
42         Ftemp = feval(OF,Pu(:,i),Data);
43         if Ftemp <= F(i)
44             P1(:,i) = Pu(:,i);
45             F(i) = Ftemp;
46         end
47     end
48     % direct search
49     if P.NM > 0
50         if mod(k,P.NMmod) == 0
51             if P.NMchoice == 1
52                 [ign,nnn] = sort(F);
53             elseif P.NMchoice == 2
```

```
54                    nnn = randperm(P.nP);
55               else
56                    error('choice not allowed')
57               end
58               for ni = 1:P.NMn
59                    auxF = F(nnn(ni)); diff = 1e7;
60                    while diff > P.NMpres
61                        paramS = P1(:,nnn(ni));
62                        NMsol = fminsearch(z,paramS,optionsA);
63                        NMsol = repair( NMsol,Data);
64                        Ftemp = calibOF(NMsol,Data);
65                        if Ftemp < F(nnn(ni))
66                            P1(:,nnn(ni)) = NMsol;
67                            F(nnn(ni)) = Ftemp;
68                            diff = abs(Ftemp-auxF);
69                            auxF = Ftemp;
70                        else
71                            break
72                        end
73                    end
74                end
75           end
76       end
77       % find best
78       [Fbest,ibest] = min(F);
79       Fbv(k) = Fbest;
80       xbest = P1(:,ibest);
81   end
82   fprintf('standard dev. of solutions %4.3f\n',std(F))
```

Similarly, we coded PSO in a function PSO.

Listing 15.31. C-OptionCalibration/M/PSO.m

```
1   function [xbest,Fbest,Fbv] = PSO(OF,Data,PS)
2   % PSO.m -- version 2011-01-07
3   if PS.NM>0
4       optionsA = optimset('Display','off','MaxIter',PS.NMiter,...
5                            'MaxFunEvals',PS.NMiter);
6       z = @(param)calibOF(param,Data);
7   end
8
9   d    = PS.d; iner = PS.iner;
10  Fbv = NaN(PS.nG,1);   % best F-value over generations
11  F   = zeros(PS.nP,1); % vector of F-values members of population
12
13  v = PS.cv * randn(d,PS.nP); % initialize velocity
14
15  % construct starting population
16  hi_lo = Data.Dc(:,2)-Data.Dc(:,1);
17  P = diag(hi_lo) * rand(PS.d,PS.nP);
18  for i = 1:Data.d, P(i,:) = P(i,:) + Data.Dc(i,1); end
19
20  % ... and evaluate population
21  for i = 1:PS.nP
22      F(i) = feval(OF,P(:,i),Data);
```

```
23 end
24 Pbest = P;   Fbest = F;   [Gbest,gbest] = min(F);
25
26 for k = 1:PS.nG
27     v = iner*v + PS.c1 * rand(d,PS.nP) .* (Pbest - P) + ...
28         PS.c2*rand(d,PS.nP) .* (Pbest(:,gbest)*ones(1,PS.nP)-P);
29     v = min(v, PS.vmax); v = max(v,-PS.vmax);
30     P = P + v;
31     for i = 1:PS.nP
32         P(:,i) = repair(P(:,i),Data);
33         F(i) = feval(OF,P(:,i),Data);
34         if isnan(F(i)), F(i)=1e7; end
35     end
36     I = F < Fbest;
37     Fbest(I) = F(I); Pbest(:,I) = P(:,I);
38     [Gbest,gbest] = min(Fbest); Fbv(k) = Gbest;
39     % direct search
40     if PS.NM>0
41         if mod(k,PS.NMmod) == 0
42             if PS.NMchoice==1
43                 [ign,nnn] = sort(F);
44             elseif PS.NMchoice==2
45                 nnn = randperm(PS.nP);
46             else
47                 error('choice not allowed')
48             end
49             for ni=1:PS.NMn
50                 auxF = F(nnn(ni)); diff = 1e7;
51                 while diff > PS.NMpres
52                     paramS = P(:,nnn(ni));
53                     NMsol = fminsearch(z,paramS,optionsA);
54                     NMsol = repair(NMsol,Data);
55                     Ftemp = calibOF(NMsol,Data);
56                     if Ftemp < F(nnn(ni))
57                         P(:,nnn(ni)) = NMsol;
58                         if Ftemp < Fbest(nnn(ni))
59                             Pbest(:,nnn(ni)) = NMsol;
60                             Fbest(nnn(ni)) = Ftemp;
61                         end
62                         F(nnn(ni)) = Ftemp;
63                         diff = abs(Ftemp-auxF);
64                         auxF = Ftemp;
65                     else
66                         break
67                     end
68
69                 end
70             end
71         end
72         I = F < Fbest;
73         Fbest(I)    = F(I);
74         Pbest(:,I) = P(:,I);
75         [Gbest,gbest] = min(Fbest);
76         Gbest = Gbest(1); gbest = gbest(1);
77         Fbv(k) = Gbest;
78     end
79 end
```

```
80 xbest = Pbest(:,gbest);
81 Fbest = Gbest;
82 fprintf('Standard dev. of solutions %4.3f\n',std(Fbest))
83 end
```

A complete example follows. We start by choosing a model and setting true parameters for it. Then we compute prices0 with the functions that use quad.

Listing 15.32. C-OptionCalibration/M/calibrate.m

```
1  % calibrate.m -- version 2010-11-29
2  %% choose a model
3  model = 'heston';
4  %model = 'bates';
5  %model = 'bsm';
6  %model = 'merton';
7  %% set true parameters and compute true prices
8  S = 100; q = 0.02; r = 0.02;
9  XX = 75:5:125; TT = [1/12 3/12 6/12 9/12 1 2 3];
10 nS = length(XX); nT = length(TT); prices0 = NaN(nS,nT);
11 if strcmp(model,'heston')
12     v0    = 0.2^2;    % current variance
13     vT    = 0.2^2;    % long-run variance (theta in paper)
14     rho   = -0.7;     % correlation
15     k     = 1;        % mean reversion speed (kappa in paper)
16     sigma = 0.5;      % vol of vol
17     for kk = 1:length(XX)
18         for tt = 1:length(TT)
19             prices0(kk,tt) = ...
20                 callHestoncf(S,XX(kk),TT(tt),r,q,v0,vT,rho,k,
                       sigma);
21         end
22     end
23     minP = [0.05^2  0.05^2 -1 0.01 0.01]';
24     maxP = [0.90^2  0.90^2  1 5.00 5.00]';
25 elseif strcmp(model,'bates')
26     v0    = 0.2^2;    % current variances
27     vT    = 0.2^2;    % long-run variance (theta in paper)
28     rho   = -0.3;     % correlation
29     k     = 1.0;      % mean reversion speed (kappa in paper)
30     sigma = 0.3;      % vol of vol
31     lambda = 0.2;     % intensity of jumps;
32     muJ   = -0.1;     % mean of jumps;
33     vJ    = 0.1^2;    % variance of jumps;
34     for kk = 1:length(XX)
35         for tt = 1:length(TT)
36             prices0(kk,tt) = callBatescf(S,XX(kk),TT(tt), ...
37                             r,q,v0,vT,rho,k,sigma,lambda,muJ,vJ);
38         end
39     end
40     minP = [0.05^2  0.05^2 -1 0.01 0.01  0.00 -0.25  0.00^2]';
41     maxP = [1.00^2  1.00^2  1 5.00 5.00  0.50  0.25  0.90^2]';
42 elseif strcmp(model,'bsm')
43     v     = 0.2^2;    % variance
44     for kk = 1:length(XX)
```

```
45          for tt = 1:length(TT)
46              prices0(kk,tt) = callBSMcf(S,XX(kk),TT(tt),r,q,v);
47          end
48      end
49      minP = [0.01^2]';
50      maxP = [2.00^2]';
51  elseif strcmp(model,'merton')
52      v      = 0.2^2;    % variance (volatility squared)
53      lambda = 0.2;      % intensity of jumps;
54      muJ    = -0.03;    % mean of jumps;
55      vJ     = 0.03^2;   % variance of jumps;
56      for kk = 1:length(XX)
57          for tt = 1:length(TT)
58              prices0(kk,tt) = callMertoncf(S,XX(kk),TT(tt), ...
59                                  r,q,v,lambda,muJ,vJ);
60          end
61      end
62      minP = [0.05^2  0.00 -0.25 0.05^2]';
63      maxP = [1.00^2  0.50  0.25 0.90^2]';
64  else
65      error('model not specified')
```

Then we set up the structure `Data` that holds all the variables necessary to compute the objective function.

Listing 15.33. C-OptionCalibration/M/calibrate.m

```
66  % add noise
67  %prices0 = prices0 .* (randn(nS,nT)*0.001+1);
68
69  %% nodes/weights for integration
70  from = 0; to = 200; N = 50;
71  [x,w] = GLnodesweights(N);
72  [x,w] = changeInterval(x, w, -1, 1, from, to);
73  % collect all in Data structure
74  Data.model = model;
75  Data.S     = S;
76  Data.q     = q;
77  Data.r     = r;
78  Data.prices0 = prices0;
79  Data.XX    = XX;
80  Data.TT    = TT;
81  Data.x     = x;
```

Finally, we decide on the settings for DE (the matrix `P1`) and the settings for PSO (the matrix `P2`); then we can run the algorithms.

Listing 15.34. C-OptionCalibration/M/calibrate.m

```
66  Data.w     = w;
67  Data.Dc    = [minP maxP];
68  Data.d     = length(minP);
69  % DE settings (P1)
```

```
70 P1.nP = 25;    P1.nG = 50;
71 P1.CR = 0.95; P1.F  = 0.5;
72 P1.d = length(minP);
73 P1.NM = 1;           % do direct search (DS)? 1 = yes, 0 = no
74 P1.NMpres = 0.001; % when to stop DS
75 P1.NMiter =   100; % maximum iterations for DS
76 P1.NMmod = 10;       % how often to do DS (mod 10: every 10 it.)
77 P1.NMn = 2;          % how many searchers
78 P1.NMchoice = 1;     % what searchers: 1 = elite, 2 = random
79 % PS settings (P2)
80 P2.nP = 25; P2.nG = 50;
81 P2.d = length(minP);
82 P2.cv = 0.1;         % inital velocity
83 P2.vmax = 0.5;       % maximum (absolute) velocity
84 P2.iner = 0.7;       % inertia weight
85 P2.c1 = 1;           % weight personal best
86 P2.c2 = 2;           % weight alltime best
87 P2.NM = 1;           % do direct search (DS)? 1 = yes, 0 = no
88 P2.NMpres = 0.001; % when to stop DS
89 P2.NMiter =   100; % maximum iterations for DS
90 P2.NMmod = 10;       % how often to do DS (mod 10: every 10 it.)
91 P2.NMn = 2;          % how many searchers
92 P2.NMchoice = 1;     % what searchers: 1 = elite, 2 = random
93
94 % run DE
95 fprintf('\nDifferential Evolution \n')
96 tic, [solA,FbestA,FbvA] = DE(@calibOF,Data,P1);toc
97 [meanE,maxE] = calibOF(solA,Data)
98 % run PS
99 fprintf('\nParticle Swarm \n')
```

Repairing solutions

The matrix Dc, that is passed with Data, holds the minimum and maximum levels for the parameters. These values were used only for generating the initial solutions. We can also use the information as actual bounds of the parameters. If a parameter lies outside this range, we reflect it back into its boundaries. This can be done with simple arithmetic operators; see Algorithm 66.

Algorithm 66 Repairing a solution x by reflection.

1: set upper bound x^{hi} and lower bound x^{lo} (a is a temporary variable)
2: compute $a = x - x^{hi}$ # repair upper bound
3: compute $a = a + |a|$
4: compute $x = x - a$
5: compute $a = x^{lo} - x$ # repair lower bound
6: compute $a = a + |a|$
7: compute $x = x + a$
8: compute $x = ((x + x^{lo}) + |x - x^{lo}|)/2$ # final check: is new x above lower bound?
9: compute $x = ((x + x^{hi}) - |x - x^{hi}|)/2$ # final check: is new x below upper bound?

We have used the fact that the maximum operator $\max(a, b)$ and minimum operator $\min(a, b)$ can be replaced with

$$\max(a,b) = \frac{a+b}{2} + \left|\frac{a-b}{2}\right|, \quad \min(a,b) = \frac{a+b}{2} - \left|\frac{a-b}{2}\right|$$

which works also on vectors. This mechanism is coded as a function `repair` that is called after new solutions are created, but before they are evaluated in DE and PSO.

15.3.3. Two experiments

We briefly describe experiments on the Heston model and the Bates model; more details can be found in Gilli and Schumann (2011).[2]

We start by creating artificial data sets: the spot price S_0 is 100, the risk-free rate r is 2%, there are no dividends. We compute prices for strikes X from 80 to 120 in steps of size 2, and maturities τ of $1/12$, $3/12$, $6/12$, $9/12$, 1, 2 and 3 years. Hence our surface comprises $21 \times 7 = 147$ prices. Given a set of parameters, we compute option prices and store them as the true prices. Then we run each of our methods 10 times to solve problem 15.24 and see if we can recover the parameters; the setup implies that a perfect fit is possible. The parameters for the Heston model come from the following table (each column is one parameter set):

$\sqrt{v_0}$	0.3	0.3	0.3	0.3	0.4	0.2	0.5	0.6	0.7	0.8
$\sqrt{\theta}$	0.3	0.3	0.2	0.2	0.2	0.4	0.5	0.3	0.3	0.3
ρ	−0.3	−0.7	−0.9	0.0	−0.5	−0.5	0.0	−0.5	−0.5	−0.5
κ	2.0	0.2	3.0	3.0	0.2	0.2	0.5	3.0	2.0	1.0
σ	1.5	1.0	0.5	0.5	0.8	0.8	3.0	1.0	1.0	1.0

For the Bates model, we use the following parameter sets:

$\sqrt{v_0}$	0.3	0.3	0.3	0.3	0.4	0.2	0.5	0.6	0.7	0.8
$\sqrt{\theta}$	0.3	0.3	0.2	0.2	0.2	0.4	0.5	0.3	0.3	0.3
ρ	−0.3	−0.7	−0.9	0.0	−0.5	−0.5	0.0	−0.5	−0.5	−0.5
κ	2.0	0.2	3.0	3.0	0.2	0.2	0.5	3.0	2.0	1.0
σ	0.3	0.5	0.5	0.5	0.8	0.8	1.0	1.0	1.0	1.0
λ	0.1	0.1	0.2	0.2	0.2	0.2	0.2	0.2	0.2	0.2
μ_J	−0.1	−0.1	−0.1	−0.1	−0.1	−0.1	−0.1	−0.1	−0.1	−0.1
σ_J	0.1	0.1	0.1	0.1	0.1	0.1	0.1	0.1	0.1	0.1

---

[2] The implementation was slightly different there, but that does not change the results.

With ten different parameter sets for each model and with ten restarts for each parameter set, we have 100 results for each optimization method. For each restart, we store the value of the objective function (the mean percentage error; Eq. (15.24)), and the corresponding parameter estimates. For the latter, we compute absolute errors, that is,

$$\text{error} = |\,\text{estimated parameter} - \text{true parameter}\,|.$$

Below we look at the distributions of these errors.

All algorithms are coded with Matlab, for the direct search we use Matlab's fminsearch. We ran a number of preliminary experiments to find effective parameter values for the algorithms. For DE, the F-parameter should be set to around 0.3–0.5 (we use 0.5); very low or high values typically impaired performance. The CR-parameter had less influence, but levels close to unity worked best; each new candidate solution is then likely changed in many dimensions. For PSO, the main task is to accelerate convergence. Velocity should not be allowed to become too high; therefore, inertia should be below unity (we set it to 0.7); we also restricted maximum absolute velocity to 0.2. The stopping criterion for DE and PSO is a fixed number of function evaluations (population size × generations); we run three settings,

$$
\begin{array}{ll}
1250 & (25\times50)\,, \\
5{,}000 & (50\times100)\,, \\
20{,}000 & (100\times200)\,.
\end{array}
$$

An alternative stopping criterion is to halt the algorithm once the diversity within the population—as measured, for instance, by the range of objective function or parameter values—falls below a tolerance level. This strategy works fine for DE where the solutions generally converge rapidly, but leads to longer run times for PSO.

For the hybrid methods, we use a population of 25 solutions, and run 50 generations. Every 10 generations, one or three solutions are selected, either the best solutions ("elitists") or random solutions. These solutions are then used as the starting values of a direct search. This search comprises repeated applications of Nelder–Mead, restricted to 200 iterations each, until no further improvement can be achieved; "further improvement" is a decrease in the objective function greater than 0.1%. Note that all the settings can be passed through the structures Data and P (see the Matlab script calibrate.m).

Results: Heston model
Price errors
Below we plot the distributions of price errors in percentage points. Increasingly darker gray stands for more function evaluations. On the left, we have DE; in the middle, we have PSO; on the right, the hybrid based on DE.

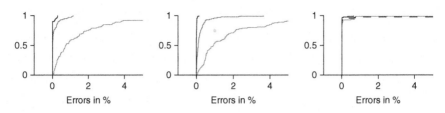

Both DE and PSO, with increasing computational resources, eventually give solutions with a zero error. The performance of the PSO-based hybrid was very similar to that based on DE, even though there was a slight advantage for DE. With DE the population converged faster and hence it mattered little for the hybrid whether the solutions for the direct search were chosen by quality or randomly. This can be taken from the right panel in the above picture. There are actually four curves: the dashed lines are from random searchers, the solid lines from elite searchers. Do not try to identify a specific distribution; they are essentially the same. We see that there are a few rare outliers (the long tails to the upside), but generally the hybrid performed very well. When the hybrid was based on PSO, then direct search that started with the best population members performed better than randomly-chosen members.

Parameter errors

So we can get a good fit of the model (i.e., a low average price error). But what about the parameters?

The figure below shows the distributions of absolute errors in the parameters for $\sqrt{v_0}$ (left), $\sqrt{\theta}$ (middle), and ρ (right).

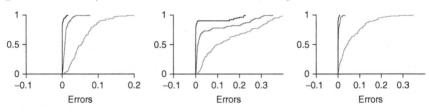

Below, we have the distributions of absolute errors in the parameters for κ (left), and σ (right).

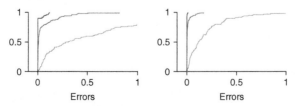

We see that the parameter estimates roughly mirror the convergence behavior of the objective function values. With increasing computational resources (indicated by darker gray), the distributions converge on zero.

In some case, though, there remain large errors; for instance, when we look at the long-run variance.

The investigate this behavior, we pool all the solutions and plot the errors in the objective function (i.e., the fit in terms of pricing error) against the parameter errors. The following panel shows the results. In the upper panel: $\sqrt{v_0}$ (left), $\sqrt{\theta}$ (middle), and ρ (right). In the lower panel: κ (left), and σ (right). All plots have the price error on the x-axis, the parameter error on the y-axis.

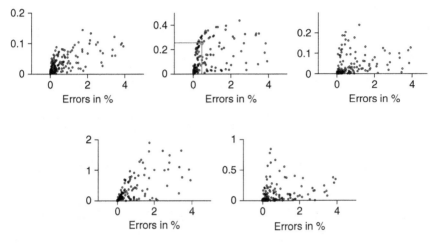

For illustration, in the middle upper panel (long-run volatility) we have singled out one point. The price error is less than 0.5% (i.e., perfectly acceptable), but the error in the volatility is 25%, which is a large number when interpreted financially.

Results: Bates model
Price errors
Again, we start with a plot of the price errors in percentage points. Again, on the left DE; in the middle PSO; on the right the hybrid based on DE. We see convergence, but slower this time. This should be expected to some extent since the model is more complicated (has more parameters).

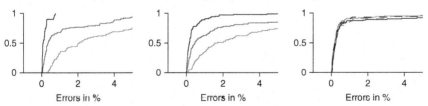

Parameter errors
Again, we also look at the errors in the parameters. The next figure shows the distributions of absolute errors in the parameters for $\sqrt{v_0}$ (left), $\sqrt{\theta}$ (middle), and ρ (right).

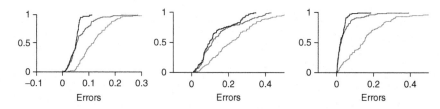

Next, we have the distributions of absolute errors in the parameters for κ (left), and σ (right).

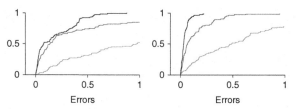

Finally, the figures below shows the distributions of absolute errors in the jump parameters: λ (left), μ_J (middle), and σ_J (right).

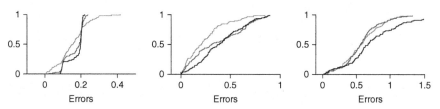

Remarkably, there seems to be no convergence for these parameters, even as we increase the number of function evaluations (i.e., let the algorithms search longer).

We again plot the errors in the objective function (on the x-axes) against the average pricing errors (i.e., the realized objective function value). Below: $\sqrt{v_0}$ (left), $\sqrt{\theta}$ (middle), and ρ (right).

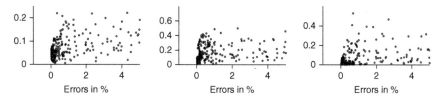

Below: κ (left), and σ (right).

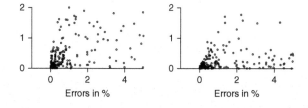

Below: λ (left), μ_J (middle), and σ_J (right).

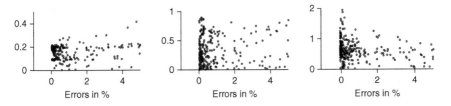

So for the Bates model, those parameters that are also in the Heston model are estimated less precisely; but for the jump parameters (λ, μ_J, and σ_J) there is essentially no convergence. No convergence in the parameters does not mean we cannot get a good fit; see the figures above. This non-convergence is to some extent due to our choice of parameters. Experiments with Merton's model (not reported) showed that for "small" mean jumps μ_J of magnitude −10% or −20%, it is difficult to recover parameters precisely because many parameter values give price errors of practically zero. In other words, the numerical optimization is fine, we can well fit the prices, but we cannot accurately identify the different parameters. In any case, parameter values of the magnitude used here have been reported in the literature (e.g., in Schoutens, Simons, and Tistaert, 2004; or in Detlefsen and Härdle, 2007). The numerical precision improves for large jumps. This is consistent with existing studies. He, Kennedy, Coleman, Forsyth, Li, and Vetzal (2006) for instance report relatively precise estimates for a mean jump size of −90%, yet at some point, this begs the question how much reason we should impose on the parameters. An advantage of theoretical models over simple interpolatory schemes is the interpretability of parameters. If we can only fit option prices by unrealistic parameters, or cannot identify the parameters with any meaningful accuracy, there is little advantage in using such models.

15.4. Final remarks

In this chapter we have investigated the calibration of option pricing models. For more complex models, we have shown how to calibrate the parameters of a model with heuristic techniques, and that we can improve the performance of these methods by adding a Nelder–Mead direct search. While good price fits could be achieved with all methods, the convergence of parameter estimates was much slower; for the jump parameters of the Bates model, there was no convergence. This, it must be stressed, is not a problem of the optimization technique, but it stems from the model. In comparison, parameters of the Heston model could be estimated more easily.

In empirical studies on option pricing models (e.g., Bakshi, Cao, and Chen, 1997; or Schoutens, Simons, and Tistaert, 2004), the calibration is often taken for granted; it is rarely discussed whether, for instance, restarts of an optimization routine with different starting values would have resulted in different parameter estimates, and how such different estimates would have influenced the studies' results. (In Gilli and Schumann (2010a) we showed that standard gradient-based methods often fail for the kinds of calibration problems discussed in this chapter, and that restarts with different starting values can lead to very different solutions.) Different parameter values may lead to good overall fits in terms of prices, but these different parameters may well imply different Greeks, or have a more marked influence on prices of exotic options. Hence, empirical studies that look, for example, into hedging performance should take into account the sensitivity of their results with respect to calibration. With luck, all that is added is another layer of noise; but the relevance of optimization is to be investigated by empirical testing, not by conjecturing. Such testing is straightforward: we just need to rerun our empirical tests many times, each time also rerunning our calibration with alternative starting values and, hence, get an idea of the sensitivity of outcomes with respect to optimization quality. Ideally, optimization quality in-sample should be evaluated jointly with empirical, out-of-sample performance of the model; see Gilli and Schumann (2010d).

Our findings underline the point raised in Gilli and Schumann (2010e) that modelers in quantitative finance should be skeptical of purely-numerical precision. Model risk is a still underappreciated aspect in quantitative finance (and one that had better not be handled by rigorous mathematical modeling). For instance, Schoutens, Simons, and Tistaert (2004) showed that the choice of an option pricing model can have a large impact on the prices of exotic options, even though all models were calibrated to the same market data. (Unfortunately, different calibration criteria lead to different results; see Detlefsen and Härdle, 2007). In the same vein, Jessen and Poulsen (2009) find that different models, when calibrated to plain vanilla options, exhibit widely differing pricing performance when used to explain actual prices of barrier options. Our results suggest that the lowly numerical optimization itself can make a difference. How important this difference is needs to be assessed empirically.

15.A. Quadrature rules for infinity

There are Gauss rules if the integrals are defined from or to infinity. We may have

$$\int_0^\infty f(x)\mathrm{d}x \qquad \text{or} \qquad \int_{-\infty}^\infty f(x)\mathrm{d}x.$$

The relevant Gauss rules here are called Gauss–Laguerre, and Gauss–Hermite. For Gauss–Laguerre we use the following trick:

$$\int_0^\infty f(x)\,\mathrm{d}x = \int_0^\infty e^x e^{-x} f(x)\,\mathrm{d}x \simeq \sum e^x w f(x);$$

thus, we weight the function with another function, e^{-x}, that rapidly decays to zero.

For Gauss–Hermite, we use

$$\int_{-\infty}^\infty f(x)\,\mathrm{d}x = \int_{-\infty}^\infty e^{x^2} e^{-x^2} f(x)\,\mathrm{d}x \simeq \sum e^{x^2} w f(x).$$

We can proceed as before with the Gauss–Legendre quadrature. For the Laguerre polynomials, we have the recurrence

$$(n+1)\varphi_{n+1}^{\mathrm{La}} = (2n+1-x)\varphi_n^{\mathrm{La}} - n\varphi_{n-1}^{\mathrm{La}},$$

or

$$\varphi_n^{\mathrm{La}} = \underbrace{-\frac{1}{n}}_{\alpha_n} x\varphi_{n-1}^{\mathrm{La}} + \underbrace{\frac{2n-1}{n}}_{\beta_n} x\varphi_{n-1}^{\mathrm{La}} - \underbrace{\frac{n-1}{n}}_{\gamma_n}\varphi_{n-2}^{\mathrm{La}}.$$

From these we obtain $\delta_n = 2n-1$, and $\eta_n = n$.

For the Hermite polynomials, we have the relation

$$\varphi_{n+1}^{\mathrm{H}} = 2x\varphi_n^{\mathrm{H}} - 2n\varphi_{n-1}^{\mathrm{H}},$$

and so

$$\varphi_n^{\mathrm{H}} = \underbrace{2}_{\alpha_n} x\varphi_{n-1}^{\mathrm{H}} - \underbrace{2(n-1)}_{\gamma_n}\varphi_{n-2}^{\mathrm{H}}.$$

Thus, we have $\delta_n = 0$, and $\eta_n = \sqrt{n/2}$.

We will need the integrals of the weights functions:

$$\int_0^\infty e^{-\zeta x} = \frac{1}{\zeta}$$

$$\int_{-\infty}^\infty e^{-\zeta x^2} = \sqrt{\frac{\pi}{\zeta}}.$$

For $\zeta = 1$, we get the integrals 1 and $\sqrt{\pi}$.

Listing 15.35. C-OptionCalibration/M/GLanodesweights.m

```
1  function [x,w] = GLanodesweights(n)
2  % GLanodesweights    -- version 2010-10-24
3  % (G_auss La_guerre...)
```

```
 4  delta = 2*(1:n)-1; eta = 1:(n-1);
 5  A = diag(delta) + diag(eta,1) + diag(eta,-1);
 6  [V,D] = eig(A);
 7  x = diag(D);
 8  % Matlab does not guaranty sorted eigenvalues
 9  [x,i] = sort(x);
10  % weights: for Laguerre, integral from 0 to infty = 1
11  w = V(1,i) .^ 2;
```

Listing 15.36. C-OptionCalibration/M/GHnodesweights.m

```
 1  function [x,w] = GHnodesweights(n)
 2  % GHnodesweights.m  -- version 2010-11-07
 3  % (G_auss H_ermite...)
 4  eta = sqrt((1:(n-1)) / 2);
 5  A = diag(eta,1) + diag(eta,-1);
 6  [V,D] = eig(A);
 7  x = diag(D);
 8  % Matlab does not guaranty sorted eigenvalues
 9  [x,i] = sort(x);
10  % weights: for Hermite, integral from -inf to inf = sqrt of pi
11  w = sqrt(pi) * V(1,i) .^ 2;
```

We can now repeat Example 15.3.

Listing 15.37. C-OptionCalibration/M/integrateGauss2.m

```
 1  % integrateGauss2.m -- version 2010-10-24
 2  % goal: to compute N(b)
 3  b = 2;
 4
 5  % number of nodes
 6  n = 20;
 7  % replace minus infinity by ...
 8  lowerLim = -10;
 9  % compute nodes/weights
10  [x,w] = GLnodesweights(n);
11  % change interval of integration
12  [x,w] = changeInterval(x, w, -1, 1, lowerLim, b);
13
14
15  [x2,w2] = GLanodesweights(n);
16
17  % result of integration
18  ourResultGLegendre = w*GaussF(x)
19  ourResultGLaguerre = w2 * (exp(x2).* GaussF(-(x2-b)))
20
21  % result of normcdf from Statistics Toolbox
22  MatlabResult = normcdf(b)
23
24  abs(ourResultGLegendre-MatlabResult)
25  abs(ourResultGLaguerre-MatlabResult)
```

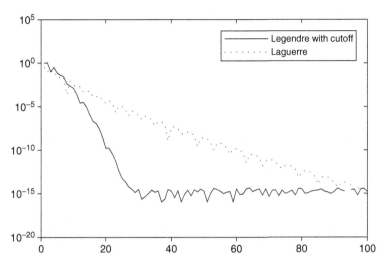

Figure 15.8 Errors for Gauss–Legendre and Gauss–Laguerre compared with normcdf.

Figure 15.8 compares the absolute error of Gauss–Laguerre with the more straightforward Gauss–Legendre (with $-\infty$ replaced by -10). We see that with more than, say, 10 nodes, the error for the latter approach is actually smaller.

Bibliography

Abramowitz, Milton and Irene A. Stegun, eds. 1965. *Handbook of Mathematical Functions*. Dover.

Acker, Daniella and Nigel W. Duck. 2007. "Reference-Day Risk and the Use of Monthly Returns Data." *Journal of Accounting, Auditing and Finance* 22(4):527–557.

Adams, Douglas. 1979. *The Hitch Hiker's Guide to the Galaxy*. Pan Books.

Akaike, Hirotugu. 1974. "A New Look at the Statistical Model Identification." *IEEE Transactions on Automatic Control* AC-19(6):716–723.

Albrecher, Hansjörg, Philipp Mayer, Wim Schoutens, and Jurgen Tistaert. 2007. "The Little Heston Trap." *Wilmott Magazine* pp. 83–92.

Althöfer, Ingo and Klaus-Uwe Koschnick. 1991. "On the Convergence of 'Threshold Accepting.'" *Applied Mathematics and Optimization* 24(1):183–195.

Armstrong, J. Scott. 1978. "Forecasting with Econometric Methods: Folklore Versus Fact." *Journal of Business* 51(4):549–564.

Artzner, Philippe, Freddy Delbaen, Jean-Marc Eber, and David Heath. 1999. "Coherent Measures of Risk." *Mathematical Finance* 9(3):203–228.

Bachelier, Louis. 1900. "Théorie de la spéculation." *Annales Scientifiques de l'École Normale Supérieure* 3(17):21–86.

Bailey, Ralph W. 1994. "Polar Generation of Random Variates with the t-Distribution." *Mathematics of Computation* 62(206):779–781.

Bakshi, Gurdip, Charles Cao, and Zhiwu Chen. 1997. "Empirical Performance of Alternative Option Pricing Models." *Journal of Finance* 52(5):2003–2049.

Bakshi, Gurdip and Dilip B. Madan. 2000. "Spanning and Derivative-Security Valuation." *Journal of Financial Economics* 55(2):205–238.

Bali, Turan G., K. Ozgur Demirtas, and Haim Levy. 2009. "Is There an Intertemporal Relation Between Downside Risk and Expected Returns?" *Journal of Financial and Quantitative Analysis* 44(4):883–909.

Bank for International Settlements (BIS). 2005. Zero-Coupon Yield Curves: Technical Documentation. BIS Papers 25 Bank for International Settlements.

Barr, Richard S., Bruce L. Golden, James P. Kelly, Mauricio G. C. Resende, and William R. Stewart. 1995. "Designing and Reporting on Computational Experiments with Heuristic Methods." *Journal of Heuristics* 1(1):9–32.

Barrett, Richard, Michael Berry, Tony F. Chan, James Demmel, June Donato, Jack Dongarra, Victor Eijkhout, Roldan Pozo, Charles Romine, and Henk van der Vorst. 1994. *Templates for the Solution of Linear Systems: Building Blocks for Iterative Methods*. Philadelphia, PA: SIAM.

Barsky, Robert B. and J. Bradford DeLong. 1993. "Why Does the Stock Market Fluctuate?" *Quarterly Journal of Economics* 108(2):291–312.

Bates, David S. 1996. "Jumps and Stochastic Volatility: Exchange Rate Processes Implicit in Deutsche Mark Options." *Review of Financial Studies* 9(1):69–107.

Bates, David S. 2003. "Empirical Option Pricing: A Retrospection." *Journal of Econometrics* 116(1–2):387–404.

Bates, Douglas and Martin Maechler. 2010. *Matrix: Sparse and Dense Matrix Classes and Methods*. R package version 0.999375-42.

Bera, Anil K., Matthew L. Higgins, and Lee Sangkyu. 1992. "Interaction between Autocorrelation and Conditional Heteroscedasticity: A Random-Coefficient Approach." *Journal of Business and Economics Statistics* 10(2):133–142.

Best, Michael J. and Robert R. Grauer. 1991. "On the Sensitivity of Mean–Variance-Efficient Portfolios to Changes in Asset Means: Some Analytical and Computational Results." *Review of Financial Studies* 4(2):315–342.

Biglova, Almira, Sergio Ortobelli, Svetlozar Rachev, and Stoyan Stoyanov. 2004. "Different Approaches to Risk Estimation in Portfolio Theory." *Journal of Portfolio Management* 31(1):103–112.

Birattari, Mauro, Luis Paquete, Thomas Stützle, and Klaus Varrentrapp. 2001. Classification of Metaheuristics and Design of Experiments for the Analysis of Components. Technical Report AIDA-2001-05 Intellektik, Technische Universität Darmstadt, Germany.

Björck, Åke. 1996. *Numerical Methods for Least Squares Problems.* Philadelphia, PA: SIAM.

Black, Fischer and Myron Scholes. 1973. "The Pricing of Options and Corporate Liabilities." *Journal of Political Economy* 81(3):637–654.

Black, Fischer and Robert Jones. 1987. "Simplifying Portfolio Insurance." *Journal of Portfolio Management* 14(1):48–51.

Blume, Marshall E. 1971. "On the Assessment of Risk." *Journal of Finance* 26(1):1–10.

Board, John L.G. and Charles M.S. Sutcliffe. 1994. "Estimation Methods in Portfolio Selection and the Effectiveness of Short Sales Restrictions: UK Evidence." *Management Science* 40(4):516–534.

Bolder, David and David Stréliski. 1999. "Yield Curve Modelling at the Bank of Canada." *Bank of Canada Technical Report* 84.

Bollerslev, Tim. 1986. "Generalized Autoregressive Conditional Heteroscedasticity." *Journal of Econometrics* 31(3):307–327.

Box, George Edward Pelham and Mervin Edgar Muller. 1958. "A Note on the Generation of Random Normal Deviates." *Annals of Mathematical Statistics* 29(2):610–611.

Boyd, Stephen and Lieven Vandenberghe. 2004. *Convex Optimization.* Cambridge University Press.

Boyle, Phelim P. and Ken Seng Tan. 1997. Quasi-Monte Carlo Methods. In *Proceedings AFIR Colloquium Cairns, Australia, August 13–15.* pp. 1–23.

Brandimarte, Paolo. 2006. *Numerical Methods in Finance and Economics—A Matlab-Based Introduction.* 2nd ed. Wiley.

Brandt, Michael W. 2009. Portfolio Choice Problems. In *Handbook of Financial Econometrics,* ed. Yacine Aït-Sahalia and Lars P. Hansen. Vol. 1, chapter 5, Elsevier, pp. 269–336.

Britten-Jones, Mark. 1999. "The Sampling Error in Estimates of Mean–Variance Efficient Portfolio Weights." *Journal of Finance* 54(2):655–671.

Broadie, Mark. 1993. "Computing Efficient Frontiers Using Estimated Parameters." *Annals of Operations Research* 45(1):21–58.

Brooks, Chris. 2008. *Introductory Econometrics for Finance.* 2nd ed. Cambridge University Press.

Brown, Byron W. and Myles Hollander. 1977. *Statistics: A Biomedical Introduction.* New York: Wiley.

Cairns, Andrew J.G. 1998. "Descriptive Bond-Yield and Forward-Rate Models for the British Government Securities' Market." *British Actuarial Journal* 4(2):265–321.

Campbell, Murray, Jr. A. Joseph Hoane, and Feng-hsiung Hsu. 2001. Deep Blue. Technical report.

Carr, Peter and Dilip B. Madan. 1999. "Option Valuation Using the Fast Fourier Transform." *Journal of Computational Finance* 2(4):61–73.

Chambers, John M. 2008. *Software for Data Analysis.* Springer.

Chan, Louis K. C., Jason Karceski, and Josef Lakonishok. 1999. "On Portfolio Optimization: Forecasting Covariances and Choosing the Risk Model." *Review of Financial Studies* 12(5):937–974.

Chan, Louis K. C. and Josef Lakonishok. 1992. "Robust Measurement of Beta Risk." *Journal of Financial and Quantitative Analysis* 27(2):265–282.

Chan, Tony F., Gene H. Golub, and Randall J. LeVeque. 1983. "Algorithms for Computing the Sample Variance: Analysis and Recommendations." *American Statistician* 37(3): 242–247.

Chekhlov, Alexei, Stanislav Uryasev, and Michael Zabarankin. 2005. "Drawdown Measure in Portfolio Optimization." *International Journal of Theoretical and Applied Finance* 8(1):13–58.

Cherubini, Umberto, Elisa Luciano, and Walter Vecchiato. 2004. *Copula Methods in Finance*. Wiley.

Chiarella, Carl and Andrew Ziogas. 2005. "Evaluation of American Strangles." *Journal of Economic Dynamics and Control* 29(1–2):31–62.

Chopra, Vijay K., Chris R. Hensel, and Andrew L. Turner. 1993. "Massaging Mean–Variance Inputs: Returns from Alternative Global Investment Strategies in the 1980s." *Management Science* 39(7):845–855.

Chourdakis, Kyriakos. 2005. "Option Pricing Using the Fractional FFT." *Journal of Computational Finance* 8(2):1–18.

Christoffersen, Peter F. 2003. *Elements of Financial Risk Management*. Elsevier Science.

Cohen, Kalman J. and Jerry A. Pogue. 1967. "An Empirical Evaluation of Alternative Portfolio-Selection Models." *Journal of Business* 40(2):166–193.

Coles, L. Stephen. 1994. "Computer Chess: The Drosophila of AI." *AI Expert Magazine* .

Cont, Rama. 2001. "Empirical Properties of Asset Returns: Stylized Facts and Statistical Issues." *Quantitative Finance* 1:223–236.

Cont, Rama and José da Fonseca. 2002. "Dynamics of Implied Volatility Surfaces." *Quantitative Finance* 2(2):45–60.

Cox, John C., Stephen A. Ross, and Mark Rubinstein. 1979. "Option Pricing: A Simplified Approach." *Journal of Financial Economics* 7(3):229–263.

Cuthbertson, Keith and Dirk Nitzsche. 2005. *Quantitative Financial Economics*. 2nd ed. Wiley.

Dacorogna, Michel M., Ramazan Gençay, Ulrich A. Müller, Richard B. Olsen, and Olivier V. Pictet. 2001. *An Introduction to High-frequency Finance*. Academic Press.

Davis, Philip J. and Philip Rabinowitz. 2007. *Methods of Numerical Integration*. 2nd ed. Dover.

Dawes, Robyn M. 1979. "The Robust Beauty of Improper Linear Models in Decision Making." *American Psychologist* 34(7):571–582.

Dawes, Robyn M. 1994. *House of Cards—Psychology and Psychotherapy Built on Myth*. Free Press.

De Bondt, Werner F. M. and Richard Thaler. 1985. "Does the Stock Market Overreact?" *Journal of Finance* 40(3):793–805.

De Pooter, Michiel. 2007. "Examining the Nelson–Siegel Class of Term Structure Models." *Tinbergen Institute Discussion Paper 2007-043/4*.

Dembo, Ron S. 1991. "Scenario Optimization." *Annals of Operations Research* 30(1): 63–80.

DeMiguel, Victor, Lorenzo Garlappi, and Raman Uppal. 2009. "Optimal versus Naive Diversification: How Inefficient is the 1/N Portfolio Strategy?" *Review of Financial Studies* 22(5):1915–1953.

Dennis, John E. Jr. and Robert B. Schnabel. 1983. *Numerical Methods for Unconstrained Optimization and Nonlinear Equations*. Series in Computational Mathematics. Englewood Cliffs, NJ: Prentice-Hall.

Derman, Emanuel and Iraj Kani. 1994. "The Volatility Smile and Its Implied Tree." *Goldman Sachs Quantitative Strategies Research Notes*.

Detlefsen, Kai and Wolfgang K. Härdle. 2007. "Calibration Risk for Exotic Options." *Journal of Derivatives* 14(4):47–63.

Devroye, Luc. 1986. *Non-Uniform Random Variate Generation*. Springer.

Devroye, Luc. 1996. Random Variate Generation in One Line of Code. In *Proceedings of the 1996 Winter Simulation Conference*, ed. J.M. Charnes, D.J. Morris, D.T. Brunner and J.J. Swain.

di Tollo, Giacomo and Dietmar Maringer. 2009. Metaheuristics for the Index Tracking Problem. In *Metaheuristics in the Service Industry*, ed. Martin J. Geiger, Walter Habenicht, Marc Sevaux and Kenneth Sörensen. Springer.

Dickey, David A. and Wayne A. Fuller. 1979. "Distribution of Estimators for Time Series Regressions with a Unit Root." *Journal of the American Statistical Association* 74(366): 427–431.

Diebold, Francis X. and Canlin Li. 2006. "Forecasting the Term Structure of Government Bond Yields." *Journal of Econometrics* 130(2):337–364.

Dimitrov, Valentin and Suresh Govindaraj. 2007. "Reference-Day Risk: Observations and Extensions." *Journal of Accounting, Auditing and Finance* 22(4):559–572.

Dimson, Elroy, Paul Marsh, and Mike Staunton. 2002. *Triumph of the Optimists: 101 Years of Global Investment Returns*. Princeton University Press.

Dorigo, Marco, Gianni Di Caro, and Luca M. Gambardella. 1999. "Ant Algorithms for Discrete Optimization." *Artificial Life* 5(2):137–172.

Dueck, Gunter and Peter Winker. 1992. "New Concepts and Algorithms for Portfolio Choice." *Applied Stochastic Models and Data Analysis* 8(3):159–178.

Dueck, Gunter and Tobias Scheuer. 1990. "Threshold Accepting. A General Purpose Optimization Algorithm Superior to Simulated Annealing." *Journal of Computational Physics* 90(1):161–175.

Duffie, Darrell, Jun Pan, and Kenneth Singleton. 2000. "Transform Analysis and Asset Pricing for Affine Jump–Diffusions." *Econometrica* 68(6):1343–1376.

Dulmage, Andrew Lloyd and Nathan Saul Mendelsohn. 1963. "Two Algorithms for Bipartite Graphs." *SIAM Journal* 11:183–194.

Dupire, Bruno. 1994. "Pricing with a Smile." *Risk* 7(1):18–20.

Eberhart, Russell C. and James Kennedy. 1995. A New Optimizer Using Particle Swarm Theory. In *Proceedings of the Sixth International Symposium on Micromachine and Human Science*. Nagoya, Japan: pp. 39–43.

Eddelbuettel, Dirk and Khanh Nguyen. 2010. *RQuantLib: R interface to the QuantLib library*. R package version 0.3.4.

Elton, Edwin J. and Martin J. Gruber. 1973. "Estimating the Dependence Structure of Share Prices—Implications for Portfolio Selection." *Journal of Finance* 28(5): 1203–1232.

Elton, Edwin J., Martin J. Gruber, and Thomas J. Urich. 1978. "Are Betas Best?" *Journal of Finance* 33(5):1375–1384.

Embrechts, Paul, Alexander J. McNeil, and Daniel Straumann. 1999. "Correlation: Pitfalls and Alternatives." *Risk* 12(5):69–71.

Embrechts, Paul, Filip Lindskog, and Alexander McNeil. 2003. Modelling Dependence with Copulas and Applications to Risk Management. In *Handbook of Heavy Tailed Distributions in Finance*, ed. S. Rachev. chapter 8, Elsevier, pp. 329–384.

Engle, Robert F. 1982. "Autoregressive Conditional Heteroscedasticity with Estimates of the Variance of United Kingdom Inflation." *Econometrica* 50(4):987–1008.

Engle, Robert F. 2002. "New Frontiers for ARCH Models." *Journal of Applied Econometrics* 17:425–446.

Engle, Robert F. and Victor K. Ng. 1993. "Measuring and Testing the Impact of News on Volatility." *Journal of Finance* 48(5):1749–1778.

Fama, Eugene F. and Kenneth R. French. 1993. "Common Risk Factors in the Returns on Stocks and Bonds." *Journal of Financial Economics* 33(1):3–56.

Fama, Eugene F. and Kenneth R. French. 2004. "The Capital Asset Pricing Model: Theory and Evidence." *Journal of Economic Perspectives* 18(3):25–46.

Fang, Fang and Cornelis W. Oosterlee. 2008. "A Novel Pricing Method for European Options Based on Fourier-Cosine Series Expansions." *SIAM Journal on Scientific Computing* 31(2):826–848.

Fang, Kai-tai, Yu Tang, Dietmar Maringer, and Peter Winker. 2006. "Lower Bounds and Stochastic Optimization for Uniform Design with Three and Four Levels." *Mathematics of Computation* 75(254):859–878.

Farlow, Stanley J. 1982. *Partial Differential Equations for Scientists and Engineers*. Wiley (Dover reprint).

Frankfurter, George M., Herbert E. Phillips, and John P. Seagle. 1971. "Portfolio Selection: The Effects of Uncertain Means, Variances, and Covariances." *Journal of Financial and Quantitative Analysis* 6(5):1251–1262.

Frimannslund, Lennart and Trond Steihaug. 2004. "A New Generating Set Search Method for Unconstrained Optimisation." University of Bergen, Norway.

Fusai, Gianluca and Andrea Roncoroni. 2008. *Implementing Models in Quantitative Finance: Methods and Cases*. Springer.

Gaivoronski, Alexei A. and Georg Pflug. 2005. "Value-at-Risk in Portfolio Optimization: Properties and Computational Approach." *Journal of Risk* 7(2):1–31.

Gander, Walter and Walter Gautschi. 2000. "Adaptive Quadrature—Revisited." *Bit* 40(1): 84–101.

Gatheral, Jim. 2006. *The Volatility Surface*. Wiley.

Gelfand, Saul B. and Sanjoy K. Mitter. 1985. Analysis of Simulated Annealing for Optimization. Technical Report LIDS-P-1494 MIT.

Geman, Stuart and Donald Geman. 1984. "Stochastic Relaxation, Gibbs Distributions, and the Bayesian Restoration of Images." *IEEE Transactions on Pattern Analysis and Machine Intelligence* 6(6):721–741.

Genest, Christian, Kilani Ghoudi, and Louis-Paul Rivest. 1995. "A Semiparametric Estimation Procedure of Dependence Parameters in Multivariate Families of Distributions." *Biometrika* 82(3):543–552.

Gentle, James E. 2009. *Computational Statistics*. Statistics and Computing Springer.

Gentleman, Robert and Ross Ihaka. 2000. "Lexical Scope and Statistical Computing." *Journal of Computational and Graphical Statistics* 9(3):491–508.

Genton, Marc G. and Elvezio Ronchetti. 2008. Robust Prediction of Beta. In *Computational Methods in Financial Engineering—Essays in Honour of Manfred Gilli*, ed. Erricos J. Kontoghiorghes, Berç Rustem and Peter Winker. Springer.

Gigerenzer, Gerd. 2004. Fast and Frugal Heuristics: The Tools of Bounded Rationality. In *Blackwell Handbook of Judgment and Decision Making*, ed. Derek J. Koehler and Nigel Harvey. chapter 4, Blackwell Publishing, pp. 62–88.

Gigerenzer, Gerd. 2008. "Why Heuristics Work." *Perspectives on Psychological Science* 3(1): 20–29.

Gill, Philip E., Walter Murray, and Margaret H. Wright. 1986. *Practical Optimization*. Amsterdam: Elsevier.

Gilli, Manfred. 1992. "Causal Ordering and Beyond." *International Economic Review* 33(4):957–971.

Gilli, Manfred, Dietmar Maringer, and Peter Winker. 2008. Applications of Heuristics in Finance. In *Handbook on Information Technology in Finance*, ed. Detlef Seese, Christof Weinhardt and Frank Schlottmann. Springer.

Gilli, Manfred and Enrico Schumann. 2010a. Calibrating the Heston Model with Differential Evolution. In *EvoApplications 2010, Part II*, ed. Cecilia Di Chio, Anthony Brabazon, Gianni Di Caro, Marc Ebner and Muddassar Farooq. Number 6025 *in* "Lecture Notes in Computer Science" Springer pp. 242–250.

Gilli, Manfred and Enrico Schumann. 2010b. "Distributed Optimisation of a Portfolio's Omega." *Parallel Computing* 36(7):381–389.

Gilli, Manfred and Enrico Schumann. 2010c. "A Note on 'Good Starting Values' in Numerical Optimisation." *COMISEF Working Paper Series No. 44.* Available from http://comisef.eu/?q=working_papers.

Gilli, Manfred and Enrico Schumann. 2010d. "Optimal Enough?" *Journal of Heuristics* forthcoming. Available from http://dx.doi.org/10.1007/s10732-010-9138-y.

Gilli, Manfred and Enrico Schumann. 2010e. "Optimization in Financial Engineering—An Essay on 'Good' Solutions and Misplaced Exactitude." *Journal of Financial Transformation* 28:117–122.

Gilli, Manfred and Enrico Schumann. 2010f. Portfolio Optimization with "Threshold Accepting": a Practical Guide. In *Optimizing Optimization: The Next Generation of Optimization Applications and Theory,* ed. Stephen E. Satchell. Elsevier.

Gilli, Manfred and Enrico Schumann. 2010g. Robust Regression with Optimisation Heuristics. In *Natural Computing in Computational Finance,* ed. Anthony Brabazon, Michael O'Neill, Dietmar Maringer, and Nikolaos Thomaidis. Vol. 3 Springer.

Gilli, Manfred and Enrico Schumann. 2011. Calibrating Option Pricing Models with Heuristics. In *Natural Computing in Computational Finance,* ed. Anthony Brabazon and Michael O'Neill. Vol. 4 Springer (forthcoming).

Gilli, Manfred and Enrico Schumann. forthcoming. "Risk–Reward Optimisation for Long-Run Investors: an Empirical Analysis." *European Actuarial Journal.* Available from http://www.actuaries.org/Munich2009/Programme_EN.cfm.

Gilli, Manfred, Enrico Schumann, Giacomo di Tollo, and Gerda Cabej. 2011. "Constructing Long/Short Portfolios with the Omega Ratio." *Journal of Asset Management* 12(2):94–108.

Gilli, Manfred and Evis Këllezi. 2002. The Threshold Accepting Heuristic for Index Tracking. In *Financial Engineering, E-Commerce and Supply Chain,* ed. P. Pardalos and V. K. Tsitsiringos. Applied Optimization Series Kluwer Academic Publishers, Boston pp. 1–18.

Gilli, Manfred, Evis Këllezi, and Hilda Hysi. 2006. "A Data-Driven Optimization Heuristic for Downside Risk Minimization." *Journal of Risk* 8(3):1–18.

Gilli, Manfred, Evis Këllezi, and Giorgio Pauletto. 2002. "Solving Finite Difference Schemes Arising in Trivariate Option Pricing." *Journal of Economic Dynamics and Control* 26(9–10):1499–1515.

Gilli, Manfred and Myriam Garbely. 1996. "Matchings, Covers, and Jacobian Matrices." *Journal of Economic Dynamics and Control* 20(9–10):1541–1556.

Gilli, Manfred and Peter Winker. 2003. "A Global Optimization Heuristic for Estimating Agent Based Models." *Computational Statistics & Data Analysis* 42(3):299–312.

Glasserman, Paul. 2004. *Monte Carlo Methods in Financial Engineering.* Springer.

Glosten, Lawrence R., Ravi Jagannathan, and David E. Runkle. 1993. "On the Relation Between the Expected Value and the Volatility of the Nominal Excess Return on Stocks." *Journal of Finance* 48(5):1779–1801.

Glover, Fred. 1986. "Future Paths for Integer Programming and Links to Artificial Intelligence." *Computers and Operations Research* 13(5):533–549.

Glover, Fred and Manuel Laguna. 1997. *Tabu Search.* Kluwer.

Goldstein, Daniel G. and Gerd Gigerenzer. 2009. "Fast and Frugal Forecasting." *International Journal of Forecasting* 25(4):760–772.

Golub, Gene H. and Charles F. Van Loan. 1989. *Matrix Computations.* Johns Hopkins University Press.

Golub, Gene H. and John H. Welsch. 1969. "Calculation of Gauss Quadrature Rules." *Mathematics of Computation* 23(106):221–230.

Gordon, Myron J. 1962. *The Investment, Financing and Valuation of the Corporation.* Homewood, Ill.: Irwin.

Goss, Simon, Serge Aron, Jean Louis Deneubourg, and Jacques Marie Pasteels. 1989. "Self-organized Shortcuts in the Argentine Ant." *Naturwissenschaften* 76(12):579–581.

Greene, William H. 2008. *Econometric Analysis.* 6th ed. Prentice Hall.

Grinold, Richard C. and Ronald N. Kahn. 2008. *Active Portfolio Management.* 2nd ed. McGraw-Hill.

Gurkaynak, Refet S., Brian Sack, and Jonathan H. Wright. 2006. "The U.S. Treasury Yield Curve: 1961 to the Present." *Federal Reserve Board Finance and Economics Discussion Series* 2006-28.

Gutjahr, Walter J. 2000. "A Graph-based Ant System and its Convergence." *Future Generation Computer Systems* 16(9):873–888.

Hale, Nicholas and Lloyd N. Trefethen. 2008. "New Quadrature Formulas from Conformal Maps." *SIAM Journal of Numerical Analysis* 46(2):930–948.

Hamida, Sana Ben and Rama Cont. 2005. "Recovering Volatility from Option Prices by Evolutionary Optimization." *Journal of Computational Finance* 8(4):1–2.

Hampel, Frank R., Elvezio M. Ronchetti, Peter J. Rousseeuw, and Werner A. Stahel. 1986. *Robust Statistics: The Approach Based on Influence Functions.* Wiley.

Hankin, Robin K.S. 2005. "Recreational Mathematics with R: Introducing the 'magic' Package." *R News* 5(1):48–51.

Harrison, Paul and Harold H. Zhang. 1999. "An Investigation of the Risk and Return Relation at Long Horizons." *Review of Economics and Statistics* 81(3):399–408.

Hastings, W. Keith. 1970. "Monte Carlo Sampling Methods Using Markov Chains and Their Applications." *Biometrika* 57(1):97–109.

He, Changhong, J. Shannon Kennedy, Thomas F. Coleman, Peter A. Forsyth, Yuying Li, and Kenneth R. Vetzal. 2006. "Calibration and Hedging under Jump Diffusion." *Review of Derivatives Research* 9(1):1–35.

Heath, Michael T. 2005. *Scientific Computing: An Introductory Survey.* 2nd ed. McGraw-Hill.

Heston, Steven L. 1993. "A Closed-Form Solution for Options with Stochastic Volatility with Applications to Bonds and Currency Options." *Review of Financial Studies* 6(2):327–343.

Higham, Desmond J. 2002. "Nine Ways to Implement the Binomial Method for Option Valuation in MATLAB." *SIAM Review* 44(4):661–677.

Higham, Desmond J. 2004. *An Introduction to Financial Option Valuation.* Cambridge University Press.

Hillier, Frederick S. 1983. "Heuristics: A Gambler's Roll." *Interfaces* 13(3):9–12.

Holland, John H. 1992. *Adaptation in Natural and Artificial Systems: An Introductory Analysis with Applications to Biology, Control and Artificial Intelligence.* MIT Press.

Hooke, Robert and Terry A. Jeeves. 1961. "'Direct search' Solution of Numerical and Statistical Problems." *Journal of ACM* 8(2):212–229.

Hoos, Holger H. and Thomas Stützle. 2004. *Stochastic Local Search: Foundations and Applications.* Morgan Kaufmann.

Hotelling, Harold and Margaret Richards Pabst. 1936. "Rank Correlation and Tests of Significance Involving No Assumption of Normality." *Annals of Mathematical Statistics* 7(1):29–43.

Hsu, Feng-hsiung. 2007. "Cracking Go." *IEEE Spectrum* 44(10):50–55.

Hull, John. 2008. *Options, Futures, and Other Derivatives.* 7th ed. Prentice Hall.

Hull, John and Alan White. 1998. "Incorporating Volatility Updating with the Historical Simulation Method for Value at Risk." *Journal of Risk* 1(1):5–19.

Hyndman, Rob J. and Yanan Fan. 1996. "Sample Quantiles in Statistical Packages." *American Statistician* 50(4):361–365.

Iacus, Stefano M. 2008. *Simulation and Inference for Stochastic Differential Equations.* Springer.

Ince, Ozgur S. and R. Burt Porter. 2006. "Individual Equity Return Data from Thomson Datastream: Handle with Care!" *Journal of Financial Research* 29(4):463–479.

Ingersoll, Jonathan E. 1987. *Theory of Financial Decision Making*. Rowman & Littlefield.

Jabbour, George M., Marat V. Kramin, and Stephen D. Young. 2001. "Two-State Option Pricing: Binomial Models Revisited." *Journal of Futures Markets* 21(11):987–1001.

Jaschke, Stefan, Richard Stehle, and Stephan Wernicke. 2000. "Arbitrage und die Gültigkeit des Barwertprinzips im Markt für Bundeswertpapiere." *Zeitschrift für betriebswirtschaftliche Forschung* 52(8):440–468.

Jessen, Cathrine and Rolf Poulsen. 2009. Empirical Performance of Models for Barrier Option Valuation. Technical report University of Copenhagen.

Jobson, J. Dave and Bob Korkie. 1980. "Estimation for Markowitz Efficient Portfolios." *Journal of the American Statistical Association* 75(371):544–554.

Jondeau, Eric, Ser-Huang Poon, and Michael Rockinger. 2007. *Financial Modeling Under Non-Gaussian Distributions*. Springer.

Jones, Owen, Robert Maillardet, and Andrew Robinson. 2009. *Introduction to Scientific Programming and Simulation Using R*. CRC Press.

Jorion, Philippe. 1985. "International Portfolio Diversification with Estimation Risk." *Journal of Business* 58(3):259–278.

Jorion, Philippe. 1986. "Bayes–Stein Estimation for Portfolio Analysis." *Journal of Financial and Quantitative Analysis* 21(3):279–292.

Joshi, Mark S. 2008. *C++ Design Patterns and Derivatives Pricing*. 2nd ed. Cambridge University Press.

Kamal, Michael and Emuanel Derman. 1999. "When You Cannot Hedge Continuously: The Corrections of Black–Scholes." *Risk* 1(12):82–85.

Keating, Con and Bill Shadwick. 2002. "An Introduction to Omega." *AIMA Newsletter*.

Kempf, Alexander and Christoph Memmel. 2006. "Estimating the Global Minimum Variance Portfolio." *Schmalenbach Business Review* 58(4):332–348.

Khuman, Anil S., Dietmar Maringer, and Nick Constantinou. 2008. Constant Proportion Portfolio Insurance: Statistical Properties and Practical Implications. working paper CCFEA WP023-08 University of Essex.

Kilin, Fiodar. 2007. "Accelerating the Calibration of Stochastic Volatility Models." *Centre for Practical Quantitative Finance Working Paper Series No. 6*.

Kim, Gew-rae and Harry M. Markowitz. 1989. "Investment Rules, Margin and Market Volatility." *Journal of Portfolio Management* 16:45–52.

Kirkpatrick, Scott, C. Daniel Gelatt, and Mario P. Vecchi. 1983. "Optimization by Simulated Annealing." *Science* 220(4598):671–680.

Kirman, Alan P. 1991. Epidemics of Opinion and Speculative Bubbles in Financial Markets. In *Money and Financial Markets*, ed. M. Taylor. London: Macmillan.

Kirman, Alan P. 1992. "Whom or What Does the Representative Individual Represent?" *Journal of Economic Perspectives* 6(2):117–136.

Kirman, Alan P. 1993. "Ants, Rationality, and Recruitment." *Quarterly Journal of Economics* 108(1):137–156.

Klemkosky, Robert C. and John D. Martin. 1975. "The Adjustment of Beta Forecasts." *Journal of Finance* 30(4):1123–1128.

Kloeden, Peter E. and Eckhard Platen. 1999. *The Numerical Solution of Stochastic Differential Equations*. Springer. corrected 3rd printing.

Knez, Peter J. and Mark J. Ready. 1997. "On the Robustness of Size and Book-to-Market in Cross-Sectional Regressions." *Journal of Finance* 52(4):1355–1382.

Konno, Hiroshi, Hiroshi Shirakawa, and Hiroaki Yamazaki. 1993. "A Mean–Absolute Deviation-Skewness Portfolio Optimization Model." *Annals of Operations Research* 45:205–220.

Konno, Hiroshi and Ken-Ichi Suzuki. 1995. "A Mean–Variance–Skewness Portfolio Optimization Model." *Journal of the Operations Research Society of Japan* 38(2): 173–187.

Lagarias, Jeffrey C., James A. Reeds, Margareth H. Wright, and Paul E. Wright. 1999. "Convergence Behavior of the Nelder–Mead Simplex Algorithm in Low Dimensions." *SIAM Journal of Optimization* 9(1):112–147.

Lawson, Charles L. and Richard J. Hanson. 1974. *Solving Least Squares Problems.* Englewood Cliffs, NJ: Prentice-Hall.

LeBaron, Blake. 2000. "Agent-Based Computational Finance: Suggested Readings and Early Research." *Journal of Economic Dynamics and Control* 24(5–7):679–702.

LeBaron, Blake. 2006. Agent-Based Computational Finance. In *Handbook of Computational Economics Volume II*, ed. Leigh Tesfatsion and Kenneth L. Judd. Elsevier, pp. 1187–1233.

Leland, Hayne E. and Mark Rubinstein. 1976. The Evolution of Portfolio Insurance. In *Portfolio Insurance: A Guide to Dynamic Hedging*, ed. D.L. Luskin. Wiley.

Lewellen, Jonathan and Jay Shanken. 2002. "Learning, Asset-Pricing Tests, and Market Efficiency." *Journal of Finance* 57(3):1113–1145.

Lewis, Alan L. 2000. *Option Valuation under Stochastic Volatility.* Finance Press.

Lo, Andrew W. 2008. *Hedge Funds—An Analytic Perspective.* Princeton University Press.

Lovie, Alexander D. and Patricia Lovie. 1986. "The Flat Maximum Effect and Linear Scoring Models for Prediction." *Journal of Forecasting* 5(3):159–168.

Luenberger, David G. 1998. *Investment Science.* Oxford: Oxford University Press.

Lunde, Asger and Peter Reinhard Hansen. 2005. "A Forecast Comparison of Volatility Models: Does Anything Beat a GARCH(1,1)?" *Journal of Applied Econometrics* 20(7): 873–889.

Madan, Dilip B. 2001. "On the Modelling of Option Prices." *Quantitative Finance* 1(5):481.

Makridakis, Spyros and Michèle Hibon. 2000. "The M3-Competition: Results, Conclusions and Implications." *International Journal of Forecasting* 16(4):451–476.

Makridakis, Spyros, Michèle Hibon, and Claus Moser. 1979. "Accuracy of Forecasting: An Empirical Investigation." *Journal of the Royal Statistical Society. Series A (General)* 142(2):97–145.

Manaster, Steven and Gary Koehler. 1982. "The Calculation of Implied Variances from the Black–Scholes Model: A Note." *Journal of Finance* 37(1):227–230.

Manousopoulos, Polychronis and Michalis Michalopoulos. 2009. "Comparison of Non-linear Optimization Algorithms for Yield Curve Estimation." *European Journal of Operational Research* 192(2):594–602.

Marazzi, Alfio. 1992. *Algorithms, Routines and S-functions for Robust Statistics.* Wadsworth & Brooks/Cole.

Maringer, Dietmar. 2004. "Finding the Relevant Risk Factors for Asset Pricing." *Computational Statistics & Data Analysis* 47(2):339–352.

Maringer, Dietmar. 2005a. "Distribution Assumptions and Risk Constraints in Portfolio Optimization." *Computational Management Science* 2(2):139–153.

Maringer, Dietmar. 2005b. *Portfolio Management with Heuristic Optimization.* Springer.

Maringer, Dietmar. 2008a. Constrained Index Tracking Under Loss Aversion Using Differential Evolution. In *Natural Computing in Computational Finance*, ed. Anthony Brabazon and Michael O'Neill. Springer.

Maringer, Dietmar. 2008b. Risk Preferences and Loss Aversion in Portfolio Optimization. In *Computational Methods in Financial Engineering—Essays in Honour of Manfred Gilli*, ed. Erricos J. Kontoghiorghes, Berç Rustem and Peter Winker. Springer.

Maringer, Dietmar and Evdoxia Pliota. 2008a. Clustering of Extreme Events: Application of Time-Varying Threshold and VaR Estimation. Technical report University of Essex.

Maringer, Dietmar and Evdoxia Pliota. 2008b. Value at Risk Estimation at Work: The Problem of Sample Length Choice. Technical report University of Essex.

Maringer, Dietmar and Evdoxia Pliota. 2008c. Value at Risk Estimation at Work: The Problem of Threshold Choice. Technical report University of Essex.

Maringer, Dietmar and Olufemi Oyewumi. 2007. "Index Tracking with Constrained Portfolios." *Intelligent Systems in Accounting, Finance & Management* 15(1):57–71.

Maringer, Dietmar and Panos Parpas. 2009. "Global Optimization of Higher Order Moments in Portfolio Selection." *Journal of Global Optimization* 43(2–3):219–230.

Maringer, Dietmar and Tikesh Ramtohul. 2011. Rebalancing Triggers for the CPPI Using Genetic Programming. Technical report University of Basel.

Markowitz, Harry M. 1952. "Portfolio Selection." *Journal of Finance* 7(1):77–91.

Markowitz, Harry M. 1959. *Portfolio Selection*. New York: Wiley.

Marsaglia, George. 1991. "Normal (Gaussian) Random Variables for Supercomputers." *Journal of Supercomputing* 5:49–55.

Marsaglia, George. 1995. "The Marsaglia Random Number CDROM including the Diehard Battery of Tests of Randomness."

Marsaglia, George and Wai Wan Tsang. 2000. "The Ziggurat Method for Generating Random Variables." *Journal of Statistical Software* 5(8):1–7.

Martin, R. Douglas and Timothy T. Simin. 2003. "Outlier-Resistant Estimates of Beta." *Financial Analysts Journal* 59(5):56–69.

MathWorks. 2002. "Accelerating MATLAB—The MATLAB JIT-Accelerator." *MATLAB Digest* 10(5).

Matsumoto, Makoto and Takuji Nishimura. 1998. "Mersenne Twister: A 623-dimensionally Equidistributed Uniform Pseudorandom Number Generator." *ACM Transactions on Modeling and Computer Simulations* 8(1):3–30.

McNeil, Alexander J., Rüdiger Frey, and Paul Embrechts. 2005. *Quantitative Risk Management: Concepts, Techniques and Tools*. Princeton University Press.

Merton, Robert C. 1973. "Theory of Rational Option Pricing." *Bell Journal of Economics and Management Science* 4(1):141–183.

Merton, Robert C. 1976. "Option Pricing when Underlying Stock Returns are Discontinuous." *Journal of Financial Economics* 3(1–2):125–144.

Metropolis, Nicholas C., Arianna W. Rosenbluth, Marshall N. Rosenbluth, Augusta H. Teller, and Edward Teller. 1953. "Equations of State Calculation by Fast Computing Machines." *Journal of Chemical Physics* 21(6):1087–1092.

Metropolis, Nicholas C. and Stanislaw M. Ulam. 1949. "The Monte Carlo Method." *Journal of the American Statistical Association* 44(247):335–341.

Michalewicz, Zbigniew and David B. Fogel. 2004. *How to Solve it: Modern Heuristics*. Springer.

Michaud, Richard O. 1989. "The Markowitz Optimization Enigma: Is 'Optimized' Optimal?" *Financial Analysts Journal* 45(1):31–42.

Mikhailov, Sergei and Ulrich Nögel. 2003. "Heston's Stochastic Volatility Model Implementation, Calibration and Some Extensions." *Wilmott Magazine* pp. 74–79.

Miller, John H. and Scott E. Page. 2007. *Complex Adaptive Systems. An Introduction to Computational Models of Social Life*. Princeton University Press.

Moler, Cleve B. 2004. *Numerical Computing with MATLAB*. SIAM. Available online from http://www.mathworks.com/moler/index_ncm.html.

Morgenstern, Oskar. 1963. *On the Accuracy of Economic Observations*. 2nd ed. Princeton University Press.

Moscato, Pablo. 1989. On Evolution, Search, Optimization, Genetic Algorithms and Martial Arts—Towards Memetic Algorithms. Technical Report 790 CalTech California Institute of Technology.

Moscato, Pablo and José F. Fontanari. 1990. "Stochastic Versus Deterministic Update in Simulated Annealing." *Physics Letters A* 146(4):204–208.

Müller, Robert. 2002. "Zur Berechnung der Obligationenrenditen im Statistischen Monatsheft der SNB." *SNB Quartalsheft* (2):64–73.

Murray, William, ed. 1972. *Numerical Methods for Unconstrained Optimization*. Academic Press.

Nelder, John A. and Roger Mead. 1965. "A Simplex Method for Function Minimization." *Computer Journal* 7(4):308–313.

Nelson, Charles R. and Andrew F. Siegel. 1987. "Parsimonious Modeling of Yield Curves." *Journal of Business* 60(4):473–489.

Nelson, Daniel B. 1991. "Conditional Heteroskedasticity in Asset Returns: A New Approach." *Econometrica* 59(2):347–70.

Niederreiter, Harald. 1992. *Random Number Generation and Quasi-Monte Carlo Methods.* Society for Industrial Mathematics.

Nocedal, Jorge and Stephen J. Wright. 2006. *Numerical Optimization.* 2nd ed. Springer.

Pearl, Judea. 1984. *Heuristics.* Addison-Wesley.

Perold, Andre F. 1986. Constant Portfolio Insurance. working paper Harvard Business School.

Petersen, Kaare Brandt and Michael Syskind Pedersen. 2008. "The Matrix Cookbook.". Version 20081110.

Pólya, George. 1957. *How to Solve it.* 2nd ed. Princeton University Press.

Powell, Michael J.D. 1972. Problems Related to Unconstrained Optimization. In *Numerical Methods for Unconstrained Optimization*, ed. W. Murray. Academic Press.

Price, Kenneth M., Rainer M. Storn, and Jouni A. Lampinen. 2005. *Differential Evolution— A practical approach to global optimization.* Springer.

R Development Core Team. 2008. *R: A Language and Environment for Statistical Computing.* Vienna, Austria: R Foundation for Statistical Computing. ISBN 3-900051-07-0.

Rebonato, Riccardo and Peter Jäckel. 1999. "The most general methodology to create a valid correlation matrix for risk management and option pricing purposes." Available online from http://www.riccardorebonato.co.uk/papers/ValCorMat.pdf.

Ripley, Brian D. 1987. *Stochastic Simulation.* Wiley.

Rockafellar, R. Tyrrell and Stanislav Uryasev. 2000. "Optimization of Conditional Value-at-Risk." *Journal of Risk* 2(3):21–41.

Rosenblatt, Murray. 1956. "Remarks on Some Nonparametric Estimates of a Density Function." *Annals of Mathematical Statistics* 27:832–835.

Rousseeuw, Peter J. 1984. "Least Median of Squares Regression." *Journal of the American Statistical Association* 79(388):871–880.

Rousseeuw, Peter J. 1997. Introduction to Positive-Breakdown Methods. In *Handbook of Statistics*, ed. G.S. Maddala and C.R. Rao. Vol. 15, chapter 5, Elsevier.

Rousseeuw, Peter J. and Katrien Van Driessen. 2005. "Computing LTS Regression for Large Data Sets." *Data Mining and Knowledge Discovery* 12(1):29–45.

Roy, Arthur D. 1952. "Safety First and the Holding of Assets." *Econometrica* 20(3): 431–449.

Rubinstein, Mark. 1994. "Implied Binomial Trees." *Journal of Finance* 49(3):771–818.

Rudolf, Markus, Hans-Jürgen Wolter, and Heinz Zimmermann. 1999. "A linear model for tracking error minimization." *Journal of Banking & Finance* 23(1):85–103.

Rudolph, Günter. 1994. "Convergence Analysis of Canonical Genetic Algorithms." *IEEE Transactions on Neural Networks* 5(1):96–101.

Ruppert, David. 1992. "Computing S-estimators for regression and multivariate location/ dispersion." *Journal of Computational and Graphical Statistics* 1(3):253–270.

Saad, Yousef. 1996. *Iterative Meethods for Sparse Linear Systems.* Boston, MA: PWS Publishing Co.

Salibian-Barrera, Matías and Víctor Yohai. 2006. "A Fast Algorithm for S-Regression Estimates." *Journal of Computational and Graphical Statistics* 15(2):414–427.

Schlottmann, Frank and Detlef Seese. 2004. Modern Heuristics for Finance Problems: A Survey of Selected Methods and Applications. In *Handbook of Computational and Numerical Methods in Finance*, ed. Svetlozar T. Rachev. Birkhäuser.

Schoutens, Wim. 2003. *Lévy Processes in Finance: Pricing Financial Derivatives.* Wiley.

Schoutens, Wim, Erwin Simons, and Jurgen Tistaert. 2004. "A Perfect Calibration! Now What?" *Wilmott Magazine*.

Schumann, Enrico. 2010. Essays on Practical Financial Optimisation, PhD thesis. University of Geneva.

Schuur, Peter C. 1997. "Classification of Acceptance Criteria for the Simulated Annealing Algorithm." *Mathematics of Operations Research* 22(2):266–275.

Schwager, Jack D. 1993. *Market Wizards*. HarperBusiness.

Schwarz, Gideon. 1978. "Estimating the Dimensions of a Model." *Annals of Statistics* 6(2):461–464.

Sharpe, William F. 1992. "Asset Allocation: Management Style and Performance Measurement." *Journal of Portfolio Management* 18(2):7–19.

Silverman, Bernard W. 1986. *Density Estimation for Statistics and Data Analysis*. London: Chapman and Hall.

Smith, G.D. 1985. *Numerical Solution of Partial Differential Equations: Finite Difference Methods*. 3rd ed. Oxford University Press.

Sortino, Frank, Robert van der Meer, and Auke Plantinga. 1999. "The Dutch Triangle." *Journal of Portfolio Management* 26(1):50–58.

Spendley, William, George R. Hext, and Francis R. Himsworth. 1962. "Sequential Application of Simplex Designs in Optimisation and Evolutionary Operation." *Technometrics* 4(4):441–461.

Staunton, Mike. 2003. "From Floating Points to Binomial Trees." *Wilmott Magazine* 1: 44–47.

Storn, Rainer M. and Kenneth V. Price. 1997. "Differential Evolution—A Simple and Efficient Heuristic for Global Optimization over Continuous Spaces." *Journal of Global Optimization* 11(4):341–359.

Stoyanov, Stoyan V., Svetlozar T. Rachev, and Frank J. Fabozzi. 2007. "Optimal Financial Portfolios." *Applied Mathematical Finance* 14(5):401–436.

Stützle, Thomas and Marco Dorigo. 2002. "A Short Convergence Proof for a Class of Ant Colony Optimization Algorithms." *IEEE Transactions On Evolutionary Computation* 6(4):358–365.

Svensson, Lars E.O. 1994. "Estimating and Interpreting Forward Interest Rates: Sweden 1992–1994." *IMF Working Paper 94/114*.

Taillard, Eric D., Luca M. Gambardella, Michel Gendreau, and Jean-Yves Potvin. 2000. "Adaptive Memory Programming: A Unified View of Metaheuristics." *European Journal of Operational Research* 135(1):1–16.

Talbi, El-Ghazali. 2002. "A Taxonomy of Hybrid Metaheuristics." *Journal of Heuristics* 8(5):541–564.

Tan, Ken Seng and Phelim P. Boyle. 1997. Applications of Scrambled Low Discrepancy Sequences To Exotic Options. In *Proceedings AFIR Colloquium Cairns, Australia, August 13–15*. pp. 885–917.

Taylor, Malcom S. and Janes R. Thompson. 1986. "A Data Based Algorithm for the Generation of Random Vectors." *Computational Statistics & Data Analysis* 4:93–101.

Tesfatsion, Leigh and Kenneth L. Judd, eds. 2006. *Handbook of Computational Economics. Volume 2: Agent-Based Computational Economics*. Amsterdam: Elsevier.

Timmermann, Allan. 1993. "How Learning in Financial Markets Generates Excess Volatility and Predictability in Stock Prices." *Quarterly Journal of Economics* 108(4):1135–1145.

Timmermann, Allan. 1996. "Excess Volatility and Predictability of Stock Returns in Autoregressive Dividend Models with Learning." *Review of Economic Studies* 63(4):523–558.

Tobin, James. 1958. "Liquidity Preference as a Behavior Towards Risk." *Review of Economic Studies* 25(2):65–86.

Torczon, Virginia J. 1989. Multi-directional Search: A Direct Search Algorithm for Parallel Machines, PhD thesis. Rice University.

Torczon, Virginia J. 1997. "On the Convergence of Pattern Search Algorithms." *SIAM Journal of Optimization* 7(1):1–25.

Trefethen, Lloyd N. 2008a. "Is Gauss Quadrature Better than Clenshaw–Curtis?" *SIAM Review* 50(1):67–87.

Trefethen, Lloyd N. 2008b. Numerical Analysis. In *Princeton Companion to Mathematics*, ed. Timothy Gowers, June Barrow-Green and Imre Leader. Princeton University Press.

Tufte, Edward R. 2001. *The Visual Display of Quantitative Information*. 2nd ed. Graphics Press.

Turlach, Berwin A. and Andreas Weingessel. 2007. *quadprog: Functions to solve Quadratic Programming Problems*. R package version 1.4-11.

Tversky, Amos and Daniel Kahneman. 1974. "Judgment under Uncertainty: Heuristics and Biases." *Science* 185(4157):1124–1131.

Ulam, Stanislaw M., Robert D. Richtmyer, and John von Neumann. 1947. Statistical Methods in Neutron Diffusion. report LAMS–551, Los Alamos Scientific Laboratory.

van den Bergh, Frans and Andries P. Engelbrecht. 2006. "A Study of Particle Swarm Optimization Particle Trajectories." *Information Sciences* 176(8):937–971.

Vasicek, Oldrich A. 1973. "A Note on the Cross-Sectional Information in Bayesian Estimation of Security Betas." *Journal of Finance* 28(5):1233–1239.

Venables, William N. and Brian D. Ripley. 2000. *S Programming*. Springer.

Venables, William N. and Brian D. Ripley. 2002. *Modern Applied Statistics with S*. 4th ed. Springer.

von Neumann, John and Herman H. Goldstine. 1947. "Numerical Inverting of Matrices of High Order." *Bulletin of the American Mathematical Society* 53(11):1021–1099.

Wets, Roger J.-B. and Stephen W. Bianchi. 2006. Term and Volatility Structures. In *Handbook of Asset and Liability Management*, ed. Stavros A. Zenios and William T. Ziemba. Vol. 1 North-Holland.

Wilf, Herbert S. 1978. *Mathematics for the Physical Sciences*. Dover.

Wilmott, Paul, Jeff Dewynne, and Sam Howison. 1993. *Option Pricing*. Oxford Financial Press.

Windcliff, Heath and Phelim P. Boyle. 2004. "The 1/n Pension Investment Puzzle." *North American Actuarial Journal* 8(3):32–45.

Winker, Peter. 2001. *Optimization Heuristics in Econometrics: Applications of Threshold Accepting*. Wiley.

Winker, Peter and Dietmar Maringer. 2007a. "The Hidden Risks of Optimizing Portfolios under Value at Risk." *Journal of Risk* 9(4):1–19.

Winker, Peter and Dietmar Maringer. 2007b. The Threshold Accepting Optimisation Algorithm in Economics and Statistics. In *Optimisation, Econometric and Financial Analysis*, ed. Erricos John Kontoghiorghes and Cristian Gatu. Vol. 9 of *Advances in Computational Management Science* Springer pp. 107–125.

Winker, Peter and Dietmar Maringer. 2009. "The Convergence of Estimators based on Heuristics: Theory and Application to a GARCH Model." *Computational Statistics* 24(3):522–550.

Winker, Peter and Kai-tai Fang. 1997. "Application of Threshold-Accepting to the Evaluation of the Discrepancy of a Set of Points." *SIAM Journal on Numerical Analysis* 34(5): 2028–2042.

Winker, Peter and Manfred Gilli. 2004. "Applications of Optimization Heuristics to Estimation and Modelling Problems." *Computational Statistics & Data Analysis* 47(2):211–223.

Winker, Peter, Manfred Gilli, and Vahidin Jeleskovic. 2007. "An Objective Function for Simulation Based Inference on Exchange Rate Data." *Journal of Economic Interaction and Coordination* 2(2):125–145.

Wright, Margaret H. 1996. Direct Search Methods: Once Scorned, Now Respectable. In *Numerical Analysis 1995 (Proceedings of the 1995 Dundee Biennial Conference in*

Numerical Analysis, ed. D.F. Griffiths and G.A. Watson. Addison Wesley Longman pp. 191–208.

Wright, Margaret H. 2000. What, If Anything, Is New in Optimization. Technical Report 00-4-08 Computing Sciences Research Center, Bell Laboratories Murray Hill, New Jersey 07974:. http://cm.bell-labs.com/cm/cs/doc/00/4-08.ps.gz.

Youngs, Edward A. and Elliot M. Cramer. 1971. "Some Results Relevant to Choice of Sum and Sum-of-Product Algorithms." *Technometrics* 13(3):657–665.

Zanakis, Stelios H. and James R. Evans. 1981. "Heuristic "Optimization": Why, When, and How to Use It." *Interfaces* 11(5):84–91.

Zeileis, Achim and Christian Kleiber. 2009. "Approximate Replication of High-Breakdown Robust Regression Techniques." *Journal of Economic and Social Measurement* 34(2–3):191–203.

Zhang, Jin and Dietmar Maringer. 2009. Index Mutual Fund Replication. In *Natural Computing in Computational Finance Vol. 3*, ed. Anthony Brabazon, Michael O'Neill and Dietmar Maringer. Springer.

Index

Printed in the United States
By Bookmasters